THEORY AND MEASUREMENT OF CONSUMER DEMAND

Volume 2

STUDIES IN MATHEMATICAL AND MANAGERIAL ECONOMICS

Editor

HENRI THEIL

VOLUME 21

NORTH-HOLLAND PUBLISHING COMPANY
AMSTERDAM · NEW YORK · OXFORD

THEORY AND MEASUREMENT OF CONSUMER DEMAND

Volume 2

by

HENRI THEIL

Center for Mathematical Studies in Business and Economics
The University of Chicago

1976

NORTH-HOLLAND PUBLISHING COMPANY
AMSTERDAM · NEW YORK · OXFORD

Library of Congress Catalog Card Number - 75-21978

Hardbound :
ISBN North-Holland 0 7204 3322 3
ISBN American Elsevier 0 444 10913 7
Paperback :
ISBN North-Holland 0 7204 3808 X
ISBN American Elsevier 0 444 10971 4

Publishers :

NORTH-HOLLAND PUBLISHING COMPANY
AMSTERDAM · NEW YORK · OXFORD

Sole distributors for the U.S.A. and Canada :

ELSEVIER / NORTH-HOLLAND INC.
52 VANDERBILT AVENUE
NEW YORK, N.Y. 10017

Sole distributors for other countries :

NORTH-HOLLAND PUBLISHING COMPANY
P.O. Box 211
Amsterdam

PRINTED IN THE U.S.A.

INTRODUCTION TO THE SERIES

This is a series of books concerned with the quantitative approach to problems in the social and administrative sciences. The studies are in particular in the overlapping areas of mathematical economics, econometrics, operational research, and management science. Also, the mathematical and statistical techniques which belong to the apparatus of modern social and administrative sciences have their place in this series. A well-balanced mixture of pure theory and practical applications is envisaged, which ought to be useful for universities and for research workers in business and government.

The Editor hopes that the volumes of this series, all of which relate to such a young and vigorous field of research activity, will contribute to the exchange of scientific information at a truly international level.

THE EDITOR

PREFACE

The publication of this volume completes my book on the theory and measurement of consumer demand. The book has become much larger than I originally anticipated. Its completion comes as a relief.

Contents of Volume 2

Whereas Volume 1 consists of a theoretical part (Chapters 1 to 4) and an empirical part (Chapters 5 and 6), Volume 2 has four parts, some of which are both theoretical and empirical.

The first part of Volume 2 (Chapters 7 to 10) discusses the specification and estimation of conditional demand models as well as the application of these models to the demand for meats in the United States. Chapter 7 describes conditional demand equations under block-independence, including the second-moment model for the disturbances of these equations. Block-independence is relaxed in Chapter 8 to blockwise dependence (weak separability); the last section of Chapter 8 describes an extension to utility maximization in a multiperiod framework. The empirical work discussed in these two chapters is based on the assumption of predetermined price changes. This is replaced by predetermined quantity changes in Chapter 9. Both price and quantity changes become endogenous in Chapter 10.

The second part (Chapters 11 and 12) is theoretical; it considers the consumer's basket as a whole, rather than the individual goods. Chapter 11 deals with such matters as the measurement of the change in the quality of consumption, Bortkiewicz's theorem, and the decomposition of the change in demand (in terms of real-income, substitution and disturbance components) in the n-dimensional commodity space. Chapter 12 presents the preference independence transformation and the axioms on which it is based. This procedure yields transformed goods so that the marginal utility of each such good is independent of the consumption of the others in the neighborhood of the budget-constrained utility maximum.

The third part (Chapters 13 and 14) is mainly empirical. Chapter 13 applies the preference independence transformation to two estimated models: the 14-commodity model of Chapter 6 and the conditional model for meats of Chapter 7. Changes in the quantity (volume) and quality of consumption are considered in Chapter 14. This chapter also provides a systematic analysis of the decomposition of such summary measures between and within commodity groups.

The final part (Chapters 15 and 16) is partly theoretical and partly empirical. Given that each transformed good obtained from the preference independence transformation has an independent marginal utility (independent of the consumption of the other transformed goods), what can be said about the behavior of these marginal utilities over time? This question leads to the subject of equivalent income changes, which is discussed in Chapter 15, along with the associated analysis of the income flexibility and the own-price elasticity of the demand for a commodity group under various conditions. Chapter 16 concludes with transitions between budget shares. In both chapters the theoretical results are applied to the data on meats.

The Presentation of the Empirical Results

Too frequently, econometricians try numerous functional forms for their equations and report only those which they consider "successful." In this book (both volumes), the disclosure of empirical results is essentially complete. The main exception is the extension of the data base for meats in Chapter 7 from 1950–1966 to 1950–1972 when it became apparent that there would be a separate Volume 2 which would not come out before 1976. The empirical results for the shorter period are not reported. Another exception is the two-dimensional decomposition of the log-changes in the quality index for the 14-commodity basket in Section 14.5. The standard errors of the estimated components are large; the estimates are therefore uninteresting and are not reported.

Acknowledgments for Volume 2

I want to express my appreciation to Messrs. William A. Barnett (Federal Reserve Board, Washington, D. C.) and Angus Deaton (Cambridge University), who made comments on parts of the manuscript; Messrs. Ronald A. Brooks and Anthony J. Finizza, whose dissertations served as starting points for topics analyzed in this volume; Mrs. Kathleen Dunne Masulis, who continued her work for the first volume by typing successive drafts of the second and reading the proofs under trying circumstances; and Mrs. Marjorie Walters, who assisted Mrs. Masulis. I am also glad to acknowledge financial support from the National Science Foundation (Grant GS-41319X).

Chicago, Illinois
February 1976

Henri Theil

TABLE OF CONTENTS

LIST OF TABLES

Chapter 7

Chapter 9

Chapter 10

Chapter 13

Chapter 14

Chapter 15

CHAPTER 16

LIST OF FIGURES

Chapter 15

Chapter 16

TECHNICAL NOTES

Chapters, sections and subsections

This volume consists of Chapters 7 to 16, which are a continuation of Chapters 1 to 6 in Volume 1. Each chapter consists of one or more opening paragraphs and a number of sections, with Section 7.2 the second section of Chapter 7. Most sections contain an opening paragraph and several (unnumbered) subsections.

Formulas, figures and tables

Formulas are indicated by two numbers, the first referring to the section and the second to the order of occurrence. Thus, eq. (3.2) is the second equation in the third section of some chapter. Whenever reference is made to eq. (3.2), it is always to the equation in the same chapter except when the contrary is stated.

Tables and figures are indicated by two numbers, the first referring to the *chapter* and the second to the order of occurrence: Table 7.10 is the tenth table in Chapter 7, Figure 11.9 is the ninth figure in Chapter 11. To facilitate finding a table or figure, its page number is frequently mentioned. The page number is always given for tables and figures in Volume 1.

Matrices, vectors and logarithms

Matrices are indicated by boldface uppercase letters (like $\mathbf{A}$), column vectors by boldface lowercase letters ($\mathbf{a}$), and row vectors by boldface lowercase letters with a prime added ($\mathbf{a}'$) to indicate that they are transposes of the corresponding column vectors. All logarithms are natural logarithms.

CHAPTER 7

CONDITIONAL DEMAND MODELS UNDER BLOCK-INDEPENDENCE

The empirical results described in Chapters 5 and 6 are based on a classification of the consumer's basket in terms of relatively broad commodity groups. Although this is frequently sufficient when the analysis is macro-oriented, it will also occur that the interest is confined to detail within one single group. The commodities of such a group are usually specific substitutes. We shall therefore use the Rotterdam Model rather than models which rely on an assumption of additive utility.

The theory in this chapter is developed under the conditions of block-independence and predetermined price changes, and it is applied to the demand for meats in the United States. Chapters 8 to 10 provide extensions under weaker conditions.

7.1 Conditional Demand Equations

Our starting point is the Rotterdam Model for block-independence with G groups of commodities, $S_1, \ldots, S_G$. If the ith commodity is part of S_g, its demand equation is

$$(1.1) \qquad \bar{w}_{it} Dq_{it} = \mu_i DQ_t + \sum_{j \in S_g} \nu_{ij} \left(Dp_{jt} - \sum_{k=1}^{n} \mu_k Dp_{kt} \right) + \varepsilon_{it}$$

In Section 2.3 we defined the following concepts for commodity groups:

$$(1.2) \qquad DQ_{gt} = \sum_{i \in S_g} \frac{\bar{w}_{it}}{\bar{W}_{gt}} Dq_{it} \quad \text{where} \quad \bar{W}_{gt} = \sum_{i \in S_g} \bar{w}_{it}$$

$$(1.3) \qquad DP'_{gt} = \sum_{i \in S_g} \frac{\mu_i}{M_g} Dp_{it} \quad \text{where} \quad M_g = \sum_{i \in S_g} \mu_i$$

By summation of (1.1) over $i \in S_g$ we derived a demand equation for the group,

$$\bar{W}_{gt}DQ_{gt} = M_g DQ_t + \phi M_g\left(DP'_{gt} - \sum_{k=1}^{n} \mu_k Dp_{kt}\right) + E_{gt} \tag{1.4}$$

where

$$E_{gt} = \sum_{i \in S_g} \varepsilon_{it} \tag{1.5}$$

Conditional Demand Equations

The results summarized above show how the n-equation system can be simplified to a G-equation system of the preference independence type by omitting all details within each group. We now proceed in the opposite direction by asking what can be said about the behavior of demand within a group, given that of the group as a whole. To answer this question we multiply (1.4) by μ_i/M_g for $i \in S_g$, which exists because $M_g > 0$ holds under block-independence:

$$\frac{\mu_i}{M_g}\bar{W}_{gt}DQ_{gt} = \mu_i DQ_t + \phi\mu_i\left(DP'_{gt} - \sum_{k=1}^{n} \mu_k Dp_{kt}\right) + \frac{\mu_i}{M_g}E_{gt}$$

Subtract this from (1.1):

$$\bar{w}_{it}Dq_{it} - \frac{\mu_i}{M_g}\bar{W}_{gt}DQ_{gt} = \sum_{j \in S_g} \nu_{ij}\left(Dp_{jt} - \sum_{k=1}^{n} \mu_k Dp_{kt}\right) + \varepsilon_{it} - \phi\mu_i\left(DP'_{gt} - \sum_{k=1}^{n} \mu_k Dp_{kt}\right) - \frac{\mu_i}{M_g}E_g$$

We use the fact that the sum over $j \in S_g$ of ν_{ij} equals $\phi\mu_i$ (because of the block-independence) to simplify this equation to

$$\bar{w}_{it}Dq_{it} = \frac{\mu_i}{M_g}\bar{W}_{gt}DQ_{gt} + \sum_{j \in S_g} \nu_{ij}(Dp_{jt} - DP'_{gt}) + \varepsilon_{it}^{g} \tag{1.6}$$

where

$$\varepsilon_{it}^{g} = \varepsilon_{it} - \frac{\mu_i}{M_g}E_{gt} \tag{1.7}$$

A comparison of (1.6) with (1.1) shows that we have the same variable on the left but that the two quantities pertaining to the consumer's budget as a whole,

$$DQ_t = \sum_{k=1}^{n} \bar{w}_{kt}Dq_{kt} \quad \text{and} \quad \sum_{k=1}^{n} \mu_k Dp_{kt}$$

do not appear in the right-hand side of (1.6). In fact, the variables of that equation are exclusively concerned with the group S_g to which the ith commodity belongs. This equation is the *conditional demand equation* of the ith commodity, given the demand for S_g. The set of equations (1.6) for all $i \in S_g$ is an allocation model within S_g, which may be clarified as follows:

(1) The log-change in real income is replaced by $\bar{W}_{gt}DQ_{gt}$. This is the left-hand variable in the demand equation (1.4) of the commodity group S_g and it has two interpretations: the volume component of the change in the budget share of S_g and the contribution of S_g to the log-change in real income. The former interpretation follows from

$$\bar{W}_{gt}DQ_{gt} = \sum_{i \in S_g} \bar{w}_{it}Dq_{it}$$

and the latter from

$$\sum_{g=1}^{G} \bar{W}_{gt}DQ_{gt} = \sum_{g=1}^{G} \bar{W}_{gt} \sum_{i \in S_g} \frac{\bar{w}_{it}}{\bar{W}_{gt}} Dq_{it} = DQ_t$$

(2) The price log-change Dp_{jt} is deflated in (1.6) by the marginal index DP'_{gt} of the commodity group, not by the marginal index of the complete basket which occurs in (1.1).

(3) The price coefficients are the same in (1.1) and (1.6), but the marginal share μ_i of (1.1) is replaced by the *conditional marginal share* μ_i/M_g in (1.6). The latter share answers the question: If income increases by one dollar, so that the amount spent on S_g increases by M_g dollars, what proportion of these M_g dollars is allocated to the ith commodity?

(4) Equation (1.7) states that the disturbance of (1.6) is obtained from that of (1.1) by subtracting the ith marginal proportion of the disturbance E_{gt} of the commodity group. Using (1.5) and (1.3) we conclude

$$\sum_{i \in S_g} \varepsilon_{it}^{g} = 0 \tag{1.8}$$

which clearly illustrates the role of (1.6) as an allocation model within the commodity group S_g.

Conditional Demand Equations in Absolute Prices

The price term of (1.6) can be written as

$$\sum_{j \in S_g} \nu_{ij}Dp_{jt} - \phi\mu_i \sum_{j \in S_g} \frac{\mu_j}{M_g} Dp_{jt} = \sum_{j \in S_g} \pi_{ij}^{g}Dp_{jt} \tag{1.9}$$

where π_{ij}^g is the $(i, j)^{\text{th}}$ element of the *conditional Slutsky matrix* $[\pi_{ij}^g]$ of the commodity group S_g, defined as

$$\pi_{ij}^g = \nu_{ij} - \phi M_g \frac{\mu_i}{M_g} \frac{\mu_j}{M_g} \qquad i, j \in S_g \tag{1.10}$$

Substitution of the right-hand side of (1.9) in (1.6) gives the absolute price version of the conditional demand equation of the ith commodity:

$$\bar{w}_{it} Dq_{it} = \frac{\mu_i}{M_g} \bar{W}_{gt} DQ_{gt} + \sum_{j \in S_g} \pi_{ij}^g Dp_{jt} + \varepsilon_{it}^g \tag{1.11}$$

The following sum rule follows from (1.10):

$$\sum_{j \in S_g} \pi_{ij}^g = 0 \qquad i \in S_g \tag{1.12}$$

This should be compared with

$$\sum_{j=1}^{n} \pi_{ij} = 0 \qquad i = 1, \ldots, n \tag{1.13}$$

where π_{ij} is the unconditional Slutsky coefficient:

$$\pi_{ij} = \nu_{ij} - \phi \mu_i \mu_j \tag{1.14}$$

By subtracting (1.14) from (1.10) we obtain

$$\pi_{ij}^g - \pi_{ij} = -\phi \mu_i \mu_j \left(\frac{1}{M_g} - 1 \right) \qquad i, j \in S_g \tag{1.15}$$

Since $0 < M_g < 1$ holds for $G > 1$ under block-independence, this shows that each conditional Slutsky coefficient is algebraically larger than the corresponding unconditional coefficient if the two commodities involved (the ith and the jth) have both positive or both negative marginal shares. For $i = j$ the difference (1.15) is always positive unless $\mu_i = 0$. If S_g consists of n_g commodities, its conditional Slutsky matrix is symmetric and negative semidefinite with rank $n_g - 1$. This can be proved straightforwardly along the lines of the analogous proposition in Section 2.4 by means of the symmetry and negative definiteness of the $n_g \times n_g$ price coefficient matrix $[\nu_{ij}]$ of S_g, which is a principal submatrix of the $n \times n$ price coefficient matrix.

The Second-Moment Model for Conditional Demand Equations

Equation (7.14) of Section 2.7 states that the covariances of the demand disturbances are proportional to the corresponding Slutsky coefficients:

$$\text{cov}(\varepsilon_{it}, \varepsilon_{jt}) = \sigma^2 \frac{\pi_{ij}}{\phi} \tag{1.16}$$

We shall prove in the next subsection:

$$\text{cov}(\varepsilon^g_{it}, \varepsilon^h_{jt}) = \begin{cases} \sigma^2 \dfrac{\pi^g_{ij}}{\phi} & \text{if} \quad i \in S_g,\ j \in S_h,\ g = h \\ 0 & \text{if} \quad i \in S_g,\ j \in S_h,\ g \neq h \end{cases} \tag{1.17}$$

We shall also prove:

$$\text{cov}(\varepsilon^g_{it}, E_{ht}) = 0 \qquad i \in S_g;\ g, h = 1, \ldots, G \tag{1.18}$$

The first line of (1.17) is the conditional version of (1.16). The second states that all conditional demand disturbances belonging to commodities of different groups are uncorrelated, and (1.18) states that each such disturbance is also uncorrelated with the disturbances of all commodity groups. When the disturbance distribution is multivariate normal, as it is under the theory of rational random behavior of Section 2.8, these zero-correlation properties imply stochastic independence. On comparing this result with the other terms in the right-hand sides of (1.4) and (1.6), we conclude that there is a complete separation of $G+1$ different demand models: the model (1.4) for commodity groups and G conditional demand models (1.6), one for each group. Equivalently, the allocation of the budget is described here as consisting of a number of independent steps. First, the consumer allocates his total expenditure on commodity groups. As (1.4) shows, this requires knowledge only of the log-changes in real income and in the marginal price indexes of the groups. Second, he allocates the expenditure on each commodity group to the separate commodities, which requires knowledge only of data for the group in view of (1.6). This second step actually consists of G stochastically independent steps, one for each group, which are also independent of the first step when the zero-correlation property of (1.17) and (1.18) is strengthened to stochastic independence.

The result (1.18) for $g=h$ is of particular importance for statistical estimation. In Section 7.2 we shall apply (1.11) to data on meats, treating $\bar{W}_{gt}DQ_{gt}$ as a predetermined variable, which would be unsatisfactory if $\bar{W}_{gt}DQ_{gt}$ were actually correlated with the disturbance of (1.11). Since (1.4) implies that E_{gt} is the random component of $\bar{W}_{gt}DQ_{gt}$, (1.18) guarantees that there is no such correlation under the conditions of the second-moment model.[1]

Derivations for the Second-Moment Model

We use eqs. (7.24) and (7.27) of Section 2.7 to express the conditional demand disturbance (1.7) in terms of the specific substitution components of the disturbances ε_{it} and E_{gt}:

$$\varepsilon_{it}^{g} = \bar{\varepsilon}_{it} - \mu_i \bar{E}_t - \frac{\mu_i}{M_g}(\bar{E}_{gt} - M_g \bar{E}_t)$$

Hence,

$$\varepsilon_{it}^{g} = \bar{\varepsilon}_{it} - \frac{\mu_i}{M_g} \bar{E}_{gt} \tag{1.19}$$

which proves that each conditional demand disturbance is the same function of the specific substitution components of the disturbances ε_{it} and E_{gt} as it is of these disturbances themselves. Note that we may regard the second term in (1.19), $-\mu_i \bar{E}_{gt}/M_g$, as the general substitution component of the conditional disturbance; it is concerned with the competition of all commodities of S_g for an incremental dollar spent on S_g. Under this interpretation the conditional and unconditional disturbances of the ith commodity have the same specific substitution component $\bar{\varepsilon}_{it}$.

Next consider eq. (7.22) of Section 2.7,

$$\operatorname{cov}(\bar{\varepsilon}_{it}, \bar{\varepsilon}_{jt}) = \sigma^2 \frac{\nu_{ij}}{\phi} \tag{1.20}$$

and sum both sides over $j \in S_g$ to obtain the covariance of $\bar{\varepsilon}_{it}$ and $\bar{E}_{gt}$:

$$\operatorname{cov}(\bar{\varepsilon}_{it}, \bar{E}_{gt}) = \begin{cases} \sigma^2 \mu_i & \text{if } i \in S_g \\ 0 & \text{if } i \in S_h, \quad g \neq h \end{cases} \tag{1.21}$$

Here use is made of the block structure of $[\nu_{ij}]$. This result should be compared with eqs. (7.25) and (7.30) of Section 2.7:

$$\operatorname{cov}(\bar{\varepsilon}_{it}, \bar{E}_t) = \sigma^2 \mu_i \qquad i = 1, \dots, n \tag{1.22}$$

$$\operatorname{cov}(\bar{E}_{gt}, \bar{E}_t) = \sigma^2 M_g \qquad g = 1, \dots, G \tag{1.23}$$

[1] POLLAK (1971, footnote 8 on p. 427) considered the question of whether the total expenditure on a commodity group can be viewed as a predetermined variable in a conditional demand equation, but he provided no answer. The result described here provides a positive answer under the conditions stated.

Note that (1.21) does and (1.22) does not require a block-independence specification.

For $g \neq h$, eq. (1.17) follows directly from (1.19), (1.20), (1.21) and the block-independence. To prove (1.17) for $g=h$ we write its left-hand side as

$$\operatorname{cov}\left(\bar{\varepsilon}_{it} - \frac{\mu_i}{M_g}\bar{E}_{gt}, \bar{\varepsilon}_{jt} - \frac{\mu_j}{M_g}\bar{E}_{gt}\right) = \operatorname{cov}(\bar{\varepsilon}_{it}, \bar{\varepsilon}_{jt}) + \frac{\mu_i\mu_j}{M_g^2}\operatorname{var}\bar{E}_{gt} - \frac{\mu_j}{M_g}\operatorname{cov}(\bar{\varepsilon}_{it}, \bar{E}_{gt}) - \frac{\mu_i}{M_g}\operatorname{cov}(\bar{\varepsilon}_{jt}, \bar{E}_{gt})$$

The first term on the right is given in (1.20). The second is equal to $\sigma^2\mu_i\mu_j/M_g$ in view of eq. (7.29) of Section 2.7, and the third to $-\sigma^2\mu_i\mu_j/M_g$ in view of (1.21). The fourth term is equal to the third. When these results are added, we obtain (1.17) for $g=h$ after using (1.10).

To prove (1.18) we write its left-hand side as

$$\operatorname{cov}\left(\bar{\varepsilon}_{it} - \frac{\mu_i}{M_g}\bar{E}_{gt}, \bar{E}_{ht} - M_h\bar{E}_t\right) \tag{1.24}$$

For $g \neq h$ this is, under block-independence, equal to

$$-M_h\operatorname{cov}(\bar{\varepsilon}_{it}, \bar{E}_t) + \frac{\mu_i M_h}{M_g}\operatorname{cov}(\bar{E}_{gt}, \bar{E}_t)$$

which vanishes in view of (1.22) and (1.23). For $g=h$ we can write (1.24) as

$$\operatorname{cov}(\bar{\varepsilon}_{it}, \bar{E}_{gt}) - M_g\operatorname{cov}(\bar{\varepsilon}_{it}, \bar{E}_t) - \frac{\mu_i}{M_g}\operatorname{var}\bar{E}_{gt} + \mu_i\operatorname{cov}(\bar{E}_{gt}, \bar{E}_t)$$

The successive values of these four terms are μ_i, $-\mu_i M_g$, $-\mu_i$ and $\mu_i M_g$, apart from the common factor σ^2, so that their sum vanishes.

7.2 The Demand for Meats in the United States: (1) Data and the Absolute Price Version

The theoretical results of Section 7.1 will now be applied to the demand for meats in the United States under the assumption that these are block-independent of all other commodities. The findings of this section are an extension of work done by Finizza (1971), who analyzed data for the years 1950–1966, to the period 1950–1972.

Basic Data

The first four columns of Table 7.1 contain the retail prices of four meats: Beef, Pork, Chicken, and Lamb.[1] Note that the price of Chicken declined from about 60 cents per pound around 1950 to about 40 cents in 1960 and then remained virtually constant. The prices of the three other meats were all much higher in the early 1970s than in 1950.

The next four columns of the table give the per capita consumption of the four meats in pounds per year (retail cut equivalent for Beef, Pork and Lamb, ready-to-cook weight for Chicken). The figures indicate that the consumption of Pork and Lamb fluctuated within rather narrow limits, whereas that of Beef and Chicken increased substantially. Note that our four meats do not include veal and turkey; no price data are available for these two meats in the earlier years of the sample period. Veal and turkey are of minor importance, and we shall therefore define "total meat" or "meat as a whole" in terms of the four meats of Table 7.1. The consumption of veal declined to about two pounds per capita per year in 1972. The consumption of turkey has increased over time, but it is largely seasonal (the holidays in November and December), particularly in the earlier years.

The last two columns of Table 7.1 contain the Bureau of Labor Statistics (BLS) consumer price index with base 100 in 1967, which will be needed in later chapters, and total per capita consumption in current dollars, which is needed for the computation of budget shares.

Derived Data

The budget shares of the four meats ($w_{1t}, \ldots, w_{4t}$) are given in the first four columns of Table 7.2. They are obtained by multiplying corresponding prices and quantities of Table 7.1 and dividing by the relevant figure in the

---

[1] The retail prices are from *Farm-Retail Spreads for Food Products*, Miscellaneous Publication No. 741 of the Economic Research Service of the U.S. Department of Agriculture (U.S.D.A.), pp. 112–116 and 128. The consumption data (next four columns of Table 7.1) are from *Food Consumption, Prices, and Expenditures*, Agricultural Economic Report No. 138 of the Economic Research Service of the U.S.D.A. (1968), pp. 59 and 61, and *Supplement for 1972* of this report, p. 17. The extra decimal place for Lamb is obtained by dividing the total civilian consumption of all lamb produced (*Livestock and Meat Statistics*, U.S.D.A. Statistical Bulletin No. 522, p. 209) by the civilian population (ibidem, p. 206) and multiplying this ratio by the conversion factor .89 (*Supplement for 1972* of Agricultural Economic Report No. 138, p. 16). The last column is obtained by dividing total personal consumption expenditures (*Survey of Current Business*) by the civilian resident population.

TABLE 7.1

BASIC DATA ON MEATS: UNITED STATES, 1950–1972

	Retail meat prices (cents per pound)				Per capita meat consumption (pounds per year)				BLS price index	Per capita consumption (current dollars)
	Beef	Pork	Chicken	Lamb	Beef	Pork	Chicken	Lamb		
1950	74.6	53.8	57.0	73.2	50.1	64.3	20.6	3.53	72.06	1267
1951	87.3	57.8	59.7	81.4	44.3	66.8	21.7	3.05	77.82	1361
1952	85.7	56.2	60.0	79.2	49.1	67.4	22.1	3.71	79.54	1408
1953	68.4	62.1	58.4	68.2	61.3	59.0	21.9	4.19	80.14	1469
1954	67.8	63.4	52.5	68.8	62.9	55.8	22.8	4.08	80.48	1481
1955	66.8	53.6	54.3	66.6	64.0	62.1	21.3	4.13	80.22	1561
1956	65.4	51.4	47.3	67.1	66.2	62.6	24.4	3.96	81.43	1606
1957	69.9	59.4	46.0	71.0	65.1	56.9	25.5	3.75	84.26	1664
1958	80.2	63.8	45.3	77.3	61.6	56.0	28.1	3.73	86.59	1684
1959	82.0	56.3	41.1	73.2	61.9	62.9	28.9	4.23	87.27	1775
1960	80.2	55.9	41.6	72.3	64.3	60.4	28.1	4.26	88.65	1826
1961	78.4	58.4	37.3	68.4	65.8	57.6	30.0	4.54	89.60	1850
1962	81.7	58.8	39.4	72.3	66.2	59.1	30.0	4.60	90.63	1933
1963	78.5	56.6	38.6	74.2	69.9	60.9	30.7	4.34	91.75	2011
1964	76.5	55.9	37.8	73.5	73.9	60.8	31.1	3.74	92.95	2121
1965	80.1	65.8	39.0	79.2	73.6	54.6	33.4	3.33	94.50	2259
1966	82.4	74.0	41.2	85.6	77.1	54.1	36.1	3.55	97.25	2411
1967	82.6	67.2	38.1	87.2	78.8	59.6	37.2	3.46	100.00	2520
1968	86.6	67.4	39.8	92.9	81.2	61.5	37.4	3.33	104.21	2720
1969	96.2	74.3	42.1	100.7	82.0	60.4	39.1	3.07	109.80	2910
1970	98.6	78.0	40.6	105.5	84.1	61.8	41.5	2.90	116.30	3062
1971	104.3	70.3	41.0	109.9	83.6	67.9	41.4	2.81	121.30	3267
1972	113.8	83.2	41.4	118.3	85.8	62.6	42.9	2.95	125.30	3519

last column of that table. The fifth column of Table 7.2 contains the total-meat budget share $W_{gt}=w_{1t}+\cdots+w_{4t}$. The last four columns give the conditional budget shares within meats, w_{it}/W_{gt} for $i=1,\ldots,4$. The meat group is indicated by S_g.

Table 7.3 contains the left-hand variables of the demand equations and the price log-changes of the four meats. By summing $\bar{w}_{it}Dq_{it}$ over $i=1,\ldots,4$ we obtain $\bar{W}_{gt}DQ_{gt}$, the volume component of ΔW_{gt} or, equivalently, the total-meat contribution to the log-change in real per capita income. Next, by dividing $\bar{W}_{gt}DQ_{gt}$ by $\bar{W}_{gt}$ (which is found by averaging successive entries of the fifth column of Table 7.2) we obtain DQ_{gt}, the log-change in the volume of total-meat consumption per capita, which is shown in the last column of Table 7.3. This log-change was predominantly positive in the period considered here; there are only six negative DQ_{gt}'s out of a total of 22. The total log-change from 1950 to 1972 is obtained by summing all figures in the last column of Table 7.3, which gives .339.[1] This amounts to an increase in the volume of total-meat consumption per capita of about 40 percent. On the other hand, the total-meat budget share declined substantially, from almost .07 in 1950 to less than .05 in the mid-1960s, after which it remained approximately constant (see Table 7.2). The conditional budget shares show an increasing trend for Beef and mostly decreasing trends for the three other meats.

A comparison of the price log-changes of Table 7.3 with those of Tables 5.2 and 5.3 for the Dutch and British commodity groups (pages 182–183 of Volume 1) reveals that the prices of meats are subject to larger annual changes. But the left-hand variables of Table 7.3 take values much closer to zero than those of Tables 5.2 and 5.3. This is so because these variables are quantity components of changes in smaller budget shares. The average budget shares of the four meats in the 23-year period 1950–1972 are

(2.1)

Beef: .02763	Chicken: .00675
Pork: .01940	Lamb: .00152

Estimation of the Conditional Demand Equations in Absolute Prices

Consider eq. (1.11),

---

[1] For any positive variable x the log-change from $t=0$ to $t=T$ is obtained by summing $Dx_t=\log(x_t/x_{t-1})$ over $t=1,\ldots,T$.

TABLE 7.2

BUDGET SHARES AND CONDITIONAL BUDGET SHARES OF MEATS

	Budget shares					Conditional budget shares			
	Beef	Pork	Chicken	Lamb	Total meat	Beef	Pork	Chicken	Lamb
1950	2.951	2.731	.927	.204	6.813	43.31	40.09	13.61	2.99
1951	2.842	2.837	.952	.182	6.814	41.71	41.64	13.97	2.68
1952	2.988	2.690	.942	.209	6.829	43.76	39.39	13.79	3.06
1953	2.855	2.495	.871	.195	6.415	44.50	38.89	13.57	3.03
1954	2.880	2.389	.808	.190	6.266	45.95	38.12	12.90	3.02
1955	2.739	2.132	.741	.176	5.788	47.32	36.84	12.80	3.04
1956	2.696	2.003	.719	.165	5.583	48.28	35.88	12.87	2.96
1957	2.735	2.031	.705	.160	5.631	48.57	36.07	12.52	2.84
1958	2.933	2.121	.756	.171	5.981	49.04	35.46	12.64	2.86
1959	2.859	1.995	.669	.174	5.697	50.18	35.01	11.74	3.06
1960	2.825	1.850	.640	.169	5.483	51.52	33.73	11.68	3.08
1961	2.788	1.818	.605	.168	5.378	51.84	33.80	11.24	3.12
1962	2.798	1.798	.611	.172	5.379	52.01	33.42	11.37	3.20
1963	2.729	1.714	.589	.160	5.192	52.55	33.01	11.35	3.08
1964	2.665	1.602	.554	.130	4.951	53.83	32.36	11.19	2.62
1965	2.610	1.590	.577	.117	4.894	53.33	32.50	11.78	2.39
1966	2.635	1.661	.617	.126	5.039	52.30	32.96	12.24	2.50
1967	2.583	1.589	.562	.120	4.854	53.21	32.74	11.59	2.47
1968	2.585	1.524	.547	.114	4.770	54.20	31.95	11.47	2.38
1969	2.711	1.542	.566	.106	4.925	55.04	31.31	11.49	2.16
1970	2.708	1.574	.550	.100	4.933	54.90	31.92	11.16	2.03
1971	2.669	1.461	.520	.095	4.745	56.26	30.80	10.95	1.99
1972	2.775	1.480	.505	.099	4.859	57.11	30.46	10.39	2.04

Note. All entries are to be divided by 100.

$$\bar{w}_{it}Dq_{it} = \frac{\mu_i}{M_g}\bar{W}_{gt}DQ_{gt} + \sum_{j \in S_g} \pi^g_{ij}Dp_{jt} + \varepsilon^g_{it} \tag{2.2}$$

where S_g = meat and $i, j = 1$ (Beef), 2 (Pork), 3 (Chicken), and 4 (Lamb). It follows from (1.12) that we may eliminate one of the conditional Slutsky coefficients in (2.2) by deflating by the corresponding price:

$$\bar{w}_{it}Dq_{it} = \frac{\mu_i}{M_g}\bar{W}_{gt}DQ_{gt} + \sum_{j=1}^{3} \pi^g_{ij}(Dp_{jt} - Dp_{4t}) + \varepsilon^g_{it} \tag{2.3}$$

This equation should be compared with the corresponding unconditional

TABLE 7.3

QUANTITY COMPONENTS OF BUDGET SHARE CHANGES AND PRICE LOG-CHANGES OF MEATS AND THE LOG-CHANGE IN THE VOLUME OF TOTAL MEAT CONSUMPTION

	$\bar{w}_{1t}Dq_{1t}$	$\bar{w}_{2t}Dq_{2t}$	$\bar{w}_{3t}Dq_{3t}$	$\bar{w}_{4t}Dq_{4t}$	Dp_{1t}	Dp_{2t}	Dp_{3t}	Dp_{4t}	DQ
1950–51	−.356	.106	.049	−.028	15.72	7.17	4.63	10.62	−3.
1951–52	.300	.025	.017	.038	−1.85	−2.81	.50	−2.74	5.
1952–53	.648	−.345	−.008	.025	−22.55	9.98	−2.70	−14.95	4.8
1953–54	.074	−.136	.034	−.005	−.88	2.07	−10.65	.88	−.5
1954–55	.049	.242	−.053	.002	−1.49	−16.79	3.37	−3.25	3.9
1955–56	.092	.017	.099	−.007	−2.12	−4.19	−13.80	.75	3.5
1956–57	−.045	−.193	.031	−.009	6.65	14.47	−2.79	5.65	−3.8
1957–58	−.157	−.033	.071	−.001	13.75	7.15	−1.53	8.50	−2.0
1958–59	.014	.239	.020	.022	2.22	−12.51	−9.73	−5.45	5.0
1959–60	.108	−.078	−.018	.001	−2.22	−.71	1.21	−1.24	.2
1960–61	.065	−.087	.041	.011	−2.27	4.38	−10.91	−5.55	.5
1961–62	.017	.046	.000	.002	4.12	.68	5.48	5.55	1.2
1962–63	.150	.053	.014	−.010	−4.00	−3.81	−2.05	2.59	3.9
1963–64	.150	−.003	.007	−.022	−2.58	−1.24	−2.09	−.95	2.6
1964–65	−.011	−.172	.040	−.014	4.60	16.31	3.13	7.47	−3.1
1965–66	.122	−.015	.046	.008	2.83	11.74	5.49	7.77	3.2
1966–67	.057	.157	.018	−.003	.24	−9.64	−7.82	1.85	4.6
1967–68	.078	.049	.003	−.004	4.73	.30	4.37	6.33	2.6
1968–69	.026	−.028	.025	−.009	10.51	9.75	5.62	8.06	.2
1969–70	.069	.036	.033	−.006	2.46	4.86	−3.63	4.66	2.6
1970–71	−.016	.143	−.001	−.003	5.62	−10.39	.98	4.09	2.5
1971–72	.071	−.120	.018	.005	8.72	16.85	.97	7.37	−.5

Notes. All entries are to be divided by 100. The subscript i of $\bar{w}_{it}Dq_{it}$ and Dp_{it} refers to Beef ($i=$ Pork ($i=2$), Chicken ($i=3$), and Lamb ($i=4$). The last column contains the log-change in total m consumption per capita.

demand equation for $n=4$:

$$\bar{w}_{it}Dq_{it} = \mu_i DQ_t + \sum_{j=1}^{3} \pi_{ij}(Dp_{jt} - Dp_{4t}) + \varepsilon_{it} \tag{2.4}$$

The second-moment theory of Section 7.1 implies that we can interpret $\bar{W}_{gt}DQ_{gt}$ as a predetermined variable in (2.3), which means that we can estimate (2.3) in the same way that we estimated (2.4) in Sections 5.2 and 5.3. So we compute least-squares estimates of the conditional marginal shares and Slutsky coefficients by regressing $\bar{w}_{it}Dq_{it}$ on $\bar{W}_{gt}DQ_{gt}$ and the three deflated price log-changes which occur in (2.3). The results are shown in the upper half of Table 7.4. Note that the two conditional Slutsky coefficients of Beef and Pork are close to each other, and that they have relatively

TABLE 7.4

FIRST SET OF ESTIMATES OF CONDITIONAL MARGINAL SHARES AND SLUTSKY COEFFICIENTS OF MEATS

	Conditional marginal share	Conditional Slutsky coefficients			
		Unconstrained estimates			
Beef	.761 (.058)	−.0122 (.0030)	.0106 (.0012)	.0018 (.0014)	−.0002 (.0038)
Pork	.141 (.053)	.0098 (.0027)	−.0129 (.0011)	.0025 (.0013)	.0006 (.0035)
Chicken	.041 (.021)	.0007 (.0011)	.0016 (.0004)	−.0049 (.0005)	.0026 (.0014)
Lamb	.057 (.011)	.0017 (.0006)	.0007 (.0002)	.0006 (.0003)	−.0030 (.0007)
		Symmetry-constrained estimates			
Beef	.746 (.053)	−.0137 (.0011)	.0100 (.0009)	.0021 (.0005)	.0016 (.0006)
Pork	.146 (.048)		−.0127 (.0009)	.0020 (.0004)	.0007 (.0002)
Chicken	.051 (.020)			−.0048 (.0005)	.0007 (.0003)
Lamb	.057 (.011)				−.0030 (.0007)

small standard errors. This agrees with the symmetry of the conditional Slutsky matrix.

Changes in tastes can be handled by adding a constant to the right-hand side of (2.3). The least-squares estimates of these constants are shown below. The standard errors are such that there is little reason to add such constants to (2.3).

(2.5)

Beef:	.00021 (.00014)	Chicken:	.00003 (.00005)
Pork:	−.00018 (.00013)	Lamb:	−.00006 (.00003)

The test statistic (3.27) of Section 5.3 for Slutsky symmetry takes a very low value, .56, when applied to (2.3).[1] The symmetry-constrained estimates, obtained from eq. (3.23) of the same section, are given in the lower half of Table 7.4. The latent roots of the symmetric estimate of the conditional Slutsky matrix are 0, −.0040, −.0070 and −.0233, which shows that this matrix is negative semidefinite with rank 3. Note that the standard errors of

[1] For the computation of this statistic, the matrix (3.28) of Section 5.3 is replaced by a matrix of the same form with $\bar{w}_1/\bar{W}_g$, $\bar{w}_2/\bar{W}_g$ and $\bar{w}_3/\bar{W}_g$ substituted for a, b and c, where $\bar{w}_1$, $\bar{w}_2$ and $\bar{w}_3$ are the average budget shares of Beef, Pork and Chicken shown in (2.1) and $\bar{W}_g=.05531$ is the average total-meat budget share.

most of the conditional Slutsky coefficients are small compared with the corresponding estimates. This is largely due to the sizable and frequently opposite price changes of the four meats (see Table 7.3).

The matrix of mean squares and products of the residuals associated with the symmetry-constrained estimates of (2.3) is

$$(2.6) \qquad 10^{-6}\begin{bmatrix} .2096 & -.1757 & -.0353 & .0013 \\ & .1763 & .0069 & -.0075 \\ & & .0295 & -.0011 \\ & & & .0073 \end{bmatrix} \begin{matrix} \text{Beef} \\ \text{Pork} \\ \text{Chicken} \\ \text{Lamb} \end{matrix}$$

7.3 The Demand for Meats in the United States: (2) An Alternative Parametrization

The left-hand variables in the conditional equation (2.3) and the unconditional equation (2.4) are the same; both are quantity components of changes in budget shares. But when we consider conditional demand equations, it is natural to analyze changes in conditional budget shares also.

The Change in a Conditional Budget Share

Consider the decomposition of $\Delta w_{it} = w_{it} - w_{i,t-1}$ given in eq. (1.11) of Section 2.1:

$$(3.1) \qquad \Delta w_{it} = \bar{w}_{it} Dp_{it} + \bar{w}_{it} Dq_{it} - \bar{w}_{it} Dm_t + O_3$$

We sum both sides over $i \in S_g$,

$$(3.2) \qquad \Delta W_{gt} = \bar{W}_{gt} DP_{gt} + \bar{W}_{gt} DQ_{gt} - \bar{W}_{gt} Dm_t + O_3$$

where DP_{gt} is the budget-share-weighted mean of the price log-changes of the commodities of S_g:

$$(3.3) \qquad DP_{gt} = \sum_{i \in S_g} \frac{\bar{w}_{it}}{\bar{W}_{gt}} Dp_{it}$$

This DP_{gt} should be compared with the marginally weighted mean given in (1.3).

Equation (3.2) provides a decomposition of the budget share change of a commodity group similar to (3.1). It will be used in the next subsection to prove the following decomposition for the change in a conditional budget share ($i \in S_g$):

$$(3.4) \qquad \Delta\left(\frac{w_{it}}{W_{gt}}\right) = \frac{\bar{w}_{it}}{\bar{W}_{gt}} Dp_{it} + \frac{\bar{w}_{it}}{\bar{W}_{gt}} Dq_{it} - \frac{\bar{w}_{it}}{\bar{W}_{gt}} (DP_{gt} + DQ_{gt}) + O_3$$

The successive terms on the right are the components of the change in the ith conditional budget share due to the changes in the ith price, the ith quantity, and the amount spent on the commodity group.[1] So, if we want a conditional demand model whose left-hand variables are quantity components of changes in conditional budget shares, all we have to do is divide both sides of (1.6) by $\bar{W}_{gt}$:

$$(3.5) \qquad \frac{\bar{w}_{it}}{\bar{W}_{gt}} Dq_{it} = \frac{\mu_i}{M_g} DQ_{gt} + \sum_{j \in S_g} \frac{\nu_{ij}}{\bar{W}_{gt}} (Dp_{jt} - DP'_{gt}) + \frac{\varepsilon^g_{it}}{\bar{W}_{gt}}$$

The first term on the right is the conditional marginal share multiplied by the log-change in the volume index of the commodity group. This is an obvious within-group extension of the real-income term $\mu_i DQ_t$ of the unconditional demand equation. Also note that the left-hand variable is, in view of (1.2), the contribution of the ith commodity to DQ_{gt}.

Derivations

Multiply (3.2) by $\bar{w}_{it}/\bar{W}_{gt}$,

$$\frac{\bar{w}_{it}}{\bar{W}_{gt}} \Delta W_{gt} = \bar{w}_{it} DP_{gt} + \bar{w}_{it} DQ_{gt} - \bar{w}_{it} Dm_t + O_3$$

and subtract this from (3.1):

$$\Delta w_{it} - \frac{\bar{w}_{it}}{\bar{W}_{gt}} \Delta W_{gt} = \bar{w}_{it} Dp_{it} + \bar{w}_{it} Dq_{it} - \bar{w}_{it} (DP_{gt} + DQ_{gt}) + O_3$$

The right-hand side is a multiple $\bar{W}_{gt}$ of that of (3.4), apart from an O_3 term. To verify (3.4) we must prove that the left-hand sides agree in the same way:

$$(3.6) \qquad \Delta w_{it} - \frac{\bar{w}_{it}}{\bar{W}_{gt}} \Delta W_{gt} = \bar{W}_{gt} \, \Delta\left(\frac{w_{it}}{W_{gt}}\right) + O_3$$

[1] The interpretation of the third component may be verified by means of eq. (2.5) of Section 2.2, which shows that the income components in (3.1) and (3.2) may be written as $-\bar{w}_{it}$ or $-\bar{W}_{gt}$ multiplied by $DP_t + DQ_t$, where $DP_t = \sum_k \bar{w}_{kt} Dp_{kt}$, apart from an O_3 term which can be merged with the O_3 term on the far right in these two equations.

For this purpose we consider

$$\Delta\left(\frac{w_{it}}{W_{gt}}\right)=\frac{w_{it}}{W_{gt}}-\frac{w_{i,t-1}}{W_{g,t-1}}=\frac{w_{it}W_{g,t-1}-W_{gt}w_{i,t-1}}{W_{gt}W_{g,t-1}} \tag{3.7}$$

The numerator of the third member can be written as

$$(\bar{w}_{it}+\tfrac{1}{2}\Delta w_{it})(\bar{W}_{gt}-\tfrac{1}{2}\Delta W_{gt})-(\bar{W}_{gt}+\tfrac{1}{2}\Delta W_{gt})(\bar{w}_{it}-\tfrac{1}{2}\Delta w_{it})$$

which equals $\bar{W}_{gt}\Delta w_{it}-\bar{w}_{it}\Delta W_{gt}$. Hence (3.7) becomes

$$\Delta\left(\frac{w_{it}}{W_{gt}}\right)=\frac{\bar{W}_{gt}\Delta w_{it}-\bar{w}_{it}\Delta W_{gt}}{W_{gt}W_{g,t-1}}=\frac{\bar{W}_{gt}\Delta w_{it}-\bar{w}_{it}\Delta W_{gt}}{\bar{W}_{gt}^2-\frac{1}{4}(\Delta W_{gt})^2}$$

Since $(\Delta W_{gt})^2=O_2$, this proves

$$\Delta\left(\frac{w_{it}}{W_{gt}}\right)=\frac{\bar{W}_{gt}\Delta w_{it}-\bar{w}_{it}\Delta W_{gt}}{\bar{W}_{gt}^2}+O_3$$

from which (3.6) follows immediately.

The Modified Conditional Demand Model

Let us define

$$v_{ij}^*=\frac{v_{ij}}{\bar{W}_{gt}} \qquad \varepsilon_{it}^*=\frac{\varepsilon_{it}^g}{\bar{W}_{gt}} \qquad i,j\in S_g \tag{3.8}$$

so that (3.5) is simplified to

$$\frac{\bar{w}_{it}}{\bar{W}_{gt}}Dq_{it}=\frac{\mu_i}{M_g}DQ_{gt}+\sum_{j\in S_g}v_{ij}^*(Dp_{jt}-DP'_{gt})+\varepsilon_{it}^* \tag{3.9}$$

We shall refer to the matrix $[v_{ij}^*]$, which is of order $n_g\times n_g$ when S_g consists of n_g commodities, as the *modified price coefficient matrix* of the commodities of S_g. This matrix is obtained from the corresponding $n_g\times n_g$ submatrix $[v_{ij}]$ by multiplication by the positive scalar $1/\bar{W}_{gt}$. Hence $[v_{ij}^*]$ is symmetric and negative definite. The constraint $\sum v_{ij}=\phi\mu_i$ (sum over $j\in S_g$) for each $i\in S_g$ implies

$$\sum_{j\in S_g}v_{ij}^*=\frac{\phi\mu_i}{\bar{W}_{gt}} \qquad i\in S_g \tag{3.10}$$

Summation of (3.10) over $i \in S_g$ gives

$$\sum_{i \in S_g} \sum_{j \in S_g} \nu_{ij}^* = \frac{\phi M_g}{\bar{W}_{gt}} \tag{3.11}$$

Now divide (1.4) by $\bar{W}_{gt}$:

$$DQ_{gt} = \frac{M_g}{\bar{W}_{gt}} DQ_t + \frac{\phi M_g}{\bar{W}_{gt}} \left(DP'_{gt} - \sum_{k=1}^{n} \mu_k Dp_{kt} \right) + \frac{E_{gt}}{\bar{W}_{gt}} \tag{3.12}$$

Since we have DQ_{gt} on the left, $\phi M_g / \bar{W}_{gt}$ is the own-price elasticity of the commodity group S_g. Therefore, (3.11) implies that under block-independence *the sum of all n_g^2 modified price coefficients of the commodities of S_g is equal to the own-price elasticity of the demand for the group.*

The Parametrization Implied by the Modified Model

When we use (3.9) and treat the ν_{ij}^*'s as constant over time, we implicitly assume that the original ν_{ij}'s are proportional to $\bar{W}_{gt}$ in view of (3.8). [A strictly consistent notation would require a t subscript attached to these ν_{ij}'s, but we shall not do this in order to keep the notation simple.] In other words, (3.9) amounts to a parametrization which differs from (1.6). So, when we apply (3.9) to the demand for meats, as will be done in the subsection immediately following the next, we assume that the ν_{ij}'s of meats vary proportionally to the total-meat budget share. Whether this is an adequate approximation is an empirical question. Recall that the constancy which was assumed for the ν_{ij}'s in Section 2.2 is a matter of convenience, not of dogma.

To simplify procedures we treat the marginal shares as constant, so that DQ_{gt} has a constant coefficient in (3.9), and we assume that the income flexibility varies proportionally to $\bar{W}_{gt}$. This insures that the two sides of both (3.10) and (3.11) are constants. Going back to Table 7.2 for the application to meats, we see that the proportionality to $\bar{W}_{gt}$ implies that ϕ takes declining absolute values from the early 1950s to the mid-1960s and then remains approximately constant. Since real per capita income had an increasing trend during the period considered here, this means that $1/\phi$ (the income elasticity of the marginal utility of income) increased in absolute value while real income also increased. Note that this is not in agreement with Frisch's conjecture quoted in Section 1.5. Also note that the idea of proportional changes in the ν_{ij}'s and ϕ is similar to the procedure described in Section 3.3, where we formulated a generalization of the Rotterdam

Model. The normalized price coefficient

$$\mu_{ij} = \frac{\nu_{ij}}{\phi} \tag{3.13}$$

is a constant both when ν_{ij} and ϕ are proportional to $\bar{W}_{gt}$ and also under condition (3.12) of Section 3.3.

The Absolute Price Version of the Modified Model

Consider the price term of (3.9), using (3.10),

$$\sum_{j \in S_g} \nu_{ij}^* Dp_{jt} - \frac{\phi \mu_i}{\bar{W}_{gt}} \sum_{j \in S_g} \frac{\mu_j}{M_g} Dp_{jt} = \sum_{j \in S_g} \pi_{ij}^* Dp_{jt} \tag{3.14}$$

where

$$\pi_{ij}^* = \nu_{ij}^* - \frac{\phi M_g}{\bar{W}_{gt}} \frac{\mu_i}{M_g} \frac{\mu_j}{M_g} \qquad i, j \in S_g \tag{3.15}$$

is the *modified conditional Slutsky coefficient* of the ith and the jth commodities. Substitution of the right-hand side of (3.14) in (3.9) gives

$$\frac{\bar{w}_{it}}{\bar{W}_{gt}} Dq_{it} = \frac{\mu_i}{M_g} DQ_{gt} + \sum_{j \in S_g} \pi_{ij}^* Dp_{jt} + \varepsilon_{it}^* \tag{3.16}$$

This is the absolute price version of (3.9). It follows from (1.8) and (3.8) that the disturbances of these two equations give zero when summed over $i \in S_g$:

$$\sum_{i \in S_g} \varepsilon_{it}^* = 0 \tag{3.17}$$

On comparing (3.15) with (1.10) and (3.8) we conclude

$$\pi_{ij}^* = \frac{\pi_{ij}^g}{\bar{W}_{gt}} \qquad i, j \in S_g \tag{3.18}$$

This shows that the new parametrization treats the original conditional Slutsky coefficients as varying proportionally to $\bar{W}_{gt}$. Also, in view of (1.12),

$$\sum_{j \in S_g} \pi_{ij}^* = 0 \qquad i \in S_g \tag{3.19}$$

It is readily verified that the $n_g \times n_g$ modified conditional Slutsky matrix is symmetric and negative semidefinite with rank $n_g - 1$.

Application to Meats

We now interpret S_g as meat and use (3.19) to write (3.16) as

$$\frac{\bar{w}_{it}}{\bar{W}_{gt}} Dq_{it} = \frac{\mu_i}{M_g} DQ_{gt} + \sum_{j=1}^{3} \pi_{ij}^* (Dp_{jt} - Dp_{4t}) + \varepsilon_{it}^* \tag{3.20}$$

We assume that the disturbances (the ε*'s) have a constant contemporaneous covariance matrix. The estimation procedure for (3.20) is then virtually identical to that for (2.3); the only modifications necessary are a division by $\bar{W}_{gt}$ of the left-hand variable and of the first variable on the right. This leads to the least-squares estimates which are shown in the upper part of Table 7.5. Notice that the estimates of the modified conditional Slutsky coefficients are almost 20 times larger than their predecessors of Table 7.4. This is in agreement with the division by the total-meat budget share $\bar{W}_{gt}$ in (3.18), which varies between .05 and .07. When constants are added to (3.20), least squares yields the following estimates of their values:

(3.21)

Beef:	.0045 (.0022)	Chicken:	.0006 (.0009)
Pork:	−.0042 (.0020)	Lamb:	−.0010 (.0005)

The implied t ratios are somewhat larger than those of (2.5), but they do not

TABLE 7.5

SECOND SET OF ESTIMATES OF CONDITIONAL MARGINAL SHARES AND SLUTSKY COEFFICIENTS OF MEATS

	Conditional marginal share	Modified conditional Slutsky coefficients			
		Unconstrained estimates			
Beef	.712 (.055)	−.197 (.048)	.176 (.020)	.026 (.023)	−.005 (.063)
Pork	.192 (.049)	.157 (.043)	−.219 (.018)	.050 (.020)	.012 (.057)
Chicken	.046 (.022)	.009 (.019)	.030 (.008)	−.087 (.009)	.048 (.025)
Lamb	.050 (.012)	.030 (.010)	.013 (.004)	.012 (.005)	−.055 (.014)
		Symmetry-constrained estimates			
Beef	.692 (.049)	−.227 (.019)	.164 (.014)	.033 (.009)	.029 (.010)
Pork	.199 (.044)		−.214 (.014)	.038 (.007)	.012 (.004)
Chicken	.059 (.021)			−.084 (.009)	.013 (.005)
Lamb	.050 (.012)				−.055 (.014)

present cogent evidence that the use of constant terms is appropriate. Given the limited economic meaning of such terms, we shall therefore suppress them.

The test statistic for Slutsky symmetry takes a low value, .65, for (3.20). The symmetry-constrained estimates are shown in the lower half of Table 7.5. The latent roots of the symmetric estimate of the modified conditional Slutsky matrix are 0, −.071, −.123 and −.385; hence this estimate is negative semidefinite with rank 3. The matrix of mean squares and products of the residuals corresponding to the symmetry-constrained estimates of (3.20) is

$$(3.22) \qquad 10^{-6}\begin{bmatrix} 54.10 & -43.26 & -9.94 & -.90 \\ & 43.11 & 1.36 & -1.21 \\ & & 8.91 & -.33 \\ & & & 2.44 \end{bmatrix} \begin{matrix} \text{Beef} \\ \text{Pork} \\ \text{Chicken} \\ \text{Lamb} \end{matrix}$$

Note that this matrix cannot be directly compared with (2.6) because (2.3) and (3.20) have different left-hand variables.

Choosing Between the Two Parametrizations

In order to decide which parametrization, (2.3) or (3.20), is to be preferred, we apply the tests against nonzero means and autocorrelation described in Section 5.6 and we compute information inaccuracies. The test statistics are shown in the first two lines of Table 7.6. The values of the statistics for

TABLE 7.6

RESIDUAL TEST STATISTICS AND AVERAGE INFORMATION INACCURACIES

	(2.3)	(3.20)	No-change extrapolation
Test against			
nonzero means	3.24	4.65	
autocorrelation	6.84	6.60	
Information inaccuracies:*			
all four meats	236.7	196.3	337.2
Beef	141.7	109.1	221.2
Pork	127.4	94.7	165.1
Chicken	47.0	42.1	71.0
Lamb	43.8	45.1	58.6

* Average information inaccuracies of the 22-year sample period, all to be multiplied by 10^{-6}.

zero means are both acceptable for $\chi^2(3)$. Those for autocorrelation are both close to the theoretical value 6 and far from the limits 0 and 12.

The last five lines of Table 7.6 contain average information inaccuracies for the conditional budget shares of meats. These are averages over $t=1,\dots,T$ of

$$I_t = \sum_{i=1}^{4} \frac{w_{it}}{W_{gt}} \log \frac{w_{it}/W_{gt}}{\hat{w}_{it}/\hat{W}_{gt}} \tag{3.23}$$

$$I_{it} = \frac{w_{it}}{W_{gt}} \log \frac{w_{it}/W_{gt}}{\hat{w}_{it}/\hat{W}_{gt}} + \left(1 - \frac{w_{it}}{W_{gt}}\right) \log \frac{1 - w_{it}/W_{gt}}{1 - \hat{w}_{it}/\hat{W}_{gt}} \tag{3.24}$$

In the last column of the table $\hat{w}_{it}/\hat{W}_{gt}$ is specified as $w_{i,t-1}/W_{g,t-1}$, which is no-change extrapolation, and in the two other columns as the estimate obtained from (2.3) or (3.20). It follows from (3.4) that the estimate based on (3.20) can be computed by subtracting a residual from the corresponding observed conditional budget share. In the case of (2.3) we have to divide the residual by $\bar{W}_{gt}$ before it is subtracted.

The results shown in Table 7.6 indicate that both parametrizations have a fit substantially better than that of no-change extrapolation. They also show that (3.20) has a better fit than (2.3), particularly with respect to Beef and Pork; no correction for loss of degrees of freedom is needed for this comparison, because both specifications use the same number of unconstrained parameters. We shall therefore use (3.20) in the sequel, which means that the conditional Slutsky coefficients are considered as varying proportionally to $\bar{W}_{gt}$.

One might perhaps think that the criterion (3.23), which is formulated in terms of *conditional* budget shares, will favor (3.20) to (2.3) because the left-hand variable of (3.20) is the quantity component of the change in such a share and that of (2.3) is the quantity component of the change in an *unconditional* budget share. This argument is not satisfactory. Both (2.3) and (3.20) are conditional demand equations for meats; they differ as to whether the conditional Slutsky coefficients are or are not constant. In neither case is the estimation based on minimizing the average of (3.23) over t. The constrained generalized least-squares method minimizes a quadratic form in the residuals subject to the constraints implied by Slutsky symmetry; the matrix of this quadratic form is determined by the variances and covariances of the disturbances. On the other hand, if we apply the quadratic approximation given in eq. (1.4) of Section 5.1 to the information inaccuracy (3.23), we obtain a weighted sum of squares of residuals for both (2.3) and (3.20). This amounts to a quadratic form with a diagonal matrix, which differs from the matrix of the quadratic form that is minimized.

Conditional Income Elasticities

By dividing a conditional marginal share by the corresponding conditional budget share, we obtain the ratio of the income elasticity of the good to that of the group to which it belongs:

$$\frac{\mu_i/M_g}{\bar{w}_{it}/\bar{W}_{gt}} = \frac{\mu_i/\bar{w}_{it}}{M_g/\bar{W}_{gt}} \qquad i \in S_g \tag{3.25}$$

We shall refer to this ratio as the *conditional income elasticity* of the ith commodity within the group S_g. The budget-share-weighted mean of these elasticities is equal to 1:

$$\sum_{i \in S_g} \frac{\bar{w}_{it}}{\bar{W}_{gt}} \frac{\mu_i/\bar{w}_{it}}{M_g/\bar{W}_{gt}} = 1 \tag{3.26}$$

Using the symmetry-constrained estimates of the conditional marginal shares of Table 7.5 and the average budget shares given in (2.1), we obtain the following estimates of the conditional income elasticities of the four meats:

(3.27) Beef: 1.39 Pork: .57 Chicken: .49 Lamb: 1.80

This indicates that, within meat, Beef and Lamb are luxuries and Pork and Chicken are necessities. The qualification "within meat" is obviously important; to obtain estimates of the unconditional income elasticities we have to multiply the four figures in (3.27) by the income elasticity of the meat group.

Conditional income elasticities are useful when the analyst is interested in the effect of a change in the consumption volume of the commodity group on a conditional budget share. By substituting either (1.6) or (3.9) for the term containing Dq_{it} in the decomposition (3.4), we find that the DQ_{gt} term of this decomposition becomes

$$\left(\frac{\mu_i}{M_g} - \frac{\bar{w}_{it}}{\bar{W}_{gt}}\right) DQ_{gt} \tag{3.28}$$

Hence, other things being equal, an increase in the demand for the commodity group ($DQ_{gt}>0$) raises or lowers the ith conditional budget share depending on whether $\mu_i/M_g \gtrless \bar{w}_{it}/\bar{W}_{gt}$. Since the inequalities

$$\frac{\mu_i}{M_g} \gtrless \frac{\bar{w}_{it}}{\bar{W}_{gt}} \quad \text{and} \quad \frac{\mu_i/\bar{w}_{it}}{M_g/\bar{W}_{gt}} \gtrless 1$$

are equivalent, the implication is that an increase in the demand for S_g raises the conditional budget shares of those of its commodities that have conditional income elasticities larger than 1. This applies to Beef and Lamb in (3.27), but not to Pork and Chicken.

7.4 The Demand for Meats in the United States: (3) The Second-Moment Model

The Connecting Parameter

Application of the second-moment model (1.17) for $i, j \in S_g$ to the disturbances defined in (3.8) gives

$$\text{cov}\,(\varepsilon_{it}^*, \varepsilon_{jt}^*) = \frac{\sigma^2}{\phi \bar{W}_{gt}^2}\, \pi_{ij}^g$$

In view of (3.18) this may be written as

$$\text{(4.1)} \qquad \text{cov}\,(\varepsilon_{it}^*, \varepsilon_{jt}^*) = \frac{\sigma^2}{\phi \bar{W}_{gt}}\, \pi_{ij}^* \qquad i, j \in S_g$$

Recall that we treat π_{ij}^* as a constant in (3.16) and ϕ as varying proportionally to $\bar{W}_{gt}$. Therefore, if we postulate that the ε^*'s have a constant contemporaneous covariance matrix [which we did when estimating (3.20) by least squares and constrained generalized least squares], the implication is that σ also varies proportionally to $\bar{W}_{gt}$. So we may write (4.1) in the form

$$\text{(4.2)} \qquad \text{cov}\,(\varepsilon_{it}^*, \varepsilon_{jt}^*) = -\frac{\pi_{ij}^*}{\gamma} \qquad i, j \in S_g$$

where

$$\text{(4.3)} \qquad \gamma = -\frac{\phi \bar{W}_{gt}}{\sigma^2}$$

is a positive constant.

If we consider unconditional rather than conditional demand equations, $\bar{W}_{gt}$ becomes 1 because S_g is the group of all n commodities. We may then write (4.2) and (4.3) as

$$\pi_{ij} = -\gamma \operatorname{cov}(\varepsilon_{it}, \varepsilon_{jt}) \quad \text{where} \quad \gamma = -\frac{\phi}{\sigma^2} \tag{4.4}$$

Hence γ is a parameter which connects the coefficients of the first- and the second-moment models (the Slutsky coefficients and the covariances of the disturbances). We shall therefore refer to γ as the *connecting parameter*. The two-sided nature of this parameter is also evident from the second equation in (4.4); it shows that γ involves ϕ, which is a first-moment parameter, and also σ^2, which is the basic variance measure of the second-moment model (1.16). In our application to meats we shall work with the γ definition (4.3).

Verification of the Second-Moment Model for Meats

Let us approximate the modified conditional Slutsky coefficient in the right-hand side of (4.2) by its symmetry-constrained estimate (Table 7.5), and the covariance on the left by the corresponding mean product of the residuals associated with these estimates. The matrix of these mean squares and products of residuals is given in (3.22).

Equation (4.2) amounts to a proportionality of the disturbance covariances and the corresponding Slutsky coefficients. If it is valid, we should expect an approximate proportionality when these parameters are replaced by the estimates mentioned in the previous paragraph. The evidence is shown in Figure 7.1 by means of 10 small circles, each of which corresponds to one of the four variances or to one of the six covariances.[1] The four circles in the positive quadrant refer to the four variances and the corresponding diagonal elements of the modified conditional Slutsky matrix; they are indicated by B, P, C and L for Beef, Pork, Chicken and Lamb, respectively. [Note that the variable measured horizontally is *minus* the modified conditional Slutsky coefficient.] The six circles to the left of the vertical axis all refer to covariances, with BP indicating that of Beef and Pork.

Evidently, the 10 points are not far from the upward sloping straight

[1] Figure 7.1 is similar to Figure 6.3 (page 317 of Volume 1) with two exceptions: the scales of Figure 7.1 are not logarithmic and the variable measured vertically includes the variances as well as the covariances.

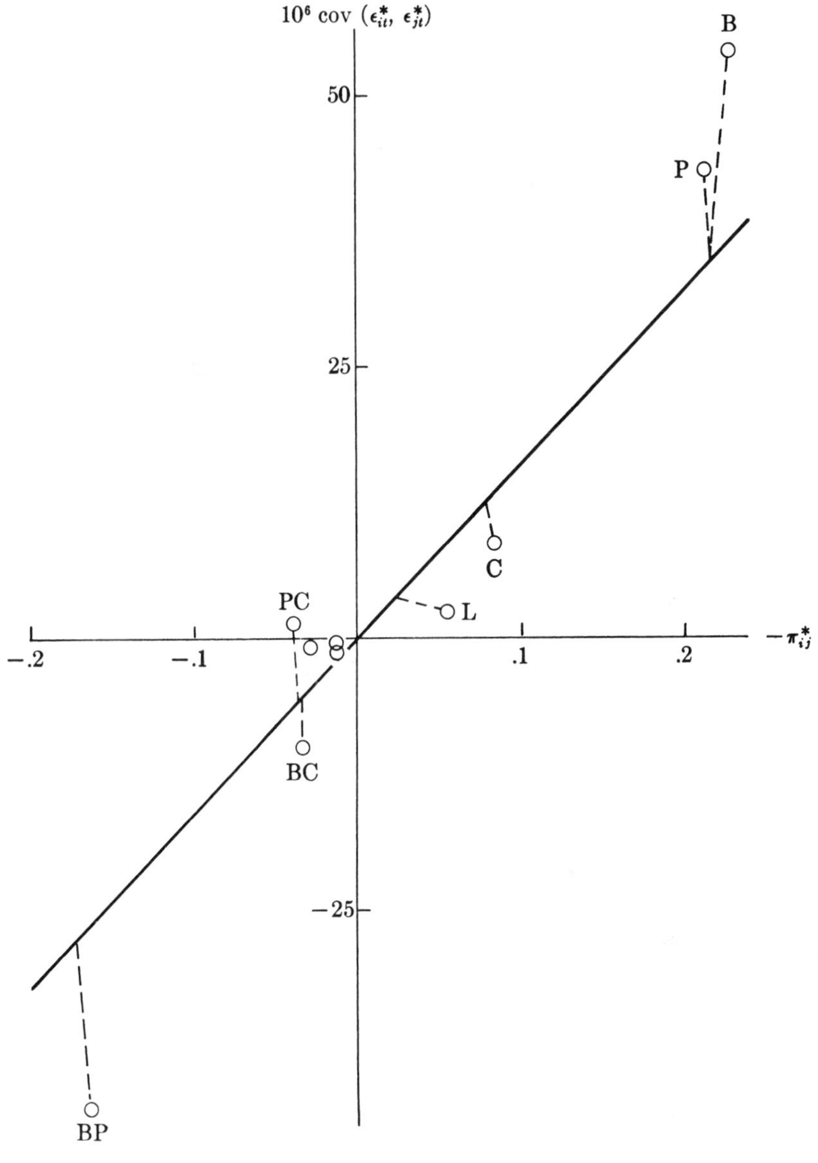

Fig. 7.1 Verification of the second-moment model for meats

line through the origin, which is encouraging for the second-moment model. [The broken lines in the figure will be explained in Section 7.5.] Approximately the same picture emerges when we use the symmetry-constrained estimates of Table 7.4 and the matrix (2.6), which correspond to the parametrization (2.2).

The objective of this section is to develop a maximum-likelihood procedure for the parameters of the first- and second-moment models jointly under the assumption of normally distributed disturbances. Numerical estimates for meats are discussed in Section 7.5.

Notation

Under the proportionality (4.2) we can write (3.20) as

$$\frac{\bar{w}_{it}}{\bar{W}_{gt}} Dq_{it} = \frac{\mu_i}{M_g} DQ_{gt} - \gamma \sum_{j=1}^{3} \omega_{ij} (Dp_{jt} - Dp_{4t}) + \varepsilon_{it}^* \tag{4.5}$$

where γ is defined in (4.3) and

$$\omega_{ij} = \operatorname{cov}(\varepsilon_{it}^*, \varepsilon_{jt}^*) \tag{4.6}$$

We define $\mathbf{\Omega}$ as the 3×3 matrix $[\omega_{ij}]$, corresponding to Beef, Pork and Chicken. Then (4.5) for $i=1$, 2 and 3 can be written in matrix form,

$$\mathbf{z}_t = \boldsymbol{\mu}_0 DQ_{gt} - \gamma \mathbf{\Omega} \mathbf{p}_t + \boldsymbol{\varepsilon}_t \tag{4.7}$$

where

(4.8)

$$\mathbf{z}_t = \begin{bmatrix} \bar{w}_{1t} Dq_{1t}/\bar{W}_{gt} \\ \bar{w}_{2t} Dq_{2t}/\bar{W}_{gt} \\ \bar{w}_{3t} Dq_{3t}/\bar{W}_{gt} \end{bmatrix} \quad \boldsymbol{\mu}_0 = \begin{bmatrix} \mu_1/M_g \\ \mu_2/M_g \\ \mu_3/M_g \end{bmatrix} \quad \mathbf{p}_t = \begin{bmatrix} Dp_{1t} - Dp_{4t} \\ Dp_{2t} - Dp_{4t} \\ Dp_{3t} - Dp_{4t} \end{bmatrix} \quad \boldsymbol{\varepsilon}_t = \begin{bmatrix} \varepsilon_{1t}^* \\ \varepsilon_{2t}^* \\ \varepsilon_{3t}^* \end{bmatrix}$$

It may be verified that (4.7) is a conditional version of eq. (8.6) of Section 6.8 when the second-moment model is applied to the latter equation.

The Log-Likelihood Function

If $\boldsymbol{\varepsilon}_1, \ldots, \boldsymbol{\varepsilon}_T$ are independent random drawings from a three-dimensional normal population with zero means and covariance matrix $\mathbf{\Omega}$, the logarithmic likelihood function associated with (4.7) is

$$\log L = -\tfrac{3}{2} T \log 2\pi + \tfrac{1}{2} T \log |\mathbf{\Omega}^{-1}| - \tfrac{1}{2} \sum_{t=1}^{T} (\mathbf{z}_t - \boldsymbol{\mu}_0 DQ_{gt} + \gamma \mathbf{\Omega} \mathbf{p}_t)' \mathbf{\Omega}^{-1} (\mathbf{z}_t - \boldsymbol{\mu}_0 DQ_{gt} + \gamma \mathbf{\Omega} \mathbf{p}_t) \tag{4.9}$$

The parameters γ and $\boldsymbol{\mu}_0$ occur only in the quadratic term which is shown in the second line. It will prove convenient to write this term in two alternative ways:

$$(4.10)\quad -\tfrac{1}{2}\sum_{t=1}^{T}(\mathbf{z}_t-\boldsymbol{\mu}_0 DQ_{gt})'\,\boldsymbol{\Omega}^{-1}(\mathbf{z}_t-\boldsymbol{\mu}_0 DQ_{gt})$$
$$-\tfrac{1}{2}\gamma^2\sum_{t=1}^{T}\mathbf{p}_t'\boldsymbol{\Omega}\mathbf{p}_t-\gamma\sum_{t=1}^{T}\mathbf{z}_t'\mathbf{p}_t+\gamma\boldsymbol{\mu}_0'\sum_{t=1}^{T}(DQ_{gt})\,\mathbf{p}_t$$

and

$$(4.11)\quad -\tfrac{1}{2}\sum_{t=1}^{T}\mathbf{z}_t'\boldsymbol{\Omega}^{-1}\mathbf{z}_t-\tfrac{1}{2}\boldsymbol{\mu}_0'\boldsymbol{\Omega}^{-1}\boldsymbol{\mu}_0\sum_{t=1}^{T}(DQ_{gt})^2+\boldsymbol{\mu}_0'\boldsymbol{\Omega}^{-1}\sum_{t=1}^{T}(DQ_{gt})\,\mathbf{z}_t$$
$$-\tfrac{1}{2}\gamma^2\sum_{t=1}^{T}\mathbf{p}_t'\boldsymbol{\Omega}\mathbf{p}_t-\gamma\sum_{t=1}^{T}\mathbf{z}_t'\mathbf{p}_t+\gamma\boldsymbol{\mu}_0'\sum_{t=1}^{T}(DQ_{gt})\,\mathbf{p}_t$$

First-Order Derivatives of the Log-Likelihood Function

The first-order derivatives of $\log L$ with respect to γ and $\boldsymbol{\mu}_0$ are obtained by differentiating (4.11):

$$(4.12)\quad \frac{\partial \log L}{\partial \gamma}=-\gamma\sum_{t=1}^{T}\mathbf{p}_t'\boldsymbol{\Omega}\mathbf{p}_t-\sum_{t=1}^{T}\mathbf{z}_t'\mathbf{p}_t+\boldsymbol{\mu}_0'\sum_{t=1}^{T}(DQ_{gt})\,\mathbf{p}_t$$

$$(4.13)\quad \frac{\partial \log L}{\partial \boldsymbol{\mu}_0}=-\boldsymbol{\Omega}^{-1}\boldsymbol{\mu}_0\sum_{t=1}^{T}(DQ_{gt})^2+\boldsymbol{\Omega}^{-1}\sum_{t=1}^{T}(DQ_{gt})\mathbf{z}_t+\gamma\sum_{t=1}^{T}(DQ_{gt})\,\mathbf{p}_t$$

For the derivative with respect to $\boldsymbol{\Omega}^{-1}$ we have, as is shown in the next subsection,

$$(4.14)\quad \frac{\partial \log L}{\partial \boldsymbol{\Omega}^{-1}}=\tfrac{1}{2}T\,(\gamma^2\boldsymbol{\Omega}\mathbf{E}'\mathbf{E}\boldsymbol{\Omega}+\boldsymbol{\Omega}-\mathbf{M}_0)'$$

where

$$(4.15)\quad \mathbf{E}'\mathbf{E}=\frac{1}{T}\sum_{t=1}^{T}\mathbf{p}_t\mathbf{p}_t'$$

$$(4.16)\quad \mathbf{M}_0=\frac{1}{T}\sum_{t=1}^{T}(\mathbf{z}_t-\boldsymbol{\mu}_0 DQ_{gt})\,(\mathbf{z}_t-\boldsymbol{\mu}_0 DQ_{gt})'$$

The 3×3 matrix $\mathbf{M}_0$ consists of the mean squares and products of the left-hand variables corrected for the effect of the change in the volume of total-meat consumption. The matrix $\mathbf{E}'\mathbf{E}$ consists of the mean squares and products of the three deflated price log-changes, and $\mathbf{E}$ may be interpreted as any 3×3 matrix which satisfies (4.15). Note that $\mathbf{M}_0$ involves the unknown parameter vector $\boldsymbol{\mu}_0$; the zero subscript serves as a reminder of this fact. The matrix $\mathbf{E}$ does not involve unknown parameters.

Both $\mathbf{M}_0$ and $\mathbf{E}'\mathbf{E}$ are moment matrices and are hence symmetric and positive semidefinite. We shall assume that both are nonsingular, so that $\mathbf{E}$ is then also nonsingular and

$$\text{(4.17)} \qquad \mathbf{E}\mathbf{M}_0\mathbf{E}' \quad \text{is symmetric and positive definite}$$

If $\mathbf{E}'\mathbf{E}$ were singular, there would be a linear relationship among the deflated price log-changes, implying that the least-squares regressions based on (3.20) are impossible owing to multicollinearity. If $\mathbf{M}_0$ were singular for some $\boldsymbol{\mu}_0$, there would be a nontrivial linear combination of the three left-hand variables which depends only on DQ_{gt}, not on the price log-changes.

Derivations

We imposed symmetry on $\boldsymbol{\Omega}$ in (4.10) and (4.11). If symmetry were not imposed, the last term in (4.10) would change from $\gamma\boldsymbol{\mu}_0' \sum_t (DQ_{gt}) \mathbf{p}_t$, which does not involve $\boldsymbol{\Omega}$, to the much more complicated expression

$$\tfrac{1}{2}\gamma\boldsymbol{\mu}_0' \sum_{t=1}^{T} (DQ_{gt})\,\mathbf{p}_t + \tfrac{1}{2}\gamma \sum_{t=1}^{T} (DQ_{gt})\,\mathbf{p}_t'\boldsymbol{\Omega}'\boldsymbol{\Omega}^{-1}\boldsymbol{\mu}_0$$

which does depend on $\boldsymbol{\Omega}$. Considerations of simplicity thus suggest that we should maximize the likelihood function with respect to a symmetry-constrained $\boldsymbol{\Omega}$ (or $\boldsymbol{\Omega}^{-1}$). However, this is less convenient in other respects, particularly with regard to the second term of (4.9) which involves the determinant of $\boldsymbol{\Omega}^{-1}$, and we shall therefore not impose symmetry on $\boldsymbol{\Omega}^{-1}$ when differentiating $\log L$ with respect to this matrix. This may seem inconsistent; if we use symmetry in (4.10), we should also impose it on $\boldsymbol{\Omega}^{-1}$ in the differentiation procedure. Nevertheless, it will appear that we can safely proceed in this apparently contradictory manner. Maximization of the likelihood function with respect to an unconstrained $\boldsymbol{\Omega}^{-1}$ can never lead to a lower value of this function than maximization with respect to a symmetry-constrained $\boldsymbol{\Omega}^{-1}$. If it turns out that the former maximum problem yields a symmetric maximizing $\boldsymbol{\Omega}^{-1}$ in spite of the fact that this symmetry was not imposed, we know that the solution is the maximum-likelihood solution. We shall be able to conclude from eq. (4.24) below that this is indeed the case.

Write $d(\log L)$ for the change in $\log L$ caused by $d\boldsymbol{\Omega}^{-1}$. The contribution of the second term in (4.9) to $d(\log L)$ is

$$\tfrac{1}{2}T \sum_{i=1}^{3} \sum_{j=1}^{3} \omega_{ji}\, d\omega^{ij} = \tfrac{1}{2}T \operatorname{tr}(d\boldsymbol{\Omega}^{-1})\,\boldsymbol{\Omega} \tag{4.18}$$

because the derivative of $\log|\boldsymbol{\Omega}^{-1}|$ with respect to $\boldsymbol{\Omega}^{-1}=[\omega^{ij}]$ is $\boldsymbol{\Omega}'$. For the third term of (4.9) we use (4.10) and $d\boldsymbol{\Omega}=-\boldsymbol{\Omega}(d\boldsymbol{\Omega}^{-1})\,\boldsymbol{\Omega}$. The contribution of this term to $d(\log L)$ is then

$$\begin{aligned}
&-\tfrac{1}{2}\sum_{t=1}^{T}(\mathbf{z}_t-\boldsymbol{\mu}_0 DQ_{gt})'\,d\boldsymbol{\Omega}^{-1}(\mathbf{z}_t-\boldsymbol{\mu}_0 DQ_{gt})+\tfrac{1}{2}\gamma^2\sum_{t=1}^{T}\mathbf{p}_t'\boldsymbol{\Omega}\,(d\boldsymbol{\Omega}^{-1})\,\boldsymbol{\Omega}\mathbf{p}_t\\
&\quad=-\tfrac{1}{2}\operatorname{tr} d\boldsymbol{\Omega}^{-1}\left[\sum_{t=1}^{T}(\mathbf{z}_t-\boldsymbol{\mu}_0 DQ_{gt})(\mathbf{z}_t-\boldsymbol{\mu}_0 DQ_{gt})'-\gamma^2\boldsymbol{\Omega}\left(\sum_{t=1}^{T}\mathbf{p}_t\mathbf{p}_t'\right)\boldsymbol{\Omega}\right]\\
&\quad=-\tfrac{1}{2}T\operatorname{tr} d\boldsymbol{\Omega}^{-1}(\mathbf{M}_0-\gamma^2\boldsymbol{\Omega}\mathbf{E}'\mathbf{E}\boldsymbol{\Omega})
\end{aligned}$$

We add this to (4.18),

$$d(\log L)=\tfrac{1}{2}T\operatorname{tr} d\boldsymbol{\Omega}^{-1}(\gamma^2\boldsymbol{\Omega}\mathbf{E}'\mathbf{E}\boldsymbol{\Omega}+\boldsymbol{\Omega}-\mathbf{M}_0) \tag{4.19}$$

from which (4.14) follows immediately. Note that the right-hand side of (4.14) is a symmetric matrix if $\boldsymbol{\Omega}$ is symmetric.

Equating the First-Order Derivatives to Zero

To obtain maximum-likelihood estimators of the parameters, we equate all first-order derivatives of the log-likelihood function to zero. In the case of (4.12) and (4.13) this gives

$$\begin{bmatrix} \sum_t \mathbf{p}_t'\boldsymbol{\Omega}\mathbf{p}_t & -\sum_t (DQ_{gt})\,\mathbf{p}_t' \\ -\sum_t (DQ_{gt})\,\mathbf{p}_t & \boldsymbol{\Omega}^{-1}\sum_t (DQ_{gt})^2 \end{bmatrix} \begin{bmatrix} \gamma \\ \boldsymbol{\mu}_0 \end{bmatrix} = \begin{bmatrix} -\sum_t \mathbf{p}_t'\mathbf{z}_t \\ \boldsymbol{\Omega}^{-1}\sum_t (DQ_{gt})\,\mathbf{z}_t \end{bmatrix} \tag{4.20}$$

where all summations are over $t=1,\ldots,T$, and γ, $\boldsymbol{\mu}_0$ and $\boldsymbol{\Omega}$ are to be interpreted as maximum-likelihood estimators. Note that (4.20) is a linear equation system in the γ and $\boldsymbol{\mu}_0$ estimators (given $\boldsymbol{\Omega}$).

In view of (4.14) the derivatives of $\log L$ with respect to all ω^{ij}'s vanish if and only if

$$\gamma^2\boldsymbol{\Omega}\mathbf{E}'\mathbf{E}\boldsymbol{\Omega}+\boldsymbol{\Omega}-\mathbf{M}_0=\mathbf{0} \tag{4.21}$$

Since $\mathbf{E}$ is nonsingular, this equation is equivalent to that obtained by pre- and postmultiplication by $\mathbf{E}$ and $\mathbf{E}'$, respectively:

$$\gamma^2(\mathbf{E}\boldsymbol{\Omega}\mathbf{E}')^2+\mathbf{E}\boldsymbol{\Omega}\mathbf{E}'-\mathbf{E}\mathbf{M}_0\mathbf{E}'=\mathbf{0} \tag{4.22}$$

This is a quadratic equation in the matrix $\mathbf{E\Omega E'}$. Its solution is described in the next subsection and the results can be summarized as follows. Since $\mathbf{EM_0E'}$ is symmetric and positive definite [as stated in (4.17)], it can be diagonalized,

$$\mathbf{EM_0E'} = \mathbf{FGF'} \tag{4.23}$$

where $\mathbf{F}$ is a 3×3 orthogonal matrix whose columns are characteristic vectors of $\mathbf{EM_0E'}$ and $\mathbf{G}$ is a 3×3 diagonal matrix whose diagonal elements are the latent roots of $\mathbf{EM_0E'}$. These roots, to be written g_1, g_2 and g_3, are positive because $\mathbf{EM_0E'}$ is positive definite. The solution of (4.22) is

$$\mathbf{\Omega} = (\mathbf{E}^{-1}\mathbf{F})\,\mathbf{H}(\mathbf{E}^{-1}\mathbf{F})' \tag{4.24}$$

where $\mathbf{H}$ is a 3×3 diagonal matrix whose i^{th} diagonal element is

$$h_i = \frac{-1 + \sqrt{1 + 4\gamma^2 g_i}}{2\gamma^2} \qquad i = 1, 2, 3 \tag{4.25}$$

The $\mathbf{\Omega}$ solution (4.24) is evidently symmetric, so that it is indeed the maximum-likelihood estimator. Also, since the estimates of the modified conditional Slutsky coefficients are computed as $-\gamma\mathbf{\Omega}$, it is thus unnecessary to impose symmetry on these coefficients in the present approach. Note finally that the coefficient h_i defined in (4.25) is the positive solution of the quadratic equation

$$\gamma^2 x^2 + x - g_i = 0 \tag{4.26}$$

This equation is identical to (4.22) when we replace $\mathbf{E\Omega E'}$ by the scalar x and $\mathbf{EM_0E'}$ by its ith latent root.

More Derivations

Write $\mathbf{I}_3$ for the 3×3 unit matrix and consider

$$\left(\gamma\mathbf{E\Omega E'} + \frac{1}{2\gamma}\mathbf{I}_3\right)^2 = \gamma^2(\mathbf{E\Omega E'})^2 + \mathbf{E\Omega E'} + \frac{1}{4\gamma^2}\mathbf{I}_3$$

This shows that we can write (4.22) in the form

$$\left(\gamma\mathbf{E\Omega E'} + \frac{1}{2\gamma}\mathbf{I}_3\right)^2 = \mathbf{EM_0E'} + \frac{1}{4\gamma^2}\mathbf{I}_3 = \mathbf{FGF'} + \frac{1}{4\gamma^2}\mathbf{I}_3 \tag{4.27}$$

where the last step is based on (4.23). Using $\mathbf{FF}'=\mathbf{I}_3$, we can write (4.27) as

$$\left(\gamma\mathbf{E\Omega E}' + \frac{1}{2\gamma}\mathbf{I}_3\right)^2 = \mathbf{F}\left(\mathbf{G} + \frac{1}{4\gamma^2}\mathbf{I}_3\right)\mathbf{F}' \tag{4.28}$$

which shows that the matrix on the left has characteristic vectors equal to the columns of $\mathbf{F}$ and latent roots equal to the diagonal elements of the diagonal matrix $\mathbf{G}+(4\gamma^2)^{-1}\mathbf{I}_3$. But the square of a square matrix has the same characteristic vectors as the matrix itself, and latent roots equal to the squares of the roots of that matrix. Therefore, (4.28) implies

$$\gamma\mathbf{E\Omega E}' + \frac{1}{2\gamma}\mathbf{I}_3 = \mathbf{F}\left(\mathbf{G} + \frac{1}{4\gamma^2}\mathbf{I}_3\right)^{1/2}\mathbf{F}' \tag{4.29}$$

where the diagonal matrix on the right consists of elements that are square roots of the corresponding elements of $\mathbf{G}+(4\gamma^2)^{-1}\mathbf{I}_3$. Note that we should take positive square roots because of the required positive definiteness of the $\mathbf{\Omega}$ estimator and the positive sign of γ.

Finally, noting that $(2\gamma)^{-1}\mathbf{I}_3$ in the left-hand side of (4.29) can be written as $(2\gamma)^{-1}\mathbf{FF}'$, we have

$$\gamma\mathbf{E\Omega E}' = \mathbf{F}\left[\left(\mathbf{G} + \frac{1}{4\gamma^2}\mathbf{I}_3\right)^{1/2} - \frac{1}{2\gamma}\mathbf{I}_3\right]\mathbf{F}'$$

or, after multiplying by $1/\gamma$,

$$\mathbf{E\Omega E}' = \mathbf{FHF}' \tag{4.30}$$

where $\mathbf{H}$ is the 3×3 diagonal matrix whose i^{th} diagonal element is defined in (4.25). The result (4.24) follows immediately from (4.30).

7.5 The Demand for Meats in the United States: (4) Estimates Under the Second-Moment Model

The estimation procedure described in the previous section is not linear in γ, $\boldsymbol{\mu}_0$ and $\mathbf{\Omega}$, so that an iterative procedure is needed. It is possible to simplify this procedure so that the iterations are confined to γ and $\mathbf{\Omega}$, after which the $\boldsymbol{\mu}_0$ estimate is obtained from the converged γ and $\mathbf{\Omega}$ estimates. The estimates are discussed first; the mathematics behind the procedure is explained thereafter.

Maximum-Likelihood Estimates

The converged estimate of γ is

$$\hat{\gamma} = 6.26 \times 10^3 \tag{5.1}$$

and those of the conditional marginal shares and the modified conditional Slutsky coefficients are shown in the middle part of Table 7.7 below the

TABLE 7.7

THIRD SET OF ESTIMATES OF CONDITIONAL MARGINAL SHARES AND SLUTSKY COEFFICIENTS OF MEATS

	Conditional marginal share	Modified conditional Slutsky coefficients			
		Symmetry-constrained estimates			
Beef	.692 (.049)	−.227 (.019)	.164 (.014)	.033 (.009)	.029 (.010)
Pork	.199 (.044)		−.214 (.014)	.038 (.007)	.012 (.004)
Chicken	.059 (.021)			−.084 (.009)	.013 (.005)
Lamb	.050 (.012)				−.055 (.014)
		First set of maximum-likelihood estimates			
Beef	.703	−.216	.173	.034	.008
Pork	.201		−.216	.035	.007
Chicken	.058			−.079	.009
Lamb	.039				−.024
		Second set of maximum-likelihood estimates			
Beef	.6841	−.2294	.1720	.0390	.0185
Pork	.2094		−.2145	.0368	.0057
Chicken	.0643			−.0776	.0017
Lamb	.0422				−.0258

symmetry-constrained estimates, which are reproduced from Table 7.5. [The last four lines of Table 7.7 will be discussed in Section 7.6.] No standard errors of maximum-likelihood estimates are computed. Since imposing the second-moment model (if valid) reduces the sampling variability of the estimator, we may use the standard errors in the first four lines of Table 7.7 as a guide for evaluating the accuracy of the maximum-likelihood estimates.

The estimates in the middle part of Table 7.7 are close to the corresponding values in the upper part except for the coefficients which involve Lamb. The second-moment model reduces the conditional marginal share of Lamb by a little over 20 percent. It has an even more sizable impact on the four modified conditional Slutsky coefficients involving Lamb, which are all forced in zero direction. We shall consider this in more detail in the next subsection.

Imposing the second-moment model amounts to projecting the 10 points represented by circles in Figure 7.1 on the straight line through the origin which corresponds to the maximum-likelihood estimates. The "projection paths" are indicated by broken lines in the figure.[1] Notice that the horizontal coordinates of the projections of B, P and C in the positive quadrant (corresponding to the diagonal Slutsky coefficients of Beef, Pork and Chicken) are rather close to the horizontal coordinates of the corresponding circles, and that the differences between their vertical coordinates are proportionately much larger. This means that the maximum-likelihood and symmetry-constrained estimates of these modified conditional Slutsky coefficients are pairwise closer to each other than the maximum-likelihood and symmetry-constrained estimates of the corresponding disturbance variances.[2] For Lamb (L in the positive quadrant) we have a much larger difference between the horizontal coordinates of the circle and its projeciton.

Comparison of First- and Second-Moment Information

The symmetry-constrained estimates of the diagonal elements of the modified conditional Slutsky matrix in Table 7.7 have t ratios well above 10 for Beef and Pork, about 10 for Chicken, and only about 4 for Lamb. The symmetry-constrained estimates of the disturbance variances have asymptotic t ratios of about 3.3 for each of the four meats.[3] Consequently, when

---

[1] The projections of B and P are identical in three places (see the middle part of Table 7.7) and are therefore represented by the same point on the line through the origin.

[2] The symmetry-constrained estimate of a disturbance variance is a mean square of residuals associated with the symmetry-constrained coefficient estimates. The maximum-likelihood estimate of a disturbance variance is obtained from (4.24); this estimate is not a mean square of maximum-likelihood residuals. The mean squares and products of the latter residuals will be considered in Section 7.7.

[3] See THEIL (1971, p. 128), who proves that under normality with T observations the least-squares estimator $\hat{v}$ of the disturbance variance v has a sampling variance equal to $2v^2/T$ for large T. The implied t ratio is thus $\hat{v}$ divided by $(2v^2/T)^{1/2}$, which becomes $(T/2)^{1/2}$ (equal to $\sqrt{11} \approx 3.3$ for $T=22$) when we approximate v by $\hat{v}$. The symmetry-constrained estimator has the same asymptotic property.

we impose the second-moment model by requiring that the estimates of these variances be proportional to those of the diagonal Slutsky elements, we should expect that the symmetry-constrained estimates of these elements carry much more weight than the corresponding variance estimates for Beef, Pork and Chicken, and that this is not so for Lamb. In other words, we expect that the first-moment information (on Slutsky coefficients) conveyed by the symmetry-constrained estimates dominates the second-moment information (on disturbance variances) in the case of Beef, Pork and Chicken, and that there is no such domination in the case of Lamb.

To analyze this in more detail we reproduce the matrix (3.22) of the mean squares and products of the residuals associated with the symmetry-constrained coefficient estimates:

$$(5.2) \qquad 10^{-6}\begin{bmatrix} 54.10 & -43.26 & -9.94 & -.90 \\ & 43.11 & 1.36 & -1.21 \\ & & 8.91 & -.33 \\ & & & 2.44 \end{bmatrix} \begin{matrix} \text{Beef} \\ \text{Pork} \\ \text{Chicken} \\ \text{Lamb} \end{matrix}$$

The second-moment model implies that the population counterparts of the

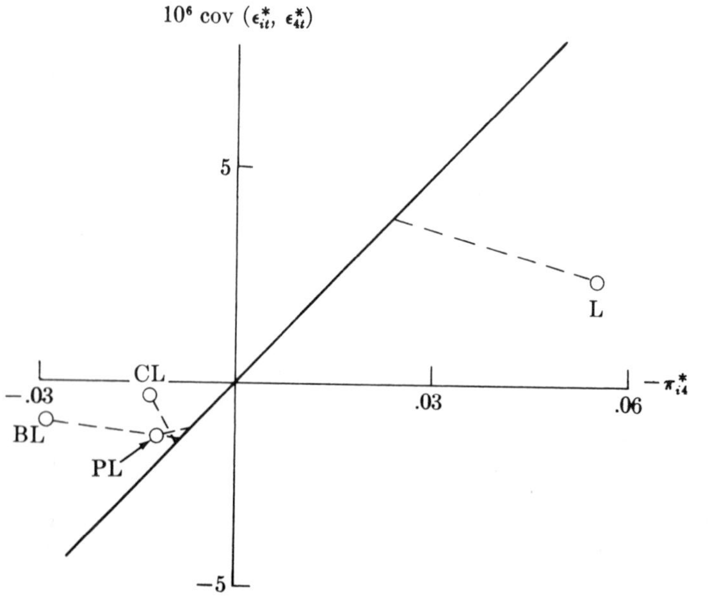

Fig. 7.2 Second moments involving Lamb

diagonal elements of (5.2) are proportional to those of the diagonal Slutsky estimates in the first four lines of Table 7.7. Let us compare the diagonal elements for Beef and Pork with that for Chicken. In (5.2) the former are about five or six times larger than the latter, whereas this ratio is less than 3 in the upper part of Table 7.7. In the middle part of the table, where the second-moment model is imposed, this ratio is still less than 3. This illustrates the domination of the first-moment information (the Slutsky estimates in the upper part of Table 7.7) in the case of Beef, Pork and Chicken.

Next compare the diagonal elements for Beef and Pork with that for Lamb. In (5.2) the former two are both on the order of 20 times larger than the latter. In the upper part of Table 7.7 this ratio is about 4, and in the middle part about 9, which is roughly equal to the geometric mean of 20 and 4. This illustrates that in the case of Lamb there is no clear domination of either the first- or the second-moment information.

The small mean square for Lamb in (5.2) implies that the residuals of this meat tend to be close to zero. Their mean products with the three other sets of residuals must therefore also be close to zero. The result is that the maximum-likelihood estimates of all modified conditional Slutsky coefficients involving Lamb are forced in zero direction. This is illustrated in Figure 7.2, which is an enlarged version of Figure 7.1 for Lamb only. All four projection paths are in the direction of the vertical axis. Also notice that the broken lines tend to be more horizontal than those in Figure 7.1 for meats other than Lamb. This illustrates the relative importance of the second-moment information for the coefficients involving Lamb.

Elimination of the Conditional Marginal Share Estimates

The remainder of this section concerns an iteration procedure which does not involve the vector $\boldsymbol{\mu}_0$. The result will also be convenient for a generalization to be discussed in Section 10.6.

We start by normalizing the vector $[DQ_{g1} \cdots DQ_{gT}]$ so that it has unit length. This yields

$$c_t = \frac{DQ_{gt}}{\left[\sum_{s=1}^{T} (DQ_{gs})^2\right]^{1/2}} \qquad t = 1, \ldots, T \tag{5.3}$$

with the c_t's obviously satisfying

$$\sum_{t=1}^{T} c_t^2 = 1 \tag{5.4}$$

We define $\mathbf{z}_0$ and $\mathbf{p}_0$ as the weighted sums of $\mathbf{z}_1, \ldots, \mathbf{z}_T$ and $\mathbf{p}_1, \ldots, \mathbf{p}_T$, respectively, with the c_t's as weights:

$$\mathbf{z}_0 = \sum_{t=1}^{T} c_t \mathbf{z}_t \qquad \mathbf{p}_0 = \sum_{t=1}^{T} c_t \mathbf{p}_t \tag{5.5}$$

The following property follows from (5.4):

$$\sum_{t=1}^{T} c_t (\mathbf{z}_t - c_t \mathbf{z}_0) = \sum_{t=1}^{T} c_t (\mathbf{p}_t - c_t \mathbf{p}_0) = \mathbf{0} \tag{5.6}$$

Next consider the second equation of (4.20),

$$-\gamma \sum_{t=1}^{T} (DQ_{gt})\, \mathbf{p}_t + \mathbf{\Omega}^{-1} \boldsymbol{\mu}_0 \sum_{t=1}^{T} (DQ_{gt})^2 = \mathbf{\Omega}^{-1} \sum_{t=1}^{T} (DQ_{gt})\, \mathbf{z}_t$$

which we solve for $\boldsymbol{\mu}_0$:

$$\boldsymbol{\mu}_0 = \frac{1}{\sum_{t=1}^{T} (DQ_{gt})^2} \sum_{t=1}^{T} DQ_{gt} (\mathbf{z}_t + \gamma \mathbf{\Omega} \mathbf{p}_t) \tag{5.7}$$

This implies

$$\begin{aligned} \boldsymbol{\mu}_0 DQ_{gt} &= \frac{DQ_{gt}}{\sum_{s=1}^{T} (DQ_{gs})^2} \sum_{s=1}^{T} DQ_{gs} (\mathbf{z}_s + \gamma \mathbf{\Omega} \mathbf{p}_s) \\ &= c_t \sum_{s=1}^{T} c_s (\mathbf{z}_s + \gamma \mathbf{\Omega} \mathbf{p}_s) = c_t (\mathbf{z}_0 + \gamma \mathbf{\Omega} \mathbf{p}_0) \end{aligned}$$

where the second step is based on (5.3) and the third on (5.5). So we have

$$\mathbf{z}_t - \boldsymbol{\mu}_0 DQ_{gt} = (\mathbf{z}_t - c_t \mathbf{z}_0) - c_t \gamma \mathbf{\Omega} \mathbf{p}_0 \tag{5.8}$$

which shows that the left-hand vector $\mathbf{z}_t$ corrected for the effect of DQ_{gt} can be written as the sum of $\mathbf{z}_t - c_t \mathbf{z}_0$, which is a known vector because it is determined by observations on variables, and a vector which involves γ and $\mathbf{\Omega}$.

We shall use (5.8) to eliminate $\boldsymbol{\mu}_0$. Note that the effect of DQ_{gt} on the left should be interpreted as the estimated effect, and $\boldsymbol{\mu}_0$ as the estimate of the true $\boldsymbol{\mu}_0$, because (5.7) is derived from (4.20) which is obtained by equating a first-order derivative of the log-likelihood function to zero. Similarly, γ and $\mathbf{\Omega}$ in (5.8) are estimates too.

Two Matrices of Mean Squares and Products

We define

$$\mathbf{Z}_0 = \frac{1}{T}\sum_{t=1}^{T} (\mathbf{z}_t - c_t\mathbf{z}_0)(\mathbf{z}_t - c_t\mathbf{z}_0)' \tag{5.9}$$

and $\mathbf{E}_0$ as any 3×3 matrix which satisfies

$$\mathbf{E}_0'\mathbf{E}_0 = \frac{1}{T}\sum_{t=1}^{T} (\mathbf{p}_t - c_t\mathbf{p}_0)(\mathbf{p}_t - c_t\mathbf{p}_0)' \tag{5.10}$$

We assume that the matrices on the right in these two equations are both positive definite. In the case of (5.10) this amounts to the assumption that the $3\times T$ matrix

$$[\mathbf{p}_1 - c_1\mathbf{p}_0 \dots \mathbf{p}_T - c_T\mathbf{p}_0] \tag{5.11}$$

has full row rank. If (5.11) has a lower rank, a row vector $\mathbf{x}'\neq\mathbf{0}$ exists so that $\mathbf{x}'\mathbf{p}_t - c_t\mathbf{x}'\mathbf{p}_0 = 0$ for each t. This means that there is a nontrivial linear combination of the deflated price log-changes at t which is proportional to c_t and hence, in view of (5.3), also proportional to DQ_{gt}, which amounts to multicollinearity of the right-hand variables in (3.20).

Similarly, positive definiteness of $\mathbf{Z}_0$ defined in (5.9) is equivalent to full row rank of the $3\times T$ matrix

$$[\mathbf{z}_1 - c_1\mathbf{z}_0 \dots \mathbf{z}_T - c_T\mathbf{z}_0] \tag{5.12}$$

If the rank of this matrix is less than 3, there is a nontrivial linear combination of the three elements of $\mathbf{z}_t$ which is proportional to DQ_{gt}. The reader may want to compare these developments with the discussion below (4.17).

The Estimate of $\boldsymbol{\Omega}$

Using (5.4) and (5.5), we find that (5.9) and (5.10) may be written as

$$\mathbf{Z}_0 = \frac{1}{T}\sum_{t=1}^{T} \mathbf{z}_t\mathbf{z}_t' - \frac{1}{T}\mathbf{z}_0\mathbf{z}_0' \tag{5.13}$$

$$\mathbf{E}_0'\mathbf{E}_0 = \frac{1}{T}\sum_{t=1}^{T} \mathbf{p}_t\mathbf{p}_t' - \frac{1}{T}\mathbf{p}_0\mathbf{p}_0' = \mathbf{E}'\mathbf{E} - \frac{1}{T}\mathbf{p}_0\mathbf{p}_0' \tag{5.14}$$

where the second equal sign in (5.14) is based on (4.15). Furthermore,

$\mathbf{M}_0$ defined in (4.16) can be written as

$$\text{(5.15)} \qquad \mathbf{M}_0 = \mathbf{Z}_0 + \gamma^2 \boldsymbol{\Omega} \left(\frac{1}{T} \mathbf{p}_0 \mathbf{p}_0' \right) \boldsymbol{\Omega}$$

To prove this we use (5.8) to write $\mathbf{M}_0$ as the sum of four terms:

$$\frac{1}{T} \sum_{t=1}^{T} (\mathbf{z}_t - c_t \mathbf{z}_0)(\mathbf{z}_t - c_t \mathbf{z}_0)' + \gamma^2 \boldsymbol{\Omega} \mathbf{p}_0 \mathbf{p}_0' \boldsymbol{\Omega} \frac{1}{T} \sum_{t=1}^{T} c_t^2$$
$$- \gamma \boldsymbol{\Omega} \mathbf{p}_0 \frac{1}{T} \sum_{t=1}^{T} c_t (\mathbf{z}_t - c_t \mathbf{z}_0)' - \left[\gamma \boldsymbol{\Omega} \mathbf{p}_0 \frac{1}{T} \sum_{t=1}^{T} c_t (\mathbf{z}_t - c_t \mathbf{z}_0)' \right]'$$

It follows from (5.6) that the last two terms vanish. The first term equals $\mathbf{Z}_0$ defined in (5.9) and the second can be simplified, in view of (5.4), as shown in (5.15).

We now substitute (5.15) in (4.21),

$$\gamma^2 \boldsymbol{\Omega} \mathbf{E}' \mathbf{E} \boldsymbol{\Omega} + \boldsymbol{\Omega} - \mathbf{Z}_0 - \gamma^2 \boldsymbol{\Omega} \left(\frac{1}{T} \mathbf{p}_0 \mathbf{p}_0' \right) \boldsymbol{\Omega} = \mathbf{0}$$

and use (5.14) to simplify this to

$$\text{(5.16)} \qquad \gamma^2 \boldsymbol{\Omega} \mathbf{E}_0' \mathbf{E}_0 \boldsymbol{\Omega} + \boldsymbol{\Omega} - \mathbf{Z}_0 = \mathbf{0}$$

Next we proceed along the lines of eqs. (4.21) and ff. So we premultiply (5.16) by $\mathbf{E}_0$ and postmultiply by the transpose of $\mathbf{E}_0$,

$$\gamma^2 (\mathbf{E}_0 \boldsymbol{\Omega} \mathbf{E}_0')^2 + \mathbf{E}_0 \boldsymbol{\Omega} \mathbf{E}_0' - \mathbf{E}_0 \mathbf{Z}_0 \mathbf{E}_0' = \mathbf{0}$$

which we write as

$$\text{(5.17)} \qquad \left(\gamma \mathbf{E}_0 \boldsymbol{\Omega} \mathbf{E}_0' + \frac{1}{2\gamma} \mathbf{I}_3 \right)^2 = \mathbf{E}_0 \mathbf{Z}_0 \mathbf{E}_0' + \frac{1}{4\gamma^2} \mathbf{I}_3$$
$$= \mathbf{F}_0 \mathbf{G}_0 \mathbf{F}_0' + \frac{1}{4\gamma^2} \mathbf{F}_0 \mathbf{F}_0'$$

where $\mathbf{F}_0$ is a 3×3 orthogonal matrix whose columns are characteristic vectors of $\mathbf{E}_0 \mathbf{Z}_0 \mathbf{E}_0'$, and $\mathbf{G}_0$ is a 3×3 diagonal matrix whose diagonal elements are latent roots of $\mathbf{E}_0 \mathbf{Z}_0 \mathbf{E}_0'$. Since $\mathbf{Z}_0$ is positive definite and $\mathbf{E}_0$ is nonsingular (because of the positive definiteness of $\mathbf{E}_0' \mathbf{E}_0$), these roots are all positive.

The further developments are a straightforward extension of the analysis in the last subsection of Section 7.4, leading to

$$\boldsymbol{\Omega} = (\mathbf{E}_0^{-1}\mathbf{F}_0)\,\mathbf{H}_0(\mathbf{E}_0^{-1}\mathbf{F}_0)' \tag{5.18}$$

where $\mathbf{H}_0$ is a 3×3 diagonal matrix whose i^{th} diagonal element is

$$h_{0i} = \frac{-1 + \sqrt{1 + 4\gamma^2 g_{0i}}}{2\gamma^2} \qquad i = 1, 2, 3 \tag{5.19}$$

with g_{0i} defined as the ith diagonal element of $\mathbf{G}_0$.

The Estimate of the Connecting Parameter

Consider the first equation of (4.20):

$$\gamma \sum_{t=1}^{T} \mathbf{p}_t'\boldsymbol{\Omega}\mathbf{p}_t = -\sum_{t=1}^{T} \mathbf{p}_t'(\mathbf{z}_t - \boldsymbol{\mu}_0 DQ_{gt}) \tag{5.20}$$

Next use (5.8) and (5.5):

$$\begin{aligned}\sum_{t=1}^{T} \mathbf{p}_t'(\mathbf{z}_t - \boldsymbol{\mu}_0 DQ_{gt}) &= \sum_{t=1}^{T} \mathbf{p}_t'(\mathbf{z}_t - c_t\mathbf{z}_0) - \gamma \sum_{t=1}^{T} c_t\mathbf{p}_t'\boldsymbol{\Omega}\mathbf{p}_0 \\ &= \sum_{t=1}^{T} \mathbf{p}_t'(\mathbf{z}_t - c_t\mathbf{z}_0) - \gamma\mathbf{p}_0'\boldsymbol{\Omega}\mathbf{p}_0\end{aligned} \tag{5.21}$$

This shows that we may write (5.20) as

$$\gamma\left(\frac{1}{T}\sum_{t=1}^{T} \mathbf{p}_t'\boldsymbol{\Omega}\mathbf{p}_t - \frac{1}{T}\mathbf{p}_0'\boldsymbol{\Omega}\mathbf{p}_0\right) = -\frac{1}{T}\sum_{t=1}^{T} \mathbf{p}_t'(\mathbf{z}_t - c_t\mathbf{z}_0) \tag{5.22}$$

The left-hand side is a multiple γ of

$$\begin{aligned}\frac{1}{T}\sum_{t=1}^{T} \mathbf{p}_t'\boldsymbol{\Omega}\mathbf{p}_t - \frac{1}{T}\mathbf{p}_0'\boldsymbol{\Omega}\mathbf{p}_0 &= \operatorname{tr}\boldsymbol{\Omega}\left(\frac{1}{T}\sum_{t=1}^{T} \mathbf{p}_t\mathbf{p}_t' - \frac{1}{T}\mathbf{p}_0\mathbf{p}_0'\right) \\ &= \operatorname{tr}\boldsymbol{\Omega}\mathbf{E}_0'\mathbf{E}_0 = \operatorname{tr}\mathbf{E}_0\boldsymbol{\Omega}\mathbf{E}_0'\end{aligned} \tag{5.23}$$

where the second step is based on (5.14). So (5.22) is simplified to

$$\gamma \operatorname{tr}\mathbf{E}_0\boldsymbol{\Omega}\mathbf{E}_0' = -\frac{1}{T}\sum_{t=1}^{T} \mathbf{p}_t'(\mathbf{z}_t - c_t\mathbf{z}_0) \tag{5.24}$$

The Computational Procedure

The procedure starts with $\mathbf{Z}_0$ and $\mathbf{E}_0$ calculated from (5.13) and (5.14). A simple symmetric specification of $\mathbf{E}_0$ is the 3×3 matrix whose characteristic vectors are equal to those of $\mathbf{E}_0'\mathbf{E}_0$ and whose latent roots are the positive square roots of the latent roots of $\mathbf{E}_0'\mathbf{E}_0$. We then compute the product $\mathbf{E}_0\mathbf{Z}_0\mathbf{E}_0'$ and its characteristic vectors (the columns of $\mathbf{F}_0$) and latent roots g_{01}, g_{02} and g_{03}. These results are all determined by observations on variables and hence do not change in the successive iterations.

As an initial estimate of $\mathbf{\Omega}$ we take the leading 3×3 submatrix of (5.2), the matrix of mean squares and products of the residuals corresponding to the symmetry-constrained coefficient estimates of Section 7.3. Since (5.24) is a linear equation in the γ estimate conditionally on $\mathbf{\Omega}$, this initial $\mathbf{\Omega}$ value yields a first γ estimate which is substituted in (5.19). The implied values of h_{01}, h_{02} and h_{03} are substituted in (5.18), after which the iteration between (5.18), (5.19) and (5.24) is continued until convergence. Once converged estimates of γ and $\mathbf{\Omega}$ are obtained, these are substituted in (5.7) to yield the implied estimates of the conditional marginal shares.

For the data considered here about 300 iterations are needed to obtain convergence in eight decimal places. This is much larger than the number of iterations needed for the computations described in Chapters 5 and 6.

7.6 The Demand for Meats in the United States: (5) A Relative Price Version

Equation (3.15) can be used to obtain the modified price coefficients of the meats from their conditional marginal shares and Slutsky coefficients:

$$(6.1) \qquad v_{ij}^* = \pi_{ij}^* + \frac{\phi M_g}{\bar{W}_{gt}} \frac{\mu_i}{M_g} \frac{\mu_j}{M_g} \qquad i, j \in S_g$$

The right-hand side contains $\phi M_g/\bar{W}_{gt}$, which is the own-price elasticity in the demand equation (3.12) for meat as a whole. So we could estimate $\phi M_g/\bar{W}_{gt}$ by estimating (3.12), but note that this equation contains the marginal shares of all n commodities in its price deflator. We shall therefore confine ourselves to a rough informal estimate. The ϕ estimate of the preferred specification given in eq. (7.1) of Section 6.7 is between $-.6$ and $-.7$. The income elasticity $M_g/\bar{W}_{gt}$ of meat in the United States between 1950 and 1972 is almost certainly less than 1. So let us approximate:

$$\frac{\phi M_g}{\bar{W}_{gt}} \approx -\tfrac{1}{2} \tag{6.2}$$

When this numerical value and the maximum-likelihood estimates in the middle part of Table 7.7 are substituted in (6.1), we obtain the figures shown in the first four lines of Table 7.8. They indicate that Beef, Pork and Chicken are pairwise specific substitutes, as one would expect them to be. However, the off-diagonal elements in the fourth column (corresponding to Lamb) are close to zero and not even uniformly positive. Indeed, the estimates

TABLE 7.8

ESTIMATES OF MODIFIED PRICE COEFFICIENTS AND PRICE ELASTICITIES OF MEATS

	Beef	Pork	Chicken	Lamb
	Preliminary estimates of modified price coefficients			
Beef	−.463	.103	.014	−.006
Pork		−.236	.030	.003
Chicken			−.080	.008
Lamb				−.025
	Maximum-likelihood estimates of modified price coefficients			
Beef	−.5286	.0804	.0109	0
Pork		−.2425	.0282	0
Chicken			−.0802	0
Lamb				−.0270
	Implied price elasticities			
Beef	−1.06	.16	.02	0
Pork	.23	−.69	.08	0
Chicken	.09	.23	−.66	0
Lamb	0	0	0	−.98

suggest that specific substitution is confined to Beef, Pork and Chicken, and that Lamb is unrelated to these three meats in terms of the Hessian matrix of the consumer's utility function. This could be interpreted in the sense that Beef, Pork and Chicken are the dominant meats among which specific competition takes place, whereas minor meats such as Lamb occupy a separate position. Whatever the merits of this line of thought, it is certainly in agreement with the approach of Section 6.6 to apply Occam's razor and to simplify the model in the direction of preference independence as far as the data permit.

Implications of the Preference Independence Assumption on Lamb

When Lamb is preference-independent of all other commodities, we have $\nu_{i4}=0$ and hence also $\nu_{i4}^*=0$ if $i\neq 4$, so that we can use the conditional equation (3.9) in relative prices. For $i=1$, 2 and 3 (Beef, Pork and Chicken) this equation takes the form

$$\text{(6.3)} \qquad \frac{\bar{w}_{it}}{\bar{W}_{gt}} Dq_{it} = \frac{\mu_i}{M_g} DQ_{gt} + \sum_{j=1}^{3} \nu_{ij}^* (Dp_{jt} - DP'_{gt}) + \varepsilon_{it}^*$$

because $j=4$ can now be deleted from the summation on the right. For Lamb, the equation can be simplified, in view of (3.10), to

$$\text{(6.4)} \qquad \frac{\bar{w}_{4t}}{\bar{W}_{gt}} Dq_{4t} = \frac{\mu_4}{M_g} DQ_{gt} + \frac{\phi\mu_4}{\bar{W}_{gt}} (Dp_{4t} - DP'_{gt}) + \varepsilon_{4t}^*$$

Write $\pi_{ij}^* = -\gamma\omega_{ij}$ in accordance with (4.2) and (4.6). When we combine this with (6.1) and impose $\nu_{i4}^*=0$ for $i<4$, we obtain

$$0 = -\gamma\omega_{i4} + \frac{\phi M_g}{\bar{W}_{gt}} \frac{\mu_i}{M_g} \frac{\mu_4}{M_g} \qquad i = 1, 2, 3$$

In view of (4.3) this is equivalent to

$$0 = \frac{\bar{W}_{gt}}{\sigma^2} \omega_{i4} + \frac{M_g}{\bar{W}_{gt}} \frac{\mu_i}{M_g} \frac{\mu_4}{M_g} \qquad i = 1, 2, 3$$

which can also be written as

$$\text{(6.5)} \qquad \frac{\mu_i}{M_g} = \frac{\bar{W}_{gt}^2}{\sigma^2 \mu_4} (-\omega_{i4}) \qquad i = 1, 2, 3$$

Since μ_i/M_g and $-\omega_{i4} = \omega_{i1} + \omega_{i2} + \omega_{i3}$ are the ith elements of the vectors $\boldsymbol{\mu}_0$ and $\boldsymbol{\Omega\iota}$, respectively, where $\boldsymbol{\iota} = [1 \quad 1 \quad 1]'$, we can write (6.5) in matrix form as

$$\text{(6.6)} \qquad \boldsymbol{\mu}_0 = \delta\boldsymbol{\Omega\iota} \quad \text{where} \quad \delta = \frac{\bar{W}_{gt}^2}{\sigma^2 \mu_4}$$

Recall from the discussion below (4.1) that σ is treated as varying proportionally to $\bar{W}_{gt}$. The implication is that δ is a (positive) constant.

We conclude from (6.6) that the preference independence assumption on Lamb implies that $\boldsymbol{\mu}_0$ can be expressed in terms of $\boldsymbol{\Omega}$ and the scalar parameter δ. Therefore, (4.7) may now be written as

$$\mathbf{z}_t = \delta\boldsymbol{\Omega}\mathbf{q}_t - \gamma\boldsymbol{\Omega}\mathbf{p}_t + \boldsymbol{\varepsilon}_t \tag{6.7}$$

where

$$\mathbf{q}_t = (DQ_{gt})\boldsymbol{\iota} = [DQ_{gt} \;\; DQ_{gt} \;\; DQ_{gt}]' \tag{6.8}$$

A New Maximum-Likelihood Estimator

Using (6.7), we find that the log-likelihood function (4.9) is changed into

$$\begin{aligned} \log L = &-\tfrac{3}{2}T\log 2\pi + \tfrac{1}{2}T\log|\boldsymbol{\Omega}^{-1}| \\ &- \tfrac{1}{2}\sum_{t=1}^{T}(\mathbf{z}_t - \delta\boldsymbol{\Omega}\mathbf{q}_t + \gamma\boldsymbol{\Omega}\mathbf{p}_t)'\,\boldsymbol{\Omega}^{-1}(\mathbf{z}_t - \delta\boldsymbol{\Omega}\mathbf{q}_t + \gamma\boldsymbol{\Omega}\mathbf{p}_t) \end{aligned} \tag{6.9}$$

which is now to be maximized by varying γ, δ and $\boldsymbol{\Omega}$. So we differentiate with respect to γ and δ:

$$\frac{\partial \log L}{\partial\gamma} = -\gamma\sum_{t=1}^{T}\mathbf{p}_t'\boldsymbol{\Omega}\mathbf{p}_t + \delta\sum_{t=1}^{T}\mathbf{p}_t'\boldsymbol{\Omega}\mathbf{q}_t - \sum_{t=1}^{T}\mathbf{z}_t'\mathbf{p}_t \tag{6.10}$$

$$\frac{\partial \log L}{\partial\delta} = \gamma\sum_{t=1}^{T}\mathbf{p}_t'\boldsymbol{\Omega}\mathbf{q}_t - \delta\sum_{t=1}^{T}\mathbf{q}_t'\boldsymbol{\Omega}\mathbf{q}_t + \sum_{t=1}^{T}\mathbf{z}_t'\mathbf{q}_t \tag{6.11}$$

When the right-hand sides are equated to zero, we obtain two equations which are linear in the γ and δ estimates conditionally on $\boldsymbol{\Omega}$. Note that we treat the $\boldsymbol{\Omega}$ estimate as symmetric in these two equations. As in the analogous analysis of Section 7.4, it will appear that the estimate obtained is symmetric in spite of the fact that no symmetry is imposed when $\log L$ is differentiated with respect to $\boldsymbol{\Omega}^{-1}$.

The expression in the second line of (6.9), insofar as it involves $\boldsymbol{\Omega}$, can be written as

$$\begin{aligned} &-\tfrac{1}{2}\sum_{t=1}^{T}\mathbf{z}_t'\boldsymbol{\Omega}^{-1}\mathbf{z}_t - \tfrac{1}{2}\sum_{t=1}^{T}(\delta\mathbf{q}_t - \gamma\mathbf{p}_t)'\,\boldsymbol{\Omega}\,(\delta\mathbf{q}_t - \gamma\mathbf{p}_t) \\ &\quad = -\tfrac{1}{2}\operatorname{tr}\boldsymbol{\Omega}^{-1}\sum_{t=1}^{T}\mathbf{z}_t\mathbf{z}_t' - \tfrac{1}{2}\operatorname{tr}\boldsymbol{\Omega}\sum_{t=1}^{T}(\delta\mathbf{q}_t - \gamma\mathbf{p}_t)(\delta\mathbf{q}_t - \gamma\mathbf{p}_t)' \end{aligned} \tag{6.12}$$

We define

$$\mathbf{Z}_* = \frac{1}{T}\sum_{t=1}^{T}\mathbf{z}_t\mathbf{z}_t' \tag{6.13}$$

and $\mathbf{E}_*$ as any 3×3 matrix which satisfies

$$\mathbf{E}_*'\mathbf{E}_* = \frac{1}{T}\sum_{t=1}^{T} (\delta\mathbf{q}_t - \gamma\mathbf{p}_t)(\delta\mathbf{q}_t - \gamma\mathbf{p}_t)' \tag{6.14}$$

so that the right-hand side of (6.12) is simplified to

$$-\tfrac{1}{2}T \operatorname{tr} \mathbf{\Omega}^{-1}\mathbf{Z}_* - \tfrac{1}{2}T \operatorname{tr} \mathbf{\Omega}\mathbf{E}_*'\mathbf{E}_* \tag{6.15}$$

In the next subsection we differentiate (6.15) and the second (determinantal) term in (6.9) with respect to $\mathbf{\Omega}^{-1}$, and we equate the sum of these derivatives to a zero matrix. This leads to an $\mathbf{\Omega}$ estimator of a form similar to (4.24):

$$\mathbf{\Omega} = (\mathbf{E}_*^{-1}\mathbf{F}_*)\,\mathbf{H}_*\,(\mathbf{E}_*^{-1}\mathbf{F}_*)' \tag{6.16}$$

Here $\mathbf{F}_*$ is a 3×3 orthogonal matrix whose columns are characteristic vectors of the matrix $\mathbf{E}_*\mathbf{Z}_*\mathbf{E}_*'$ and $\mathbf{H}_*$ is a 3×3 diagonal matrix whose diagonal elements are

$$h_i^* = -\tfrac{1}{2} + \sqrt{\tfrac{1}{4} + g_i^*} \qquad i = 1, 2, 3 \tag{6.17}$$

where g_1^*, g_2^* and g_3^* are the latent roots of $\mathbf{E}_*\mathbf{Z}_*\mathbf{E}_*'$. Note that the solution (6.16) is a symmetric matrix.

Derivations for the Maximum-Likelihood Estimator

When $\mathbf{\Omega}^{-1}$ changes by $d\mathbf{\Omega}^{-1}$, the effect on the matrix (6.15) is

$$\begin{aligned} -\tfrac{1}{2}T \operatorname{tr}(d\mathbf{\Omega}^{-1})\,\mathbf{Z}_* - \tfrac{1}{2}T \operatorname{tr}(d\mathbf{\Omega})\,\mathbf{E}_*'\mathbf{E}_* \\ = -\tfrac{1}{2}T \operatorname{tr} d\mathbf{\Omega}^{-1}(\mathbf{Z}_* - \mathbf{\Omega}\mathbf{E}_*'\mathbf{E}_*\mathbf{\Omega}) \end{aligned} \tag{6.18}$$

where the equal sign is based on

$$\operatorname{tr}(d\mathbf{\Omega})\,\mathbf{E}_*'\mathbf{E}_* = -\operatorname{tr}\mathbf{\Omega}(d\mathbf{\Omega}^{-1})\,\mathbf{\Omega}\mathbf{E}_*'\mathbf{E}_* = -\operatorname{tr}(d\mathbf{\Omega}^{-1})\,\mathbf{\Omega}\mathbf{E}_*'\mathbf{E}_*\mathbf{\Omega}$$

To obtain the total effect of $d\mathbf{\Omega}^{-1}$ on $\log L$ we must add to (6.18) the effect on the second right-hand term in (6.9). This effect is given in (4.18), since the term containing $|\mathbf{\Omega}^{-1}|$ is the same in (4.9) and (6.9). The result is

$$\frac{\partial \log L}{\partial \mathbf{\Omega}^{-1}} = \tfrac{1}{2}T\,(\mathbf{\Omega}\mathbf{E}_*'\mathbf{E}_*\mathbf{\Omega} + \mathbf{\Omega} - \mathbf{Z}_*)' \tag{6.19}$$

which should be compared with (4.14).

The estimate of $\mathbf{\Omega}$ is found by equating the right-hand side of (6.19) to a zero matrix,

$$\mathbf{\Omega E}_*'\mathbf{E}_*\mathbf{\Omega} + \mathbf{\Omega} - \mathbf{Z}_* = \mathbf{0} \tag{6.20}$$

We premultiply this by $\mathbf{E}_*$ and postmultiply by $\mathbf{E}_*'$:

$$(\mathbf{E}_*\mathbf{\Omega E}_*')^2 + \mathbf{E}_*\mathbf{\Omega E}_*' - \mathbf{E}_*\mathbf{Z}_*\mathbf{E}_*' = \mathbf{0} \tag{6.21}$$

Equations (6.20) and (6.21) are equivalent when $\mathbf{E}_*$ is nonsingular. If $\mathbf{E}_*$ is singular, so is $\mathbf{E}_*'\mathbf{E}_*$ defined in (6.14), which implies multicollinearity among the right-hand variables of (6.7). This singularity will be excluded. We also assume that the three variables represented in $\mathbf{z}_t$ are not linearly dependent, so that $\mathbf{Z}_*$ defined in (6.13) and hence also $\mathbf{E}_*\mathbf{Z}_*\mathbf{E}_*'$ are symmetric positive definite.

Equation (6.21) should be compared with (4.22). The further developments are a straightforward extension of those described at the end of Section 7.4, and the results have been summarized in the last paragraph of the previous subsection. Note that (6.17) is the positive solution of the quadratic equation

$$x^2 + x - g_i^* = 0 \qquad i = 1, 2, 3 \tag{6.22}$$

which is obtained from (6.21) by replacing $\mathbf{E}_*\mathbf{\Omega E}_*'$ by the scalar x and $\mathbf{E}_*\mathbf{Z}_*\mathbf{E}_*'$ by its ith latent root.

The Computational Procedure

The computations differ from those described at the end of Section 7.5 to the extent that the characteristic vectors (the columns of $\mathbf{F}_*$) and the associated roots depend on estimates of parameters. Hence their calculation is part of the iterative procedure. The only matrix which does not change in the iterations is $\mathbf{Z}_*$ defined in (6.13).

As an initial value of $\mathbf{\Omega}$ we take the maximum-likelihood estimate of Section 7.5, which is equal to the estimated Slutsky matrix in the middle part of Table 7.7 on page 32, multiplied by minus the reciprocal of the γ estimate (5.1). This $\mathbf{\Omega}$ is substituted in the right-hand sides of (6.10) and (6.11), which are then equated to zero and solved for γ and δ. These solutions are substituted in (6.14) to yield $\mathbf{E}_*$, which is defined as the symmetric 3×3 matrix with the same characteristic vectors as those of $\mathbf{E}_*'\mathbf{E}_*$ and latent roots equal to the positive square roots of the latent roots of $\mathbf{E}_*'\mathbf{E}_*$. We then compute $\mathbf{E}_*\mathbf{Z}_*\mathbf{E}_*'$ and its latent roots and characteristic vectors (g_1^*, g_2^*, g_3^* and the columns of $\mathbf{F}_*$), followed by h_i^* of (6.17) and $\mathbf{\Omega}$

TABLE 7.9

SUMMARY OF ITERATIONS

Iteration	$10^5\,\gamma$	$10^3\,\delta$	$10^{13}\,\omega_{11}$	$10^{13}\,\omega_{22}$	$10^{13}\,\omega_{33}$
0	651403582	250686500	352549301	329995005	120279441
1000	613269677	228913078	373960161	349702004	126520558
2000	612811400	227236109	374365281	349965965	126601085
3000	612776480	227109169	374396180	349986094	126607225
4000	612773836	227099564	374398519	349987618	126607690
5000	612773636	227098837	374398696	349987734	126607726
6000	612773621	227098782	374398710	349987742	126607728
7000	612773620	227098778	374398711	349987743	126607728
8000	612773620	227098778	374398711	349987743	126607728
9000	612773620	227098778	374398711	349987743	126607728
10000	612773620	227098778	374398711	349987743	126607728
	$-10^{13}\,\omega_{12}$	$-10^{14}\,\omega_{13}$	$-10^{14}\,\omega_{23}$	$10^8\,\mathrm{tr}\,\mathbf{A}_2\mathbf{\Omega}^{-1}$	
0	264598849	606502292	570475536		
1000	280456312	636171602	600954147	300935644	
2000	280618438	636420239	601306807	300070855	
3000	280630800	636439191	601333696	300005362	
4000	280631736	636440626	601335732	300000406	
5000	280631807	636440735	601335886	300000031	
6000	280631812	636440743	601335898	300000002	
7000	280631813	636440744	601335899	300000000	
8000	280631813	636440744	601335899	300000000	
9000	280631813	636440744	601335899	300000000	
10000	280631813	636440744	601335899	300000000	

as shown in (6.16). These values of γ, δ and $\mathbf{\Omega}$ are shown in the line "iteration 0" of Table 7.9. After substituting the $\mathbf{\Omega}$ thus obtained in (6.10) and (6.11) we obtain new values for γ and δ, and so on until the procedure converges. The converged estimates of δ and $\mathbf{\Omega}$ are used to obtain the estimate of $\boldsymbol{\mu}_0$ from (6.6).

The convergence is by far the slowest of all the iterative procedures described in this book. A comparison of the successive lines of Table 7.9 shows that, for most of the estimates, convergence in an extra decimal place requires an additional 1000 iterations. The column of figures under $\mathrm{tr}\,\mathbf{A}_2\mathbf{\Omega}^{-1}$ is discussed in Section 7.7.

This slow convergence agrees with a similar experience described by Chow (1968) in simultaneous-equation estimation. He suggests Newton's method, which requires the second-order derivatives of the log-likelihood function. Other methods exist which do not require these derivatives. Some provide the Hessian of the log-likelihood function at the point of convergence, which may be used to obtain asymptotic standard errors. See POWELL (1964) and STEWART (1967) as well as the articles quoted by these authors.

Discussion of the New Maximum-Likelihood Estimates

The converged estimates of γ and δ are

$$\hat{\gamma} = 6.128 \times 10^3 \qquad \hat{\delta} = 2.271 \times 10^5 \tag{6.23}$$

Notice that this γ estimate differs from its predecessor (5.1) by only about 2 percent.

The new estimates of the conditional marginal shares and Slutsky coefficients are shown, with an extra decimal place, in the last four lines of Table 7.7 on page 32. The agreement with the corresponding estimates in the middle part of the table is close in most cases. Using the average budget shares (2.1), we find the following conditional income elasticities based on the new maximum-likelihood estimates of the conditional marginal shares:

(6.24) Beef: 1.37 Pork: .60 Chicken: .53 Lamb: 1.54

These elasticities are rather close to those given in (3.27), which were derived from the symmetry-constrained estimates without the second-moment model. The largest discrepancy is for Lamb. The new estimate of its conditional income elasticity is about 15 percent below the corresponding figure in (3.27), which is due to the lower estimate of the conditional marginal share.

The Implied Own-Price Elasticity of Total Meat

Since $v^*_{4j}=0$ for $j<4$, summation of (6.1) for $i=4$ over $j=1$, 2 and 3 gives

$$0 = \sum_{j=1}^{3} \pi^*_{4j} + \frac{\phi M_g}{\bar{W}_{gt}} \frac{\mu_4}{M_g}\left(1 - \frac{\mu_4}{M_g}\right)$$

It follows from (3.19) that the first term on the right may be written as $-\pi^*_{44}$, so that we obtain an expression for the own-price elasticity of total-meat consumption:

$$\frac{\phi M_g}{\bar{W}_{gt}} = \frac{\pi^*_{44}}{\dfrac{\mu_4}{M_g}\left(1 - \dfrac{\mu_4}{M_g}\right)} \tag{6.25}$$

Substitution of the two estimates in the last line of Table 7.7 gives

$$\text{(6.26)} \qquad \text{Estimate of } \frac{\phi M_g}{\bar{W}_{gt}} = -.6393$$

which is larger in absolute value than the informal estimate (6.2) that was used for the preliminary estimates of the v_{ij}^*'s in the first four lines of Table 7.8. It is interesting to note that the preference independence assumption on Lamb enables us to estimate the own-price elasticity of the demand for meat as a whole. This estimation procedure does not involve an analysis of total-meat consumption in terms of real income and a deflated meat price index.

The Implied Price Coefficients and Elasticities of the Four Meats

Application of (6.26) in conjunction with (6.1) and the maximum-likelihood estimates in the last four rows of Table 7.7 gives the maximum-likelihood estimates of the v_{ij}^*'s. These are shown in the middle part of Table 7.8. They are rather close to the corresponding figures in the first four lines except for v_{11}^*. The discrepancy in this particular case is due to that between (6.2) and (6.26) combined with the large conditional marginal share of Beef. As (6.1) shows, we obtain v_{ij}^* from π_{ij}^* by adding a multiple $\phi M_g/\bar{W}_{gt}$ of the product of the ith and j^{th} conditional marginal shares, and this product takes by far the largest value for $i=j=1$. A major cause of the discrepancy between (6.2) and (6.26) is the relatively large Slutsky estimate (.009) for Chicken and Lamb in the middle part of Table 7.7. Since the conditional marginal shares of these two meats are small, a large absolute value of $\phi M_g/\bar{W}_{gt}$ is needed in (6.1) to force v_{34}^* to be zero.

It follows from (6.3) that the price elasticities of the demand for the ith meat are obtained by dividing each v_{ij}^* by the ith conditional budget share. These elasticities, based on the average budget shares (2.1), are shown in the last four lines of Table 7.8. Thus, the estimated own-price elasticity of the demand for Beef is -1.06 and the estimated elasticities of this demand with respect to the deflated prices of Pork and Chicken are .16 and .02, respectively.

7.7 The Demand for Meats in the United States: (6) A Test for the Second-Moment Model

This section describes a likelihood ratio test for the second-moment model. Since the validity of this model is an important issue, we shall apply the test to the specifications of both Section 7.5 and Section 7.6. The discussion starts with a property of the maximum-likelihood residuals which is used for the test.

Mean Squares and Products of the Maximum-Likelihood Residuals

Consider the $\mathbf{\Omega}$ estimate obtained from (4.24) or, equivalently, from (5.18). This estimate is not identical to the matrix of mean squares and products of the maximum-likelihood residuals (the residuals associated with the maximum-likelihood coefficient estimates). The latter matrix is obtained from

$$\text{(7.1)} \qquad \mathbf{A}_1 = \frac{1}{T}\sum_{t=1}^{T} (\mathbf{z}_t - \boldsymbol{\mu}_0 DQ_{gt} + \gamma\mathbf{\Omega}\mathbf{p}_t)(\mathbf{z}_t - \boldsymbol{\mu}_0 DQ_{gt} + \gamma\mathbf{\Omega}\mathbf{p}_t)'$$

where γ, $\boldsymbol{\mu}_0$ and $\mathbf{\Omega}$ stand for the maximum-likelihood estimates of Section 7.5.

Table 7.10 contains four sets of residual mean squares and products. Those in the first four lines correspond to the least-squares coefficient estimates of Section 7.3; these coefficient estimates are shown in the upper half of Table 7.5 on page 19. The next four lines of Table 7.10 contain the residual mean squares and products associated with the symmetry-constrained coefficient estimates in the lower half of Table 7.5; these figures are reproduced from the matrix (3.22). Next is the matrix (7.1) in enlarged 4×4 form. The last matrix, to be discussed in the subsection immediately following the next, refers to the specification of Section 7.6. The table shows that corresponding elements are mostly close to each other. As could be expected, mean squares of residuals tend to increase when more constraints are imposed on the coefficients.

Although $\mathbf{A}_1$, defined in (7.1), differs from the maximum-likelihood estimate of $\mathbf{\Omega}$, there is a simple trace relation between the two matrices. In the next subsection we prove

$$\text{(7.2)} \qquad \operatorname{tr} \mathbf{A}_1\mathbf{\Omega}^{-1} = 3$$

where $\mathbf{\Omega}$ is to be interpreted as the maximum-likelihood estimate. The number 3 on the right is the order (3×3) of the matrices $\mathbf{A}_1$ and $\mathbf{\Omega}$. We may interpret (7.2), which is useful as a check on the computations, in the sense that $\mathbf{A}_1$ has a "size" which agrees with that of the maximum-likelihood estimate. It should be compared with the scalar unbiasedness criterion $\operatorname{tr}\hat{\mathbf{\Omega}}\mathbf{\Omega}^{-1}$ used in Section 6.5.

TABLE 7.10

MEAN SQUARES AND PRODUCTS OF RESIDUALS

	Beef	Pork	Chicken	Lamb
		Least squares		
Beef	52.63	−42.54	−9.11	−.99
Pork		42.39	1.28	−1.12
Chicken			8.15	−.32
Lamb				2.43
		Symmetry-constrained		
Beef	54.10	−43.26	−9.94	−.90
Pork		43.11	1.36	−1.21
Chicken			8.91	−.33
Lamb				2.44
		Maximum likelihood, Section 7.5		
Beef	53.44	−43.52	−9.24	−.68
Pork		43.69	1.12	−1.30
Chicken			9.15	−1.03
Lamb				3.01
		Maximum likelihood, Section 7.6		
Beef	54.95	−44.03	−9.49	−1.43
Pork		43.49	1.21	−.67
Chicken			9.55	−1.27
Lamb				3.37

Note. All entries are to be multiplied by 10^{-6}.

Proof of the Trace Relation

To prove (7.2) we write the right-hand side of (7.1) as the sum of four terms,

$$\frac{1}{T}\sum_{t=1}^{T}(\mathbf{z}_t - \boldsymbol{\mu}_0 DQ_{gt})(\mathbf{z}_t - \boldsymbol{\mu}_0 DQ_{gt})' = \mathbf{M}_0 \qquad \text{[see (4.16)]} \tag{7.3}$$

$$\gamma^2\boldsymbol{\Omega}\left(\frac{1}{T}\sum_{t=1}^{T}\mathbf{p}_t\mathbf{p}_t'\right)\boldsymbol{\Omega} = \gamma^2\boldsymbol{\Omega}\mathbf{E}'\mathbf{E}\boldsymbol{\Omega} \qquad \text{[see (4.15)]} \tag{7.4}$$

$$\gamma\boldsymbol{\Omega}\frac{1}{T}\sum_{t=1}^{T}\mathbf{p}_t(\mathbf{z}_t - \boldsymbol{\mu}_0 DQ_{gt})' \tag{7.5}$$

plus a fourth term which is equal to the transpose of (7.5). By adding the four terms, postmultiplying by $\mathbf{\Omega}^{-1}$ and taking the trace we find

$$\text{(7.6)} \qquad \operatorname{tr}\mathbf{A}_1\mathbf{\Omega}^{-1} = \operatorname{tr}\mathbf{M}_0\mathbf{\Omega}^{-1} + \gamma^2 \operatorname{tr}\mathbf{\Omega}\mathbf{E}'\mathbf{E} + \frac{2\gamma}{T}\sum_{t=1}^{T} (\mathbf{z}_t - \boldsymbol{\mu}_0 DQ_{gt})'\,\mathbf{p}_t$$

where the last term, which results from (7.5) and its transpose, is based on

$$\begin{aligned}\operatorname{tr}\mathbf{\Omega}\left[\sum_{t=1}^{T} \mathbf{p}_t(\mathbf{z}_t - \boldsymbol{\mu}_0 DQ_{gt})'\right]\mathbf{\Omega}^{-1} &= \operatorname{tr}\mathbf{\Omega}^{-1}\mathbf{\Omega}\sum_{t=1}^{T} \mathbf{p}_t(\mathbf{z}_t - \boldsymbol{\mu}_0 DQ_{gt})' \\ &= \operatorname{tr}\sum_{t=1}^{T} \mathbf{p}_t(\mathbf{z}_t - \boldsymbol{\mu}_0 DQ_{gt})' \\ &= \sum_{t=1}^{T} (\mathbf{z}_t - \boldsymbol{\mu}_0 DQ_{gt})'\,\mathbf{p}_t\end{aligned}$$

Next we use $\sum_t \mathbf{p}_t'\mathbf{\Omega}\mathbf{p}_t = \operatorname{tr}\mathbf{\Omega}\sum_t \mathbf{p}_t\mathbf{p}_t' = T\operatorname{tr}\mathbf{\Omega}\mathbf{E}'\mathbf{E}$ to write (5.20) as

$$\gamma T \operatorname{tr}\mathbf{\Omega}\mathbf{E}'\mathbf{E} = -\sum_{t=1}^{T} \mathbf{p}_t'(\mathbf{z}_t - \boldsymbol{\mu}_0 DQ_{gt})$$

which we substitute in the last term of (7.6):

$$\begin{aligned}\operatorname{tr}\mathbf{A}_1\mathbf{\Omega}^{-1} &= \operatorname{tr}\mathbf{M}_0\mathbf{\Omega}^{-1} - \gamma^2\operatorname{tr}\mathbf{\Omega}\mathbf{E}'\mathbf{E} \\ &= \operatorname{tr}(\mathbf{M}_0 - \gamma^2\mathbf{\Omega}\mathbf{E}'\mathbf{E}\mathbf{\Omega})\,\mathbf{\Omega}^{-1}\end{aligned}$$

This is equal to $\operatorname{tr}\mathbf{\Omega}\mathbf{\Omega}^{-1} = 3$ in view of (4.21).

Extension to the Specification of Section 7.6

The mean squares and products of the maximum-likelihood residuals of the model (6.7) are obtained from

$$\text{(7.7)} \qquad \mathbf{A}_2 = \frac{1}{T}\sum_{t=1}^{T} [\mathbf{z}_t - \mathbf{\Omega}(\delta\mathbf{q}_t - \gamma\mathbf{p}_t)]\,[\mathbf{z}_t - \mathbf{\Omega}(\delta\mathbf{q}_t - \gamma\mathbf{p}_t)]'$$

where γ, δ and $\mathbf{\Omega}$ are maximum-likelihood estimates. The matrix $\mathbf{A}_2$ in enlarged 4×4 form is shown in the last four lines of Table 7.10.

We have

$$\text{(7.8)} \qquad \operatorname{tr}\mathbf{A}_2\mathbf{\Omega}^{-1} = 3$$

which is similar to (7.2). The convergence of this trace toward 3 is shown in Table 7.9. To prove (7.8) we use (6.13) and (6.14):

$$\text{(7.9)} \qquad \operatorname{tr}\mathbf{A}_2\mathbf{\Omega}^{-1} = \operatorname{tr}\mathbf{Z}_*\mathbf{\Omega}^{-1} + \operatorname{tr}\mathbf{\Omega}\mathbf{E}_*'\mathbf{E}_* - \frac{2}{T}\sum_{t=1}^{T} \mathbf{z}_t'(\delta\mathbf{q}_t - \gamma\mathbf{p}_t)$$

Recall that the derivatives (6.10) and (6.11) are equated to zero. This implies

$$-\gamma \sum_{t=1}^{T} \mathbf{z}_t'\mathbf{p}_t = \gamma^2 \sum_{t=1}^{T} \mathbf{p}_t'\mathbf{\Omega}\mathbf{p}_t - \gamma\delta \sum_{t=1}^{T} \mathbf{p}_t'\mathbf{\Omega}\mathbf{q}_t$$

$$\delta \sum_{t=1}^{T} \mathbf{z}_t'\mathbf{q}_t = -\gamma\delta \sum_{t=1}^{T} \mathbf{p}_t'\mathbf{\Omega}\mathbf{q}_t + \delta^2 \sum_{t=1}^{T} \mathbf{q}_t'\mathbf{\Omega}\mathbf{q}_t$$

By adding these two equations we obtain

$$\begin{aligned}\sum_{t=1}^{T} \mathbf{z}_t'(\delta\mathbf{q}_t - \gamma\mathbf{p}_t) &= \sum_{t=1}^{T} (\delta\mathbf{q}_t - \gamma\mathbf{p}_t)'\,\mathbf{\Omega}\,(\delta\mathbf{q}_t - \gamma\mathbf{p}_t)\\ &= \operatorname{tr}\mathbf{\Omega} \sum_{t=1}^{T} (\delta\mathbf{q}_t - \gamma\mathbf{p}_t)(\delta\mathbf{q}_t - \gamma\mathbf{p}_t)'\\ &= T \operatorname{tr}\mathbf{\Omega}\mathbf{E}_*'\mathbf{E}_*\end{aligned}$$

This proves that (7.9) can be simplified to

$$\operatorname{tr}\mathbf{A}_2\mathbf{\Omega}^{-1} = \operatorname{tr}(\mathbf{Z}_* - \mathbf{\Omega}\mathbf{E}_*'\mathbf{E}_*\mathbf{\Omega})\,\mathbf{\Omega}^{-1}$$

which is equal to $\operatorname{tr}\mathbf{\Omega}\mathbf{\Omega}^{-1} = 3$ in view of (6.20).

A Likelihood Ratio Test for the Second-Moment Model

The maximum value of the log-likelihood function (4.9) is obtained by substituting the maximum-likelihood estimates for the parameter values. The quadratic form in the second line of (4.9) can be written as

$$-\tfrac{1}{2}\operatorname{tr}\mathbf{\Omega}^{-1} \sum_{t=1}^{T} (\mathbf{z}_t - \boldsymbol{\mu}_0 DQ_{gt} + \gamma\mathbf{\Omega}\mathbf{p}_t)(\mathbf{z}_t - \boldsymbol{\mu}_0 DQ_{gt} + \gamma\mathbf{\Omega}\mathbf{p}_t)'$$

which equals $-\frac{1}{2}T\operatorname{tr}\mathbf{\Omega}^{-1}\mathbf{A}_1$ in view of (7.1) when parameters are replaced by estimates. It follows from (7.2) that this expression can be simplified to $-3T/2$. Therefore, the maximum of (4.9) is

$$-\tfrac{3}{2}T\log 2\pi e - \tfrac{1}{2}T\log|\hat{\mathbf{\Omega}}_{ML}| \tag{7.10}$$

where $\hat{\mathbf{\Omega}}_{ML}$ is used here as an explicit symbol for the maximum-likelihood estimator of $\mathbf{\Omega}$.

We obtain the unconstrained maximum of the log-likelihood function by imposing neither the second-moment model nor Slutsky symmetry. The value of this unconstrained maximum is

$$-\tfrac{3}{2}T\log 2\pi e - \tfrac{1}{2}T\log|\hat{\mathbf{\Omega}}_{LS}| \tag{7.11}$$

where $\hat{\mathbf{\Omega}}_{LS}$ is the least-squares estimator of $\mathbf{\Omega}$ (the leading 3×3 submatrix of the first matrix in Table 7.10). By subtracting (7.11) from (7.10) and taking antilogs we obtain the likelihood ratio for testing the second-moment model:

$$l = \frac{|\hat{\mathbf{\Omega}}_{LS}|^{T/2}}{|\hat{\mathbf{\Omega}}_{ML}|^{T/2}} \tag{7.12}$$

The specification of Section 7.6 requires consideration of the log-likelihood function (6.9). The quadratic form in the second line of (6.9) can be written as $-\frac{1}{2}T\,\mathrm{tr}\,\mathbf{\Omega}^{-1}\mathbf{A}_2$, where $\mathbf{A}_2$ is defined in (7.7). It is readily verified that this results in the same likelihood ratio (7.12) except that $\hat{\mathbf{\Omega}}_{ML}$ must now be interpreted according to the model of Section 7.6.

Applications of the Test

The test will be based on the asymptotic χ^2 distribution of $-2\log l$. To determine the number of degrees of freedom we note that the unconstrained maximum-likelihood procedure (which is least squares in this case) adjusts 18 parameters: three conditional marginal shares, nine modified conditional Slutsky coefficients, three disturbance variances, and three disturbance covariances. The model of Section 7.5 adjusts 10 parameters: γ, $\boldsymbol{\mu}_0$ (three elements) and $\mathbf{\Omega}$ (six, given the symmetry of the $\mathbf{\Omega}$ estimator). Therefore, the χ^2 distribution has $18-10=8$ degrees of freedom for the model of Section 7.5.

The determinant of the 3×3 matrix $\hat{\mathbf{\Omega}}_{LS}$ in the first three lines of Table 7.10 is 8.24×10^{-16} and that of $\hat{\mathbf{\Omega}}_{ML}$ of Section 7.5 is 14.32×10^{-16}, which yields a likelihood ratio of 2.28×10^{-3} for $T=22$. The implied value of $-2\log l$ is 12.2, which is less than 13.4, the 10 percent point of $\chi^2(8)$. For the model of Section 7.6 we obtain a determinant of $\hat{\mathbf{\Omega}}_{ML}$ equal to 17.00×10^{-16}, which lowers the likelihood ratio to 3.47×10^{-4} and raises $-2\log l$ to 15.9. The relevant χ^2 distribution is now $\chi^2(10)$ because the number of parameters adjusted in Section 7.6 is two below that of Section 7.5, the three-element vector $\boldsymbol{\mu}_0$ being eliminated at the expense of the scalar δ. Since the 10 percent point of $\chi^2(10)$ is 16.0, the second-moment model is acceptable at the 10 percent significance level under both specifications.

It should be noted that we obtain the same value for the likelihood ratio when the 3×3 matrix $\mathbf{\Omega}$ does not refer to Beef, Pork and Chicken but to any other selection of three of the four meats. To prove this we take the $\mathbf{\Omega}$ used above, $[\omega_{ij}]$ with $i, j=1, 2$ and 3, and we add (without changing the value of the determinant) the sum of the first two columns to the third. This yields the following determinant:

$$\begin{vmatrix} \omega_{11} & \omega_{12} & \omega_{11}+\omega_{12}+\omega_{13} \\ \omega_{21} & \omega_{22} & \omega_{21}+\omega_{22}+\omega_{23} \\ \omega_{31} & \omega_{32} & \omega_{31}+\omega_{32}+\omega_{33} \end{vmatrix} = \begin{vmatrix} \omega_{11} & \omega_{12} & -\omega_{14} \\ \omega_{21} & \omega_{22} & -\omega_{24} \\ \omega_{31} & \omega_{32} & -\omega_{34} \end{vmatrix} = - \begin{vmatrix} \omega_{11} & \omega_{12} & \omega_{14} \\ \omega_{21} & \omega_{22} & \omega_{24} \\ \omega_{31} & \omega_{32} & \omega_{34} \end{vmatrix}$$

Next, in the determinant in the third member, add the sum of the first two rows to the third. This gives, after similar rearrangements,

$$(7.13) \qquad |\mathbf{\Omega}| = \begin{vmatrix} \omega_{11} & \omega_{12} & \omega_{14} \\ \omega_{21} & \omega_{22} & \omega_{24} \\ \omega_{41} & \omega_{42} & \omega_{44} \end{vmatrix}$$

The determinant on the right is that of $\mathbf{\Omega}$ with Chicken rather than Lamb deleted. By applying (7.13) to the determinants of $\hat{\mathbf{\Omega}}_{LS}$ and $\hat{\mathbf{\Omega}}_{ML}$ in (7.12) we find that the value of the likelihood ratio is independent of the choice of the deleted meat.

7.8 The Second-Moment Model Reconsidered

Comparison of the Second-Moment Models of Chapters 6 and 7

Recall that the likelihood ratio test of Section 6.8 was much less favorable for the second-moment model than the numerical values described above (although the evidence shown in Figure 6.3 was encouraging for this model). In the last subsection of Section 6.8 we surmised that observational errors could have caused the failure of the data to pass the test. The estimates of σ^2, derived in the next paragraph, seem to confirm this. When there are observational errors, they are combined with the behavioral disturbances and tend to raise the residual mean squares, thus leading to a larger estimate of σ^2.

To estimate σ^2 we use (4.3), $\gamma = -\phi \bar{W}_{gt}/\sigma^2$. When we substitute the estimate given in (6.23) for γ, a value of the order $-.6$ for ϕ, and the average total-meat budget share obtained from (2.1) for $\bar{W}_{gt}$, the implied value of σ^2 is

$$(8.1) \qquad \sigma^2 \approx 5 \times 10^{-6}$$

This is indeed much smaller than the estimates in eqs. (8.16) and (8.17) of Section 6.8, both of which exceed 10^{-4}.

Aggregation Over Consumers

We now return to Section 4.4, where conditions were derived under which the second-moment model is applicable to per capita data. The approach amounts to writing ε_{ic}, the disturbance of the demand for the ith commodity by the cth consumer, as the sum of a national component, ζ_i, and a personal component, ζ_{ic}. Similarly, $\sigma^2 = \sigma_0^2 + \sigma_1^2$, where σ_0^2 refers to the national and σ_1^2 to the personal component of the microdisturbances. When we have a per capita demand model for a sufficiently large group of consumers, the associated second-moment model is formulated in terms of σ_0^2 rather than σ^2. Also, for any pair of consumers (the cth and the dth, $c \neq d$) and for any commodity (the ith), the correlation coefficient of the microdisturbances ε_{ic} and ε_{id} equals $\rho = \sigma_0^2/\sigma^2$, independent of the subscripts c, d and i.

Since (8.1) is derived from per capita data, it is an estimate of σ_0^2; we shall adhere to this notation in the aggregation analysis which follows. The question arises whether we can draw numerical conclusions on ρ and σ^2 from this σ_0^2 estimate. Since the aggregation conditions of Section 4.4 are rather restrictive, it makes little sense to strive for generality. We shall therefore confine ourselves to equations of the preference-independent type,

$$\bar{w}_{it} Dq_{it} = \mu_i DQ_t + \phi\mu_i \left(Dp_{it} - \sum_{k=1}^{n} \mu_k Dp_{kt} \right) + \varepsilon_{it} \tag{8.2}$$

This equation should be interpreted as referring to an individual consumer; the subscript c is suppressed in order not to overburden the notation.

Multiple Correlation Coefficients of Demand Equations

We shall use the multiple correlation coefficient of an individual demand equation as a tool for obtaining an idea of the order of magnitude of σ^2. This requires an assessment of the degree to which the behavior of the left-hand variable is accounted for by income and prices. Since it is somewhat easier to speculate on a multiple correlation coefficient when we have Dq_{it} on the left, we divide (8.2) by $\bar{w}_{it}$. This gives an equation that describes the log-change in the consumer's demand for the ith commodity:

$$Dq_{it} = E_i x_{it} + \frac{\varepsilon_{it}}{\bar{w}_{it}} \tag{8.3}$$

Here $E_i = \mu_i / \bar{w}_{it}$ is the income elasticity of the ith commodity and x_{it} is the tth observation on a mixed income-price variable:

$$x_{it} = DQ_t + \phi \left(Dp_{it} - \sum_{k=1}^{n} \mu_k Dp_{kt} \right) \tag{8.4}$$

As the E_i notation (without subscript t) indicates, we shall ignore changes in this elasticity over time.

Write R_i for the population value of the multiple correlation coefficient associated with (8.3) for a set of T successive annual observations. Since there is no constant term in (8.3), we shall define R_i in terms of second moments around zero. As is well known, the ratio of R_i^2 to $1-R_i^2$ is then equal to the mean square of the "systematic part" of the equation divided by the second moment of the disturbance $\varepsilon_{it}/\bar{w}_{it}$; this second moment is of course identical to the variance because the disturbance has zero mean. We ignore the variation over time of $\bar{w}_{it}$ in $\varepsilon_{it}/\bar{w}_{it}$ by writing this ratio as ε_{it}/w_i. Thus, applying the second-moment model to the individual consumer (with σ^2 rather than σ_0^2), we have

$$\frac{R_i^2}{1-R_i^2} = \frac{E_i^2 k_i}{\sigma^2 \mu_i (1-\mu_i)/w_i^2}$$

where k_i is the mean square of the variable (8.4) over the T observations. Using $E_i = \mu_i/w_i$, we can simplify this result to

$$\text{(8.5)} \qquad \frac{R_i^2}{1-R_i^2} = \frac{k_i}{\sigma^2} \frac{\mu_i}{1-\mu_i}$$

which shows that the budget share and the income elasticity disappear from the right-hand side.

Numerical Speculation

The mean square k_i will be different for different values of i, because x_{it} involves the change in the deflated i^{th} price besides the change in real income. However, mean squares of deflated annual price log-changes of most commodities are probably within relatively narrow limits. To the extent that this is true, (8.5) implies that R_i tends to increase with μ_i. This is a plausible result: the fit of a demand equation tends to be better when the commodity is more important as measured by its marginal share.

We proceed to consider a commodity with a marginal share $\mu_i = .01$, so that the right-hand side of (8.5) becomes approximately $k_i/100\sigma^2$. Recall that the left-hand variable of (8.3) is the annual change in the logarithm of the ith quantity for an individual consumer. The associated R_i for a commodity of this size will probably be in the range from .3 to .5, which implies that the left-hand side of (8.5) varies from one-tenth to one-third.

Hence,

$$\tfrac{1}{10} < \frac{k_i}{100\,\sigma^2} < \tfrac{1}{3}$$

which is equivalent to

(8.6) $$(.03)\,k_i < \sigma^2 < (.1)\,k_i$$

On the assumption that individual real incomes and relative prices typically change by about 5 to 10 percent per year, we may put the root-mean-square of the income-price variable (8.4) at a little over .05 to almost .15. Taking the square, we obtain a k_i between about .003 and .02. By combining this with (8.6) we obtain

(8.7) $$10^{-4} \lesssim \sigma^2 \lesssim 2 \times 10^{-3}$$

Obviously, this wide interval is only a rough guess for the order of magnitude of σ^2. But it does suggest, when compared with (8.1), that σ_0^2 is only a small fraction of σ^2. The implication is that the demand correlation between consumers, $\rho = \sigma_0^2/\sigma^2$, is probably not more than a few percentage points and perhaps even less.

CHAPTER 8

BLOCKWISE DEPENDENCE

Chapter 7 is based on the utility specification

$$u(\mathbf{q}) = u_1(\mathbf{q}_1) + \cdots + u_G(\mathbf{q}_G)$$

where $\mathbf{q}_g$ is the vector of quantities that fall under the commodity group S_g. This amounts to an additive separation of utility in terms of G groups. In this chapter we relax this assumption by postulating separability but not additivity. The theory is formulated in terms of the equations of the Rotterdam Model. Section 8.6 describes applications to the demand for meats in the United States. Section 8.7 outlines an extension of the Rotterdam Model for utility maximization over time.

8.1 The Utility Structure of Blockwise Dependence

We assume that the n commodities of the basket can be allocated to G groups $S_1, \ldots, S_G$ in such a way that (1) each commodity belongs to exactly one group and (2) the utility function can be written as an increasing function $f(\ )$ of G partial utility functions, each involving the quantities of only one group:

$$u(\mathbf{q}) = f(u_1(\mathbf{q}_1), \ldots, u_G(\mathbf{q}_G)) \tag{1.1}$$

This specification, that of *blockwise dependence*, contains the block-independence assumption as a special case for the $f(\ )$ which is the sum of the partial utility functions. It is also known as the case of *weak separability* of the G groups; see, for example, GOLDMAN and UZAWA (1964). Reference should also be made to BARTEN (1971), who derived some of the results described in this chapter.

Note that (1.1) amounts to a restriction on the consumer's preferences if and only if at least one group consists of two or more commodities. When all groups consist of one commodity each, (1.1) becomes

$$u(\mathbf{q}) = f(u_1(q_1), u_2(q_2), \ldots, u_n(q_n)) \tag{1.2}$$

of which the following specification is an example:

$$u(\mathbf{q}) = f(\log q_1, \log q_2, \ldots, \log q_n)$$

This specification is equivalent to a reformulation of the utility function in terms of the logarithms of the quantities, which clearly implies no restriction at all on the consumer's preferences. It is interesting to compare (1.2) with the corresponding case for block-independence,

$$u(\mathbf{q}) = u_1(q_1) + u_2(q_2) + \cdots + u_n(q_n)$$

which amounts to preference independence and which is the strongest version of block-independence.

Second-Order Derivatives of the Utility Function

It is assumed throughout this book that the utility function has continuous derivatives up to the third order. Here we extend this assumption to the $G+1$ functions $f(\ )$ and $u_g(\ )$ for $g = 1, \ldots, G$.

By differentiating (1.1) with respect to q_i we obtain

$$\text{(1.3)} \qquad \frac{\partial u}{\partial q_i} = \frac{\partial f}{\partial u_g} \frac{\partial u_g}{\partial q_i} \quad \text{if} \quad i \in S_g$$

after which we differentiate $\partial u / \partial q_i$ with respect to the quantity q_j of a good that belongs to a different group S_h,

$$\text{(1.4)} \qquad \frac{\partial^2 u}{\partial q_i \partial q_j} = \frac{\partial^2 f}{\partial u_g \partial u_h} \frac{\partial u_g}{\partial q_i} \frac{\partial u_h}{\partial q_j} = \frac{\dfrac{\partial^2 f}{\partial u_g \partial u_h}}{\dfrac{\partial f}{\partial u_g} \dfrac{\partial f}{\partial u_h}} \frac{\partial u}{\partial q_i} \frac{\partial u}{\partial q_j}$$

where the last step is based on (1.3). Note that $\partial f / \partial u_g$ and $\partial f / \partial u_h$ are positive because $f(\ )$ is by assumption an increasing function of its G arguments. Also note that the second-order derivative of $f(\ )$ with respect to u_g and u_h is symmetric in g and h because $f(\ )$ has continuous derivatives of the third order.

Next we divide (1.4) by $p_i p_j$ and apply the equilibrium condition $\partial u / \partial q_i = \lambda p_i$ to the third member of (1.4):

$$\text{(1.5)} \qquad \frac{\partial^2 u}{\partial (p_i q_i) \partial (p_j q_j)} = \lambda^2 \frac{\dfrac{\partial^2 f}{\partial u_g \partial u_h}}{\dfrac{\partial f}{\partial u_g} \dfrac{\partial f}{\partial u_h}} \qquad \begin{array}{c} i \in S_g \\ j \in S_h \\ g \neq h \end{array}$$

Hence, if we select two commodities (the ith and the jth) in two different groups, an additional dollar spent on either good has the same effect on the marginal utility of one dollar spent on the other, for any pair of commodities that we select in these two groups. For example, if food and clothing are two such commodity groups, an extra dollar spent on either bread or butter has the same effect on the marginal utility of one dollar spent on any commodity of the clothing group. This shows that the utility interaction of commodities of different groups is a matter of the groups rather than the individual commodities, which should clarify the term blockwise dependence. Under the stronger condition of block-independence such interactions of different groups are all zero, because $f(\ )$ is then linear and its second-order derivative in (1.5) vanishes.

It follows from (1.1) and (1.3) that if i and j both belong to S_g, the corresponding second-order derivative of $u(\ )$ involves an extra term equal to $\partial f/\partial u_g$ multiplied by $\partial^2 u_g/\partial q_i \partial q_j$. Hence (1.5) for $g=h$ becomes

$$\frac{\partial^2 u}{\partial (p_i q_i)\,\partial (p_j q_j)} = \lambda^2 \frac{\partial^2 f/\partial u_g^2}{(\partial f/\partial u_g)^2} + \frac{\partial f}{\partial u_g} \frac{\partial^2 u_g}{\partial (p_i q_i)\,\partial (p_j q_j)} \tag{1.6}$$

which in contrast to (1.5) depends on the subscripts i and j of the individual commodities.

The Hessian of the Utility Function in Expenditure Terms

Write n_g for the number of commodities of S_g, so that $n_1 + \cdots + n_G = n$. We arrange the commodities so that those of S_1 come first, those of S_2 next, and so on.

The left-hand sides of (1.5) and (1.6) are elements of $\mathbf{P}^{-1}\mathbf{U}\mathbf{P}^{-1}$, the Hessian matrix of the utility function in expenditure terms, where $\mathbf{P}$ is the $n \times n$ diagonal matrix which contains the prices of the n commodities in the diagonal and $\mathbf{U}$ is the Hessian of the utility function in quantity terms. With $\boldsymbol{\iota}_g$ defined as the column vector which consists of n_g unit elements, we use (1.5) and (1.6) to write the Hessian in expenditure terms as

$$\mathbf{P}^{-1}\mathbf{U}\mathbf{P}^{-1} = k \begin{bmatrix} \mathbf{V}_1 & c_{12}\boldsymbol{\iota}_1\boldsymbol{\iota}_2' & \cdots & c_{1G}\boldsymbol{\iota}_1\boldsymbol{\iota}_G' \\ c_{21}\boldsymbol{\iota}_2\boldsymbol{\iota}_1' & \mathbf{V}_2 & \cdots & c_{2G}\boldsymbol{\iota}_2\boldsymbol{\iota}_G' \\ \vdots & \vdots & & \vdots \\ c_{G1}\boldsymbol{\iota}_G\boldsymbol{\iota}_1' & c_{G2}\boldsymbol{\iota}_G\boldsymbol{\iota}_2' & \cdots & \mathbf{V}_G \end{bmatrix} \tag{1.7}$$

where k and c_{gh} are scalars and $\mathbf{V}_g$ is an $n_g \times n_g$ matrix:

$$k = \frac{\lambda}{\phi m} \tag{1.8}$$

$$c_{gh} = \phi\lambda m \frac{\dfrac{\partial^2 f}{\partial u_g \partial u_h}}{\dfrac{\partial f}{\partial u_g}\dfrac{\partial f}{\partial u_h}} \quad \text{if} \quad g \neq h \tag{1.9}$$

$$\mathbf{V}_g = \phi\lambda m \frac{\partial^2 f/\partial u_g^2}{(\partial f/\partial u_g)^2} \boldsymbol{\iota}_g \boldsymbol{\iota}_g' + \frac{\phi m}{\lambda}\frac{\partial f}{\partial u_g}\left[\frac{\partial^2 u_g}{\partial(p_i q_i)\,\partial(p_j q_j)}\right] \tag{1.10}$$

The expression in brackets in (1.10) stands for the $n_g \times n_g$ Hessian matrix of the group utility function $u_g(\;)$ in expenditure terms. Since $\mathbf{P}^{-1}\mathbf{U}\mathbf{P}^{-1}$ is symmetric negative definite and $k<0$, the matrices $\mathbf{V}_1, \ldots, \mathbf{V}_G$ are symmetric positive definite.

We obtain a more compact notation by introducing

$$\mathbf{C} = \begin{bmatrix} 0 & c_{12} & \cdots & c_{1G} \\ c_{21} & 0 & \cdots & c_{2G} \\ \vdots & \vdots & & \vdots \\ c_{G1} & c_{G2} & \cdots & 0 \end{bmatrix} \tag{1.11}$$

which is a symmetric $G \times G$ matrix whose off-diagonal elements are defined in (1.9). Then (1.7) may be written as

$$\mathbf{P}^{-1}\mathbf{U}\mathbf{P}^{-1} = k(\mathbf{V} + \mathbf{J}\mathbf{C}\mathbf{J}') \tag{1.12}$$

where $\mathbf{V}$ is an $n \times n$ block-diagonal matrix and $\mathbf{J}$ is of order $n \times G$:

$$\mathbf{V} = \begin{bmatrix} \mathbf{V}_1 & \mathbf{0} & \cdots & \mathbf{0} \\ \mathbf{0} & \mathbf{V}_2 & \cdots & \mathbf{0} \\ \vdots & \vdots & & \vdots \\ \mathbf{0} & \mathbf{0} & \cdots & \mathbf{V}_G \end{bmatrix} \qquad \mathbf{J} = \begin{bmatrix} \boldsymbol{\iota}_1 & \mathbf{0} & \cdots & \mathbf{0} \\ \mathbf{0} & \boldsymbol{\iota}_2 & \cdots & \mathbf{0} \\ \vdots & \vdots & & \vdots \\ \mathbf{0} & \mathbf{0} & \cdots & \boldsymbol{\iota}_G \end{bmatrix} \tag{1.13}$$

The Inverse of the Hessian

It will prove convenient to introduce, for $g=1, \ldots, G$, the vector $\mathbf{a}_g$ and the scalar α_g defined as

$$\mathbf{a}_g = \mathbf{V}_g^{-1}\boldsymbol{\iota}_g \qquad \alpha_g = \boldsymbol{\iota}_g'\mathbf{a}_g = \boldsymbol{\iota}_g'\mathbf{V}_g^{-1}\boldsymbol{\iota}_g > 0 \tag{1.14}$$

where the inequality sign on the far right is based on the positive definiteness of $\mathbf{V}_g$. So, with $\mathbf{V}$ and $\mathbf{J}$ defined in (1.13), we have

$$\mathbf{V}^{-1}\mathbf{J} = \begin{bmatrix} \mathbf{a}_1 & \mathbf{0} & \cdots & \mathbf{0} \\ \mathbf{0} & \mathbf{a}_2 & \cdots & \mathbf{0} \\ \vdots & \vdots & & \vdots \\ \mathbf{0} & \mathbf{0} & \cdots & \mathbf{a}_G \end{bmatrix} \qquad \mathbf{J}'\mathbf{V}^{-1}\mathbf{J} = \begin{bmatrix} \alpha_1 & 0 & \cdots & 0 \\ 0 & \alpha_2 & \cdots & 0 \\ \vdots & \vdots & & \vdots \\ 0 & 0 & \cdots & \alpha_G \end{bmatrix} \tag{1.15}$$

In the next subsection we shall invert both sides of (1.12) with the following result:

$$\text{(1.16)} \qquad \mathbf{PU}^{-1}\mathbf{P} = \frac{1}{k}(\mathbf{V}^{-1} + \mathbf{V}^{-1}\mathbf{JC}^*\mathbf{J}'\mathbf{V}^{-1})$$

Here $\mathbf{C}^*$ is the symmetric $G \times G$ matrix

$$\text{(1.17)} \qquad \mathbf{C}^* = \mathbf{D}(\mathbf{D}+\mathbf{C})^{-1}\,\mathbf{D} - \mathbf{D}$$

where $\mathbf{D}$ is the inverse of the diagonal matrix $\mathbf{J}'\mathbf{V}^{-1}\mathbf{J}$ shown in (1.15):

$$\text{(1.18)} \qquad \mathbf{D} = (\mathbf{J}'\mathbf{V}^{-1}\mathbf{J})^{-1}$$

So, using the expression for $\mathbf{V}^{-1}\mathbf{J}$ which is given in (1.15), we conclude that (1.16) can be written in partitioned form,

(1.19)

$$\mathbf{PU}^{-1}\mathbf{P} = \frac{1}{k}\begin{bmatrix} \mathbf{V}_1^{-1} + c_{11}^*\mathbf{a}_1\mathbf{a}_1' & c_{12}^*\mathbf{a}_1\mathbf{a}_2' & \cdots & c_{1G}^*\mathbf{a}_1\mathbf{a}_G' \\ c_{21}^*\mathbf{a}_2\mathbf{a}_1' & \mathbf{V}_2^{-1} + c_{22}^*\mathbf{a}_2\mathbf{a}_2' & \cdots & c_{2G}^*\mathbf{a}_2\mathbf{a}_G' \\ \vdots & \vdots & & \vdots \\ c_{G1}^*\mathbf{a}_G\mathbf{a}_1' & c_{G2}^*\mathbf{a}_G\mathbf{a}_2' & \cdots & \mathbf{V}_G^{-1} + c_{GG}^*\mathbf{a}_G\mathbf{a}_G' \end{bmatrix}$$

where c_{gh}^* is the $(g, h)^{\text{th}}$ element of $\mathbf{C}^*$. On comparing this result with (1.7) we conclude that the Hessian of the utility function in expenditure terms and the inverse of this Hessian are similar in that the off-diagonal blocks are all matrices of unit rank. When blockwise dependence is strengthened to block-independence, we have $\mathbf{C}=\mathbf{0}$ in view of (1.9) and (1.11). It follows from (1.17) that this implies $\mathbf{C}^*=\mathbf{0}$, so that (1.19) becomes a block-diagonal matrix with the inverses of $\mathbf{V}_1, \ldots, \mathbf{V}_G$ in the diagonal blocks. Note that $\mathbf{C}=\mathbf{0}$ both implies and is implied by $\mathbf{C}^*=\mathbf{0}$; this also follows from (1.17).

Derivations

We write (1.17) in the form

$$\mathbf{C}^* = \mathbf{D}(\mathbf{D}+\mathbf{C})^{-1}\,[\mathbf{D} - (\mathbf{D}+\mathbf{C})] = -\,\mathbf{D}(\mathbf{D}+\mathbf{C})^{-1}\,\mathbf{C}$$

which shows that (1.16) can be written as

$$k\mathbf{PU}^{-1}\mathbf{P} = \mathbf{V}^{-1} - \mathbf{V}^{-1}\mathbf{JD}(\mathbf{D}+\mathbf{C})^{-1}\,\mathbf{CJ}'\mathbf{V}^{-1}$$

We premultiply the right-hand side of this equation by the expression in parentheses in (1.12):

$$\begin{aligned}(\mathbf{V}+\mathbf{JCJ}')\,[\mathbf{V}^{-1} - \mathbf{V}^{-1}\mathbf{JD}(\mathbf{D}+\mathbf{C})^{-1}\,\mathbf{CJ}'\mathbf{V}^{-1}]& \\ = \mathbf{I} + \mathbf{JCJ}'\mathbf{V}^{-1} &- \mathbf{JD}(\mathbf{D}+\mathbf{C})^{-1}\,\mathbf{CJ}'\mathbf{V}^{-1} \\ &- \mathbf{JC}(\mathbf{J}'\mathbf{V}^{-1}\mathbf{JD})\,(\mathbf{D}+\mathbf{C})^{-1}\,\mathbf{CJ}'\mathbf{V}^{-1}\end{aligned}$$

We use $\mathbf{J}'\mathbf{V}^{-1}\mathbf{J}\mathbf{D}=\mathbf{I}$, which follows from (1.18), to simplify the last term and then combine the last two terms:

$$\mathbf{I}+\mathbf{J}\mathbf{C}\mathbf{J}'\mathbf{V}^{-1}-\mathbf{J}(\mathbf{D}+\mathbf{C})(\mathbf{D}+\mathbf{C})^{-1}\mathbf{C}\mathbf{J}'\mathbf{V}^{-1}=\mathbf{I}$$

This completes the proof that (1.16) gives the inverse of (1.12).

The $G\times G$ matrix $\mathbf{D}+\mathbf{C}$, the inverse of which occurs in (1.17), takes the following form in view of (1.11), (1.15) and (1.18):

$$(1.20)\qquad \mathbf{D}+\mathbf{C}=(\mathbf{J}'\mathbf{V}^{-1}\mathbf{J})^{-1}+\mathbf{C}=\begin{bmatrix} 1/\alpha_1 & c_{12} & \dots & c_{1G} \\ c_{21} & 1/\alpha_2 & \dots & c_{2G} \\ \vdots & \vdots & & \vdots \\ c_{G1} & c_{G2} & \dots & 1/\alpha_G \end{bmatrix}$$

This is a positive definite $G\times G$ matrix. To verify this statement we postmultiply the expression in parentheses in (1.12), which is positive definite because $\mathbf{P}^{-1}\mathbf{U}\mathbf{P}^{-1}$ is negative definite and $k<0$, by the matrix product $\mathbf{V}^{-1}\mathbf{J}\mathbf{D}$ and premultiply by the transpose of this product:

$$(\mathbf{V}^{-1}\mathbf{J}\mathbf{D})'(\mathbf{V}+\mathbf{J}\mathbf{C}\mathbf{J}')\mathbf{V}^{-1}\mathbf{J}\mathbf{D}=\mathbf{D}\mathbf{J}'\mathbf{V}^{-1}\mathbf{J}\mathbf{D}+\mathbf{D}\mathbf{J}'\mathbf{V}^{-1}\mathbf{J}\mathbf{C}\mathbf{J}'\mathbf{V}^{-1}\mathbf{J}\mathbf{D}$$

It follows from (1.18) that this may be simplified to

$$(1.21)\qquad (\mathbf{V}^{-1}\mathbf{J}\mathbf{D})'(\mathbf{V}+\mathbf{J}\mathbf{C}\mathbf{J}')\mathbf{V}^{-1}\mathbf{J}\mathbf{D}=\mathbf{D}+\mathbf{C}$$

Given that $\mathbf{V}+\mathbf{J}\mathbf{C}\mathbf{J}'$ is positive definite, $\mathbf{D}+\mathbf{C}$ must also be positive definite if $\mathbf{V}^{-1}\mathbf{J}\mathbf{D}$ has full column rank. This is indeed the case, because $\mathbf{J}$ has full column rank and the diagonal elements of the diagonal matrix $\mathbf{D}$ are the reciprocals of the α's, which are all positive [see (1.14)].

8.2 The Rotterdam Model Under Blockwise Dependence

Recall from eq. (5.17) of Section 1.5 that the price coefficient matrix of the Rotterdam Model, to be written $\mathbf{N}$, is proportional to the inverse of the Hessian in expenditure terms, $\mathbf{N}=(\lambda/m)\mathbf{P}\mathbf{U}^{-1}\mathbf{P}$. On combining this with (1.16) and (1.8) we obtain

$$(2.1)\qquad \phi^{-1}\mathbf{N}=\mathbf{V}^{-1}+\mathbf{V}^{-1}\mathbf{J}\mathbf{C}^*\mathbf{J}'\mathbf{V}^{-1}$$

or, using (1.19),

$$(2.2)\qquad \phi^{-1}\mathbf{N}=\begin{bmatrix} \mathbf{V}_1^{-1}+c_{11}^*\mathbf{a}_1\mathbf{a}_1' & c_{12}^*\mathbf{a}_1\mathbf{a}_2' & \dots & c_{1G}^*\mathbf{a}_1\mathbf{a}_G' \\ c_{21}^*\mathbf{a}_2\mathbf{a}_1' & \mathbf{V}_2^{-1}+c_{22}^*\mathbf{a}_2\mathbf{a}_2' & \dots & c_{2G}^*\mathbf{a}_2\mathbf{a}_G' \\ \vdots & \vdots & & \vdots \\ c_{G1}^*\mathbf{a}_G\mathbf{a}_1' & c_{G2}^*\mathbf{a}_G\mathbf{a}_2' & \dots & \mathbf{V}_G^{-1}+c_{GG}^*\mathbf{a}_G\mathbf{a}_G' \end{bmatrix}$$

In (2.1) and (2.2) we have the normalized price coefficient matrix on the left, each element of **N** being divided by ϕ, which is the sum of all elements of **N**. The off-diagonal blocks on the right in (2.2) show that under blockwise dependence the price coefficients ν_{ij} of commodities which belong to different groups ($i \in S_g, j \in S_h, g \neq h$) form a matrix of unit rank. In this section we analyze the implications of this property for the demand equations of the Rotterdam Model.

Marginal Shares and Conditional Marginal Shares

Write the constraint $\sum_j \nu_{ij} = \phi\mu_i$ in the form

$$\sum_{j=1}^{n} \frac{\nu_{ij}}{\phi} = \mu_i \qquad i = 1, \dots, n \tag{2.3}$$

This implies that the sum of all n elements in the ith row of the right-hand matrix in (2.2) equals μ_i. Let us apply this summation to each of the first n_1 rows in (2.2) corresponding to the commodity group S_1. This gives a sum vector consisting of n_1 elements,

$$\begin{aligned}(\mathbf{V}_1^{-1} + c_{11}^* \mathbf{a}_1 \mathbf{a}_1') \boldsymbol{\iota}_1 + (c_{12}^* \mathbf{a}_1 \mathbf{a}_2') \boldsymbol{\iota}_2 + \dots + (c_{1G}^* \mathbf{a}_1 \mathbf{a}_G') \boldsymbol{\iota}_G \\ = \mathbf{a}_1 + c_{11}^* \alpha_1 \mathbf{a}_1 + c_{12}^* \alpha_2 \mathbf{a}_1 + \dots + c_{1G}^* \alpha_G \mathbf{a}_1\end{aligned}$$

where the equal sign is based on (1.14). Since each element of this sum vector equals μ_i for some $i \in S_1$, this must be the vector of all marginal shares that fall under S_1.

More generally, summation of all elements in each of the n_g rows in (2.2) that correspond to S_g gives

$$\left(1 + \sum_{h=1}^{G} c_{gh}^* \alpha_h\right) \mathbf{a}_g = \boldsymbol{\mu}_g \tag{2.4}$$

where $\boldsymbol{\mu}_g$ is the n_g-element vector of the marginal shares of the commodities of S_g,

$$\boldsymbol{\mu} = [\boldsymbol{\mu}_1' \quad \boldsymbol{\mu}_2' \quad \dots \quad \boldsymbol{\mu}_G']' \tag{2.5}$$

with $\boldsymbol{\mu}$ defined as the marginal share vector of all n commodities. Next premultiply (2.4) by the transpose of $\boldsymbol{\iota}_g$ and use (1.14),

$$\left(1 + \sum_{h=1}^{G} c_{gh}^* \alpha_h\right) \alpha_g = M_g \tag{2.6}$$

where

$$M_g = \boldsymbol{\iota}_g' \boldsymbol{\mu}_g = \sum_{i \in S_g} \mu_i \tag{2.7}$$

is the marginal share of the commodity group S_g.

Therefore, if the expression in parentheses in (2.4) and (2.6) does not vanish, we have the following result for the vector of conditional marginal shares of S_g:

$$[\mu_i / M_g] = \frac{1}{M_g} \boldsymbol{\mu}_g = \frac{1}{\alpha_g} \mathbf{a}_g \tag{2.8}$$

Zero Marginal Shares of Commodity Groups

If the expression in parentheses in (2.4) vanishes, the marginal shares of all commodities of S_g are zero and so is their sum, $M_g = 0$. This possibility should not be excluded. We have $M_g > 0$ for each g under block-independence, but this inequality does not hold under the weaker assumption of blockwise dependence. For example, take the case of blockwise dependence for groups consisting of one commodity each as discussed below (1.2). No constraints on the consumer's preferences are implied in such a case, so that the one-commodity groups may have zero marginal shares. In fact, both $M_g = 0$ and $M_g < 0$ are possible under blockwise dependence, as will be explained in remark (3) on page 73.

If M_g vanishes, it is inappropriate to define a conditional marginal share as μ_i / M_g, as is done in (2.8). However, it follows from (1.14) and the positive definiteness of $\mathbf{V}_g$ that the third member of (2.8) is well defined under all circumstances. We shall therefore replace (2.8) by

$$[\mu_i^g] = \tilde{\boldsymbol{\mu}}_g = \frac{1}{\alpha_g} \mathbf{a}_g \tag{2.9}$$

where $\tilde{\boldsymbol{\mu}}_g$ is the n_g-element vector of the conditional marginal shares of S_g, which exists when M_g vanishes. We obviously have

$$\mu_i = \mu_i^g M_g \quad \text{if} \quad i \in S_g \tag{2.10}$$

or, in words, the marginal share of a good is equal to its conditional marginal share of the total marginal share of the group. Also, in view of (1.14), the conditional marginal shares add up to 1 for each group:

$$\sum_{i \in S_g} \mu_i^g = \boldsymbol{\iota}_g' \tilde{\boldsymbol{\mu}}_g = 1 \qquad g = 1, \ldots, G \tag{2.11}$$

Price Coefficients and Conditional Marginal Shares

It follows from (2.2) that the $n_g \times n_h$ price coefficient submatrix which corresponds to two different groups S_g and S_h is $\phi c^*_{gh}\mathbf{a}_g\mathbf{a}'_h$. On comparing this with (2.9) we conclude

$$\nu_{ij} = N_{gh}\mu^g_i\mu^h_j \quad \text{if} \quad i \in S_g,\ j \in S_h,\ g \neq h \tag{2.12}$$

where

$$N_{gh} = \phi c^*_{gh}\alpha_g\alpha_h \quad \text{if} \quad g \neq h \tag{2.13}$$

Hence, *when i and j belong to different groups, their price coefficient ν_{ij} is proportional to the product of their conditional marginal shares.* The proportionality constant (N_{gh}) depends on the groups to which they belong. In the case of block-independence we have $\mathbf{C}^* = \mathbf{0}$ and hence $N_{gh} = 0$ for $g \neq h$, so that the ν_{ij}'s considered in (2.12) all vanish.

Next, for $i \in S_g$, sum ν_{ij} over $j \in S_g$,

$$\sum_{j \in S_g} \nu_{ij} = \sum_{j=1}^{n} \nu_{ij} - \sum_{h \neq g} \sum_{j \in S_h} \nu_{ij} = \phi\mu_i - \mu^g_i \sum_{h \neq g} N_{gh}$$

where the last step is based on (2.11) and (2.12). The result can be written in the more convenient form

$$\sum_{j \in S_g} \nu_{ij} = N_{gg}\mu^g_i \quad \text{if} \quad i \in S_g \tag{2.14}$$

where

$$N_{gg} = \phi M_g - \sum_{h \neq g} N_{gh} \qquad g = 1, \ldots, G \tag{2.15}$$

Equation (2.14) states that, *for each $i \in S_g$, the sum of the ν_{ij}'s of its own group is proportional to its conditional marginal share.* The proportionality constant (N_{gg}) is, in general, different for different groups. Under block-independence (2.15) is simplified to $N_{gg} = \phi M_g$, so that (2.14) amounts to the familiar result

$$\sum_{j \in S_g} \nu_{ij} = \phi M_g \mu^g_i = \phi\mu_i \quad \text{if} \quad i \in S_g \tag{2.16}$$

Demand Equations Under Blockwise Dependence

Consider the substitution term in the ith demand equation ($i \in S_g$) of the Rotterdam Model:

$$\sum_{h=1}^{G} \sum_{j \in S_h} \nu_{ij}\left(Dp_{jt} - \sum_{k=1}^{n} \mu_k Dp_{kt}\right)$$

We use a double summation (first over groups, then over commodities within groups) in order to separate this term into two components: one which contains only the log-changes in the deflated prices of S_g,

$$\sum_{j \in S_g} \nu_{ij} (Dp_{jt} - \sum_{k=1}^{n} \mu_k Dp_{kt}) \tag{2.17}$$

and a second which involves all other deflated prices. It follows from (2.12) that the latter component can be written as

$$\mu_i^g \sum_{h \neq g} N_{gh} \sum_{j \in S_h} \mu_j^h \left(Dp_{jt} - \sum_{k=1}^{n} \mu_k Dp_{kt} \right) = \mu_i^g \sum_{h \neq g} N_{gh} \left(DP'_{ht} - \sum_{k=1}^{n} \mu_k Dp_{kt} \right) \tag{2.18}$$

where

$$DP'_{gt} = \sum_{i \in S_g} \mu_i^g Dp_{it} \qquad g = 1, \ldots, G \tag{2.19}$$

The definition (2.19) is equivalent to eq. (1.3) of Section 7.1 but formulated in terms of the conditional marginal shares (2.9).

On combining (2.18) with the other component of the substitution term given in (2.17) we obtain the following demand equation for $i \in S_g$:

$$\bar{w}_{it} Dq_{it} = \mu_i DQ_t + \sum_{j \in S_g} \nu_{ij} \left(Dp_{jt} - \sum_{k=1}^{n} \mu_k Dp_{kt} \right) + \mu_i^g \sum_{h \neq g} N_{gh} \left(DP'_{ht} - \sum_{k=1}^{n} \mu_k Dp_{kt} \right) + \varepsilon_{it} \tag{2.20}$$

Therefore, under blockwise dependence each demand equation contains the changes in the relative prices of commodities of groups other than its own, but in a very special way, viz., as *marginally weighted price indexes of commodity groups.* This result makes the blockwise dependence visible at the level of the demand equations for the individual goods.

Under block-independence we have the constraint (2.16), which may be formulated as a proportionality (for each $i \in S_g$) of the sum of the ν_{ij}'s over $j \in S_g$ to the ith conditional marginal share, with ϕM_g as proportionality constant. It follows from (2.14) that the ν_{ij}'s shown in (2.20) are subject to the same proportionality except that the proportionality constant is N_{gg} rather than ϕM_g. The properties of the N_{gh}'s will be considered in Section 8.3.

The Number of Unconstrained Parameters

The particular way in which the commodity prices of other groups (S_h with $h \neq g$) occur in (2.20) results, in general, in a reduction of the number of unconstrained parameters. Given the symmetry of N_{gh} with respect to g and h which is implied by (2.13), there are $\frac{1}{2}G(G-1)$ unconstrained N_{gh}'s with $g \neq h$. Since the N_{gg}'s are determined by these N_{gh}'s and by ϕ and the M_g's in view of (2.15), we thus have a total of $\frac{1}{2}G(G-1)$ unconstrained coefficients N_{gh} in addition to ϕ and the marginal shares. [The analysis of the N_{gh}'s in Section 8.3 will confirm this count.] Also, given (2.14) and the symmetry of $[\nu_{ij}]$, there are $\frac{1}{2}n_g(n_g-1)$ unconstrained ν_{ij}'s in (2.20) for all $i \in S_g$. Therefore, apart from ϕ and the marginal shares, the total number of unconstrained parameters in the demand model (2.20) for $i=1, \ldots, n$ is

$$(2.21) \quad \tfrac{1}{2}G(G-1) + \tfrac{1}{2}\sum_{g=1}^{G} n_g(n_g-1) = \tfrac{1}{2}G(G-1) + \tfrac{1}{2}\sum_{g=1}^{G} n_g^2 - \tfrac{1}{2}n$$

Since $(1/G)\sum_g n_g^2$ is the second moment of the numbers of commodities of the G groups, and since $(1/G)\sum_g n_g = n/G$ is the corresponding mean, we have

$$\frac{1}{G}\sum_{g=1}^{G} n_g^2 = \frac{1}{G}\sum_{g=1}^{G}\left(n_g - \frac{n}{G}\right)^2 + \left(\frac{n}{G}\right)^2$$

This shows that the right-hand side of (2.21) is equal to

$$\tfrac{1}{2}G(G-1) + (\tfrac{1}{2}G)\frac{1}{G}\sum_{g=1}^{G}\left(n_g - \frac{n}{G}\right)^2 + \frac{n^2}{2G} - \tfrac{1}{2}n$$

which can be written more conveniently as

$$(2.22) \qquad (\tfrac{1}{2}G)\frac{1}{G}\sum_{g=1}^{G}\left(n_g - \frac{n}{G}\right)^2 + h(G, n)$$

where

$$(2.23) \qquad h(G, n) = \tfrac{1}{2}G(G-1) + \tfrac{1}{2}n\left(\frac{n}{G} - 1\right)$$

We conclude from (2.22) that – apart from ϕ and the marginal shares – the number of unconstrained parameters can be written as the sum of two terms. The first is a multiple $\frac{1}{2}G$ of the variance of the numbers of commodities of the G groups. It shows that, given G and n, the more unequal the numbers $n_1, \ldots, n_g$ are, the larger is the number of unconstrained parameters.

The other component of (2.22) as specified in (2.23) depends only on the number of groups (G) and the total number of commodities (n). The extreme cases are $G=1$ (no grouping) and $G=n$ (all groups consist of one commodity), for which (2.23) yields

$$(2.24) \qquad h(1, n) = h(n, n) = \tfrac{1}{2}n(n-1)$$

This suggests that, for given n, $h(\ )$ is minimized at some value of G between these limits. The matter is pursued in the next subsection, which shows that $h(G, n)$ for given n is minimized, approximately, when the average number of commodities per group, n/G, equals $(2n)^{1/3}$. Therefore, if the objective is to minimize the number of unknown parameters, the average number of commodities per group should increase with the total number (n) but at a much slower rate.

As an example, take $n=32$ for which $(2n)^{1/3}=4$, so that there are 32 commodities and eight groups. If all groups consist of four commodities, we have a total number of unconstrained parameters equal to 76 from (2.22) and (2.23). When there is block-independence, so that the N_{gh}'s disappear and the first term on the right in (2.23) is replaced by zero, this number becomes 48. These two numbers amount to reductions of about 85 and 90 percent, respectively, below the 496 unconstrained parameters which (2.24) implies for $G=1$ and $G=n$ at $n=32$. Again, note that this count of parameters does not include ϕ and the marginal shares.

Derivations

To simplify the analysis of $h(\ )$ defined in (2.23) we treat G as continuously variable. So we differentiate $h(\ )$ with respect to G:

$$\frac{\partial h}{\partial G} = G - \tfrac{1}{2} - \tfrac{1}{2}\frac{n^2}{G^2} \tag{2.25}$$

For $n \geq 2$ this derivative is negative at $G=1$ and positive at $G=n$. So we equate (2.25) to zero, $G-\frac{1}{2}-\frac{1}{2}(n/G)^2=0$, which we multiply by $-2n/G$:

$$\left(\frac{n}{G}\right)^3 + \frac{n}{G} - 2n = 0 \tag{2.26}$$

This is a cubic equation in n/G, the average number of commodities per group, with one real root; see, for example, TURNBULL (1947, pp. 118–121). This root, which provides the unique solution to our minimum problem, is

$$\frac{n}{G} = \left(n + \sqrt{n^2 + \tfrac{1}{27}}\right)^{1/3} + \left(n - \sqrt{n^2 + \tfrac{1}{27}}\right)^{1/3} \tag{2.27}$$

For large n this amounts to $n/G \approx (2n)^{1/3}$, which is obtained by expanding the right-hand side according to powers of n.

8.3 Group Demand and Conditional Demand

By summing (2.12) over $i \in S_g$ and $j \in S_h$ and applying (2.11), we find that N_{gh} for $g \neq h$ is equal to the sum of all $n_g n_h$ price coefficients which correspond to all commodities of S_g and S_h. It follows from (2.14) that this is also true for $g = h$. Therefore,

$$N_{gh} = \sum_{i \in S_g} \sum_{j \in S_h} v_{ij} \qquad g, h = 1, \ldots, G \tag{3.1}$$

In view of the definition of **J** in (1.13) this means that N_{gh} is the $(g, h)^{\text{th}}$ element of the $G \times G$ matrix

$$[N_{gh}] = \mathbf{J}'\mathbf{N}\mathbf{J} \tag{3.2}$$

Using (1.14) and (2.2), we conclude that this implies

$$N_{gh} = \begin{cases} \phi\alpha_g + \phi c_{gg}^* \alpha_g^2 & \text{if} \quad g = h \\ \phi c_{gh}^* \alpha_g \alpha_h & \text{if} \quad g \neq h \end{cases} \tag{3.3}$$

which is an extension of (2.13).

The discussion starts with demand equations for commodity groups, which will appear to have the N_{gh}'s as price coefficients, after which we turn to conditional demand equations for commodities within their groups.

The Demand for Commodity Groups

The demand equation for the group S_g is obtained by summing (2.20) over $i \in S_g$. Consider then the first price term in (2.20), which contains Dp_{jt} with $j \in S_g$. Using (2.14) and the symmetry of $[v_{ij}]$, we find that the sum over $i \in S_g$ of this term is

$$\begin{aligned} \sum_{j \in S_g} \left(\sum_{i \in S_g} v_{ij} \right) \left(Dp_{jt} - \sum_{k=1}^{n} \mu_k Dp_{kt} \right) &= N_{gg} \sum_{j \in S_g} \mu_j^g \left(Dp_{jt} - \sum_{k=1}^{n} \mu_k Dp_{kt} \right) \\ &= N_{gg} \left(DP'_{gt} - \sum_{k=1}^{n} \mu_k Dp_{kt} \right) \end{aligned}$$

Therefore, by summing (2.20) over $i \in S_g$ we obtain the following demand equation for the commodity group S_g:

$$\bar{W}_{gt} DQ_{gt} = M_g DQ_t + \sum_{h=1}^{G} N_{gh} \left(DP'_{ht} - \sum_{k=1}^{n} \mu_k Dp_{kt} \right) + E_{gt} \tag{3.4}$$

where $\bar{W}_{gt}$, DQ_{gt} and E_{gt} are defined in eqs. (1.2) and (1.5) of Section 7.1.

Equation (3.4) for $g=1,\ldots,G$ amounts to a demand equation system of the Rotterdam Model with the N_{gh}'s as price coefficients. It is the "uppercase version" of the demand model for the individual goods,

$$\bar{w}_{it}Dq_{it} = \mu_i DQ_t + \sum_{j=1}^{n} v_{ij}\left(Dp_{jt} - \sum_{k=1}^{n} \mu_k Dp_{kt}\right) + \varepsilon_{it} \tag{3.5}$$

Recall that the constraint on the marginal shares of (3.5) is $\sum_i \mu_i = 1$. For (3.4) we have the analogous constraint $\sum_g M_g = 1$. The next subsection shows that the constraints on the price coefficients of (3.4) and (3.5) are also completely analogous.

It is interesting to compare this result with the demand equation for S_g under block-independence given in eq. (1.4) of Section 7.1,

$$\bar{W}_{gt}DQ_{gt} = M_g DQ_t + \phi M_g\left(DP'_{gt} - \sum_{k=1}^{n} \mu_k Dp_{kt}\right) + E_{gt} \tag{3.6}$$

which is the uppercase version of the preference-independent demand equation for an individual good:

$$\bar{w}_{it}Dq_{it} = \mu_i DQ_t + \phi\mu_i\left(Dp_{it} - \sum_{k=1}^{n} \mu_k Dp_{kt}\right) + \varepsilon_{it} \tag{3.7}$$

Thus, whereas summation of equations for individual commodities gives a group demand equation of the preference independence type under block-independence, it yields the group demand equation (3.4) of the general Rotterdam Model type under the weaker assumption of blockwise dependence.

The Price Coefficient Matrix of the Commodity Groups

The constraints on the $n \times n$ price coefficient matrix $[v_{ij}]$ of (3.5) are symmetry, negative definiteness and $\sum_j v_{ij} = \phi\mu_i$ for each i (sum over $j=1,\ldots,n$). Below are four remarks, the first two of which show that the $G \times G$ matrix $[N_{gh}]$ of (3.4) is subject to analogous constraints.

(1) Equation (2.15) can be written as

$$\sum_{h=1}^{G} N_{gh} = \phi M_g \qquad g = 1,\ldots,G \tag{3.8}$$

This is a proportionality of the sum of the price coefficients in (3.4) to the corresponding marginal share, with ϕ as proportionality constant, which is the counterpart of $\sum_j \nu_{ij}=\phi\mu_i$ for (3.5). Also, summation of (3.8) over g gives

$$\sum_{g=1}^{G}\sum_{h=1}^{G} N_{gh}=\phi \tag{3.9}$$

which is the group version of $\sum_i \sum_j \nu_{ij}=\phi$.

(2) Since **J** defined in (1.13) has full column rank, eq. (3.2) extends the symmetry and negative definiteness of the $n\times n$ price coefficient matrix $\mathbf{N}=[\nu_{ij}]$ to the $G\times G$ matrix $[N_{gh}]$ of the commodity groups. Hence the diagonal elements $N_{11},\ldots, N_{GG}$ are all negative.

(3) Symmetry, negative definiteness and (3.8) are the only constraints on $[N_{gh}]$. Hence the number of unconstrained N_{gh}'s is $\frac{1}{2}G(G-1)$, in agreement with the discussion preceding (2.21). These constraints do not exclude the possibility that the left-hand side of (3.8) is positive or zero for some g, implying $M_g\leq 0$.

(4) The definition of specific substitution and complementarity can also be extended to commodity groups: if N_{gh} is positive (negative), the groups S_g and S_h are defined as specific substitutes (complements). Each group is its own specific complement because $N_{gg}<0$. It follows from (2.12) that if i and j belong to different groups, their specific substitution or complementarity relation is the same as that of the groups when their conditional marginal shares have equal signs. [Note that when the group is inferior but the commodity is not, $M_g<0<\mu_i$, the conditional marginal share is negative whereas the unconditional share is positive.] Also, (3.6) shows that under block-independence no group is a specific substitute or complement of any other group. This, too, is a straightforward extension of (3.7) for individual goods.

The Inverse of the Price Coefficient Matrix of the Groups

By inverting (2.1) and using (1.12) and (1.16) we obtain

$$\phi\mathbf{N}^{-1}=\mathbf{V}+\mathbf{JCJ}'=\frac{1}{k}\mathbf{P}^{-1}\mathbf{UP}^{-1} \tag{3.10}$$

The first and third members of this equation constitute the familiar proportionality of the inverse of the $n\times n$ price coefficient matrix to the Hessian of the utility function in expenditure terms.

The question arises whether the inverse of the $G\times G$ matrix $[N_{gh}]$ of the groups, to be written $[N^{gh}]$, has a similar proportionality property. For this purpose we premultiply the first two members of (3.10) by the matrix $(\mathbf{J}'\mathbf{N}\mathbf{J})^{-1}\,\mathbf{J}'\mathbf{N}$ and postmultiply by $\mathbf{V}^{-1}\mathbf{J}(\mathbf{J}'\mathbf{V}^{-1}\mathbf{J})^{-1}$:

$$\phi(\mathbf{J}'\mathbf{N}\mathbf{J})^{-1} = (\mathbf{J}'\mathbf{V}^{-1}\mathbf{J})^{-1} + \mathbf{C} \tag{3.11}$$

It follows from (3.2) that the matrix on the left is $[\phi N^{gh}]$. The right-hand side is given in (1.20), so that

$$[\phi N^{gh}] = \begin{bmatrix} 1/\alpha_1 & c_{12} & \dots & c_{1G} \\ c_{21} & 1/\alpha_2 & \dots & c_{2G} \\ \vdots & \vdots & & \vdots \\ c_{G1} & c_{G2} & \dots & 1/\alpha_G \end{bmatrix} \tag{3.12}$$

To interpret this result we introduce the $n \times G$ matrix $\tilde{\mathbf{M}}$ consisting of zeros and conditional marginal shares:

$$\tilde{\mathbf{M}} = \begin{bmatrix} \tilde{\boldsymbol{\mu}}_1 & \mathbf{0} & \dots & \mathbf{0} \\ \mathbf{0} & \tilde{\boldsymbol{\mu}}_2 & \dots & \mathbf{0} \\ \vdots & \vdots & & \vdots \\ \mathbf{0} & \mathbf{0} & \dots & \tilde{\boldsymbol{\mu}}_G \end{bmatrix} \tag{3.13}$$

Each row of $\tilde{\mathbf{M}}$ corresponds to a commodity, each column to a group. The element in the ith row and the gth column is the ith conditional marginal share if $i \in S_g$; it is zero when $i \in S_h$ and $g \neq h$. In the next subsection we prove

$$\tilde{\mathbf{M}}'(\mathbf{V} + \mathbf{J}\mathbf{C}\mathbf{J}')\,\tilde{\mathbf{M}} = \begin{bmatrix} 1/\alpha_1 & c_{12} & \dots & c_{1G} \\ c_{21} & 1/\alpha_2 & \dots & c_{2G} \\ \vdots & \vdots & & \vdots \\ c_{G1} & c_{G2} & \dots & 1/\alpha_G \end{bmatrix} \tag{3.14}$$

On comparing this with (3.10) and (3.12) we find

$$[\phi N^{gh}] = \frac{1}{k}\,\tilde{\mathbf{M}}'(\mathbf{P}^{-1}\mathbf{U}\mathbf{P}^{-1})\,\tilde{\mathbf{M}} \tag{3.15}$$

or, in scalar form for $g, h = 1, \ldots, G$:

$$\phi N^{gh} = \frac{1}{k} \sum_{i \in S_g} \sum_{j \in S_h} \mu_i^g \mu_j^h \frac{\partial^2 u}{\partial(p_i q_i)\,\partial(p_j q_j)} \tag{3.16}$$

This shows that the elements of $[N^{gh}]$ are proportional to the marginally weighted means of the corresponding second-order derivatives of the utility function in expenditure terms.

Derivations

Using (2.9), we find that (3.13) can be written as

$$\tilde{\mathbf{M}} = \begin{bmatrix} (1/\alpha_1)\mathbf{a}_1 & \mathbf{0} & \dots & \mathbf{0} \\ \mathbf{0} & (1/\alpha_2)\mathbf{a}_2 & \dots & \mathbf{0} \\ \vdots & \vdots & & \vdots \\ \mathbf{0} & \mathbf{0} & \dots & (1/\alpha_G)\mathbf{a}_G \end{bmatrix} \tag{3.17}$$

and hence, using (1.15) also,

$$\tilde{\mathbf{M}} = \mathbf{V}^{-1}\mathbf{J}(\mathbf{J}'\mathbf{V}^{-1}\mathbf{J})^{-1} \tag{3.18}$$

This proves

$$\mathbf{J}'\tilde{\mathbf{M}} = \mathbf{I} \tag{3.19}$$

which can also be verified from (3.13) and (1.13). Note that (3.18) implies that $\tilde{\mathbf{M}}$ depends only on $\mathbf{V}$, so that $\tilde{\mathbf{M}}$ is independent of the c_{gh}'s which occur in the Hessian (1.7). Therefore, when these c_{gh}'s are all replaced by zero, which means that blockwise dependence is strengthened to block-independence, we obtain exactly the same conditional marginal shares, provided only that the diagonal blocks $(\mathbf{V}_1, \dots, \mathbf{V}_G)$ in the Hessian (1.7) remain unchanged.

From (3.18) and (3.19) we have

$$\tilde{\mathbf{M}}'\mathbf{V}\tilde{\mathbf{M}} = (\mathbf{J}'\mathbf{V}^{-1}\mathbf{J})^{-1} \tag{3.20}$$

$$\tilde{\mathbf{M}}'\mathbf{J}\mathbf{C}\mathbf{J}'\tilde{\mathbf{M}} = \mathbf{C} \tag{3.21}$$

We obtain (3.14) by adding these two equations and using (1.11) for $\mathbf{C}$ and (1.15) for $\mathbf{J}'\mathbf{V}^{-1}\mathbf{J}$.

The Case of Two Commodity Groups

For $G=2$ we have $N_{11}=\phi M_1 - N_{12}$ and $N_{22}=\phi M_2 - N_{12}$ in view of (3.8) and the symmetry of $[N_{gh}]$. Hence the 2×2 price coefficient matrix of the commodity groups is determined by ϕ, the two marginal shares, and the off-diagonal element N_{12}:

$$[N_{gh}] = \begin{bmatrix} \phi M_1 - N_{12} & N_{12} \\ N_{12} & \phi M_2 - N_{12} \end{bmatrix} \tag{3.22}$$

To insure that this matrix is negative definite we require that its determinant value be positive:

$$(\phi M_1 - N_{12})(\phi M_2 - N_{12}) - N_{12}^2 > 0$$

This is equivalent to $\phi^2 M_1 M_2 - \phi(M_1+M_2)N_{12} > 0$ and hence, since $\phi<0$ and $M_1+M_2=1$, to

$$N_{12} > \phi M_1 M_2 \tag{3.23}$$

If either M_1 or M_2 is zero or negative, the two groups must be specific substitutes ($N_{12}>0$). For the leading element of (3.22) we have under (3.23):

$$\phi M_1 - N_{12} < \phi M_1 - \phi M_1 M_2 = \phi M_1(1-M_2) = \phi M_1^2 \leq 0$$

This proves that (3.22) has negative diagonal elements under (3.23). Hence, given the positive determinant, we may conclude that (3.23) insures that (3.22) is a negative definite matrix.

We use the first row of (3.22) to write the substitution term of the demand equation (3.4) for S_1 as

$$(\phi M_1 - N_{12})\left(DP'_{1t} - \sum_{k=1}^{n} \mu_k Dp_{kt}\right) + N_{12}\left(DP'_{2t} - \sum_{k=1}^{n} \mu_k Dp_{kt}\right)$$

Since the price deflator $\sum_k \mu_k Dp_{kt}$ equals $M_1 DP'_{1t} + M_2 DP'_{2t}$, we may write this substitution term as

$$\begin{aligned}(\phi M_1 - N_{12})&[(1-M_1)\,DP'_{1t} - M_2 DP'_{2t}] \\ &+ N_{12}[(1-M_2)\,DP'_{2t} - M_1 DP'_{1t}] \\ &= (\phi M_1 - N_{12})\,M_2\,(DP'_{1t} - DP'_{2t}) + N_{12}M_1\,(DP'_{2t} - DP'_{1t})\end{aligned}$$

which can be simplified to $(\phi M_1 M_2 - N_{12})(DP'_{1t} - DP'_{2t})$. Therefore, in the two-group case we can write the demand equation (3.4) for S_1 as

$$\bar{W}_{1t} DQ_{1t} = M_1 DQ_t + (\phi M_1 M_2 - N_{12})\,(DP'_{1t} - DP'_{2t}) + E_{1t} \tag{3.24}$$

The equation for S_2 is the same except that the subscripts 1 and 2 are to be interchanged.

The substitution term in (3.24) is a multiple $\phi M_1 M_2 - N_{12}$ of the log-change in the ratio of the marginally weighted price indexes of the two groups, and (3.23) implies that this multiple is negative. Its absolute value is larger when the groups are specific substitutes ($N_{12}>0$) than when they are specific complements, given $\phi<0$ and M_1, $M_2>0$.

Conditional Demand Equations

We multiply (3.4) by the ith conditional marginal share,

$$\mu_i^g \bar{W}_{gt} DQ_{gt} = \mu_i DQ_t + \mu_i^g \sum_{h=1}^{G} N_{gh}\left(DP'_{ht} - \sum_{k=1}^{n} \mu_k Dp_{kt}\right) + \mu_i^g E_{gt}$$

and subtract this from (2.20):

$$\bar{w}_{it}Dq_{it} = \mu_i^g \bar{W}_{gt} DQ_{gt} + \sum_{j \in S_g} \nu_{ij}\left(Dp_{jt} - \sum_{k=1}^{n} \mu_k Dp_{kt}\right) - \mu_i^g N_{gg}\left(DP'_{gt} - \sum_{k=1}^{n} \mu_k Dp_{kt}\right) + \varepsilon_{it} - \mu_i^g E_{gt}$$

It follows from (2.14) that this can be simplified to

$$\bar{w}_{it}Dq_{it} = \mu_i^g \bar{W}_{gt} DQ_{gt} + \sum_{j \in S_g} \nu_{ij}(Dp_{jt} - DP'_{gt}) + \varepsilon_{it}^g \tag{3.25}$$

where

$$\varepsilon_{it}^g = \varepsilon_{it} - \mu_i^g E_{gt} \qquad i \in S_g \tag{3.26}$$

Equation (3.25) is the ith conditional demand equation under blockwise dependence. Note that, apart from the special notation for the conditional marginal shares, its form is identical to that of its block-independent counterpart given in eq. (1.6) of Section 7.1.

Remarks:

(1) When we apply (3.25) to each $i \in S_g$, we obtain an allocation model within S_g that contains n_g^2 price coefficients ν_{ij}. Under block-independence the sum of these coefficients equals ϕM_g. It follows from (3.1) that under blockwise dependence this sum equals N_{gg}, which is the own-price coefficient in the demand equation (3.4) for the commodity group. This amounts to a direct generalization, since ϕM_g is the own-price coefficient in (3.6).

(2) As in eq. (3.25) of Section 7.3, we define the conditional income elasticity of the ith good within its group as the ratio of its conditional marginal share to its conditional budget share. The budget-share-weighted average of these elasticities is 1 for each group:

$$\sum_{i \in S_g} \frac{\bar{w}_{it}}{\bar{W}_{gt}} \frac{\mu_i^g}{\bar{w}_{it}/\bar{W}_{gt}} = 1 \tag{3.27}$$

(3) The decomposition (3.4) of Section 7.3 also holds under blockwise dependence. Substitution of the conditional equation (3.25) for the term involving Dq_{it} in this decomposition yields a DQ_{gt} term equal to

$$\left(\mu_i^g - \frac{\bar{w}_{it}}{\bar{W}_{gt}}\right) DQ_{gt} \tag{3.28}$$

which is the extension of the analogous term (3.28) of Section 7.3. Hence an increase in the demand for a commodity group ($DQ_{gt} > 0$) raises the conditional budget shares of those of its components that have conditional income elasticities larger than 1. This is exactly as it is in the case of block-independence, but note that when the group is inferior ($M_g < 0$), conditional income elasticities exceeding 1 amount to negative unconditional elasticities which exceed that of the group in absolute value.

(4) The extension of the modified conditional model of Section 7.3 to blockwise dependence is considered in Section 8.6.

8.4 Demand Equations in Absolute Prices and the Second-Moment Model

In this section we turn to demand equations in absolute prices,

$$\bar{w}_{it} Dq_{it} = \mu_i DQ_t + \sum_{j=1}^{n} \pi_{ij} Dp_{jt} + \varepsilon_{it} \tag{4.1}$$

where

$$\pi_{ij} = \nu_{ij} - \phi \mu_i \mu_j \qquad i, j = 1, \ldots, n \tag{4.2}$$

is the $(i, j)^{\text{th}}$ Slutsky coefficient, which satisfies

$$\sum_{j=1}^{n} \pi_{ij} = 0 \qquad i = 1, \ldots, n \tag{4.3}$$

Such equations in absolute prices can be formulated for conditional as well as unconditional demand and also for group demand. It will be convenient to start with commodity groups.

Demand Equations for Groups in Absolute Prices

Write the price deflator in (3.4) as

$$\sum_{k=1}^{n} \mu_k Dp_{kt} = \sum_{h=1}^{G} M_h DP'_{ht} \tag{4.4}$$

so that we can write the substitution term of (3.4), using (3.8), as

$$\sum_{h=1}^{G} N_{gh} DP'_{ht} - \phi M_g \sum_{h=1}^{G} M_h DP'_{ht} = \sum_{h=1}^{G} \Pi_{gh} DP'_{ht} \tag{4.5}$$

where

$$\Pi_{gh} = N_{gh} - \phi M_g M_h \qquad g, h = 1, \ldots, G \tag{4.6}$$

is the Slutsky coefficient of the groups S_g and S_h. Substitution of (4.5) in (3.4) gives

$$\bar{W}_{gt} DQ_{gt} = M_g DQ_t + \sum_{h=1}^{G} \Pi_{gh} DP'_{ht} + E_{gt} \tag{4.7}$$

which is the demand equation for S_g in absolute prices.

Equations (4.6) and (4.7) are the uppercase versions of (4.2) and (4.1), respectively. By applying (3.8) we find

$$\sum_{h=1}^{G} \Pi_{gh} = 0 \qquad g = 1, \ldots, G \tag{4.8}$$

which should be compared with (4.3). Also, using (4.6) and the negative definiteness of $[N_{gh}]$, we can easily verify that the $G \times G$ Slutsky matrix $[\Pi_{gh}]$ of the commodity groups is symmetric negative semidefinite with rank $G-1$.

Conditional Demand Equations in Absolute Prices

Next use (2.14) to write the substitution term of (3.25) as

$$\sum_{j \in S_g} \nu_{ij} Dp_{jt} - N_{gg}\mu_i^g \sum_{j \in S_g} \mu_j^g Dp_{jt} = \sum_{j \in S_g} \pi_{ij}^g Dp_{jt} \tag{4.9}$$

where

$$\pi_{ij}^g = \nu_{ij} - N_{gg}\mu_i^g \mu_j^g \qquad i, j \in S_g \tag{4.10}$$

is the conditional Slutsky coefficient of the ith and j^{th} commodities within their group S_g. Substitution of (4.9) in (3.25) gives the absolute price version of the conditional demand model:

$$\bar{w}_{it} Dq_{it} = \mu_i^g \bar{W}_{gt} DQ_{gt} + \sum_{j \in S_g} \pi_{ij}^g Dp_{jt} + \varepsilon_{it}^g \tag{4.11}$$

Equations (4.10) and (4.11) are equivalent to (1.10) and (1.11), respectively, of Section 7.1 except that ϕM_g is replaced by N_{gg} in (4.10). This replacement agrees with the roles played by ϕM_g and N_{gg} in remark (1) below (3.26). Application of (2.14) gives

$$\sum_{j \in S_g} \pi_{ij}^g = 0 \qquad i \in S_g \tag{4.12}$$

which agrees with eq. (1.12) of Section 7.1. It is readily verified that (4.10) is the $(i, j)^{\text{th}}$ element of a symmetric negative semidefinite conditional Slutsky matrix whose order is $n_g \times n_g$ and whose rank is $n_g - 1$.

Unconditional Demand Equations in Absolute Prices

We proceed to consider the unconditional demand equation (2.20). Using (2.14), we write the price term in the first line as

$$\sum_{j \in S_g} \nu_{ij} Dp_{jt} - N_{gg}\mu_i^g \sum_{j=1}^{n} \mu_j Dp_{jt}$$

When we add the price term in the second line to this expression, we obtain

$$\sum_{j\in S_g} \nu_{ij} Dp_{jt} + \mu_i^g \sum_{h\neq g} N_{gh} \sum_{j\in S_h} \mu_j^h Dp_{jt} - \mu_i^g \left(\sum_{h=1}^{G} N_{gh}\right) \sum_{j=1}^{n} \mu_j Dp_{jt}$$

The sum in parentheses in the third term equals ϕM_g in view of (3.8), so that it becomes $\phi\mu_i$ when it is multiplied by the ith conditional marginal share. So we arrive at the following expression for the substitution term of (2.20):

$$\sum_{j\in S_g} \nu_{ij} Dp_{jt} + \mu_i^g \sum_{h\neq g} N_{gh} \sum_{j\in S_h} \mu_j^h Dp_{jt} - \phi\mu_i \sum_{j=1}^{n} \mu_j Dp_{jt} \tag{4.13}$$

This result shows that (2.20) can be written in the form (4.1) if we define

$$\pi_{ij} = \begin{cases} \nu_{ij} - \phi\mu_i\mu_j & \text{if } i\in S_g \text{ and } j\in S_g \\ N_{gh}\mu_i^g\mu_j^h - \phi\mu_i\mu_j & \text{if } i\in S_g,\ j\in S_h,\ g\neq h \end{cases} \tag{4.14}$$

It follows from (4.6) that the expression in the second line equals

$$(N_{gh} - \phi M_g M_h)\,\mu_i^g\mu_j^h = \Pi_{gh}\mu_i^g\mu_j^h$$

Using (4.10) also, we write the expression in the first line of (4.14) as

$$\nu_{ij} - N_{gg}\mu_i^g\mu_j^g + (N_{gg} - \phi M_g^2)\,\mu_i^g\mu_j^g = \pi_{ij}^g + \Pi_{gg}\mu_i^g\mu_j^g$$

We conclude that the π_{ij}'s can be expressed in terms of conditional Slutsky coefficients (within the groups) and Slutsky coefficients of the groups multiplied by conditional marginal shares:

$$\pi_{ij} = \begin{cases} \pi_{ij}^g + \Pi_{gg}\mu_i^g\mu_j^g & \text{if } i\in S_g \text{ and } j\in S_g \\ \Pi_{gh}\mu_i^g\mu_j^h & \text{if } i\in S_g,\ j\in S_h,\ g\neq h \end{cases} \tag{4.15}$$

The Unconditional Slutsky Coefficients Under Blockwise Dependence

Equation (4.15) implies several interesting properties for the π_{ij}'s under blockwise dependence. The first line is an extension of eq. (1.15) of Section 7.1. This follows from $\Pi_{gg}=\phi M_g(1-M_g)$, which is implied by (4.6) under the stronger condition of block-independence. Since $[\Pi_{gh}]$ satisfies (4.8) and is negative semidefinite with rank $G-1$, Π_{gg} in the first line of (4.15) is negative. This shows that conditional Slutsky coefficients with equal subscripts are algebraically larger than the corresponding π_{ii} except when the ith conditional marginal share vanishes.

The second line of (4.15) may be viewed as a "Slutsky version" of (2.12). It implies that Slutsky coefficients of commodities belonging to different groups are proportional to the product of their conditional marginal shares.

If M_g and M_h do not vanish, this amounts to a proportionality of π_{ij} to $\mu_i\mu_j$ with Π_{gh}/M_gM_h as proportionality constant, which may be used as a tool for verifying whether there is blockwise dependence on the basis of an estimated version of (4.1).

Using (4.12), we obtain, after summation of (4.15) over $j \in S_h$:

$$\sum_{j \in S_h} \pi_{ij} = \Pi_{gh}\mu_i^g \qquad i \in S_g;\ g, h = 1, \ldots, G \tag{4.16}$$

For $g=h$ this is the Slutsky version of (2.14), and for $g \neq h$ it is the Slutsky version of the equation obtained by summing (2.12) over $j \in S_h$. When we sum (4.16) over $h=1, \ldots, G$ and apply (4.8), we obtain $\sum_j \pi_{ij}=0$ (sum over $j=1, \ldots, n$). This agrees with (4.3). By summing (4.16) over $i \in S_g$ we find

$$\sum_{i \in S_g} \sum_{j \in S_h} \pi_{ij} = \Pi_{gh} \qquad g, h = 1, \ldots, G \tag{4.17}$$

which is the Slutsky version of (3.1).

The Second-Moment Model Under Blockwise Dependence

The second-moment model in the form of eq. (7.14) of Section 2.7 is

$$\operatorname{cov}(\varepsilon_{it}, \varepsilon_{jt}) = \sigma^2 \frac{\pi_{ij}}{\phi} \tag{4.18}$$

The covariance of the disturbances E_{gt} and E_{ht} in the group demand equations (3.4) and (4.7) is obtained by summing (4.18) over $i \in S_g$ and $j \in S_h$. Using (4.17), we obtain

$$\operatorname{cov}(E_{gt}, E_{ht}) = \sigma^2 \frac{\Pi_{gh}}{\phi} \qquad g, h = 1, \ldots, G \tag{4.19}$$

which is the uppercase version of (4.18). On combining (4.18) and (4.19) with (4.15), we find

$$\operatorname{cov}(\varepsilon_{it}, \varepsilon_{jt}) = \mu_i^g \mu_j^h \operatorname{cov}(E_{gt}, E_{ht}) \quad \text{if} \quad i \in S_g, j \in S_h,\ g \neq h \tag{4.20}$$

Hence the demand disturbances of commodities of different groups have a covariance equal to that of their groups multiplied by the product of their conditional marginal shares.

In the next subsection we prove

$$\operatorname{cov}(\varepsilon_{it}^g, \varepsilon_{jt}^h) = \begin{cases} \sigma^2 \dfrac{\pi_{ij}^g}{\phi} & \text{if} \quad i \in S_g,\ j \in S_h,\ g = h \\ 0 & \text{if} \quad i \in S_g,\ j \in S_h,\ g \neq h \end{cases} \tag{4.21}$$

as well as

$$\text{(4.22)} \qquad \operatorname{cov}(\varepsilon_{it}^g, E_{ht}) = 0 \qquad i \in S_g;\ g, h = 1, \ldots, G$$

These results are identical to those given in eqs. (1.17) and (1.18) of Section 7.1 except that the conditional Slutsky coefficient in (4.21) is as defined in (4.10). We conclude that the separation of the allocation models for groups and for commodities within groups applies equally to block-independence and to blockwise dependence. The only major difference is that in the latter case we have log-changes in the deflated price indexes of all G groups in the group demand equation (3.4).

Derivations for the Second-Moment Model

We write our disturbances as sums of specific and general substitution components, so that the conditional disturbance (3.26) becomes

$$\varepsilon_{it}^g = \bar{\varepsilon}_{it} - \mu_i \bar{E}_t - \mu_i^g (\bar{E}_{gt} - M_g \bar{E}_t)$$

This can be simplified to

$$\text{(4.23)} \qquad \varepsilon_{it}^g = \bar{\varepsilon}_{it} - \mu_i^g \bar{E}_{gt}$$

which is an extension of eq. (1.19) of Section 7.1 with a similar interpretation.

Next consider eq. (7.22) of Section 2.7,

$$\text{(4.24)} \qquad \operatorname{cov}(\bar{\varepsilon}_{it}, \bar{\varepsilon}_{jt}) = \sigma^2 \frac{v_{ij}}{\phi}$$

and sum both sides over $j \in S_h$, using (2.12) and (2.14):

$$\text{(4.25)} \qquad \operatorname{cov}(\bar{\varepsilon}_{it}, \bar{E}_{ht}) = \sigma^2 \mu_i^g \frac{N_{gh}}{\phi} \qquad i \in S_g;\ g, h = 1, \ldots, G$$

Summation over $i \in S_g$ gives

$$\text{(4.26)} \qquad \operatorname{cov}(\bar{E}_{gt}, \bar{E}_{ht}) = \sigma^2 \frac{N_{gh}}{\phi} \qquad g, h = 1, \ldots, G$$

By combining (4.24) and (4.26) with (2.12) we obtain

$$\text{(4.27)} \qquad \operatorname{cov}(\bar{\varepsilon}_{it}, \bar{\varepsilon}_{jt}) = \mu_i^g \mu_j^h \operatorname{cov}(\bar{E}_{gt}, \bar{E}_{ht}) \quad \text{if} \quad i \in S_g, j \in S_h,\ g \neq h$$

which should be compared with (4.20).

We use (4.23) to write the left-hand side of (4.22) as

$$\operatorname{cov}(\bar{\varepsilon}_{it} - \mu_i^g \bar{E}_{gt}, \bar{E}_{ht} - M_h \bar{E}_t)$$
$$= \sigma^2 \mu_i^g \frac{N_{gh}}{\phi} - \mu_i^g \left(\sigma^2 \frac{N_{gh}}{\phi}\right) - M_h(\sigma^2 \mu_i) + \mu_i^g M_h (\sigma^2 M_g)$$

where the terms on the right are obtained by successive application of (4.25), (4.26) and eqs. (7.25) and (7.30) of Section 2.7. These four terms sum to zero, which proves (4.22).

To verify (4.21) we write its left-hand side as

$$\operatorname{cov}\left(\bar{\varepsilon}_{it} - \mu_i^g \bar{E}_{gt}, \bar{\varepsilon}_{jt} - \mu_j^h \bar{E}_{ht}\right)$$

In view of (4.24) to (4.26) this is equal to

$$\frac{\sigma^2}{\phi}\left(v_{ij} - N_{gh}\mu_i^g \mu_j^h\right)$$

It follows from (2.12) that this expression vanishes for $g \neq h$ and from (4.10) that it is a multiple σ^2/ϕ of the $(i,j)^{\text{th}}$ conditional Slutsky coefficient for $g=h$, in agreement with (4.21).

8.5 Further Comparisons with Block-Independence

We concluded below (3.19) that the conditional marginal shares are not affected when blockwise dependence is strengthened to block-independence in such a way that the c_{gh}'s in (1.7) are replaced by zeros while $\mathbf{V}_1, \ldots, \mathbf{V}_G$ remain as they are. In this section we consider similar properties for the price coefficients and the conditional Slutsky coefficients.

Analysis of Price Coefficients

Write $\mathbf{N}_g$ for the $n_g \times n_g$ submatrix of $[v_{ij}]$ which corresponds to S_g. It follows from (2.2) that this matrix equals

$$\mathbf{N}_g = \phi\mathbf{V}_g^{-1} + \phi c_{gg}^* \mathbf{a}_g \mathbf{a}_g' = \phi\mathbf{V}_g^{-1} + \phi c_{gg}^* \alpha_g^2 \tilde{\boldsymbol{\mu}}_g \tilde{\boldsymbol{\mu}}_g' \tag{5.1}$$

where the second step is based on (2.9). Next we use (3.3) to write this result as

$$\mathbf{N}_g = \phi\mathbf{V}_g^{-1} + (N_{gg} - \phi\alpha_g)\,\tilde{\boldsymbol{\mu}}_g \tilde{\boldsymbol{\mu}}_g'$$

which may also be written as

$$\mathbf{N}_g = \phi\mathbf{V}_g^{-1} + \left(N_{gg} - \frac{1}{N^{gg}}\right)\tilde{\boldsymbol{\mu}}_g \tilde{\boldsymbol{\mu}}_g' \tag{5.2}$$

in view of (3.12).

When there is block-independence, the $G \times G$ matrix $[N_{gh}]$ is diagonal and N^{gg} is equal to the reciprocal of $N_{gg} = \phi M_g$. In that case the expression in parentheses in (5.2) vanishes. This expression does not vanish under the weaker assumption of blockwise dependence. Hence, given unchanged matrices $\phi^{-1}\mathbf{V}_1, \ldots, \phi^{-1}\mathbf{V}_G$, changing blockwise dependence into block-independence by replacing the c_{gh}'s in (1.7) by zeros affects the price coefficients in the blocks around the diagonal. The effect amounts to the addition of a scalar multiple of the matrix $\tilde{\boldsymbol{\mu}}_g\tilde{\boldsymbol{\mu}}_g'$. It is interesting to compare this with the effect on the off-diagonal block corresponding to S_g and $S_h (g \neq h)$. Under block-independence such a block is a zero matrix, but it is $N_{gh}\tilde{\boldsymbol{\mu}}_g\tilde{\boldsymbol{\mu}}_h'$ under blockwise dependence in view of (2.12). Therefore, given unchanged matrices $\phi^{-1}\mathbf{V}_1, \ldots, \phi^{-1}\mathbf{V}_G$, the difference between the $(g, h)^{\text{th}}$ submatrix of the $[\nu_{ij}]$ of block-independence and that of blockwise dependence is a scalar multiple of the matrix $\tilde{\boldsymbol{\mu}}_g\tilde{\boldsymbol{\mu}}_h'$, both for $g = h$ and for $g \neq h$.

Recall from the last subsection of Section 2.5 that when we apply a monotonic transformation of the utility function, each ν_{ij} is raised by a multiple (independent of i and j) of the product $\mu_i\mu_j$. This can be used to simplify (5.2). If M_g does not vanish, we may write the $(i, j)^{\text{th}}$ element of the second matrix on the right as

$$(5.3) \qquad \frac{N_{gg} - 1/N^{gg}}{M_g^2} \mu_i\mu_j$$

which is a multiple of $\mu_i\mu_j$. By selecting an appropriate nonlinear transformation of the utility function we can modify and even eliminate this term. We shall use this device in Section 8.6 to simplify the analysis of the meat group. Note that this device can be used for only one group because such transformations yield only one degree of freedom.

Analysis of Conditional Slutsky Coefficients

It follows from (4.10) that the $n_g \times n_g$ conditional Slutsky matrix of S_g can be written as

$$(5.4) \qquad [\pi_{ij}^g] = \mathbf{N}_g - N_{gg}\tilde{\boldsymbol{\mu}}_g\tilde{\boldsymbol{\mu}}_g' = \phi\mathbf{V}_g^{-1} - \frac{1}{N^{gg}}\tilde{\boldsymbol{\mu}}_g\tilde{\boldsymbol{\mu}}_g'$$

where the second step is based on (5.2). Since $1/N^{gg} = \phi\alpha_g$ in view of (3.12), and since (1.14) states that α_g equals a quadratic form in $\boldsymbol{\iota}_g$ with the inverse of $\mathbf{V}_g$ as matrix, we can write (5.4) as

$$(5.5) \qquad [\pi_{ij}^g] = \phi\mathbf{V}_g^{-1} - \phi(\boldsymbol{\iota}_g'\mathbf{V}_g^{-1}\boldsymbol{\iota}_g)\tilde{\boldsymbol{\mu}}_g\tilde{\boldsymbol{\mu}}_g'$$

We concluded from (3.18) that the conditional marginal shares are the same under block-independence and under blockwise dependence, provided that $\mathbf{V}_1, \ldots, \mathbf{V}_G$ are unchanged. It is readily verified that this proviso is equivalent to unchanged matrices $\phi^{-1}\mathbf{V}_1, \ldots, \phi^{-1}\mathbf{V}_G$. Since (5.5) implies that the conditional Slutsky matrix of S_g is determined by $\tilde{\boldsymbol{\mu}}_g$ and $\phi^{-1}\mathbf{V}_g$, we may conclude that both the conditional marginal shares and the conditional Slutsky coefficients take the same values under block-independence and under blockwise dependence if the matrices $\phi^{-1}\mathbf{V}_1, \ldots, \phi^{-1}\mathbf{V}_G$ are the same under these two specifications.

8.6 The Demand for Meats in the United States: (7) The Case of Blockwise Dependence

In Chapter 7 we assumed that Beef, Pork, Chicken and Lamb constitute a four-commodity group which satisfies the block-independence assumption. In this section we relax this to blockwise dependence and we analyze whether the empirical results obtained in Chapter 7 are also applicable under this weaker assumption. For the approach of Section 7.2 this is obviously the case, since eq. (2.2) of that section is identical to (4.11) – apart from the notation used for the conditional marginal shares – and since (4.22) implies that $\bar{W}_{gt}DQ_{gt}$ is predetermined in (4.11) under the normality assumption. So the first object of analysis is the modified model of Section 7.3.

The Modified Conditional Model Under Blockwise Dependence

In Section 7.3 we divided the ith conditional demand equation by the budget share of the group, so that the left-hand variable is the quantity component of the change in the ith conditional budget share. Now apply this to (3.25),

$$\text{(6.1)} \qquad \frac{\bar{w}_{it}}{\bar{W}_{gt}} Dq_{it} = \mu_i^g DQ_{gt} + \sum_{j \in S_g} v_{ij}^* (Dp_{jt} - DP'_{gt}) + \varepsilon_{it}^*$$

where

$$\text{(6.2)} \qquad v_{ij}^* = \frac{v_{ij}}{\bar{W}_{gt}} \qquad \varepsilon_{it}^* = \frac{\varepsilon_{it}^g}{\bar{W}_{gt}} \qquad i, j \in S_g$$

Next use (2.14),

$$\text{(6.3)} \qquad \sum_{j \in S_g} v_{ij}^* = \frac{N_{gg}}{\bar{W}_{gt}} \mu_i^g \qquad i \in S_g$$

and sum this over $i \in S_g$:

$$\text{(6.4)} \qquad \sum_{i \in S_g} \sum_{j \in S_g} v_{ij}^* = \frac{N_{gg}}{\bar{W}_{gt}}$$

Also divide (3.4) by $\bar{W}_{gt}$:

$$\text{(6.5)} \qquad DQ_{gt} = \frac{M_g}{\bar{W}_{gt}} DQ_t + \sum_{h=1}^{G} \frac{N_{gh}}{\bar{W}_{gt}} \left(DP'_{ht} - \sum_{k=1}^{n} \mu_k Dp_{kt} \right) + \frac{E_{gt}}{\bar{W}_{gt}}$$

Hence, if S_g is meat, $N_{gg}/\bar{W}_{gt}$ is the own-price elasticity in the demand equation (6.5) for total meat, and (6.4) implies that the sum of all modified price coefficients of the four meats is equal to this own-price elasticity. It is easily verified that (6.3) to (6.5) are a direct extension of eqs. (3.10) to (3.12) of Section 7.3.

The absolute price version of (6.1) is

$$\frac{\bar{w}_{it}}{\bar{W}_{gt}} Dq_{it} = \mu_i^g DQ_{gt} + \sum_{j \in S_g} \pi_{ij}^* Dp_{jt} + \varepsilon_{it}^* \tag{6.6}$$

The modified conditional Slutsky coefficients are obtained by dividing (4.10) by $\bar{W}_{gt}$:

$$\pi_{ij}^* = \frac{\pi_{ij}^g}{\bar{W}_{gt}} = v_{ij}^* - \frac{N_{gg}}{\bar{W}_{gt}} \mu_i^g \mu_j^g \qquad i, j \in S_g \tag{6.7}$$

This is an immediate extension of eqs. (3.15) and (3.16) of Section 7.3. The reader may want to verify that the estimates shown in Table 7.5 on page 19 are all applicable under the assumption of blockwise dependence, with meat being one of the G groups.

In Sections 7.4 and 7.5 we applied the second-moment model. Using (4.21) and (6.2), we find that the covariances of the disturbances of the model (6.6) can be written as

$$\operatorname{cov}(\varepsilon_{it}^*, \varepsilon_{jt}^*) = \frac{\sigma^2}{\phi \bar{W}_{gt}^2} \pi_{ij}^g$$

and hence, using (6.7) also, as

$$\operatorname{cov}(\varepsilon_{it}^*, \varepsilon_{jt}^*) = \frac{\sigma^2}{\phi \bar{W}_{gt}} \pi_{ij}^* \qquad i, j \in S_g \tag{6.8}$$

This is identical to eq. (4.1) of Section 7.4 except that, obviously, π_{ij}^* is now specified as in (6.7). Again, it is straightforward to verify that the estimates obtained in Section 7.5 also apply under blockwise dependence.

A Special Form of Blockwise Dependence

In Section 7.6 we obtained preliminary estimates of the modified price coefficients from

$$v_{ij}^* = \pi_{ij}^* + \frac{\phi M_g}{\bar{W}_{gt}} \frac{\mu_i}{M_g} \frac{\mu_j}{M_g}$$

by means of informal estimates of ϕ and the total-meat income elasticity $M_g/\bar{W}_{gt}$. The result was that the implied estimates of the off-diagonal price coefficients involving Lamb are close to zero, and we decided to make Lamb preference-independent of all other goods. It is evident from (6.7) that we cannot proceed in this way under blockwise dependence, because the own-price elasticity of meat is now $N_{gg}/\bar{W}_{gt}$, which is not equal to the product of ϕ and $M_g/\bar{W}_{gt}$.

Let us modify the approach of Section 7.6 by postulating that (1) there is blockwise dependence with G groups, S_g being defined as consisting of the four meats, and (2) the group utility function $u_g(\ )$ of meats takes the form

$$u_g(q_1, \ldots, q_4) = u_A(q_1, q_2, q_3) + u_B(q_4) \tag{6.9}$$

where q_1, q_2 and q_3 are the quantities of Beef, Pork and Chicken, respectively, and q_4 is the quantity of Lamb. Thus, there is blockwise dependence for meat and $G-1$ other commodity groups, and within meat there is block-independence with respect to the group utility function $u_g(\ )$. This utility specification is of the type proposed by PEARCE (1961, 1964).

Utility Derivatives Implied by the Special Form

To verify what this specification implies for the Hessian of $u(\ )$ we consider (1.6),

$$\frac{\partial^2 u}{\partial(p_i q_i)\,\partial(p_j q_j)} = \lambda^2 \frac{\partial^2 f/\partial u_g^2}{(\partial f/\partial u_g)^2} + \frac{\partial f}{\partial u_g} \frac{\partial^2 u_g}{\partial(p_i q_i)\,\partial(p_j q_j)}$$

where $i, j = 1, \ldots, 4$. It follows from (6.9) that the second term on the right vanishes for $i=4, j\neq 4$ and $i\neq 4, j=4$. Since the first term is a constant with respect to i and j, we conclude that the marginal utilities of a dollar spent on Beef, Pork and Chicken will change by the same amount when an extra dollar is spent on Lamb. Similarly, the marginal utility of a dollar spent on Lamb changes by the same amount when an extra dollar is spent on either Beef or Pork or Chicken.

Note that exactly the same result emerges [see (1.5) and the discussion below that equation] when we have two meat groups, one consisting of Beef, Pork and Chicken and the other of Lamb. This is not really surprising. Let us write S_1 for meat, so that the utility specification (1.1) under condition (6.9) becomes

$$u = f(u_A + u_B, u_2, \ldots, u_G) \tag{6.10}$$

This shows that utility can also be written as a function of $G+1$ group utility functions:

$$u = f^*(u_A, u_B, u_2, \ldots, u_G) \tag{6.11}$$

Hence we have two alternative interpretations under (6.9), with meats as either one group or two. Both interpretations are equally valid, and we shall indeed use both in the next subsection.

Conditional Demand Equations Implied by the Special Form

Consider (4.15) for different groups:

$$\pi_{ij} = \Pi_{gh}\mu_i^g\mu_j^h \quad \text{if} \quad i \in S_g, j \in S_h, \ g \neq h \tag{6.12}$$

We apply this to the two-group interpretation of meats, with S_g defined as the three-meat group ($i=1$, Beef; 2, Pork; 3, Chicken) and S_h as Lamb ($j=4$). If the marginal shares of these two groups do not vanish, we can write (6.12) as

$$\pi_{i4} = c\mu_i\mu_4 \qquad i = 1, 2, 3 \tag{6.13}$$

where

$$c = \frac{\Pi_{gh}}{M_g M_h} \tag{6.14}$$

Next combine (6.13) with $\nu_{ij}=\pi_{ij}+\phi\mu_i\mu_j$ to obtain

$$\nu_{i4} = (\phi + c)\,\mu_i\mu_4 \qquad i = 1, 2, 3 \tag{6.15}$$

We proved at the end of Section 2.5 that, if the utility function is monotonically transformed, each ν_{ij} is raised by a positive or negative multiple of $\mu_i\mu_j$ which does not involve i and j. By selecting an appropriate nonlinear transformation we can thus insure that the three ν_{i4}'s of (6.15) become zero. Note that this does not mean that Lamb becomes a preference-independent good. The ν_{i4}'s with $i>4$ (nonmeats) are different from zero as shown in (2.12), but these ν's do not occur in our conditional demand equations.

It is also possible to derive this result more directly. For this purpose we return to (3.25) with S_g interpreted as the four-meat group. Using (6.15) and the symmetry of $[\nu_{ij}]$, we write the substitution term of (3.25) for Lamb as

$$(\phi + c)\,\mu_4 \sum_{i=1}^{3} \mu_i(Dp_{it} - DP'_{gt}) + \nu_{44}(Dp_{4t} - DP'_{gt}) \tag{6.16}$$

The first term in (6.16) is a multiple $(\phi+c)\mu_4$ of

$$\sum_{i \in S_g} \mu_i(Dp_{it} - DP'_{gt}) - \mu_4(Dp_{4t} - DP'_{gt})$$
$$= M_g \sum_{i \in S_g} \mu_i^g(Dp_{it} - DP'_{gt}) - \mu_4(Dp_{4t} - DP'_{gt})$$

Since the first term on the right vanishes, we can simplify (6.16) to

$$(6.17) \qquad [\nu_{44} - (\phi + c)\,\mu_4^{2}]\,(Dp_{4t} - DP'_{gt})$$

This shows that the conditional demand equation for Lamb does not contain the relative prices of the three other meats and that the original own-price coefficient ν_{44} is raised by $-(\phi+c)\mu_4^2$. If we apply the analogous modification to the ν's of (6.15), they all become zero.

Extension to the Modified Conditional Demand Model

We continue with the four-meat interpretation of S_g. The developments of the previous subsection imply that, after the utility function has been monotonically transformed, so that $\nu_{i4}=0$ for $i<4$, the conditional equation (3.25) for Beef, Pork or Chicken ($i=1, 2, 3$) takes the form

$$\bar{w}_{it} Dq_{it} = \mu_i^g \bar{W}_{gt} DQ_{gt} + \sum_{j=1}^{3} \nu_{ij}\,(Dp_{jt} - DP'_{gt}) + \varepsilon_{it}^g$$

or, after dividing both sides by $\bar{W}_{gt}$,

$$(6.18) \qquad \frac{\bar{w}_{it}}{\bar{W}_{gt}} Dq_{it} = \mu_i^g DQ_{gt} + \sum_{j=1}^{3} \nu_{ij}^*\,(Dp_{jt} - DP'_{gt}) + \varepsilon_{it}^*$$

For Lamb we have $\nu_{4j}=\nu_{j4}=0$ for $j<4$, so that (2.14) implies that ν_{44} equals N_{gg} multiplied by the conditional marginal share of Lamb. We may summarize these properties, after dividing by $\bar{W}_{gt}$, as

$$(6.19) \qquad \nu_{i4}^* = \begin{cases} \dfrac{N_{gg}}{\bar{W}_{gt}}\,\mu_4^g & \text{if} \quad i = 4 \\ 0 & \text{if} \quad i < 4 \end{cases}$$

so that the equation for Lamb becomes

$$(6.20) \qquad \frac{\bar{w}_{4t}}{\bar{W}_{gt}} Dq_{4t} = \mu_4^g DQ_{gt} + \frac{N_{gg}}{\bar{W}_{gt}}\,\mu_4^g\,(Dp_{4t} - DP'_{gt}) + \varepsilon_{4t}^*$$

Apart from the replacement of ϕM_g by N_{gg} in (6.20), this equation and (6.18) are equivalent to eqs. (6.4) and (6.3), respectively, of Section 7.6.

Next combine (6.7) and (6.19),

$$\pi_{i4}^* = -\frac{N_{gg}}{\bar{W}_{gt}}\,\mu_i^g \mu_4^g \qquad i = 1, 2, 3$$

and apply (6.8) also:

$$\text{(6.21)}\qquad \operatorname{cov}(\varepsilon_{it}^*, \varepsilon_{4t}^*) = -\frac{\sigma^2 N_{gg}}{\phi \bar{W}_{gt}^2}\,\mu_i^g\mu_4^g \qquad i = 1, 2, 3$$

The left-hand side equals $\omega_{i4} = -\omega_{i1} - \omega_{i2} - \omega_{i3}$ in the notation of Section 7.6 and is hence equal to the ith element of $-\boldsymbol{\Omega\iota}$. The expression on the right is the ith element of $-(1/\delta)\boldsymbol{\mu}_0$, where $\boldsymbol{\mu}_0$ is the vector of conditional marginal shares (of Beef, Pork and Chicken) and

$$\text{(6.22)}\qquad \delta = \frac{\phi \bar{W}_{gt}}{\sigma^2 \mu_4^g N_{gg}/\bar{W}_{gt}} = \frac{\phi \bar{W}_{gt}}{\sigma^2 v_{44}^*}$$

where the second step is based on (6.19). We thus have $\boldsymbol{\mu}_0 = \delta\boldsymbol{\Omega\iota}$, as in eq. (6.6) of Section 7.6, and the present δ is obtained from its predecessor by substituting N_{gg} for ϕM_g. This proves that the estimates obtained in Section 7.6 are valid under blockwise dependence if the group utility function of meats takes the form (6.9).

8.7 Extension to Utility Maximization Over Time

In this section we apply the assumption of blockwise dependence to a multiperiod utility function. The analysis shows that the (static) demand model for current expenditures on n commodities may be viewed as a conditional allocation model, given the decision on total current consumption.

A Multiperiod Generalization

Let $\mathbf{q}_t = [q_{it}]$ be the n-element quantity vector of the current period t. We extend the theory by assuming that the consumer has a horizon of three periods (the generalization to any other horizon is obvious), so that $\mathbf{q}_t$, $\mathbf{q}_{t+1}$ and $\mathbf{q}_{t+2}$ are the quantity vectors which appear as arguments of the multiperiod utility function. In particular, let this function take the form

$$\text{(7.1)}\qquad u(\mathbf{q}_t, \mathbf{q}_{t+1}, \mathbf{q}_{t+2}) = f(u_1(\mathbf{q}_t), u_2(\mathbf{q}_{t+1}, \mathbf{q}_{t+2}))$$

This multiperiod utility specification was considered by Koopmans (1960) and Koopmans, Diamond and Williamson (1964), who referred to it as "weak time perspective."

Assume that (7.1) is to be maximized subject to

$$\text{(7.2)}\qquad \sum_{s=t}^{t+2}\sum_{i=1}^{n} p_{is}q_{is} = m$$

where p_{is} is the price of the ith commodity in period s and m is the total amount available for spending in the three periods. We introduce

$$\text{(7.3)}\qquad \mathbf{p} = \begin{bmatrix} \mathbf{p}_t \\ \mathbf{p}_{t+1} \\ \mathbf{p}_{t+2} \end{bmatrix} \qquad \mathbf{q} = \begin{bmatrix} \mathbf{q}_t \\ \mathbf{q}_{t+1} \\ \mathbf{q}_{t+2} \end{bmatrix}$$

where $\mathbf{p}_t = [p_{it}]$. Then (7.2) takes the familiar form $\mathbf{p}'\mathbf{q} = m$ and the left-hand side of (7.1) may be written as $u(\mathbf{q})$.

A Blockwise Dependence Interpretation

It is immediately seen that $u(\mathbf{q})$ as specified in (7.1) may be viewed as a special case of (1.1) with two blocks: current consumption ($\mathbf{q}_t$) and future consumption ($\mathbf{q}_{t+1}$, $\mathbf{q}_{t+2}$). Write S_1 for the group whose quantities are represented in $\mathbf{q}_t$ and S_2 for the group whose quantities are elements of $\mathbf{q}_{t+1}$ and $\mathbf{q}_{t+2}$. We thus have $G = 2$, which suggests that (3.4) for $g = 1$ is now the demand equation for total current consumption,

$$\text{(7.4)}\qquad \bar{W}_{1t} DQ_{1t} = M_1 DQ_t + \sum_{h=1}^{2} N_{1h}\left(DP'_{ht} - \sum_{k=1}^{n} \mu_k Dp_{kt}\right) + E_{1t}$$

or, after dividing by $\bar{W}_{1t}$,

$$\text{(7.5)}\qquad DQ_{1t} = \frac{M_1}{\bar{W}_{1t}} DQ_t + \sum_{h=1}^{2} \frac{N_{1h}}{\bar{W}_{1t}}\left(DP'_{ht} - \sum_{k=1}^{n} \mu_k Dp_{kt}\right) + \frac{E_{1t}}{\bar{W}_{1t}}$$

The left-hand side of (7.5) is the log-change in the volume of total current consumption and $M_1/\bar{W}_{1t}$ is the elasticity of this volume with respect to the "three-period income" m shown in (7.2).

Since DQ_{1t} of (7.5) may be identified with the log-change in real income of the one-period model, this approach also suggests that (6.1) for $g = 1$ provides the demand equation for the current consumption of the ith commodity:

$$\text{(7.6)}\qquad \frac{\bar{w}_{it}}{\bar{W}_{1t}} Dq_{it} = \mu_i^1 DQ_{1t} + \sum_{j \in S_1} \nu_{ij}^* (Dp_{jt} - DP'_{1t}) + \varepsilon_{it}^*$$

The variable on the left is the quantity component of the change in w_{it}/W_{1t}, which is now the share of the ith commodity in total current expenditures.

Two Implications

Two important conclusions follow from (7.5) and (7.6). First, (4.22) and (6.2) show that the disturbances of these two demand equations are uncorrelated, and hence independent when their distribution is normal. Therefore, the blockwise dependent form of the multiperiod utility specification (7.1) combined with the normal decision distribution of the theory of rational random behavior (Section 2.8) implies that *the log-change in real income* (DQ_{1t}) *is a predetermined variable in the allocation model* (7.6) *for current expenditures*. We have postulated this on earlier occasions; the present result shows how it can be justified within the framework of utility maximization over time.

The second conclusion concerns the income flexibility of the one-period model, which is equal to the sum of all price coefficients of that model. So consider the sum of the price coefficients in (7.6) for all $i \in S_1$, using (6.4):

$$\sum_{i \in S_1} \sum_{j \in S_1} \nu_{ij}^* = \frac{N_{11}}{\bar{W}_{1t}} \tag{7.7}$$

On comparing this with (7.5) we find that *the income flexibility of the allocation model for current expenditures is equal to the own-price elasticity of total current consumption.*

Comments on Price Deflators

Although the above conclusions are correct, some comments are in order. In a multiperiod framework it is not satisfactory to write the price deflator in the form $\sum_k \mu_k Dp_{kt}$, as was done in (7.4) and (7.5), because this deflator involves price log-changes in future periods also. The simplest way to approach this problem is by means of (3.24), which is the demand equation for S_1 in the case $G=2$ and which contains a substitution term equal to a negative multiple of $DP'_{1t} - DP'_{2t}$. Here DP'_{1t} is the marginally weighted mean of $Dp_{1t}, \ldots, Dp_{nt}$, which occurs as the price deflator of the allocation model (7.6) of current expenditures. But how should we interpret DP'_{2t}?

The Rotterdam Model measures prices logarithmically from the level of period $t-1$: $\log(p_{it}/p_{i,t-1}) = Dp_{it}$. Thus, the prices of period $t+1$ are

$$\log \frac{p_{i,t+1}}{p_{i,t-1}} = \log \frac{p_{it}}{p_{i,t-1}} + \log \frac{p_{i,t+1}}{p_{it}} = Dp_{it} + Dp_{i,t+1}$$

and, more generally, those of period $s = t, t+1, \ldots$ are

$$\log \frac{p_{is}}{p_{i,t-1}} = \sum_{r=t}^{s} Dp_{ir} \tag{7.8}$$

Therefore, in a three-period framework we have

$$(7.9)\quad DP'_{2t} = \sum_{i=1}^{n} \theta_i (Dp_{it} + Dp_{i,t+1}) + \sum_{i=1}^{n} \theta_{n+i} (Dp_{it} + Dp_{i,t+1} + Dp_{i,t+2})$$

where $\theta_1, \ldots, \theta_n$ are conditional marginal shares for spending in $t+1$ and $\theta_{n+1}, \ldots, \theta_{2n}$ are analogous shares for $t+2$, all under the condition that money is spent in either $t+1$ or $t+2$. The shares $\theta_1, \ldots, \theta_{2n}$ add up to 1.

Thus, DP'_{2t} is a price index of future spending in log-change form and $DP'_{1t} - DP'_{2t}$ in (3.24) is, in the present context, a measure of the relative difference between current and future price levels. The deflator $\sum_k \mu_k Dp_{kt}$ in (7.4) and (7.5) should be read as $M_1 DP'_{1t} + M_2 DP'_{2t}$, the marginally weighted mean of the price deflator DP'_{1t} in the current allocation model (7.6) and DP'_{2t} defined in (7.9).

Concluding Comments

A plea can be made for the idea that future prices and incomes should be discounted, so that the left-hand side of (7.2) becomes

$$(7.10)\quad \sum_{s=t}^{t+2} e^{-\rho(s-t)} \sum_{i=1}^{n} p_{is} q_{is}$$

where ρ is the discount rate. This is equivalent to multiplying p_{is} by the discount factor $e^{-\rho(s-t)}$, which changes the price variable (7.8) into

$$(7.11)\quad \log \frac{e^{-\rho(s-t)}\, p_{is}}{p_{i,t-1}} = -\rho(s-t) + \sum_{r=t}^{s} Dp_{ir}$$

and the price index (7.9) of future spending into

$$(7.12)\quad DP'_{2t} = \sum_{i=1}^{n} \theta_i (-\rho + Dp_{it} + Dp_{i,t+1}) + \sum_{i=1}^{n} \theta_{n+i} (-2\rho + Dp_{it} + Dp_{i,t+1} + Dp_{i,t+2})$$

The terms involving ρ in (7.12) can be simplified to

$$(7.13)\quad -\rho\left(\sum_{i=1}^{n} \theta_i + 2\sum_{i=1}^{n} \theta_{n+i}\right) = -\rho\left(1 + \sum_{i=1}^{n} \theta_{n+i}\right)$$

where the equal sign is based on $\theta_1 + \cdots + \theta_{2n} = 1$. Note that the sum of the θ's in the right-hand side of (7.13) is the conditional marginal share of total consumption in $t+2$, given that money is spent in either $t+1$ or $t+2$.

Therefore, in the case of discounting we have to correct the DP'_{2t} of (7.9) by means of (7.13), which implies that discounting has a substitution effect on the decision regarding total current versus total future spending. But note that discounting also affects the right-hand side of (7.2), which becomes the present value of the flow of disposable income. Thus, discounting has both a substitution and a real-income effect or, more precisely, the multiperiod version of a real-income effect.

The approach can be extended to include variable discount rates and problems of uncertainty as to the future behavior of income and prices. Labor-leisure decisions may also be considered; see BARNETT (1974) for such an analysis based on the Rotterdam Model. These developments are beyond the scope of this volume. For our purposes it is sufficient to conclude that, in a multiperiod framework under the assumption that current and future consumption are blockwise dependent, (1) the one-period Rotterdam Model can be interpreted as a conditional allocation model for current expenditures, (2) the log-change in the volume of total current consumption is a predetermined variable in this model, and (3) the income flexibility of this model can be identified with the own-price elasticity of total current consumption.

CHAPTER 9

QUANTITY CHANGES AS PREDETERMINED VARIABLES

In Section 4.5 we decided to treat prices as predetermined variables because they are determined by retailers on the basis of cost considerations, independently of the consumption of the various goods. In Section 9.1 a model is developed which suggests that this approach is not satisfactory for agricultural goods, such as the meats considered in Chapters 7 and 8, and that it is preferable to treat the quantities as predetermined variables. This approach is pursued in the present chapter. It is extended in Chapter 10, where both prices and quantities are treated as endogenous variables.

9.1 The Case of Predetermined Quantities

Supply and Demand

Let i be an agricultural good and assume, as usual, that per capita consumption (q_{it} in year t) is determined by per capita income (m_t) and prices, apart from a random disturbance (η_{it}):

(1.1) $$q_{it} = f_i(m_t, p_{1t}, \ldots, p_{nt}) + \eta_{it}$$

Assume further that the farmers' supply of this good, also measured per capita of the population, is determined by current and lagged cost factors ($C_t, C_{t-1}, \ldots$) and by lagged values of the prices:

(1.2) $$q'_{it} = g_i(C_t, C_{t-1}, \ldots, p_{1,t-k_1}, \ldots, p_{n,t-k_n}) + \eta'_{it}$$

Here q'_{it} stands for the per capita supply of the ith good in year t, $k_1, \ldots, k_n$ for positive time lags, and η'_{it} for the supply disturbance.

We assume that the cost factor C_t is neither directly nor indirectly affected by current consumption (q_{it})[1] and that the demand and supply disturbances are stochastically independent. Specifically, when T is the number of

[1] The argument which follows is not affected when the supply equation contains other exogenous variables besides C_t, such as the population and the number of farms.

years included in the sample, the T demand disturbance vectors $[\eta_{1t}\ \eta_{2t}\ \ldots]$ and the T supply disturbance vectors $[\eta'_{1t}\ \eta'_{2t}\ \ldots]$ for $t=1,\ldots,T$ are $2T$ independent random vectors. Then, if the market is cleared in every year (i.e., if $q_{it}=q'_{it}$ for each t), the supply equation makes the ith quantity predetermined in the demand-and-supply system, because this equation describes the quantity in terms of current exogenous (C_t) and lagged variables ($C_{t-1}, p_{1,t-k_1}, \ldots$) and a disturbance ($\eta'_{it}$) which is independent of the demand disturbances. The role of prices is now to insure that the market is indeed cleared, which makes them endogenous in the demand-and-supply system.

This model, which implies predetermined quantities rather than prices, may be considered as originating with the Danish economist E. P. MACKEPRANG, who regressed prices on quantities in his doctoral dissertation in 1906.[1] In this chapter we take the assumption of predetermined quantities as valid; we shall come back to it in Section 10.1.

A Log-change Formulation

In contrast to (1.1), the demand equations of the Rotterdam Model are not formulated in terms of levels but in terms of log-changes. The extension of (1.1) and (1.2) is straightforward when we imagine that the supply equations are also in log-changes, with additive disturbances ε'_{it}. Market clearance is then defined as the equality of the log-changes in supply and demand; stochastic independence is assumed for the demand disturbances ε_{it} and the supply disturbances ε'_{it}, and so on. The result is that Dq_{it} becomes predetermined and Dp_{it} becomes endogenous.

Consider then the absolute price version of the ith demand equation:

$$\bar{w}_{it}Dq_{it} = \mu_i DQ_t + \sum_{j=1}^{n} \pi_{ij}Dp_{jt} + \varepsilon_{it}$$

Using the constraint $\sum_j \pi_{ij}=0$, we write this as

$$\bar{w}_{it}Dq_{it} = \mu_i DQ_t + \sum_{j=1}^{n-1} \pi_{ij}(Dp_{jt} - Dp_{nt}) + \varepsilon_{it} \tag{1.3}$$

for $i=1,\ldots,n-1$. [As usual, we delete the nth equation because it is obtained by summing (1.3) over $i=1,\ldots,n-1$.] In our present approach we thus have a predetermined variable Dq_{it} on the left and n endogenous variables $Dp_{1t},\ldots,Dp_{nt}$ on the right.

---

[1] See WOLD's (1969) description of Mackeprang's work, and also FOX (1958, Chapter 1, and 1968) and STIGLER (1954) for other historical surveys in this area.

Extension to the Conditional Demand for Meats

Consider eqs. (3.20) of Section 7.3 and (4.6) of Section 7.4:

$$\frac{\bar{w}_{it}}{\bar{W}_{gt}} Dq_{it} = \frac{\mu_i}{M_g} DQ_{gt} + \sum_{j=1}^{3} \pi_{ij}^* (Dp_{jt} - Dp_{4t}) + \varepsilon_{it}^* \tag{1.4}$$

$$\omega_{ij} = \operatorname{cov}(\varepsilon_{it}^*, \varepsilon_{jt}^*) \tag{1.5}$$

We use the vector notation (4.8) of Section 7.4,

(1.6)

$$\mathbf{z}_t = \begin{bmatrix} \bar{w}_{1t} Dq_{1t}/\bar{W}_{gt} \\ \bar{w}_{2t} Dq_{2t}/\bar{W}_{gt} \\ \bar{w}_{3t} Dq_{3t}/\bar{W}_{gt} \end{bmatrix} \qquad \boldsymbol{\mu}_0 = \begin{bmatrix} \mu_1/M_g \\ \mu_2/M_g \\ \mu_3/M_g \end{bmatrix} \qquad \mathbf{p}_t = \begin{bmatrix} Dp_{1t} - Dp_{4t} \\ Dp_{2t} - Dp_{4t} \\ Dp_{3t} - Dp_{4t} \end{bmatrix} \qquad \boldsymbol{\varepsilon}_t = \begin{bmatrix} \varepsilon_{1t}^* \\ \varepsilon_{2t}^* \\ \varepsilon_{3t}^* \end{bmatrix}$$

to write (1.4) for $i = 1$, 2 and 3 as

$$\mathbf{z}_t = \boldsymbol{\mu}_0 DQ_{gt} + \boldsymbol{\Pi}\mathbf{p}_t + \boldsymbol{\varepsilon}_t \tag{1.7}$$

where

$$\boldsymbol{\Pi} = \begin{bmatrix} \pi_{11}^* & \pi_{12}^* & \pi_{13}^* \\ \pi_{21}^* & \pi_{22}^* & \pi_{23}^* \\ \pi_{31}^* & \pi_{32}^* & \pi_{33}^* \end{bmatrix} = \begin{bmatrix} \boldsymbol{\pi}_1' \\ \boldsymbol{\pi}_2' \\ \boldsymbol{\pi}_3' \end{bmatrix} \begin{matrix} \text{Beef} \\ \text{Pork} \\ \text{Chicken} \end{matrix} \tag{1.8}$$

Here $\boldsymbol{\pi}_i$ in the third member is the transpose of the ith row of $\boldsymbol{\Pi}$.

Predetermined Quantity Components of Budget Share Changes

It will be convenient to treat $\bar{w}_{it}$ in (1.3) as predetermined; this is basically equivalent to what we did in Section 5.5 (see page 221 of Volume 1) when we used the observed $\bar{w}_{it}$'s to generate extrapolations. This means that predetermined quantity log-changes (Dq_{it}) imply and are implied by predetermined quantity components of budget share changes ($\bar{w}_{it} Dq_{it}$). Since DQ_t equals the sum of $\bar{w}_{it} Dq_{it}$ over all i, this is also a predetermined variable. Note that this property of DQ_t is implied by the present approach; there is no need to derive it from the second-moment model under blockwise dependence assumptions in a multiperiod framework, as we did in Section 8.7. In this chapter the second-moment model will not be used for purposes of estimation.

In the same way, if $\bar{w}_{it}$ is predetermined, $\bar{W}_{gt} = \sum_i \bar{w}_{it}$ is also predetermined and hence so is the quantity component of the change in the conditional budget share in (1.4). The log-change in the volume index of meat consumption is

$$DQ_{gt} = \sum_{i=1}^{4} \frac{\bar{w}_{it}}{\bar{W}_{gt}} Dq_{it} = \iota_3' \mathbf{z}_t + \frac{\bar{w}_{4t}}{\bar{W}_{gt}} Dq_{4t} \tag{1.9}$$

where $\iota_3 = [1 \ \ 1 \ \ 1]'$; the subscript 4 refers to Lamb. We conclude from (1.9) that DQ_{gt} is also predetermined.

Review of Some Earlier Results

For the estimation procedure of Section 9.2 we shall need some further notation and results developed in Section 7.5. It is convenient to collect them here.

In eq. (5.3) of Section 7.5 we defined c_t as the ratio of DQ_{gt} to the length of the vector $[DQ_{g1} \dots DQ_{gT}]$. This can be written as

$$c_t = qDQ_{gt} \quad \text{where} \quad q = \left[\sum_{t=1}^{T} (DQ_{gt})^2\right]^{-1/2} \tag{1.10}$$

The c_t's have unit length,

$$\sum_{t=1}^{T} c_t^2 = 1 \tag{1.11}$$

which is eq. (5.4) of Section 7.5.

We shall also need eqs. (5.5) and (5.6) of the same section,

$$\mathbf{z}_0 = \sum_{t=1}^{T} c_t \mathbf{z}_t \qquad \mathbf{p}_0 = \sum_{t=1}^{T} c_t \mathbf{p}_t \tag{1.12}$$

$$\sum_{t=1}^{T} c_t (\mathbf{z}_t - c_t \mathbf{z}_0) = \sum_{t=1}^{T} c_t (\mathbf{p}_t - c_t \mathbf{p}_0) = \mathbf{0} \tag{1.13}$$

as well as eqs. (5.9) and (5.13) of that section:

$$\mathbf{Z}_0 = \frac{1}{T} \sum_{t=1}^{T} (\mathbf{z}_t - c_t \mathbf{z}_0)(\mathbf{z}_t - c_t \mathbf{z}_0)' = \frac{1}{T} \sum_{t=1}^{T} \mathbf{z}_t \mathbf{z}_t' - \frac{1}{T} \mathbf{z}_0 \mathbf{z}_0' \tag{1.14}$$

A Limit Condition

To prove the asymptotic properties that will be described in Section 9.2 we shall assume that, as $T \to \infty$, the mean squares and products of the quantity components of the conditional budget share changes converge in probability to finite limits. This refers to all four meats. Hence, using (1.9), we have a 4×4 limit matrix,

$$\operatorname*{plim}_{T \to \infty} \frac{1}{T} \sum_{t=1}^{T} \begin{bmatrix} \mathbf{z}_t \\ DQ_{gt} - \iota_3' \mathbf{z}_t \end{bmatrix} [\mathbf{z}_t' \quad DQ_{gt} - \iota_3' \mathbf{z}_t] = \bar{\mathbf{W}} \tag{1.15}$$

which we assume to be positive definite. An implication is

$$\underset{T\to\infty}{\text{plim}}\ \frac{1}{T}\sum_{t=1}^{T}(DQ_{gt})^2 = \boldsymbol{\iota}_4'\overline{\mathbf{W}}\boldsymbol{\iota}_4 > 0 \tag{1.16}$$

where $\boldsymbol{\iota}_4 = [1 \ \ 1 \ \ 1 \ \ 1]'$.

Next we use (1.12) and (1.10) in the following steps:

$$\mathbf{z}_0 = \sum_{t=1}^{T} c_t \mathbf{z}_t = \left[\sum_{t=1}^{T}(DQ_{gt})^2\right]^{-1/2} \sum_{t=1}^{T}(DQ_{gt})\,\mathbf{z}_t$$
$$= \sqrt{T}\left[\frac{1}{T}\sum_{t=1}^{T}(DQ_{gt})^2\right]^{-1/2} \frac{1}{T}\sum_{t=1}^{T}(DQ_{gt})\,\mathbf{z}_t$$

This shows that, as $T\to\infty$, $(1/T)\,\mathbf{z}_0\mathbf{z}_0'$ converges in probability to the leading 3×3 submatrix of $(\boldsymbol{\iota}_4'\overline{\mathbf{W}}\boldsymbol{\iota}_4)^{-1}\,\overline{\mathbf{W}}\boldsymbol{\iota}_4\boldsymbol{\iota}_4'\overline{\mathbf{W}}$. Hence $\mathbf{Z}_0$ defined in (1.14) has a probability limit equal to the leading 3×3 submatrix of

$$\overline{\mathbf{W}} - \frac{1}{\boldsymbol{\iota}_4'\overline{\mathbf{W}}\boldsymbol{\iota}_4}\overline{\mathbf{W}}\boldsymbol{\iota}_4\boldsymbol{\iota}_4'\overline{\mathbf{W}} \tag{1.17}$$

which implies that the limit matrix $\overline{\mathbf{Z}}_0$ of $\mathbf{Z}_0$ is symmetric positive definite:

$$\underset{T\to\infty}{\text{plim}}\ \mathbf{Z}_0 = \overline{\mathbf{Z}}_0 \quad \text{(symmetric positive definite)} \tag{1.18}$$

To prove this we premultiply the 4×4 matrix (1.17) by a vector $\mathbf{x}'$ and we postmultiply by $\mathbf{x}$:

$$\mathbf{x}'\overline{\mathbf{W}}\mathbf{x} - \frac{(\mathbf{x}'\overline{\mathbf{W}}\boldsymbol{\iota}_4)^2}{\boldsymbol{\iota}_4'\overline{\mathbf{W}}\boldsymbol{\iota}_4} = \frac{1}{\boldsymbol{\iota}_4'\overline{\mathbf{W}}\boldsymbol{\iota}_4}\left[(\boldsymbol{\iota}_4'\overline{\mathbf{W}}\boldsymbol{\iota}_4)\,(\mathbf{x}'\overline{\mathbf{W}}\mathbf{x}) - (\mathbf{x}'\overline{\mathbf{W}}\boldsymbol{\iota}_4)^2\right]$$

The expression on the right is positive for any $\mathbf{x}$ which is not a scalar multiple of $\boldsymbol{\iota}_4$. Therefore, any principal submatrix of the symmetric matrix (1.17), including $\overline{\mathbf{Z}}_0$, is symmetric positive definite.

It will also be assumed that $\mathbf{Z}_0$ is positive definite for finite T; see the discussion below eq. (5.10) of Section 7.5.

9.2 Quantity Changes Used as Instrumental Variables

This section develops an estimation method, based on the use of quantity changes as instrumental variables, for the parameter matrices $\boldsymbol{\mu}_0$ and $\boldsymbol{\Pi}$ of (1.7). [More precisely, the instrumental variables used are the quantity components of the conditional budget share changes.] The estimator of $\boldsymbol{\Pi}$

is not symmetric; we shall therefore refer to the estimator derived below as the unconstrained instrumental-variable estimator. A symmetry-constrained version is developed in Section 9.4.

Elimination of the Conditional Marginal Shares

We postmultiply (1.7) by $(T^{-1}\mathbf{z}_t)'$ and sum over t:

$$\frac{1}{T}\sum_{t=1}^{T} \mathbf{z}_t\mathbf{z}_t' = \boldsymbol{\mu}_0 \frac{1}{T}\sum_{t=1}^{T} (DQ_{gt})\,\mathbf{z}_t' + \boldsymbol{\Pi}\frac{1}{T}\sum_{t=1}^{T} \mathbf{p}_t\mathbf{z}_t' + \frac{1}{T}\sum_{t=1}^{T} \boldsymbol{\varepsilon}_t\mathbf{z}_t'$$

It follows from (1.10) and (1.12) that this can be simplified to

$$\frac{1}{T}\sum_{t=1}^{T} \mathbf{z}_t\mathbf{z}_t' = \frac{1}{qT}\boldsymbol{\mu}_0\mathbf{z}_0' + \boldsymbol{\Pi}\frac{1}{T}\sum_{t=1}^{T} \mathbf{p}_t\mathbf{z}_t' + \frac{1}{T}\sum_{t=1}^{T} \boldsymbol{\varepsilon}_t\mathbf{z}_t' \tag{2.1}$$

Next multiply (1.7) by c_t and sum over t, using (1.12):

$$\mathbf{z}_0 = \boldsymbol{\mu}_0 \sum_{t=1}^{T} c_t DQ_{gt} + \boldsymbol{\Pi}\mathbf{p}_0 + \sum_{t=1}^{T} c_t\boldsymbol{\varepsilon}_t = \frac{1}{q}\boldsymbol{\mu}_0 + \boldsymbol{\Pi}\mathbf{p}_0 + \sum_{t=1}^{T} c_t\boldsymbol{\varepsilon}_t \tag{2.2}$$

where the second step is based on (1.10) and (1.11). We conclude from (2.2) that $\boldsymbol{\mu}_0$ can be expressed as

$$\boldsymbol{\mu}_0 = q\mathbf{z}_0 - q\boldsymbol{\Pi}\mathbf{p}_0 - q\sum_{t=1}^{T} c_t\boldsymbol{\varepsilon}_t \tag{2.3}$$

which we substitute in (2.1):

$$\frac{1}{T}\sum_{t=1}^{T} \mathbf{z}_t\mathbf{z}_t' - \frac{1}{T}\mathbf{z}_0\mathbf{z}_0' = \boldsymbol{\Pi}\left(\frac{1}{T}\sum_{t=1}^{T} \mathbf{p}_t\mathbf{z}_t' - \frac{1}{T}\mathbf{p}_0\mathbf{z}_0'\right) + \frac{1}{T}\sum_{t=1}^{T} \boldsymbol{\varepsilon}_t(\mathbf{z}_t - c_t\mathbf{z}_0)'$$

We use (1.14) to simplify this to

$$\mathbf{Z}_0 = \boldsymbol{\Pi}\mathbf{L} + \frac{1}{T}\sum_{t=1}^{T} \boldsymbol{\varepsilon}_t(\mathbf{z}_t - c_t\mathbf{z}_0)' \tag{2.4}$$

where $\mathbf{L}$ is a 3×3 matrix:

$$\mathbf{L} = \frac{1}{T}\sum_{t=1}^{T} \mathbf{p}_t\mathbf{z}_t' - \frac{1}{T}\mathbf{p}_0\mathbf{z}_0' \tag{2.5}$$

Equation (2.4) contains only $\boldsymbol{\Pi}$ as an unknown parameter matrix, which is achieved by using (2.2) to eliminate $\boldsymbol{\mu}_0$. Recall that we used eqs. (5.7) and (5.8) of Section 7.5 for a similar purpose, but note that the latter equations differ from (2.1) to (2.5) in that the present $\boldsymbol{\Pi}$ and $\boldsymbol{\mu}_0$ stand for parameters, not for estimates of parameters. In this chapter it is important to use different symbols for estimates and parameters.

The Unconstrained Instrumental-Variable Estimator

In our present approach $\mathbf{z}_t$ and DQ_{gt} are predetermined, and so is c_t in view of (1.10). Hence the disturbance term in (2.4) has zero expectation conditionally on the predetermined variables. When we use these as instrumental variables by replacing the disturbance term by its expectation, (2.4) becomes an estimation equation of the form $\mathbf{Z}_0 = \hat{\mathbf{\Pi}}\mathbf{L}$. This yields the instrumental-variable estimator of $\mathbf{\Pi}$,

$$\hat{\mathbf{\Pi}} = \mathbf{Z}_0 \mathbf{L}^{-1} \tag{2.6}$$

provided that the 3×3 matrix $\mathbf{L}$ is nonsingular. For $\boldsymbol{\mu}_0$ we proceed in the same way by means of (2.3) after replacing the disturbance term by its conditional expectation (zero) and $\mathbf{\Pi}$ by $\hat{\mathbf{\Pi}}$:

$$\hat{\boldsymbol{\mu}}_0 = q\mathbf{z}_0 - q\hat{\mathbf{\Pi}}\mathbf{p}_0 \tag{2.7}$$

Note that this estimation procedure is asymmetric in the sense that the instrumental variables used are the three elements of $\mathbf{z}_t$ defined in (1.6), with Lamb excluded, and DQ_{gt} (or, equivalently, c_t). However, there is no real asymmetry, because (1.9) shows that the quantity component of the conditional budget share change of Lamb is a linear combination of DQ_{gt} and the elements of $\mathbf{z}_t$.

The Existence and Consistency of the Estimator

The ith row of the 3×3 disturbance matrix in (2.4) has zero expectation conditionally on the predetermined variables. Its covariance matrix is

$$\frac{1}{T^2} \sum_{s=1}^{T} \sum_{t=1}^{T} (\mathbf{z}_s - c_s\mathbf{z}_0)\, \mathscr{E}(\varepsilon_{is}^*\varepsilon_{it}^*)\, (\mathbf{z}_t - c_t\mathbf{z}_0)' \tag{2.8}$$

$$= \frac{\omega_{ii}}{T^2} \sum_{t=1}^{T} (\mathbf{z}_t - c_t\mathbf{z}_0)(\mathbf{z}_t - c_t\mathbf{z}_0)' = \frac{\omega_{ii}}{T} \mathbf{Z}_0$$

where the first step is based on (1.5) and the assumed serial independence of the disturbances, and the second on (1.14). It follows from (1.18) that, as $T \to \infty$, (2.8) converges to $(\omega_{ii}/T)\bar{\mathbf{Z}}_0$ and hence to a zero matrix. Therefore, each row of the disturbance matrix in (2.4) converges in probability to zero. The asymptotic version of (2.4) thus states that $\bar{\mathbf{Z}}_0$ equals $\mathbf{\Pi}$ postmultiplied by the probability limit of $\mathbf{L}$, which implies that the latter limit must be nonsingular. Hence $\hat{\mathbf{\Pi}}$ defined in (2.6) exists for large T and is a consistent estimator of $\mathbf{\Pi}$.

By subtracting (2.3) from (2.7) we obtain

$$\hat{\boldsymbol{\mu}}_0 - \boldsymbol{\mu}_0 = q \sum_{t=1}^{T} c_t \boldsymbol{\varepsilon}_t - q (\hat{\mathbf{\Pi}} - \mathbf{\Pi}) \mathbf{p}_0 \tag{2.9}$$

This equation describes the sampling error of the $\boldsymbol{\mu}_0$ estimator as consisting of two parts, with the second resulting from the substitution of $\hat{\mathbf{\Pi}}$ for $\mathbf{\Pi}$ in (2.7), while the first would be the sampling error of $\hat{\boldsymbol{\mu}}_0$ if we had used the true $\mathbf{\Pi}$ in (2.7). It is shown in the subsection immediately following the next that both parts converge in probability to zero as $T \to \infty$, which establishes the consistency of $\hat{\boldsymbol{\mu}}_0$.

Note that we have treated $\mathbf{z}_t$ and c_t as nonstochastic in the derivation of the covariance matrix (2.8). This amounts to assuming that these variables are purely exogenous, which is stronger than predetermined. The same asymptotic results can be derived under the weaker condition when $\boldsymbol{\varepsilon}_1, \dots, \boldsymbol{\varepsilon}_T$ are independent random drawings from the same distribution with zero means and covariance matrix $[\omega_{ij}]$, but we shall proceed along the lines of (2.8) for reasons of simplicity.

The Asymptotic Behavior of the Estimator of $\mathbf{\Pi}$

By postmultiplying (2.4) by $\mathbf{L}^{-1}$ we obtain

$$\mathbf{\Pi} = \mathbf{Z}_0 \mathbf{L}^{-1} - \frac{1}{T} \sum_{t=1}^{T} \boldsymbol{\varepsilon}_t (\mathbf{z}_t - c_t \mathbf{z}_0)' \mathbf{L}^{-1}$$

which we subtract from (2.6):

$$\hat{\mathbf{\Pi}} - \mathbf{\Pi} = \frac{1}{T} \sum_{t=1}^{T} \boldsymbol{\varepsilon}_t (\mathbf{z}_t - c_t \mathbf{z}_0)' \mathbf{L}^{-1} \tag{2.10}$$

To analyze the asymptotic behavior of this sampling error we define

$$\mathbf{a}_t' = \frac{1}{T} (\mathbf{z}_t - c_t \mathbf{z}_0)' \bar{\mathbf{Z}}_0^{-1} \qquad t = 1, \dots, T \tag{2.11}$$

It follows from (1.13), (1.14) and (1.18) that these vectors satisfy

$$\sum_{t=1}^{T} c_t \mathbf{a}_t = \mathbf{0} \tag{2.12}$$

$$\operatorname*{plim}_{T \to \infty} T \sum_{t=1}^{T} \mathbf{a}_t \mathbf{a}_t' = \bar{\mathbf{Z}}_0^{-1} \tag{2.13}$$

The discussion below (2.8) shows that, as $T \to \infty$, $\mathbf{L}^{-1}$ converges in probability to the inverse of $\mathbf{\Pi}^{-1}\bar{\mathbf{Z}}_0$. Hence (2.10) is asymptotically equivalent to

$$\hat{\mathbf{\Pi}} - \mathbf{\Pi} = \frac{1}{T} \sum_{t=1}^{T} \boldsymbol{\varepsilon}_t (\mathbf{z}_t - c_t \mathbf{z}_0)' \, \bar{\mathbf{Z}}_0^{-1} \mathbf{\Pi} = \sum_{t=1}^{T} \boldsymbol{\varepsilon}_t \mathbf{a}_t' \mathbf{\Pi} \tag{2.14}$$

where the second step is based on (2.11).

It follows from (1.6) and (1.8) that (2.14) may be written as

$$\hat{\boldsymbol{\pi}}_i - \boldsymbol{\pi}_i = \mathbf{\Pi}' \sum_{t=1}^{T} \mathbf{a}_t \varepsilon_{it}^* \qquad i = 1, 2, 3 \tag{2.15}$$

This is equivalent to

$$\begin{bmatrix} \hat{\boldsymbol{\pi}}_1 - \boldsymbol{\pi}_1 \\ \hat{\boldsymbol{\pi}}_2 - \boldsymbol{\pi}_2 \\ \hat{\boldsymbol{\pi}}_3 - \boldsymbol{\pi}_3 \end{bmatrix} = \sum_{t=1}^{T} \begin{bmatrix} \mathbf{\Pi}'\mathbf{a}_t & \mathbf{0} & \mathbf{0} \\ \mathbf{0} & \mathbf{\Pi}'\mathbf{a}_t & \mathbf{0} \\ \mathbf{0} & \mathbf{0} & \mathbf{\Pi}'\mathbf{a}_t \end{bmatrix} \begin{bmatrix} \varepsilon_{1t}^* \\ \varepsilon_{2t}^* \\ \varepsilon_{3t}^* \end{bmatrix} = \sum_{t=1}^{T} [\mathbf{I}_3 \otimes (\mathbf{\Pi}'\mathbf{a}_t)] \, \boldsymbol{\varepsilon}_t$$

Therefore,

$$\hat{\boldsymbol{\pi}} - \boldsymbol{\pi} = \sum_{t=1}^{T} [\mathbf{I}_3 \otimes (\mathbf{\Pi}'\mathbf{a}_t)] \, \boldsymbol{\varepsilon}_t \tag{2.16}$$

where $\hat{\boldsymbol{\pi}}$ and $\boldsymbol{\pi}$ are the matrices $\hat{\mathbf{\Pi}}$ and $\mathbf{\Pi}$, respectively, written as nine-element column vectors:

$$\hat{\boldsymbol{\pi}} = [\hat{\boldsymbol{\pi}}_1' \quad \hat{\boldsymbol{\pi}}_2' \quad \hat{\boldsymbol{\pi}}_3']' \qquad \boldsymbol{\pi} = [\boldsymbol{\pi}_1' \quad \boldsymbol{\pi}_2' \quad \boldsymbol{\pi}_3']' \tag{2.17}$$

The Asymptotic Behavior of the Conditional Marginal Share Estimator

It is shown in the next subsection that (2.9) is asymptotically equivalent to

$$\hat{\boldsymbol{\mu}}_0 - \boldsymbol{\mu}_0 = q \sum_{t=1}^{T} c_t \boldsymbol{\varepsilon}_t + \mathbf{A}(\hat{\boldsymbol{\pi}} - \boldsymbol{\pi}) \tag{2.18}$$

where $\mathbf{A}$ is a fixed (nonrandom) 3×9 matrix to be specified in (2.24). Hence the second term in the right-hand side converges in probability to zero as $T \to \infty$ in view of the consistency of $\hat{\boldsymbol{\pi}}$.

To establish the consistency of $\hat{\boldsymbol{\mu}}_0$ it is thus sufficient to prove that the first right-hand term in (2.18) also converges to zero. This term has zero expectation and the following covariance matrix:

$$q^2 \sum_{s=1}^{T} \sum_{t=1}^{T} c_s c_t \mathscr{E}(\boldsymbol{\varepsilon}_s \boldsymbol{\varepsilon}_t') = q^2 \mathbf{\Omega} \sum_{t=1}^{T} c_t^2$$

It follows from (1.10) and (1.11) that this can be simplified to

$$\mathscr{V}\left[q \sum_{t=1}^{T} c_t \boldsymbol{\varepsilon}_t\right] = \left[\sum_{t=1}^{T} (DQ_{gt})^2\right]^{-1} \mathbf{\Omega} \tag{2.19}$$

which converges to a zero matrix as $T \to \infty$ in view of (1.16). By applying Chebyshev's inequality we conclude that the first term on the right in (2.18) converges in probability to its expectation (zero).

Derivations for the Conditional Marginal Shares

We use (1.10) and (1.12) in the following steps:

$$q\mathbf{z}_0 = q^2 \sum_{t=1}^{T} (DQ_{gt})\, \mathbf{z}_t = \left[\frac{1}{T} \sum_{t=1}^{T} (DQ_{gt})^2\right]^{-1} \frac{1}{T} \sum_{t=1}^{T} (DQ_{gt})\, \mathbf{z}_t$$

It thus follows from (1.15) that $q\mathbf{z}_0$ has a probability limit equal to the leading three-element subvector of $(\mathbf{\iota}_4' \overline{\mathbf{W}} \mathbf{\iota}_4)^{-1}\, \overline{\mathbf{W}} \mathbf{\iota}_4$. We shall write $\mathbf{b}$ for this limit vector,

(2.20) $$\operatorname*{plim}_{T\to\infty} q\mathbf{z}_0 = \mathbf{b} = [b_i]$$

and note that the ith element of $\mathbf{b}$ is the coefficient in

(2.21) $$\frac{\bar{w}_{it}}{\overline{W}_{gt}} Dq_{it} = b_i DQ_{gt} + \text{residual}$$

which is the least-squares regression of the quantity component of the change in the conditional budget share of the ith meat on DQ_{gt} for $T \to \infty$.

Next we use (1.8) in

$$-q(\hat{\mathbf{\Pi}} - \mathbf{\Pi})\, \mathbf{p}_0 = -q \begin{bmatrix} (\hat{\boldsymbol{\pi}}_1 - \boldsymbol{\pi}_1)' \mathbf{p}_0 \\ (\hat{\boldsymbol{\pi}}_2 - \boldsymbol{\pi}_2)' \mathbf{p}_0 \\ (\hat{\boldsymbol{\pi}}_3 - \boldsymbol{\pi}_3)' \mathbf{p}_0 \end{bmatrix} = -q \begin{bmatrix} \mathbf{p}_0' (\hat{\boldsymbol{\pi}}_1 - \boldsymbol{\pi}_1) \\ \mathbf{p}_0' (\hat{\boldsymbol{\pi}}_2 - \boldsymbol{\pi}_2) \\ \mathbf{p}_0' (\hat{\boldsymbol{\pi}}_3 - \boldsymbol{\pi}_3) \end{bmatrix}$$

Since the third member can be written as

$$\begin{bmatrix} -q\mathbf{p}_0' & \mathbf{0} & \mathbf{0} \\ \mathbf{0} & -q\mathbf{p}_0' & \mathbf{0} \\ \mathbf{0} & \mathbf{0} & -q\mathbf{p}_0' \end{bmatrix} \begin{bmatrix} \hat{\boldsymbol{\pi}}_1 - \boldsymbol{\pi}_1 \\ \hat{\boldsymbol{\pi}}_2 - \boldsymbol{\pi}_2 \\ \hat{\boldsymbol{\pi}}_3 - \boldsymbol{\pi}_3 \end{bmatrix}$$

we can conclude

(2.22) $$-q(\hat{\mathbf{\Pi}} - \mathbf{\Pi})\, \mathbf{p}_0 = [\mathbf{I}_3 \otimes (-q\mathbf{p}_0')]\, (\hat{\boldsymbol{\pi}} - \boldsymbol{\pi})$$

Furthermore, (2.3) implies

(2.23) $$-q\mathbf{p}_0 = \mathbf{\Pi}^{-1} \left(\boldsymbol{\mu}_0 - q\mathbf{z}_0 + q \sum_{t=1}^{T} c_t \boldsymbol{\varepsilon}_t\right)$$

We concluded below (2.19) that $q \sum_t c_t \boldsymbol{\varepsilon}_t$ converges in probability to a zero vector as $T \to \infty$; hence (2.20) and (2.23) imply that $-q\mathbf{p}_0$ converges in probability to $\mathbf{\Pi}^{-1}(\boldsymbol{\mu}_0-\mathbf{b})$. Therefore, the vector (2.22) is asymptotically equivalent to $\mathbf{A}(\hat{\boldsymbol{\pi}}-\boldsymbol{\pi})$ when $\mathbf{A}$ is defined as

$$\mathbf{A} = \mathbf{I}_3 \otimes [\mathbf{\Pi}^{-1}(\boldsymbol{\mu}_0 - \mathbf{b})]' \tag{2.24}$$

This leads directly to (2.18).

The Asymptotic Distribution of the Estimator

It follows from (2.16) and (2.18) that $\hat{\boldsymbol{\pi}}$ and $\hat{\boldsymbol{\mu}}_0$ have an asymptotic distribution with means $\boldsymbol{\pi}$ and $\boldsymbol{\mu}_0$. This asymptotic distribution is normal when $\boldsymbol{\varepsilon}_1, \ldots, \boldsymbol{\varepsilon}_T$ are normally distributed. It is shown in the next subsection that the asymptotic covariance matrix is

(2.25)

$$\mathscr{V}\begin{bmatrix}\hat{\boldsymbol{\pi}}\\ \hat{\boldsymbol{\mu}}_0\end{bmatrix} = \begin{bmatrix} \frac{1}{T}\boldsymbol{\Omega}\otimes(\mathbf{\Pi}'\bar{\mathbf{Z}}_0^{-1}\mathbf{\Pi}) & \frac{1}{T}\boldsymbol{\Omega}\otimes[\mathbf{\Pi}'\bar{\mathbf{Z}}_0^{-1}(\boldsymbol{\mu}_0-\mathbf{b})] \\ \frac{1}{T}\boldsymbol{\Omega}\otimes[(\boldsymbol{\mu}_0-\mathbf{b})'\,\bar{\mathbf{Z}}_0^{-1}\mathbf{\Pi}] & (\alpha_0+\alpha_1)\,\boldsymbol{\Omega} \end{bmatrix}$$

where α_0 and α_1 are scalars:

$$\alpha_0 = \left[\sum_{t=1}^{T}(DQ_{gt})^2\right]^{-1} \qquad \alpha_1 = \frac{1}{T}(\boldsymbol{\mu}_0-\mathbf{b})'\,\bar{\mathbf{Z}}_0^{-1}(\boldsymbol{\mu}_0-\mathbf{b}) \tag{2.26}$$

The matrix (2.25) in conjunction with (1.16) and (2.26) shows that the asymptotic variances are all of order $1/T$.

It is interesting to note that the asymptotic covariance matrix of $\hat{\boldsymbol{\mu}}_0$ is a scalar multiple $(\alpha_0+\alpha_1)$ of the contemporaneous covariance matrix of the disturbances. It will appear that the α_0 component results from the first right-hand term in (2.18) and the α_1 component from the second.

Proof of the Asymptotic Covariance Matrix

To obtain the asymptotic covariance matrix of $\hat{\boldsymbol{\pi}}$ we postmultiply the right-hand side of (2.16) by its transpose and then take the expectation:

$$\sum_{s=1}^{T}\sum_{t=1}^{T}[\mathbf{I}_3\otimes(\mathbf{\Pi}'\mathbf{a}_s)]\,\mathscr{E}(\boldsymbol{\varepsilon}_s\boldsymbol{\varepsilon}_t')\,[\mathbf{I}_3\otimes(\mathbf{a}_t'\mathbf{\Pi})]$$

This may be written as

$$\sum_{t=1}^{T}[\mathbf{I}_3\otimes(\mathbf{\Pi}'\mathbf{a}_t)]\,(\boldsymbol{\Omega}\otimes 1)\,[\mathbf{I}_3\otimes(\mathbf{a}_t'\mathbf{\Pi})] = \boldsymbol{\Omega}\otimes\left[\mathbf{\Pi}'\left(\sum_{t=1}^{T}\mathbf{a}_t\mathbf{a}_t'\right)\mathbf{\Pi}\right]$$

Hence (2.13) implies that $\sqrt{T}(\hat{\boldsymbol{\pi}}-\boldsymbol{\pi})$ has a limiting distribution with covariance matrix $\boldsymbol{\Omega}\otimes(\boldsymbol{\Pi}'\bar{\mathbf{Z}}_0^{-1}\boldsymbol{\Pi})$, in agreement with (2.25).

Next we use (2.16) in

$$\begin{aligned}\sum_{t=1}^{T} c_t\mathscr{E}[\boldsymbol{\varepsilon}_t(\hat{\boldsymbol{\pi}}-\boldsymbol{\pi})'] &= \sum_{t=1}^{T}\sum_{s=1}^{T} c_t\mathscr{E}(\boldsymbol{\varepsilon}_t\boldsymbol{\varepsilon}_s')[\mathbf{I}_3\otimes(\mathbf{a}_s'\boldsymbol{\Pi})] \\ &= \boldsymbol{\Omega}\sum_{t=1}^{T} c_t[\mathbf{I}_3\otimes(\mathbf{a}_t'\boldsymbol{\Pi})] \\ &= \boldsymbol{\Omega}\left[\mathbf{I}_3\otimes\left(\sum_{t=1}^{T} c_t\mathbf{a}_t'\boldsymbol{\Pi}\right)\right]\end{aligned}$$

The matrix in the last line vanishes in view of (2.12), so that

$$\sum_{t=1}^{T} c_t\mathscr{E}[\boldsymbol{\varepsilon}_t(\hat{\boldsymbol{\pi}}-\boldsymbol{\pi})'] = \mathbf{0} \tag{2.27}$$

The lower-left submatrix in (2.25) is obtained by postmultiplying (2.18) by the transpose of (2.16), which yields the sum of two terms, and then taking the expectation. The expectation of the first term vanishes in view of (2.27) and that of the second is

$$\begin{aligned}\mathbf{A}\mathscr{V}(\hat{\boldsymbol{\pi}}) &= \left(\mathbf{I}_3\otimes[\boldsymbol{\Pi}^{-1}(\boldsymbol{\mu}_0-\mathbf{b})]'\right)\left[\frac{1}{T}\boldsymbol{\Omega}\otimes(\boldsymbol{\Pi}'\bar{\mathbf{Z}}_0^{-1}\boldsymbol{\Pi})\right] \\ &= \frac{1}{T}\boldsymbol{\Omega}\otimes[(\boldsymbol{\mu}_0-\mathbf{b})'\,\bar{\mathbf{Z}}_0^{-1}\boldsymbol{\Pi}]\end{aligned} \tag{2.28}$$

where the first equal sign is based on (2.24). Finally, to obtain $\mathscr{V}(\hat{\boldsymbol{\mu}}_0)$ we postmultiply (2.18) by its transpose and take the expectation. It follows from (2.27) that this yields the covariance matrix of $q\sum_t c_t\boldsymbol{\varepsilon}_t$, which equals $\alpha_0\boldsymbol{\Omega}$ in view of (2.19) and (2.26), plus $\mathbf{A}\mathscr{V}(\hat{\boldsymbol{\pi}})\mathbf{A}'$. The latter matrix is $\alpha_1\boldsymbol{\Omega}$ with α_1 defined in (2.26), which may be verified by postmultiplying (2.28) by $\mathbf{A}'$.

We conclude by stressing that these are all large-sample results based on the approximations (2.16) and (2.18). Equation (2.18) is asymptotically equivalent to the exact equation (2.9) in the sense that, as $T\to\infty$, $\sqrt{T}$ times the right-hand side of (2.18) converges in distribution to $\sqrt{T}$ times that of (2.9). There is a similar relationship between (2.16) and (2.10).

A Consistent Estimator of the Disturbance Covariance Matrix

Consider the 6×6 matrix of mean squares and products of two sets of variables,

(2.29)

$$\frac{1}{T}\sum_{t=1}^{T}\begin{bmatrix}\mathbf{z}_t - c_t\mathbf{z}_0\\ \mathbf{p}_t - c_t\mathbf{p}_0\end{bmatrix}[(\mathbf{z}_t - c_t\mathbf{z}_0)' \qquad (\mathbf{p}_t - c_t\mathbf{p}_0)'] = \begin{bmatrix}\mathbf{Z}_0 & \mathbf{L}'\\ \mathbf{L} & \mathbf{E}_0'\mathbf{E}_0\end{bmatrix}$$

where the lower-right submatrix ($\mathbf{E}_0'\mathbf{E}_0$) is based on eq. (5.10) of Section 7.5, while the off-diagonal blocks follow from (1.12), (1.13) and (2.5):

$$\frac{1}{T}\sum_{t=1}^{T}(\mathbf{p}_t - c_t\mathbf{p}_0)(\mathbf{z}_t - c_t\mathbf{z}_0)'$$

$$= \frac{1}{T}\sum_{t=1}^{T}\mathbf{p}_t\mathbf{z}_t' - \frac{1}{T}\sum_{t=1}^{T}c_t\mathbf{p}_t\mathbf{z}_0' - \mathbf{p}_0\frac{1}{T}\sum_{t=1}^{T}c_t(\mathbf{z}_t - c_t\mathbf{z}_0)'$$

$$= \frac{1}{T}\sum_{t=1}^{T}\mathbf{p}_t\mathbf{z}_t' - \frac{1}{T}\mathbf{p}_0\mathbf{z}_0' = \mathbf{L}$$

Next we use (1.10) to write the tth residual vector as

(2.30)

$$\mathbf{z}_t - \hat{\boldsymbol{\mu}}_0 DQ_{gt} - \hat{\boldsymbol{\Pi}}\mathbf{p}_t = \mathbf{z}_t - \frac{c_t}{q}\hat{\boldsymbol{\mu}}_0 - \hat{\boldsymbol{\Pi}}\mathbf{p}_t = (\mathbf{z}_t - c_t\mathbf{z}_0) - \hat{\boldsymbol{\Pi}}(\mathbf{p}_t - c_t\mathbf{p}_0)$$

where the second step is based on (2.7). We define the estimator of $\boldsymbol{\Omega}$ as the matrix of mean squares and products of the residuals,

$$\hat{\boldsymbol{\Omega}} = \frac{1}{T}\sum_{t=1}^{T}(\mathbf{z}_t - \hat{\boldsymbol{\mu}}_0 DQ_{gt} - \hat{\boldsymbol{\Pi}}\mathbf{p}_t)(\mathbf{z}_t - \hat{\boldsymbol{\mu}}_0 DQ_{gt} - \hat{\boldsymbol{\Pi}}\mathbf{p}_t)'$$

$$= \mathbf{Z}_0 + \hat{\boldsymbol{\Pi}}\mathbf{E}_0'\mathbf{E}_0\hat{\boldsymbol{\Pi}}' - \hat{\boldsymbol{\Pi}}\mathbf{L} - \mathbf{L}'\hat{\boldsymbol{\Pi}}'$$

where the second equal sign is based on (2.30) and (2.29). It follows from (2.6) that this result can be simplified to

(2.31)
$$\hat{\boldsymbol{\Omega}} = \hat{\boldsymbol{\Pi}}\mathbf{E}_0'\mathbf{E}_0\hat{\boldsymbol{\Pi}}' - \mathbf{Z}_0$$

Using (1.7), we can write the residual vector (2.30) as

$$\boldsymbol{\varepsilon}_t - DQ_{gt}(\hat{\boldsymbol{\mu}}_0 - \boldsymbol{\mu}_0) - (\hat{\boldsymbol{\Pi}} - \boldsymbol{\Pi})\,\mathbf{p}_t$$

which shows, given the consistency of $\hat{\boldsymbol{\mu}}_0$ and $\hat{\boldsymbol{\Pi}}$, that (2.30) converges in distribution to $\boldsymbol{\varepsilon}_t$ as $T \to \infty$. Hence Khintchine's theorem implies that $\hat{\boldsymbol{\Omega}}$ is a consistent estimator of $\boldsymbol{\Omega}$ if $\boldsymbol{\varepsilon}_1, \ldots, \boldsymbol{\varepsilon}_T$ are independently and identically distributed.

An Estimate of the Asymptotic Covariance Matrix

To estimate the unknown parameters in the asymptotic covariance matrix (2.25) we substitute $\hat{\mathbf{\Omega}}$ for $\mathbf{\Omega}$ and, using (2.7), the vector $\hat{\boldsymbol{\mu}}_0 - q\mathbf{z}_0 = -q\hat{\mathbf{\Pi}}\mathbf{p}_0$ for $\boldsymbol{\mu}_0 - \mathbf{b}$. This amounts to a replacement of parameters by consistent estimators [see (2.20)]. The estimator of (2.25) is

$$(2.32)\qquad \begin{bmatrix} \dfrac{1}{T}\hat{\mathbf{\Omega}} \otimes (\hat{\mathbf{\Pi}}'\mathbf{Z}_0^{-1}\hat{\mathbf{\Pi}}) & -\dfrac{q}{T}\hat{\mathbf{\Omega}} \otimes (\hat{\mathbf{\Pi}}'\mathbf{Z}_0^{-1}\hat{\mathbf{\Pi}}\mathbf{p}_0) \\ -\dfrac{q}{T}\hat{\mathbf{\Omega}} \otimes (\mathbf{p}_0'\hat{\mathbf{\Pi}}'\mathbf{Z}_0^{-1}\hat{\mathbf{\Pi}}) & (\alpha_0 + \hat{\alpha}_1)\,\hat{\mathbf{\Omega}} \end{bmatrix}$$

Here $\hat{\alpha}_1$ is an estimator of α_1 defined in (2.26),

$$(2.33)\qquad \hat{\alpha}_1 = \frac{q^2}{T}\,\mathbf{p}_0'\hat{\mathbf{\Pi}}'\mathbf{Z}_0^{-1}\hat{\mathbf{\Pi}}\mathbf{p}_0 = \frac{1}{T}\left[\sum_{t=1}^{T}(DQ_{gt})^2\right]^{-1}\mathbf{p}_0'\hat{\mathbf{\Pi}}'\mathbf{Z}_0^{-1}\hat{\mathbf{\Pi}}\mathbf{p}_0$$

where the second step is based on (1.10).

The matrix (2.32), when multiplied by T, is a consistent estimator of T times the asymptotic covariance matrix (2.25). This follows from the convergence in probability of $\hat{\mathbf{\Omega}}$, $\hat{\mathbf{\Pi}}$, $\mathbf{Z}_0$ and $-q\hat{\mathbf{\Pi}}\mathbf{p}_0$ to $\mathbf{\Omega}$, $\mathbf{\Pi}$, $\bar{\mathbf{Z}}_0$ and $\boldsymbol{\mu}_0 - \mathbf{b}$, respectively.

9.3 The Demand for Meats in the United States: (8) Unconstrained Instrumental-Variable Estimates

In this section we apply the estimation procedure of Section 9.2 to the data on meats. The approach may be viewed as the predetermined-quantity counterpart of the least-squares analysis of Section 7.3, which is an unconstrained (not symmetry-constrained) procedure based on the assumption of predetermined prices.

Discussion of the Estimates

The point estimates and their asymptotic standard errors are given in the lower half of Table 9.1 below the unconstrained (least-squares) estimates of Table 7.5 on page 19. To obtain estimates and their asymptotic standard errors for the coefficients involving Lamb, we apply the linear constraints that are used to eliminate them. Details are provided at the end of this section.

The new estimates of the conditional marginal shares are rather close to their predecessors except for Lamb, which has an instrumental-variable esti-

TABLE 9.1

UNCONSTRAINED INSTRUMENTAL-VARIABLE ESTIMATES OF CONDITIONAL MARGINAL SHARES AND SLUTSKY COEFFICIENTS OF MEATS

	Conditional marginal share	Modified conditional Slutsky coefficients			
		Unconstrained estimates of Table 7.5			
Beef	.712 (.055)	−.197 (.048)	.176 (.020)	.026 (.023)	−.005 (.063)
Pork	.192 (.049)	.157 (.043)	−.219 (.018)	.050 (.020)	.012 (.057)
Chicken	.046 (.022)	.009 (.019)	.030 (.008)	−.087 (.009)	.048 (.025)
Lamb	.050 (.012)	.030 (.010)	.013 (.004)	.012 (.005)	−.055 (.014)
		Unconstrained instrumental-variable estimates			
Beef	.669 (.073)	−.307 (.090)	.171 (.030)	.046 (.029)	.090 (.116)
Pork	.191 (.060)	.186 (.074)	−.236 (.025)	.043 (.024)	.007 (.096)
Chicken	.060 (.028)	.033 (.035)	.037 (.012)	−.106 (.011)	.036 (.045)
Lamb	.081 (.022)	.088 (.027)	.028 (.009)	.017 (.009)	−.133 (.035)

mate that exceeds the least-squares value by about 60 percent. The new estimates of the diagonal Slutsky coefficients are all larger than the corresponding figures in the first four lines of the table, particularly for Lamb. The new off-diagonal estimates are all positive; they satisfy Slutsky symmetry rather closely.

The residual moment matrix (2.31) is shown, in enlarged 4×4 form, in

TABLE 9.2

MEAN SQUARES AND PRODUCTS OF RESIDUALS

	Beef	Pork	Chicken	Lamb	Beef	Pork	Chicken	Lamb
	Least-squares, Table 7.10				*Symmetry-constrained, Table 7.10*			
Beef	52.63	−42.54	−9.11	−.99	54.10	−43.26	−9.94	−.90
Pork		42.39	1.28	−1.12		43.11	1.36	−1.21
Chicken			8.15	−.32			8.91	−.33
Lamb				2.43				2.44
	Instrumental variables, unconstrained				*Instrumental variables, symmetry-constrained*			
Beef	69.92	−49.49	−14.10	−6.33	69.92	−48.24	−15.36	−6.32
Pork		47.32	2.80	−.64		47.39	2.52	−1.67
Chicken			10.56	.74			11.24	1.60
Lamb				6.22				6.39

Note. All entries are to be multiplied by 10^{-6}.

Table 9.2 below the corresponding least-squares estimate (reproduced from Table 7.10 on page 50). The new estimates of $\omega_{11},\dots,\omega_{44}$ exceed their predecessors, which is one reason why the asymptotic standard errors of the instrumental-variable estimates in Table 9.1 exceed those of the least-squares estimates. The right half of Table 9.2 refers to symmetry-constrained estimates and will be discussed in Section 9.4.

Alternative Expressions for the Estimators of $\mathbf{\Pi}$

Table 9.1 suggests that the instrumental-variable estimate of $\mathbf{\Pi}$ exhibits a greater price sensitivity of demand than the least-squares estimate. To analyze this more formally it is convenient to use a different notation. We write (1.7), using (1.10) and (2.3), as

$$\mathbf{z}_t = \frac{c_t}{q}\boldsymbol{\mu}_0 + \mathbf{\Pi}\mathbf{p}_t + \boldsymbol{\varepsilon}_t = c_t\mathbf{z}_0 + \mathbf{\Pi}(\mathbf{p}_t - c_t\mathbf{p}_0) + \boldsymbol{\varepsilon}_t - c_t\sum_{s=1}^{T} c_s\boldsymbol{\varepsilon}_s$$

This can also be written in the form

$$\mathbf{z}_t - c_t\mathbf{z}_0 = \mathbf{\Pi}(\mathbf{p}_t - c_t\mathbf{p}_0) + \boldsymbol{\varepsilon}_t - c_t\boldsymbol{\varepsilon}_0 \tag{3.1}$$

where

$$\boldsymbol{\varepsilon}_0 = \sum_{t=1}^{T} c_t\boldsymbol{\varepsilon}_t \tag{3.2}$$

We transpose (3.1) and write the result for $t=1,\dots,T$ as

$$\mathbf{Y} = \mathbf{X}\mathbf{\Pi}' + \begin{bmatrix}(\boldsymbol{\varepsilon}_1 - c_1\boldsymbol{\varepsilon}_0)'\\ \vdots \\ (\boldsymbol{\varepsilon}_T - c_T\boldsymbol{\varepsilon}_0)'\end{bmatrix} \tag{3.3}$$

where

$$\mathbf{Y} = \begin{bmatrix}(\mathbf{z}_1 - c_1\mathbf{z}_0)'\\ \vdots \\ (\mathbf{z}_T - c_T\mathbf{z}_0)'\end{bmatrix} \qquad \mathbf{X} = \begin{bmatrix}(\mathbf{p}_1 - c_1\mathbf{p}_0)'\\ \vdots \\ (\mathbf{p}_T - c_T\mathbf{p}_0)'\end{bmatrix} \tag{3.4}$$

On comparing (3.4) with (2.29) we conclude

$$\frac{1}{T}\begin{bmatrix}\mathbf{Y}'\mathbf{Y} & \mathbf{Y}'\mathbf{X}\\ \mathbf{X}'\mathbf{Y} & \mathbf{X}'\mathbf{X}\end{bmatrix} = \begin{bmatrix}\mathbf{Z}_0 & \mathbf{L}'\\ \mathbf{L} & \mathbf{E}_0'\mathbf{E}_0\end{bmatrix} \tag{3.5}$$

from which it follows directly that (2.6) can be written as

$$\hat{\mathbf{\Pi}} = \mathbf{Y}'\mathbf{Y}(\mathbf{X}'\mathbf{Y})^{-1} \tag{3.6}$$

The least-squares estimator of $\mathbf{\Pi}$, to be written $\hat{\mathbf{\Pi}}_{LS}$, has a similar form:

$$\hat{\mathbf{\Pi}}_{LS} = \mathbf{Y}'\mathbf{X}(\mathbf{X}'\mathbf{X})^{-1} \tag{3.7}$$

To verify this we note that the least-squares procedure of Section 7.3 can be viewed as the instrumental-variable method which is based on DQ_{gt} and $\mathbf{p}_t$ as the tth observation on four instrumental variables. Since DQ_{gt} is proportional to c_t in view of (1.10), this means that in the least-squares estimation equations (the normal equations) the vector $\boldsymbol{\varepsilon}_0$ defined in (3.2) is replaced by zero. Also consider

$$\sum_{t=1}^{T} (\mathbf{p}_t - c_t\mathbf{p}_0)\,\boldsymbol{\varepsilon}_t' = \sum_{t=1}^{T} \mathbf{p}_t\boldsymbol{\varepsilon}_t' - \mathbf{p}_0\boldsymbol{\varepsilon}_0'$$

which becomes $\sum_t \mathbf{p}_t\boldsymbol{\varepsilon}_t'$ when $\boldsymbol{\varepsilon}_0$ is replaced by zero. On comparing this with (3.3), with zero substituted for $\boldsymbol{\varepsilon}_0$, we conclude that using $\mathbf{p}_1, \ldots, \mathbf{p}_T$ as the other instrumental variables is equivalent to estimating $\mathbf{\Pi}'$ of (3.3) by least squares, which yields the transpose of (3.7).

A Canonical Correlation Comparison

To compare the price sensitivity of demand implied by the estimators (3.6) and (3.7) we consider $\bar{r}^2$, the mean square canonical correlation coefficient of the two sets of variables whose observations are arranged in the matrices $\mathbf{X}$ and $\mathbf{Y}$. When both sets consist of three variables, as is the case here, this coefficient is defined as

$$\bar{r}^2 = \tfrac{1}{3}\,\mathrm{tr}\,\mathbf{X}(\mathbf{X}'\mathbf{X})^{-1}\,\mathbf{X}'\mathbf{Y}(\mathbf{Y}'\mathbf{Y})^{-1}\,\mathbf{Y}' \tag{3.8}$$

This $\bar{r}^2$ is the mean square of r_1, r_2 and r_3, the three canonical correlation coefficients of the $\mathbf{X}$ variables and the $\mathbf{Y}$ variables, so that $0 \le \bar{r}^2 \le 1$. See Theil (1971, pp. 317–321) for further details.

If $\hat{\mathbf{\Pi}}$ and $\hat{\mathbf{\Pi}}_{LS}$ were identical, the product matrix $\hat{\mathbf{\Pi}}^{-1}\hat{\mathbf{\Pi}}_{LS}$ would be $\mathbf{I}_3$ with a trace equal to 3. It follows from (3.6) and (3.7) that this trace actually is

$$\mathrm{tr}\,\mathbf{X}'\mathbf{Y}(\mathbf{Y}'\mathbf{Y})^{-1}\,\mathbf{Y}'\mathbf{X}(\mathbf{X}'\mathbf{X})^{-1} = \mathrm{tr}\,\mathbf{X}(\mathbf{X}'\mathbf{X})^{-1}\,\mathbf{X}'\mathbf{Y}(\mathbf{Y}'\mathbf{Y})^{-1}\,\mathbf{Y}'$$

Hence, in view of (3.8),

$$\mathrm{tr}\,\hat{\mathbf{\Pi}}^{-1}\hat{\mathbf{\Pi}}_{LS} = 3\bar{r}^2 \tag{3.9}$$

which is ≤ 3 because $\bar{r}^2 \le 1$. This shows that the estimated price sensitivity of demand computed from $\hat{\mathbf{\Pi}}$ exceeds that computed from $\hat{\mathbf{\Pi}}_{LS}$ on the basis of a trace function that should be compared with similar traces used in eqs. (5.12) of Section 6.5 and (7.2) of Section 7.7.

Disturbance Covariances and the Conditional Marginal Share of Lamb

The 4×4 disturbance covariance matrix is obtained from the 3×3 matrix $\mathbf{\Omega}$ by premultiplication by $\mathbf{I}_*$ and postmultiplication by the transpose of $\mathbf{I}_*$, which is the following 4×3 matrix:

$$\text{(3.10)} \qquad \mathbf{I}_* = \begin{bmatrix} 1 & 0 & 0 \\ 0 & 1 & 0 \\ 0 & 0 & 1 \\ \cdots & \cdots & \cdots \\ -1 & -1 & -1 \end{bmatrix} = \begin{bmatrix} \mathbf{I}_3 \\ -\mathbf{\iota}_3' \end{bmatrix}$$

The last column of the lower-left 4×4 matrix in Table 9.2 is thus derived directly from the 3×3 matrix (2.31).

The conditional marginal share of Lamb is computed as 1 minus the sum of the three other shares. This implies that the asymptotic covariance matrix of these four shares is obtained from that of the three shares by bordering by a row and a column so that each of the four rows and each of the four columns have zero sum. It follows from (2.32) and (3.10) that the estimate of this 4×4 asymptotic covariance matrix is

$$\text{(3.11)} \qquad (\alpha_0 + \hat{\alpha}_1)\, \mathbf{I}_* \hat{\mathbf{\Omega}} \mathbf{I}_*'$$

The asymptotic standard errors in the first column and the last four rows of Table 9.1 are the square roots of the diagonal elements of the matrix (3.11). For the data considered here we have $\alpha_0 = 44.3$ and $\hat{\alpha}_1 = 31.8$. Since the α_1 component results from the use of $\hat{\mathbf{\Pi}}$ in (2.7), we conclude that a little over 40 percent of the estimated asymptotic covariance matrix of the conditional marginal share estimates can be attributed to the occurrence of $\hat{\mathbf{\Pi}}$ in their estimation equation.

Slutsky Estimates Involving Lamb

The 4×4 matrix of modified conditional Slutsky coefficients can be written as $\mathbf{I}_* \mathbf{\Pi} \mathbf{I}_*'$. It is shown in the next paragraph that the 16 elements of this matrix can also be written in column form as

$$\text{(3.12)} \qquad [\pi_{11}^* \dots \pi_{14}^* \quad \pi_{21}^* \dots \pi_{24}^* \quad \pi_{31}^* \dots \pi_{34}^* \quad \pi_{41}^* \dots \pi_{44}^*]' = (\mathbf{I}_* \otimes \mathbf{I}_*)\, \boldsymbol{\pi}$$

so that the estimate of the left-hand vector has, in view of (2.32), an estimated asymptotic covariance matrix of the form

$$\text{(3.13)} \qquad \frac{1}{T} (\mathbf{I}_* \mathbf{\Omega} \mathbf{I}_*') \otimes (\mathbf{I}_* \hat{\mathbf{\Pi}}' \mathbf{Z}_0^{-1} \hat{\mathbf{\Pi}} \mathbf{I}_*')$$

The asymptotic standard errors in the last four rows and columns of Table 9.1 are computed as the square roots of the diagonal elements of the 16×16 matrix (3.13).

To prove (3.12) we consider the left-hand vector as consisting of four subvectors:

$$[\pi_{i1}^* \dots \pi_{i4}^*]' \qquad i = 1, \dots, 4 \tag{3.14}$$

For $i=1$, 2 and 3 the vector (3.14) equals $\mathbf{I}_* \boldsymbol{\pi}_i$, where $\boldsymbol{\pi}_i$ is defined in (1.8). Hence the leading 12-element subvector of (3.12) is

$$\begin{bmatrix} \mathbf{I}_* & \mathbf{0} & \mathbf{0} \\ \mathbf{0} & \mathbf{I}_* & \mathbf{0} \\ \mathbf{0} & \mathbf{0} & \mathbf{I}_* \end{bmatrix} \boldsymbol{\pi} = (\mathbf{I}_3 \otimes \mathbf{I}_*)\, \boldsymbol{\pi} \tag{3.15}$$

The vector (3.14) for $i=4$ is

$$\begin{bmatrix} \pi_{41}^* \\ \pi_{42}^* \\ \pi_{43}^* \\ \pi_{44}^* \end{bmatrix} = \begin{bmatrix} -1 & 0 & 0 & -1 & 0 & 0 & -1 & 0 & 0 \\ 0 & -1 & 0 & 0 & -1 & 0 & 0 & -1 & 0 \\ 0 & 0 & -1 & 0 & 0 & -1 & 0 & 0 & -1 \\ 1 & 1 & 1 & 1 & 1 & 1 & 1 & 1 & 1 \end{bmatrix} \boldsymbol{\pi} \tag{3.16}$$

$$= -[\mathbf{I}_* \quad \mathbf{I}_* \quad \mathbf{I}_*]\, \boldsymbol{\pi} = -(\boldsymbol{\iota}_3' \otimes \mathbf{I}_*)\, \boldsymbol{\pi}$$

By combining (3.15) and (3.16) we obtain

$$\begin{bmatrix} \mathbf{I}_3 \otimes \mathbf{I}_* \\ -\boldsymbol{\iota}_3' \otimes \mathbf{I}_* \end{bmatrix} \boldsymbol{\pi} = \left(\begin{bmatrix} \mathbf{I}_3 \\ -\boldsymbol{\iota}_3' \end{bmatrix} \otimes \mathbf{I}_* \right) \boldsymbol{\pi} = (\mathbf{I}_* \otimes \mathbf{I}_*)\, \boldsymbol{\pi}$$

which completes the proof of (3.12).

9.4 The Demand for Meats in the United States: (9) Symmetry-Constrained Instrumental-Variable Estimates

In this section we extend the instrumental-variable method to include testing and imposing Slutsky symmetry. The approach may be viewed as the predetermined-quantity counterpart of the Slutsky symmetry analysis of Section 7.3.

Testing Slutsky Symmetry

The symmetry condition on the matrix (1.8) can be written in the form

$\mathbf{R}\pi = \mathbf{0}$ when $\mathbf{R}$ is specified as the following 3×9 matrix:

$$
(4.1) \qquad \mathbf{R} = \begin{bmatrix} \overset{\pi^*_{11}}{0} & \overset{\pi^*_{12}}{1} & \overset{\pi^*_{13}}{0} & \overset{\pi^*_{21}}{-1} & \overset{\pi^*_{22}}{0} & \overset{\pi^*_{23}}{0} & \overset{\pi^*_{31}}{0} & \overset{\pi^*_{32}}{0} & \overset{\pi^*_{33}}{0} \\ 0 & 0 & 1 & 0 & 0 & 0 & -1 & 0 & 0 \\ 0 & 0 & 0 & 0 & 0 & 1 & 0 & -1 & 0 \end{bmatrix}
$$

If $\mathbf{R}\pi = \mathbf{0}$ is valid, $\mathbf{R}\hat{\pi}$ equals $\mathbf{R}(\hat{\pi} - \pi)$, which has an asymptotic normal distribution with zero mean and covariance matrix $\mathbf{R}\mathscr{V}(\hat{\pi})\,\mathbf{R}'$ when the disturbances are normally distributed. Therefore, the quadratic form

$$
(4.2) \qquad \hat{\pi}'\mathbf{R}'[\mathbf{R}\mathscr{V}(\hat{\pi})\,\mathbf{R}']^{-1}\,\mathbf{R}\hat{\pi}
$$

is asymptotically distributed as $\chi^2(3)$ under the null hypothesis of Slutsky symmetry.

With $\mathscr{V}(\hat{\pi})$ approximated in accordance with (2.32),

$$
(4.3) \qquad \mathscr{V}(\hat{\pi}) \approx \frac{1}{T}\,\hat{\mathbf{\Omega}} \otimes (\hat{\mathbf{\Pi}}'\mathbf{Z}_0^{-1}\hat{\mathbf{\Pi}})
$$

we obtain .25 for (4.2) from the meat data. This is far from significant for $\chi^2(3)$ at any reasonable level of significance. There is little reason for refining this χ^2 test to an F test, as we did in Section 5.3, because the instrumental-variable theory of Section 9.2 is asymptotic and the F test is asymptotically equivalent to a χ^2 test.

The Symmetry-Constrained Instrumental-Variable Estimator

The constrained instrumental-variable estimator of π is defined as

$$
(4.4) \qquad \hat{\pi}^* = \hat{\pi} - \mathscr{V}(\hat{\pi})\,\mathbf{R}'[\mathbf{R}\mathscr{V}(\hat{\pi})\,\mathbf{R}']^{-1}\,\mathbf{R}\hat{\pi}
$$

which satisfies $\mathbf{R}\hat{\pi}^* = \mathbf{0}$. The associated estimator of $\boldsymbol{\mu}_0$ is based on (2.3),

$$
(4.5) \qquad \hat{\boldsymbol{\mu}}_0^* = q\mathbf{z}_0 - q\hat{\mathbf{\Pi}}^*\mathbf{p}_0
$$

where $\hat{\mathbf{\Pi}}^*$ is $\hat{\pi}^*$ written in 3×3 matrix form:

$$
(4.6) \qquad \hat{\mathbf{\Pi}}^* = [\hat{\pi}_1^* \quad \hat{\pi}_2^* \quad \hat{\pi}_3^*]'
$$

By subtracting (2.7) from (4.5) we obtain

$$
(4.7) \qquad \hat{\boldsymbol{\mu}}_0^* - \hat{\boldsymbol{\mu}}_0 = -q(\hat{\mathbf{\Pi}}^* - \hat{\mathbf{\Pi}})\,\mathbf{p}_0
$$

Equation (4.4) can be written as

$$
(4.8) \qquad \hat{\pi}^* = \mathbf{B}\hat{\pi} \quad \text{where} \quad \mathbf{B} = \mathbf{I}_9 - \mathscr{V}(\hat{\pi})\,\mathbf{R}'[\mathbf{R}\mathscr{V}(\hat{\pi})\,\mathbf{R}']^{-1}\,\mathbf{R}
$$

with $\mathbf{I}_9$ defined as the 9×9 unit matrix. The results (4.7) and (4.8) show that the constrained instrumental-variable estimators of $\boldsymbol{\pi}$ and $\boldsymbol{\mu}_0$ can be obtained from the unconstrained estimators by means of a linear transformation.

Discussion of the Constrained Estimates

Table 9.3 contains the symmetry-constrained instrumental-variable estimates, based on the approximation (4.3), below the corresponding estimates of Table 7.5 on page 19. The new estimate of the 4×4 matrix of modified conditional Slutsky coefficients has latent roots equal to 0, −.131, −.198 and −.456, so that this estimate is negative semidefinite with rank 3. The symmetry-constrained instrumental-variable estimates of the conditional marginal shares are close to the corresponding unconstrained estimates of Table 9.1. The derivation of the asymptotic standard errors in the lower half of Table 9.3 is described in the subsections which follow. They are all larger than the corresponding standard errors in the upper half, but the differences between the corresponding t ratios tend to be smaller.

Figure 9.1 provides an illustration of the two sets of symmetry-constrained Slutsky estimates, with those of Table 7.5 measured horizontally and the instrumental-variable estimates measured vertically. The upward sloping straight line has an angle of 45 degrees with respect to both axes. The 10 points appear to be scattered around a steeper line, which illustrates that the

TABLE 9.3

SYMMETRY-CONSTRAINED INSTRUMENTAL-VARIABLE ESTIMATES OF CONDITIONAL MARGINAL SHARES AND SLUTSKY COEFFICIENTS OF MEATS

	Conditional marginal share	Modified conditional Slutsky coefficients			
		Symmetry-constrained estimates of Table 7.5			
Beef	.692 (.049)	−.227 (.019)	.164 (.014)	.033 (.009)	.029 (.010)
Pork	.199 (.044)		−.214 (.014)	.038 (.007)	.012 (.004)
Chicken	.059 (.021)			−.084 (.009)	.013 (.005)
Lamb	.050 (.012)				−.055 (.014)
		Symmetry-constrained instrumental-variable estimates			
Beef	.669 (.057)	−.306 (.031)	.171 (.018)	.047 (.013)	.089 (.027)
Pork	.183 (.047)		−.239 (.015)	.040 (.008)	.028 (.009)
Chicken	.067 (.024)			−.105 (.011)	.018 (.009)
Lamb	.081 (.022)				−.135 (.035)

assumption of predetermined quantity changes implies an estimated price sensitivity of demand exceeding that of predetermined price changes. This agrees with the results obtained for the unconstrained estimates in Section 9.3.

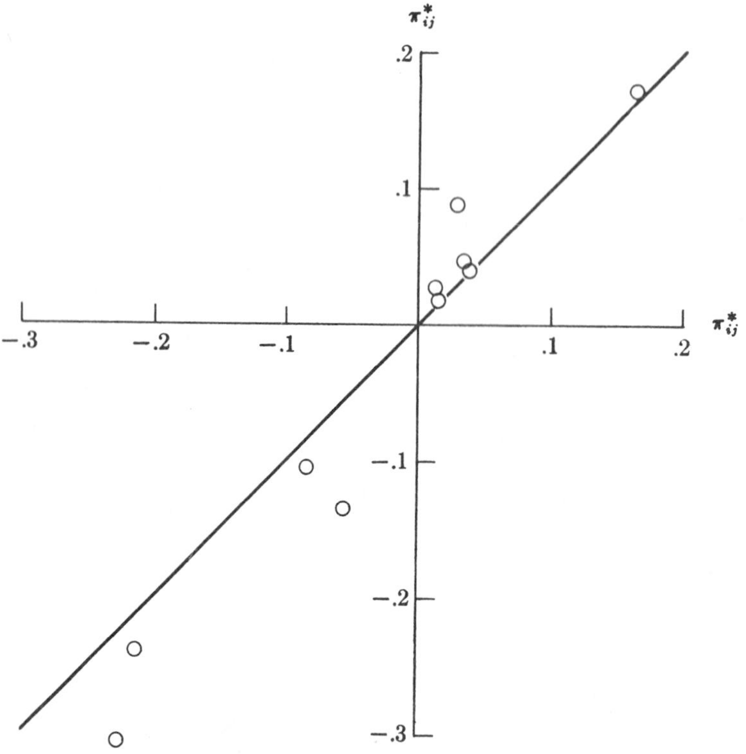

Fig. 9.1 Estimates of modified conditional Slutsky coefficients under predetermined price changes (horizontal) and predetermined quantity changes (vertical)

The tth residual vector associated with the symmetry-constrained coefficient estimates is

$$\mathbf{z}_t - \hat{\boldsymbol{\mu}}_0^* DQ_{gt} - \hat{\boldsymbol{\Pi}}^*\mathbf{p}_t = \mathbf{z}_t - \frac{c_t}{q}\hat{\boldsymbol{\mu}}_0^* - \hat{\boldsymbol{\Pi}}^*\mathbf{p}_t \tag{4.9}$$
$$= (\mathbf{z}_t - c_t\mathbf{z}_0) - \hat{\boldsymbol{\Pi}}^*(\mathbf{p}_t - c_t\mathbf{p}_0)$$

where the first step is based on (1.10) and the second on (4.5). So, using (2.29), we have the following symmetry-constrained estimate of $\boldsymbol{\Omega}$:

$$\hat{\boldsymbol{\Omega}}^* = \mathbf{Z}_0 + \hat{\boldsymbol{\Pi}}^*\mathbf{E}_0'\mathbf{E}_0\hat{\boldsymbol{\Pi}}^* - \hat{\boldsymbol{\Pi}}^*\mathbf{L} - \mathbf{L}'\hat{\boldsymbol{\Pi}}^* \tag{4.10}$$

This estimate is shown in enlarged 4×4 form in the lower-right corner of Table 9.2 on page 109. It is evidently close to the unconstrained instrumental-variable estimate in the lower left.

The Sampling Error of the Constrained Estimator

To evaluate the asymptotic distribution of the symmetry-constrained estimators of $\boldsymbol{\pi}$ and $\boldsymbol{\mu}_0$ we consider the sampling error first. The definition of $\mathbf{B}$ in (4.8) shows that $\mathbf{R}\boldsymbol{\pi}=\mathbf{0}$ implies $\mathbf{B}\boldsymbol{\pi}=\boldsymbol{\pi}$. By subtracting $\boldsymbol{\pi}=\mathbf{B}\boldsymbol{\pi}$ from $\hat{\boldsymbol{\pi}}^*=\mathbf{B}\hat{\boldsymbol{\pi}}$ we obtain

$$\hat{\boldsymbol{\pi}}^* - \boldsymbol{\pi} = \mathbf{B}(\hat{\boldsymbol{\pi}} - \boldsymbol{\pi}) \tag{4.11}$$

which expresses the sampling error of $\hat{\boldsymbol{\pi}}^*$ in terms of that of the unconstrained estimator. Similarly, by subtracting (2.3) from (4.5) we obtain

$$\hat{\boldsymbol{\mu}}_0^* - \hat{\boldsymbol{\mu}}_0 = q \sum_{t=1}^{T} c_t \boldsymbol{\varepsilon}_t - q\,(\hat{\boldsymbol{\Pi}}^* - \boldsymbol{\Pi})\,\mathbf{p}_0 \tag{4.12}$$

It may be verified along the lines of (2.22) to (2.24) that the second right-hand term of (4.12) is asymptotically equivalent to $\mathbf{A}(\hat{\boldsymbol{\pi}}^*-\boldsymbol{\pi})$, where $\mathbf{A}$ is defined in (2.24). Hence, using (4.11) also, we obtain the following asymptotic approximation of (4.12):

$$\hat{\boldsymbol{\mu}}_0^* - \boldsymbol{\mu}_0 = q \sum_{t=1}^{T} c_t \boldsymbol{\varepsilon}_t + \mathbf{AB}\,(\hat{\boldsymbol{\pi}} - \boldsymbol{\pi}) \tag{4.13}$$

The Asymptotic Distribution of the Constrained Estimator

Recall from the discussion preceding (2.19) that the first right-hand term in (4.13) has zero expectation. Recall also that $\hat{\boldsymbol{\pi}}$ has an asymptotic distribution with mean $\boldsymbol{\pi}$. It thus follows from (4.11) and (4.13) that the constrained estimators of $\boldsymbol{\pi}$ and $\boldsymbol{\mu}_0$ have an asymptotic distribution with means equal to the corresponding parameters. Recall further that the asymptotic distribution of the unconstrained estimators is normal when $\boldsymbol{\varepsilon}_1, \ldots, \boldsymbol{\varepsilon}_T$ are normally distributed. We conclude from (4.11) and (4.13) that the asymptotic distribution of the constrained estimators is normal under the same condition.

The asymptotic covariance matrix of these estimators is derived in the next subsection. To summarize the result we write (2.25) as

$$\mathscr{V}\begin{bmatrix}\hat{\boldsymbol{\pi}} \\ \hat{\boldsymbol{\mu}}_0\end{bmatrix} = \begin{bmatrix}\mathscr{V}(\hat{\boldsymbol{\pi}}) & \mathbf{C}' \\ \mathbf{C} & \mathscr{V}(\hat{\boldsymbol{\mu}}_0)\end{bmatrix} \tag{4.14}$$

where

$$\mathscr{V}(\hat{\boldsymbol{\pi}}) = \frac{1}{T}\,\boldsymbol{\Omega} \otimes (\boldsymbol{\Pi}'\bar{\mathbf{Z}}_0^{-1}\boldsymbol{\Pi}) \tag{4.15}$$

$$\mathscr{V}(\hat{\boldsymbol{\mu}}_0) = (\alpha_0 + \alpha_1)\,\boldsymbol{\Omega} \tag{4.16}$$

$$\mathbf{C} = \frac{1}{T}\,\boldsymbol{\Omega} \otimes [(\boldsymbol{\mu}_0 - \mathbf{b})'\,\bar{\mathbf{Z}}_0^{-1}\boldsymbol{\Pi}] = \mathbf{A}\mathscr{V}(\hat{\boldsymbol{\pi}}) \qquad \text{[see (2.28)]} \tag{4.17}$$

The asymptotic covariance matrix of the constrained estimator is

$$\mathscr{V}\begin{bmatrix}\hat{\boldsymbol{\pi}}^* \\ \hat{\boldsymbol{\mu}}_0^*\end{bmatrix} = \begin{bmatrix}\mathscr{V}(\hat{\boldsymbol{\pi}}) - \mathscr{V}(\hat{\boldsymbol{\pi}})\,\mathbf{D}\mathscr{V}(\hat{\boldsymbol{\pi}}) & \mathbf{C}' - \mathscr{V}(\hat{\boldsymbol{\pi}})\mathbf{D}\mathbf{C}' \\ \mathbf{C} - \mathbf{C}\mathbf{D}\mathscr{V}(\hat{\boldsymbol{\pi}}) & \mathscr{V}(\hat{\boldsymbol{\mu}}_0) - \mathbf{C}\mathbf{D}\mathbf{C}'\end{bmatrix} \tag{4.18}$$

where $\mathbf{D}$ is a symmetric positive semidefinite matrix of order 9×9:

$$\mathbf{D} = \mathbf{R}'[\mathbf{R}\mathscr{V}(\hat{\boldsymbol{\pi}})\,\mathbf{R}']^{-1}\,\mathbf{R} \tag{4.19}$$

The result (4.18) clearly shows how the asymptotic sampling variances are reduced when the symmetry constraint is imposed.

The symmetry-constrained estimates of $\boldsymbol{\pi}$ and $\boldsymbol{\mu}_0$ are thus consistent, which insures that the residual vector (4.9) converges in distribution to $\boldsymbol{\varepsilon}_t$ as $T \to \infty$. Hence Khintchine's theorem implies that (4.10) provides a consistent estimate of $\boldsymbol{\Omega}$ if $\boldsymbol{\varepsilon}_1, \ldots, \boldsymbol{\varepsilon}_T$ are independently and identically distributed.

Proof of the Asymptotic Covariance Matrix

The asymptotic covariance matrix of $\hat{\boldsymbol{\pi}}^*$ equals $\mathbf{B}\mathscr{V}(\hat{\boldsymbol{\pi}})\,\mathbf{B}'$ in view of (4.11). By substituting the $\mathbf{B}$ definition of (4.8) and using (4.19) for $\mathbf{D}$ we obtain the leading submatrix of (4.18).

To verify the other submatrices of (4.18) we use (4.8) and (4.19) to write $\mathbf{B}$ and its transpose as

$$\mathbf{B} = \mathbf{I}_9 - \mathscr{V}(\hat{\boldsymbol{\pi}})\,\mathbf{D} \qquad \mathbf{B}' = \mathbf{I}_9 - \mathbf{D}\mathscr{V}(\hat{\boldsymbol{\pi}}) \tag{4.20}$$

and we consider

$$\mathbf{A}\mathbf{B}\mathscr{V}(\hat{\boldsymbol{\pi}}) = \mathbf{A}[\mathbf{I}_9 - \mathscr{V}(\hat{\boldsymbol{\pi}})\,\mathbf{D}]\,\mathscr{V}(\hat{\boldsymbol{\pi}}) = \mathbf{A}\mathscr{V}(\hat{\boldsymbol{\pi}})\,[\mathbf{I}_9 - \mathbf{D}\mathscr{V}(\hat{\boldsymbol{\pi}})]$$

The last member equals $\mathbf{C}\mathbf{B}'$ in view of (4.17) and (4.20). Therefore,

$$\mathbf{A}\mathbf{B}\mathscr{V}(\hat{\boldsymbol{\pi}})\,\mathbf{B}' = \mathbf{C}(\mathbf{B}')^2 = \mathbf{C}\mathbf{B}' = \mathbf{C} - \mathbf{C}\mathbf{D}\mathscr{V}(\hat{\boldsymbol{\pi}}) \tag{4.21}$$

where the second step is based on $(\mathbf{B}')^2 = \mathbf{B}'$, which may be verified by means of (4.20) and (4.19). Finally, we postmultiply (4.21) by $\mathbf{A}'$:

$$\mathbf{A}\mathbf{B}\mathscr{V}(\hat{\boldsymbol{\pi}})\,\mathbf{B}'\mathbf{A}' = \mathbf{C}\mathbf{A}' - \mathbf{C}\mathbf{D}\mathscr{V}(\hat{\boldsymbol{\pi}})\,\mathbf{A}' = \mathbf{C}\mathbf{A}' - \mathbf{C}\mathbf{D}\mathbf{C}' \tag{4.22}$$

The lower-left submatrix of (4.18) is obtained by postmultiplying the right-hand side of (4.13) by the transpose of (4.11) and taking the expectation. This gives $\mathbf{AB}\mathscr{V}(\hat{\pi})\,\mathbf{B}'$ in view of (2.27), after which (4.21) completes the proof for this submatrix. For the lower-right submatrix of (4.18) we proceed similarly with (4.13) and its transpose. Applying (2.27) again, we find that this submatrix is equal to the covariance matrix of $q\sum_t c_t\varepsilon_t$, which is given in (2.19), plus the matrix (4.22). The proof of (4.18) is then completed by using (2.24), (2.26) and (4.17) for $\mathbf{CA}'$.

An Estimate of the Asymptotic Covariance Matrix

Symmetry-constrained estimates are used to approximate the submatrices of (4.18). This amounts to the following modification of (2.32):

(4.23) $$\text{Estimate of } \mathscr{V}(\hat{\pi}) = \frac{1}{T}\hat{\mathbf{\Omega}}^* \otimes (\hat{\mathbf{\Pi}}^*\mathbf{Z}_0^{-1}\hat{\mathbf{\Pi}}^*)$$

(4.24) $$\text{Estimate of } \mathbf{C} = -\frac{q}{T}\hat{\mathbf{\Omega}}^* \otimes (\mathbf{p}_0'\hat{\mathbf{\Pi}}^*\mathbf{Z}_0^{-1}\hat{\mathbf{\Pi}}^*)$$

(4.25) $$\text{Estimate of } \mathscr{V}(\hat{\boldsymbol{\mu}}_0) = (\alpha_0 + \hat{\alpha}_1^*)\,\hat{\mathbf{\Omega}}^*$$

where

(4.26) $$\hat{\alpha}_1^* = \frac{1}{T}\left[\sum_{t=1}^{T}(DQ_{gt})^2\right]^{-1} \mathbf{p}_0'\hat{\mathbf{\Pi}}^*\mathbf{Z}_0^{-1}\hat{\mathbf{\Pi}}^*\mathbf{p}_0$$

which is the constrained version of $\hat{\alpha}_1$ defined in (2.33). The matrix $\mathbf{D}$ given in (4.19) is approximated by the substitution of the right-hand side of (4.23) for $\mathscr{V}(\hat{\pi})$. The asymptotic standard errors in the lower part of Table 9.3, insofar as they refer to elements of $\boldsymbol{\pi}$ and $\boldsymbol{\mu}_0$, are computed as the square roots of the diagonal elements of the matrix (4.18), approximated as described above.

To obtain the asymptotic covariance matrix of the constrained estimates of the four conditional marginal shares, we enlarge $\mathscr{V}(\hat{\boldsymbol{\mu}}_0)-\mathbf{CDC}'$ in (4.18) by a fourth row and column so that the 4×4 matrix which results has zero row and column sums. For the estimated version, this amounts to replacing $\hat{\mathbf{\Omega}}^*$ in (4.24) and (4.25) by $\mathbf{I}_*\hat{\mathbf{\Omega}}^*$ and $\mathbf{I}_*\hat{\mathbf{\Omega}}^*\mathbf{I}_*'$, respectively. For the four constrained Slutsky estimates involving Lamb we combine (3.16) with (4.18). This yields an asymptotic covariance matrix of order 4×4,

$$(\boldsymbol{\iota}_3'\otimes\mathbf{I}_*)\,[\mathscr{V}(\hat{\pi}) - \mathscr{V}(\hat{\pi})\,\mathbf{D}\mathscr{V}(\hat{\pi})]\,(\boldsymbol{\iota}_3\otimes\mathbf{I}_*')$$

from which the four asymptotic standard errors can be computed by means of the approximations described in the previous paragraph.

9.5 The Rotterdam Model in Reciprocal Form

Using the left-hand variables of the Rotterdam Model as instrumental variables is one way of estimating the model when these variables are predetermined. An alternative is to rearrange the equations of the model so that the endogenous price log-changes are on the left and the $\bar{w}_{it}Dq_{it}$'s are on the right. This procedure is considered below. Although it does not lead to an estimation procedure that is simpler than the instrumental-variable method, it does provide valuable insights.

The Reciprocal Equations of the Rotterdam Model

We consider the unconditional relative price version of the Rotterdam Model. The ith demand equation ($i=1,\dots,n$) is then

$$\bar{w}_{it}Dq_{it} = \mu_i DQ_t + \sum_{j=1}^{n} \nu_{ij}\left(Dp_{jt} - \sum_{k=1}^{n} \mu_k Dp_{kt}\right) + \varepsilon_{it} \tag{5.1}$$

We write $\mathbf{N}$, $\boldsymbol{\mu}$ and $\boldsymbol{\iota}$ for, respectively, the $n\times n$ price coefficient matrix $[\nu_{ij}]$, the n-element column vector $[\mu_i]$ of marginal shares, and the column vector which consists of n unit elements. The constraint $\sum_j \nu_{ij}=\phi\mu_i$ for each i can then be written as $\mathbf{N}\boldsymbol{\iota}=\phi\boldsymbol{\mu}$. We premultiply this by $(\phi\mathbf{N})^{-1}$,

$$\mathbf{N}^{-1}\boldsymbol{\mu} = \frac{1}{\phi}\boldsymbol{\iota} \tag{5.2}$$

or, in scalar form,

$$\sum_{j=1}^{n} \nu^{ij}\mu_j = \frac{1}{\phi} \qquad i = 1,\dots,n \tag{5.3}$$

where ν^{ij} is the $(i,j)^{\text{th}}$ element of $\mathbf{N}^{-1}$.

Next write (5.1) in matrix form:

$$\begin{bmatrix} \bar{w}_{1t}Dq_{1t} \\ \vdots \\ \bar{w}_{nt}Dq_{nt} \end{bmatrix} = (DQ_t)\,\boldsymbol{\mu} + \mathbf{N}\begin{bmatrix} Dp_{1t} - \sum_k \mu_k Dp_{kt} \\ \vdots \\ Dp_{nt} - \sum_k \mu_k Dp_{kt} \end{bmatrix} + \begin{bmatrix} \varepsilon_{1t} \\ \vdots \\ \varepsilon_{nt} \end{bmatrix}$$

We premultiply this by $\mathbf{N}^{-1}$, using (5.2). The result may be written as

$$\begin{bmatrix} Dp_{1t} - \sum_k \mu_k Dp_{kt} \\ \vdots \\ Dp_{nt} - \sum_k \mu_k Dp_{kt} \end{bmatrix} = \mathbf{N}^{-1}\begin{bmatrix} \bar{w}_{1t}Dq_{1t} \\ \vdots \\ \bar{w}_{nt}Dq_{nt} \end{bmatrix} - \frac{DQ_t}{\phi}\boldsymbol{\iota} - \mathbf{N}^{-1}\begin{bmatrix} \varepsilon_{1t} \\ \vdots \\ \varepsilon_{nt} \end{bmatrix}$$

or, in scalar form for $i=1,\dots,n$, as

$$(5.4) \qquad Dp_{it} - \sum_{j=1}^{n} \mu_j Dp_{jt} = \sum_{j=1}^{n} \nu^{ij} \bar{w}_{jt} Dq_{jt} - \frac{1}{\phi} DQ_t + \zeta_{it}$$

where

$$(5.5) \qquad \zeta_{it} = -\sum_{j=1}^{n} \nu^{ij} \varepsilon_{jt} \qquad i = 1,\dots,n$$

Equation (5.4) accomplishes our goal of rearranging (5.1) so that the endogenous price log-changes are on the left. We shall refer to (5.4) for $i=1,\dots,n$ as the *reciprocal equations* of the Rotterdam Model. This terminology reflects the interchanged position of prices and quantities as well as the occurrence of the elements of $\mathbf{N}^{-1}$, the inverse of the price coefficient matrix, among the parameters of (5.4).

Problems in Estimating Reciprocal Equations

The left-hand variable of (5.4) is a deflated price log-change. This should cause no surprise, because demand theory is in terms of relative prices, but it does mean that we have unknown parameters (the μ's) in the left-hand side of the reciprocal equations. This makes the estimation of (5.4) more complicated. One might think that the problem can be solved by adding $\sum_j \mu_j Dp_{jt}$ to both sides,

$$(5.6) \qquad Dp_{it} = \sum_{j=1}^{n} \mu_j Dp_{jt} + \sum_{j=1}^{n} \nu^{ij} \bar{w}_{jt} Dq_{jt} - \frac{1}{\phi} DQ_t + \zeta_{it}$$

and running a regression of Dp_{it} on all right-hand variables. However, this does not work because the latter variables include Dp_{it}.

Another problem is the linear dependence of the disturbances of (5.4). The marginally weighted average of the ζ's vanishes,

$$(5.7) \qquad \sum_{i=1}^{n} \mu_i \zeta_{it} = 0$$

which follows from

$$\sum_{i=1}^{n} \mu_i \zeta_{it} = -\sum_{j=1}^{n} \left(\sum_{i=1}^{n} \mu_i \nu^{ij} \right) \varepsilon_{jt} = -\frac{1}{\phi} \sum_{j=1}^{n} \varepsilon_{jt} = 0$$

where the first step is based on (5.5), the second on (5.3) and the symmetry of $[\nu^{ij}]$, and the third on

$$(5.8) \qquad \sum_{i=1}^{n} \varepsilon_{it} = 0$$

which is the linear dependence of the disturbances of (5.1).

Note the difference between the linear dependences (5.7) and (5.8). In (5.8) we have no unknown parameters, but in (5.7) we have the unknown μ's which also occur in the left-hand side of (5.4). So we have two problems when estimating (5.4) which we did not have in the previous sections when we developed the instrumental-variable method. Since the latter method appears to be satisfactory under the assumption of predetermined $\bar{w}_{it}Dq_{it}$'s, we devote the remainder of this section to the economic structure of the reciprocal equations rather than their statistical estimation.

The Interpretation of the Reciprocal Equations

The reciprocal equations have a very simple economic interpretation. Consider eqs. (6.2) and (6.6) of Section 1.6,

$$(5.9) \quad d(\log\lambda) = \frac{1}{\phi}\left[d(\log m) - \sum_{k=1}^{n} w_k d(\log p_k)\right] - \sum_{k=1}^{n} \mu_k d(\log p_k)$$

$$(5.10) \quad d\left(\log\frac{\partial u}{\partial q_i}\right) = \sum_{j=1}^{n} v^{ij} w_j d(\log q_j)$$

where $(m, \mathbf{p})$ is deleted for notational convenience. By subtracting (5.9) from (5.10) we obtain

$$d\left(\log\frac{\partial u}{\partial q_i}\right) - d(\log\lambda) = \sum_{k=1}^{n} \mu_k d(\log p_k) + \sum_{j=1}^{n} v^{ij} w_j d(\log q_j) - \frac{1}{\phi}\left[d(\log m) - \sum_{k=1}^{n} w_k d(\log p_k)\right]$$

The right-hand side of this equation is the infinitesimal version of that of (5.6). By identifying the left-hand sides in the same way, we can conclude that (5.6) or, equivalently, the reciprocal equation (5.4), is simply the first-order equilibrium condition $\partial u/\partial q_i = \lambda p_i$ written in log-change form.

The coefficients of the reciprocal equations also have a simple interpretation. The v^{ij}'s of (5.4) form a matrix $[v^{ij}]$ which is directly, rather than inversely, proportional to the Hessian matrix of the utility function in expenditure terms; this follows from eq. (5.20) of Section 1.5. Equation (5.3) shows that the coefficients $v^{i1}, \ldots, v^{in}$ of the $\bar{w}_{jt}Dq_{jt}$'s in (5.4) have a marginally weighted average equal to $1/\phi$, which is the income elasticity of the marginal utility of income. Also, the coefficient of DQ_t in (5.4) is minus the same elasticity, which holds for each of the n reciprocal equations, whereas the coefficient μ_i of DQ_t in (5.1) depends on i. We conclude that the reciprocal equations and their coefficients have indeed a simple interpretation and several attractive features, which makes a more detailed analysis worthwhile.

Reciprocal Slutsky Coefficients

Consider the absolute price version of (5.1),

$$\bar{w}_{it}Dq_{it} = \mu_i DQ_t + \sum_{j=1}^{n} \pi_{ij} Dp_{jt} + \varepsilon_{it} \tag{5.11}$$

where $\pi_{ij} = \nu_{ij} - \phi\mu_i\mu_j$ is the $(i, j)^{\text{th}}$ Slutsky coefficient. We write this in matrix form, with $[\pi_{ij}]$ for the $n \times n$ Slutsky matrix, as

$$[\pi_{ij}] = \mathbf{N} - \phi\boldsymbol{\mu}\boldsymbol{\mu}' \tag{5.12}$$

We obtain (5.11) from (5.1) by combining price terms. We now proceed in the same way for (5.4) by combining the first two terms on the right, using $DQ_t = \sum_j \bar{w}_{jt} Dq_{jt}$. This gives

$$Dp_{it} - \sum_{j=1}^{n} \mu_j Dp_{jt} = \sum_{j=1}^{n} \pi^{ij} \bar{w}_{jt} Dq_{jt} + \zeta_{it} \tag{5.13}$$

where

$$\pi^{ij} = \nu^{ij} - \frac{1}{\phi} \qquad i, j = 1, \ldots, n \tag{5.14}$$

which will be called the $(i, j)^{\text{th}}$ *reciprocal Slutsky coefficient*. This term is explained in the next subsection.

The reciprocal Slutsky coefficients form an $n \times n$ matrix $[\pi^{ij}]$, the reciprocal Slutsky matrix,

$$[\pi^{ij}] = \mathbf{N}^{-1} - \frac{1}{\phi}\boldsymbol{\iota}\boldsymbol{\iota}' \tag{5.15}$$

which is symmetric negative semidefinite with rank $n-1$. This follows from the fact that it is obtained from the Slutsky matrix (5.12) by pre- and post-multiplication by the symmetric nonsingular matrix $\mathbf{N}^{-1}$,

$$[\pi^{ij}] = \mathbf{N}^{-1} [\pi_{ij}] \, \mathbf{N}^{-1} \tag{5.16}$$

which may be verified by means of (5.2) and (5.12).

The singularity of the matrix (5.15) follows directly from (5.2) and $\boldsymbol{\iota}'\boldsymbol{\mu} = 1$,

$$\left(\mathbf{N}^{-1} - \frac{1}{\phi}\boldsymbol{\iota}\boldsymbol{\iota}'\right)\boldsymbol{\mu} = \frac{1}{\phi}\boldsymbol{\iota} - \frac{1}{\phi}\boldsymbol{\iota} = \mathbf{0}$$

or, in scalar form,

$$\sum_{j=1}^{n} \pi^{ij}\mu_j = 0 \qquad i = 1, \ldots, n \tag{5.17}$$

Hence the reciprocal Slutsky coefficients $\pi^{i1}, \ldots, \pi^{in}$ of (5.13) have a zero marginally weighted average. This should be compared with the constraint $\sum_j \pi_{ij} = 0$ on the Slutsky coefficients of (5.11).

Two Inverse Relationships

The reciprocal Slutsky matrix owes its name to the fact that it is a reflexive generalized inverse of the Slutsky matrix. Such an inverse of a matrix $\mathbf{A}_1$ is any matrix $\mathbf{A}_2$ which satisfies

$$\mathbf{A}_1\mathbf{A}_2\mathbf{A}_1 = \mathbf{A}_1 \qquad \mathbf{A}_2\mathbf{A}_1\mathbf{A}_2 = \mathbf{A}_2 \tag{5.18}$$

Let $\mathbf{A}_1$ be the Slutsky matrix (5.12) and $\mathbf{A}_2$ its reciprocal (5.15). To verify (5.18) we consider

$$\mathbf{A}_1\mathbf{A}_2 = (\mathbf{N} - \phi\boldsymbol{\mu}\boldsymbol{\mu}')\left(\mathbf{N}^{-1} - \frac{1}{\phi}\boldsymbol{\iota}\boldsymbol{\iota}'\right) = \mathbf{I} - \boldsymbol{\mu}\boldsymbol{\iota}' \tag{5.19}$$

where the second step is based on (5.2), $\mathbf{N}\boldsymbol{\iota} = \phi\boldsymbol{\mu}$ and $\boldsymbol{\mu}'\boldsymbol{\iota} = 1$. Next postmultiply (5.19) by $\mathbf{A}_1$,

$$\mathbf{A}_1\mathbf{A}_2\mathbf{A}_1 = (\mathbf{I} - \boldsymbol{\mu}\boldsymbol{\iota}')(\mathbf{N} - \phi\boldsymbol{\mu}\boldsymbol{\mu}') = \mathbf{N} - \phi\boldsymbol{\mu}\boldsymbol{\mu}' = \mathbf{A}_1$$

and premultiply (5.19) by $\mathbf{A}_2$:

$$\mathbf{A}_2\mathbf{A}_1\mathbf{A}_2 = \left(\mathbf{N}^{-1} - \frac{1}{\phi}\boldsymbol{\iota}\boldsymbol{\iota}'\right)(\mathbf{I} - \boldsymbol{\mu}\boldsymbol{\iota}') = \mathbf{N}^{-1} - \frac{1}{\phi}\boldsymbol{\iota}\boldsymbol{\iota}' = \mathbf{A}_2$$

These two results in conjunction with (5.18) confirm that $[\pi_{ij}]$ and $[\pi^{ij}]$ are reflexive generalized inverses of each other.

Another inverse relation is

$$\begin{bmatrix} [\pi_{ij}] & \boldsymbol{\mu} \\ \boldsymbol{\mu}' & 0 \end{bmatrix} \begin{bmatrix} [\pi^{ij}] & \boldsymbol{\iota} \\ \boldsymbol{\iota}' & 0 \end{bmatrix} = \mathbf{I} \tag{5.20}$$

where $\mathbf{I}$ on the right has $n+1$ rows and columns. Using (5.12) and (5.15), we can write this in the equivalent form

$$\begin{bmatrix} \mathbf{N} - \phi\boldsymbol{\mu}\boldsymbol{\mu}' & \boldsymbol{\mu} \\ \boldsymbol{\mu}' & 0 \end{bmatrix} \begin{bmatrix} \mathbf{N}^{-1} - (1/\phi)\,\boldsymbol{\iota}\boldsymbol{\iota}' & \boldsymbol{\iota} \\ \boldsymbol{\iota}' & 0 \end{bmatrix} = \mathbf{I}$$

which is easily verified by means of (5.19). We conclude from (5.20) that the Slutsky matrix bordered by marginal shares is the (ordinary) inverse of the reciprocal Slutsky matrix bordered by units.

The Distribution of the Disturbances

The disturbance ζ_{it} of (5.4) and (5.13) is defined in (5.5) as a linear combination of the disturbances $\varepsilon_{1t}, \ldots, \varepsilon_{nt}$ of the model (5.1) with constant weights. Hence, if the ε's have zero expectations and zero lagged covariances and a constant contemporaneous covariance matrix, the ζ's have the same properties. Also, if the ε's are normally distributed, the ζ's are normally distributed too.

Consider the second-moment model in the form of eq. (7.14) of Section 2.7:

$$\text{(5.21)} \qquad \operatorname{cov}(\varepsilon_{it}, \varepsilon_{jt}) = \sigma^2 \frac{\pi_{ij}}{\phi} \qquad i, j = 1, \ldots, n$$

The right-hand side is the $(i, j)^{\text{th}}$ element of $(\sigma^2/\phi)\,[\pi_{ij}]$. It follows from (5.5) that the covariance matrix of $[\zeta_{1t} \ldots \zeta_{nt}]$ is obtained from this matrix by pre- and postmultiplication by $-\mathbf{N}^{-1}$. Hence, using (5.16), we obtain

$$\text{(5.22)} \qquad \operatorname{cov}(\zeta_{it}, \zeta_{jt}) = \sigma^2 \frac{\pi^{ij}}{\phi} \qquad i, j = 1, \ldots, n$$

which shows that the disturbance covariances of the reciprocal equations are proportional to the corresponding reciprocal Slutsky coefficients, with the same proportionality constant (σ^2/ϕ) as we have in (5.21) for the Rotterdam Model in its standard form.

Preference Independence and Block-Independence

Under preference independence we have $v_{ii} = \phi\mu_i$ and $v_{ij} = 0$ for $i \neq j$, so that

$$\text{(5.23)} \qquad v^{ij} = \begin{cases} 1/\phi\mu_i & \text{if} \quad i = j \\ 0 & \text{if} \quad i \neq j \end{cases}$$

which implies that (5.4) can be simplified to

$$\text{(5.24)} \qquad Dp_{it} - \sum_{j=1}^{n} \mu_j Dp_{jt} = \frac{\bar{w}_{it} Dq_{it}}{\phi\mu_i} - \frac{1}{\phi} DQ_t + \zeta_{it} \quad \text{where} \quad \zeta_{it} = -\frac{\varepsilon_{it}}{\phi\mu_i}$$

The first term on the right equals Dq_{it} multiplied by the ratio of $1/\phi$, the income elasticity of the marginal utility of income, to the income elasticity $\mu_i/\bar{w}_{it}$ of the ith commodity. The reciprocal of this ratio was discussed at the end of Section 1.5.

By combining (5.23) with (5.14) we find the reciprocal Slutsky coefficients:

$$\pi^{ij} = \phi^{-1}\left(\frac{1}{\mu_i} - 1\right) \quad \text{if} \quad i = j \qquad (5.25)$$
$$- \phi^{-1} \quad \text{if} \quad i \neq j$$

Hence, under preference independence, all off-diagonal elements of the reciprocal Slutsky matrix are equal to the absolute value of the income elasticity of the marginal utility of income. The second-moment model (5.22) thus implies that all disturbance covariances ($i \neq j$) take the same negative value, $-\sigma^2/\phi^2$.

Next consider block-independence with G commodity groups, $S_1, \ldots, S_G$. Since ν^{ij} vanishes when i and j belong to different groups, we can confine the summation over j in the right-hand side of (5.4) to $j \in S_g$ when i belongs to S_g:

$$Dp_{it} - \sum_{j=1}^{n} \mu_j Dp_{jt} = \sum_{j \in S_g} \nu^{ij} \bar{w}_{jt} Dq_{jt} - \frac{1}{\phi} DQ_t + \zeta_{it} \qquad (5.26)$$

Similarly, (5.3) becomes

$$\sum_{j \in S_g} \nu^{ij} \mu_j = \frac{1}{\phi} \quad \text{if} \quad i \in S_g \qquad (5.27)$$

It is also easily verified that, if i and j belong to different groups, their reciprocal Slutsky coefficient equals $-1/\phi$. This agrees with the second line of (5.25).

Reciprocal Equations of Commodity Groups Under Block-Independence

We multiply (5.26) by the conditional marginal share μ_i/M_g and sum over $i \in S_g$. The left-hand side becomes

$$\sum_{i \in S_g} \frac{\mu_i}{M_g}\left(Dp_{it} - \sum_{j=1}^{n} \mu_j Dp_{jt}\right) = DP'_{gt} - \sum_{j=1}^{n} \mu_j Dp_{jt}$$

For the first term on the right we obtain, using (5.27) and the symmetry of $[\nu^{ij}]$,

$$\frac{1}{M_g} \sum_{j \in S_g} \left(\sum_{i \in S_g} \mu_i \nu^{ij}\right) \bar{w}_{jt} Dq_{jt} = \frac{1}{\phi M_g} \sum_{j \in S_g} \bar{w}_{jt} Dq_{jt} = \frac{\bar{W}_{gt} DQ_{gt}}{\phi M_g}$$

Therefore, when (5.26) is weighted proportionally to the marginal shares of the commodities of S_g, the result is

$$DP'_{gt} - \sum_{j=1}^{n} \mu_j Dp_{jt} = \frac{\bar{W}_{gt} DQ_{gt}}{\phi M_g} - \frac{1}{\phi} DQ_t + Z_{gt} \tag{5.28}$$

where

$$Z_{gt} = \sum_{i \in S_g} \frac{\mu_i}{M_g} \zeta_{it} \tag{5.29}$$

Equation (5.28) is the reciprocal equation for the group S_g under block-independence. Note that it is the uppercase version of the preference-independent reciprocal equation (5.24).

Conditional Reciprocal Equations Under Block-Independence

Next we subtract (5.28) from (5.26). The result may be written as

$$Dp_{it} - DP'_{gt} = \sum_{j \in S_g} v^{ij} \bar{w}_{jt} Dq_{jt} - \frac{\bar{W}_{gt} DQ_{gt}}{\phi M_g} + \zeta_{it}^g \tag{5.30}$$

where

$$\zeta_{it}^g = \zeta_{it} - Z_{gt} \quad \text{if} \quad i \in S_g \tag{5.31}$$

Equation (5.30) is the conditional reciprocal equation of the ith commodity within its group (S_g) under block-independence. The ith price log-change on the left is deflated, not by the marginal price index of the basket, but by that of the commodity group. The first term on the right is identical to that of the unconditional equation (5.26). The second terms differ. In (5.26) it is $-DQ_t$ multiplied by the reciprocal of ϕ. In the conditional equation (5.30) it is $-DQ_{gt}$ multiplied by the reciprocal of $\phi M_g / \bar{W}_{gt}$, which is the own-price elasticity of the demand for S_g under block-independence.

In the next section we derive the reciprocal models (5.28) and (5.30) from the corresponding demand models under weaker conditions.

9.6 Extensions of the Reciprocal Approach to Blockwise Dependence

The analysis which follows applies the reciprocal approach to three layers of demand models under blockwise dependence: the unconditional model for the n commodities of the basket, the G conditional models for commodities within groups, and the model for the G groups. It will prove convenient to consider these models in reverse order.

Reciprocal Equations of Commodity Groups

Our starting point is eq. (3.4) of Section 8.3,

$$(6.1) \qquad \bar{W}_{gt} DQ_{gt} = M_g DQ_t + \sum_{h=1}^{G} N_{gh} \left(DP'_{ht} - \sum_{k=1}^{n} \mu_k Dp_{kt} \right) + E_{gt}$$

which is the uppercase version of (5.1). By applying the approach of (5.2) through (5.5) to (6.1) we obtain

$$(6.2) \qquad DP'_{gt} - \sum_{j=1}^{n} \mu_j Dp_{jt} = \sum_{h=1}^{G} N^{gh} \bar{W}_{ht} DQ_{ht} - \frac{1}{\phi} DQ_t + Z_{gt}$$

where N^{gh} is the $(g, h)^{\text{th}}$ element of $[N_{gh}]^{-1}$, the inverse of the $G \times G$ price coefficient matrix of the groups, and

$$(6.3) \qquad Z_{gt} = - \sum_{h=1}^{G} N^{gh} E_{ht} \qquad g = 1, \ldots, G$$

Equation (6.2) is the reciprocal equation of S_g under blockwise dependence. It contains (5.28) as a special case for block-independence, because N^{gh} then vanishes for $g \neq h$ and it is equal to $1/\phi M_g$ for $g = h$. It is shown in (6.15) below that the disturbance Z_{gt} is obtained from the corresponding ζ_{it}'s by weighting with conditional marginal shares, in agreement with (5.29).

Conditional Reciprocal Equations

Next consider the conditional demand equation (3.25) of Section 8.3,

$$(6.4) \qquad \bar{w}_{it} Dq_{it} = \mu_i^g \bar{W}_{gt} DQ_{gt} + \sum_{j \in S_g} v_{ij} (Dp_{jt} - DP'_{gt}) + \varepsilon_{it}^g$$

and recall from eq. (3.1) of Section 8.3 that the sum of the v_{ij}'s which occur in (6.4) for all $i \in S_g$ equals N_{gg}, the own-price coefficient in (6.1). This N_{gg} thus takes the place of ϕ in the model (5.1), and $\bar{W}_{gt} DQ_{gt}$ similarly replaces DQ_t. So, when we apply the approach of (5.2) through (5.5) to (6.4), we obtain

$$(6.5) \qquad Dp_{it} - DP'_{gt} = \sum_{j \in S_g} v^{gij} \bar{w}_{jt} Dq_{jt} - \frac{\bar{W}_{gt} DQ_{gt}}{N_{gg}} + \zeta_{it}^g$$

where v^{gij} is the $(i, j)^{\text{th}}$ element of the inverse of the $n_g \times n_g$ price coefficient submatrix $[v_{ij}]$, the rows and columns of which correspond to the commodities of S_g, and

$$(6.6) \qquad \zeta_{it}^g = - \sum_{j \in S_g} v^{gij} \varepsilon_{jt}^g \quad \text{if} \quad i \in S_g$$

Equation (6.5) is the conditional reciprocal equation of the ith good within its group under blockwise dependence. The coefficient of $-DQ_{gt}$ is the reciprocal of $N_{gg}/\bar{W}_{gt}$, the own-price elasticity of the demand for the group S_g. Under block-independence this becomes the reciprocal of $\phi M_g/\bar{W}_{gt}$. Also, the $n \times n$ price coefficient matrix $\mathbf{N}$ is then block-diagonal, and the inverse of each diagonal block is identical to the corresponding submatrix of $\mathbf{N}^{-1} = [\nu^{ij}]$, so that the first superscript of ν^{gij} can be deleted. This leads to (5.30).

Unconditional Reciprocal Equations

Using $\sum_j \bar{w}_{jt} Dq_{jt} = \bar{W}_{gt} DQ_{gt}$, where the summation is over $j \in S_g$, we obtain the following result by adding (6.2) and (6.5):

$$(6.7) \qquad Dp_{it} - \sum_{j=1}^{n} \mu_j Dp_{jt} = \sum_{j \in S_g} \left(\nu^{gij} - \frac{1}{N_{gg}} + N^{gg} \right) \bar{w}_{jt} Dq_{jt}$$
$$+ \sum_{h \neq g} N^{gh} \bar{W}_{ht} DQ_{ht} - \frac{1}{\phi} DQ_t + \zeta_{it}^g + Z_{gt}$$

This can be written in the form (5.4) when we specify

$$(6.8) \qquad \zeta_{it} = \zeta_{it}^g + Z_{gt} \quad \text{if} \quad i \in S_g$$

which agrees with (5.31), and

$$(6.9) \qquad \nu^{ij} = \begin{cases} \nu^{gij} - \dfrac{1}{N_{gg}} + N^{gg} & \text{if} \quad i \in S_g \text{ and } j \in S_g \\ N^{gh} & \text{if} \quad i \in S_g, j \in S_h, \; g \neq h \end{cases}$$

Equation (6.7) makes the blockwise dependence visible at the level of the unconditional reciprocal equations for the individual goods. Under the stronger condition of block-independence we have

$$\nu^{gij} = \nu^{ij} \qquad N^{gg} = \frac{1}{\phi M_g} \qquad N^{gh} = 0 \quad \text{for} \quad g \neq h$$

so that (6.7) is then simplified to (5.26).

Note also that (6.9) specifies the inverse of the $n \times n$ price coefficient matrix under blockwise dependence. The elements of this inverse are equal to the corresponding element N^{gh} of the group inverse except for the diagonal blocks. These blocks involve (in addition to N^{gg}) the inverse of the price coefficient matrix within the group as well as the corresponding diagonal element of $[N_{gh}]$.

Some Marginally Weighted Averages

The uppercase version of (5.3) is

$$\sum_{h=1}^{G} N^{gh}M_h = \frac{1}{\phi} \qquad g = 1, \ldots, G \tag{6.10}$$

Similarly, within each group we have

$$\sum_{j \in S_g} v^{gij}\mu_j^g = \frac{1}{N_{gg}} \quad \text{if} \quad i \in S_g \tag{6.11}$$

which follows directly from the fact that under blockwise dependence ϕ is replaced by N_{gg} when we operate within S_g.

By combining (6.9) with (6.11) we obtain

$$\sum_{j \in S_g} v^{ij}\mu_j^g = N^{gg} \quad \text{if} \quad i \in S_g \tag{6.12}$$

This is the reciprocal version of eq. (2.14) of Section 8.2, which states that, for each $i \in S_g$, the sum of v_{ij} over $j \in S_g$ is equal to N_{gg} multiplied by the ith conditional marginal share. Note that under block-independence both (6.11) and (6.12) are equivalent to (5.27) when the latter equation is divided by M_g.

Equations (6.10) to (6.12) concern marginally weighted averages of inverted price coefficients. They have immediate implications for the identically weighted averages of the disturbances of the corresponding reciprocal equations. Using the symmetry of $[N^{gh}]$ as well as (6.3), (6.10) and $\sum_h E_{ht} = 0$, we obtain

$$\sum_{g=1}^{G} M_g Z_{gt} = 0 \tag{6.13}$$

which is the uppercase version of (5.7). Within groups we have

$$\sum_{i \in S_g} \mu_i^g \zeta_{it}^g = 0 \tag{6.14}$$

which may be verified by means of (6.6) and (6.11). Finally, by multiplying (6.8) by the ith conditional marginal share, summing over $i \in S_g$ and using (6.14), we obtain

$$\sum_{i \in S_g} \mu_i^g \zeta_{it} = Z_{gt} \tag{6.15}$$

This is the extension of (5.29) to blockwise dependence.

Reciprocal Slutsky Coefficients of Commodity Groups

We can write (6.2) in the equivalent form

$$DP'_{gt} - \sum_{j=1}^{n} \mu_j Dp_{jt} = \sum_{h=1}^{G} \Pi^{gh} \bar{W}_{ht} DQ_{ht} + Z_{gt} \tag{6.16}$$

where

$$\Pi^{gh} = N^{gh} - \frac{1}{\phi} \qquad g, h = 1, \ldots, G \tag{6.17}$$

is the reciprocal Slutsky coefficient of the groups S_g and S_h. It is the upper-case version of (5.14).

It is a matter of straightforward algebra to verify that $[\Pi^{gh}]$ has properties similar to $[\pi^{ij}]$. In particular, $[\Pi^{gh}]$ is a reflexive generalized inverse of $[\Pi_{gh}]$, defined in eq. (4.6) of Section 8.4, and it is symmetric negative semidefinite with rank $G-1$. The cause of the singularity is

$$\sum_{h=1}^{G} \Pi^{gh} M_h = 0 \tag{6.18}$$

which follows directly from (6.10) and (6.17).

Conditional Reciprocal Slutsky Coefficients

Similarly, we can write (6.5) as

$$Dp_{it} - DP'_{gt} = \sum_{j \in S_g} \pi^{gij} \bar{w}_{jt} Dq_{jt} + \zeta_{it}^{g} \tag{6.19}$$

where

$$\pi^{gij} = \nu^{gij} - \frac{1}{N_{gg}} \quad \text{if} \quad i, j \in S_g \tag{6.20}$$

is the conditional reciprocal Slutsky coefficient of i and j within their group. The matrix of these coefficients, $[\pi^{gij}]$, is of order $n_g \times n_g$. It is a reflexive generalized inverse of the conditional Slutsky matrix whose $(i, j)^{\text{th}}$ element is shown in eq. (4.10) of Section 8.4; it is symmetric negative semidefinite with rank $n_g - 1$ and satisfies

$$\sum_{j \in S_g} \pi^{gij} \mu_j^g = 0 \quad \text{if} \quad i \in S_g \tag{6.21}$$

which may be verified from (6.11) and (6.20).

Unconditional Reciprocal Slutsky Coefficients

In the same way, we can write (6.7) in the form (5.13) when we specify π^{ij} for i and j both $\in S_g$ as

$$\nu^{gij} - \frac{1}{N_{gg}} + N^{gg} - \frac{1}{\phi}$$

and as $N^{gh} - 1/\phi$ for $i \in S_g$, $j \in S_h$, $g \neq h$. On comparing this with (6.17) and (6.20) we conclude that this amounts to

$$\text{(6.22)} \qquad \pi^{ij} = \begin{cases} \pi^{gij} + \Pi^{gg} & \text{if } i \in S_g \text{ and } j \in S_g \\ \Pi^{gh} & \text{if } i \in S_g, j \in S_h,\ g \neq h \end{cases}$$

This result is the reciprocal version of eq. (4.15) of Section 8.4. The reciprocal Slutsky coefficient π^{ij} of two commodities belonging to different groups is equal to the reciprocal Slutsky coefficient of their groups. For any pair of commodities within a group we have to add the relevant conditional reciprocal Slutsky coefficient. Note the similarity to (6.9).

The Second-Moment Model

Equations (6.3) and (6.6) express the disturbances of the reciprocal equations (for groups and for commodities within groups) in terms of the corresponding demand disturbances. The implications of the second-moment model for the latter disturbances are shown in eqs. (4.19) to (4.22) of Section 8.4. Using the group version and the within-group version of (5.16),

$$\text{(6.23)} \qquad [\Pi^{gh}] = [N^{gh}]\,[\Pi_{gh}]\,[N^{gh}]$$

$$\text{(6.24)} \qquad [\pi^{gij}] = [\nu^{gij}]\,[\pi^g_{ij}]\,[\nu^{gij}]$$

we thus obtain the second-moment model for the disturbances of the reciprocal equations for groups,

$$\text{(6.25)} \qquad \operatorname{cov}(Z_{gt}, Z_{ht}) = \sigma^2 \frac{\Pi^{gh}}{\phi} \qquad g, h = 1, \dots, G$$

and for commodities within groups,

$$\text{(6.26)} \qquad \operatorname{cov}(\zeta^g_{it}, \zeta^h_{jt}) = \begin{cases} \sigma^2 \dfrac{\pi^{gij}}{\phi} & \text{if } i \in S_g, j \in S_h,\ g = h \\ 0 & \text{if } i \in S_g, j \in S_h,\ g \neq h \end{cases}$$

as well as

$$\text{(6.27)} \qquad \operatorname{cov}(\zeta^g_{it}, Z_{ht}) = 0 \qquad i \in S_g;\ g, h = 1, \dots, G$$

By combining these three results with (6.8) we obtain

$$\operatorname{cov}(\zeta_{it}, \zeta_{jt}) = \begin{cases} \sigma^2 \dfrac{\pi^{gij} + \Pi^{gg}}{\phi} & \text{if} \quad i \in S_g \text{ and } j \in S_g \\[2ex] \sigma^2 \dfrac{\Pi^{gh}}{\phi} & \text{if} \quad i \in S_g, j \in S_h, \; g \neq h \end{cases}$$

This amounts to $\operatorname{cov}(\zeta_{it}, \zeta_{jt}) = \sigma^2 \pi^{ij}/\phi$ with π^{ij} defined in (6.22), in agreement with (5.22).

CHAPTER 10

ENDOGENOUS PRICE AND QUANTITY CHANGES

In Section 9.1 we argued that in the case of agricultural goods it is preferable to treat quantities rather than prices as predetermined variables. We return to this issue in Section 10.1, where both prices and quantities are introduced as endogenous variables. This approach is pursued under the second-moment model; it leads to an estimation method which is applied to the demand for meats in Section 10.5.

10.1 A Second-Moment Model with Endogenous Price and Quantity Changes

Consider again the demand-and-supply system (1.1) and (1.2) of Section 9.1:

$$q_{it} = f_i(m_t, p_{1t}, \ldots, p_{nt}) + \eta_{it} \tag{1.1}$$

$$q'_{it} = g_i(C_t, C_{t-1}, \ldots, p_{1,t-k_1}, \ldots, p_{n,t-k_n}) + \eta'_{it} \tag{1.2}$$

We concluded in Section 9.1 that, if the market is cleared in every year ($q_{it} = q'_{it}$) and if the demand and supply disturbances are independent, q_{it} is predetermined by the supply equation. The crucial point is that prices occur in (1.2) only in lagged form. If the supply equation contains current prices, as is the case in

$$q'_{it} = h_i(C_t, C_{t-1}, \ldots, p_{1t}, p_{1,t-1}, \ldots, p_{nt}, p_{n,t-1}, \ldots) + \eta''_{it} \tag{1.3}$$

then it is no longer true that the quantities are predetermined even when $q_{it} = q'_{it}$ and when the demand and supply disturbances are independent. In the system (1.1) and (1.3) both prices and quantities are endogenous.

Outline of the Approach and Notation

In this chapter we shall treat the price and quantity log-changes of the Rotterdam Model as endogenous variables. This is done within the context of the second-moment model as will be explained in the next subsection; the simple parametrization which is selected is justified in Section 10.2

by means of a particular supply model. The log-change in real income (DQ_t) will be treated as predetermined. This is justified by means of the result, obtained in Section 8.7, that under appropriate blockwise dependence conditions in a multiperiod framework DQ_t is a predetermined variable in the allocation model for current expenditures.

We write this model in the form of eq. (1.3) of Section 9.1,

$$\bar{w}_{it}Dq_{it} = \mu_i DQ_t + \sum_{j=1}^{n-1} \pi_{ij}(Dp_{jt} - Dp_{nt}) + \varepsilon_{it} \tag{1.4}$$

where $i=1,\ldots,n-1$, the nth equation again being deleted. We write the second-moment model (7.14) of Section 2.7 as $\pi_{ij} = -\gamma\omega_{ij}$, where $\gamma = -\phi/\sigma^2$ and ω_{ij} is the covariance of ε_{it} and ε_{jt}. So, if we impose this model on (1.4), this equation becomes

$$\bar{w}_{it}Dq_{it} = \mu_i DQ_t - \gamma \sum_{j=1}^{n-1} \omega_{ij}(Dp_{jt} - Dp_{nt}) + \varepsilon_{it} \tag{1.5}$$

or, in matrix form (for $i=1,\ldots,n-1$),

$$\mathbf{z}_t = \boldsymbol{\mu}_0 DQ_t - \gamma\boldsymbol{\Omega}\mathbf{p}_t + \boldsymbol{\varepsilon}_t \tag{1.6}$$

where $\boldsymbol{\Omega}$ is the covariance matrix of $[\varepsilon_{1t}\ldots\varepsilon_{n-1,t}]$ and $\mathbf{z}_t$, $\boldsymbol{\mu}_0$, $\mathbf{p}_t$ and $\boldsymbol{\varepsilon}_t$ are $(n-1)$-element column vectors whose i^{th} elements are $\bar{w}_{it}Dq_{it}$, μ_i, $Dp_{it} - Dp_{nt}$ and ε_{it}, respectively.

Note that (1.6) is an unconditional version of eq. (4.7) of Section 7.4, with γ as specified in eq. (4.4) of that section. We shall find it attractive to work with the full basket; in Sections 10.4 to 10.6 we will return to the notation for meats.

A Second-Moment Model Which Allows Endogenous Price Changes

If DQ_t and the price log-changes are all predetermined, we obtain the following equation by taking the expectations of both sides of (1.6):

$$\mathscr{E}\mathbf{z}_t = \boldsymbol{\mu}_0 DQ_t - \gamma\boldsymbol{\Omega}\mathbf{p}_t$$

If only DQ_t is predetermined, this is to be changed into

$$\mathscr{E}\mathbf{z}_t = \boldsymbol{\mu}_0 DQ_t - \gamma\boldsymbol{\Omega}\mathscr{E}\mathbf{p}_t \tag{1.7}$$

Note that, as in Chapter 9, expectations should be considered as conditional expectations, given the values of the predetermined variables at t.

We subtract (1.7) from (1.6),

$$\mathbf{z}_t - \mathscr{E}\mathbf{z}_t + \gamma\mathbf{\Omega}(\mathbf{p}_t - \mathscr{E}\mathbf{p}_t) = \boldsymbol{\varepsilon}_t \tag{1.8}$$

postmultiply by the transpose of $\boldsymbol{\varepsilon}_t$ and then take the expectation:

$$\mathscr{E}[(\mathbf{z}_t - \mathscr{E}\mathbf{z}_t)\,\boldsymbol{\varepsilon}_t'] + \gamma\mathbf{\Omega}\mathscr{E}[(\mathbf{p}_t - \mathscr{E}\mathbf{p}_t)\,\boldsymbol{\varepsilon}_t'] = \mathbf{\Omega}$$

This can be simplified to

$$\mathscr{E}(\mathbf{z}_t\boldsymbol{\varepsilon}_t') + \gamma\mathbf{\Omega}\mathscr{E}(\mathbf{p}_t\boldsymbol{\varepsilon}_t') = \mathbf{\Omega} \tag{1.9}$$

because the matrices $(\mathscr{E}\mathbf{z}_t)\,\boldsymbol{\varepsilon}_t'$ and $(\mathscr{E}\mathbf{p}_t)\,\boldsymbol{\varepsilon}_t'$ have zero expectations.

As in Chapter 9 (see page 97), we shall consider $\bar{w}_{it}$ as predetermined, so that the $\bar{w}_{it}Dq_{it}$'s and hence also $\mathbf{z}_t$ are predetermined if and only if the Dq_{it}'s are predetermined. In that special case the first left-hand term of (1.9) vanishes. If, on the other hand, the price log-changes are all predetermined, the second term of (1.9) vanishes. Both cases are covered by

$$\mathscr{E}(\mathbf{z}_t\boldsymbol{\varepsilon}_t') = (1-\theta)\,\mathbf{\Omega} \qquad \gamma\mathbf{\Omega}\mathscr{E}(\mathbf{p}_t\boldsymbol{\varepsilon}_t') = \theta\mathbf{\Omega} \tag{1.10}$$

where θ is a scalar. This is a simple extension of the second-moment model which satisfies (1.9) and which allows both price and quantity changes to be endogenous at the expense of one additional parameter (θ).

The Degree of Price-Disturbance Dependence

The model (1.10) implies that at $\theta=0$ each element of $\mathbf{p}_t$ is uncorrelated with the disturbances at t. If the random variation is multivariate normal, this amounts to stochastic independence, so that $\theta=0$ then implies and is implied by a predetermined $\mathbf{p}_t$. In the same way, $\theta=1$ implies and is implied by a predetermined $\mathbf{z}_t$ under normality.

When θ increases from 0 to 1, the covariances of the $\mathbf{z}_t$ and $\boldsymbol{\varepsilon}_t$ elements move toward zero. This follows from the first equation in (1.10). By premultiplying the second equation by $(\gamma\mathbf{\Omega})^{-1}$ we obtain

$$\mathscr{E}(\mathbf{p}_t\boldsymbol{\varepsilon}_t') = \frac{\theta}{\gamma}\mathbf{I} \tag{1.11}$$

which shows that, as θ increases from 0 to 1, the covariances of the corresponding elements of $\mathbf{p}_t$ and $\boldsymbol{\varepsilon}_t$ move upward, starting from zero. We shall therefore refer to θ as the *degree of price-disturbance dependence* of the model (1.10).

A Complete Variance-Covariance Specification

Note that (1.10) is an incomplete covariance specification. Both $\mathbf{z}_t$ and $\mathbf{p}_t$ are now random; their complete covariance matrix, which is square of order $2n-2$, is needed for the maximum-likelihood method described in Section 10.3. We specify the covariance matrix of $\mathbf{z}_t$ and $\gamma\mathbf{\Omega}\mathbf{p}_t$ as

$$\mathscr{V}\begin{bmatrix}\mathbf{z}_t\\ \gamma\mathbf{\Omega}\mathbf{p}_t\end{bmatrix}=\begin{bmatrix}\delta_{11}\mathbf{\Omega} & \delta_{12}\mathbf{\Omega}\\ \delta_{12}\mathbf{\Omega} & \delta_{22}\mathbf{\Omega}\end{bmatrix}=\mathbf{\Delta}\otimes\mathbf{\Omega} \tag{1.12}$$

where $\mathbf{\Delta}$ is a symmetric 2×2 matrix:

$$\mathbf{\Delta}=\begin{bmatrix}\delta_{11} & \delta_{12}\\ \delta_{12} & \delta_{22}\end{bmatrix} \tag{1.13}$$

To analyze the relationship between (1.10) and (1.12) we write (1.8) as

$$\boldsymbol{\varepsilon}_t=[\mathbf{I}\quad\mathbf{I}]\begin{bmatrix}\mathbf{z}_t-\mathscr{E}\mathbf{z}_t\\ \gamma\mathbf{\Omega}(\mathbf{p}_t-\mathscr{E}\mathbf{p}_t)\end{bmatrix} \tag{1.14}$$

Hence the covariance matrix of $\boldsymbol{\varepsilon}_t$ is obtained from that of $\mathbf{z}_t$ and $\gamma\mathbf{\Omega}\mathbf{p}_t$ by premultiplication by the $(n-1)\times(2n-2)$ matrix $[\mathbf{I}\quad\mathbf{I}]$ and postmultiplication by the transpose of this matrix. This shows that (1.12) is compatible with $\mathscr{V}(\boldsymbol{\varepsilon}_t)=\mathbf{\Omega}$ if and only if

$$\delta_{11}+2\delta_{12}+\delta_{22}=1 \tag{1.15}$$

Similarly, by postmultiplying $\mathbf{z}_t$ and $\gamma\mathbf{\Omega}\mathbf{p}_t$ by the transpose of (1.14) and taking the expectations, we find that (1.12) is compatible with (1.10) if and only if

$$\delta_{11}+\delta_{12}=1-\theta \qquad \delta_{12}+\delta_{22}=\theta \tag{1.16}$$

Note that (1.15) is implied by (1.16). Also note that, whereas there is only one additional parameter (θ) in (1.10), there are two in (1.12). These are the two parameters which determine the matrix $\mathbf{\Delta}$, given its symmetry and the constraint (1.15).

The Fixed-Price and the Fixed-Quantity Limits of the Model

Since $\mathbf{\Delta}\otimes\mathbf{\Omega}$ in (1.12) is a covariance matrix, $\mathbf{\Delta}$ must be positive semidefinite. This implies $\delta_{11}\geq 0$, $\delta_{22}\geq 0$ and

$$\delta_{12}^2\leq\delta_{11}\delta_{22} \tag{1.17}$$

so that $\delta_{12}=0$ when either $\delta_{11}=0$ or $\delta_{22}=0$.

If δ_{22} vanishes, (1.12) implies that $\mathbf{p}_t$ has a zero random component. This special case will be referred to as the *fixed-price limit* of the model (1.12). For $\delta_{11}=0$ we have a zero random component of $\mathbf{z}_t$; this is the *fixed-quantity limit*. It follows from (1.16) that the fixed-price limit implies $\theta=0$ (because $\delta_{12}=0$ if $\delta_{22}=0$) and hence, given (1.10), $\mathscr{E}(\mathbf{p}_t\boldsymbol{\varepsilon}_t')=\mathbf{0}$. But the fixed-price limit is not implied by $\theta=0$, since $\delta_{22}>0$ is possible in spite of $\theta=0$; this is the case in which δ_{22} and $-\delta_{12}$ take the same positive value. We have a similar result for the other limiting case, $\theta=1$ being implied by $\delta_{11}=\delta_{12}=0$ but also by $\delta_{11}=-\delta_{12}>0$.

10.2 A Natural Conjugate Supply Model

In this section we derive the covariance specification (1.12) by combining the demand equations of the Rotterdam Model with a particular supply model.

A Supply Model in Log-changes

The initial specification of the supply model is

$$Dq_{it} = k_{it} + \sum_{j=1}^{n} c_{ij} Dp_{jt} + \varepsilon_{it}' \qquad i = 1, \ldots, n \tag{2.1}$$

which is a log-change version of (1.3), with k_{it} representing the combined effect at t of all predetermined variables.[1] The coefficient c_{ij} measures the current (nonlagged) effect of a change in the jth price on the supply of the ith good. The left-hand variable is the log-change in the supply of the ith good, but since we shall equate this to the log-change in demand, no special symbol is needed.

We assume that the disturbance ε_{it}' in (2.1) has zero expectation conditionally on the predetermined k_{it} and DQ_t. So, by taking expectations of both sides of (2.1) and subtracting the result from (2.1), we obtain

$$Dq_{it} - \mathscr{E}(Dq_{it}) = \sum_{j=1}^{n} c_{ij} [Dp_{jt} - \mathscr{E}(Dp_{jt})] + \varepsilon_{it}' \tag{2.2}$$

This shows the relationship between the random components of the variables which is implied by the supply model.

---

[1] These variables may include lagged price log-changes and exogenous variables such as the log-changes in the population and the number of farms (see footnote 1 on page 95).

Supply-and-Demand Interaction

Next consider the ith demand equation in absolute prices:

$$\bar{w}_{it}Dq_{it} = \mu_i DQ_t + \sum_{j=1}^{n} \pi_{ij}Dp_{jt} + \varepsilon_{it} \tag{2.3}$$

Again, take the expectation and subtract the result from (2.3):

$$\bar{w}_{it}\left[Dq_{it} - \mathscr{E}(Dq_{it})\right] = \sum_{j=1}^{n} \pi_{ij}\left[Dp_{jt} - \mathscr{E}(Dp_{jt})\right] + \varepsilon_{it} \tag{2.4}$$

The variances and covariances of the random components of the price and quantity log-changes are obtained by combining (2.2) and (2.4) for $i=1,\dots,n$. A slight simplification is obtained by multiplying (2.2) by $\bar{w}_{it}$,

$$\bar{w}_{it}\left[Dq_{it} - \mathscr{E}(Dq_{it})\right] = \bar{w}_{it} \sum_{j=1}^{n} c_{ij}\left[Dp_{jt} - \mathscr{E}(Dp_{jt})\right] + \bar{w}_{it}\varepsilon'_{it} \tag{2.5}$$

because (2.4) and (2.5) have the same variables on the left. However, the price terms on the right, with their different sets of coefficients (π_{ij} and c_{ij}), present a major problem. A drastic simplification is needed to make further progress.

A Particular Supply Model

This simplification consists of assuming that $\bar{w}_{it}c_{ij}$ in (2.5) is a non-positive multiple (independent of i and j) of the Slutsky coefficient π_{ij}; a justification is given in the subsection immediately following the next. We can then write (2.5) as

$$\bar{w}_{it}\left[Dq_{it} - \mathscr{E}(Dq_{it})\right] = -s_1 \sum_{j=1}^{n} \pi_{ij}\left[Dp_{jt} - \mathscr{E}(Dp_{jt})\right] + \eta_{it} \tag{2.6}$$

where $s_1 \geq 0$ and $\eta_{it} = \bar{w}_{it}\varepsilon'_{it}$. We also assume that $[\eta_{1t}\dots\eta_{nt}]$ has a covariance matrix equal to a nonnegative multiple s_2 of that of $[\varepsilon_{1t}\dots\varepsilon_{nt}]$ and that the two sets of disturbances are uncorrelated:

$$\text{cov}(\eta_{it}, \eta_{jt}) = s_2\omega_{ij} \qquad i,j=1,\dots,n \tag{2.7}$$

$$\text{cov}(\eta_{it}, \varepsilon_{jt}) = 0 \qquad i,j=1,\dots,n \tag{2.8}$$

The model (2.6) to (2.8) involves two coefficients (s_1 and s_2) in addition to those which occur in the demand equations. Assume that this model is true and that the second-moment model $\pi_{ij} = -\gamma\omega_{ij}$ is also true. It is shown in the next subsection that this implies the covariance specification (1.12) for the following values of the δ's:

$$(2.9) \qquad \delta_{11} = \frac{s_1^2 + s_2}{(1+s_1)^2} \qquad \delta_{12} = \frac{s_1 - s_2}{(1+s_1)^2} \qquad \delta_{22} = \frac{1 + s_2}{(1+s_1)^2}$$

Substituting $s_1 = s_2 = 0$ gives $\delta_{11} = \delta_{12} = 0$ and $\delta_{22} = 1$, which is the fixed-quantity limit of (1.12). This agrees with (2.1), because $s_1 = 0$ implies that each c_{ij} vanishes and $s_2 = 0$ implies that the disturbance of (2.1) is zero with unit probability, so that Dq_{it} equals the predetermined k_{it}. When s_1 increases, suppliers react to price changes with increasing intensity. It follows from (2.9) that we obtain the fixed-price limit, $\delta_{11} = 1$ and $\delta_{12} = \delta_{22} = 0$, in the limit for $s_1 \to \infty$, provided s_2 remains constant. This proviso may be relaxed to the condition that s_1 increases faster than $\sqrt{s_2}$.

Derivations

We combine (2.4) and (2.6) in matrix form:

$$(2.10) \qquad \begin{bmatrix} 1 & -1 \\ -1 & -s_1 \end{bmatrix} \begin{bmatrix} \bar{w}_{it}[Dq_{it} - \mathscr{E}(Dq_{it})] \\ \sum_j \pi_{ij}[Dp_{jt} - \mathscr{E}(Dp_{jt})] \end{bmatrix} = \begin{bmatrix} \varepsilon_{it} \\ -\eta_{it} \end{bmatrix}$$

Since we have

$$\begin{bmatrix} 1 & -1 \\ -1 & -s_1 \end{bmatrix}^{-1} = \frac{1}{1+s_1} \begin{bmatrix} s_1 & -1 \\ -1 & -1 \end{bmatrix}$$

the solution of (2.10) is

$$(2.11) \qquad \bar{w}_{it}[Dq_{it} - \mathscr{E}(Dq_{it})] = \frac{\eta_{it} + s_1 \varepsilon_{it}}{1 + s_1} \qquad i = 1, \ldots, n$$

$$(2.12) \qquad \sum_{j=1}^{n} \pi_{ij}[Dp_{jt} - \mathscr{E}(Dp_{jt})] = \frac{\eta_{it} - \varepsilon_{it}}{1 + s_1} \qquad i = 1, \ldots, n$$

Using $\mathscr{E}(\varepsilon_{it}\varepsilon_{jt}) = \omega_{ij}$ as well as (2.7) and (2.8), we thus obtain

$$(2.13) \qquad \text{cov}(\bar{w}_{it}Dq_{it}, \bar{w}_{jt}Dq_{jt}) = \frac{s_1^2 + s_2}{(1+s_1)^2}\,\omega_{ij}$$

$$(2.14) \qquad \text{cov}\left(\sum_{k=1}^{n} \pi_{ik}Dp_{kt}, \sum_{k=1}^{n} \pi_{jk}Dp_{kt}\right) = \frac{1 + s_2}{(1+s_1)^2}\,\omega_{ij}$$

$$(2.15) \qquad \text{cov}\left(\bar{w}_{it}Dq_{it}, \sum_{k=1}^{n} \pi_{jk}Dp_{kt}\right) = -\frac{s_1 - s_2}{(1+s_1)^2}\,\omega_{ij}$$

A comparison with (1.12) shows that (2.13) confirms the δ_{11} specification of (2.9). For (2.14) and (2.15) we use

$$\sum_{k=1}^{n} \pi_{jk} Dp_{kt} = \sum_{k=1}^{n-1} \pi_{jk}(Dp_{kt} - Dp_{nt}) = -\gamma \sum_{k=1}^{n-1} \omega_{jk}(Dp_{kt} - Dp_{nt})$$

which is the jth element of the vector $-\gamma\mathbf{\Omega p}_t$. The verification of δ_{12} and δ_{22} from (2.14) and (2.15) is then straightforward.

The Supply Model and the Theory of the Firm

The additional parameters which occur in the supply model (2.6) to (2.8) are s_1, which measures the suppliers' response to price changes relative to the demand response [compare (2.6) with (2.4)], and s_2, which is the basic variance measure of the supply disturbances relative to the demand disturbances. To explain this model we apply the theory of the firm under perfect competition. It is true that perfect competition is not a realistic assumption for the economy as a whole, but when it is confined to meats (as will be done in Section 10.5), it becomes more acceptable since individual meat producers have little influence on the prices of their products and production factors.

We follow MALINVAUD (1972, pp. 55–64) by assuming that the firm's objective is to maximize the net value of its production, which equals the value of the outputs minus the value of the inputs, subject to the constraints implied by its production function. If this function satisfies appropriate regularity conditions, several results emerge which are directly comparable with those of consumer demand theory. For example, when the price of a good increases, the supply of this good cannot decrease. This implies $c_{ii} \geq 0$ in (2.1), which agrees with $-s_1\pi_{ii} \geq 0$ in (2.6). Slutsky symmetry is another example. To clarify this we write $w_i d(\log q_i) = (p_i/m)\, dq_i$ for the infinitesimal version of $\bar{w}_{it} Dq_{it}$ in (2.6), so that this equation implies

$$\frac{\partial q_i}{\partial p_j} = -\frac{s_1 m}{p_i p_j}\pi_{ij}$$

where $\partial q_i/\partial p_j$ here is the derivative of the supply of the ith good with respect to the jth price. This derivative is evidently symmetric in i and j because of the symmetry of $[\pi_{ij}]$. The second-moment model (2.7) for the supply disturbances is another extension of the corresponding model for demand theory, the covariance $s_2\omega_{ij}$ being proportional to the coefficient $-s_1\pi_{ij}$ in (2.6) if π_{ij} equals $-\gamma\omega_{ij}$.

Be this as it may, some obvious questions arise. Why should the supply response to price changes be a scalar multiple of the demand response $[\pi_{ij}]$? After all, the demand response to price changes is determined by the consumer's utility function and by income and prices, whereas the supply response involves matters of production technology. How can we relate such different determining factors to each other?

Comparison with Bayesian Inference

The simplest way to answer these questions is by means of an analogy from Bayesian inference. This type of inference uses a prior density function to formalize prior judgments on unknown parameters. The posterior density function is then obtained by multiplying the prior density by the likelihood function. The procedure typically requires extensive integration, which in many cases is analytically intractable. Numerical integration is then necessary, but this is usually practical only when there are very few parameters. Sometimes, however, elegant solutions emerge if the analyst is willing to formulate prior judgments in a particular way, viz., so that the prior density function is a "natural conjugate" of the likelihood function. For example, such a natural conjugate prior distribution of a parameter may be the normal distribution, in which case the analyst still has two degrees of freedom (the mean and the variance of this normal distribution) to express his prior judgments.

Using a natural conjugate prior distribution is a device to make Bayesian inference more operational. This procedure may distort the analyst's true prior judgments, but there are many situations in which the analyst decides that these judgments are adequately approximated by a natural conjugate distribution. It should also be taken into consideration that the model which yields the likelihood function is usually not perfect either. Typically, it is a tractable model which promises to be in reasonable agreement with the process that generates the data. Posterior distributions are the result of two ingredients: the prior distribution and the likelihood function. It is clearly unreasonable to require one ingredient to be perfect when the other is not.

By analogy, we consider (2.6) to (2.8) a *natural conjugate supply model* associated with the Rotterdam consumer demand model. The purpose of this supply model is to enable the analyst to make both price and quantity changes endogenous in a tractable way, in agreement with the idea of supply and demand interaction. By combining (2.6) to (2.8) with the demand equations of the Rotterdam Model it is possible, to a certain extent, to estimate demand response while taking this interaction into account.

How Accurate Is the Natural Conjugate Supply Model?

In spite of these limited claims it is certainly conceivable that the price terms of the supply model are not greatly in error when s_1 is specified appropriately. We should expect that an increase in the price of beef raises the supply of this meat. This agrees with $-s_1\pi_{ii}>0$ in (2.6) when $s_1>0$. We should also expect that, other things remaining constant, this price increase reduces the supply of pork. This is implied by (2.6) when the consumers treat beef and pork as substitutes in Hicks's sense, because $s_1>0$ implies $-s_1\pi_{ij}<0$ when i stands for beef and j for pork. Although π_{ij} refers specifically to the consumers' response to price changes, there are many cases in which the sign of this coefficient is also applicable (when multiplied by $-s_1<0$) to the suppliers' response.

It is also appropriate to compare using a natural conjugate supply model with the alternative of designing a full-fledged supply model. If our interest concerns demand rather than supply, as is the case in this book, it is not at all obvious that the latter alternative should be preferred. The natural conjugate supply model contains only two coefficients (s_1 and s_2) in addition to those of the demand model, whereas a full-fledged supply model will involve many more. Even if the latter model gives a better description of supply responses in principle, its larger number of unknown coefficients will lead to a more serious problem of sampling errors (and possibly also observational errors of the additional variables that are needed). Such errors can affect the coefficient estimates of the demand equations adversely. Basically, this argument is the same as that used at the end of Section 3.7 for the merits of price and real-income indexes which minimize the use of unknown parameters.

The Degree of Price-Disturbance Dependence Under the Supply Model

By adding δ_{12} and δ_{22} of (2.9) and using (1.16) we obtain

$$\theta = \delta_{12} + \delta_{22} = \frac{1}{1+s_1} \tag{2.16}$$

This shows that the degree of price-disturbance dependence of the model (1.10) depends on s_1 but not on s_2. Recall from the discussion below (1.16) that $\mathbf{\Delta}$ defined in (1.13) is determined by two parameters. The natural conjugate supply model implies that these two may be identified with s_1 and s_2.

By combining (2.16) with $s_1 \geq 0$ we find that the degree of price-disturbance dependence cannot be outside the interval (0, 1):

$$0 \leq \theta \leq 1 \tag{2.17}$$

Note that this constraint is not implied by the positive semidefiniteness of $\mathbf{\Delta}$, which allows $\delta_{11}+\delta_{12}<0$ and $\delta_{12}+\delta_{22}<0$. Both inequalities yield a θ outside (0, 1) in view of (1.16).

It follows from (2.16) and (2.9) that $s_1=0$ implies $\theta=1$ and $\delta_{11}=-\delta_{12}=s_2$. The fixed-quantity limit thus requires the additional condition $s_2=0$. When s_1 and s_2 increase indefinitely so that s_2/s_1^2 converges to a constant c, δ_{22} and $-\delta_{12}$ converge to c also. The fixed-price limit requires $c=0$. These results should be compared with the discussion below (1.17).

The Random Components of the Deflated Price Log-changes

Equation (2.12) expresses the random component of $\sum_j \pi_{ij} Dp_{jt}$ in terms of the ith supply and demand disturbances. Let us write it for $i=1,\ldots,n$ in matrix form,

$$[\pi_{ij}]\begin{bmatrix} Dp_{1t}-\mathscr{E}(Dp_{1t}) \\ \vdots \\ Dp_{nt}-\mathscr{E}(Dp_{nt}) \end{bmatrix} = \frac{1}{1+s_1}\begin{bmatrix} \eta_{1t}-\varepsilon_{1t} \\ \vdots \\ \eta_{nt}-\varepsilon_{nt} \end{bmatrix} \tag{2.18}$$

where $[\pi_{ij}]$ is the $n\times n$ Slutsky matrix.

We have $\mathbf{N}^{-1}[\pi_{ij}]=\mathbf{I}-\boldsymbol{\iota}\boldsymbol{\mu}'$ in view of eqs. (5.2) and (5.12) of Section 9.5 or, in scalar terms,

$$\sum_{k=1}^{n} \nu^{ik}\pi_{kj} = \begin{cases} 1-\mu_j & \text{if} \quad i=j \\ -\mu_j & \text{if} \quad i\neq j \end{cases} \tag{2.19}$$

Hence, by premultiplying (2.18) by $\mathbf{N}^{-1}=[\nu^{ik}]$, we obtain

(2.20)
$$Dp_{it}-\sum_{k=1}^{n}\mu_k Dp_{kt}-\mathscr{E}\left(Dp_{it}-\sum_{k=1}^{n}\mu_k Dp_{kt}\right)=\frac{1}{1+s_1}\sum_{k=1}^{n}\nu^{ik}(\eta_{kt}-\varepsilon_{kt})$$

The left-hand side is the random component of the marginally deflated price log-change of the ith good, so that (2.20) implies that this component is a weighted sum of the n differences between corresponding supply and demand disturbances.

The Covariance Matrix of the Deflated Price Log-changes

The right-hand side of (2.20) is the ith element of the vector

$$\frac{1}{1+s_1}\mathbf{N}^{-1}[\eta_{1t}-\varepsilon_{1t}\ldots\eta_{nt}-\varepsilon_{nt}]' \tag{2.21}$$

The covariance matrix of $[\eta_{1t}-\varepsilon_{1t} \ldots \eta_{nt}-\varepsilon_{nt}]$ is

$$(1+s_2)\,[\omega_{ij}] = \frac{(1+s_2)\,\sigma^2}{\phi}\,[\pi_{ij}]$$

where the first expression is based on (2.7) and (2.8), and the second on eq. (7.14) of Section 2.7. Hence the covariance matrix of the vector (2.21) is

$$\frac{1+s_2}{(1+s_1)^2}\,\frac{\sigma^2}{\phi}\,\mathbf{N}^{-1}[\pi_{ij}]\,\mathbf{N}^{-1} = \delta_{22}\,\frac{\sigma^2}{\phi}\,[\pi^{ij}]$$

where the equal sign is based on (2.9) and eq. (5.16) of Section 9.5. Since (2.20) contains the ith element of (2.21), we have thus proved

$$\text{(2.22)} \qquad \operatorname{cov}\left(Dp_{it} - \sum_{k=1}^{n} \mu_k Dp_{kt},\, Dp_{jt} - \sum_{k=1}^{n} \mu_k Dp_{kt}\right) = \delta_{22}\sigma^2\,\frac{\pi^{ij}}{\phi}$$

which states that the covariance of the random components of the ith and j^{th} deflated price log-changes is proportional to the corresponding reciprocal Slutsky coefficient, with $\delta_{22}\sigma^2/\phi$ as proportionality constant.

The fixed-quantity limit is an interesting special case. We then have $\delta_{22}=1$, so that the right-hand side of (2.22) becomes $\sigma^2\pi^{ij}/\phi$, which is identical to that of eq. (5.22) of Section 9.5. This is as it should be, because if the $\bar{w}_{jt}Dq_{jt}$'s are predetermined, as we assumed in Section 9.5, the ζ's in eqs. (5.4) and (5.22) of that section are the random components of the deflated price log-changes. Hence (2.22) provides a generalization of the second-moment model of the reciprocal equations for the case in which the quantity log-changes are also endogenous.

Covariances of Deflated Price Log-changes and Demand Disturbances

To derive the covariances of the marginally deflated price log-changes and the demand disturbances we multiply (2.20) by ε_{jt} and take the expectation. Using (2.8), (2.16) and $\pi_{ij}=-\gamma\omega_{ij}$, we obtain

$$-\frac{1}{1+s_1}\sum_{k=1}^{n} \nu^{ik}\mathscr{E}(\varepsilon_{kt}\varepsilon_{jt}) = -\,\theta\sum_{k=1}^{n}\nu^{ik}\omega_{kj} = \frac{\theta}{\gamma}\sum_{k=1}^{n}\nu^{ik}\pi_{kj}$$

Hence, using (2.19) also, we find

$$\text{(2.23)} \qquad \operatorname{cov}\left(Dp_{it} - \sum_{k=1}^{n}\mu_k Dp_{kt},\, \varepsilon_{jt}\right) = \begin{cases} \dfrac{\theta}{\gamma}(1-\mu_j) & \text{if } i=j \\[2ex] -\dfrac{\theta}{\gamma}\mu_j & \text{if } i\neq j \end{cases}$$

For $j \neq n$ this implies

$$\operatorname{cov}\left(Dp_{nt} - \sum_{k=1}^{n} \mu_k Dp_{kt}, \varepsilon_{jt}\right) = -\frac{\theta}{\gamma}\mu_j$$

which we subtract from (2.23):

$$\operatorname{cov}(Dp_{it} - Dp_{nt}, \varepsilon_{jt}) = \begin{cases} \dfrac{\theta}{\gamma} & \text{if} \quad i = j < n \\ 0 & \text{if} \quad i \neq j < n \end{cases} \tag{2.24}$$

This is identical to (1.11), because the elements of $\mathbf{p}_t$ and $\boldsymbol{\varepsilon}_t$ in (1.11) are $Dp_{it} - Dp_{nt}$ and ε_{it} for $i = 1, \ldots, n-1$.

10.3 A Maximum-Likelihood Approach

In this section we consider the maximum-likelihood method under the assumption that our random variables are independently and normally distributed with covariances of the form implied by (1.12). It turns out that, owing to the presence of incidental parameters, this estimation method yields no useful results. The pragmatic reader who is interested in positive rather than negative results may wish to proceed directly to Section 10.4.

The Log-Likelihood Function

The present theory implies that both $\mathbf{z}_t$ and $\mathbf{p}_t$ of (1.12) are random vectors, each containing $n-1$ elements. We assume that the vector pairs $(\mathbf{z}_1, \mathbf{p}_1), \ldots, (\mathbf{z}_T, \mathbf{p}_T)$ are T independent random drawings from $(2n-2)$-variate normal distributions. Note that these distributions are not identical, since the expectations $(\mathscr{E}\mathbf{z}_t, \mathscr{E}\mathbf{p}_t)$ are functions of t.

It is shown in the next subsection that the log-likelihood function can be written as

$$\begin{aligned} \log L = & -(n-1)T\log 2\pi + (n-1)T\log\gamma - \tfrac{1}{2}(n-1)T\log|\Delta| \\ & -\tfrac{1}{2}\sum_{t=1}^{T}\begin{bmatrix}\mathbf{z}_t - \mathscr{E}\mathbf{z}_t \\ \mathbf{p}_t - \mathscr{E}\mathbf{p}_t\end{bmatrix}'\begin{bmatrix}\mathbf{I} & \mathbf{0} \\ \mathbf{0} & \gamma\boldsymbol{\Omega}\end{bmatrix}(\boldsymbol{\Delta}^{-1}\otimes\boldsymbol{\Omega}^{-1})\begin{bmatrix}\mathbf{I} & \mathbf{0} \\ \mathbf{0} & \gamma\boldsymbol{\Omega}\end{bmatrix}\begin{bmatrix}\mathbf{z}_t - \mathscr{E}\mathbf{z}_t \\ \mathbf{p}_t - \mathscr{E}\mathbf{p}_t\end{bmatrix}\end{aligned} \tag{3.1}$$

Remarks:

(1) The function (3.1) is to be maximized by varying all unknown parameters: γ, $\boldsymbol{\mu}_0$, $\boldsymbol{\Omega}$, $\boldsymbol{\Delta}$ as well as $\mathscr{E}\mathbf{z}_1, \ldots, \mathscr{E}\mathbf{z}_T, \mathscr{E}\mathbf{p}_1, \ldots, \mathscr{E}\mathbf{p}_T$. The last $2T$ vectors are "incidental parameters"; their number is not fixed but increases as the number of observations (T) increases.

(2) The maximization of (3.1) is subject to constraints. The matrix $\mathbf{\Delta}$ must be symmetric and, in view of (1.15), its elements must add up to 1. We also have eq. (1.7),

$$\mathscr{E}\mathbf{z}_t = \boldsymbol{\mu}_0 DQ_t - \gamma\mathbf{\Omega}\mathscr{E}\mathbf{p}_t \qquad t = 1, \ldots, T \tag{3.2}$$

which imposes constraints on the incidental parameters. Note that $\boldsymbol{\mu}_0$ occurs in (3.2) but not in (3.1).

(3) The occurrence of $\mathbf{\Delta}^{-1}$ in (3.1) implies that we have to exclude the fixed-price and fixed-quantity limits, because in both cases $\mathbf{\Delta}$ has a row and a column consisting of zero elements. However, these two limit models may be approached arbitrarily closely without violating the nonsingularity condition on $\mathbf{\Delta}$.

Derivation of the Log-Likelihood Function

Since we have

$$\begin{bmatrix} \mathbf{z}_t \\ \mathbf{p}_t \end{bmatrix} = \begin{bmatrix} \mathbf{I} & \mathbf{0} \\ \mathbf{0} & (\gamma\mathbf{\Omega})^{-1} \end{bmatrix} \begin{bmatrix} \mathbf{z}_t \\ \gamma\mathbf{\Omega}\mathbf{p}_t \end{bmatrix}$$

the covariance matrix of $(\mathbf{z}_t, \mathbf{p}_t)$ follows directly from (1.12):

$$\mathscr{V}\begin{bmatrix} \mathbf{z}_t \\ \mathbf{p}_t \end{bmatrix} = \begin{bmatrix} \mathbf{I} & \mathbf{0} \\ \mathbf{0} & (\gamma\mathbf{\Omega})^{-1} \end{bmatrix} (\mathbf{\Delta} \otimes \mathbf{\Omega}) \begin{bmatrix} \mathbf{I} & \mathbf{0} \\ \mathbf{0} & (\gamma\mathbf{\Omega})^{-1} \end{bmatrix} \tag{3.3}$$

If $\mathbf{\Delta}$ is nonsingular, the inverse of this matrix is

$$\left(\mathscr{V}\begin{bmatrix} \mathbf{z}_t \\ \mathbf{p}_t \end{bmatrix}\right)^{-1} = \begin{bmatrix} \mathbf{I} & \mathbf{0} \\ \mathbf{0} & \gamma\mathbf{\Omega} \end{bmatrix} (\mathbf{\Delta}^{-1} \otimes \mathbf{\Omega}^{-1}) \begin{bmatrix} \mathbf{I} & \mathbf{0} \\ \mathbf{0} & \gamma\mathbf{\Omega} \end{bmatrix} \tag{3.4}$$

For $\mathbf{A}$ and $\mathbf{B}$ of order $m \times m$ and $n \times n$, respectively, the determinant of $\mathbf{A} \otimes \mathbf{B}$ equals $|\mathbf{A}|^n\, |\mathbf{B}|^m$. Since the order of $\mathbf{\Delta}$ is 2×2 and that of $\mathbf{\Omega}$ is $(n-1) \times (n-1)$, we thus obtain from (3.3):

$$\left|\mathscr{V}\begin{bmatrix} \mathbf{z}_t \\ \mathbf{p}_t \end{bmatrix}\right| = \frac{1}{\gamma^{n-1}\,|\mathbf{\Omega}|}\, |\mathbf{\Delta}|^{n-1}\, |\mathbf{\Omega}|^2 \,\frac{1}{\gamma^{n-1}\,|\mathbf{\Omega}|} = \gamma^{2-2n}\, |\mathbf{\Delta}|^{n-1}$$

Hence,

$$\log\left|\mathscr{V}\begin{bmatrix} \mathbf{z}_t \\ \mathbf{p}_t \end{bmatrix}\right| = -\,2\,(n-1)\log\gamma + (n-1)\log|\mathbf{\Delta}| \tag{3.5}$$

Under normality, the log-likelihood function is the sum of three terms. The first is $\log 2\pi$ multiplied by $-\frac{1}{2}$ times the number of degrees of freedom prior to the estimation. This number is $2(n-1)\,T$. The second is $-\frac{1}{2}T$ times the logarithm of the determinant given in (3.5). The third is $-\frac{1}{2}$ times the sum of T quadratic forms based on the inverted covariance matrix (3.4). The result is shown in (3.1).

Estimation of the Incidental Parameters

We start the maximization of $\log L$ by varying the incidental parameters, for which purpose we can confine ourselves to the quadratic form in the second line of (3.1). We have

$$\begin{bmatrix} \mathbf{I} & \mathbf{0} \\ \mathbf{0} & \gamma\mathbf{\Omega} \end{bmatrix} \begin{bmatrix} \mathbf{z}_t - \mathscr{E}\mathbf{z}_t \\ \mathbf{p}_t - \mathscr{E}\mathbf{p}_t \end{bmatrix} = \begin{bmatrix} \mathbf{z}_t - \mathscr{E}\mathbf{z}_t \\ \gamma\mathbf{\Omega}(\mathbf{p}_t - \mathscr{E}\mathbf{p}_t) \end{bmatrix} = \begin{bmatrix} \mathbf{z}_t - \boldsymbol{\mu}_0 DQ_t + \gamma\mathbf{\Omega}\mathscr{E}\mathbf{p}_t \\ \gamma\mathbf{\Omega}\mathbf{p}_t - \gamma\mathbf{\Omega}\mathscr{E}\mathbf{p}_t \end{bmatrix}$$

where the second step is based on (3.2). We may write this result as

$$(3.6) \qquad \begin{bmatrix} \mathbf{I} & \mathbf{0} \\ \mathbf{0} & \gamma\mathbf{\Omega} \end{bmatrix} \begin{bmatrix} \mathbf{z}_t - \mathscr{E}\mathbf{z}_t \\ \mathbf{p}_t - \mathscr{E}\mathbf{p}_t \end{bmatrix} = \begin{bmatrix} \mathbf{z}_t - \boldsymbol{\mu}_0 DQ_t \\ \gamma\mathbf{\Omega}\mathbf{p}_t \end{bmatrix} + \begin{bmatrix} 1 \\ -1 \end{bmatrix} \otimes (\gamma\mathbf{\Omega}\mathscr{E}\mathbf{p}_t)$$

Note that the right-hand side of this equation separates the incidental parameters from the others. Let us write it as $\mathbf{a}_t + \mathbf{b}_t$, where

$$(3.7) \qquad \mathbf{a}_t = \begin{bmatrix} \mathbf{z}_t - \boldsymbol{\mu}_0 DQ_t \\ \gamma\mathbf{\Omega}\mathbf{p}_t \end{bmatrix} \qquad \mathbf{b}_t = \begin{bmatrix} 1 \\ -1 \end{bmatrix} \otimes (\gamma\mathbf{\Omega}\mathscr{E}\mathbf{p}_t)$$

The expression after the summation sign in (3.1) can then be written as

$$(\mathbf{a}_t + \mathbf{b}_t)' (\mathbf{\Delta}^{-1} \otimes \mathbf{\Omega}^{-1}) (\mathbf{a}_t + \mathbf{b}_t)$$

Note that this is the only component of $\log L$ which contains $\mathscr{E}\mathbf{p}_t$. Also note that $\mathbf{a}_t'(\mathbf{\Delta}^{-1} \otimes \mathbf{\Omega}^{-1})\,\mathbf{a}_t$ does not involve $\mathscr{E}\mathbf{p}_t$. Therefore, given the factor $-\frac{1}{2}$ before the summation sign in (3.1), maximizing $\log L$ with respect to $\mathscr{E}\mathbf{p}_t$ is equivalent to minimizing

$$(3.8) \qquad \mathbf{b}_t'(\mathbf{\Delta}^{-1} \otimes \mathbf{\Omega}^{-1})\,\mathbf{b}_t + 2\mathbf{b}_t'(\mathbf{\Delta}^{-1} \otimes \mathbf{\Omega}^{-1})\,\mathbf{a}_t$$

It is shown in the next subsection that the expression (3.8) is equal to a positive multiple of

$$(3.9) \qquad \tfrac{1}{2}\gamma(\mathscr{E}\mathbf{p}_t)'\,\mathbf{\Omega}\mathscr{E}\mathbf{p}_t + (\mathscr{E}\mathbf{p}_t)'\,[\theta(\mathbf{z}_t - \boldsymbol{\mu}_0 DQ_t) - (1-\theta)\,\gamma\mathbf{\Omega}\mathbf{p}_t]$$

Since this is to be minimized for variations in $\mathscr{E}\mathbf{p}_t$, we differentiate with respect to this vector:

$$\gamma\mathbf{\Omega}\mathscr{E}\mathbf{p}_t + \theta(\mathbf{z}_t - \boldsymbol{\mu}_0 DQ_t) - (1-\theta)\,\gamma\mathbf{\Omega}\mathbf{p}_t$$

By equating this to zero we obtain

$$\text{(3.10)} \qquad \text{Estimate of } \gamma\mathbf{\Omega}\mathscr{E}\mathbf{p}_t = -\theta(\mathbf{z}_t - \boldsymbol{\mu}_0 DQ_t) + (1-\theta)\gamma\mathbf{\Omega}\mathbf{p}_t$$

from which the implied estimate of $\mathscr{E}\mathbf{p}_t$ is obtained by premultiplication by $(\gamma\mathbf{\Omega})^{-1}$, and that of $\mathscr{E}\mathbf{z}_t$ from (3.2).

Derivations for the Incidental Parameters

Write δ^{ij} for the $(i, j)^{\text{th}}$ element of $\mathbf{\Delta}^{-1}$. Hence,

$$\begin{bmatrix} \delta^{11} & \delta^{12} \\ \delta^{12} & \delta^{22} \end{bmatrix} = \frac{1}{|\mathbf{\Delta}|}\begin{bmatrix} \delta_{22} & -\delta_{12} \\ -\delta_{12} & \delta_{11} \end{bmatrix}$$

from which we derive, using (1.16),

$$\text{(3.11)} \qquad \delta^{11} - \delta^{12} = (\delta_{22} + \delta_{12})\,|\mathbf{\Delta}^{-1}| = \theta\,|\mathbf{\Delta}^{-1}|$$

$$\text{(3.12)} \qquad \delta^{12} - \delta^{22} = -(\delta_{12} + \delta_{11})\,|\mathbf{\Delta}^{-1}| = -(1-\theta)\,|\mathbf{\Delta}^{-1}|$$

Subtraction gives

$$\text{(3.13)} \qquad \delta^{11} - 2\delta^{12} + \delta^{22} = |\mathbf{\Delta}^{-1}|$$

Using (3.7), we write the first term of (3.8) as

$$\left([1 \quad -1] \otimes (\gamma\mathbf{\Omega}\mathscr{E}\mathbf{p}_t)'\right)(\mathbf{\Delta}^{-1} \otimes \mathbf{\Omega}^{-1})\left[\begin{pmatrix} 1 \\ -1 \end{pmatrix} \otimes (\gamma\mathbf{\Omega}\mathscr{E}\mathbf{p}_t)\right]$$
$$= \left([1 \quad -1]\,\mathbf{\Delta}^{-1}\begin{bmatrix} 1 \\ -1 \end{bmatrix}\right)(\gamma\mathbf{\Omega}\mathscr{E}\mathbf{p}_t)'\,\mathbf{\Omega}^{-1}(\gamma\mathbf{\Omega}\mathscr{E}\mathbf{p}_t)$$

The quadratic form within large parentheses in the second line is equal to the left-hand side of (3.13). Therefore,

$$\text{(3.14)} \qquad \mathbf{b}_t'(\mathbf{\Delta}^{-1} \otimes \mathbf{\Omega}^{-1})\,\mathbf{b}_t = \gamma^2\,|\mathbf{\Delta}^{-1}|\,(\mathscr{E}\mathbf{p}_t)'\,\mathbf{\Omega}\mathscr{E}\mathbf{p}_t$$

The second term of (3.8) can similarly be written as

$$\text{(3.15)} \qquad 2\left([1 \quad -1] \otimes (\gamma\mathbf{\Omega}\mathscr{E}\mathbf{p}_t)'\right)(\mathbf{\Delta}^{-1} \otimes \mathbf{\Omega}^{-1})\begin{bmatrix} \mathbf{z}_t - \boldsymbol{\mu}_0 DQ_t \\ \gamma\mathbf{\Omega}\mathbf{p}_t \end{bmatrix}$$

To evaluate this expression we consider

$$\left([1 \quad -1] \otimes (\gamma\mathbf{\Omega}\mathscr{E}\mathbf{p}_t)'\right)(\mathbf{\Delta}^{-1} \otimes \mathbf{\Omega}^{-1}) = \left([1 \quad -1]\,\mathbf{\Delta}^{-1}\right) \otimes (\gamma\mathscr{E}\mathbf{p}_t)'$$
$$= [\delta^{11} - \delta^{12} \quad \delta^{12} - \delta^{22}] \otimes (\gamma\mathscr{E}\mathbf{p}_t)'$$

which is equal to $\gamma|\mathbf{\Delta}^{-1}|\,[\theta(\mathscr{E}\mathbf{p}_t)' \quad -(1-\theta)\,(\mathscr{E}\mathbf{p}_t)']$ in view of (3.11) and (3.12). By substituting this in (3.15) we obtain

$$2\gamma\,|\mathbf{\Delta}^{-1}|\,[\theta(\mathscr{E}\mathbf{p}_t)'\,(\mathbf{z}_t - \boldsymbol{\mu}_0 DQ_t) - (1-\theta)\,(\mathscr{E}\mathbf{p}_t)'\,(\gamma\mathbf{\Omega}\mathbf{p}_t)]$$

When this is added to (3.14) a multiple $2\gamma|\mathbf{\Delta}^{-1}|$ of the expression (3.9) results.

Substitution of the Estimated Incidental Parameters

We proceed to substitute the estimate (3.10) in (3.6),

$$\begin{bmatrix} \mathbf{I} & \mathbf{0} \\ \mathbf{0} & \gamma\mathbf{\Omega} \end{bmatrix} \begin{bmatrix} \mathbf{z}_t - \mathscr{E}\mathbf{z}_t \\ \mathbf{p}_t - \mathscr{E}\mathbf{p}_t \end{bmatrix} = \begin{bmatrix} \mathbf{z}_t - \boldsymbol{\mu}_0 DQ_t \\ \gamma\mathbf{\Omega}\mathbf{p}_t \end{bmatrix} + \begin{bmatrix} -\theta(\mathbf{z}_t - \boldsymbol{\mu}_0 DQ_t) + (1-\theta)\gamma\mathbf{\Omega}\mathbf{p}_t \\ \theta(\mathbf{z}_t - \boldsymbol{\mu}_0 DQ_t) - (1-\theta)\gamma\mathbf{\Omega}\mathbf{p}_t \end{bmatrix}$$

$$= \begin{bmatrix} (1-\theta)(\mathbf{z}_t - \boldsymbol{\mu}_0 DQ_t + \gamma\mathbf{\Omega}\mathbf{p}_t) \\ \theta(\mathbf{z}_t - \boldsymbol{\mu}_0 DQ_t + \gamma\mathbf{\Omega}\mathbf{p}_t) \end{bmatrix}$$

which can be written more conveniently as

$$(3.16) \qquad \begin{bmatrix} \mathbf{I} & \mathbf{0} \\ \mathbf{0} & \gamma\mathbf{\Omega} \end{bmatrix} \begin{bmatrix} \mathbf{z}_t - \mathscr{E}\mathbf{z}_t \\ \mathbf{p}_t - \mathscr{E}\mathbf{p}_t \end{bmatrix} = \begin{bmatrix} 1-\theta \\ \theta \end{bmatrix} \otimes (\mathbf{z}_t - \boldsymbol{\mu}_0 DQ_t + \gamma\mathbf{\Omega}\mathbf{p}_t)$$

Therefore, when this substitution is made, the expression after the summation sign in (3.1) becomes the product of two quadratic forms,

$$(3.17) \qquad [1-\theta \quad \theta]\,\mathbf{\Delta}^{-1} \begin{bmatrix} 1-\theta \\ \theta \end{bmatrix} = 1$$

and

$$(3.18) \qquad (\mathbf{z}_t - \boldsymbol{\mu}_0 DQ_t + \gamma\mathbf{\Omega}\mathbf{p}_t)'\,\mathbf{\Omega}^{-1}(\mathbf{z}_t - \boldsymbol{\mu}_0 DQ_t + \gamma\mathbf{\Omega}\mathbf{p}_t)$$

To verify the equal sign in (3.17) we write (1.16) as

$$[1 \quad 1]\,\mathbf{\Delta} = [1-\theta \quad \theta]$$

or $[1 \quad 1] = [1-\theta \quad \theta]\,\mathbf{\Delta}^{-1}$. Postmultiplication by $[1-\theta \quad \theta]'$ gives 1 on the left and the quadratic form (3.17) on the right. This proves the equal sign of (3.17) and, hence, that the quadratic form (3.18) equals the expression after the summation sign in (3.1) when the estimate (3.10) is substituted in the log-likelihood function.

We conclude that when this function is maximized by varying the incidental parameters subject to (3.2), the resulting maximum – which is still a function of the other parameters – becomes

$$(3.19) \qquad -(n-1)\,T\log 2\pi + (n-1)\,T\log\gamma - \tfrac{1}{2}(n-1)\,T\log|\mathbf{\Delta}|$$
$$- \tfrac{1}{2}\sum_{t=1}^{T} (\mathbf{z}_t - \boldsymbol{\mu}_0 DQ_t + \gamma\mathbf{\Omega}\mathbf{p}_t)'\,\mathbf{\Omega}^{-1}(\mathbf{z}_t - \boldsymbol{\mu}_0 DQ_t + \gamma\mathbf{\Omega}\mathbf{p}_t)$$

Note that this function contains $\mathbf{\Delta}$ only in determinantal form; the matrix no longer occurs in the quadratic form. Since the logarithm of $|\mathbf{\Delta}|$ is multiplied by a negative number, we can raise the value of the function (3.19) arbitrarily by letting $\mathbf{\Delta}$ approach singularity. Hence the likelihood function has no finite maximum. The matrix $\mathbf{\Delta}$ can approach singularity when either δ_{11} or δ_{22} moves toward zero, or when $\pm\delta_{12}$ moves toward the geometric mean of δ_{11} and δ_{22} (both positive). This shows that $\mathbf{\Delta}$ has no unique maximum-likelihood estimator.

The situation is different when $\mathbf{\Delta}$ is assumed to be known, because the third term of (3.19) then becomes a known constant. However, when we maximize (3.19) thus modified with respect to the remaining parameters, the result will be completely independent of $\mathbf{\Delta}$, which is not particularly reassuring.

Concluding Comments

It is not unknown that the maximum-likelihood method faces difficulties when there are incidental parameters. Consider the following, much simpler, example.[1] Let there be T independent normal random variables $x_1, \dots, x_T$ with unknown means $\theta_1, \dots, \theta_T$ and the same positive but otherwise unknown variance σ^2. The θ's are thus the incidental parameters in this problem. The log-likelihood function is

$$(3.20) \qquad -\tfrac{1}{2}T\log 2\pi - \tfrac{1}{2}T\log\sigma^2 - \frac{1}{2\sigma^2}\sum_{t=1}^{T}(x_t-\theta_t)^2$$

When we differentiate this function with respect to $\theta_1, \dots, \theta_T$ and equate the derivatives to zero, we obtain $\hat{\theta}_t = x_t$ for each t, where $\hat{\theta}_t$ is the estimate of θ_t produced by the maximum-likelihood method. Subsequent differentiation with respect to σ^2 yields

$$(3.21) \qquad \hat{\sigma}^2 = \frac{1}{T}\sum_{t=1}^{T}(x_t-\hat{\theta}_t)^2$$

which is zero because $\hat{\theta}_t = x_t$ for each t. Thus $\hat{\sigma}^2 = 0$ in spite of the prior specification that σ^2 is positive. This may be compared with the singularity of the $\mathbf{\Delta}$ "estimator" obtained by maximizing (3.19). There is another similarity in that (3.20) does not have a finite maximum.

[1] See KENDALL and STUART (1967, p. 61 and also pp. 375–418). A detailed account of econometric problems which arise when several variables in an equation have random components has been given by MALINVAUD (1970, Chapter 10).

It is also interesting to compare the log-likelihood function with that of the fixed-price model. The latter function is

$$(3.22)\qquad \log L = -\tfrac{1}{2}(n-1)\,T\log 2\pi - \tfrac{1}{2}T\log|\boldsymbol{\Omega}| - \tfrac{1}{2}\sum_{t=1}^{T}(\mathbf{z}_t - \boldsymbol{\mu}_0 DQ_t + \gamma\boldsymbol{\Omega}\mathbf{p}_t)'\,\boldsymbol{\Omega}^{-1}(\mathbf{z}_t - \boldsymbol{\mu}_0 DQ_t + \gamma\boldsymbol{\Omega}\mathbf{p}_t)$$

which is the unconditional version of eq. (4.9) of Section 7.4. The present log-likelihood function is (3.1), but it should be understood that the right-hand side of (3.2) is substituted for $\mathscr{E}\mathbf{z}_t$; this shows how γ, $\boldsymbol{\mu}_0$, $\boldsymbol{\Omega}$ and $\mathscr{E}\mathbf{p}_t$ occur in the quadratic term. The differences between the two log-likelihood functions are striking; they are not at all confined to the occurrence of incidental parameters in (3.1). The only parameter matrix in the logarithmic term of (3.22) is $\boldsymbol{\Omega}$. In the case of (3.1) there is no $\boldsymbol{\Omega}$ in the logarithmic term, but we do have γ in this term (besides $\boldsymbol{\Delta}$) which occurs in (3.22) only in the quadratic term.

10.4 A Conditionally Consistent Estimation Method

This section develops an estimation method which, conditionally on the degree of price-disturbance dependence (θ), yields consistent estimators. The conditional nature of the procedure implies that we have to specify a certain value of θ or that we work with alternative values. It will appear that the method, although it is not maximum likelihood, is a simple extension of the maximum-likelihood method of Section 7.4.

Notation

Since we shall want to compare the new results with those of Section 7.4, it is convenient to use the notation of that section. So we replace (1.6) by

$$(4.1)\qquad \mathbf{z}_t = \boldsymbol{\mu}_0 DQ_{gt} - \gamma\boldsymbol{\Omega}\mathbf{p}_t + \boldsymbol{\varepsilon}_t$$

where DQ_{gt} is the log-change in the volume of total-meat consumption and $\mathbf{z}_t = [\bar{w}_{it}Dq_{it}/\bar{W}_{gt}]$ is the vector of the quantity components of the changes in the conditional budget shares of Beef, Pork and Chicken.[1] All vectors in (4.1) contain three elements and the order of $\boldsymbol{\Omega}$ is 3×3; the relevant symbols are as defined in eqs. (4.3) and (4.8) of Section 7.4.

[1] When we formulate this conditional version in terms of the natural conjugate supply model of Section 10.2, this has to be done by means of conditional supply equations. Such equations are described in Section 14.7; the specific case of meats is considered in Section 14.9.

By subtracting $\boldsymbol{\mu}_0 DQ_{gt}$ from both sides of (4.1) we obtain the left-hand variable corrected for the effect of the change in the volume of total-meat consumption:

$$\mathbf{z}_t - \boldsymbol{\mu}_0 DQ_{gt} = -\gamma\boldsymbol{\Omega}\mathbf{p}_t + \boldsymbol{\varepsilon}_t \tag{4.2}$$

The matrix of mean squares and products of these corrected variables is

$$\mathbf{M}_0 = \frac{1}{T}\sum_{t=1}^{T} (\mathbf{z}_t - \boldsymbol{\mu}_0 DQ_{gt})(\mathbf{z}_t - \boldsymbol{\mu}_0 DQ_{gt})' \tag{4.3}$$

and that of the deflated price log-changes, $Dp_{it} - Dp_{4t}$ for $i=1$, 2 and 3, is

$$\mathbf{E}'\mathbf{E} = \frac{1}{T}\sum_{t=1}^{T} \mathbf{p}_t\mathbf{p}_t' \tag{4.4}$$

The definitions (4.3) and (4.4) are identical to eqs. (4.16) and (4.15), respectively, of Section 7.4.

We shall use the second-moment model in the form (1.10) and in particular its implication (1.11),

$$\mathscr{E}(\mathbf{p}_t\boldsymbol{\varepsilon}_t') = \frac{\theta}{\gamma}\mathbf{I}_3 \tag{4.5}$$

where $\mathbf{I}_3$ is the 3×3 unit matrix.

An Estimation Equation for the Conditional Marginal Shares

Recall that we treated DQ_t as predetermined in (1.6), using a blockwise dependence specification in a multiperiod framework. In the same way we treat DQ_{gt} as predetermined in (4.1), using a blockwise dependence specification in the one-period framework with meats constituting one of the commodity groups.

Now multiply (4.1) by DQ_{gt}, sum over t, and multiply by $1/T$:

(4.6)

$$\frac{1}{T}\sum_{t=1}^{T} (DQ_{gt})\mathbf{z}_t = \boldsymbol{\mu}_0\frac{1}{T}\sum_{t=1}^{T} (DQ_{gt})^2 - \gamma\boldsymbol{\Omega}\frac{1}{T}\sum_{t=1}^{T} (DQ_{gt})\mathbf{p}_t + \frac{1}{T}\sum_{t=1}^{T} (DQ_{gt})\boldsymbol{\varepsilon}_t$$

Since DQ_{gt} is predetermined, the last term on the right has zero expectation. Let us replace this term by its expectation, so that (4.6) can be written as

$$\boldsymbol{\mu}_0\frac{1}{T}\sum_{t=1}^{T} (DQ_{gt})^2 = \frac{1}{T}\sum_{t=1}^{T} DQ_{gt}(\mathbf{z}_t + \gamma\boldsymbol{\Omega}\mathbf{p}_t) \tag{4.7}$$

This will be interpreted as an estimation equation for $\boldsymbol{\mu}_0$. It can be used to obtain an estimate of $\boldsymbol{\mu}_0$ when estimates of γ and $\boldsymbol{\Omega}$ are available.

Note that (4.7) is identical to the second equation of the vector equation (4.20) of Section 7.4, which was obtained by equating the derivative of the log-likelihood function with respect to $\boldsymbol{\mu}_0$ to zero. Hence the algebraic results are the same, but (4.7) is not obtained by maximizing a likelihood function.

An Estimation Equation for the Connecting Parameter

Postmultiply (4.2) by $(T^{-1}\mathbf{p}_t)'$ and sum over t:

$$\frac{1}{T}\sum_{t=1}^{T}(\mathbf{z}_t - \boldsymbol{\mu}_0 DQ_{gt})\,\mathbf{p}_t' = -\gamma\boldsymbol{\Omega}\frac{1}{T}\sum_{t=1}^{T}\mathbf{p}_t\mathbf{p}_t' + \frac{1}{T}\sum_{t=1}^{T}\boldsymbol{\varepsilon}_t\mathbf{p}_t'$$

In view of (4.4), this may be written as

$$\frac{1}{T}\sum_{t=1}^{T}(\mathbf{z}_t - \boldsymbol{\mu}_0 DQ_{gt})\,\mathbf{p}_t' = -\gamma\boldsymbol{\Omega}\mathbf{E}'\mathbf{E} + \frac{1}{T}\sum_{t=1}^{T}\boldsymbol{\varepsilon}_t\mathbf{p}_t' \tag{4.8}$$

Now take the trace of both sides, using $\operatorname{tr}\mathbf{ab}' = \operatorname{tr}\mathbf{b}'\mathbf{a} = \mathbf{b}'\mathbf{a}$ for any pair of vectors $\mathbf{a}$, $\mathbf{b}$ consisting of an equal number of elements:

$$\frac{1}{T}\sum_{t=1}^{T}\mathbf{p}_t'(\mathbf{z}_t - \boldsymbol{\mu}_0 DQ_{gt}) = -\gamma\operatorname{tr}\boldsymbol{\Omega}\mathbf{E}'\mathbf{E} + \frac{1}{T}\sum_{t=1}^{T}\mathbf{p}_t'\boldsymbol{\varepsilon}_t \tag{4.9}$$

Since $\mathbf{p}_t\boldsymbol{\varepsilon}_t'$ has expectation $(\theta/\gamma)\,\mathbf{I}_3$ in view of (4.5), $\mathbf{p}_t'\boldsymbol{\varepsilon}_t = \operatorname{tr}\mathbf{p}_t\boldsymbol{\varepsilon}_t'$ has an expectation equal to $3\theta/\gamma$. When we substitute this expectation in (4.9), an estimation equation for γ results:

$$\frac{1}{T}\sum_{t=1}^{T}\mathbf{p}_t'(\mathbf{z}_t - \boldsymbol{\mu}_0 DQ_{gt}) = -\gamma\operatorname{tr}\boldsymbol{\Omega}\mathbf{E}'\mathbf{E} + \frac{3\theta}{\gamma} \tag{4.10}$$

Note that the derivation of (4.10) from (4.9) amounts to an extension of the instrumental-variable method. If $\mathbf{p}_t$ were used as an instrumental-variable vector, the last term in (4.9) would be replaced by zero in the instrumental-variable estimation equation. But this term has nonzero expectation under the present model, which is in conflict with the instrumental-variable assumptions. The procedure is generalized by (4.10), which replaces the term by its nonzero expectation.

An Estimation Equation for Ω

Next postmultiply (4.2) by $T^{-1}(\mathbf{z}_t - \boldsymbol{\mu}_0 DQ_{gt})'$ and sum over t. The left-hand side becomes $\mathbf{M}_0$ defined in (4.3), so that we obtain

$$\mathbf{M}_0 = -\gamma\boldsymbol{\Omega}\frac{1}{T}\sum_{t=1}^{T}\mathbf{p}_t(\mathbf{z}_t - \boldsymbol{\mu}_0 DQ_{gt})' + \frac{1}{T}\sum_{t=1}^{T}\boldsymbol{\varepsilon}_t(\mathbf{z}_t - \boldsymbol{\mu}_0 DQ_{gt})' \tag{4.11}$$

The first term on the right is $-\gamma\mathbf{\Omega}$ postmultiplied by the transpose of the left-hand side of (4.8). So, using the right-hand side of (4.8), we write this term as

$$\gamma^2\mathbf{\Omega E'E\Omega} - \gamma\mathbf{\Omega}\frac{1}{T}\sum_{t=1}^{T}\mathbf{p}_t\boldsymbol{\varepsilon}_t' \tag{4.12}$$

For the second term in the right-hand side of (4.11) we use (4.2):

$$\frac{1}{T}\sum_{t=1}^{T}\boldsymbol{\varepsilon}_t\boldsymbol{\varepsilon}_t' - \frac{1}{T}\sum_{t=1}^{T}\boldsymbol{\varepsilon}_t\mathbf{p}_t'(\gamma\mathbf{\Omega})' \tag{4.13}$$

By adding (4.12) and (4.13), we find that (4.11) can be written as

(4.14)
$$\mathbf{M}_0 = \gamma^2\mathbf{\Omega E'E\Omega} + \frac{1}{T}\sum_{t=1}^{T}\boldsymbol{\varepsilon}_t\boldsymbol{\varepsilon}_t' - \gamma\mathbf{\Omega}\frac{1}{T}\sum_{t=1}^{T}\mathbf{p}_t\boldsymbol{\varepsilon}_t' - \left(\gamma\mathbf{\Omega}\frac{1}{T}\sum_{t=1}^{T}\mathbf{p}_t\boldsymbol{\varepsilon}_t'\right)'$$

The last three terms in this equation involve disturbances. The first of these, $(1/T)\sum_t\boldsymbol{\varepsilon}_t\boldsymbol{\varepsilon}_t'$, has expectation $\mathscr{V}(\boldsymbol{\varepsilon}_t)=\mathbf{\Omega}$. The expectation of the second is $-\theta\mathbf{\Omega}$ in view of (4.5). Since this is symmetric, the third term has the same expectation. So we obtain, by replacing these three terms by their expectations,

$$\gamma^2\mathbf{\Omega E'E\Omega} + (1-2\theta)\,\mathbf{\Omega} - \mathbf{M}_0 = \mathbf{0} \tag{4.15}$$

which is the estimation equation for $\mathbf{\Omega}$.

Comparison with the Fixed-Price Limit

Recall from the discussion below (4.7) that this estimation equation is identical to the corresponding maximum-likelihood equation of Section 7.4. This holds for any value of θ because θ does not occur in (4.7).

Equation (4.15) should be compared with eq. (4.21) of Section 7.4,

$$\gamma^2\mathbf{\Omega E'E\Omega} + \mathbf{\Omega} - \mathbf{M}_0 = \mathbf{0} \tag{4.16}$$

which was obtained by equating the derivative of the log-likelihood function with respect to $\mathbf{\Omega}^{-1}$ to zero. At $\theta=0$ the two equations, (4.15) and (4.16), are identical. So, if the fixed-price limit is used, which implies $\theta=0$, the estimation equation (4.15) is equivalent to the maximum-likelihood equation (4.16).

The maximum-likelihood equation for γ under the fixed-price limit is obtained from eq. (4.20) of Section 7.4:

$$\gamma\sum_{t=1}^{T}\mathbf{p}_t'\mathbf{\Omega}\mathbf{p}_t = -\sum_{t=1}^{T}\mathbf{p}_t'(\mathbf{z}_t - \boldsymbol{\mu}_0 DQ_{gt})$$

This is equivalent to the estimation equation (4.10) at $\theta=0$ because

$$\text{(4.17)} \qquad \operatorname{tr} \boldsymbol{\Omega}\mathbf{E}'\mathbf{E} = \operatorname{tr} \boldsymbol{\Omega} \frac{1}{T} \sum_{t=1}^{T} \mathbf{p}_t \mathbf{p}_t' = \frac{1}{T} \sum_{t=1}^{T} \mathbf{p}_t' \boldsymbol{\Omega} \mathbf{p}_t$$

We conclude that the approach based on the estimation equations (4.7), (4.10) and (4.15) is identical to maximum likelihood under the conditions of the fixed-price limit.

The Conditional Nature of the Estimator and Its Consistency

The matrix equation (4.15) consists of as many scalar equations as there are $\boldsymbol{\Omega}$ elements to be estimated. This is also true for (4.7) and (4.10) with respect to $\boldsymbol{\mu}_0$ and γ, respectively. The problem of how to obtain estimates from these equations is considered in Section 10.6. Note that there is no estimation equation for θ. This parameter has to be specified numerically, which means that the estimators of γ, $\boldsymbol{\mu}_0$ and $\boldsymbol{\Omega}$ are conditional estimators.

In the next subsection we prove that these estimators are consistent under two assumptions (and, of course, conditionally on θ). First, as $T \to \infty$, the second moments

$$\frac{1}{T} \sum_{t=1}^{T} (DQ_{gt})^2 \quad \text{and} \quad \frac{1}{T} \sum_{t=1}^{T} \mathscr{E}\mathbf{p}_t (\mathscr{E}\mathbf{p}_t)'$$

converge to finite limits, the first limit being a positive scalar and the second a positive definite 3×3 matrix. Second, the vectors

$$\text{(4.18)} \qquad \mathbf{v}_t = \begin{bmatrix} \mathbf{z}_t - \mathscr{E}\mathbf{z}_t \\ \gamma\boldsymbol{\Omega}(\mathbf{p}_t - \mathscr{E}\mathbf{p}_t) \end{bmatrix}$$

for $t=1,\ldots,T$ are independent random drawings from a six-dimensional distribution with zero means and a covariance matrix of the form (1.12) for some symmetric positive semidefinite 2×2 matrix $\boldsymbol{\Lambda}$ which satisfies (1.15). In contrast to the maximum-likelihood approach of Section 10.3, we do not assume that this distribution is normal.

Recall from (1.14) that $\boldsymbol{\varepsilon}_t$ equals $[\mathbf{I} \quad \mathbf{I}]\, \mathbf{v}_t$, with $\mathbf{I}=\mathbf{I}_3$ in the case discussed here. The second assumption thus implies that $\boldsymbol{\varepsilon}_1,\ldots,\boldsymbol{\varepsilon}_T$ are independent random drawings from a three-dimensional distribution with zero means and covariance matrix $\boldsymbol{\Omega}$.

Proof of the Conditional Consistency

To prove the conditional consistency it is sufficient to show that the terms which have been replaced by their expectations converge in probability to these expectations as $T \to \infty$. In the case of (4.6) this term is the average over t of $(DQ_{gt})\,\boldsymbol{\varepsilon}_t$, which is a random vector with zero expectation and a covariance matrix equal to

$$\frac{1}{T^2}\sum_{s=1}^{T}\sum_{t=1}^{T} DQ_{gs}DQ_{gt}\mathscr{E}(\boldsymbol{\varepsilon}_s\boldsymbol{\varepsilon}_t') = \frac{1}{T^2}\sum_{t=1}^{T}(DQ_{gt})^2\,\mathscr{E}(\boldsymbol{\varepsilon}_t\boldsymbol{\varepsilon}_t')$$
$$= T^{-1}\boldsymbol{\Omega}\left[\frac{1}{T}\sum_{t=1}^{T}(DQ_{gt})^2\right]$$

where the first step is based on the serial independence of the $\boldsymbol{\varepsilon}$'s and their zero means. Given the assumption on the limiting behavior of the mean square of $DQ_{g1},\ldots, DQ_{gT}$, the factor T^{-1} in the second line insures that the covariance matrix converges to zero as $T \to \infty$. It then follows from Chebyshev's inequality that the disturbance term of (4.6) converges in probability to its expectation (zero).

Next consider (4.14). The second term on the right is the average of T random variables, $\boldsymbol{\varepsilon}_1\boldsymbol{\varepsilon}_1',\ldots, \boldsymbol{\varepsilon}_T\boldsymbol{\varepsilon}_T'$, which are independently and identically distributed. Khintchine's theorem implies that this average converges in probability to the expectation of these variables, $\mathscr{E}(\boldsymbol{\varepsilon}_t\boldsymbol{\varepsilon}_t')=\boldsymbol{\Omega}$. The third term in (4.14) may be written as

$$-\gamma\boldsymbol{\Omega}\frac{1}{T}\sum_{t=1}^{T}(\mathscr{E}\mathbf{p}_t)\,\boldsymbol{\varepsilon}_t' - \gamma\boldsymbol{\Omega}\frac{1}{T}\sum_{t=1}^{T}(\mathbf{p}_t - \mathscr{E}\mathbf{p}_t)\,\boldsymbol{\varepsilon}_t'$$

In the next subsection we prove

$$\text{(4.19)} \qquad \operatorname*{plim}_{T\to\infty}\frac{1}{T}\sum_{t=1}^{T}(\mathscr{E}\mathbf{p}_t)\,\boldsymbol{\varepsilon}_t' = \mathbf{0}$$

$$\text{(4.20)} \qquad \operatorname*{plim}_{T\to\infty}\frac{1}{T}\sum_{t=1}^{T}\gamma\boldsymbol{\Omega}(\mathbf{p}_t - \mathscr{E}\mathbf{p}_t)\,\boldsymbol{\varepsilon}_t' = \theta\boldsymbol{\Omega}$$

so that the third term of (4.14) has probability limit $-\theta\boldsymbol{\Omega}$. Since the fourth term is the transpose of the third, the sum of the three disturbance terms in (4.14) has $(1-2\theta)\,\boldsymbol{\Omega}$ as its probability limit, which is identical to the expectation used in (4.15).

The disturbance term of (4.9) may be written as

$$\text{(4.21)} \qquad \operatorname{tr}\frac{1}{T}\sum_{t=1}^{T}\mathbf{p}_t\boldsymbol{\varepsilon}_t' = \operatorname{tr}(\gamma\boldsymbol{\Omega})^{-1}\gamma\boldsymbol{\Omega}\frac{1}{T}\sum_{t=1}^{T}\mathbf{p}_t\boldsymbol{\varepsilon}_t'$$

The trace on the right is that of the matrix obtained by postmultiplying $(\gamma\boldsymbol{\Omega})^{-1}$ by minus the third term of (4.14). We proved in the previous paragraph that this term has probability limit $-\theta\mathbf{\Omega}$, so that (4.21) converges in probability to the trace of $(\gamma\mathbf{\Omega})^{-1}(\theta\mathbf{\Omega})=(\theta/\gamma)\,\mathbf{I}_3$, which is $3\theta/\gamma$ in agreement with the expectation used in (4.10).

Derivations

The $(i,j)^{\text{th}}$ element of the 3×3 matrix in the left-hand side of (4.19) is

$$\frac{1}{T}\sum_{t=1}^{T}\left[\mathscr{E}(Dp_{it}-Dp_{4t})\right]\varepsilon_{jt}^{*} \tag{4.22}$$

This is a random variable with zero mean. Using the serial independence and the zero means of the ε's, we find for its variance:

$$\frac{1}{T^2}\sum_{t=1}^{T}\left[\mathscr{E}(Dp_{it}-Dp_{4t})\right]^2\mathscr{E}\varepsilon_{jt}^{*2}=\frac{\omega_{jj}}{T}\left(\frac{1}{T}\sum_{t=1}^{T}\left[\mathscr{E}(Dp_{it}-Dp_{4t})\right]^2\right)$$

The right-hand side is a multiple ω_{jj}/T of a diagonal element of the matrix $(1/T)\sum_t \mathscr{E}\mathbf{p}_t(\mathscr{E}\mathbf{p}_t)'$. These diagonal elements converge by assumption to finite positive numbers as $T\to\infty$, so that the multiplication by ω_{jj}/T insures that the variance of (4.22) converges to zero. Application of Chebyshev's inequality completes the proof of (4.19).

With $\mathbf{v}_t$ defined in (4.18), consider

$$\frac{1}{T}\sum_{t=1}^{T}\gamma\mathbf{\Omega}(\mathbf{p}_t-\mathscr{E}\mathbf{p}_t)\,\boldsymbol{\varepsilon}_t'=[\mathbf{0}\quad\mathbf{I}_3]\left(\frac{1}{T}\sum_{t=1}^{T}\mathbf{v}_t\mathbf{v}_t'\right)\begin{bmatrix}\mathbf{I}_3\\ \mathbf{I}_3\end{bmatrix} \tag{4.23}$$

The matrix $(1/T)\sum_t \mathbf{v}_t\mathbf{v}_t'$ is the average of T independently and identically distributed random variables and, hence, converges in probability to $\mathscr{V}(\mathbf{v}_t)$ given in (1.12). Using (1.16), we find that the right-hand side of (4.23) converges in probability to $\theta\mathbf{\Omega}$, in agreement with (4.20).

10.5 The Demand for Meats in the United States: (10) The Case of Endogenous Price and Quantity Changes

Table 10.1 contains the estimates of the conditional marginal shares and the modified conditional Slutsky coefficients for θ increments of .1 from 0 to 1, with B, P, C and L standing for Beef, Pork, Chicken and Lamb. The estimates of the connecting parameter and the disturbance covariance matrix are given in Table 10.2; an extra decimal place is provided, which enables the reader to obtain more precision for the Slutsky estimates (by means of $\pi_{ij}^{*}=-\gamma\omega_{ij}$) if he desires such precision. The procedure for deriving the estimates is described in Section 10.6.

TABLE 10.1

ESTIMATES OF CONDITIONAL MARGINAL SHARES AND SLUTSKY COEFFICIENTS OF MEATS AT DIFFERENT DEGREES OF PRICE-DISTURBANCE DEPENDENCE

θ	Conditional marginal shares				Modified conditional Slutsky coefficients: Diagonal coefficients				Off-diagonal coefficients					
	B	P	C	L	B	P	C	L	BP	BC	BL	PC	PL	CL
0	703	201	58	39	−216	−216	−79	−24	173	34	8	35	7	9
.1	700	199	59	41	−222	−218	−82	−31	174	36	13	37	8	10
.2	698	197	60	44	−229	−221	−86	−39	174	37	19	38	9	11
.3	695	196	61	48	−236	−223	−88	−50	173	37	26	38	11	13
.4	691	194	62	53	−245	−225	−91	−64	172	37	36	39	14	15
.5	686	192	63	60	−256	−227	−94	−83	170	37	49	39	17	17
.6	680	189	63	68	−270	−229	−97	−106	168	37	65	40	21	20
.7	672	186	63	79	−287	−231	−100	−136	165	36	86	40	26	24
.8	662	183	63	92	−308	−235	−103	−175	161	34	113	41	33	28
.9	649	178	63	110	−335	−238	−108	−224	155	32	147	41	42	34
1	632	173	63	133	−371	−243	−113	−289	148	30	193	41	53	42

Note. All entries are to be multiplied by 10^{-3}.

TABLE 10.2

ESTIMATES OF THE CONNECTING PARAMETER AND OF DISTURBANCE COVARIANCES OF MEATS AT DIFFERENT DEGREES OF PRICE-DISTURBANCE DEPENDENCE

θ	γ	Disturbance variances				Disturbance covariances					
		B	P	C	L	BP	BC	BL	PC	PL	CL
0	6263	3447	3442	1258	383	−2769	−548	−130	−565	−108	−145
.1	6875	3232	3174	1200	448	−2527	−520	−185	−532	−115	−148
.2	7364	3108	2994	1163	535	−2357	−498	−252	−509	−128	−155
.3	7725	3060	2881	1145	652	−2240	−482	−338	−495	−146	−167
.4	7948	3087	2826	1147	811	−2163	−472	−452	−489	−173	−186
.5	8023	3194	2825	1169	1031	−2122	−465	−606	−491	−212	−213
.6	7948	3394	2880	1215	1337	−2113	−462	−819	−501	−266	−252
.7	7725	3711	2997	1291	1764	−2134	−463	−1114	−520	−342	−307
.8	7364	4183	3185	1403	2371	−2183	−466	−1533	−550	−451	−386
.9	6875	4876	3465	1567	3256	−2261	−471	−2145	−595	−610	−501
1	6263	5925	3881	1811	4613	−2368	−475	−3083	−659	−854	−677

Note. The values shown for the variances and covariances (all entries except those in the first column) are to be multiplied by 10^{-8}.

An Overview of the Estimates

The estimates at $\theta=0$ are obviously identical to the first set of maximum-likelihood estimates in Table 7.7 on page 32. None of the estimates changes in sign when θ increases from 0 to 1. The behavior is either monotonic, or increasing until a maximum and then decreasing, or decreasing until a minimum and then increasing. The estimate of the connecting parameter (γ in the first column of Table 10.2) is a symmetric function of θ with a maximum at $\theta = \frac{1}{2}$. We shall prove in Section 10.6 that this is necessarily so; it serves as a useful check on the computations.

The estimates of the conditional marginal shares of Beef and Pork decline gradually when θ increases from 0 to 1, whereas those of Chicken and Lamb increase. For Lamb the increase is quite large. The tables show that the behavior of all coefficients involving Lamb, including the Slutsky and covariance estimates, differs from that of the coefficients not involving Lamb.

Comparison with the Estimates of Section 7.3

It is instructive to compare the estimates at various values of θ with those obtained when the second-moment model is not imposed. Table 10.3 contains the symmetry-constrained estimates of Table 7.5 on page 19 in the first four lines, followed by the conditional estimates at $\theta = .4$. Equation (2.16) shows that $\theta = .4$ corresponds to $s_1 = 1\frac{1}{2}$, which amounts to a supply response to price changes exceeding the demand response by a factor $1\frac{1}{2}$. Note that this refers to the short-term response; k_{it} in (2.1) may include lagged price log-changes.

The conditional marginal share estimates in the first four lines of Table 10.3 are very close to those at $\theta = .4$. The Slutsky estimates at $\theta = .4$ are somewhat, but not very much, larger than those in the first four lines. This result could be expected. We know from Section 9.3 that the instrumental-variable approach based on the assumption of predetermined $\bar{w}_{it} Dq_{it}$'s yields an estimated price sensitivity of demand exceeding that of Table 7.5 (which is based on the assumption of predetermined Dp_{it}'s). Since $\theta = .4$ is almost halfway between the fixed-price and fixed-quantity limits, we should expect that its Slutsky estimates show more price sensitivity than those of Table 7.5. This is confirmed by the first eight lines of Table 10.3.

Comparison with the Instrumental-Variable Estimates of Section 9.4

The next 12 lines of Table 10.3 contain the symmetry-constrained instrumental-variable estimates of Table 9.3 on page 115 and the conditional estimates at $\theta = .7$ and .8. Using their average, $\theta = .75$, we conclude from (2.16) that this implies $s_1 = \frac{1}{3}$, so that the price response of the suppliers is one-third of that of the consumers.

TABLE 10.3

SIX SETS OF ESTIMATES OF CONDITIONAL MARGINAL SHARES AND SLUTSKY COEFFICIENTS OF MEATS

	Conditional marginal share	Modified conditional Slutsky coefficients			
		Symmetry-constrained estimates of Table 7.5			
Beef	.692	−.227	.164	.033	.029
Pork	.199		−.214	.038	.012
Chicken	.059			−.084	.013
Lamb	.050				−.055
		Estimates at $\theta = .4$			
Beef	.691	−.245	.172	.037	.036
Pork	.194		−.225	.039	.014
Chicken	.062			−.091	.015
Lamb	.053				−.064
		Estimates at $\theta = .7$			
Beef	.672	−.287	.165	.036	.086
Pork	.186		−.231	.040	.026
Chicken	.063			−.100	.024
Lamb	.079				−.136
		Symmetry-constrained instrumental-variable estimates			
Beef	.669	−.306	.171	.047	.089
Pork	.183		−.239	.040	.028
Chicken	.067			−.105	.018
Lamb	.081				−.135
		Estimates at $\theta = .8$			
Beef	.662	−.308	.161	.034	.113
Pork	.183		−.235	.041	.033
Chicken	.063			−.103	.028
Lamb	.092				−.175
		Estimates at $\theta = 1$			
Beef	.632	−.371	.148	.030	.193
Pork	.173		−.243	.041	.053
Chicken	.063			−.113	.042
Lamb	.133				−.289

Table 10.3 shows that, for the conditional marginal shares and Slutsky estimates which do not involve Lamb, the instrumental-variable estimates are rather close to the conditional estimates at $\theta = .8$. For the estimates which involve Lamb, the instrumental-variable estimates are closer to the

conditional estimates at $\theta=.7$. This reflects the fact that the conditional estimates involving Lamb change faster than the other estimates when θ increases.

Since the instrumental-variable estimates are based on the assumption of predetermined $\bar{w}_{it}Dq_{it}$'s, it is appropriate to compare them with the conditional estimates at $\theta=1$ also. The latter estimates are given in the last four lines of Table 10.3. This leads to a further increase of the diagonal Slutsky estimates, which is modest for Pork and Chicken but quite large for Lamb. By dividing this Lamb estimate at $\theta=1$ by the conditional budget share of Lamb, we obtain about -10 for the own-Slutsky elasticity of meat,[1] which is an unrealistic value.

The Second-Moment Model with Predetermined Quantity Changes

The estimates at $\theta=1$ are illustrated in Figure 10.1, which is similar to Figure 7.1 on page 25. Modified conditional Slutsky coefficients (multiplied by -1) are measured horizontally and the corresponding disturbance variances and covariances vertically. The 10 small circles are based on the symmetry-constrained instrumental-variable estimates of these two sets of parameters (see Table 9.2 on page 109 for the estimates of the disturbance covariances). The upward sloping straight line through the origin contains the estimates obtained when the second-moment model is imposed for $\theta=1$, and the broken lines show how the instrumental-variable estimates are affected by this model. Note that these lines for the disturbance variance of Lamb and the covariance of Beef and Lamb are almost parallel to the line through the origin. The considerable lengths of these two broken lines imply that imposing the second-moment model for $\theta=1$ has a substantial effect on the value of the corresponding estimates. For Beef, Pork and Chicken the effect is more moderate. The Pork/Lamb and Chicken/Lamb points in Figure 10.1 are too close to the origin to permit an adequate display of their projection paths.

These results indicate that, if the degree of price-disturbance dependence is considered large, θ being close to 1, the approach of the natural conjugate supply model may yield unsatisfactory estimates. It is then preferable to abandon the second-moment model and to use the instrumental-variable approach of Sections 9.2 to 9.4. To understand why the coefficients involving

---

1 This follows from eq. (3.16) of Section 7.3. The budget shares used are the averages shown in (2.1) of Section 7.2.

Lamb are so sensitive to changes in θ for the data used here, we go back to Section 7.5, where we found that the impact of the second-moment information is much greater for the Lamb coefficients than for those which do not involve Lamb. It is therefore not surprising to find that, if the second-

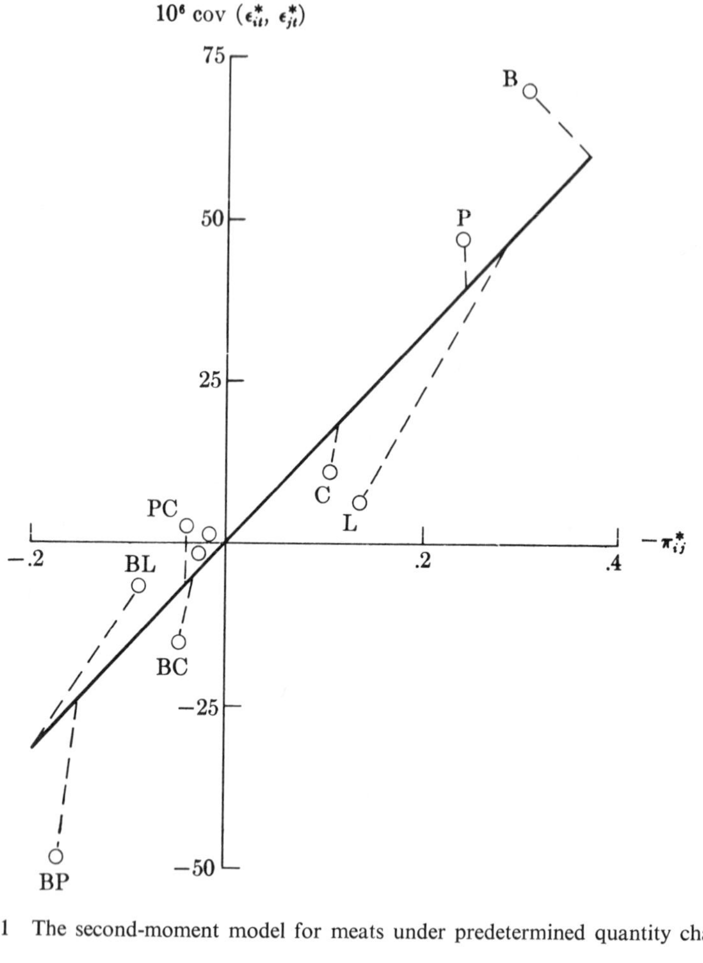

Fig. 10.1 The second-moment model for meats under predetermined quantity changes

moment model is generalized to (1.10), the associated parameter θ also has a greater impact on the Lamb coefficients. On the other hand, as the first eight lines of Table 10.3 show, this does not necessarily have an adverse effect on the estimates as long as θ takes more moderate values.

10.6 The Conditionally Consistent Estimates

Review of Some Earlier Results

To obtain the estimates shown in Tables 10.1 and 10.2 we use eqs. (5.13) to (5.15) of Section 7.5:

$$\mathbf{Z}_0 = \frac{1}{T}\sum_{t=1}^{T} \mathbf{z}_t\mathbf{z}_t' - \frac{1}{T}\mathbf{z}_0\mathbf{z}_0' \tag{6.1}$$

$$\mathbf{E}_0'\mathbf{E}_0 = \mathbf{E}'\mathbf{E} - \frac{1}{T}\mathbf{p}_0\mathbf{p}_0' \tag{6.2}$$

$$\mathbf{M}_0 = \mathbf{Z}_0 + \gamma^2\mathbf{\Omega}\left(\frac{1}{T}\mathbf{p}_0\mathbf{p}_0'\right)\mathbf{\Omega} \tag{6.3}$$

Following the derivation of eq. (5.16) of Section 7.5, we write (4.15) as

$$\gamma^2\mathbf{\Omega}\mathbf{E}_0'\mathbf{E}_0\mathbf{\Omega} + (1-2\theta)\,\mathbf{\Omega} - \mathbf{Z}_0 = \mathbf{0}$$

which is equivalent to

$$\gamma^2\,(\mathbf{E}_0\mathbf{\Omega}\mathbf{E}_0')^2 + (1-2\theta)\,\mathbf{E}_0\mathbf{\Omega}\mathbf{E}_0' - \mathbf{E}_0\mathbf{Z}_0\mathbf{E}_0' = \mathbf{0} \tag{6.4}$$

because $\mathbf{E}_0$ is nonsingular [see the discussion below eq. (5.10) of Section 7.5].

The Estimate of $\mathbf{\Omega}$

To solve (6.4) for $\mathbf{\Omega}$ we write it in the form

$$\begin{aligned}\left(\gamma\mathbf{E}_0\mathbf{\Omega}\mathbf{E}_0' + \frac{1-2\theta}{2\gamma}\mathbf{I}_3\right)^2 &= \mathbf{E}_0\mathbf{Z}_0\mathbf{E}_0' + \frac{(1-2\theta)^2}{4\gamma^2}\mathbf{I}_3 \\ &= \mathbf{F}_0\mathbf{G}_0\mathbf{F}_0' + \frac{(1-2\theta)^2}{4\gamma^2}\mathbf{F}_0\mathbf{F}_0'\end{aligned} \tag{6.5}$$

where $\mathbf{F}_0$ is a 3×3 orthogonal matrix whose columns are characteristic vectors of $\mathbf{E}_0\mathbf{Z}_0\mathbf{E}_0'$ and $\mathbf{G}_0$ is a 3×3 diagonal matrix whose diagonal elements are latent roots of this matrix. Note that $\mathbf{F}_0$ and $\mathbf{G}_0$ are identical to the matrices $\mathbf{F}_0$ and $\mathbf{G}_0$ in eq. (5.17) of Section 7.5.

The left-hand matrix in parentheses in (6.5) can then be written as

$$\gamma\mathbf{E}_0\mathbf{\Omega}\mathbf{E}_0' + \frac{1-2\theta}{2\gamma}\mathbf{I}_3 = \mathbf{F}_0\left[\mathbf{G}_0 + \frac{(1-2\theta)^2}{4\gamma^2}\mathbf{I}_3\right]^{1/2}\mathbf{F}_0' \tag{6.6}$$

When we write $\mathbf{I}_3$ on the left as $\mathbf{F}_0\mathbf{F}_0'$, we obtain

$$\mathbf{\Omega}(\theta) = (\mathbf{E}_0^{-1}\mathbf{F}_0)\,\mathbf{H}_0\,(\mathbf{E}_0^{-1}\mathbf{F}_0)' \tag{6.7}$$

where $\mathbf{H}_0$ is the 3×3 diagonal matrix whose diagonal elements are

$$h_{0i} = \frac{-(1-2\theta) + \sqrt{(1-2\theta)^2 + 4\gamma^2 g_{0i}}}{2\gamma^2} \qquad i = 1, 2, 3 \tag{6.8}$$

with g_{0i} defined as the ith diagonal element of $\mathbf{G}_0$. The notation $\mathbf{\Omega}(\theta)$ is used in (6.7) to indicate that this is the $\mathbf{\Omega}$ estimate at the selected value of θ. Note that (6.8) is the positive solution of the quadratic equation

$$\gamma^2 x^2 + (1-2\theta)\, x - g_{0i} = 0 \qquad i = 1, 2, 3 \tag{6.9}$$

which is equivalent to (6.4) when we replace $\mathbf{E}_0\mathbf{\Omega}\mathbf{E}_0'$ by x and $\mathbf{E}_0\mathbf{Z}_0\mathbf{E}_0'$ by its ith latent root.

The Estimate of the Connecting Parameter

We use eq. (5.21) of Section 7.5 to write (4.10) as

$$\frac{1}{T}\sum_{t=1}^{T} \mathbf{p}_t'(\mathbf{z}_t - c_t\mathbf{z}_0) = -\gamma\left(\operatorname{tr}\mathbf{\Omega}\mathbf{E}'\mathbf{E} - \frac{1}{T}\mathbf{p}_0'\mathbf{\Omega}\mathbf{p}_0\right) + \frac{3\theta}{\gamma} \tag{6.10}$$

In view of (6.2) the expression in parentheses on the right can be simplified to

$$\operatorname{tr}\mathbf{\Omega}\left(\mathbf{E}'\mathbf{E} - \frac{1}{T}\mathbf{p}_0\mathbf{p}_0'\right) = \operatorname{tr}\mathbf{\Omega}\mathbf{E}_0'\mathbf{E}_0 = \operatorname{tr}\mathbf{E}_0\mathbf{\Omega}\mathbf{E}_0'$$

So, when we define

$$k = \frac{1}{T}\sum_{t=1}^{T} \mathbf{p}_t'(\mathbf{z}_t - c_t\mathbf{z}_0) \tag{6.11}$$

we can write (6.10) as

$$k = -\gamma \operatorname{tr}\mathbf{E}_0\mathbf{\Omega}\mathbf{E}_0' + \frac{3\theta}{\gamma} \tag{6.12}$$

which is identical to eq. (5.24) of Section 7.5 at $\theta = 0$. Note also that k defined in (6.11) is equal to the trace of $\mathbf{L}$ defined in eq. (2.5) of Section 9.2.

Multiplication of (6.12) by γ yields a quadratic equation in γ,

$$\gamma^2 \operatorname{tr}\mathbf{E}_0\mathbf{\Omega}\mathbf{E}_0' + k\gamma - 3\theta = 0$$

with the following pair of solutions:

$$\gamma = \frac{-k \pm \sqrt{k^2 + 12\theta \operatorname{tr}\mathbf{E}_0\mathbf{\Omega}\mathbf{E}_0'}}{2 \operatorname{tr}\mathbf{E}_0\mathbf{\Omega}\mathbf{E}_0'} \tag{6.13}$$

It is shown in the next paragraph that the positive square root is to be selected. Hence the estimate of γ, to be written $\gamma(\theta)$, is equal to

$$\gamma(\theta) = \frac{-k + \sqrt{k^2 + 12\theta \operatorname{tr} \mathbf{E}_0 \mathbf{\Omega} \mathbf{E}_0'}}{2 \operatorname{tr} \mathbf{E}_0 \mathbf{\Omega} \mathbf{E}_0'} \tag{6.14}$$

The γ estimate at $\theta=0$ is given in eq. (5.24) of Section 7.5. Using (6.11), we can write this estimate as

$$\gamma(0) = \frac{-k}{\operatorname{tr} \mathbf{E}_0 \mathbf{\Omega} \mathbf{E}_0'} \tag{6.15}$$

Since the trace in the denominator is positive, this means that k must be negative: $-k=|k|$. So, if we select the negative square root in (6.13), the numerator at $\theta=0$ becomes $|k|-\sqrt{k^2}=0$, which is contradicted by (6.15). If we select the positive square root, the right-hand side of (6.13) at $\theta=0$ becomes

$$\frac{|k| + \sqrt{k^2}}{2 \operatorname{tr} \mathbf{E}_0 \mathbf{\Omega} \mathbf{E}_0'} = \frac{2|k|}{2 \operatorname{tr} \mathbf{E}_0 \mathbf{\Omega} \mathbf{E}_0'} = \frac{-k}{\operatorname{tr} \mathbf{E}_0 \mathbf{\Omega} \mathbf{E}_0'}$$

which agrees with (6.15). Since the estimation equations are continuous in θ, we must take the positive square root for each value of θ.

The Behavior of the Estimated Connecting Parameter

The following result is proved in the next subsection:

$$\frac{3}{2\gamma(\theta)} = k + \operatorname{tr}\left[\mathbf{G}_0 + \frac{(1-2\theta)^2}{4\gamma(\theta)^2}\mathbf{I}_3\right]^{1/2} \tag{6.16}$$

Recall that $\mathbf{G}_0$ is diagonal and that its diagonal elements are the latent roots of $\mathbf{E}_0 \mathbf{Z}_0 \mathbf{E}_0'$. This means that $\mathbf{G}_0$ is determined by observations on variables and hence that it is independent of θ. The same holds for k defined in (6.11). Therefore, (6.16) implies

$$\frac{3}{2\gamma(\theta)} \geq k + \operatorname{tr} \mathbf{G}_0^{1/2} \tag{6.17}$$

with the equal sign applying if and only if $\theta=\frac{1}{2}$. This proves that the γ estimate has a unique maximum at $\theta=\frac{1}{2}$, in agreement with the results shown in the first column of Table 10.2.

Note further that the expression $(1-2\theta)^2$ remains unchanged when θ is replaced by $1-\theta$:

$$[1-2(1-\theta)]^2=(-1+2\theta)^2=(1-2\theta)^2$$

Since θ occurs in (6.16) only in the forms $\gamma(\theta)$ and $(1-2\theta)^2$, this proves

$$\gamma(\theta)=\gamma(1-\theta) \tag{6.18}$$

Hence the γ estimate is a symmetric function around $\theta=\frac{1}{2}$, which also agrees with Table 10.2.

Derivations

To prove (6.16) we take the trace of the matrix equation (6.6). On the left we obtain

$$\gamma \operatorname{tr} \mathbf{E}_0\mathbf{\Omega}\mathbf{E}_0' + \frac{3(1-2\theta)}{2\gamma} \tag{6.19}$$

The trace of the right-hand side is

$$\operatorname{tr} \mathbf{F}_0\left[\mathbf{G}_0 + \frac{(1-2\theta)^2}{4\gamma^2}\mathbf{I}_3\right]^{1/2}\mathbf{F}_0' = \operatorname{tr} \mathbf{F}_0'\mathbf{F}_0\left[\mathbf{G}_0 + \frac{(1-2\theta)^2}{4\gamma^2}\mathbf{I}_3\right]^{1/2}$$

which can be simplified to

$$\operatorname{tr}\left[\mathbf{G}_0 + \frac{(1-2\theta)^2}{4\gamma^2}\mathbf{I}_3\right]^{1/2} \tag{6.20}$$

because $\mathbf{F}_0$ is an orthogonal matrix. The trace of (6.6) is then obtained by equating (6.19) to (6.20). The result may be written as

$$\gamma \operatorname{tr} \mathbf{E}_0\mathbf{\Omega}\mathbf{E}_0' - \frac{3\theta}{\gamma} = -\frac{3}{2\gamma} + \operatorname{tr}\left[\mathbf{G}_0 + \frac{(1-2\theta)^2}{4\gamma^2}\mathbf{I}_3\right]^{1/2}$$

The expression on the left is equal to the right-hand side of (6.12), apart from sign. Therefore,

$$-k=-\frac{3}{2\gamma} + \operatorname{tr}\left[\mathbf{G}_0 + \frac{(1-2\theta)^2}{4\gamma^2}\mathbf{I}_3\right]^{1/2}$$

which proves (6.16).

The Computational Procedure

The numerical procedure is a continuation of that described at the end of Section 7.5. The estimates shown in Tables 10.1 and 10.2 are obtained by means of θ increments of .05. Substitution of $\gamma(0)$ and $\theta=.05$ in (6.8) and (6.7) yields an initial value of $\mathbf{\Omega}(.05)$. This $\mathbf{\Omega}$ and $\theta=.05$ are substituted in (6.14), after which the iteration between (6.7) and (6.14) is continued until convergence. The $\boldsymbol{\mu}_0$ estimate is then obtained from (4.7). Next, to obtain estimates at $\theta=.1$, we substitute the converged value of $\gamma(.05)$ and $\theta=.1$ in (6.8) and (6.7), then substitute the $\mathbf{\Omega}$ thus obtained in (6.14), and so on.

For each θ value 300 iterations have been used. The symmetry property (6.18) is satisfied to five decimal places.

CHAPTER 11

STATISTICAL AND GEOMETRIC APPROACHES TO DEMAND THEORY

In this chapter we turn from individual commodities to the consumer's basket as a whole. One of the objectives is to pursue the statistical interpretations which are suggested by the frequent occurrence of averages. Examples are the log-change in real income, $\sum_i \bar{w}_{it} Dq_{it}$, the log-change in the cost-of-living index, $\sum_i \bar{w}_{it} Dp_{it}$, and the log-change in the marginal price index, $\sum_i \mu_i Dp_{it}$, all of which are weighted means of price or quantity log-changes. Another objective is to provide a geometric interpretation of demand and its components in the n-dimensional commodity space.

It is assumed throughout this chapter that price log-changes are predetermined when the second-moment model is discussed. Extensions to the natural conjugate supply model of Section 10.2 are described in Section 12.8.

11.1 The Price-Quantity Covariance

It will prove convenient to denote first-order moments of log-changes by uppercase symbols in agreement with the notation DQ_t for $\sum_i \bar{w}_{it} Dq_{it}$. Also, we shall add a prime when the weights are marginal rather than budget shares, which agrees with the notation for the marginal price index of the group S_g in eq. (3.14) of Section 2.3,

$$DP'_{gt} = \sum_{i \in S_g} \frac{\mu_i}{M_g} DP_{it}$$

Thus, the log-change in the cost-of-living index and that in the marginal price index will be written as

$$(1.1) \qquad DP_t = \sum_{i=1}^{n} \bar{w}_{it} Dp_{it} \qquad DP'_t = \sum_{i=1}^{n} \mu_i Dp_{it}$$

The Covariance of the Price and Quantity Log-changes

The substitution effect of price changes implies, in imprecise terms, that commodities whose prices increase by more than the average tend to be subject to a declining demand. We should therefore expect that in most cases price changes and quantity changes are negatively correlated. To analyze this more systematically we consider the weighted covariance of the price and quantity log-changes,

$$\begin{matrix} Dp_{1t} & Dp_{2t} & \dots & Dp_{nt} \\ Dq_{1t} & Dq_{2t} & \dots & Dq_{nt} \end{matrix}$$

with the averages of the budget shares in $t-1$ and t as weights:

$$\bar{w}_{1t} \quad \bar{w}_{2t} \quad \dots \quad \bar{w}_{nt}$$

This weighted covariance, to be called the *price-quantity covariance* for short, is equal to

$$\Gamma_t = \sum_{i=1}^{n} \bar{w}_{it}(Dp_{it} - DP_t)(Dq_{it} - DQ_t) \tag{1.2}$$

where DP_t and DQ_t are the corresponding means (with $\bar{w}_{it}$'s as weights) of the two variables.

Since the value of a covariance is not affected when only one of the two variables is measured as a deviation from the mean, we can write Γ_t in the equivalent form

$$\Gamma_t = \sum_{i=1}^{n} \bar{w}_{it}(Dp_{it} - DP_t)\, Dq_{it} = \sum_{i=1}^{n} (Dp_{it} - DP_t)\, \bar{w}_{it} Dq_{it} \tag{1.3}$$

The third member shows that Γ_t is equal to a weighted sum of the left-hand variables of the demand equations of the Rotterdam Model, with weights equal to the log-changes in the corresponding relative prices. The deflator used here to obtain these relative prices is the cost-of-living index.

The Factors Determining the Price-Quantity Covariance Under Preference Independence

We proceed to evaluate Γ_t in the special case of preference independence, so that the ith demand equation can then be written as

$$\bar{w}_{it} Dq_{it} = \mu_i DQ_t + \phi \mu_i (Dp_{it} - DP'_t) + \varepsilon_{it} \tag{1.4}$$

The main reason for considering this special case is that it is much simpler than the general case; we shall consider the general case at the end of this section.

Substitution of the right-hand side of (1.4) in the third member of (1.3) gives

$$\begin{aligned} \Gamma_t = {} & DQ_t \sum_{i=1}^{n} \mu_i (Dp_{it} - DP_t) \\ & + \phi \sum_{i=1}^{n} \mu_i (Dp_{it} - DP_t)(Dp_{it} - DP'_t) + \sum_{i=1}^{n} (Dp_{it} - DP_t)\varepsilon_{it} \end{aligned} \tag{1.5}$$

The first term on the right can be simplified to $DQ_t(DP'_t - DP_t)$, and the third to $\sum_i Dp_{it}\varepsilon_{it}$ because $DP_t \sum_i \varepsilon_{it} = 0$. Hence,

$$\Gamma_t = (DP'_t - DP_t)\,DQ_t + \phi\Pi'_t + \sum_{i=1}^{n} Dp_{it}\varepsilon_{it} \tag{1.6}$$

where

$$\Pi'_t = \sum_{i=1}^{n} \mu_i (Dp_{it} - DP'_t)^2 \tag{1.7}$$

is the marginally weighted variance of the price log-changes; this is a simple measure of the change in relative prices. Note that the corresponding term in (1.5) involves the product of $Dp_{it} - DP_t$ and $Dp_{it} - DP'_t$ rather than the square of $Dp_{it} - DP'_t$. This makes no difference when we sum them over i; to compute the marginally weighted variance it is sufficient to subtract the marginally weighted mean in only one of the two factors. Note also the prime of Π'_t and the absence of such a prime from Γ_t. This serves to stress the use of μ_i's in the former case and that of $\bar{w}_{it}$'s in the latter, similar to DP'_t and DP_t in (1.1).

The Real-Income and Substitution Components of the Price-Quantity Covariance

The second term in the right-hand side of (1.6), $\phi\Pi'_t$, corresponds to the second term of (1.4), and hence represents the substitution effect of the price changes on the price-quantity covariance. This term is negative, as could be expected, except when all prices change proportionally. In that special case the term vanishes. Actually, Γ_t is then also zero, and all three right-hand terms are individually zero, as is easily verified.

To interpret the real-income term of (1.6) we consider the case in which the prices of luxuries increase more or decrease less than those of necessities. This implies $DP'_t - DP_t > 0$, because luxuries (necessities) have larger (smaller) weights in DP'_t than in DP_t. An alternative way of looking at this is provided by

$$DP'_t - DP_t = \sum_{i=1}^{n} (\mu_i - \bar{w}_{it})\,Dp_{it} = \sum_{i=1}^{n} \bar{w}_{it}\left(\frac{\mu_i}{\bar{w}_{it}} - 1\right) Dp_{it}$$

which can be written in the equivalent form

$$DP'_t - DP_t = \sum_{i=1}^{n} \bar{w}_{it}\,(Dp_{it} - DP_t)\left(\frac{\mu_i}{\bar{w}_{it}} - 1\right) \tag{1.8}$$

The right-hand side is the budget-share-weighted covariance of the price log-changes and the income elasticities. Thus, a positive difference $DP'_t - DP_t$

amounts to a positive correlation of price log-changes and income elasticities in this particular weighted sense. Such a positive correlation may be considered as equivalent to the statement that, on average, luxuries increase in price relative to necessities.

Assuming that such a change in the price structure takes place, we may conclude that, other things being equal, the consumption of necessities is stimulated at the expense of that of luxuries; this is what the substitution effect amounts to. But suppose that other things are not equal and, specifically, that there is an increase in real income ($DQ_t > 0$). That increase will stimulate the consumption of luxuries relative to that of necessities, which – given the parallel development of prices – contributes to a positive rather than a negative sign of Γ_t. This real-income effect occurs in (1.6) as the product of $DP'_t - DP_t$ and DQ_t, both of which are positive in the case discussed here. Other sign patterns can be analyzed similarly.

The Disturbance Component Under the Second-Moment Model

The disturbance component of (1.6), $\sum_i Dp_{it}\varepsilon_{it}$, is random with zero mean if the ε's have zero mean. We continue to work with the preference independence assumption and proceed to derive the variance of the random component of Γ_t under the second-moment model of Section 2.7. This model amounts to the covariance structure given in eq. (7.13) of that section:

$$\text{(1.9)} \qquad \operatorname{cov}(\varepsilon_{it}, \varepsilon_{jt}) = \begin{cases} \sigma^2\mu_i(1-\mu_i) & \text{if } i=j \\ -\sigma^2\mu_i\mu_j & \text{if } i\neq j \end{cases}$$

This implies the following variance of $\sum_i Dp_{it}\varepsilon_{it}$:

$$\begin{aligned}\sum_{i=1}^{n}\sum_{j=1}^{n} Dp_{it}Dp_{jt}\mathscr{E}(\varepsilon_{it}\varepsilon_{jt}) &= \sigma^2\left[\sum_{i=1}^{n}\mu_i(Dp_{it})^2 - \sum_{i=1}^{n}\sum_{j=1}^{n}\mu_i\mu_j Dp_{it}Dp_{jt}\right] \\ &= \sigma^2\left[\sum_{i=1}^{n}\mu_i(Dp_{it})^2 - \left(\sum_{i=1}^{n}\mu_i Dp_{it}\right)^2\right] \\ &= \sigma^2\sum_{i=1}^{n}\mu_i(Dp_{it} - DP'_t)^2\end{aligned}$$

We can write this result as

$$\text{(1.10)} \qquad \operatorname{var}\left(\sum_{i=1}^{n} Dp_{it}\varepsilon_{it}\right) = \sigma^2\Pi'_t$$

The variance of the disturbance component of the price-quantity covariance thus appears to be proportional to the marginally weighted variance Π'_t of the price log-changes; that is, precisely the same Π_t' as that in the substitution term of (1.6).

Under the theory of rational random behavior of Section 2.8, the disturbances have a multinormal distribution. The result just obtained then implies that the random component of the price-quantity covariance is normally distributed with zero mean and a variance proportional to the marginally weighted variance of the price log-changes.

The Preference Independence Assumption Reconsidered

The above results are very simple and attractive, but it should be stressed that the restrictive assumption of preference independence has been used. If the assumption is not satisfied, we have to replace the second term in the right-hand side of (1.4) by a weighted sum of $Dp_{1t} - DP_t', \ldots, Dp_{nt} - DP_t'$ with weights equal to $\nu_{i1}, \ldots, \nu_{in}$. This implies that the component $\phi\Pi_t'$ of the price-quantity covariance in (1.6) is replaced by

$$\sum_{i=1}^{n} \sum_{j=1}^{n} \nu_{ij} (Dp_{it} - DP_t)(Dp_{jt} - DP_t')$$

which may be written as

$$\sum_{i=1}^{n} \sum_{j=1}^{n} \nu_{ij} (Dp_{it} - DP_t')(Dp_{jt} - DP_t') \tag{1.11}$$

because the difference between the two expressions is

$$(DP_t - DP_t') \sum_{i=1}^{n} \sum_{j=1}^{n} \nu_{ij} (Dp_{jt} - DP_t') = \phi (DP_t - DP_t') \sum_{j=1}^{n} \mu_j (Dp_{jt} - DP_t')$$

which is zero.

We thus find that relaxing the preference independence assumption implies that the substitution component of Γ_t becomes a negative definite quadratic form in the marginally deflated price log-changes, with the price coefficient matrix $[\nu_{ij}]$ as the negative definite matrix. This is a much less attractive expression than ϕ times the marginally weighted variance of the price log-changes. Another source of concern is the fact that, if there is no preference independence, we can no longer exclude inferior goods. When there are such goods, DP_t' ceases to be a "proper" mean because some of its weights (the μ_i's) are negative. These are sufficient reasons for exploring the possibility of transforming the demand equations so that they become of the preference independence type, as will be done in Chapter 12.

11.2 Bortkiewicz's Theorem and Extensions

When we introduced the price-quantity covariance in Section 11.1, we did so in statistical rather than economic terms. For the reader who prefers an economic approach, it will be of interest to know that the use of simple Laspeyres and Paasche indexes implies another, but very similar, covariance.

A Covariance of Price and Quantity Ratios

The Laspeyres price index which compares t and $t-1$ is

$$P_t^L = \frac{\sum_{i=1}^n p_{it} q_{i,t-1}}{\sum_{i=1}^n p_{i,t-1} q_{i,t-1}} = \sum_{i=1}^n w_{i,t-1} \frac{p_{it}}{p_{i,t-1}} \tag{2.1}$$

and the corresponding volume index is

$$Q_t^L = \frac{\sum_{i=1}^n p_{i,t-1} q_{it}}{\sum_{i=1}^n p_{i,t-1} q_{i,t-1}} = \sum_{i=1}^n w_{i,t-1} \frac{q_{it}}{q_{i,t-1}} \tag{2.2}$$

Both indexes can therefore be regarded as weighted means of price or quantity ratios with weights equal to last period's budget shares. The corresponding covariance of these ratios is

$$C_t^L = \sum_{i=1}^n w_{i,t-1} \left(\frac{p_{it}}{p_{i,t-1}} - P_t^L \right) \left(\frac{q_{it}}{q_{i,t-1}} - Q_t^L \right) \tag{2.3}$$

which may also be written as

$$C_t^L = \sum_{i=1}^n w_{i,t-1} \frac{p_{it} q_{it}}{p_{i,t-1} q_{i,t-1}} - P_t^L Q_t^L = \frac{m_t}{m_{t-1}} - P_t^L Q_t^L \tag{2.4}$$

where m_t and m_{t-1} are the amounts of total expenditure in the two periods.

Next consider the Paasche price and volume indexes:

$$P_t^P = \frac{\sum_{i=1}^n p_{it} q_{it}}{\sum_{i=1}^n p_{i,t-1} q_{it}} \qquad Q_t^P = \frac{\sum_{i=1}^n p_{it} q_{it}}{\sum_{i=1}^n p_{it} q_{i,t-1}} \tag{2.5}$$

A comparison with (2.1) and (2.2) shows that the product of the Laspeyres price index and the Paasche volume index equals m_t/m_{t-1}, and that this also holds for the product of the Laspeyres volume index and the Paasche price index. Therefore,

$$(P_t^P - P_t^L)\, Q_t^L = (Q_t^P - Q_t^L)\, P_t^L = \frac{m_t}{m_{t-1}} - P_t^L Q_t^L$$

and hence, in view of (2.4),

$$(P_t^P - P_t^L)\, Q_t^L = (Q_t^P - Q_t^L)\, P_t^L = C_t^L \tag{2.6}$$

This result is from BORTKIEWICZ (1923). It implies that if the covariance (2.3) is negative, as is very frequently the case, the Paasche price and volume indexes are both below the corresponding Laspeyres indexes.

Extension to Price Log-changes

To provide an extension of (2.6) to the indexes used in this book, we note that the Laspeyres indexes have weights of $t-1$ and that the Paasche indexes have current weights. Thus, when proceeding to the price log-changes $Dp_{1t}, \ldots, Dp_{nt}$, a natural approach is to compare the weighted mean whose weights are the current budget shares (corresponding to Paasche) with the weighted mean based on last period's shares (corresponding to Laspeyres). The difference between these two weighted means is

$$\sum_{i=1}^{n} w_{it} Dp_{it} - \sum_{i=1}^{n} w_{i,t-1} Dp_{it} = \sum_{i=1}^{n} \Delta w_{it} Dp_{it} \tag{2.7}$$

Using the decomposition

$$\begin{aligned} \Delta w_{it} &= \bar{w}_{it} Dp_{it} + \bar{w}_{it} Dq_{it} - \bar{w}_{it} Dm_t + O_3 \\ &= \bar{w}_{it}(Dp_{it} - DP_t) + \bar{w}_{it}(Dq_{it} - DQ_t) + O_3 \end{aligned} \tag{2.8}$$

we can write (2.7) as

$$\sum_{i=1}^{n} w_{it} Dp_{it} - \sum_{i=1}^{n} w_{i,t-1} Dp_{it}$$
$$= \sum_{i=1}^{n} \bar{w}_{it} Dp_{it} (Dp_{it} - DP_t) + \sum_{i=1}^{n} \bar{w}_{it} Dp_{it} (Dq_{it} - DQ_t) + O_4$$

where the O_4 term is based on the fact that the O_3 term of (2.8) is multiplied by $Dp_{it} = O_1$ in (2.7). We can write this result in the simpler form

$$\sum_{i=1}^{n} w_{it} Dp_{it} - \sum_{i=1}^{n} w_{i,t-1} Dp_{it} = \Pi_t + \Gamma_t + O_4 \tag{2.9}$$

where

$$\Pi_t = \sum_{i=1}^{n} \bar{w}_{it} (Dp_{it} - DP_t)^2 \tag{2.10}$$

is the budget-share-weighted variance of the price log-changes. It is similar to the variance (1.7), but weighted differently.

Comparison with Bortkiewicz's Theorem

There are three differences between (2.9) and (2.6). First, (2.9) contains a remainder term of the fourth order of smallness. Since Π_t and Γ_t are both O_2, the relative error in (2.9) is thus O_2, which is of the same order as that of (2.8). Second, the difference between the price indexes in (2.6) is multiplied by the Laspeyres volume index, but there is no volume index in (2.9). Third, (2.9) contains a variance of price log-changes, whereas (2.6) contains no variance, only a covariance.

To investigate the sign of the difference in the left-hand side of (2.9) we assume that there is preference independence and apply (1.6):

$$(2.11)\quad \sum_{i=1}^{n} w_{it}Dp_{it} - \sum_{i=1}^{n} w_{i,t-1}Dp_{it} = (DP_t' - DP_t)\,DQ_t + \Pi_t + \phi\Pi_t' + \sum_{i=1}^{n} Dp_{it}\varepsilon_{it} + O_4$$

To simplify the analysis further we assume that, as far as the first two moments of the price log-changes from $t-1$ to t are concerned, it makes no difference whether they use marginal or budget shares as weights. The first term on the right then vanishes and the next two become a multiple $1+\phi$ of the variance of the price log-changes (either marginally or budget-share-weighted). The empirical findings of Chapters 5 and 6 indicate that ϕ is a negative number less than 1 in absolute value, thus suggesting that the left-hand side of (2.11) is "normally" positive. Since $\sum_i w_{it}Dp_{it}$ corresponds to the Paasche price index (with current weights), this conclusion differs from that drawn below (2.6) under the condition of a negative covariance (2.3). This difference is evidently due to the fact that the use of weighted means of price log-changes results in the addition of the variance Π_t to the covariance Γ_t in (2.9).

Quantity Log-changes and Their Variance

The quantity version of (2.7) is

$$\sum_{i=1}^{n} w_{it}Dq_{it} - \sum_{i=1}^{n} w_{i,t-1}Dq_{it} = \sum_{i=1}^{n} \Delta w_{it}Dq_{it}$$

Application of (2.8) and appropriate rearrangements give an equation similar to (2.9),

(2.12)
$$\sum_{i=1}^{n} w_{it}Dq_{it} - \sum_{i=1}^{n} w_{i,t-1}Dq_{it} = K_t + \Gamma_t + O_4$$

where

(2.13)
$$K_t = \sum_{i=1}^{n} \bar{w}_{it}(Dq_{it} - DQ_t)^2$$

is the variance (budget-share-weighted) of the quantity log-changes. This variance describes the extent to which the individual quantity log-changes deviate from their weighted mean DQ_t, the log-change in real income. Equivalently, K_t is a measure of the change in the relative composition of the consumer's basket. It vanishes when the n quantities change proportionally, in which case the relative composition remains unchanged, and it takes a large positive value when the quantities show a considerable divergence in their development from $t-1$ to t.

The Informational Divergence of Successive Budget Shares

An interesting result emerges when we add eqs. (2.9) and (2.12). On the left we obtain

(2.14)
$$\sum_{i=1}^{n} w_{it}D(p_{it}q_{it}) - \sum_{i=1}^{n} w_{i,t-1}D(p_{it}q_{it}) = \sum_{i=1}^{n} (w_{it} - w_{i,t-1})(Dw_{it} + Dm_t)$$

where use is made of $D(p_{it}q_{it}) = D(w_{it}m_t) = Dw_{it} + Dm_t$. Since the terms involving Dm_t cancel each other out, the sum of the left-hand sides of (2.9) and (2.12) becomes a function of the budget shares of the two periods:

(2.15)
$$\sum_{i=1}^{n} (w_{it} - w_{i,t-1})\,Dw_{it} = \sum_{i=1}^{n} w_{it} \log \frac{w_{it}}{w_{i,t-1}} + \sum_{i=1}^{n} w_{i,t-1} \log \frac{w_{i,t-1}}{w_{it}}$$
$$= I(w_t : w_{t-1}) + I(w_{t-1} : w_t)$$

where $I(\ )$ is the information expectation defined in eq. (1.3) of Section 5.1. The sum of the two information expectations in the second line is known as the *informational divergence* of the two sets of shares; see, for example, KULLBACK (1968, p. 6).

Since information expectations and hence also the informational divergence are nonnegative, we thus have from (2.14) and (2.15):

$$\sum_{i=1}^{n} w_{it}D(p_{it}q_{it}) - \sum_{i=1}^{n} w_{i,t-1}D(p_{it}q_{it}) \geq 0$$

This is equivalent to

$$(2.16) \qquad \sum_{i=1}^{n} w_{it}Dp_{it} + \sum_{i=1}^{n} w_{it}Dq_{it} \geq \sum_{i=1}^{n} w_{i,t-1}Dp_{it} + \sum_{i=1}^{n} w_{i,t-1}Dq_{it}$$

We concluded below (2.11) that $\sum_i w_{it}Dp_{it} > \sum_i w_{i,t-1}Dp_{it}$ is "normally" true. This should be compared with (2.16), which is true under all circumstances.

It is also interesting to compare the informational divergence with the allocation discrepancy $\sum_i \bar{w}_{it}Dw_{it}$, for which purpose we consider eqs. (1.17) and (1.18) of Section 5.1:

$$(2.17) \qquad \sum_{i=1}^{n} \bar{w}_{it}Dw_{it} = DP_t + DQ_t - Dm_t$$

$$(2.18) \qquad \sum_{i=1}^{n} \bar{w}_{it}Dw_{it} = \tfrac{1}{2}I(w_t : w_{t-1}) - \tfrac{1}{2}I(w_{t-1} : w_t)$$

This shows that the informational divergence is the sum, and the allocation discrepancy is one-half of the difference, of the same information expectations.

Moments of Log-changes in Budget Shares

Recall that (2.14) and (2.15) were obtained by adding the left-hand sides of (2.9) and (2.12). We now add the right-hand sides of these equations, which gives $\Pi_t + K_t + 2\Gamma_t$, apart from an O_4 term. Therefore,

$$(2.19) \qquad I(w_t : w_{t-1}) + I(w_{t-1} : w_t) = \Pi_t + K_t + 2\Gamma_t + O_4$$

To evaluate the expression on the right, we write $w_{it} = p_{it}q_{it}/m_t$ in log-change form,

$$(2.20) \qquad \begin{aligned} Dw_{it} &= Dp_{it} + Dq_{it} - Dm_t \\ &= (Dp_{it} - DP_t) + (Dq_{it} - DQ_t) + DW_t \end{aligned}$$

where the second step is based on (2.17) and on

$$(2.21) \qquad DW_t = \sum_{i=1}^{n} \bar{w}_{it}Dw_{it}$$

As the DW_t notation indicates, the allocation discrepancy is equal to the budget-share-weighted mean of the log-changes in the budget shares.

Next write (2.20) as

$$Dw_{it} - DW_t = (Dp_{it} - DP_t) + (Dq_{it} - DQ_t) \tag{2.22}$$

Square both sides and weight the result with $\bar{w}_{it}$ $(i=1,\ldots,n)$:

$$\sum_{i=1}^{n} \bar{w}_{it}(Dw_{it} - DW_t)^2 = \Pi_t + K_t + 2\Gamma_t \tag{2.23}$$

We conclude that the budget-share-weighted variance of the log-changes in the budget shares can be expressed in terms of the similarly weighted variances and covariance of the price and quantity log-changes. Also, using (2.19), we have

$$I(w_t : w_{t-1}) + I(w_{t-1} : w_t) = \sum_{i=1}^{n} \bar{w}_{it}(Dw_{it} - DW_t)^2 + O_4 \tag{2.24}$$

Thus, apart from an O_4 term, the informational divergence of the two sets of budget shares is equal to the weighted variance of their log-changes. This should be compared with (2.21) for the allocation discrepancy, which is the other informational measure based on budget shares.

Conclusion

In the opening paragraph of this section we expressed a desire to describe Γ_t in economic rather than statistical terms. It turns out that the discussion has not diminished the importance of statistical concepts; it has even led to new statistical summary measures of the change in the consumer's basket, including the informational divergence defined in (2.15) and the three variances shown in (2.23).

The discussion has also produced a useful result for the prediction of the change in the cost of living. Suppose that quantity data become available later than price data, so that Dp_{it} is known prior to $\bar{w}_{it}$ (which involves q_{it} via $w_{it}=p_{it}q_{it}/m_t$). Hence we cannot compute the change in the cost of living, $DP_t=\sum_i \bar{w}_{it}Dp_{it}$, as soon as we know Dp_{it}. But if we know $w_{i,t-1}$, we can compute the second term in the left-hand side of (2.9), which is related to DP_t by

$$DP_t - \sum_{i=1}^{n} w_{i,t-1}Dp_{it} = \tfrac{1}{2}\sum_{i=1}^{n} \Delta w_{it}Dp_{it} \tag{2.25}$$

If an estimated demand model is available, we can use this to estimate Δw_{it} on the right. This matter is pursued in Section 13.7.

11.3 The Quality Index

Three first-order moments of the quantity and price log-changes were mentioned in the opening paragraph of this chapter: DQ_t, DP_t and DP'_t in the present notation. There is obviously a fourth, the marginally weighted average of the quantity log-changes,

$$DQ'_t = \sum_{i=1}^{n} \mu_i Dq_{it} \tag{3.1}$$

which is the object of this section.

Quality Measured by the Luxury/Necessity Composition of the Basket

The interpretation of DQ'_t is simplified when we measure it as a deviation from the log-change in real income:

$$DQ'_t - DQ_t = \sum_{i=1}^{n} (\mu_i - \bar{w}_{it})\, Dq_{it} \tag{3.2}$$

The log-change Dq_{it} on the right is multiplied by a positive coefficient $\mu_i - \bar{w}_{it}$ when the ith commodity is a luxury, and by a negative coefficient when the commodity is a necessity. Hence, when the quantity log-changes of luxuries are more positive (or less negative) than those of necessities, the difference $DQ'_t - DQ_t$ is positive. Conversely, if the quantity log-changes of luxuries are less positive or more negative than those of necessities, so that there is a shift away from luxuries toward necessities, then $DQ'_t - DQ_t$ is negative. Since we have

$$\sum_{i=1}^{n} (\mu_i - \bar{w}_{it})\, Dq_{it} = \sum_{i=1}^{n} \bar{w}_{it}\left(\frac{\mu_i}{\bar{w}_{it}} - 1\right) Dq_{it}$$

we may conclude that $DQ'_t - DQ_t$ is also equal to the budget-share-weighted covariance of the quantity log-changes and the income elasticities:

$$DQ'_t - DQ_t = \sum_{i=1}^{n} \bar{w}_{it}(Dq_{it} - DQ_t)\left(\frac{\mu_i}{\bar{w}_{it}} - 1\right) \tag{3.3}$$

This result should be compared with (1.8). A positive or negative value of $DQ'_t - DQ_t$ is equivalent to a weighted correlation of income elasticities and quantity log-changes which has the same sign.

Luxuries are more desirable than necessities from the consumer's point of view in the sense that, other things being equal, he spends a larger fraction of his income on the former commodities and a smaller fraction on the latter when his income increases. Hence, a positive (negative) sign of $DQ'_t - DQ_t$ indicates that the consumer's basket has increased (decreased) in desirability. We shall therefore refer to $DQ'_t - DQ_t$ as the log-change in the *quality index* of the consumer's basket. The implied definition of quality does not involve an outside value judgment on what is "good" for the consumer. If heroin has a higher income elasticity than pipe tobacco and if the consumer gives up the latter in favor of the former, then, other things being equal, the quality index of his commodity basket increases. This index measures the desirability of the basket from the consumer's point of view as revealed by his behavior.

Alternative Ways of Measuring Quality

There are more direct ways of measuring quality. For example, in the case of automobiles, factors such as horsepower, weight and length determine quality. They are also determining factors of the price of an automobile. This approach is in fact used in the literature on hedonic price indexes to explain price differentials; see, for example, CRAMER (1966) and GRILICHES (1971).

The approach which uses quality characteristics for each commodity becomes less practical when the analyst is interested in several commodities simultaneously. There is also the problem that certain characteristics are subjective and cannot be measured easily. It is then more attractive to summarize quality by means of a single number. One way of doing this, suggested independently by HOUTHAKKER (1952–53) and THEIL (1952–53), is by means of the average price paid. Take coffee as an example. Since high-quality coffee commands a higher price than low-quality coffee, the average price which a family pays for a pound of coffee is a measure of the quality of the coffee bought. Such an indicator can be used in a cross-section study when prices are approximately constant during a short period of time. However, this procedure is feasible only within narrowly defined commodity groups, since dimensional considerations prevent us from averaging the prices of coffee and dental services. The definition (3.2) has the advantage of being generally applicable, because it involves only dimensionless concepts (shares and quantity log-changes).

It is likely that the criterion of the average price paid is positively correlated with that based on income elasticities. In Germany, where beer is cheap relative to wine, the income elasticity of beer is only .5 and that of wine is 1.3. In Italy, where beer is expensive relative to wine, the income elasticity of beer is 1.1 and that of wine is only .7. These estimates, based on a European household survey in 1963–64, are quoted from CRAMER (1973); we refer to this article for further details.

Factors Determining the Quality Index Under Preference Independence

Under the assumption of preference independence we can express the right-hand side of (3.2) in terms of income and price changes as shown below.

$$\sum_{i=1}^{n} \frac{\mu_i}{\bar{w}_{it}} \bar{w}_{it} Dq_{it} - DQ_t$$

$$= \sum_{i=1}^{n} \frac{\mu_i}{\bar{w}_{it}} [\mu_i DQ_t + \phi\mu_i (Dp_{it} - DP'_t) + \varepsilon_{it}] - DQ_t$$

$$= \left(\sum_{i=1}^{n} \frac{\mu_i^2}{\bar{w}_{it}} - 1\right) DQ_t + \phi \sum_{i=1}^{n} \mu_i (Dp_{it} - DP'_t) \frac{\mu_i}{\bar{w}_{it}} + \sum_{i=1}^{n} \frac{\mu_i}{\bar{w}_{it}} \varepsilon_{it}$$

The coefficient of DQ_t in the last line can be interpreted as the weighted variance of the income elasticities $\mu_1/\bar{w}_{1t}, \ldots, \mu_n/\bar{w}_{nt}$ with the $\bar{w}_{it}$'s as weights:

$$\sum_{i=1}^{n} \bar{w}_{it} \left(\frac{\mu_i}{\bar{w}_{it}} - 1\right)^2 = \sum_{i=1}^{n} \frac{\mu_i^2}{\bar{w}_{it}} - 1 \tag{3.4}$$

The result is, therefore,

$$DQ'_t - DQ_t = DQ_t \sum_{i=1}^{n} \bar{w}_{it} \left(\frac{\mu_i}{\bar{w}_{it}} - 1\right)^2 + \phi \sum_{i=1}^{n} \mu_i (Dp_{it} - DP'_t) \frac{\mu_i}{\bar{w}_{it}} + \sum_{i=1}^{n} \frac{\mu_i}{\bar{w}_{it}} \varepsilon_{it} \tag{3.5}$$

which shows that the log-change in the quality index, like the price-quantity covariance Γ_t, consists of three components, to be discussed in the next subsection.

The Three Components of the Quality Index

The first component of (3.5) shows that the quality index goes up when real income increases, which should cause no surprise. Since the left-hand side is the log-change in quality and DQ_t is the log-change in real income, the coefficient of DQ_t in (3.5) has the nature of an income elasticity. More specifically, the *income elasticity of the demand for quality* is equal to the budget-share-weighted variance of the income elasticities of the n commodities. The implication is that, given a fixed nonzero value of DQ_t, the quality change is larger when the income elasticities of the n goods are more different from each other. This is intuitively appealing. When all income elasticities are equal to 1, so that the variance vanishes, an increase in real income has no effect on the quality index because $\mu_i - \bar{w}_{it}$ then vanishes for each i. If, on the other hand, some commodities have income elasticities much larger than 1 and others have elasticities much smaller than 1, an increase in real income raises the quantities of the former relative to those of the latter, and hence raises both sides of (3.2) also.

The second term in the right-hand side of (3.5) is the substitution effect of the price changes on the quality index. It is equal to a negative multiple (ϕ) of the marginally weighted covariance of the price log-changes and the income elasticities. [Note that the marginally weighted mean DP'_t is subtracted from Dp_{it} and compare this with the budget-share-weighted covariance in (1.8).] Hence, when the prices of luxuries increase relative to those of necessities, the quality index will decrease – which is as it should be.

It follows from (1.9) that the variance of the third term of (3.5) can be written as

$$\sum_{i=1}^{n}\sum_{j=1}^{n}\frac{\mu_i\mu_j}{\bar{w}_{it}\bar{w}_{jt}}\mathscr{E}(\varepsilon_{it}\varepsilon_{jt}) = \sigma^2\left[\sum_{i=1}^{n}\frac{\mu_i^3}{\bar{w}_{it}^2} - \sum_{i=1}^{n}\sum_{j=1}^{n}\frac{\mu_i^2\mu_j^2}{\bar{w}_{it}\bar{w}_{jt}}\right]$$

$$= \sigma^2\left[\sum_{i=1}^{n}\mu_i\left(\frac{\mu_i}{\bar{w}_{it}}\right)^2 - \left(\sum_{i=1}^{n}\mu_i\frac{\mu_i}{\bar{w}_{it}}\right)^2\right]$$

This may be written in the form

$$\text{(3.6)} \qquad \operatorname{var}\left(\sum_{i=1}^{n}\frac{\mu_i}{\bar{w}_{it}}\varepsilon_{it}\right) = \sigma^2\sum_{i=1}^{n}\mu_i\left(\frac{\mu_i}{\bar{w}_{it}} - \sum_{j=1}^{n}\mu_j\frac{\mu_j}{\bar{w}_{jt}}\right)^2$$

Thus, the disturbance component of the log-change in the quality index has a variance proportional to a weighted variance of the income elasticities; unlike the case of the DQ_t coefficient in (3.5), the weights here are the *marginal* rather than the budget shares.

Under the assumption of rational random behavior (Section 2.8) the ε's are normally distributed. The random component of the log-change in the quality index is then also normal, with zero mean and a variance proportional to the marginally weighted variance of the income elasticities of the n commodities.

Quantity and Quality Multiplied

Our starting point in the opening paragraph was DQ'_t defined in (3.1), but we quickly shifted our attention to $DQ'_t - DQ_t$. Since we have

$$\text{(3.7)} \qquad DQ'_t = (DQ'_t - DQ_t) + DQ_t$$

we may regard DQ'_t as the log-change in the *product* of the quality index and the index of real income. It is interesting to compare this with

$$Dm_t = DP_t + DQ_t + O_3 \tag{3.8}$$

according to which the log-change in the money value of total expenditure equals the log-change in the product of the indexes of the cost of living and real income (apart from an O_3 term). This comparison suggests that DQ'_t may also be regarded as the log-change in a value index, but with "value" interpreted differently: as quality × quantity rather than price × quantity. This interpretation will prove useful in the analysis of Section 11.4.

The expression for DQ'_t in terms of income and price changes is obtained by adding DQ_t to both sides of (3.5). The coefficient of DQ_t becomes

$$\sum_{i=1}^{n} \frac{\mu_i^2}{\bar{w}_{it}} = \sum_{i=1}^{n} \bar{w}_{it}\left(\frac{\mu_i}{\bar{w}_{it}}\right)^2 \tag{3.9}$$

This is the budget-share-weighted second moment of the income elasticities, which is larger than 1 except when all income elasticities are equal. Note that it is also equal to the marginally weighted mean of the same income elasticities:

$$\sum_{i=1}^{n} \frac{\mu_i^2}{\bar{w}_{it}} = \sum_{i=1}^{n} \mu_i \frac{\mu_i}{\bar{w}_{it}} \tag{3.10}$$

This is a weighting scheme identical to that of the variance in the right-hand side of (3.6) and of the covariance in the second right-hand term of (3.5).

We thus find that the marginally weighted mean of the income elasticities is at least equal to 1 or, equivalently, at least equal to the budget-share-weighted mean of these elasticities. No such result holds for the variances. Take the two-commodity case with

$$\bar{w}_{1t} = \tfrac{1}{2} \qquad \bar{w}_{2t} = \tfrac{1}{2} \qquad \mu_1 = \tfrac{3}{4} \qquad \mu_2 = \tfrac{1}{4} \tag{3.11}$$

so that the income elasticities are $\mu_1/\bar{w}_{1t} = 1\frac{1}{2}$, $\mu_2/\bar{w}_{2t} = \frac{1}{2}$. Their budget-share-weighted variance is $\frac{1}{4}$ and their marginally weighted variance is smaller, $\frac{3}{16}$. Next take

$$\bar{w}_{1t} = \tfrac{3}{4} \qquad \bar{w}_{2t} = \tfrac{1}{4} \qquad \mu_1 = \tfrac{1}{2} \qquad \mu_2 = \tfrac{1}{2} \tag{3.12}$$

with income elasticities $\frac{2}{3}$ and 2. Their budget-share-weighted variance is $\frac{1}{3}$ and their marginally weighted variance is larger, $\frac{4}{9}$.

The Preference Independence Assumption Reconsidered

The above results, as in Section 11.1, are confined to the case of preference independence. Relaxing this assumption forces us to replace the second term in the right-hand side of (3.5) by

$$\sum_{i=1}^{n} \sum_{j=1}^{n} v_{ij}(Dp_{it} - DP'_t) \frac{\mu_j}{\bar{w}_{jt}} \tag{3.13}$$

which is a bilinear form in the deflated price log-changes and the income elasticities with $[v_{ij}]$ as matrix. This is an even less transparent expression than the quadratic form (1.11) which we obtained for the price-quantity covariance. As in the case of this covariance, we have to face the additional complication that DP'_t is not a proper mean when there are inferior goods. This also applies to DQ'_t. These problems will be resolved by means of a preference independence transformation in Chapter 12.

11.4 The True Marginal Expenditure Index

In Section 3.4 we defined three true indexes, which are the theoretical counterparts of DP_t, DQ_t and DP'_t. Now that we have defined DQ'_t in (3.1), we should consider whether the theory of the true indexes can be extended to this fourth index, which would amount to the definition of the true marginal volume index. In this section we follow a slightly different approach by focusing on the true marginal expenditure index. This is the theoretical version of

$$DP'_t + DQ'_t = DQ_t + (DQ'_t - DQ_t) + DP'_t \tag{4.1}$$

On comparing the right-hand side of this equation with (3.7), we conclude that it equals the log-change in quantity × quality × price, with the price index marginally weighted. It should be noted that this section is similar to Section 3.4 in that preference independence is not assumed, so that inferior goods are not excluded.

Review of Three True Indexes

It will be convenient to summarize the theory of the true indexes briefly. The starting point is the function $C(U, \mathbf{p})$, which specifies the cost of utility U at the price vector $\mathbf{p}$. Two utility-price situations are considered, $(U_t, \mathbf{p}_t)$ and $(U_{t-1}, \mathbf{p}_{t-1})$. The true cost-of-living index at U and the true real-income index at $\mathbf{p}$ are defined in eqs. (4.12) and (4.16) of Section 3.4:

$$P(\mathbf{p}_t, \mathbf{p}_{t-1} \mid U) = \frac{C(U, \mathbf{p}_t)}{C(U, \mathbf{p}_{t-1})} \tag{4.2}$$

$$Q(U_t, U_{t-1} \mid \mathbf{p}) = \frac{C(U_t, \mathbf{p})}{C(U_{t-1}, \mathbf{p})} \tag{4.3}$$

The true marginal price index concerns $\partial C/\partial U$, the marginal cost of utility. In eqs. (4.20) and (4.21) of Section 3.4 we considered the additional cost of raising the utility level by dU in the two price situations:

$$C(U + dU, \mathbf{p}_t) - C(U, \mathbf{p}_t) = \frac{\partial}{\partial U} C(U, \mathbf{p}_t)\, dU \tag{4.4}$$

$$C(U + dU, \mathbf{p}_{t-1}) - C(U, \mathbf{p}_{t-1}) = \frac{\partial}{\partial U} C(U, \mathbf{p}_{t-1})\, dU \tag{4.5}$$

The ratio of these two expressions,

$$P'(\mathbf{p}_t, \mathbf{p}_{t-1} \mid U) = \frac{\dfrac{\partial}{\partial U} C(U, \mathbf{p}_t)}{\dfrac{\partial}{\partial U} C(U, \mathbf{p}_{t-1})} \tag{4.6}$$

is the true marginal price index which compares $\mathbf{p}_t$ and $\mathbf{p}_{t-1}$ at the utility level U.

Logarithmic Price Changes Proportional to Income Elasticities

As (4.4) and (4.5) indicate, the numerator and the denominator of the marginal index (4.6) are both obtained by changing the argument U of $C(\ )$ infinitesimally. So, if our objective is to define a second marginal index, it is natural to consider infinitesimal changes in the prices, which are the other arguments of $C(\ )$. Since there are n prices, we shall have to specify how they change. The developments of Section 11.3 show that the luxury/necessity distinction is of crucial importance for the quality index. Accordingly, we shall consider diverging price changes for luxuries and necessities.

Imagine that prices are different from what they are, both in $t-1$ and in t; more specifically, let the logarithmic price differences be proportional to the corresponding income elasticities in some utility-price situation $(U, \mathbf{p})$,

$$d(\log p_i) = k\frac{\mu_i^0(U, \mathbf{p})}{w_i^0(U, \mathbf{p})} \qquad i = 1, \ldots, n \tag{4.7}$$

where k is an infinitesimal proportionality constant. The specification (4.7) for $k>0$ implies that we imagine that goods which are luxuries at $(U, \mathbf{p})$ increase in price relative to necessities, both in $t-1$ and in t, and that inferior goods become cheaper. The price changes in the two periods can then be written as

$$dp_{it} = kp_{it} \frac{\mu_i^0(U, \mathbf{p})}{w_i^0(U, \mathbf{p})} \tag{4.8}$$

$$dp_{i,t-1} = kp_{i,t-1} \frac{\mu_i^0(U, \mathbf{p})}{w_i^0(U, \mathbf{p})} \tag{4.9}$$

The True Marginal Expenditure Index

We shall be interested in the change in the cost of U_t caused by the price changes (4.8),

$$C(U_t, \mathbf{p}_t + d\mathbf{p}_t) - C(U_t, \mathbf{p}_t) \quad \text{where} \quad d\mathbf{p}_t = [dp_{it}] \tag{4.10}$$

and in the change in the cost of U_{t-1} caused by (4.9),

$$C(U_{t-1}, \mathbf{p}_{t-1} + d\mathbf{p}_{t-1}) - C(U_{t-1}, \mathbf{p}_{t-1}) \quad \text{where} \quad d\mathbf{p}_{t-1} = [dp_{i,t-1}] \tag{4.11}$$

The true marginal expenditure index which compares the utility-price situations $(U_t, \mathbf{p}_t)$ and $(U_{t-1}, \mathbf{p}_{t-1})$ at $(U, \mathbf{p})$ is defined as the ratio of (4.10) to (4.11):

$$M'(U_t, \mathbf{p}_t, U_{t-1}, \mathbf{p}_{t-1} \mid U, \mathbf{p}) = \frac{C(U_t, \mathbf{p}_t + d\mathbf{p}_t) - C(U_t, \mathbf{p}_t)}{C(U_{t-1}, \mathbf{p}_{t-1} + d\mathbf{p}_{t-1}) - C(U_{t-1}, \mathbf{p}_{t-1})} \tag{4.12}$$

The prime added to M serves to indicate its "marginal" nature, similar to P' of (4.6).

The definition (4.12) amounts to the ratio of the increased costs of the prevailing utility levels in the two periods, U_t and U_{t-1}, when we imagine that the price logarithms increase proportionally to the corresponding income elasticities at $(U, \mathbf{p})$, so that luxuries become more expensive relative to necessities. Note that we have both (U_t, U_{t-1}) and $(\mathbf{p}_t, \mathbf{p}_{t-1})$ in (4.12), whereas we have either (U_t, U_{t-1}) or $(\mathbf{p}_t, \mathbf{p}_{t-1})$ – but not both – in the earlier indexes (4.2), (4.3) and (4.6). This is why (4.12) is neither a price nor a volume index but an expenditure index. In (4.2) and (4.6) we compare price vectors at a selected utility level and in (4.3) we compare utility levels at a selected price vector. In (4.12) we compare two utility-price situations at $(U, \mathbf{p})$, which is a third utility-price situation. The role of this third situation is to define the income elasticities in (4.7).

Evaluating the True Marginal Expenditure Index

Consider eq. (4.4) of Section 3.4:

$$\frac{\partial C(U, \mathbf{p})}{\partial p_i} = q_i^0(U, \mathbf{p})$$

On combining this with (4.8) we find that the expression (4.10) can be written as

$$\sum_{i=1}^{n} \left.\frac{\partial C(U_t, \mathbf{p})}{\partial p_i}\right|_{\mathbf{p}=\mathbf{p}_t} dp_{it} = k \sum_{i=1}^{n} p_{it} q_i^0(U_t, \mathbf{p}_t) \frac{\mu_i^0(U, \mathbf{p})}{w_i^0(U, \mathbf{p})}$$

$$= k m_t \sum_{i=1}^{n} w_{it} \frac{\mu_i^0(U, \mathbf{p})}{w_i^0(U, \mathbf{p})}$$

For (4.11) we obtain the same result except that t is to be replaced by $t-1$. Substitution in (4.12) then gives

$$\text{(4.13)} \qquad \frac{M'(U_t, \mathbf{p}_t, U_{t-1}, \mathbf{p}_{t-1} \mid U, \mathbf{p})}{m_t/m_{t-1}} = \frac{\sum_{i=1}^{n} \mu_i^0(U, \mathbf{p}) \dfrac{w_{it}}{w_i^0(U, \mathbf{p})}}{\sum_{i=1}^{n} \mu_i^0(U, \mathbf{p}) \dfrac{w_{i,t-1}}{w_i^0(U, \mathbf{p})}}$$

The expression on the left is the true marginal expenditure index of $(U_t, \mathbf{p}_t)$ and $(U_{t-1}, \mathbf{p}_{t-1})$ at $(U, \mathbf{p})$, expressed as a fraction of the expenditure ratio of the two periods. The numerator on the right is the weighted mean of the ratios of the budget shares at t and $(U, \mathbf{p})$, with weights equal to the marginal shares at $(U, \mathbf{p})$. The denominator is the identically weighted mean of the ratios of the budget shares at $t-1$ and $(U, \mathbf{p})$.

Special Cases

When there is no change in the budget shares, $w_{it} = w_{i,t-1}$ for each i, the right-hand side of (4.13) equals 1. The true marginal expenditure index is then equal to the expenditure ratio m_t/m_{t-1}, independent of the choice of $(U, \mathbf{p})$.

In general, however, the true marginal expenditure index does depend on the utility-price situation $(U, \mathbf{p})$ at which it is evaluated. If we select $(U, \mathbf{p}) = (U_{t-1}, \mathbf{p}_{t-1})$, the right-hand denominator in (4.13) becomes

$$\sum_{i=1}^{n} \mu_i^0(U_{t-1}, \mathbf{p}_{t-1}) \frac{w_{i,t-1}}{w_i^0(U_{t-1}, \mathbf{p}_{t-1})} = \sum_{i=1}^{n} \mu_i^0(U_{t-1}, \mathbf{p}_{t-1}) = 1$$

which implies

$$\text{(4.14)} \qquad \frac{M'(U_t, \mathbf{p}_t, U_{t-1}, \mathbf{p}_{t-1} \mid U_{t-1}, \mathbf{p}_{t-1})}{m_t/m_{t-1}} = \sum_{i=1}^{n} \mu_i^0(U_{t-1}, \mathbf{p}_{t-1}) \frac{w_{it}}{w_{i,t-1}}$$

This shows that the true marginal expenditure index evaluated at $(U_{t-1}, \mathbf{p}_{t-1})$ is equal to the product of the expenditure ratio of the two periods and the weighted arithmetic mean of the budget share ratios of these periods, with weights equal to the marginal shares of $t-1$.

Similarly, if we specify $(U, \mathbf{p}) = (U_t, \mathbf{p}_t)$, the right-hand numerator in (4.13) becomes 1, so that this equation may be written as

$$\text{(4.15)} \qquad \frac{m_t/m_{t-1}}{M'(U_t, \mathbf{p}_t, U_{t-1}, \mathbf{p}_{t-1} \mid U_t, \mathbf{p}_t)} = \sum_{i=1}^{n} \mu_i^0(U_t, \mathbf{p}_t) \frac{w_{i,t-1}}{w_{it}}$$

This means that the true marginal expenditure index evaluated at $(U_t, \mathbf{p}_t)$ is the product of the expenditure ratio and a weighted harmonic mean of the budget share ratios $w_{it}/w_{i,t-1}$, with weights equal to the marginal shares of t.

The Index at Geometric Mean Income and Prices

The most interesting result emerges when we specify $(U, \mathbf{p})$ in accordance with the particular choice that was made in Section 3.7 for the indexes (4.2), (4.3) and (4.6). This amounts to geometric mean prices,

$$\text{(4.16)} \qquad \mathbf{p}_t^* = [\sqrt{p_{i,t-1} p_{it}}]$$

and the utility level associated with geometric mean income and prices:

$$\text{(4.17)} \qquad U_t^* = u_I(m_t^*, \mathbf{p}_t^*) \quad \text{where} \quad m_t^* = \sqrt{m_{t-1} m_t}$$

In the next subsection we prove

$$\text{(4.18)} \qquad \log M'(U_t, \mathbf{p}_t, U_{t-1}, \mathbf{p}_{t-1} \mid U_t^*, \mathbf{p}_t^*) = \sum_{i=1}^{n} \mu_i^0(U_t^*, \mathbf{p}_t^*)(Dp_{it} + Dq_{it}) + O_3$$

This shows that, if the variability of the marginal shares is ignored, so that the first term on the right equals $DP'_t + DQ'_t$, both sides of (4.1) can be identified with the log-change in the true marginal expenditure index at geometric mean income and prices, apart from an error term O_3. In other words, if we imagine that the price logarithms of $t-1$ and t increase proportionally to the income elasticities at geometric mean income and prices, the logarithmic ratio of the implied increased costs of U_t and U_{t-1} equals $DP'_t + DQ'_t$ plus an O_3 term.

Derivations

We shall use the abbreviation

$$\mu_i = \mu_i^0 (U_t^*, \mathbf{p}_t^*) \qquad i = 1, \ldots, n \tag{4.19}$$

so that (4.13) at geometric mean income and prices is simplified to

$$\frac{M'(U_t, \mathbf{p}_t, U_{t-1}, \mathbf{p}_{t-1} \mid U_t^*, \mathbf{p}_t^*)}{m_t/m_{t-1}} = \frac{\sum_{i=1}^{n} \mu_i \dfrac{w_{it}}{w_i^0(U_t^*, \mathbf{p}_t^*)}}{\sum_{i=1}^{n} \mu_i \dfrac{w_{i,t-1}}{w_i^0(U_t^*, \mathbf{p}_t^*)}} \tag{4.20}$$

The numerator and denominator on the right are both weighted arithmetic means of budget share ratios. Suppose for a moment that we had weighted geometric means instead. The right-hand side of (4.20) then becomes

$$\frac{\prod_{i=1}^{n} [w_{it}/w_i^0(U_t^*, \mathbf{p}_t^*)]^{\mu_i}}{\prod_{i=1}^{n} [w_{i,t-1}/w_i^0(U_t^*, \mathbf{p}_t^*)]^{\mu_i}} = \prod_{i=1}^{n} \left(\frac{w_{it}}{w_{i,t-1}}\right)^{\mu_i} \tag{4.21}$$

When we substitute this in (4.20) and take logs, we find that $\log M'$ at geometric mean income and prices equals

$$\begin{aligned} Dm_t + \sum_{i=1}^{n} \mu_i Dw_{it} &= Dm_t + \sum_{i=1}^{n} \mu_i (Dp_{it} + Dq_{it} - Dm_t) \\ &= \sum_{i=1}^{n} \mu_i (Dp_{it} + Dq_{it}) \end{aligned}$$

After substituting (4.19) for μ_i, we obtain the right-hand side of (4.18) excluding the O_3 term. Therefore, to verify (4.18), we must prove that the occurrence of arithmetic rather than geometric means in (4.20) implies a term of order O_3.

For this purpose we define

$$1 + \delta_i = \frac{w_{it}}{w_i^0(U_t^*, \mathbf{p}_t^*)} \qquad 1 + \varepsilon_i = \frac{w_{i,t-1}}{w_i^0(U_t^*, \mathbf{p}_t^*)} \tag{4.22}$$

Since δ_i and ε_i are both O_1, the logarithm of the right-hand numerator in (4.20) can be written as

$$\log\left[\sum_{i=1}^{n} \mu_i(1+\delta_i)\right] = \log\left(1+\sum_{i=1}^{n} \mu_i\delta_i\right) = \sum_{i=1}^{n} \mu_i\delta_i - \tfrac{1}{2}\left(\sum_{i=1}^{n} \mu_i\delta_i\right)^2 + O_3$$

and the logarithm of the denominator as

$$\log\left[\sum_{i=1}^{n} \mu_i(1+\varepsilon_i)\right] = \sum_{i=1}^{n} \mu_i\varepsilon_i - \tfrac{1}{2}\left(\sum_{i=1}^{n} \mu_i\varepsilon_i\right)^2 + O_3$$

By subtracting we find the logarithm of the right-hand side of (4.20):

$$(4.23) \qquad \sum_{i=1}^{n} \mu_i(\delta_i - \varepsilon_i) - \tfrac{1}{2}\left[\left(\sum_{i=1}^{n} \mu_i\delta_i\right)^2 - \left(\sum_{i=1}^{n} \mu_i\varepsilon_i\right)^2\right] + O_3$$

We shall prove in the next paragraph that the expression in brackets is O_3, and also the following result for the first term:

$$(4.24) \qquad \sum_{i=1}^{n} \mu_i(\delta_i - \varepsilon_i) = \sum_{i=1}^{n} \mu_i Dw_{it} + O_3$$

This shows that the expression (4.23) is equal to the logarithm of the geometric mean (4.21) plus an O_3 term, which completes the proof of (4.18).

The proof of (4.24) follows from (4.22),

$$\delta_i - \varepsilon_i = \frac{\Delta w_{it}}{w_i^0(U_t^*, \mathbf{p}_t^*)} = \frac{\Delta w_{it}}{\bar{w}_{it}} + O_3 = Dw_{it} + O_3$$

where the second step is based on the proposition (proved on page 136 of Volume 1) that the ith budget share at geometric mean income and prices differs from $\bar{w}_{it}$ to the order O_2, and the third step is based on eq. (1.28) of Section 5.1. Next, using the same properties, we write

$$1 + \delta_i = \frac{w_{it}}{\bar{w}_{it}} + O_2 = 1 + \tfrac{1}{2}\frac{\Delta w_{it}}{\bar{w}_{it}} + O_2 = 1 + \tfrac{1}{2} Dw_{it} + O_2$$

Hence $\delta_i = \frac{1}{2} Dw_{it} + O_2$ and therefore $\sum_i \mu_i\delta_i = \frac{1}{2}\sum_i \mu_i Dw_{it} + O_2$, which we square:

$$(4.25) \qquad \left(\sum_{i=1}^{n} \mu_i\delta_i\right)^2 = \tfrac{1}{4}\left(\sum_{i=1}^{n} \mu_i Dw_{it}\right)^2 + O_3$$

Similarly, $\varepsilon_i = -\frac{1}{2}Dw_{it} + O_2$ and $\sum_i \mu_i \varepsilon_i = -\frac{1}{2}\sum_i \mu_i Dw_{it} + O_2$, which gives

$$\left(\sum_{i=1}^{n} \mu_i \varepsilon_i\right)^2 = \tfrac{1}{4}\left(\sum_{i=1}^{n} \mu_i Dw_{it}\right)^2 + O_3 \tag{4.26}$$

By subtracting (4.26) from (4.25) we find that the expression in brackets in (4.23) is of the third order.

11.5 The Distance from the Marginal Allocation and Some First and Second Moments

The first term in the right-hand side of (4.24) is the marginally weighted mean of the log-changes in the budget shares:

$$DW_t' = \sum_{i=1}^{n} \mu_i Dw_{it} \tag{5.1}$$

This is the marginal version of the allocation discrepancy $DW_t = \sum_i \bar{w}_{it} Dw_{it}$ given in (2.21), which has some interesting properties.

The Change in the Distance from the Marginal Allocation

When income increases but prices remain constant, all budget shares move in the direction of the corresponding marginal shares. This follows from eq. (5.24) of Section 1.5, which is simplified to

$$dw_i = (\mu_i - w_i)\, d(\log m)$$

when prices are constant. Thus, in the case of a positive income change, we have a positive dw_i for luxuries and a negative dw_i for necessities; for both kinds of goods, w_i moves in the direction of μ_i.

This simple result leads to the question of how we can measure a movement of the n budget shares toward or away from the corresponding marginal shares. One possibility is on the basis of the expected information of the message which transforms the budget shares ("prior probabilities") into the marginal shares ("posterior probabilities"). This requires that the latter shares all be nonnegative, so that we have to exclude inferior goods.

So, using the definition (1.3) of Section 5.1, we obtain

$$I(\mu : w_t) = \sum_{i=1}^{n} \mu_i \log \frac{\mu_i}{w_{it}} \tag{5.2}$$

Note that this distance measure is equal to the logarithm of the marginally weighted geometric mean of the income elasticities. To find out whether the distance of the budget from the marginal allocation has increased or decreased, we subtract from (5.2) the value at $t-1$:

$$\sum_{i=1}^{n} \mu_i \log \frac{\mu_i}{w_{it}} - \sum_{i=1}^{n} \mu_i \log \frac{\mu_i}{w_{i,t-1}} = - \sum_{i=1}^{n} \mu_i \log \frac{w_{it}}{w_{i,t-1}}$$

This proves

$$I(\mu : w_t) - I(\mu : w_{t-1}) = - DW'_t \tag{5.3}$$

where DW'_t is the marginal mean of the budget share log-changes defined in (5.1). We conclude that the budget shares move in the direction of (away from) the corresponding marginal shares when the log-changes in the budget shares have a positive (negative) marginal mean. Also note that, whereas negative marginal shares must be excluded in (5.2), there is no need to exclude them in (5.1), although DW'_t is then an "improper" mean similar to DP'_t and DQ'_t.

The Marginal Mean of the Budget Share Log-changes

We multiply (2.22) by μ_i and sum over i:

$$DW'_t - DW_t = (DP'_t - DP_t) + (DQ'_t - DQ_t) \tag{5.4}$$

This shows that, apart from the allocation discrepancy DW_t whose order is O_3, the marginal mean of the log-changes in the budget shares is equal to the log-change in the quality index plus the difference between the price index log-changes DP'_t and DP_t. Hence, to express DW'_t in terms of income and price changes under preference independence, it is sufficient to add $DP'_t - DP_t$ to the right-hand side of (3.5).

It follows from (2.17) and (2.21) that (5.4) can be written in the equivalent form

$$DW'_t = (DP'_t + DQ'_t) - Dm_t \tag{5.5}$$

The expression in parentheses is equal to the left-hand side of (4.1) and hence, in view of (4.18), equal to the log-change in the true marginal expenditure index at geometric mean income and prices plus an O_3 term. By combining this with (5.3) we conclude that, apart from an error term O_3, the change in the distance from the marginal allocation is equal to the logarithm of the ratio of m_t/m_{t-1} to this marginal expenditure index.

The Marginal Variance of the Budget Share Log-changes and the Marginal Price-Quantity Covariance

We subtract (5.4) from (2.22),

$$Dw_{it} - DW_t' = (Dp_{it} - DP_t') + (Dq_{it} - DQ_t')$$

and square both sides and weight with marginal shares:

$$\sum_{i=1}^{n} \mu_i (Dw_{it} - DW_t')^2 = \Pi_t' + K_t' + 2\Gamma_t' \tag{5.6}$$

Here Π_t' is the marginally weighted variance of the price log-changes defined in (1.7), while K_t' and Γ_t' involve quantity log-changes:

$$K_t' = \sum_{i=1}^{n} \mu_i (Dq_{it} - DQ_t')^2 \tag{5.7}$$

$$\Gamma_t' = \sum_{i=1}^{n} \mu_i (Dp_{it} - DP_t')(Dq_{it} - DQ_t') \tag{5.8}$$

Equation (5.6) is the marginal version of (2.23). It contains Γ_t', the marginal counterpart of Γ_t whose three components are shown in (1.6). The new covariance also consists of three components. To show this we write (5.8) in the equivalent form

$$\Gamma_t' = \sum_{i=1}^{n} \mu_i (Dp_{it} - DP_t')\, Dq_{it} = \sum_{i=1}^{n} \frac{\mu_i}{\bar{w}_{it}} (Dp_{it} - DP_t')\, \bar{w}_{it} Dq_{it}$$

We substitute for $\bar{w}_{it} Dq_{it}$ the right-hand side of the preference-independent demand equation,

$$\bar{w}_{it} Dq_{it} = \mu_i DQ_t + \phi \mu_i (Dp_{it} - DP_t') + \varepsilon_{it}$$

to obtain

$$\Gamma_t' = DQ_t \sum_{i=1}^{n} \mu_i (Dp_{it} - DP_t') \frac{\mu_i}{\bar{w}_{it}} + \phi \sum_{i=1}^{n} \mu_i (Dp_{it} - DP_t')^2 \frac{\mu_i}{\bar{w}_{it}} + \sum_{i=1}^{n} \frac{\mu_i}{\bar{w}_{it}} (Dp_{it} - DP_t')\, \varepsilon_{it} \tag{5.9}$$

The real-income component of Γ_t' is equal to a multiple DQ_t/ϕ of the substitution component of the log-change in the quality index given in (3.5). The substitution component of Γ_t' equals ϕ multiplied by a marginally weighted third-order moment of price log-changes and income elasticities.

Two Variances of Quantity Log-changes

The variance K_t' defined in (5.7) involves interactions of real-income, substitution and disturbance components, because it contains the square of Dq_{it}. This also holds for the budget-share-weighted variance K_t defined in (2.13). To show this more explicitly for the latter variance, we write it as

$$(5.10) \qquad K_t = \sum_{i=1}^{n} \bar{w}_{it}(Dq_{it})^2 - (DQ_t)^2 = \sum_{i=1}^{n} \frac{(\bar{w}_{it}Dq_{it})^2}{\bar{w}_{it}} - (DQ_t)^2$$

$$= \sum_{i=1}^{n} \frac{1}{\bar{w}_{it}} [\mu_i DQ_t + \phi\mu_i(Dp_{it} - DP_t') + \varepsilon_{it}]^2 - (DQ_t)^2$$

When we square the expression in brackets, we find that K_t becomes the sum of six terms, three of which concern real income, substitution and disturbances, while the other three describe the interaction of any pair of these determining factors. The component which deals exclusively with real income is

$$(5.11) \qquad (DQ_t)^2 \sum_{i=1}^{n} \frac{\mu_i^2}{\bar{w}_{it}} - (DQ_t)^2 = (DQ_t)^2 \sum_{i=1}^{n} \bar{w}_{it}\left(\frac{\mu_i}{\bar{w}_{it}} - 1\right)^2$$

This component is nonnegative and equal to a multiple DQ_t of the real-income component of the log-change in the quality index given in (3.5). The component which involves only price substitution is

$$(5.12) \qquad \phi^2 \sum_{i=1}^{n} \mu_i(Dp_{it} - DP_t')^2 \frac{\mu_i}{\bar{w}_{it}}$$

which equals ϕ multiplied by the substitution term of Γ_t' given in (5.9). The term which describes the interaction of real income and substitution is

$$(5.13) \qquad 2\phi DQ_t \sum_{i=1}^{n} \mu_i(Dp_{it} - DP_t') \frac{\mu_i}{\bar{w}_{it}}$$

which is equal to 2ϕ multiplied by the real-income component of Γ_t', and also to $2DQ_t$ multiplied by the substitution component of $DQ_t' - DQ_t$ given in (3.5). In addition, K_t contains three terms involving disturbances.

Similarly, (5.7) may be written as

$$K_t' = \sum_{i=1}^{n} \mu_i(Dq_{it})^2 - (DQ_t')^2 = \sum_{i=1}^{n} \mu_i \frac{(\bar{w}_{it}Dq_{it})^2}{\bar{w}_{it}^2} - (DQ_t')^2$$

Since the real-income component of DQ_t' is $DQ_t \sum_i \mu_i^2/\bar{w}_{it}$, we conclude that the component of K_t' which deals exclusively with real income is

$$(5.14)\quad (DQ_t)^2 \sum_{i=1}^{n} \mu_i \left(\frac{\mu_i}{\bar{w}_{it}}\right)^2 - (DQ_t)^2 \left(\sum_{i=1}^{n} \mu_i \frac{\mu_i}{\bar{w}_{it}}\right)^2 = (DQ_t)^2 \sum_{i=1}^{n} \mu_i \left(\frac{\mu_i}{\bar{w}_{it}} - \sum_{j=1}^{n} \mu_j \frac{\mu_j}{\bar{w}_{jt}}\right)^2$$

This is the marginal version of the right-hand side of (5.11). Note also that the expression in the second line of (5.14) is a multiple $(DQ_t)^2/\sigma^2$ of the variance (3.6) of the random component of $DQ_t' - DQ_t$.

The other five components of K_t' can be obtained similarly. Their derivation is straightforward, but the results lack the simplicity which characterizes the components of Γ_t in (1.6) and of $DQ_t' - DQ_t$ in (3.5). We shall return to K_t and K_t' in Section 15.3.

11.6 The Geometry of Demand

It is shown in this section how the demand equations of the Rotterdam Model can be displayed in the n-dimensional Euclidean commodity space. The importance of this geometric approach is increased by the fact that the preference independence transformation of Chapter 12 can also be illustrated geometrically in a simple and illuminating manner, as is shown in Section 12.4. It is therefore sufficient to consider here the geometric approach for the special case of preference independence, so that the demand equations take the form

$$(6.1)\quad \bar{w}_{it} Dq_{it} = \mu_i DQ_t + \phi\mu_i (Dp_{it} - DP_t') + \varepsilon_{it} \qquad i = 1, \ldots, n$$

The Budget Ellipse and the Marginal Ellipse

We define $(\mathbf{w})_\Delta$ and $(\boldsymbol{\mu})_\Delta$ as $n \times n$ diagonal matrices which contain the budget shares $\bar{w}_{it}$ and the marginal shares, respectively, in the diagonal:

$$(6.2)\quad (\mathbf{w})_\Delta = \begin{bmatrix} \bar{w}_{1t} & 0 & \ldots & 0 \\ 0 & \bar{w}_{2t} & \ldots & 0 \\ \vdots & \vdots & & \vdots \\ 0 & 0 & \ldots & \bar{w}_{nt} \end{bmatrix} \qquad (\boldsymbol{\mu})_\Delta = \begin{bmatrix} \mu_1 & 0 & \ldots & 0 \\ 0 & \mu_2 & \ldots & 0 \\ \vdots & \vdots & & \vdots \\ 0 & 0 & \ldots & \mu_n \end{bmatrix}$$

These two matrices are illustrated in Figure 11.1 by means of ellipses. This figure concerns the two-commodity case, with the horizontal axis referring to the first commodity and the vertical axis to the second. It contains the unit circle, which is the locus of all points satisfying

(6.3) $$\mathbf{u}'\mathbf{u} = 1 \quad \text{where} \quad \mathbf{u} = [u_1 \quad u_2]'$$

and two ellipses:

(6.4) $$\mathbf{u}'(\mathbf{w})_\Delta\mathbf{u} = 1 \qquad \mathbf{u}'(\boldsymbol{\mu})_\Delta\mathbf{u} = 1$$

The first ellipse will be called the budget share ellipse or, for short, the *budget ellipse*. The second is the marginal share ellipse, or the *marginal ellipse*. Since

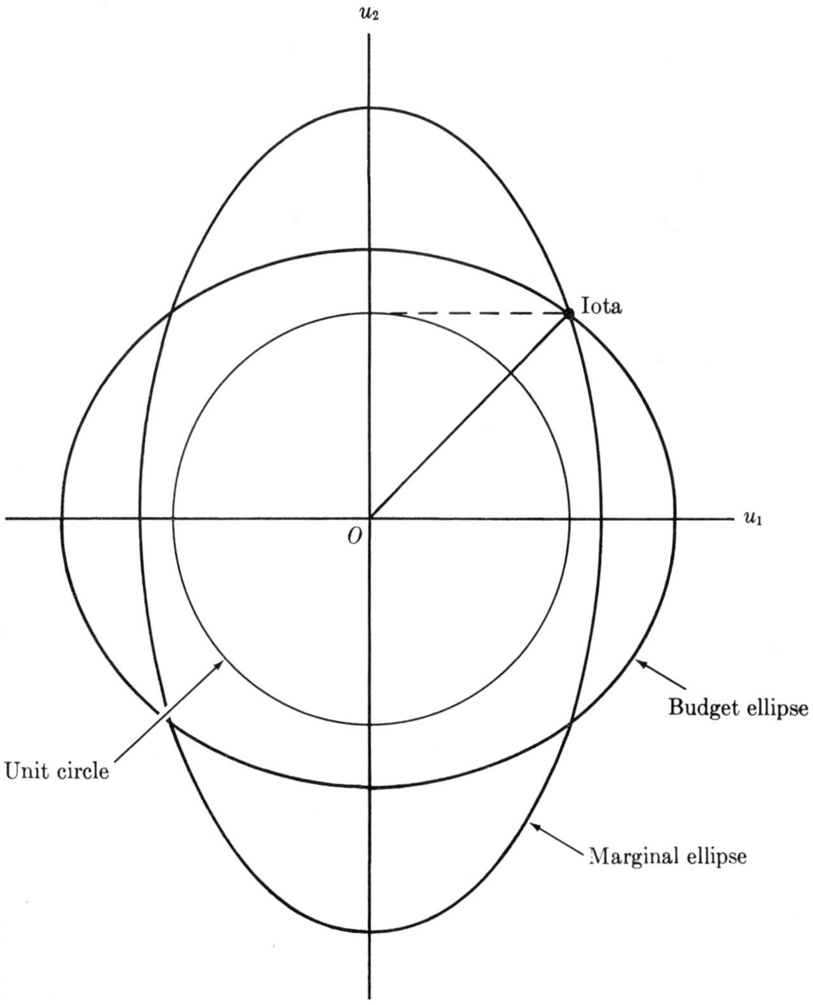

Fig. 11.1 The budget ellipse and the marginal ellipse

$(\mathbf{w})_\Delta$ and $(\boldsymbol{\mu})_\Delta$ are both diagonal matrices, the axes of the two ellipses coincide with those of the coordinate system.

We have $\sum_i \bar{w}_{it} = \sum_i \mu_i = 1$ and hence $\boldsymbol{\iota}'(\mathbf{w})_\Delta\boldsymbol{\iota} = \boldsymbol{\iota}'(\boldsymbol{\mu})_\Delta\boldsymbol{\iota} = 1$, where $\boldsymbol{\iota} = [1 \quad 1]'$. This shows that the ellipses intersect at $\mathbf{u} = \boldsymbol{\iota}$, the point whose coordinates are both 1. This point is indicated as Iota in the figure. The upward sloping straight line through this point has equal angles with the positive direction of the two axes. The horizontal broken line through Iota intersects the vertical axis at $u_1 = 0$, $u_2 = 1$, which is a point on the unit circle. This circle is wholly inside the budget ellipse, since $\mathbf{u}'(\mathbf{w})_\Delta\mathbf{u} < \mathbf{u}'\mathbf{u}$ for any $\mathbf{u} \neq \mathbf{0}$ follows from the fact that the diagonal elements of $(\mathbf{w})_\Delta$ are less than 1. The diagonal elements of $(\boldsymbol{\mu})_\Delta$ are also less than 1 under preference independence, so that the unit circle is also inside the marginal ellipse.

The extension for $n > 2$ commodities is straightforward. The commodity space is then n-dimensional and $\mathbf{u}$ has n elements, $u_1, \ldots, u_n$. This space contains a unit sphere within a budget ellipsoid and a marginal ellipsoid. The two ellipsoids intersect at Iota, the point whose n coordinates are all equal to 1.

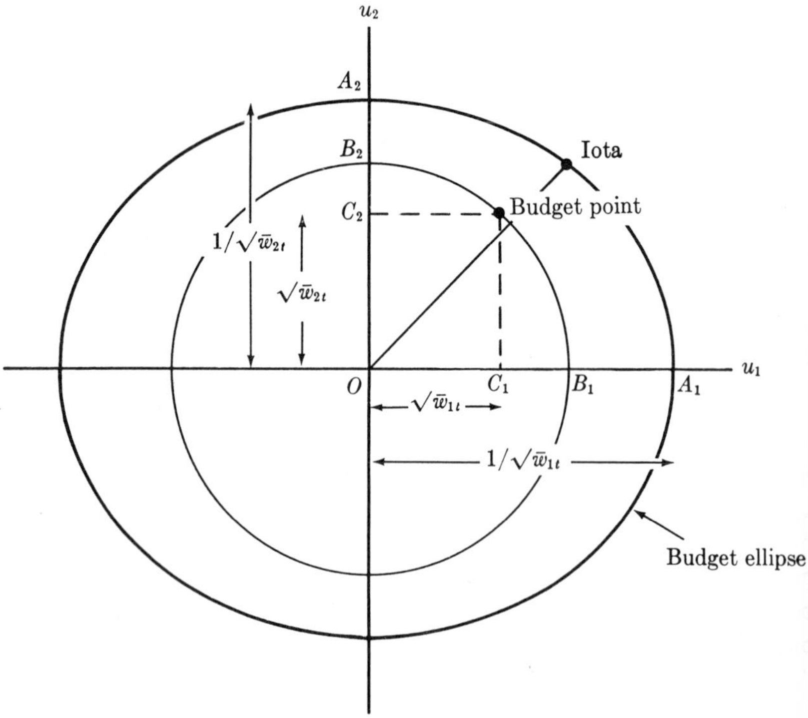

Fig. 11.2 The budget point

The Budget Point

Figure 11.2 contains the same budget ellipse and unit circle. Points A_1 and A_2 are at the intersection of the ellipse and the positive parts of the two axes. By substituting

$$\mathbf{u}=[u_1 \quad 0]' \quad \text{and} \quad \mathbf{u}=[0 \quad u_2]'$$

in $\mathbf{u}'(\mathbf{w})_\Delta\mathbf{u}=1$, we find that the distances of A_1 and A_2 from the origin are $1/\sqrt{\bar{w}_{1t}}$ and $1/\sqrt{\bar{w}_{2t}}$, respectively. Point B_1 is on the unit circle and C_1 is such that OB_1 equals the geometric mean of OA_1 and OC_1; hence $OC_1=\sqrt{\bar{w}_{1t}}$. Point C_2 is constructed on the vertical axis in the same way, so that $OC_2=\sqrt{\bar{w}_{2t}}$. The broken lines through C_1 and C_2 parallel to the axes intersect at the unit circle, because the sum of the squares of $\sqrt{\bar{w}_{1t}}$ and $\sqrt{\bar{w}_{2t}}$ equals 1. We shall refer to this point of intersection as the *budget point*. This point geometrically describes how income is allocated to the two commodities in the transition from $t-1$ to t. It does so by means of its coordinates, which are square roots of budget shares.

In the general n-commodity space the budget point is located on the unit sphere in the positive orthant of the n-dimensional space. The coordinates of this point are $\sqrt{\bar{w}_{1t}},\ldots,\sqrt{\bar{w}_{nt}}$, or $(\mathbf{w})_\Delta^{1/2}\boldsymbol{\iota}$ in vector form, where $\boldsymbol{\iota}$ is a column vector consisting of n unit elements and $(\mathbf{w})_\Delta^{1/2}$ is the $n\times n$ matrix whose elements are the positive square roots of the corresponding elements of $(\mathbf{w})_\Delta$ defined in (6.2). If O is the origin and A_i the intersection point of the budget ellipsoid with the positive part of the ith axis, the projection of the budget point on this axis is a point C_i so that OA_i and OC_i have unit geometric mean.

The Budget Transformation, the Quantity Point, and the Log-change in Real Income

Premultiplying an n-element column vector by $(\mathbf{w})_\Delta^{1/2}$ amounts to a linear transformation, which will be called the *budget transformation.* Since $(\mathbf{w})_\Delta$ is a diagonal matrix, this transformation multiplies the ith coordinate by $\sqrt{\bar{w}_{it}}$. We just found that the coordinates of the budget point are the elements of $(\mathbf{w})_\Delta^{1/2}\boldsymbol{\iota}$; hence the budget transformation changes Iota into the budget point. Also, defining $\mathbf{v}=(\mathbf{w})_\Delta^{1/2}\mathbf{u}$, we find that the budget ellipse $\mathbf{u}'(\mathbf{w})_\Delta\mathbf{u}=1$ becomes $\mathbf{v}'\mathbf{v}=1$. This shows that the budget transformation changes the budget ellipse into the unit circle. The budget transformation amounts to a 'compression" along the axes, because $\sqrt{\bar{w}_{it}}$ is less than 1 for each i.

Figure 11.3 provides another picture of the unit circle and the budget ellipse. It also contains the *quantity point* Q whose coordinates are $Dq_{1t},\ldots,$

Dq_{nt}. [When Q is based on annual data, it will normally be closer to the origin than is shown here.] The budget transformation changes Q into Q^*, the coordinates of which are

(6.5) $$\sqrt{\bar{w}_{1t}}Dq_{1t}, \ldots, \sqrt{\bar{w}_{nt}}Dq_{nt}$$

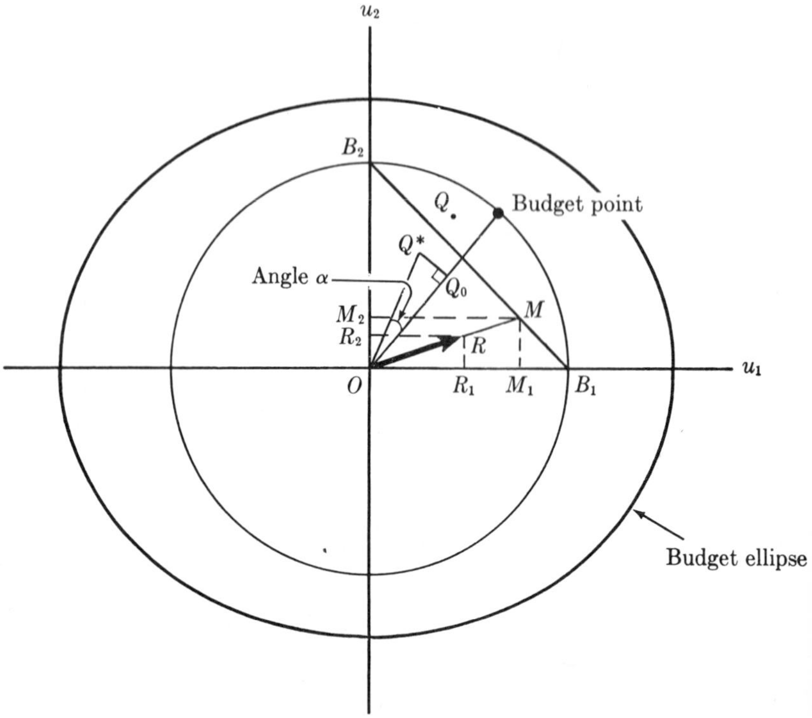

Fig. 11.3 The quantity point and the vector of real-income components of the demand equations

Consider now the angle α between the lines which connect the origin with Q^* and the budget point. Its cosine is

(6.6) $$\cos\alpha = \frac{\sum_{i=1}^{n} \sqrt{\bar{w}_{it}}\sqrt{\bar{w}_{it}}\, Dq_{it}}{\sqrt{\sum_{i=1}^{n} (\sqrt{\bar{w}_{it}})^2 \sum_{i=1}^{n} (\sqrt{\bar{w}_{it}}\, Dq_{it})^2}} = \frac{DQ_t}{\sqrt{\sum_{i=1}^{n} \bar{w}_{it}(Dq_{it})^2}}$$

The denominator in the third member is the length of the vector OQ^*. Hence (6.6) proves that OQ_0, where Q_0 is the projection of Q^* on the line from the origin to the budget point, can be identified with the log-change in real income, DQ_t.

Note that OQ_0 is to be considered nonpositive ($DQ_t \leq 0$) when Q_0 is not within the positive quadrant. Also note that Q_0 is always in the positive quadrant ($u_1, u_2 > 0$) or in the opposite quadrant ($u_1, u_2 < 0$) or in the origin ($u_1 = u_2 = 0$) because of its location on the line from the origin to the budget point. The same holds for general n when we replace quadrant by orthant.

The Variance of the Quantity Log-changes

We proceed to square (6.6),

$$\cos^2 \alpha = \frac{(DQ_t)^2}{\sum_{i=1}^{n} \bar{w}_{it}(Dq_{it})^2}$$

from which we derive

$$\sin^2 \alpha = 1 - \cos^2 \alpha = \frac{\sum_{i=1}^{n} \bar{w}_{it}(Dq_{it})^2 - (DQ_t)^2}{\sum_{i=1}^{n} \bar{w}_{it}(Dq_{it})^2}$$

This may be written as

$$\sin^2 \alpha = \frac{K_t}{\sum_{i=1}^{n} \bar{w}_{it}(Dq_{it})^2} \tag{6.7}$$

where K_t is the budget-share-weighted variance of the quantity log-changes defined in (2.13).

Taking square roots in (6.7), we find that the associated standard deviation of the quantity log-changes is equal to the distance of Q^* from the line between the origin and the budget point. As we know from the discussion below (2.13), this distance measures the change in the relative composition of the consumer's basket from $t-1$ to t.

The Real-Income Components of the Demand Model

The straight line through B_1 and B_2 in Figure 11.3 is the locus of all points in the positive quadrant whose coordinates add up to 1. For general n this line becomes an $(n-1)$-dimensional plane through the n points

$$\begin{matrix} (1, & 0, & \ldots, & 0) \\ (0, & 1, & \ldots, & 0) \\ \ldots & \ldots & \ldots & \ldots \\ (0, & 0, & \ldots, & 1) \end{matrix} \tag{6.8}$$

Point M on the line B_1B_2 has the ith marginal share as the ith coordinate. [Under preference independence all marginal shares are positive, so that M must be between B_1 and B_2.] The line OM is therefore the locus of all points for which the ith coordinate equals $\theta\mu_i$, where θ varies from 0 to 1. At R we have $\theta = DQ_t$, the distance ratios OR/OM, OR_1/OM_1 and OR_2/OM_2 all being equal to the ratio of OQ_0 to the distance between the origin and the budget point. [The latter distance is of course 1.] We conclude that the ith coordinate of R equals $\mu_i DQ_t$, which proves that the vector OR (the boldface vector in Figure 11.3), is the *vector of real-income components* of the Rotterdam Model. Note that this vector is in the negative quadrant when $DQ_t < 0$.

The Marginal Transformation, the Price Point, and the Substitution Components of the Demand Model

To describe geometrically the vector of substitution components in (6.1) we introduce the *marginal transformation*, which amounts to premultiplication by $(\boldsymbol{\mu})_\Delta^{1/2}$, the matrix whose elements are equal to the positive square roots of the corresponding elements of $(\boldsymbol{\mu})_\Delta$ defined in (6.2). This transformation changes Iota into the *marginal point* with coordinates $\sqrt{\mu_1}, \ldots, \sqrt{\mu_n}$. The marginal point is similar to the budget point in that it is located on the unit sphere in the positive orthant. By applying the marginal transformation to Iota twice, we obtain $(\mu_1, \ldots, \mu_n)$, which is point M in Figure 11.3. In what follows, we shall use primes to indicate points obtained from the marginal transformation, and we shall continue to use asterisks (as in Q^*) for those obtained from the budget transformation.

Figure 11.4 contains the unit circle and the marginal ellipse of Figure 11.1, as well as the *price point* P with coordinates $Dp_{1t}, \ldots, Dp_{nt}$. The marginal transformation changes P into P', whose i^{th} coordinate is $Dp_{it}\sqrt{\mu_i}$.[1] It is readily verified along the lines of (6.6) to (6.7), after replacing quantities by prices and budget shares by marginal shares, that DP_t' of (6.1) equals OP_0, where P_0 is the projection of P' on the line from the origin to the marginal point, and that Π_t' defined in (1.7) is equal to the square of $P'P_0$. Also, DP_t' is positive (negative) when P_0 is in the positive (negative) quadrant.

Next, to construct the *deflated price point* P_d with i^{th} coordinate equal to $Dp_{it} - DP_t'$, we subtract DP_t' from each coordinate of P. This subtraction is

[1] The marginal (budget) ellipse is shown in the figures when the marginal (budget) transformation is used, and both ellipses only when both transformations are used.

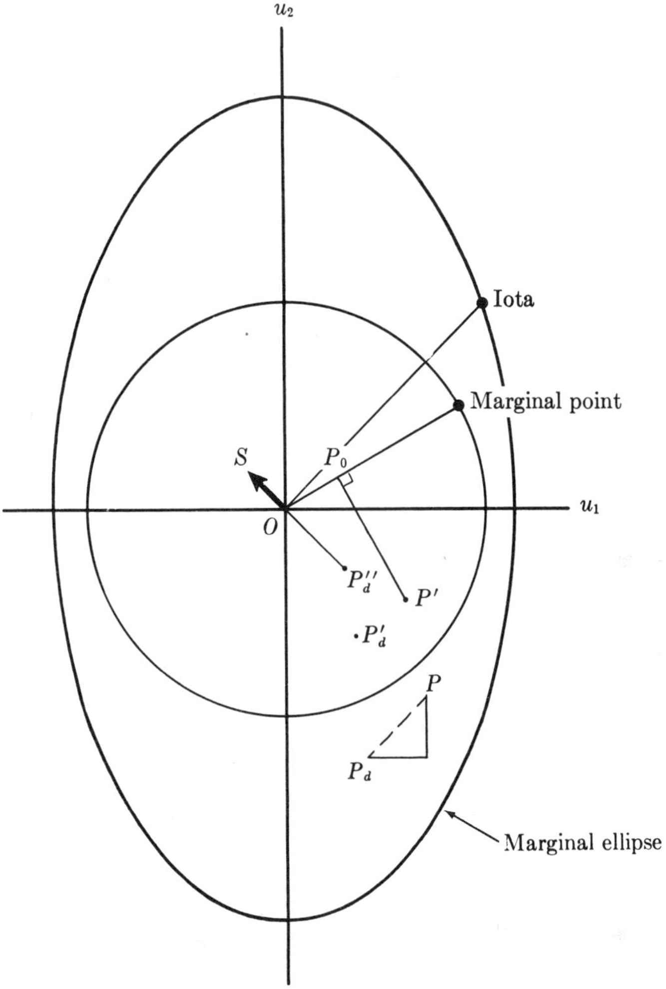

Fig. 11.4 The price point and the substitution vector of the demand equations

shown in Figure 11.4 by the vertical and horizontal line segments below P. Note that the broken line PP_d is parallel to the line from the origin to Iota, and that this parallelism also holds for $n > 2$.

Finally, to obtain the substitution term of (6.1), we apply the marginal transformation to P_d twice. This yields P_d'', whose i^{th} coordinate is

$$\sqrt{\mu_i}\sqrt{\mu_i}(Dp_{it} - DP_t') = \mu_i(Dp_{it} - DP_t') \tag{6.9}$$

The intermediate step P_d', which results from applying the marginal transformation once, is also shown in Figure 11.4.[1] Since the substitution term of (6.1) is obtained by multiplying (6.9) by the negative ϕ, the boldface vector OS is the vector of substitution components or, for short, the *substitution vector* of the Rotterdam Model.

The points S, O and P_d'' are all on the same straight line, and S and P_d'' are on opposite sides of the origin (because $\phi<0$). Also, since (6.9) gives zero when summed over i, this line is perpendicular to the line which connects the origin with Iota. In the case of general n, the points S and P_d'' are located in the $(n-1)$-dimensional plane through the origin which is perpendicular to the line from the origin to Iota. The equation of this plane is $\mathbf{\iota}'\mathbf{u}=0$; the plane is parallel to the plane $\mathbf{\iota}'\mathbf{u}=1$ which goes through the n points (6.8).

The Basic Vectors of Consumer Demand

Figure 11.5 combines Figures 11.3 and 11.4 with everything deleted that is not essential for the argument which follows.

Recall that Q^* with coordinates (6.5) is obtained by applying the budget transformation to the quantity point Q. By applying this transformation twice, similar to what was done in (6.9) by means of the marginal transformation, we obtain Q^{**}, whose i^{th} coordinate is $\bar{w}_{it}Dq_{it}$. This leads to the vector OQ^{**} of the left-hand variables in (6.1) or, for short, the *demand vector* of the Rotterdam Model. We know that $\bar{w}_{it}Dq_{it}$ has two interpretations: it is the quantity component of Δw_{it} and also the contribution of the ith commodity to the log-change in real income. The result obtained here amounts to another, geometric, interpretation: the demand vector corresponds to the point Q^{**} which is obtained from the quantity point $Q=(Dq_{1t},\ldots, Dq_{nt})$ by applying the budget transformation twice.

Three of the vectors of the model (6.1) have been introduced and are shown in Figure 11.5: the demand vector OQ^{**} and the vectors of real-income and substitution components, OR and OS. The fourth is the disturbance vector OD, where $D=(\varepsilon_{1t},\ldots, \varepsilon_{nt})$. Since the disturbances have zero sum, D is located on the line through S, O and P_d''. The point indicated by $D+S$ is obtained by adding the vectors OD and OS; the resulting sum vector is the combined effect on demand of the disturbances and the changes in relative prices. This sum vector and OR are two sides of a parallelogram

[1] The squared length of the vector OP_d' (not shown in the figure) is equal to Π_t' and the points O, P_0, P' and P_d' form a rectangle.

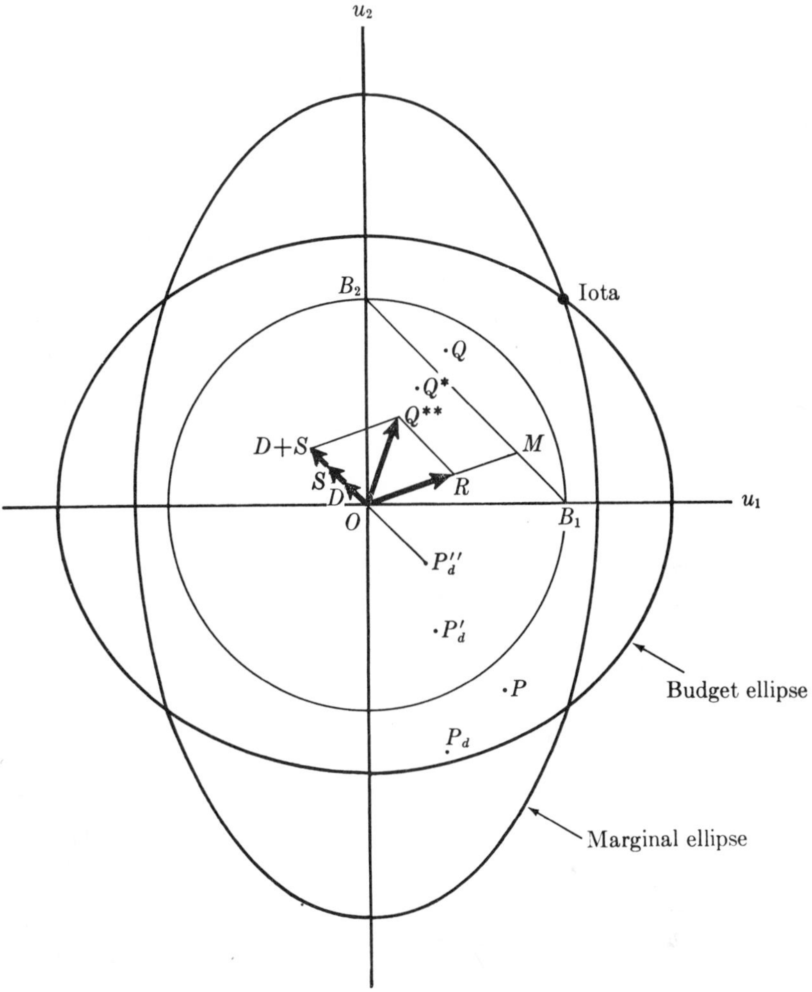

Fig. 11.5 The basic vectors of consumer demand

which yields OQ^{**}, so that this vector is described as the sum of its three components: OR for real income, OS for substitution, and OD for the disturbances. Since OD and OS are both parallel to B_1B_2, the line RQ^{**} must also be parallel to B_1B_2. This is indeed the case, because R and Q^{**} have coordinates with the same sum, DQ_t.

The zero-sum constraint on the disturbances for general n implies that OD is located in the $(n-1)$-dimensional plane through the origin which is parallel to the plane through the points (6.8). The vectors OD and OS are both in this subspace, but they need not have the same directions. The line RQ^{**} is also in an $(n-1)$-dimensional plane parallel to that which goes through the points (6.8).

The Distribution of the Disturbances

The disturbance point D in Figure 11.5 is a point that randomly fluctuates on the downward sloping line through the origin. It thus has a distribution over that line or, for general n, over the $(n-1)$-dimensional plane through the origin which is parallel to the plane through the points (6.8).

If the disturbances have zero expectation, the origin is the mean vector of this distribution. To describe the second-moment model geometrically, it is convenient to decompose the disturbances in terms of specific and general components. So we apply eqs. (7.23) and (7.24) of Section 2.7,

$$\varepsilon_{it} = \bar{\varepsilon}_{it} - \mu_i \bar{E}_t \quad \text{where} \quad \bar{E}_t = \sum_{i=1}^{n} \bar{\varepsilon}_{it} \tag{6.10}$$

and we use the covariance structure of eq. (7.22) of the same section under the specification of preference independence:

$$\operatorname{cov}(\bar{\varepsilon}_{it}, \bar{\varepsilon}_{jt}) = \begin{cases} \sigma^2 \mu_i & \text{if } i=j \\ 0 & \text{if } i \neq j \end{cases} \tag{6.11}$$

Since the general substitution component of ε_{it} is simply $-\mu_i$ multiplied by the sum of all n specific components, it is sufficient to consider the covariance structure (6.11) of the latter components. This structure amounts to a covariance matrix of the vector $\bar{\boldsymbol{\varepsilon}}_t = [\bar{\varepsilon}_{it}]$ equal to $\sigma^2(\boldsymbol{\mu})_\Delta$. Therefore, the marginal ellipse $\mathbf{u}'(\boldsymbol{\mu})_\Delta \mathbf{u} = 1$, shown in Figure 11.5, is a concentration ellipse of the specific component of the disturbance vector. If we apply the "reciprocal" marginal transformation by premultiplying $\bar{\boldsymbol{\varepsilon}}_t$ by the inverse of $(\boldsymbol{\mu})_\Delta^{1/2}$, the new vector has covariance matrix $\sigma^2 \mathbf{I}$. Thus, the transformation which changes the marginal point into Iota changes $\bar{\boldsymbol{\varepsilon}}_t$ into a vector of uncorrelated random variables with equal variance.

The theory of rational random behavior of Section 2.8 implies that $\bar{\boldsymbol{\varepsilon}}_t$ is normally distributed with zero mean vector and variances and covariances of the form (6.11). For $n=2$ this distribution can be visualized by means of a bivariate normal density on top of Figure 11.5, centered at the origin with the marginal ellipse as a concentration ellipse.

Conclusion

The above analysis shows that under preference independence the n demand equations of the Rotterdam Model can be geometrically described in terms of six elementary concepts, which include two ellipses (ellipsoids for $n>2$), two scalars, and two points:

(1) The budget ellipse $\mathbf{u}'(\mathbf{w})_\Delta\mathbf{u}=1$ describes the expenditure levels by means of the shares $\bar{w}_{1t},\dots,\bar{w}_{nt}$.

(2) The marginal ellipse $\mathbf{u}'(\boldsymbol{\mu})_\Delta\mathbf{u}=1$, the income flexibility ϕ and the parameter σ^2 of the second-moment model concern behavioral parameters. For the ellipse, it is the behavior induced by changes in real income $(\mu_1,\dots,\mu_n)$; for ϕ, it is the behavior induced by changes in relative prices (the substitution effects of price changes); for σ^2, it is the random component of behavior.

(3) The two points are the price point P and the quantity point Q. All other points that refer to the transition from $t-1$ to t are derived from these two, including the disturbance point D in Figure 11.5.

11.7 The Geometry of Summary Measures of the Consumer's Basket

We found in the previous section that the variance K_t of the quantity log-changes is equal to the square of Q^*Q_0 in Figure 11.3, and that the variance Π_t' of the price log-changes equals the square of $P'P_0$ in Figure 11.4. Both variances are among the statistical summary measures described earlier in this chapter. In this section we geometrically analyze other such measures.

The Price-Quantity Covariance

Both K_t and Π_t' are equal to the square of a line segment, and hence to an area in two dimensions. This area interpretation holds generally for second-order moments of price and quantity log-changes, including the price-quantity covariance, which we shall write as

$$\Gamma_t = \sum_{i=1}^{n} \bar{w}_{it} Dp_{it} (Dq_{it} - DQ_t) \tag{7.1}$$

Figure 11.6 contains the budget ellipse and quantity point Q of Figure 11.5. We start by constructing point Q_d with i^{th} coordinate equal to $Dq_{it}-DQ_t$. This is a matter of subtracting DQ_t (equal to OQ_0 in Figure 11.3) from each coordinate of Q. Hence the broken line QQ_d is parallel to the line from the origin to Iota. Recall that PP_d in Figure 11.4 has the same property.

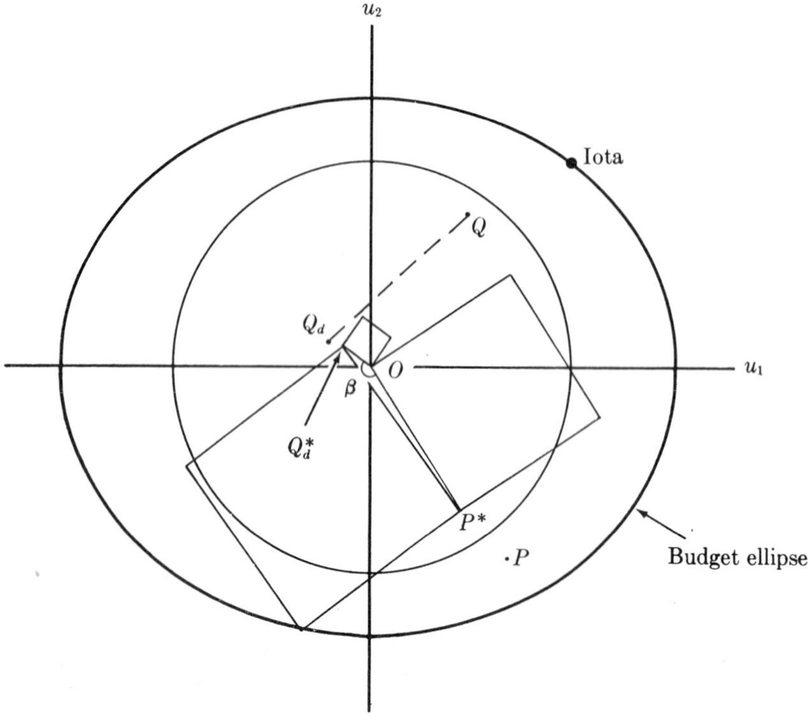

Fig. 11.6 The price-quantity covariance

Next we apply the budget transformation to P and Q_d, which gives P^* and Q_d^*, whose i^{th} coordinates are, respectively,

$$\sqrt{\bar{w}_{it}}Dp_{it} \quad \text{and} \quad \sqrt{\bar{w}_{it}}(Dq_{it} - DQ_t)$$

These two points and the associated triangle $OP^*Q_d^*$ are also shown in Figure 11.6. The angle β between OP^* and OQ_d^* has the following cosine:

$$\cos\beta = \frac{\sum_{i=1}^{n} \bar{w}_{it}Dp_{it}(Dq_{it} - DQ_t)}{\sqrt{\sum_{i=1}^{n} \bar{w}_{it}(Dp_{it})^2 \sum_{i=1}^{n} \bar{w}_{it}(Dq_{it} - DQ_t)^2}} \tag{7.2}$$

The denominator equals $(OP^*)(OQ_d^*)$, the product of the line segments OP^* and OQ_d^*. Hence, using (7.1),

$$\Gamma_t = (OP^*)(OQ_d^*)\cos\beta \tag{7.3}$$

The law of cosines states that

$$(P^*Q_d^*)^2 = (OP^*)^2 + (OQ_d^*)^2 - 2(OP^*)(OQ_d^*)\cos\beta$$

On combining this with (7.3) we obtain

$$2\Gamma_t = (OP^*)^2 + (OQ_d^*)^2 - (P^*Q_d^*)^2 \tag{7.4}$$

Hence the price-quantity covariance is equal to one-half of the area in the right-hand side. This area is obtained by subtracting the square on $P^*Q_d^*$ from the sum of the squares on OP^* and on OQ_d^*. All three squares are shown in Figure 11.6. Note that (7.4) yields a negative Γ_t when β exceeds 90 degrees, as is the case in this figure.

The Quality Index

The geometric construction of $DQ'_t = \sum_i \mu_i Dq_{it}$ is a matter of applying the marginal transformation to the quantity point, which yields Q' in Figure 11.7, the ith coordinate of which is $Dq_{it}\sqrt{\mu_i}$. It may be verified along the lines of (6.6), with budget shares replaced by marginal shares, that DQ'_t equals OQ_1, where Q_1 is the projection of Q' on the line which connects the origin with the marginal point.

Point Q_2 is located on the same line so that OQ_2 equals DQ_t, which is OQ_0 in Figure 11.3. The log-change in the quality index, $DQ'_t - DQ_t$, is thus equal to minus the distance Q_1Q_2. Hence there is a decline in quality from $t-1$ to t. This decline results from the fact that the smaller coordinate of the quantity point Q in Figure 11.7 is that of the first commodity ($Dq_{1t} < Dq_{2t}$), whose income elasticity exceeds that of the second; hence the basket has less of a luxury character in t than in $t-1$. The relative magnitude of the income elasticities can be read from Figure 11.2, which shows that $\bar{w}_{1t} < \bar{w}_{2t}$, and from Figure 11.3, where the horizontal coordinate (μ_1) of M exceeds the vertical coordinate. Therefore, $\mu_1/\bar{w}_{1t}$ is larger than $\mu_2/\bar{w}_{2t}$ in the case illustrated here.

Log-changes in Budget Shares

Figure 11.8 contains the price point P and the quantity point Q. The fourth corner of the parallelogram on O, P and Q is indicated by $P+Q$, the ith coordinate of which is $Dp_{it} + Dq_{it}$. The budget transformation changes this point into Z with coordinates

$$\sqrt{\bar{w}_{1t}}(Dp_{1t} + Dq_{1t}), \ldots, \sqrt{\bar{w}_{nt}}(Dp_{nt} + Dq_{nt})$$

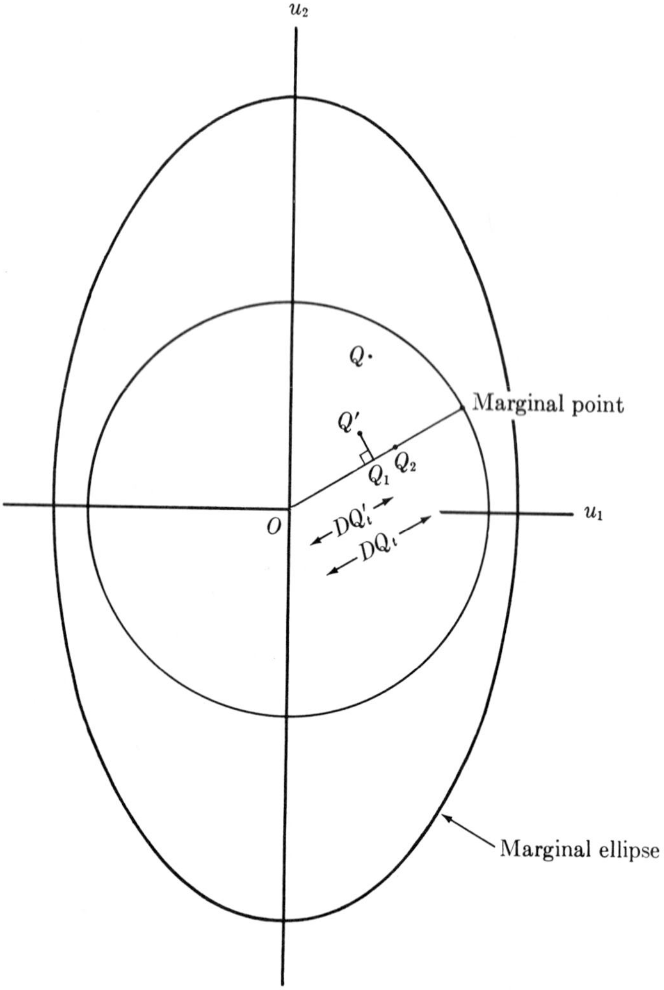

Fig. 11.7 The quality index

By proceeding along the lines of (6.6) we find that $DP_t + DQ_t$ is equal to the distance between the origin and the projection of Z on the line from the origin to the budget point. [If $DP_t + DQ_t < 0$, the projection is in the negative quadrant and the distance must be counted negatively.] We subtract this distance from each coordinate of $P+Q$, which gives W with the following coordinates:

$$(7.5) \quad Dp_{1t} + Dq_{1t} - (DP_t + DQ_t), \ldots, Dp_{nt} + Dq_{nt} - (DP_t + DQ_t)$$

The subtraction is illustrated by the broken line from $P+Q$ to W. This line is parallel to that from the origin to Iota.

It follows from (2.22) and (7.5) that the coordinates of W are the log-changes in the budget shares.[1] Next consider Figure 11.9, which illustrates DW_t', the marginal mean of these log-changes. Point W is subjected to the

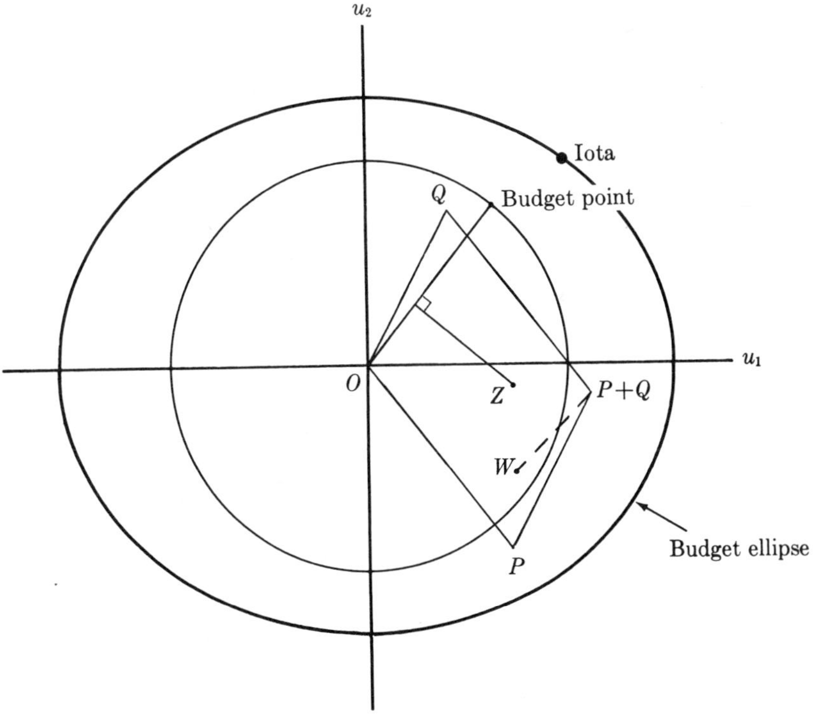

Fig. 11.8 Log-changes in budget shares

marginal transformation, which yields W' with i^{th} coordinate equal to $Dw_{it}\sqrt{\mu_i}$. We then project W' on the line from the origin to the marginal point. The distance from the origin to the projection point W_0 is DW_t' defined in (5.1), and the square of $W'W_0$ is equal to the marginally weighted variance of the budget share log-changes given in (5.6).

---

1 This and the following statements should be qualified in view of the presence of the allocation discrepancy DW_t in (2.22). However, the order of this term is O_3 and it plays an insignificant role in the figure.

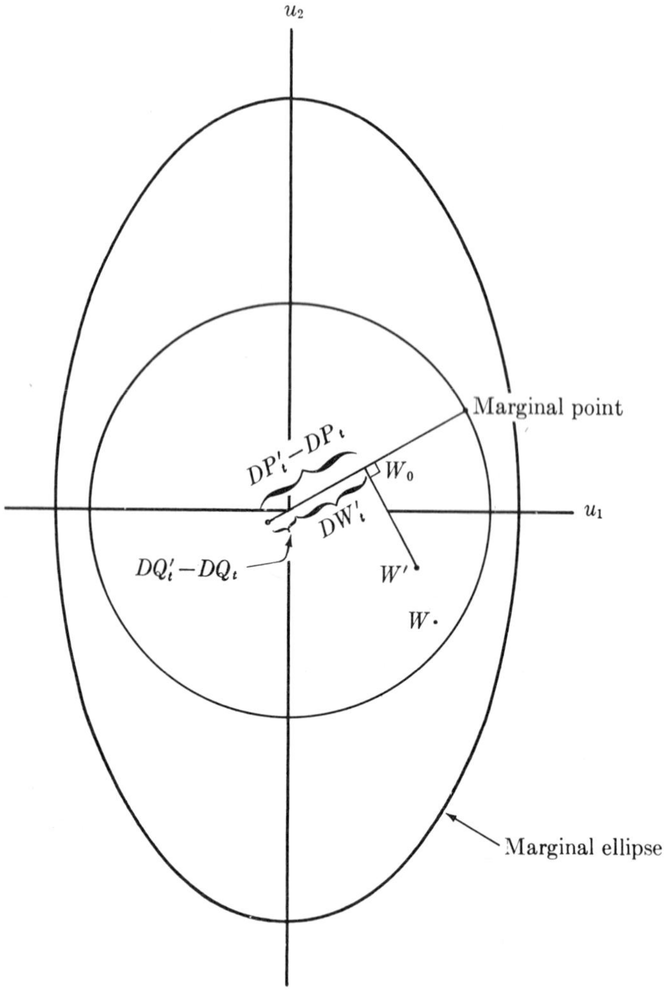

Fig. 11.9 The change in the distance from the marginal allocation

We have a positive DW_t' in Figure 11.9 because W_0 is in the positive quadrant. Hence, in view of (5.3), the distance from the marginal allocation has declined from $t-1$ to t. Also, given (5.4), DW_t' is equal to the sum of $DP_t'-DP_t$ and $DQ_t'-DQ_t$. Figure 11.9 contains $DQ_t'-DQ_t$, which is taken from Figure 11.7, on the line from the origin to the marginal point. Since $DQ_t'-DQ_t$ is negative in the case illustrated here, it is represented by a line segment in the negative quadrant, so that $DP_t'-DP_t$ exceeds DW_t'.

Further Geometric Analyses

The real-income, substitution and disturbance components of Γ_t and $DQ'_t - DQ_t$ can also be displayed geometrically, similar to the components of the demand vector OQ^{**} shown in Figure 11.5. In the case of Γ_t this amounts to adding three two-dimensional areas, each of which may be negative.

The geometric approach can also be applied to the income elasticities and their moments. Consider point $M = (\mu_1, \ldots, \mu_n)$ in Figure 11.3 and apply to this point the reciprocal budget transformation, which amounts to dividing the ith coordinate by $\sqrt{\bar{w}_{it}}$. This yields M_* with i^{th} coordinate equal to $\mu_i/\sqrt{\bar{w}_{it}}$. [An asterisk as subscript is used here to indicate the reciprocal budget transformation.] The squared length of the vector OM_* is $\sum_i \mu_i^2/\bar{w}_{it}$, which is both the marginal mean and the budget-share-weighted second moment of the income elasticities. Since this moment is at least equal to 1, M_* is never inside the unit circle; it is on the circle only if all commodities have unitary income elasticities.

When the reciprocal budget transformation is applied once more, M_* becomes M_{**} with i^{th} coordinate equal to the income elasticity $\mu_i/\bar{w}_{it}$. Next apply the marginal transformation, so that M_{**} becomes M'_{**} with coordinates of the form $\mu_i^{3/2}/\bar{w}_{it}$. The squared length of the vector OM'_{**} is

$$(OM'_{**})^2 = \sum_{i=1}^{n} \mu_i \left(\frac{\mu_i}{\bar{w}_{it}}\right)^2$$

which is the marginally weighted second moment of the income elasticities.

CHAPTER 12

THE PREFERENCE INDEPENDENCE TRANSFORMATION

In Chapters 5, 6 and 7 we made efforts to simplify demand systems in the direction of preference independence as far as the observed price-quantity data permit. The question arises, once we have reached this limit, whether it is possible to transform the system into full preference-independent form, so that utility becomes additive when formulated in terms of the implied "transformed goods." This idea is related to that of the "basic characteristics" proposed by LANCASTER (1966, 1971) and similar concepts in BECKER'S (1965) work. Another reason for such an analysis is provided by Sections 11.1 and 11.3, where we found that the price-quantity covariance and the quality index can be analyzed in a much simpler way under preference independence than otherwise.

The first attempt to transform the demand equations of the Rotterdam Model into a preference-independent system was made by THEIL (1967, Section 7.A). Subsequently BROOKS (1970) provided an alternative solution. This chapter is an extension of his work. Section 12.1 contains some ingredients for the preference independence transformation and Section 12.2 derives this transformation by means of three axioms. The later sections provide further extensions. In Section 12.7 we return to the price-quantity covariance and the quality index. Section 12.8 provides extensions based on the natural conjugate supply model of Section 10.2.

12.1 Preface to the Transformation

It will be convenient to write the $(i, j)^{\text{th}}$ price coefficient as $\phi\mu_{ij}$, where μ_{ij} is the corresponding normalized price coefficient and ϕ is the income flexibility. The ith equation of the Rotterdam Model is then

$$(1.1) \qquad \bar{w}_{it} Dq_{it} = \mu_i DQ_t + \phi \sum_{j=1}^{n} \mu_{ij} \left(Dp_{jt} - \sum_{k=1}^{n} \mu_k Dp_{kt} \right) + \varepsilon_{it}$$

The constraint $\sum_j v_{ij} = \phi\mu_i$ for each i takes the form

$$(1.2) \qquad \sum_{j=1}^{n} \mu_{ij} = \mu_i \qquad i = 1, \ldots, n$$

and $\sum_i \sum_j \nu_{ij} = \phi$ becomes

$$\sum_{i=1}^{n} \sum_{j=1}^{n} \mu_{ij} = 1 \tag{1.3}$$

The analysis which follows does not require ϕ to be constant over time. So we may allow the income flexibility to vary with the level of real income, as in eqs. (3.29) and (3.30) of Section 3.3, or to vary proportionally to the budget share of a commodity group, as in the parametrization of Section 7.3.

Matrix Notation

We introduce three n-element vectors,[1]

$$\mathbf{z}_t = \begin{bmatrix} \bar{w}_{1t} Dq_{1t} \\ \vdots \\ \bar{w}_{nt} Dq_{nt} \end{bmatrix} \qquad \boldsymbol{\pi}_t = \begin{bmatrix} Dp_{1t} \\ \vdots \\ Dp_{nt} \end{bmatrix} \qquad \boldsymbol{\varepsilon}_t = \begin{bmatrix} \varepsilon_{1t} \\ \vdots \\ \varepsilon_{nt} \end{bmatrix} \tag{1.4}$$

as well as the $n \times n$ normalized price coefficient matrix $\mathbf{M} = [\mu_{ij}]$ and the n-element marginal share vector $\boldsymbol{\mu} = [\mu_i]$. Since the price coefficient matrix prior to the normalization is symmetric negative definite, $\mathbf{M}$ is symmetric positive definite. Also, (1.2) and (1.3) can be written as

$$\mathbf{M}\boldsymbol{\iota} = \boldsymbol{\mu} \qquad \boldsymbol{\iota}'\mathbf{M}\boldsymbol{\iota} = 1 \tag{1.5}$$

where $\boldsymbol{\iota}$ is a column vector consisting of n unit elements.

Equation (1.1) for $i = 1, \ldots, n$ can now be written in matrix form,

$$\mathbf{z}_t = (DQ_t)\,\boldsymbol{\mu} + \phi \mathbf{M}(\mathbf{I} - \boldsymbol{\iota}\boldsymbol{\mu}')\,\boldsymbol{\pi}_t + \boldsymbol{\varepsilon}_t \tag{1.6}$$

where $\mathbf{I}$ is the $n \times n$ unit matrix. Using (1.5), we may write (1.6) also as

$$\mathbf{z}_t = (DQ_t)\,\mathbf{M}\boldsymbol{\iota} + \phi \mathbf{M}(\mathbf{I} - \boldsymbol{\iota}\boldsymbol{\iota}'\mathbf{M})\,\boldsymbol{\pi}_t + \boldsymbol{\varepsilon}_t \tag{1.7}$$

This equation shows how the parameters of the model are determined by the income flexibility and the normalized price coefficient matrix.

The second-moment model in the form of eq. (7.11) of Section 2.7 is

$$\operatorname{cov}(\varepsilon_{it}, \varepsilon_{jt}) = \sigma^2 \left(\frac{\nu_{ij}}{\phi} - \mu_i \mu_j \right)$$

Using the normalized price coefficient matrix, we write this as

$$\mathscr{V}(\boldsymbol{\varepsilon}_t) = \sigma^2 (\mathbf{M} - \mathbf{M}\boldsymbol{\iota}\boldsymbol{\iota}'\mathbf{M}) \tag{1.8}$$

[1] Note that the vectors $\mathbf{z}_t$ and $\boldsymbol{\varepsilon}_t$ are identical to those introduced in eq. (4.8) of Section 5.4 except that they contain n elements ($n = 4$ in Section 5.4). In the present analysis none of the demand equations is deleted.

In the analysis which follows we can allow σ to vary over time. Recall from the discussion below eq. (4.1) of Section 7.4 that we treated σ there as varying proportionally to the budget share of a commodity group.

Expenditures on Transformed Goods

Our objective is to apply a linear transformation to the model (1.7) so that the transformed counterpart of the matrix **M** becomes diagonal. This can be done in infinitely many ways, but it will always involve a transformation of the expenditures on the n commodities into expenditures on "transformed goods" in such a way that utility becomes additive in these new goods (or, at least, locally additive around the budget-constrained utility maximum). This additivity insures that the associated Hessian becomes diagonal, so that the transformed counterparts of the price coefficient matrix and of **M** are also diagonal. The economic interpretation of the transformation is that utility is written as the sum of n utilities, each corresponding to one of the consumer's basic wants and also to one transformed good which serves to satisfy the associated basic want. Examples based on data are given in Sections 13.1 and 13.2. From now on we abbreviate transformed goods as T-goods and we reserve the word "commodity" for the n original (observed) commodities.

Let each dollar spent on the jth commodity imply r_{ij} dollars spent on the ith T-good, where r_{ij} is as yet undefined ($i, j = 1, \ldots, n$). So, if $p_j q_j$ is the amount spent on the jth commodity, the expenditure on this T-good is $r_{ij} p_j q_j$ insofar as it originates with the jth commodity. Summation over j gives the total amount spent on this good:

$$\text{(1.9)} \qquad \text{Expenditure on } i^{\text{th}} \text{ T-good} = \sum_{j=1}^{n} r_{ij} p_j q_j$$

In Section 12.2 we determine the r_{ij}'s and derive other properties of the transformation by means of certain axioms. The remainder of the present section describes diagonalizations of square matrices which are used in the transformation. The reader who prefers motivation prior to algebra is advised to proceed to Section 12.2 and to go through the material which follows when reference is made to it in Section 12.2.

Diagonalization Relative to a Diagonal Matrix

The standard diagonalization of an $n \times n$ matrix **A** is

$$\text{(1.10)} \qquad (\mathbf{A} - \lambda_i \mathbf{I})\, \mathbf{v}_i = \mathbf{0} \qquad i = 1, \ldots, n$$

where $\lambda_1, \ldots, \lambda_n$ are the latent roots of **A** and $\mathbf{v}_1, \ldots, \mathbf{v}_n$ are the characteristic vectors of **A**, normalized according to

$$\mathbf{v}_i'\mathbf{v}_j = \begin{cases} 1 & \text{if } i = j \\ 0 & \text{if } i \neq j \end{cases} \tag{1.11}$$

In Section 12.2 we shall want to diagonalize the normalized price coefficient matrix **M**, not relative to the unit matrix as in (1.10), but relative to

$$(\mathbf{w})_\Delta = \begin{bmatrix} \bar{w}_{1t} & 0 & \ldots & 0 \\ 0 & \bar{w}_{2t} & \ldots & 0 \\ \vdots & \vdots & & \vdots \\ 0 & 0 & \ldots & \bar{w}_{nt} \end{bmatrix} \tag{1.12}$$

which is the diagonal budget share matrix introduced in eq. (6.2) of Section 11.6. This leads to an extension of (1.10),

$$[\mathbf{M} - \lambda_i (\mathbf{w})_\Delta]\, \mathbf{x}_i = \mathbf{0} \qquad i = 1, \ldots, n \tag{1.13}$$

with the following property of the characteristic vectors:

$$\mathbf{x}_i'(\mathbf{w})_\Delta \mathbf{x}_j = \begin{cases} 1 & \text{if } i = j \\ 0 & \text{if } i \neq j \end{cases} \tag{1.14}$$

To interpret (1.13), we recall from eq. (5.20) of Section 1.5 that the price coefficient matrix is inversely proportional to the Hessian matrix of the utility function in expenditure terms. The normalized matrix **M** obviously has the same property. The diagonal elements of $(\mathbf{w})_\Delta$ may similarly be interpreted as being proportional to the expenditures on the corresponding commodities during the transition from $t-1$ to t. Therefore, we may view (1.13) as *a diagonalization of the inverted Hessian in expenditure terms relative to the expenditure levels which prevail in* $(t-1, t)$.

Note that the use of these expenditure levels makes the diagonalization time-dependent even when the normalized price coefficient matrix is treated as a constant matrix. In fact, it is unnecessary to assume constancy for this matrix. The preference independence transformation is basically independent of the parametrization used by the Rotterdam Model,[1] but we shall find it convenient to use this model. For typographical convenience we shall refrain from using time subscripts for λ_i and $\mathbf{x}_i$, but it should be understood that they vary over time.

[1] Several models can be written in "Rotterdam format." See in particular DEATON (1974).

Comparison with the Standard Diagonalization

To compare (1.13) with (1.10) we premultiply (1.13) by $(\mathbf{w})_\Delta^{-1/2}$, the diagonal matrix whose i^{th} diagonal element is the reciprocal of the positive square root of $\bar{w}_{it}$. This gives

$$[(\mathbf{w})_\Delta^{-1/2}\,\mathbf{M} - \lambda_i(\mathbf{w})_\Delta^{1/2}]\,\mathbf{x}_i = \mathbf{0}$$

which can be written more conveniently as

$$[(\mathbf{w})_\Delta^{-1/2}\,\mathbf{M}(\mathbf{w})_\Delta^{-1/2} - \lambda_i\mathbf{I}]\,(\mathbf{w})_\Delta^{1/2}\,\mathbf{x}_i = \mathbf{0} \tag{1.15}$$

When we compare (1.15) and (1.14) with (1.10) and (1.11), respectively, we find that the two diagonalizations are identical for

$$\mathbf{A} = (\mathbf{w})_\Delta^{-1/2}\,\mathbf{M}(\mathbf{w})_\Delta^{-1/2} \qquad \mathbf{v}_i = (\mathbf{w})_\Delta^{1/2}\,\mathbf{x}_i \tag{1.16}$$

Since $\mathbf{M}$ is a symmetric positive definite matrix and $(\mathbf{w})_\Delta^{-1/2}$ is a diagonal matrix with nonzero diagonal elements, $\mathbf{A}$ as specified in (1.16) is also symmetric positive definite. Therefore, $\lambda_1, \ldots, \lambda_n$ in (1.13) and (1.15) are positive and real,

$$\lambda_i > 0 \qquad\qquad i = 1, \ldots, n \tag{1.17}$$

and the diagonalization (1.13) is unique when there are no multiple roots (equal λ's). That is, it is unique except that each characteristic vector can be arbitrarily multiplied by -1. It will appear from eqs. (3.1) and (3.2) in Section 12.3 that this qualification has no consequences for the preference independence transformation. For further details on generalized characteristic value problems see, for example, GANTMACHER (1959, pp. 310–326).

Budget Shares Expressed in Terms of Characteristic Vectors

We introduce the $n \times n$ matrix of the characteristic vectors of (1.13):

$$\mathbf{X} = [\mathbf{x}_1 \quad \mathbf{x}_2 \quad \ldots \quad \mathbf{x}_n] \tag{1.18}$$

Equation (1.14) can then be written as

$$\mathbf{X}'(\mathbf{w})_\Delta\mathbf{X} = \mathbf{I} \tag{1.19}$$

or, equivalently, as

$$\mathbf{X}'(\mathbf{w})_\Delta^{1/2}\,[\mathbf{X}'(\mathbf{w})_\Delta^{1/2}]' = \mathbf{I}$$

This proves the orthogonality of $\mathbf{K}$, defined as

$$\mathbf{K} = \mathbf{X}'(\mathbf{w})_{\Delta}^{1/2} = \mathbf{X}^{-1}(\mathbf{w})_{\Delta}^{-1/2} \tag{1.20}$$

where the second equal sign is based on (1.19).[1]

Next pre- and postmultiply (1.19) by $(\mathbf{X}')^{-1}$ and $\mathbf{X}^{-1}$, respectively:

$$(\mathbf{w})_{\Delta} = (\mathbf{X}')^{-1}\mathbf{X}^{-1} = (\mathbf{X}\mathbf{X}')^{-1} \tag{1.21}$$

This result shows that the budget shares of the commodities can be expressed in terms of the characteristic vectors of the diagonalization (1.13), and that they do not involve the roots (the λ's) of this diagonalization.

Extension to the Normalized Price Coefficients

To obtain a result for $\mathbf{M}$ similar to (1.21), we write (1.13) for $i = 1, \ldots, n$ as

$$\mathbf{M}[\mathbf{x}_1 \quad \mathbf{x}_2 \quad \ldots \quad \mathbf{x}_n] = (\mathbf{w})_{\Delta}[\mathbf{x}_1 \quad \mathbf{x}_2 \quad \ldots \quad \mathbf{x}_n]\begin{bmatrix} \lambda_1 & 0 & \ldots & 0 \\ 0 & \lambda_2 & \ldots & 0 \\ \vdots & \vdots & & \vdots \\ 0 & 0 & \ldots & \lambda_n \end{bmatrix}$$

By premultiplying this equation by $\mathbf{X}'$ we obtain $\mathbf{X}'(\mathbf{w})_{\Delta}\mathbf{X}$ postmultiplied by the diagonal matrix of the λ's on the right. Hence, using (1.19), we find

$$\mathbf{X}'\mathbf{M}\mathbf{X} = \mathbf{\Lambda} \quad \text{where} \quad \mathbf{\Lambda} = \begin{bmatrix} \lambda_1 & 0 & \ldots & 0 \\ 0 & \lambda_2 & \ldots & 0 \\ \vdots & \vdots & & \vdots \\ 0 & 0 & \ldots & \lambda_n \end{bmatrix} \tag{1.22}$$

A comparison with (1.19) shows that the transformation which changes $(\mathbf{w})_{\Delta}$ into the unit matrix changes the normalized price coefficient matrix into a diagonal matrix with positive diagonal elements [see (1.17)]. Also, by pre- and postmultiplying (1.22) by $(\mathbf{X}')^{-1}$ and $\mathbf{X}^{-1}$, respectively, we obtain

$$\mathbf{M} = (\mathbf{X}')^{-1}\mathbf{\Lambda}\mathbf{X}^{-1} \tag{1.23}$$

This shows that $\mathbf{M}$, in contrast to $(\mathbf{w})_{\Delta}$ given in (1.21), depends on both the latent roots and the characteristic vectors.

---

[1] The first equal sign implies that multiplying $\mathbf{x}_i$ by -1 changes the sign of the ith row of $\mathbf{K}$, so that there are 2^n possibilities of specifying $\mathbf{K}$. This has no real effect on the transformation; one particular choice suffices. See footnote 1 on page 234 and the discussion below (3.8).

Similarly, write (1.15) with $\mathbf{A}$ defined in (1.16) for $i=1,\ldots,n$ as

$$\mathbf{A}(\mathbf{w})_{\Delta}^{1/2}[\mathbf{x}_1\ldots\mathbf{x}_n]=(\mathbf{w})_{\Delta}^{1/2}[\mathbf{x}_1\ldots\mathbf{x}_n]\,\mathbf{\Lambda}$$

Using (1.20), we write this as

$$\mathbf{AK}'=\mathbf{K}'\mathbf{\Lambda} \tag{1.24}$$

Since $\mathbf{K}$ is orthogonal, this implies

$$\mathbf{KAK}'=\mathbf{\Lambda} \qquad \mathbf{A}=\mathbf{K}'\mathbf{\Lambda}\mathbf{K} \tag{1.25}$$

which amounts to a diagonalization of $\mathbf{A}$ leading to the same diagonal matrix $\mathbf{\Lambda}$ as that in (1.22).

The Case of Block-Independence

Suppose that the n commodities can be divided into two groups, S_1 and S_2, which are block-independent. If the commodities are appropriately arranged, the normalized price coefficient matrix and the diagonal budget share matrix can be written in partitioned form,

$$\mathbf{M}=\begin{bmatrix}\mathbf{M}_1 & \mathbf{0}\\ \mathbf{0} & \mathbf{M}_2\end{bmatrix} \qquad (\mathbf{w})_{\Delta}=\begin{bmatrix}(\mathbf{w}_1)_{\Delta} & \mathbf{0}\\ \mathbf{0} & (\mathbf{w}_2)_{\Delta}\end{bmatrix} \tag{1.26}$$

where the subscripts 1 and 2 refer to S_1 and S_2, respectively. It is readily verified that the simultaneous diagonalization (1.19) and (1.22) is satisfied by a matrix $\mathbf{X}$ with the same block structure:

$$\begin{bmatrix}\mathbf{X}_1' & \mathbf{0}\\ \mathbf{0} & \mathbf{X}_2'\end{bmatrix}\begin{bmatrix}(\mathbf{w}_1)_{\Delta} & \mathbf{0}\\ \mathbf{0} & (\mathbf{w}_2)_{\Delta}\end{bmatrix}\begin{bmatrix}\mathbf{X}_1 & \mathbf{0}\\ \mathbf{0} & \mathbf{X}_2\end{bmatrix}=\begin{bmatrix}\mathbf{I} & \mathbf{0}\\ \mathbf{0} & \mathbf{I}\end{bmatrix} \tag{1.27}$$

$$\begin{bmatrix}\mathbf{X}_1' & \mathbf{0}\\ \mathbf{0} & \mathbf{X}_2'\end{bmatrix}\begin{bmatrix}\mathbf{M}_1 & \mathbf{0}\\ \mathbf{0} & \mathbf{M}_2\end{bmatrix}\begin{bmatrix}\mathbf{X}_1 & \mathbf{0}\\ \mathbf{0} & \mathbf{X}_2\end{bmatrix}=\begin{bmatrix}\mathbf{\Lambda}_1 & \mathbf{0}\\ \mathbf{0} & \mathbf{\Lambda}_2\end{bmatrix} \tag{1.28}$$

This amounts to

$$\mathbf{X}_g'(\mathbf{w}_g)_{\Delta}\,\mathbf{X}_g=\mathbf{I} \qquad \mathbf{X}_g'\mathbf{M}_g\mathbf{X}_g=\mathbf{\Lambda}_g \qquad g=1,2 \tag{1.29}$$

Since (1.29) is equivalent to (1.19) and (1.22) but confined to S_g, this proves that the diagonalization (1.13) may be applied to each group separately under block-independence.

This result can be extended straightforwardly to any number of groups larger than two. When that number is n, so that block-independence becomes preference independence, the price coefficient matrix is diagonal as is the normalized price coefficient $\mathbf{M}$, which has the marginal shares in the diagonal. Equations (1.19) and (1.22) are then satisfied by $\mathbf{X}=(\mathbf{w})_{\Delta}^{-1/2}$ and $\lambda_i=\mu_i/\bar{w}_{it}$, the income elasticity of the ith commodity ($i=1,\ldots,n$).

Diagonalization Under Constraints

In Section 12.2 we shall want to find an $n \times n$ matrix $\mathbf{R}$ which is subject to the constraint

$$\iota'\mathbf{R} = \iota' \tag{1.30}$$

and which is such that the matrix product

$$(\mathbf{X}'\mathbf{R}^{-1})^{-1}\mathbf{\Lambda}(\mathbf{X}'\mathbf{R}^{-1}) \tag{1.31}$$

is a nonsingular diagonal matrix, with $\mathbf{X}$ and $\mathbf{\Lambda}$ defined in (1.18) and (1.22).

It is shown in the next subsection that under certain conditions (stated in the next paragraph) $\mathbf{R}$ satisfies these two properties if and only if it is of the form

$$\mathbf{R} = \mathbf{B}(\mathbf{X}^{-1}\iota)_{\Delta}\,\mathbf{X}' \tag{1.32}$$

where $\mathbf{B}$ is an arbitrary $n \times n$ permutation matrix (with exactly one unit element in each row and each column, and zeros elsewhere) and $(\mathbf{X}^{-1}\iota)_{\Delta}$ is the vector $\mathbf{X}^{-1}\iota$ written as a diagonal matrix. This notation is similar to $(\mathbf{w})_{\Delta}$ in (1.12).

Two conditions are imposed. First, $\mathbf{X}^{-1}\iota$ should have no zero elements. When it contains zero elements, $(\mathbf{X}^{-1}\iota)_{\Delta}$ is singular and so is the $\mathbf{R}$ solution (1.32), so that $\mathbf{R}^{-1}$ in (1.31) does not exist. Second, $\mathbf{\Lambda}$ should have distinct diagonal elements (no multiple roots among the λ's). Note that the solution (1.32) does not involve $\mathbf{\Lambda}$ except for this condition.

Derivations

We define

$$\mathbf{Y} = \mathbf{X}'\mathbf{R}^{-1} \tag{1.33}$$

so that the matrix product (1.31) becomes $\mathbf{Y}^{-1}\mathbf{\Lambda}\mathbf{Y} = \mathbf{D}_1$, which is required to be diagonal and nonsingular. Hence $\mathbf{\Lambda}\mathbf{Y} = \mathbf{Y}\mathbf{D}_1$ or, in scalar form,

$$\lambda_i y_{ij} = d_j y_{ij} \qquad i, j = 1, \ldots, n \tag{1.34}$$

where y_{ij} is the $(i, j)^{\text{th}}$ element of $\mathbf{Y}$ and d_j is the jth diagonal element of $\mathbf{D}_1$.

Take $j = 1$ in (1.34), $(\lambda_i - d_1)\, y_{i1} = 0$ for $i = 1, \ldots, n$. This implies $\lambda_i = d_1$ for each i for which $y_{i1} \neq 0$. Since the λ's are distinct by assumption, this means that the first column of $\mathbf{Y}$ can have at most one nonzero element. The argument can be repeated for the other columns and the result is that each has at most one nonzero element. But the existence of a nonsingular diagonal matrix $\mathbf{D}_1 = \mathbf{Y}^{-1}\mathbf{\Lambda Y}$ requires that $\mathbf{Y}$ be nonsingular. Therefore, each row and each column of $\mathbf{Y}$ must have exactly one nonzero element, which implies that $\mathbf{Y}$ can be written as $\mathbf{D}_2\mathbf{B}'$, where $\mathbf{D}_2$ is a nonsingular diagonal matrix and $\mathbf{B}$ is a permutation matrix ($\mathbf{B}'$ is also a permutation matrix). The successive diagonal elements of $\mathbf{D}_2$ are equal to the nonzero elements in the successive rows of $\mathbf{Y}$.

So, given $\mathbf{Y}=\mathbf{D}_2\mathbf{B}'$ and (1.33), we have $\mathbf{R}=(\mathbf{B}')^{-1}\,\mathbf{D}_2^{-1}\mathbf{X}'$, which can be written as

$$\mathbf{R} = \mathbf{B}\mathbf{D}_2^{-1}\mathbf{X}' \tag{1.35}$$

because permutation matrices are orthogonal. Also, $\boldsymbol{\iota}'\mathbf{B}=\boldsymbol{\iota}'$. On combining this with (1.30) we obtain $\boldsymbol{\iota}'=\boldsymbol{\iota}'\mathbf{D}_2^{-1}\mathbf{X}'$ after premultiplying (1.35) by $\boldsymbol{\iota}'$. This can be written as $\mathbf{X}^{-1}\boldsymbol{\iota}=\mathbf{D}_2^{-1}\boldsymbol{\iota}$, which is equivalent to $\mathbf{D}_2^{-1}=(\mathbf{X}^{-1}\boldsymbol{\iota})_\Delta$ because $\mathbf{D}_2$ is diagonal. By combining this with (1.35) we obtain (1.32).

12.2 An Axiomatic Approach to the Preference Independence Transformation

The First Axiom: Imposing the Budget Constraint

In (1.9) we wrote $\sum_j r_{ij}p_jq_j$ for the expenditure on a T-good. By summing over i we obtain the amount spent on all T-goods:

$$\sum_{i=1}^{n}\sum_{j=1}^{n} r_{ij}p_jq_j = \sum_{j=1}^{n}\left(\sum_{i=1}^{n} r_{ij}\right)p_jq_j$$

The first axiom states that the T-goods satisfy the budget constraint in the sense that the total amount spent on them equals $m=\sum_j p_jq_j$, for any values of m and the p's. On comparing this with the right-hand side of the above equation, we conclude that this amounts to $\sum_i r_{ij}=1$ for $j=1,\ldots,n$ or, in matrix form,

$$\boldsymbol{\iota}'\mathbf{R} = \boldsymbol{\iota}' \tag{2.1}$$

where $\mathbf{R}$ is the $n\times n$ matrix $[r_{ij}]$.

So, by dividing both sides of (1.9) by m we obtain $(w_i)_T$, the budget share of the ith T-good:

$$(w_i)_T = \sum_{j=1}^{n} r_{ij}w_j \tag{2.2}$$

In the sequel we confine ourselves to the transition from $t-1$ to t, for which (2.2) implies the following average budget share of this T-good:

$$(\bar{w}_{it})_T = \sum_{j=1}^{n} r_{ij}\bar{w}_{jt} \tag{2.3}$$

Using (2.1), we find that these shares add up to 1:

$$\sum_{i=1}^{n} (\bar{w}_{it})_T = \sum_{j=1}^{n} \left(\sum_{i=1}^{n} r_{ij} \right) \bar{w}_{jt} = \sum_{j=1}^{n} \bar{w}_{jt} = 1 .$$

It should be noted that we do not require the r_{ij}'s to be nonnegative. Doing so would deny the possibility that a commodity is detrimental with respect to the basic wants which correspond to certain T-goods. This would be quite restrictive. For example, if the enjoyment of his own garden is one of the consumer's basic wants, spending money on summer vacations elsewhere is detrimental to the satisfaction of this particular want.

Decomposition of Budget Share Changes

Consider the decomposition of the change in the budget share of the jth commodity:

$$\text{(2.4)} \qquad \Delta w_{jt} = \bar{w}_{jt} Dp_{jt} + \bar{w}_{jt} Dq_{jt} - \bar{w}_{jt} Dm_t + O_3$$

We multiply both sides by r_{ij} and sum over j. It follows from (2.2) that the left-hand side may be identified with the change in the budget share of a T-good, so that the equation obtained is a decomposition of this budget share change in terms of the price and quantity changes of the n commodities and the income change. The right-hand side, apart from the O_3 term, is

$$\text{(2.5)} \qquad \sum_{j=1}^{n} r_{ij} \bar{w}_{jt} Dp_{jt} + \sum_{j=1}^{n} r_{ij} \bar{w}_{jt} Dq_{jt} - (\bar{w}_{it})_T \, Dm_t$$

where $(\bar{w}_{it})_T$ is defined in (2.3).

The Second Axiom: Defining Price Log-changes of T-Goods

Consider the decomposition of the infinitesimal change in a budget share w_k:

$$dw_k = w_k d(\log p_k) + w_k d(\log q_k) - w_k d(\log m)$$

Let us use this decomposition for any grouping of expenditures, including commodities as well as T-goods. Then (2.4) is its finite-change approximation for the jth commodity and (2.5) is its finite-change approximation for the ith T-good. Note that this implies that the first term in (2.5) is the price component of the budget share change of this T-good. Note further that this also implies

$$\text{(2.6)} \qquad \sum_{j=1}^{n} r_{ij} \bar{w}_{jt} Dp_{jt} = (\bar{w}_{it})_T \times \text{price log-change of } i^{\text{th}} \text{ T-good}$$

because $\sum_j r_{ij}\bar{w}_{jt}Dp_{jt}$ is the T-good version of $\bar{w}_{jt}Dp_{jt}$ for the jth commodity in (2.4).

Equation (2.6) constitutes our second axiom. It equates the price component of the budget share change of each T-good to the product of the price log-change of this good and the budget share average $(\bar{w}_{it})_T$ defined in (2.3). This axiom implies the following definition of the price log-change of this T-good:

$$\text{(2.7)} \qquad \sum_{j=1}^{n} s_{ij}Dp_{jt} \quad \text{where} \quad s_{ij} = \frac{r_{ij}\bar{w}_{jt}}{(\bar{w}_{it})_T} = \frac{r_{ij}\bar{w}_{jt}}{\sum_{k=1}^{n} r_{ik}\bar{w}_{kt}}$$

Note that the s_{ij} definition involves time subscripts. In order to simplify the notation we shall use no such subscripts for s_{ij}.

Three Remarks on the Second Axiom

(1) The s_{ij} definition in (2.7) implies $\sum_j s_{ij}=1$ for each i or, equivalently,

$$\text{(2.8)} \qquad \mathbf{S}\boldsymbol{\iota} = \boldsymbol{\iota}$$

where $\mathbf{S}=[s_{ij}]$. Suppose that the prices of all n commodities change proportionately, $Dp_{it}=k$ for each i. Then $\boldsymbol{\pi}_t=k\boldsymbol{\iota}$, where $\boldsymbol{\pi}_t$ is defined in (1.4), so that $\mathbf{S}\boldsymbol{\pi}_t=k\mathbf{S}\boldsymbol{\iota}=k\boldsymbol{\iota}$ in view of (2.8). Since the definition (2.7) implies that $\mathbf{S}\boldsymbol{\pi}_t$ is the vector of price log-changes of the T-goods, this proves that, when the prices of all commodities change proportionately, the price of each T-good changes in the same proportion.

(2) If we apply the arguments leading to (2.6) and (2.7) to quantities instead of prices, we obtain $\sum_j s_{ij}Dq_{jt}$ for the quantity log-change of the ith T-good. This proves that the approach can be viewed as one which applies identical transformations to price and quantity log changes.

(3) When $(\bar{w}_{it})_T$ vanishes, s_{ij} is not defined in (2.7). The treatment of this case is postponed until the first subsection of Section 12.3. It is assumed throughout the present section that all elements of $\mathbf{S}$ exist and that this matrix is nonsingular. [As we shall be able to conclude from (2.22) below, this is equivalent to assuming that the vector $\mathbf{X}^{-1}\boldsymbol{\iota}$ contains no zero elements, $\mathbf{X}$ being defined in (1.18). This assumption is one of the two conditions described below (1.32).]

The Third Axiom: A Negative Definite Diagonal Price Coefficient Matrix

The quantity component $\sum_j r_{ij}\bar{w}_{jt}Dq_{jt}$ in (2.5) is the ith element of the vector $\mathbf{R}\mathbf{z}_t$, where $\mathbf{z}_t$ is defined in (1.4). So we obtain the demand equations for the T-goods by premultiplying (1.7) by **R**:

$$\mathbf{Rz}_t = (DQ_t)\,\mathbf{RM\iota} + \phi\mathbf{RM}(\mathbf{I} - \mathbf{\iota\iota'M})\,\boldsymbol{\pi}_t + \mathbf{R}\boldsymbol{\varepsilon}_t$$

This equation contains price log-changes of commodities ($\boldsymbol{\pi}_t$), not of T-goods ($\mathbf{S}\boldsymbol{\pi}_t$). So we write it as

$$\mathbf{Rz}_t = (DQ_t)\,\mathbf{RM\iota} + \phi\mathbf{RM}(\mathbf{I} - \mathbf{\iota\iota'M})\,\mathbf{S}^{-1}(\mathbf{S}\boldsymbol{\pi}_t) + \mathbf{R}\boldsymbol{\varepsilon}_t$$

or, more conveniently, as

$$\mathbf{Rz}_t = (DQ_t)\,\mathbf{RM\iota} + \phi\mathbf{RMS}^{-1}(\mathbf{I} - \mathbf{S\iota\iota'MS}^{-1})\,\mathbf{S}\boldsymbol{\pi}_t + \mathbf{R}\boldsymbol{\varepsilon}_t$$

The matrix in parentheses can be written as

$$\mathbf{I} - \mathbf{\iota\iota'MS}^{-1} = \mathbf{I} - \mathbf{\iota\iota'}(\mathbf{RMS}^{-1})$$

in view of (2.8) and (2.1). Also, since premultiplication of $\mathbf{S\iota} = \boldsymbol{\iota}$ by $\mathbf{S}^{-1}$ gives $\boldsymbol{\iota} = \mathbf{S}^{-1}\boldsymbol{\iota}$, we may write $DQ_t(\mathbf{RMS}^{-1})\boldsymbol{\iota}$ for the real-income term. So the transformed demand model takes the form

(2.9)
$$\mathbf{Rz}_t = DQ_t(\mathbf{RMS}^{-1})\,\boldsymbol{\iota} + \phi\mathbf{RMS}^{-1}\,[\mathbf{I} - \mathbf{\iota\iota'}(\mathbf{RMS}^{-1})]\,\mathbf{S}\boldsymbol{\pi}_t + \mathbf{R}\boldsymbol{\varepsilon}_t$$

On comparing this equation with (1.7), we conclude that the price coefficient matrix $\phi\mathbf{M}$ has been transformed into $\phi\mathbf{RMS}^{-1}$. Equivalently, the normalized price coefficient matrix **M** has been transformed into $\mathbf{RMS}^{-1}$, which occurs in the same three places in (2.9) as **M** does in (1.7). The third axiom states that $\mathbf{RMS}^{-1}$ is diagonal with positive diagonal elements, so that $\phi\mathbf{RMS}^{-1}$, the transformed price coefficient matrix, is diagonal and negative definite.

Some Invariance Properties

Before implementing the third axiom it is convenient to consider certain implications of the two earlier axioms. Several properties of the basket are invariant under the preference independence transformation:

(1) The first axiom in the form (2.1) implies that the log-change in real income is invariant. To prove this, note that this log-change is equal to the sum of the left-hand variables of the demand equations, $DQ_t = \boldsymbol{\iota}'\mathbf{z}_t$. Since $\mathbf{z}_t$ is transformed into $\mathbf{Rz}_t$, this sum after the transformation becomes

$$\boldsymbol{\iota}'(\mathbf{Rz}_t) = (\boldsymbol{\iota}'\mathbf{R})\,\mathbf{z}_t = \boldsymbol{\iota}'\mathbf{z}_t = DQ_t$$

(2) The first axiom also implies that the zero-sum property of the disturbances, $\boldsymbol{\iota}'\boldsymbol{\varepsilon}_t = 0$, is invariant, because the disturbance vector of (2.9) is $\mathbf{R}\boldsymbol{\varepsilon}_t$ and $\boldsymbol{\iota}'\mathbf{R}\boldsymbol{\varepsilon}_t = 0$ follows from $\boldsymbol{\iota}'\mathbf{R} = \boldsymbol{\iota}'$ and $\boldsymbol{\iota}'\boldsymbol{\varepsilon}_t = 0$.

(3) The log-change in the marginal price index in (1.7) is of the form $\boldsymbol{\iota}'\mathbf{M}\boldsymbol{\pi}_t$. Its transformed counterpart in (2.9) is

$$\boldsymbol{\iota}'(\mathbf{RMS}^{-1})\,\mathbf{S}\boldsymbol{\pi}_t = \boldsymbol{\iota}'\mathbf{RM}\boldsymbol{\pi}_t$$

which is independent of $\mathbf{S}$. Using (2.1), we conclude that the first axiom implies that the marginal price index is invariant.

(4) We now turn to the second axiom and write (2.6) as

$$\sum_{j=1}^{n} r_{ij}\bar{w}_{jt}Dp_{jt} = (\bar{w}_{it})_T \sum_{j=1}^{n} s_{ij}Dp_{jt} \tag{2.10}$$

The right-hand side is the transformed version of $\bar{w}_{it}Dp_{it}$. Since the log-change in the cost-of-living index equals $\sum_i \bar{w}_{it}Dp_{it}$, the log-change in the transformed cost-of-living index is equal to the sum over i of the right-hand side of (2.10). But the sum over i of the left-hand side equals $\sum_j \bar{w}_{jt}Dp_{jt}$ in view of (2.1). Therefore, the first and second axioms jointly imply that the cost-of-living index is invariant.

(5) The sum of all n^2 price coefficients is equal to the income flexibility. This is equivalent to the unit sum of all normalized price coefficients, $\boldsymbol{\iota}'\mathbf{M}\boldsymbol{\iota}=1$ in (1.5). The transformed counterpart in (2.9) has the same property,

$$\boldsymbol{\iota}'(\mathbf{RMS}^{-1})\,\boldsymbol{\iota} = \boldsymbol{\iota}'\mathbf{M}\boldsymbol{\iota} = 1$$

because $\boldsymbol{\iota}'\mathbf{R}=\boldsymbol{\iota}'$ and $\mathbf{S}^{-1}\boldsymbol{\iota}=\boldsymbol{\iota}$ (which is implied by $\mathbf{S}\boldsymbol{\iota}=\boldsymbol{\iota}$). Hence the sum of all elements of the price coefficient matrix $\phi\mathbf{RMS}^{-1}$ in (2.9) equals ϕ, which proves the invariance of the income flexibility. Note that this result, too, is implied by the first and second axioms jointly.

The Composition Matrix of the Preference Independence Transformation

Consider (2.3), $(\bar{w}_{it})_T=\sum_j r_{ij}\bar{w}_{jt}$, which shows that $r_{ij}\bar{w}_{jt}$ may be viewed as the component of $(\bar{w}_{it})_T$ that originates with the jth commodity. This $r_{ij}\bar{w}_{jt}$ links an individual T-good to an individual commodity. It is the $(i,j)^{\text{th}}$ element of the $n\times n$ matrix

$$\mathbf{T} = \mathbf{R}(\mathbf{w})_\Delta \tag{2.11}$$

where $(\mathbf{w})_\Delta$ is the diagonal budget share matrix defined in (1.12).

The matrix $\mathbf{T}$ will be called the *composition matrix* of the preference independence transformation; this term is explained in the next subsection. The sum of the elements of the ith row of $\mathbf{T}$ equals $(\bar{w}_{it})_T$, the budget share of a T-good, and the sum of the elements of the ith column equals $\bar{w}_{it}$, the budget share of a commodity:

$$\mathbf{T}\boldsymbol{\iota} = \mathbf{w}_T \quad \text{where} \quad \mathbf{w}_T = [(\bar{w}_{1t})_T \cdots (\bar{w}_{nt})_T]' \tag{2.12}$$

$$\mathbf{T}'\boldsymbol{\iota} = \mathbf{w} \quad \text{where} \quad \mathbf{w} = [\bar{w}_{1t} \cdots \bar{w}_{nt}]' \tag{2.13}$$

To prove (2.12) we postmultiply (2.11) by $\boldsymbol{\iota}$, which gives $\mathbf{T}\boldsymbol{\iota}=\mathbf{R}\mathbf{w}$, and use (2.3) to verify that the ith element of the vector $\mathbf{Rw}$ is equal to $(\bar{w}_{it})_T$. For (2.13) we use (2.11) and (2.1):

$$\boldsymbol{\iota}'\mathbf{T} = \boldsymbol{\iota}'\mathbf{R}(\mathbf{w})_\Delta = \boldsymbol{\iota}'(\mathbf{w})_\Delta = \mathbf{w}'$$

The Composition Matrix as a Tool for Identifying T-Goods

We may conclude from (2.12) that each row of **T** describes the composition of a T-good in terms of commodities and from (2.13) that each column describes the composition of a commodity in terms of T-goods. As an example, consider the following composition matrix:

$$\mathbf{T} = \begin{bmatrix} .344 & .421 & .165 \\ .136 & -.082 & 0 \\ .024 & .030 & -.038 \end{bmatrix} \begin{matrix} .930 = (\bar{w}_{1t})_T \\ .054 = (\bar{w}_{2t})_T \\ .016 = (\bar{w}_{3t})_T \end{matrix} \tag{2.14}$$

$$.504 = \bar{w}_{1t} \qquad .369 = \bar{w}_{2t} \qquad .127 = \bar{w}_{3t}$$

The column sums indicate that 50.4 percent of the budget is accounted for by the first commodity, 36.9 percent by the second, and 12.7 percent by the third. Similarly, the row sums show that 93 percent of the same budget is allocated to the first T-good, 5.4 percent to the second, and only 1.6 percent to the third.

Next consider the individual elements in the successive rows. Those in the first row are all positive, which means that the three commodities are positively represented in the first T-good. The elements in the second row show that the third commodity is not represented in the second T-good, and that the second commodity is represented negatively. This means that this T-good is a *contrast* between the first and the second commodities; the associated basic want is the pleasure of consuming the first commodity rather than the second. In the same way, the third T-good represents a contrast between the first and second commodities on one hand, and the third on the other.

The elements in each column allow a similar interpretation. Those in the first column show that the first commodity contributes positively to all three basic wants. This is not true for the other two commodities. The second contributes negatively to the second basic want, and the third negatively to the third basic want, while it yields a zero contribution to the second basic want.

This example illustrates how the composition matrix can be used to identify the nature of the T-goods. It is not the only tool which is available for this purpose; as we shall see from eq. (2.32) below, the income elasticities of the T-goods provide another tool.

R *and* S *Expressed in Terms of the Composition Matrix*

We write the vector equations (2.12) and (2.13) in diagonal matrix form,

$$(\mathbf{w}_T)_\Delta = (\mathbf{T}\boldsymbol{\iota})_\Delta \qquad (\mathbf{w})_\Delta = (\mathbf{T}'\boldsymbol{\iota})_\Delta \tag{2.15}$$

and apply this to (2.11):

$$\mathbf{R} = \mathbf{T}(\mathbf{w})_\Delta^{-1} = \mathbf{T}(\mathbf{T}'\boldsymbol{\iota})_\Delta^{-1} \tag{2.16}$$

Next write the s_{ij} definition in (2.7) in matrix form,

$$\mathbf{S} = (\mathbf{w}_T)_\Delta^{-1}\,\mathbf{R}(\mathbf{w})_\Delta$$

and apply (2.15) and (2.11):

$$\mathbf{S} = (\mathbf{T}\boldsymbol{\iota})_\Delta^{-1}\,\mathbf{R}(\mathbf{w})_\Delta = (\mathbf{T}\boldsymbol{\iota})_\Delta^{-1}\,\mathbf{T} \tag{2.17}$$

Equation (2.16) implies that each column of **R** is obtained from the corresponding column of **T** by dividing its elements by the column sum, which is the budget share of a commodity. Similarly, (2.17) shows that each row of **S** is obtained from the corresponding row of **T** by dividing by the row sum, which is the budget share of a T-good. If these budget shares are positive, corresponding elements of **R**, **S** and **T** must therefore all have the same sign. Thus, if a commodity is positively (negatively) represented in the budget share of a T-good, its price log-change also has a positive (negative) effect on the price log-change of this T-good: $s_{ij} \gtrless 0$ if and only if $r_{ij} \gtrless 0$.

The **R** and **S** matrices implied by the composition matrix (2.14) are

$$\mathbf{R} = \begin{bmatrix} .68 & 1.14 & 1.30 \\ .27 & -.22 & 0 \\ .05 & .08 & -.30 \end{bmatrix} \qquad \mathbf{S} = \begin{bmatrix} .37 & .45 & .18 \\ 2.52 & -1.52 & 0 \\ 1.50 & 1.88 & -2.38 \end{bmatrix}$$

Note that these matrices satisfy $\boldsymbol{\iota}'\mathbf{R} = \boldsymbol{\iota}'$ and $\mathbf{S}\boldsymbol{\iota} = \boldsymbol{\iota}$. Also note that the elements of **R** and **S** may be larger than 1. However, the elements of the composition matrix are always less than 1 in absolute value, as will be proved in the next section [see (3.9)].

The Solution of R

The third axiom states that $\mathbf{RMS}^{-1}$ in (2.9) must be diagonal and that its diagonal elements must be positive, which implies that it must be nonsingular. We apply the second member of (2.17) for **S**:

$$\mathbf{RMS}^{-1} = \mathbf{RM}(\mathbf{w})_\Delta^{-1}\,\mathbf{R}^{-1}(\mathbf{T}\boldsymbol{\iota})_\Delta$$

The right-hand side is the product of $\mathbf{RM}(\mathbf{w})_\Delta^{-1}\,\mathbf{R}^{-1}$ and the diagonal matrix $(\mathbf{T}\boldsymbol{\iota})_\Delta$. Since $\mathbf{RMS}^{-1}$ must be nonsingular, $(\mathbf{T}\boldsymbol{\iota})_\Delta$ must be nonsingular also. So postmultiply by the inverse of $(\mathbf{T}\boldsymbol{\iota})_\Delta$:

$$\mathbf{RMS}^{-1}(\mathbf{T}\boldsymbol{\iota})_\Delta^{-1} = \mathbf{RM}(\mathbf{w})_\Delta^{-1}\,\mathbf{R}^{-1} \tag{2.18}$$

The matrix product on the right is thus required to be the product of two nonsingular diagonal matrices, so that it must also be diagonal and nonsingular. Next apply (1.21) and (1.23),

$$\mathbf{M}(\mathbf{w})_\Delta^{-1} = (\mathbf{X}')^{-1}\boldsymbol{\Lambda}\mathbf{X}^{-1}\mathbf{X}\mathbf{X}' = (\mathbf{X}')^{-1}\boldsymbol{\Lambda}\mathbf{X}'$$

and substitute this in the right-hand side of (2.18):

$$\mathbf{RM}(\mathbf{w})_\Delta^{-1}\,\mathbf{R}^{-1} = \mathbf{R}(\mathbf{X}')^{-1}\boldsymbol{\Lambda}\mathbf{X}'\mathbf{R}^{-1} = (\mathbf{X}'\mathbf{R}^{-1})^{-1}\boldsymbol{\Lambda}(\mathbf{X}'\mathbf{R}^{-1})$$

The matrix product in the third member involves **X** and **Λ**, which are determined by **M** and $(\mathbf{w})_\Delta$ [see (1.13) and (1.14)], and the matrix **R**; hence **R** is to be selected so that this product is diagonal and nonsingular subject to the constraint (2.1). We considered this problem in (1.30) and (1.31), and obtained the solution (1.32),

$$\mathbf{R} = \mathbf{B}(\mathbf{X}^{-1}\boldsymbol{\iota})_\Delta\,\mathbf{X}'$$

where **B** is an arbitrary permutation matrix.

The occurrence of this **B** suggests that **R** is not uniquely determined, but this lack of uniqueness is actually trivial. Going back to (1.9), we conclude that choosing a different permutation matrix simply changes the order in which the T-goods are listed. So we may choose $\mathbf{B}=\mathbf{I}$ without any real loss of generality, which gives

$$\mathbf{R} = (\mathbf{X}^{-1}\boldsymbol{\iota})_\Delta\,\mathbf{X}' \tag{2.19}$$

Also recall from the discussion below (1.32) that this solution for **R** requires two conditions: the diagonal elements $\lambda_1, \ldots, \lambda_n$ of **Λ** are distinct and the vector $\mathbf{X}^{-1}\boldsymbol{\iota}$ contains no zero elements. Both conditions will be considered later in this section.

The Solution of S *and the Composition Matrix*

By combining (2.19) with (2.11) and (1.21) we obtain the solution of the composition matrix:

$$\mathbf{T} = (\mathbf{X}^{-1}\boldsymbol{\iota})_\Delta \mathbf{X}'(\mathbf{X}')^{-1}\mathbf{X}^{-1} = (\mathbf{X}^{-1}\boldsymbol{\iota})_\Delta \mathbf{X}^{-1} \tag{2.20}$$

Postmultiply this by $\boldsymbol{\iota}$:

$$\mathbf{T}\boldsymbol{\iota} = (\mathbf{X}^{-1}\boldsymbol{\iota})_\Delta \mathbf{X}^{-1}\boldsymbol{\iota} = (\mathbf{X}^{-1}\boldsymbol{\iota})_\Delta^2 \boldsymbol{\iota}$$

If we write the vector $\mathbf{T}\boldsymbol{\iota}$ in diagonal matrix form, this becomes

$$(\mathbf{T}\boldsymbol{\iota})_\Delta = (\mathbf{X}^{-1}\boldsymbol{\iota})_\Delta^2 \tag{2.21}$$

The solution of $\mathbf{S}$ is obtained from the third member of (2.17), combined with (2.20) and (2.21):

$$\mathbf{S} = (\mathbf{X}^{-1}\boldsymbol{\iota})_\Delta^{-2}(\mathbf{X}^{-1}\boldsymbol{\iota})_\Delta \mathbf{X}^{-1} = (\mathbf{X}^{-1}\boldsymbol{\iota})_\Delta^{-1}\mathbf{X}^{-1} \tag{2.22}$$

Note that this solution requires that $\mathbf{X}^{-1}\boldsymbol{\iota}$ contain no zero elements.

Next postmultiply the transpose of (2.19) by (2.22):

$$\mathbf{X}(\mathbf{X}^{-1}\boldsymbol{\iota})_\Delta(\mathbf{X}^{-1}\boldsymbol{\iota})_\Delta^{-1}\mathbf{X}^{-1} = \mathbf{I}$$

This proves

$$\mathbf{R}'\mathbf{S} = \mathbf{I} \tag{2.23}$$

which implies that the ith column of $\mathbf{R}$, which is associated with the ith commodity, is orthogonal to the jth column of $\mathbf{S}$ (associated with the jth commodity) when $i \neq j$, and that corresponding columns $(i=j)$ all have an inner product equal to 1. By taking the transpose of (2.23) we obtain $\mathbf{S}'\mathbf{R}=\mathbf{I}$, which implies $\mathbf{S}'=\mathbf{R}^{-1}$ and hence $\mathbf{R}\mathbf{S}'=\mathbf{I}$. This amounts to orthogonality of non-corresponding rows of $\mathbf{R}$ and $\mathbf{S}$ (associated with different T-goods) and unit inner products of corresponding rows.

Budget Shares of T-Goods

By combining (2.15) with (2.21) we obtain

$$(\mathbf{w}_T)_\Delta = (\mathbf{X}^{-1}\boldsymbol{\iota})_\Delta^2 \tag{2.24}$$

which proves that $(\bar{w}_{it})_T$, the ith diagonal element of $(\mathbf{w}_T)_\Delta$, is equal to the square of the corresponding element of $(\mathbf{X}^{-1}\boldsymbol{\iota})_\Delta$. This result may also be written as

$$\left[\sqrt{(\bar{w}_{1t})_T} \cdots \sqrt{(\bar{w}_{nt})_T}\right] = (\mathbf{X}^{-1}\boldsymbol{\iota})' \tag{2.25}$$

If an element of $\mathbf{X}^{-1}\boldsymbol{\iota}$ is negative, it should be interpreted as the negative square root of the budget share of the corresponding T-good. Excluding zero elements in $\mathbf{X}^{-1}\iota$, as we did for the $\mathbf{S}$ solution (2.22), thus amounts to excluding the case in which nothing is spent on a T-good. This case is considered in the first subsection of Section 12.3.

The sum of the budget shares of the T-goods is identical to the sum of the squares of their square roots. So we take the squared length of the vector (2.25),

$$(2.26)\qquad (\mathbf{X}^{-1}\iota)'(\mathbf{X}^{-1}\iota) = \iota'(\mathbf{X}')^{-1}\mathbf{X}^{-1}\iota = \iota'(\mathbf{w})_\Delta\,\iota = \sum_{i=1}^{n} \bar{w}_{it} = 1$$

where the second step is based on (1.21). This confirms that the budget shares of the T-goods add up to 1.

Square Roots of Budget Shares Are Orthogonally Transformed

We have $\mathbf{X}^{-1} = \mathbf{X}'(\mathbf{w})_\Delta$ from (1.19), so that $\mathbf{X}^{-1}\iota = \mathbf{X}'(\mathbf{w})_\Delta\,\iota$. We apply this to (2.25) after taking the transposes of both sides:

$$\begin{bmatrix} \sqrt{(\bar{w}_{1t})_T} \\ \vdots \\ \sqrt{(\bar{w}_{nt})_T} \end{bmatrix} = \mathbf{X}'(\mathbf{w})_\Delta\,\iota = \mathbf{X}'(\mathbf{w})_\Delta^{1/2} \begin{bmatrix} \sqrt{\bar{w}_{1t}} \\ \vdots \\ \sqrt{\bar{w}_{nt}} \end{bmatrix}$$

This can be written as

$$(2.27)\qquad \begin{bmatrix} \sqrt{(\bar{w}_{1t})_T} \\ \vdots \\ \sqrt{(\bar{w}_{nt})_T} \end{bmatrix} = \mathbf{K} \begin{bmatrix} \sqrt{\bar{w}_{1t}} \\ \vdots \\ \sqrt{\bar{w}_{nt}} \end{bmatrix}$$

where $\mathbf{K}$ is the orthogonal matrix (1.20).[1]

We conclude that the preference independence transformation implies an orthogonal transformation of square roots of budget shares. This result is not immediately obvious. However, recall that the budget point, with coordinates equal to the square roots of the budget shares (see Figure 11.2 on page 200), played an important role in the geometric analysis of Section 11.6. It will appear in Section 12.4 that the geometric approach is equally instructive for the preference independence transformation.

Price Coefficients and Marginal Shares of T-Goods

Using (1.23), (2.19) and (2.22), we obtain the normalized price coef-

[1] Multiplication of the ith row of $\mathbf{K}$ by -1 changes the sign of the square root of the budget share of the corresponding T-good in (2.27). This multiplication amounts to replacing $\mathbf{x}_i$ by $-\mathbf{x}_i$ (see footnote 1 on page 222).

ficient matrix of the transformed demand model (2.9):

$$\mathbf{RMS}^{-1} = (\mathbf{X}^{-1}\boldsymbol{\iota})_\Delta \, \mathbf{X}'(\mathbf{X}')^{-1}\boldsymbol{\Lambda}\mathbf{X}^{-1}\mathbf{X}(\mathbf{X}^{-1}\boldsymbol{\iota})_\Delta$$

This may be simplified to

$$\mathbf{RMS}^{-1} = (\mathbf{X}^{-1}\boldsymbol{\iota})_\Delta \, \boldsymbol{\Lambda}(\mathbf{X}^{-1}\boldsymbol{\iota})_\Delta \tag{2.28}$$

Recall from (1.17) that the diagonal matrix $\boldsymbol{\Lambda}$ contains exclusively positive elements in the diagonal. Therefore, (2.28) implies that, after the transformation, the normalized price coefficient matrix is diagonal and positive definite, as the third axiom requires, if $\mathbf{X}^{-1}\boldsymbol{\iota}$ contains no zero elements.

It follows from (2.9) that the vector of marginal shares of the T-goods, to be written $\boldsymbol{\mu}_T = [\mu_{iT}]$, is obtained by postmultiplying the diagonal matrix (2.28) by $\boldsymbol{\iota}$. This amounts to writing the diagonal of the diagonal matrix (2.28) as a column vector. Equivalently, if we write $\boldsymbol{\mu}_T$ in diagonal matrix form, it is identical to the normalized price coefficient matrix. Hence (2.28) can be extended to

$$\mathbf{RMS}^{-1} = (\mathbf{X}^{-1}\boldsymbol{\iota})_\Delta \, \boldsymbol{\Lambda}(\mathbf{X}^{-1}\boldsymbol{\iota})_\Delta = (\boldsymbol{\mu}_T)_\Delta \tag{2.29}$$

Also, since $(\mathbf{X}^{-1}\boldsymbol{\iota})_\Delta \, \boldsymbol{\iota} = \mathbf{X}^{-1}\boldsymbol{\iota}$, $\mathbf{S}^{-1}\boldsymbol{\iota} = \boldsymbol{\iota}$ and $\mathbf{M}\boldsymbol{\iota} = \boldsymbol{\mu}$, we obtain by postmultiplying (2.29) by $\boldsymbol{\iota}$:

$$\mathbf{R}\boldsymbol{\mu} = (\mathbf{X}^{-1}\boldsymbol{\iota})_\Delta \, \boldsymbol{\Lambda}\mathbf{X}^{-1}\boldsymbol{\iota} = \boldsymbol{\mu}_T \tag{2.30}$$

We conclude from (2.29) that the marginal shares of the T-goods are all positive when $\mathbf{X}^{-1}\boldsymbol{\iota}$ consists of nonzero elements. These marginal shares add up to 1, which is proved by premultiplication of the second member of (2.30) by $\boldsymbol{\iota}'$,

$$\boldsymbol{\iota}'(\mathbf{X}^{-1}\boldsymbol{\iota})_\Delta \, \boldsymbol{\Lambda}\mathbf{X}^{-1}\boldsymbol{\iota} = \boldsymbol{\iota}'(\mathbf{X}')^{-1}\boldsymbol{\Lambda}\mathbf{X}^{-1}\boldsymbol{\iota} = \boldsymbol{\iota}'\mathbf{M}\boldsymbol{\iota} = 1 \tag{2.31}$$

where the second step is based on (1.23).

The Income Elasticities of the T-Goods

We obtain the income elasticities of the T-goods, arranged as diagonal elements of a diagonal matrix, by pre- or postmultiplying the diagonal marginal share matrix $(\boldsymbol{\mu}_T)_\Delta$ by the inverse of the diagonal budget share matrix $(\mathbf{w}_T)_\Delta$. Using (2.24), (2.29) and the commutative multiplication property of diagonal matrices, we obtain

$$(\mathbf{w}_T)_\Delta^{-1} \, (\boldsymbol{\mu}_T)_\Delta = \boldsymbol{\Lambda} \tag{2.32}$$

This shows that the latent roots $\lambda_1,\ldots, \lambda_n$ of the diagonalization (1.13) are the income elasticities of the T-goods. Note that these elasticities are all positive in view of (1.17).

Recall that the solution (1.32) of **R** requires that the λ's be distinct. If two (or more) λ's are equal, the diagonalization (1.13) is not unique. If two T-goods have equal income elasticities, they cannot be identified separately. This will be further clarified along geometric lines in Section 12.4.

We showed below (2.14) how the composition matrix can be used to analyze the nature of the T-goods. The λ's provide another tool because they measure the extent to which a T-good is a luxury or a necessity.

Summary of the Transformation

The developments in the previous pages amount to a transformation of the Rotterdam Model, based on three axioms, into a demand system of the preference-independent type,

$$\bar{w}_{it}Dq_{it} = \mu_i DQ_t + \phi\mu_i(Dp_{it} - DP_t') + \varepsilon_{it} \tag{2.33}$$

where $DP_t' = \sum_k \mu_k Dp_{kt}$. The transformation changes the commodities into T-goods, accompanied by changes in the left-hand variables, the price log-changes, the disturbances, and the marginal shares. The latter shares all become positive, similar to μ_i in (2.33), except when $\mathbf{X}^{-1}\boldsymbol{\iota}$ contains zero elements (to be discussed in Section 12.3). The variables DQ_t and DP_t' and the income flexibility ϕ, all of which refer to the consumer's basket as a whole, do not change because they are invariant under the transformation.

Recall from Section 2.5 that ϕ is not invariant under monotonic transformations of the utility function. Since ϕ is invariant under the preference independence transformation, the latter transformation is thus not invariant under the former. This should come as no surprise. In the opening paragraph of this chapter we referred to efforts made to simplify demand systems in the direction of preference independence as far as the data permit; this amounts to imposing constraints on the price coefficients which insure the identification of the relative price version of the Rotterdam Model. In the next subsection we shall see how a monotonic transformation of the utility function can be used to simplify the preference independence transformation in a particular case.

Note also the different roles played by the two immediate results of the diagonalization (1.13): the matrix $\mathbf{X}$ of the characteristic vectors and the diagonal matrix $\mathbf{\Lambda}$ of the latent roots. The former is concerned with *expenditure levels* which prevail during $(t-1, t)$ and the latter with *rates of expendi-*

ture change caused by income changes. This is immediately clear for $\mathbf{\Lambda}$ in view of the interpretation of its diagonal elements as the income elasticities of the T-goods.[1] For $\mathbf{X}$ this may be verified from (1.21), (2.20) and (2.24), which show that $\mathbf{X}$ uniquely determines the budget shares of the commodities and of the T-goods and also the composition matrix which connects these two sets of shares:

$$(\mathbf{w}_T)_\Delta = (\mathbf{X}^{-1}\boldsymbol{\iota})_\Delta^2 \qquad \mathbf{T} = (\mathbf{X}^{-1}\boldsymbol{\iota})_\Delta \mathbf{X}^{-1} \qquad (\mathbf{w})_\Delta = (\mathbf{X}')^{-1}\mathbf{X}^{-1}$$

Special Cases

It follows from eqs. (1.26) to (1.29) that under block-independence the preference independence transformation can be applied to each block separately; details are provided in Sections 13.1 and 13.2. An implication is that each commodity with a preference-independent demand equation can be identified with a T-good.

A similar simplification is possible for blockwise dependence with two groups under appropriate conditions. Write eq. (2.20) of Section 8.2 in the form

$$\bar{w}_{it} Dq_{it} = \mu_i DQ_t + \sum_{j \in S_g} v_{ij}(Dp_{jt} - DP'_t) + \mu_i^g \sum_{h \neq g} N_{gh}(DP'_{ht} - DP'_t) + \varepsilon_{it}$$

Hence for $G=2$ groups the price coefficient matrix can be written as

(2.34)
$$\begin{bmatrix} \mathbf{N}_1 & N_{12}\tilde{\boldsymbol{\mu}}_1\tilde{\boldsymbol{\mu}}'_2 \\ N_{21}\tilde{\boldsymbol{\mu}}_2\tilde{\boldsymbol{\mu}}'_1 & \mathbf{N}_2 \end{bmatrix}$$

where $\mathbf{N}_g$ is the $n_g \times n_g$ price coefficient matrix within S_g and $\tilde{\boldsymbol{\mu}}_g$ is the conditional marginal share vector of this group ($g=1, 2$). Recall from eqs. (5.9) to (5.11) of Section 2.5 that, when the utility function is monotonically transformed, each price coefficient v_{ij} becomes

$$v_{ij} - \phi g_1 \mu_i \mu_j = v_{ij} - \phi g_1 M_g M_h \mu_i^g \mu_j^h$$

where $-\infty < g_1 < 1$ and $i \in S_g$, $j \in S_h$. Hence, if a monotonic transformation is applied which satisfies

(2.35)
$$\phi g_1 M_1 M_2 = N_{12}$$

[1] The matrix $\mathbf{\Lambda}$, when multiplied by the income flexibility, also provides rates of change with respect to changes in relative prices. This leads to the subject of the price elasticities of the T-goods, which is considered in Section 12.3.

the price coefficient matrix (2.34) is transformed into

$$\begin{bmatrix} \mathbf{N}_1 - N_{12}\tilde{\boldsymbol{\mu}}_1\tilde{\boldsymbol{\mu}}_1' & \mathbf{0} \\ \mathbf{0} & \mathbf{N}_2 - N_{12}\tilde{\boldsymbol{\mu}}_2\tilde{\boldsymbol{\mu}}_2' \end{bmatrix} \tag{2.36}$$

where use is made of $N_{12}=N_{21}$. So, if the diagonal blocks of (2.36) are negative definite, we can apply the preference independence transformation to each block separately. Note that (2.35) for $N_{12}\neq 0$ requires $M_1\neq 0$, $M_2\neq 0$.

12.3 Further Analysis of the Transformation

The discussion starts with the case of zero expenditures on one or more T-goods. This is followed by an analysis of the rows and columns of the matrices **R**, **S** and **T**. Next comes the second-moment model for T-goods, certain properties of their income and price elasticities, and the effect of errors and changes in the matrices **M** and $(\mathbf{w})_\Delta$ which determine the diagonalization (1.13). The last subsection describes the approach in the form originally proposed by BROOKS (1970), which amounts to a transformation of the levels of prices and quantities.

T-Goods with Zero Budget Shares

To interpret the situation in which the ith element of $\mathbf{X}^{-1}\boldsymbol{\iota}$ vanishes, we imagine that, owing to small changes in the matrices **M** and/or $(\mathbf{w})_\Delta$ in (1.13), this element moves from a small positive or negative value toward zero. It follows from (2.24) that the budget share of the corresponding T-good also moves to zero, and from (2.20) that the contributions of *all* commodities to this good move to zero as well. Hence the occurrence of a zero $(\bar{w}_{it})_T$ is not a matter of positive and negative contributions which cancel each other out.

The explanation is in terms of price changes. If the ith element of $\mathbf{X}^{-1}\boldsymbol{\iota}$ moves toward zero, the ith row of **S** given in (2.22) will consist of larger and larger values. Hence, given $Dp_{1t}, \ldots, Dp_{nt}$, the price log-change $\sum_j s_{ij}Dp_{jt}$ moves toward $\pm\infty$. If this movement is toward $+\infty$, the T-good is priced out of the market, so that nothing is spent on it in the limit. If the movement is toward $-\infty$, the T-good becomes a free good, which also means that nothing is spent on it in the limit.

Therefore, zero budget shares may be viewed as limiting cases caused by infinite price log-changes of the corresponding T-goods; a simple geometric interpretation is given in Section 12.4. Since T-goods on which nothing is spent are not interesting, we may decide to delete them. If we do so, the transform of the normalized price coefficient matrix becomes a nonsingular principal submatrix of $(\boldsymbol{\mu}_T)_\Delta$, which is diagonal with exclusively positive diagonal elements in agreement with the third axiom. Whenever it is stated in the sequel that the preference independence transformation yields positive marginal shares, this is to be interpreted in the sense that T-goods with zero budget shares are ignored.

Comments on Average Budget Shares

The critical reader will object to the reasoning in the previous subsection by pointing out that, if the price of a T-good in $t-1$ is positive and finite and if its log-change from $t-1$ to t is $\pm\infty$, this implies that its budget share in t vanishes, which is not the same as a zero value of the average budget share $(\bar{w}_{it})_T$ defined in (2.3).

Our critical reader is quite right; it is the average budget share of $t-1$ and t which is obtained from (2.24), which vanishes if and only if the shares in both $t-1$ and t are zero. However, he will rapidly agree that the point he raises is a matter of the O_3 terms that are ignored. Suppose that we do not use the average budget share $\bar{w}_{jt}$ in the decomposition (2.4), but a share of the type given in eq. (1.20) of Section 5.1:

$$\tilde{w}_{jt} = \frac{\left(\bar{w}_{jt}w_{jt}w_{j,t-1}\right)^{1/3}}{\sum_{k=1}^{n}\left(\bar{w}_{kt}w_{kt}w_{k,t-1}\right)^{1/3}}$$

The difference between $\bar{w}_{jt}$ and $\tilde{w}_{jt}$ is O_2. Since $\bar{w}_{jt}$ is multiplied by log-changes in (2.4), the effect of replacing $\bar{w}_{jt}$ by $\tilde{w}_{jt}$ is O_3 and can hence be merged with the O_3 term on the far right in (2.4). Next replace (2.3) by

$$(\tilde{w}_{it})_T = \sum_{j=1}^{n} r_{ij}\tilde{w}_{jt}$$

where $(\tilde{w}_{it})_T$ is interpreted analogously, viz., as the ratio of the cube root of

$$(\bar{w}_{it})_T\,(w_{it})_T\,(w_{i,t-1})_T = \tfrac{1}{2}\left[(w_{it})_T + (w_{i,t-1})_T\right](w_{it})_T\,(w_{i,t-1})_T$$

to the sum of all n such cube roots. Since $(\tilde{w}_{it})_T$ vanishes when the T-good has a zero budget share in either $t-1$ or t, the apparent conflict is resolved when we interpret the ith diagonal element of $(\mathbf{w}_T)_\Delta$ in (2.24) as $(\tilde{w}_{it})_T$.

The Rows of R, S *and* T

We have $\mathbf{X}^{-1}=\mathbf{X}'(\mathbf{w})_\Delta$ from (1.19), which implies $\mathbf{X}^{-1}\boldsymbol{\iota}=\mathbf{X}'\mathbf{w}$. Therefore, the diagonal matrix $(\mathbf{X}^{-1}\boldsymbol{\iota})_\Delta$ has the inner product of $\mathbf{x}_i$ and $\mathbf{w}$ as the ith diagonal element.

Write (2.20) as $\mathbf{T}=(\mathbf{X}^{-1}\boldsymbol{\iota})_\Delta\,\mathbf{X}^{-1}=(\mathbf{X}^{-1}\boldsymbol{\iota})_\Delta\,\mathbf{X}'(\mathbf{w})_\Delta$. Applying the property of $(\mathbf{X}^{-1}\boldsymbol{\iota})_\Delta$ stated in the previous paragraph, we conclude

$$\text{(3.1)} \qquad \mathbf{T} = \begin{bmatrix} (\mathbf{x}_1'\mathbf{w})\,\mathbf{x}_1'\,(\mathbf{w})_\Delta \\ \vdots \\ (\mathbf{x}_n'\mathbf{w})\,\mathbf{x}_n'\,(\mathbf{w})_\Delta \end{bmatrix}$$

Similarly, from (2.19) and (2.22), we obtain the rows of $\mathbf{R}$ and $\mathbf{S}$:

$$\text{(3.2)} \qquad \mathbf{R} = \begin{bmatrix} (\mathbf{x}_1'\mathbf{w})\,\mathbf{x}_1' \\ \vdots \\ (\mathbf{x}_n'\mathbf{w})\,\mathbf{x}_n' \end{bmatrix} \qquad \mathbf{S} = \begin{bmatrix} (\mathbf{x}_1'\mathbf{w})^{-1}\,\mathbf{x}_1'\,(\mathbf{w})_\Delta \\ \vdots \\ (\mathbf{x}_n'\mathbf{w})^{-1}\,\mathbf{x}_n'\,(\mathbf{w})_\Delta \end{bmatrix}$$

Equations (3.1) and (3.2) show that when we replace $\mathbf{x}_i$ by $-\mathbf{x}_i$, this has no effect on any of the elements of the matrices $\mathbf{R}$, $\mathbf{S}$ and $\mathbf{T}$.

Orthogonality Properties of R *and* S

Equation (2.23) implies $\mathbf{R}'=\mathbf{S}^{-1}$ and $\mathbf{S}'=\mathbf{R}^{-1}$. In the discussion following (2.23) we concluded that, for $i \neq j$, the ith and j^{th} columns of $\mathbf{R}$ and $\mathbf{S}$ are orthogonal vectors and the ith and j^{th} rows of $\mathbf{R}$ and $\mathbf{S}$ are also orthogonal vectors. These orthogonality properties refer to one vector (row or column) in $\mathbf{R}$ and another vector in $\mathbf{S}$. Are $\mathbf{R}$ and $\mathbf{S}$ themselves orthogonal matrices? Recall that we concluded from (2.27) that square roots of budget shares are orthogonally transformed, because the transformation matrix $\mathbf{K}$ in (2.27) is orthogonal.

The transformation matrix $\mathbf{R}$ of the budget shares in (2.3) is not orthogonal, but it does have this property in a weighted sense. Applying (2.19) and (1.19), we find

$$\mathbf{R}(\mathbf{w})_\Delta\,\mathbf{R}' = (\mathbf{X}^{-1}\boldsymbol{\iota})_\Delta\,\mathbf{X}'(\mathbf{w})_\Delta\,\mathbf{X}(\mathbf{X}^{-1}\boldsymbol{\iota})_\Delta = (\mathbf{X}^{-1}\boldsymbol{\iota})_\Delta^2$$

So, using (2.24) also, we obtain the first equation of

$$\text{(3.3)} \qquad \mathbf{R}(\mathbf{w})_\Delta\,\mathbf{R}' = (\mathbf{w}_T)_\Delta \qquad \mathbf{S}'(\mathbf{w}_T)_\Delta\,\mathbf{S} = (\mathbf{w})_\Delta$$

The second equation is obtained from the first by premultiplication by $\mathbf{R}^{-1}=\mathbf{S}'$ and postmultiplication by $(\mathbf{R}')^{-1}=\mathbf{S}$.

We may write (3.3) in scalar form as

$$\text{(3.4)} \qquad \sum_{k=1}^{n} \bar{w}_{kt} r_{ik} r_{jk} = \begin{cases} (\bar{w}_{it})_T & \text{if } i = j \\ 0 & \text{if } i \neq j \end{cases}$$

$$\text{(3.5)} \qquad \sum_{k=1}^{n} (\bar{w}_{kt})_T\, s_{ki} s_{kj} = \begin{cases} \bar{w}_{it} & \text{if } i = j \\ 0 & \text{if } i \neq j \end{cases}$$

The first line of (3.4) states that the weighted squared length of each row of $\mathbf{R}$ (with weights equal to the budget shares of the commodities) is equal to the budget share of the associated T-good. The second line states that any two rows of $\mathbf{R}$ (corresponding to different T-goods) are orthogonal in the same weighted sense. Equation (3.5) is similar; the rows of $\mathbf{R}$ are replaced by the columns of $\mathbf{S}$ and the two sets of budget shares are interchanged.

Orthogonality Properties of the Composition Matrix

Consider (2.11), $\mathbf{T}=\mathbf{R}(\mathbf{w})_\Delta$. On combining this with (3.3) we obtain the first equation of

(3.6) $$\mathbf{T}(\mathbf{w})_\Delta^{-1}\mathbf{T}'=(\mathbf{w}_T)_\Delta \qquad \mathbf{T}'(\mathbf{w}_T)_\Delta^{-1}\mathbf{T}=(\mathbf{w})_\Delta$$

which implies that the weighted squared length of the ith row of $\mathbf{T}$ (with weights of the form $1/\bar{w}_{jt}$) equals $(\bar{w}_{it})_T$ and that any two rows of $\mathbf{T}$ (corresponding to different T-goods) are orthogonal in the same weighted sense. The second equation of (3.6) is obtained from the first by pre- and postmultiplication by $\mathbf{T}^{-1}$ and $(\mathbf{T}')^{-1}$, respectively, followed by inversion of both sides. It states that the weighted squared length of the ith column of $\mathbf{T}$ [with weights of the form $1/(\bar{w}_{jt})_T$] equals $\bar{w}_{it}$ and that any two columns of $\mathbf{T}$ (corresponding to different commodities) are orthogonal in the same weighted sense.

Next pre- and postmultiply the first equation of (3.6) by $(\mathbf{w}_T)_\Delta^{-1/2}$:

$$(\mathbf{w}_T)_\Delta^{-1/2}\,\mathbf{T}\,(\mathbf{w})_\Delta^{-1}\,\mathbf{T}'\,(\mathbf{w}_T)_\Delta^{-1/2}=\mathbf{I}$$

This can be written as

$$[(\mathbf{w}_T)_\Delta^{-1/2}\,\mathbf{T}\,(\mathbf{w})_\Delta^{-1/2}]\,[(\mathbf{w}_T)_\Delta^{-1/2}\,\mathbf{T}\,(\mathbf{w})_\Delta^{-1/2}]'=\mathbf{I}$$

which shows that the matrix product $(\mathbf{w}_T)_\Delta^{-1/2}\,\mathbf{T}(\mathbf{w})_\Delta^{-1/2}$ is an orthogonal matrix. Applying (2.20) and (2.24), we find that this product equals

(3.7) $$(\mathbf{X}^{-1}\boldsymbol{\iota})_\Delta^{-1}\,(\mathbf{X}^{-1}\boldsymbol{\iota})_\Delta\,\mathbf{X}^{-1}\,(\mathbf{w})_\Delta^{-1/2}=\mathbf{X}^{-1}\,(\mathbf{w})_\Delta^{-1/2}=\mathbf{K}$$

where the last step is based on (1.20). Therefore,

(3.8) $$(\mathbf{w}_T)_\Delta^{-1/2}\,\mathbf{T}\,(\mathbf{w})_\Delta^{-1/2}=\mathbf{K}$$

This result is subject to the qualification that each row of the matrix $\mathbf{K}$ on the right may have to be multiplied by -1, which amounts to multiplying the corresponding column $\mathbf{x}_i$ by -1 in view of (1.20). The reason is that in (3.7) we equate square roots of budget shares of T-goods to the elements of $\mathbf{X}^{-1}\boldsymbol{\iota}$, which may be negative square roots [see the discussion below (2.25)].

However, this qualification does not affect the orthogonality of the matrix product in the left-hand side of (3.8).

Three Rules on the Row and Column Sums of the Composition Matrix

Recall that we concluded from (2.16) that each column of the transformation matrix **R** of the budget shares is obtained from the corresponding column of **T** by dividing by the column sum. Similarly, we concluded from (2.17) that each row of the transformation matrix **S** of the price log-changes is obtained from the corresponding row of **T** by dividing by the row sum. Equation (3.8) provides a third result concerning **T** and its row and column sums, dealing with the transformation matrix **K** of the square roots of the budget shares in (2.27). Subject to the qualification on signs stated below (3.8), each element of **K** is obtained from the corresponding element of **T** by dividing by the geometric mean of the corresponding row and column sums. This follows directly from (3.8) and (2.15).

Equivalently, the composition matrix becomes orthogonal when we divide each element by the geometric mean of the corresponding row and column sums. Since $\mathbf{K}'\mathbf{K}=\mathbf{I}$ implies that the sum of the squares of the elements in each column of **K** equals 1, all elements of **K** are at most equal to 1 in absolute value. Therefore, (3.8) implies

$$\left|\frac{t_{ij}}{\sqrt{(\bar{w}_{it})_T\,\bar{w}_{jt}}}\right| \leq 1$$

or, equivalently,

$$t_{ij}^2 \leq (\bar{w}_{it})_T\,\bar{w}_{jt} \qquad i,j=1,\ldots,n \tag{3.9}$$

where t_{ij} is the $(i,j)^{\text{th}}$ element of **T**. This proves that the absolute value of each element of the composition matrix is at most equal to the geometric mean of the budget share of the corresponding T-good and that of the corresponding commodity. The implication $|t_{ij}|<1$ is obvious.

The Second-Moment Model

Consider the second-moment model (1.8) associated with the demand system (1.7) prior to the transformation. Since the transformed system (2.9) has $\mathbf{R}\boldsymbol{\varepsilon}_t$ as its disturbance vector, the implied second-moment model for (2.9) is

$$\mathscr{V}(\mathbf{R}\boldsymbol{\varepsilon}_t)=\sigma^2(\mathbf{RMR}'-\mathbf{RM\iota\iota'MR}') \tag{3.10}$$

In view of (2.23) and (2.29) we have

$$\mathbf{RMR}' = (\boldsymbol{\mu}_T)_\Delta \tag{3.11}$$

We also have $\mathbf{RM\iota} = \mathbf{R\mu} = \boldsymbol{\mu}_T$ in view of (2.30). On combining this with (3.11) we find that (3.10) can be simplified to

$$\mathscr{V}(\mathbf{R}\boldsymbol{\varepsilon}_t) = \sigma^2 [(\boldsymbol{\mu}_T)_\Delta - \boldsymbol{\mu}_T\boldsymbol{\mu}_T'] \tag{3.12}$$

This shows that σ^2 is invariant under the transformation and that the variances and covariances of the transformed disturbances are proportional to $\mu_{iT}(1-\mu_{iT})$ and $-\mu_{iT}\mu_{jT}$, respectively. Hence the preference-independent form of the second-moment model applies to the T-goods.

Also, if $\boldsymbol{\varepsilon}_t$ is normally distributed, as it is under the theory of rational random behavior (Section 2.8), then the transformed disturbance vector $\mathbf{R}\boldsymbol{\varepsilon}_t$ has the same property if $\mathbf{M}$ and $(\mathbf{w})_\Delta$ are regarded as nonrandom matrices. This follows from (2.19), which expresses $\mathbf{R}$ in terms of $\mathbf{X}$, and from the fact that the columns of $\mathbf{X}$ are determined as characteristic vectors associated with $\mathbf{M}$ and $(\mathbf{w})_\Delta$.

We can write (3.11) in scalar form as

$$\sum_{h=1}^{n}\sum_{k=1}^{n} \mu_{hk} r_{ih} r_{jk} = \begin{cases} \mu_{iT} & \text{if} \quad i = j \\ 0 & \text{if} \quad i \neq j \end{cases} \tag{3.13}$$

which should be compared with (3.4). By pre- and postmultiplying (3.11) by $\mathbf{R}^{-1} = \mathbf{S}'$ and $(\mathbf{R}')^{-1} = \mathbf{S}$, respectively, we obtain

$$\mathbf{S}'(\boldsymbol{\mu}_T)_\Delta \mathbf{S} = \mathbf{M} \tag{3.14}$$

or, in scalar form,

$$\sum_{k=1}^{n} \mu_{kT} s_{ki} s_{kj} = \mu_{ij} \qquad i, j = 1, \ldots, n \tag{3.15}$$

This should be compared with (3.5).

Income Elasticities of Commodities and T-Goods

We divide both sides of (1.1) by $\bar{w}_{it}$,

$$Dq_{it} = \frac{\mu_i}{\bar{w}_{it}} DQ_t + \sum_{j=1}^{n} \frac{\phi\mu_{ij}}{\bar{w}_{it}} (Dp_{jt} - DP_t') + \frac{\varepsilon_{it}}{\bar{w}_{it}} \tag{3.16}$$

where $DP_t' = \sum_k \mu_k Dp_{kt}$. The income elasticity $\mu_i/\bar{w}_{it}$ is an element of the vector $(\mathbf{w})_\Delta^{-1}\boldsymbol{\mu} = (\mathbf{w})_\Delta^{-1}\mathbf{M\iota}$. Using (1.21) and (1.23), we find that this vector can be written as

$$(\mathbf{w})_\Delta^{-1}\boldsymbol{\mu} = \mathbf{X}\boldsymbol{\Lambda}\mathbf{X}^{-1}\boldsymbol{\iota} \tag{3.17}$$

Let us premultiply this by $\mathbf{S}$ given in (2.22),

$$\mathbf{S}(\mathbf{w})_\Delta^{-1}\boldsymbol{\mu} = (\mathbf{X}^{-1}\boldsymbol{\iota})_\Delta^{-1}\boldsymbol{\Lambda}\mathbf{X}^{-1}\boldsymbol{\iota} = \boldsymbol{\Lambda}(\mathbf{X}^{-1}\boldsymbol{\iota})_\Delta^{-1}\mathbf{X}^{-1}\boldsymbol{\iota}$$

where the second step is based on the commutative multiplication property of diagonal matrices. The third member is simply $\boldsymbol{\Lambda\iota}$, the income elasticity vector of the T-goods, because $\mathbf{X}^{-1}\boldsymbol{\iota}$ premultiplied by the inverse of $(\mathbf{X}^{-1}\boldsymbol{\iota})_\Delta$ equals $\boldsymbol{\iota}$. This proves the first equation of

$$\boldsymbol{\Lambda\iota} = \mathbf{S}(\mathbf{w})_\Delta^{-1}\boldsymbol{\mu} \qquad (\mathbf{w})_\Delta^{-1}\boldsymbol{\mu} = \mathbf{R}'\boldsymbol{\Lambda\iota} \tag{3.18}$$

The second equation is obtained from the first by premultiplication by the matrix $\mathbf{S}^{-1} = \mathbf{R}'$.

We conclude from (3.18) that premultiplication by $\mathbf{S}$ transforms the income elasticity vector of the commodities into the income elasticity vector of the T-goods, and that premultiplication by $\mathbf{R}'$ transforms the latter vector into the former. This amounts in both cases to a weighted sum:

$$\lambda_i = \sum_{j=1}^{n} s_{ij}\frac{\mu_j}{\bar{w}_{jt}} \qquad \frac{\mu_i}{\bar{w}_{it}} = \sum_{j=1}^{n} r_{ji}\lambda_j$$

Note that the weights sum to 1 (because $\mathbf{S}\boldsymbol{\iota} = \boldsymbol{\iota}$ and $\mathbf{R}'\boldsymbol{\iota} = \boldsymbol{\iota}$) but that they may be negative.

Price Elasticities of Commodities and T-Goods

The price elasticity matrix of the commodities in (3.16) is

$$\phi(\mathbf{w})_\Delta^{-1}\mathbf{M} = \phi\mathbf{X}\boldsymbol{\Lambda}\mathbf{X}^{-1} \tag{3.19}$$

where the equal sign is based on (1.21) and (1.23). Now premultiply (1.13) by $\phi(\mathbf{w})_\Delta^{-1}$:

$$[\phi(\mathbf{w})_\Delta^{-1}\mathbf{M} - \phi\lambda_i\mathbf{I}]\,\mathbf{x}_i = \mathbf{0} \qquad i = 1, \ldots, n \tag{3.20}$$

The first matrix in brackets is the price elasticity matrix (3.19), so that (3.20) implies that $\phi\lambda_i$ is a latent root of this elasticity matrix. Recall from (2.29) that the normalized price coefficient matrix of the T-goods is $(\boldsymbol{\mu}_T)_\Delta$, so that the "unnormalized" matrix is $\phi(\boldsymbol{\mu}_T)_\Delta$. It then follows from (2.32) that the price elasticity matrix of the T-goods is $\phi\boldsymbol{\Lambda}$, which is a diagonal matrix with $\phi\lambda_1, \ldots, \phi\lambda_n$ as diagonal elements. Therefore, (3.20) proves that the own-price elasticities of the T-goods are the latent roots of the (asymmetric) matrix of price elasticities of the commodities.

For any square matrix the sum of the latent roots is equal to the sum of the diagonal elements. In the case of (3.20) this gives

$$\sum_{i=1}^{n} (\phi\lambda_i) = \sum_{i=1}^{n} \frac{\phi\mu_{ii}}{\bar{w}_{it}} \tag{3.21}$$

Both sides of this equation are a sum of n own-price elasticities, on the left for T-goods and on the right for commodities. This proves that the sum of the own-price elasticities is invariant under the preference independence transformation.

Price Elasticities and the Composition Matrix

Next premultiply (3.19) by **T** defined in (2.20),

$$\mathbf{T}[\phi(\mathbf{w})_\Delta^{-1}\mathbf{M}] = \phi(\mathbf{X}^{-1}\boldsymbol{\iota})_\Delta\,\boldsymbol{\Lambda}\mathbf{X}^{-1} = \phi\boldsymbol{\Lambda}(\mathbf{X}^{-1}\boldsymbol{\iota})_\Delta\,\mathbf{X}^{-1}$$

where the last step is based on the commutative multiplication property of diagonal matrices. Since the third member equals $\phi\boldsymbol{\Lambda}\mathbf{T}$, this proves

$$\mathbf{T}[\phi(\mathbf{w})_\Delta^{-1}\mathbf{M}] = (\phi\boldsymbol{\Lambda})\,\mathbf{T} \tag{3.22}$$

or, in words, the price elasticity matrix of the commodities premultiplied by the composition matrix equals the price elasticity matrix of the T-goods postmultiplied by the composition matrix.

Finally, write (3.22) as

$$[t_{i1} \dots t_{in}]\;\phi(\mathbf{w})_\Delta^{-1}\mathbf{M} = \phi\lambda_i\,[t_{i1} \dots t_{in}]$$

or, equivalently, as

$$[t_{i1} \dots t_{in}]\;[\phi(\mathbf{w})_\Delta^{-1}\mathbf{M} - \phi\lambda_i\mathbf{I}] = \mathbf{0} \qquad i = 1, \dots, n \tag{3.23}$$

where $[t_{i1} \dots t_{in}]$ is the ith row of **T** (corresponding to the ith T-good). This proves that the rows of the composition matrix are characteristic vectors of the price elasticity matrix of the commodities. The normalization of these rows is as shown in (3.6).

The Effect of Errors in the Normalized Price Coefficients

The diagonalization (1.13) of the normalized price coefficient matrix **M** relative to the budget share matrix $(\mathbf{w})_\Delta$ requires an estimate of **M**, which is usually subject to error. To simplify the analysis of this subject we confine ourselves to infinitesimal errors.

Consider the (symmetric) matrix **A**, which is diagonalized in (1.10), and assume that its latent roots are distinct. We imagine that $\mathbf{A}$ is subject to a symmetric displacement $d\mathbf{A}$. It is proved in the next subsection that this implies displacements of the ith latent root (λ_i) and the corresponding characteristic vector ($\mathbf{v}_i$) equal to

$$d\lambda_i = \mathbf{v}_i'(d\mathbf{A})\,\mathbf{v}_i \qquad d\mathbf{v}_i = \sum_{j \neq i} \frac{\mathbf{v}_i'(d\mathbf{A})\,\mathbf{v}_j}{\lambda_i - \lambda_j}\,\mathbf{v}_j \tag{3.24}$$

Assume now that $\mathbf{A}$ and $\mathbf{v}_i$ are as specified in (1.16),

$$\mathbf{A} = (\mathbf{w})_\Delta^{-1/2}\,\mathbf{M}(\mathbf{w})_\Delta^{-1/2} \qquad \mathbf{v}_i = (\mathbf{w})_\Delta^{1/2}\,\mathbf{x}_i \tag{3.25}$$

and that the displacement $d\mathbf{A}$ is due to an error $d\mathbf{M}$ in the numerical specification of $\mathbf{M}$. Hence,

$$d\mathbf{A} = (\mathbf{w})_\Delta^{-1/2}\,(d\mathbf{M})\,(\mathbf{w})_\Delta^{-1/2} \tag{3.26}$$

from which we derive, using (3.24) and (3.25),

$$d\mathbf{x}_i = \sum_{j \neq i} \frac{\mathbf{x}_i'(d\mathbf{M})\,\mathbf{x}_j}{\lambda_i - \lambda_j}\,\mathbf{x}_j \tag{3.27}$$

This shows that, when there are two T-goods (the ith and j^{th}) which have nearly equal income elasticities, $\lambda_i - \lambda_j$ being close to zero, the corresponding columns $\mathbf{x}_i$ and $\mathbf{x}_j$ of the matrix $\mathbf{X}$ tend to have large errors even when the estimate of $\mathbf{M}$ has only moderate errors. The inner products of $\mathbf{x}_i$ and $\mathbf{x}_j$ with $\mathbf{w}$ will then also be subject to a large margin of error. Since we have $\mathbf{X}'\mathbf{w} = \mathbf{X}^{-1}\boldsymbol{\iota}$ in view of (1.19), the implication is that the ith and j^{th} elements of $\mathbf{X}^{-1}\boldsymbol{\iota}$ will be uncertain, so that the same holds for the budget shares of the two T-goods, which are equal to the squares of these elements. As (3.1) and (3.2) show, this uncertainty also applies to the corresponding rows (the ith and j^{th}) of $\mathbf{R}$, $\mathbf{S}$ and $\mathbf{T}$.

This result is not surprising. It was stated below (2.32) that two T-goods cannot be identified separately when they have equal income elasticities. We should then expect that it is difficult to distinguish between them when they have nearly equal income elasticities. This difficulty may be viewed as equivalent to the uncertainty as to the properties of these T-goods.

Note that the λ's themselves do not have this problem of uncertainty caused by near-equal λ's. On combining $d\lambda_i$ of (3.24) with $\mathbf{v}_i$ and $d\mathbf{A}$ of (3.25) and (3.26), we find that the displacement $d\lambda_i$ of the income elasticity of a T-good is equal to a quadratic form in the corresponding $\mathbf{x}_i$ with $d\mathbf{M}$ as matrix. This involves no near-zero denominator as in the case of (3.27) with a near-zero $\lambda_i - \lambda_j$.

Derivations

When $\mathbf{A}$ becomes $\mathbf{A}+d\mathbf{A}$, the equation $\mathbf{A}\mathbf{v}_i=\lambda\mathbf{v}_i$ becomes

$$(\mathbf{A}+d\mathbf{A})(\mathbf{v}_i+d\mathbf{v}_i)=(\lambda_i+d\lambda_i)(\mathbf{v}_i+d\mathbf{v}_i)$$

By subtracting $\mathbf{A}\mathbf{v}_i=\lambda_i\mathbf{v}_i$ from this equation we obtain

$$(\mathbf{A}-\lambda_i\mathbf{I})\,d\mathbf{v}_i-(d\lambda_i)\,\mathbf{v}_i=-(d\mathbf{A})\,\mathbf{v}_i \tag{3.28}$$

Next subtract $\mathbf{v}_i'\mathbf{v}_i=1$ from $(\mathbf{v}_i+d\mathbf{v}_i)'\,(\mathbf{v}_i+d\mathbf{v}_i)=1$ to obtain $\mathbf{v}_i'(d\mathbf{v}_i)=0$, and combine this with (3.28) in partitioned form:

$$\begin{bmatrix}\mathbf{A}-\lambda_i\mathbf{I} & \mathbf{v}_i\\ \mathbf{v}_i' & 0\end{bmatrix}\begin{bmatrix}d\mathbf{v}_i\\ -d\lambda_i\end{bmatrix}=\begin{bmatrix}-(d\mathbf{A})\,\mathbf{v}_i\\ 0\end{bmatrix} \tag{3.29}$$

The inverse of the $(n+1)\times(n+1)$ matrix on the left is

$$\begin{bmatrix}\sum_{j\neq i}(\lambda_j-\lambda_i)^{-1}\,\mathbf{v}_j\mathbf{v}_j' & \mathbf{v}_i\\ \mathbf{v}_i' & 0\end{bmatrix}$$

which may be verified by means of $\mathbf{v}_i'\mathbf{v}_i=1$, $\mathbf{v}_i'\mathbf{v}_j=0$ for $i\neq j$, and

$$(\mathbf{A}-\lambda_i\mathbf{I})\sum_{j\neq i}\frac{1}{\lambda_j-\lambda_i}\mathbf{v}_j\mathbf{v}_j'=\sum_{j\neq i}\frac{\lambda_j-\lambda_i}{\lambda_j-\lambda_i}\mathbf{v}_j\mathbf{v}_j'=\mathbf{I}-\mathbf{v}_i\mathbf{v}_i'$$

where the first equal sign is based on $\mathbf{A}\mathbf{v}_j=\lambda_j\mathbf{v}_j$. Therefore, the solution of (3.29) is

$$\begin{bmatrix}d\mathbf{v}_i\\ -d\lambda_i\end{bmatrix}=\begin{bmatrix}\sum_{j\neq i}(\lambda_j-\lambda_i)^{-1}\,\mathbf{v}_j\mathbf{v}_j'\\ \mathbf{v}_i'\end{bmatrix}(-d\mathbf{A})\,\mathbf{v}_i$$

which is equivalent to (3.24).

The Effect of Changes in Budget Shares

Given the normalized price coefficient matrix $\mathbf{M}$, the diagonalization (1.13) depends on the diagonal budget share matrix $(\mathbf{w})_\Delta$ with diagonal elements $\bar{w}_{1t},\ldots,\bar{w}_{nt}$. Thus, as time proceeds, $(\mathbf{w})_\Delta$ takes different values, which affects (1.13). To analyze this effect we assume that the displacement $d\mathbf{A}$ in (3.24) is due to a change $d\mathbf{w}$ in the budget share vector. It is shown in the next paragraph that the implied change in $\mathbf{x}_i$ is

$$d\mathbf{x}_i=-\tfrac{1}{2}(d\mathbf{w})_\Delta\,(\mathbf{w})_\Delta^{-1}\,\mathbf{x}_i-\tfrac{1}{2}\sum_{j\neq i}\frac{(\lambda_i+\lambda_j)\,\mathbf{x}_i'(d\mathbf{w})_\Delta\,\mathbf{x}_j}{\lambda_i-\lambda_j}\,\mathbf{x}_j \tag{3.30}$$

The first term on the right results from the fact that, given $\mathbf{v}_i$ defined in (3.25), $\mathbf{x}_i$ is affected by a change in $\mathbf{w}$. The second term results from the change in $\mathbf{v}_i$. It is this second term which is responsible for large changes in characteristic vectors which correspond to nearly equal λ's. The same conclusions apply as those drawn below (3.27) except that "large errors" should be interpreted here as large changes over time. [Obviously, we have the same large-change interpretation for (3.27) when $\mathbf{M}$ is not constant and $d\mathbf{M}$ stands for the change in $\mathbf{M}$.]

To prove (3.30) we start by postmultiplying (3.19) by $\phi^{-1}\mathbf{X}$, which gives $(\mathbf{w})_\Delta^{-1}\mathbf{MX}=\mathbf{X\Lambda}$. The ith column of this matrix equation can be written as

$$(3.31) \qquad (\mathbf{w})_\Delta^{-1}\,\mathbf{M}\mathbf{x}_i = \lambda_i \mathbf{x}_i$$

If the displacement $d\mathbf{A}$ is due to $d\mathbf{w}$, as it is in (3.30), (3.25) yields

$$d\mathbf{A} = -\tfrac{1}{2}(d\mathbf{w})_\Delta(\mathbf{w})_\Delta^{-3/2}\,\mathbf{M}(\mathbf{w})_\Delta^{-1/2} - \tfrac{1}{2}(\mathbf{w})_\Delta^{-1/2}\,\mathbf{M}(\mathbf{w})_\Delta^{-3/2}(d\mathbf{w})_\Delta$$

With $d\mathbf{A}$ thus specified we consider $\mathbf{v}_i'(d\mathbf{A})\,\mathbf{v}_j$, using (3.25) for $\mathbf{v}_i$ as well as the commutative multiplication property of $(\mathbf{w})_\Delta$ and $(d\mathbf{w})_\Delta$,

$$(3.32) \qquad \begin{aligned} \mathbf{v}_i'(d\mathbf{A})\mathbf{v}_j &= -\tfrac{1}{2}\mathbf{x}_i'\left[(d\mathbf{w})_\Delta(\mathbf{w})_\Delta^{-1}\mathbf{M} + \mathbf{M}(\mathbf{w})_\Delta^{-1}(d\mathbf{w})_\Delta\right]\mathbf{x}_j \\ &= -\tfrac{1}{2}(\lambda_i+\lambda_j)\,\mathbf{x}_i'(d\mathbf{w})_\Delta\,\mathbf{x}_j \end{aligned}$$

where the second step is based on (3.31). Consider finally the differential of $\mathbf{x}_i$, again using (3.25):

$$d\mathbf{x}_i = -\tfrac{1}{2}(d\mathbf{w})_\Delta(\mathbf{w})_\Delta^{-3/2}\,\mathbf{v}_i + (\mathbf{w})_\Delta^{-1/2}\,d\mathbf{v}_i = -\tfrac{1}{2}(d\mathbf{w})_\Delta(\mathbf{w})_\Delta^{-1}\,\mathbf{x}_i + (\mathbf{w})_\Delta^{-1/2}\,d\mathbf{v}_i$$

The result (3.30) then follows directly from (3.24) and (3.32).

Transforming Levels of Prices and Quantities

As a completely different approach, consider the idea of transforming the prices $p_1,\ldots,p_n$ of the commodities linearly into prices $x_1,\ldots,x_n$ of the T-goods, and similarly transforming the quantities $q_1,\ldots,q_n$ linearly into quantities $y_1,\ldots,y_n$ of these T-goods. In this connection, recall that we concluded in remark (2) on page 227 that in the approach discussed there the price and quantity log-changes are subject to the *same* transformation. Of course, levels of prices and quantities are not at all equivalent to their log-changes, but it is nevertheless rather easy to argue on intuitive grounds in favor of such an identical price and quantity transformation. Suppose that the jth commodity contributes nothing to the basic want which is satisfied by the ith T-good, so that the $(i,j)^{\text{th}}$ element of the transformation matrix for quantities vanishes. We should then expect that a change in p_j will not make the satisfaction of this basic want more expensive or less expensive, which means that we expect the $(i, j)^{\text{th}}$ element of the transformation matrix for prices to be zero also. On the other hand, if the jth commodity has a great deal to offer to the basic want that corresponds to the ith T-good, we should expect that the $(i, j)^{\text{th}}$ elements of both transformation matrices take large positive values.

So let us agree, tentatively, to apply the same transformation to prices and quantities:

$$\begin{aligned} x_i &= k_{i1}p_1 + \cdots + k_{in}p_n \\ y_i &= k_{i1}q_1 + \cdots + k_{in}q_n \end{aligned} \qquad i = 1, \ldots, n \tag{3.33}$$

or, in matrix form, $\mathbf{x} = \mathbf{Kp}$ and $\mathbf{y} = \mathbf{Kq}$, where $\mathbf{K} = [k_{ij}]$ is the $n \times n$ transformation matrix and $\mathbf{x} = [x_i]$, $\mathbf{y} = [y_i]$ are n-element column vectors. As in our earlier approach, we require that the budget constraint be satisfied by the T-goods. This amounts to $m = \mathbf{x}'\mathbf{y} = \mathbf{p}'\mathbf{K}'\mathbf{Kq}$, which means that the transformation matrix $\mathbf{K}$ must be orthogonal. This should come as a danger sign. The elements of an orthogonal matrix are dimensionless, because the sum of the squared elements of each row is equal to 1: $k_{i1}^2 + \cdots + k_{in}^2 = 1$. A comparison with (3.33) shows that we are multiplying the n prices as well as the n quantities by dimensionless weights. This leads to an acceptable price x_i of the ith T-good only if all n commodity prices have the same dimension and, similarly, to an acceptable y_i only if all q's have the same dimension. This condition is usually not fulfilled, because quantities of different commodities are measured in different units: pounds, gallons, pieces, etc.

It is nevertheless possible to rescue the approach based on (3.33). The reason is that the analyst is free to choose his n quantity units. He can exploit this freedom by choosing identical units for the prices and quantities of all commodities. Since the product $p_i q_i$ has the dimension of expenditure per unit of time, he can perform this by measuring both prices and quantities in a unit which equals the square root of expenditure per unit of time. That is, if 36 dollars is spent on the ith commodity in a certain year, we write $p_i = 6$ and $q_i = 6$, both in $(\$/\text{year})^{1/2}$. Thus, p_i and q_i become numerically equal, and hence both equal to the square root of $p_i q_i$, so that (3.33) can be written as

$$\begin{aligned} x_i &= k_{i1}\sqrt{p_1 q_1} + \cdots + k_{in}\sqrt{p_n q_n} \\ y_i &= k_{i1}\sqrt{p_1 q_1} + \cdots + k_{in}\sqrt{p_n q_n} \end{aligned}$$

This pair of equations implies $x_i = y_i = \sqrt{x_i y_i}$:

$$\sqrt{x_i y_i} = k_{i1}\sqrt{p_1 q_1} + \cdots + k_{in}\sqrt{p_n q_n}$$

Dividing both sides by the square root of income gives

$$\sqrt{(w_i)_T} = k_{i1}\sqrt{w_1} + \cdots + k_{in}\sqrt{w_n} \tag{3.34}$$

Given the orthogonality condition on $[k_{ij}]$, this amounts to an orthogonal transformation of square roots of budget shares. A comparison with (2.27) shows that this $[k_{ij}]$ may be identified with $\mathbf{K}$ of (1.20), in agreement with the notation used.

We conclude that the orthogonal transformation of square roots of budget shares is equivalent to an identical orthogonal transformation of prices and quantities (levels, not log-changes), after the dimension problem is solved by measuring all prices and quantities in the same unit. It should be stressed that the freedom of choice regarding the quantity units, which was alluded to at the beginning of the previous paragraph, can be used for only one period. Equation (2.27) shows that the period selected is the transition from $t-1$ to t. The quantity units described here are thus "updated" from one period to the next. This may be compared with a similar phenomenon observed in Section 3.7. We found there that DQ_t, the log-change in real income, is evaluated at the geometric means of the prices in $t-1$ and t; and that DP_t, the log-change in the cost-of-living index, is evaluated at the utility level which corresponds to the geometric means of income and prices of the same two periods. These geometric means all change as time proceeds.

12.4 The Geometry of the Transformation

In this section we describe the preference independence transformation geometrically in the n-dimensional Euclidean commodity space. The exposition is in part a continuation of Section 11.6.

The Budget Ellipse and the Price Coefficient Ellipse

Figure 12.1, which is similar to Figure 11.1 on page 199, illustrates the two-commodity case. It contains the unit circle,

$$\mathbf{u}'\mathbf{u} = 1 \quad \text{where} \quad \mathbf{u} = [u_1 \quad u_2]' \tag{4.1}$$

and two ellipses,

$$\mathbf{u}'(\mathbf{w})_\Delta\,\mathbf{u} = 1 \qquad \mathbf{u}'\mathbf{M}\mathbf{u} = 1 \tag{4.2}$$

The first ellipse is the budget ellipse of the commodities. The second is the normalized price coefficient ellipse or, for short, the *price coefficient ellipse.* Since $\mathbf{M}$ is not a diagonal matrix, the axes of the latter ellipse do not coincide

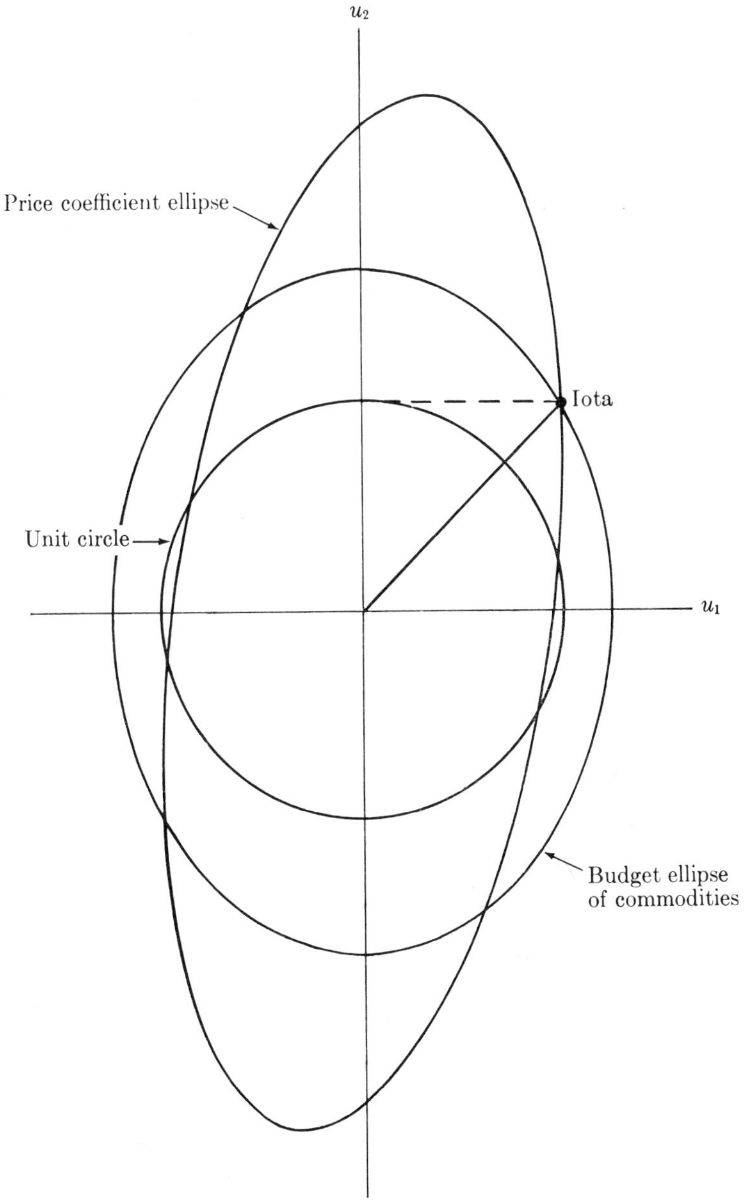

Fig. 12.1 The budget ellipse and the price coefficient ellipse

with those of the coordinate system. [This is, of course, precisely the problem to be solved.] The case illustrated here is that of specific substitution, $\nu_{12}>0$ and $\mu_{12}<0$.

It follows from $\boldsymbol{\iota}'(\mathbf{w})_\Delta \boldsymbol{\iota}=\boldsymbol{\iota}'\mathbf{M}\boldsymbol{\iota}=1$, where $\boldsymbol{\iota}=[1 \;\; 1]'$, that the two ellipses intersect at Iota. This is exactly as it is in the preference independence case illustrated in Figure 11.1. The extension to a larger number of commodities is straightforward; the vector $\mathbf{u}$ then has n elements and $\mathbf{u}'\mathbf{M}\mathbf{u}=1$ becomes the price coefficient ellipsoid. However, note that it is not necessarily true that the unit sphere is wholly inside the price coefficient ellipsoid. This is illustrated in Figure 12.1 for $n=2$, and it is in contrast to the corresponding property of the marginal ellipse in Figure 11.1.

The First Step of the Transformation: A Compression

We proceed to describe the preference independence transformation geometrically in three successive steps. For this purpose it is convenient to attach a subscript 0 to the vector $\mathbf{u}$, so that the ellipses (4.2) become

$$\mathbf{u}_0'(\mathbf{w})_\Delta \mathbf{u}_0 = 1 \qquad \mathbf{u}_0'\mathbf{M}\mathbf{u}_0 = 1 \tag{4.3}$$

We shall write u_{0i} for the ith element of $\mathbf{u}_0$.

The first step is the budget transformation,

$$\mathbf{u}_1 = (\mathbf{w})_\Delta^{1/2}\, \mathbf{u}_0 \tag{4.4}$$

which amounts to a contraction along the axes (a compression). It changes the ellipses (4.3) into

$$\mathbf{u}_1'\mathbf{u}_1 = 1 \qquad \mathbf{u}_1'\,(\mathbf{w})_\Delta^{-1/2}\,\mathbf{M}\,(\mathbf{w})_\Delta^{-1/2}\,\mathbf{u}_1 = 1 \tag{4.5}$$

The first equation shows that the budget transformation changes the budget ellipse into the unit circle (which we already know from Section 11.6). The second shows that the price coefficient ellipse is transformed into another ellipse, to be called the *compressed price coefficient ellipse*.

This new ellipse is shown in Figure 12.2. It intersects the unit circle at the budget point, which may be verified by substituting the vector $\mathbf{u}_1=(\mathbf{w})_\Delta^{1/2}\boldsymbol{\iota}$ in both equations of (4.5). This budget point is obtained from the budget ellipse along the lines of Figure 11.2 on page 200. Note that in the case illustrated here, with the budget point closer to the horizontal axis than to the vertical axis ($\bar{w}_{1t}>\bar{w}_{2t}$), the budget transformation implies a compression along the vertical axis which exceeds that along the horizontal axis.

The Second Step of the Transformation: A Rotation

It follows from (1.16) that the second equation in (4.5) can be written as $\mathbf{u}_1'\mathbf{A}\mathbf{u}_1 = 1$. So, using (1.25) also, we write (4.5) as

$$\mathbf{u}_1'\mathbf{u}_1 = 1 \qquad \mathbf{u}_1'\mathbf{K}'\mathbf{\Lambda}\mathbf{K}\mathbf{u}_1 = 1 \tag{4.6}$$

The second step of the preference independence transformation is

$$\mathbf{u}_2 = \mathbf{K}\mathbf{u}_1 \tag{4.7}$$

which changes (4.6) into

$$\mathbf{u}_2'\mathbf{u}_2 = 1 \qquad \mathbf{u}_2'\mathbf{\Lambda}\mathbf{u}_2 = 1 \tag{4.8}$$

Since **K** is orthogonal, the transformation (4.7) amounts to a rotation[1] of the axes which leaves the unit circle unchanged. The matrix of the compressed price coefficient ellipse is now diagonalized, so that the rotation is such that the new axes (u_{21} and u_{22} in Figure 12.2) coincide with the axes of this ellipse. Furthermore, it follows from (2.27) that the rotation (4.7) is the orthogonal transformation which changes the square roots of the budget shares of the commodities into those of the T-goods. This is also shown in Figure 12.2. Note that both sets of square roots of budget shares, those before as well as those after the transformation, are represented by the same budget point. The difference is the set of axes from which the coordinates of this point are measured.

This completes the discussion of Figure 12.2 except for the points *A* and *B*. These two points are considered in the subsection immediately following the next.

The Third Step of the Transformation: A Decompression

The third step is the reciprocal budget transformation based on the budget shares of the T-goods:

$$\mathbf{u}_3 = (\mathbf{w}_T)_\Delta^{-1/2}\, \mathbf{u}_2 \tag{4.9}$$

This amounts to a reciprocal contraction (a decompression) along the rotated axes. It changes the unit circle of (4.8) into $\mathbf{u}_3'(\mathbf{w}_T)_\Delta\, \mathbf{u}_3 = 1$, which is the budget ellipse of the T-goods, and $\mathbf{u}_2'\mathbf{\Lambda}\mathbf{u}_2$ into

$$\mathbf{u}_3'\,(\mathbf{w}_T)_\Delta^{1/2}\, \mathbf{\Lambda}\,(\mathbf{w}_T)_\Delta^{1/2}\, \mathbf{u}_3 = \mathbf{u}_3'\,(\mathbf{X}^{-1}\boldsymbol{\iota})_\Delta\, \mathbf{\Lambda}\,(\mathbf{X}^{-1}\boldsymbol{\iota})_\Delta\, \mathbf{u}_3 = \mathbf{u}_3'\,(\boldsymbol{\mu}_T)_\Delta\, \mathbf{u}_3$$

---

[1] The transformation is a rotation when $|\mathbf{K}| = 1$, but it involves a reflection when $|\mathbf{K}| = -1$. The latter alternative can be ruled out without loss of generality by multiplying, if necessary, $\mathbf{x}_i$ for some i by -1 (see footnote 1 on page 222).

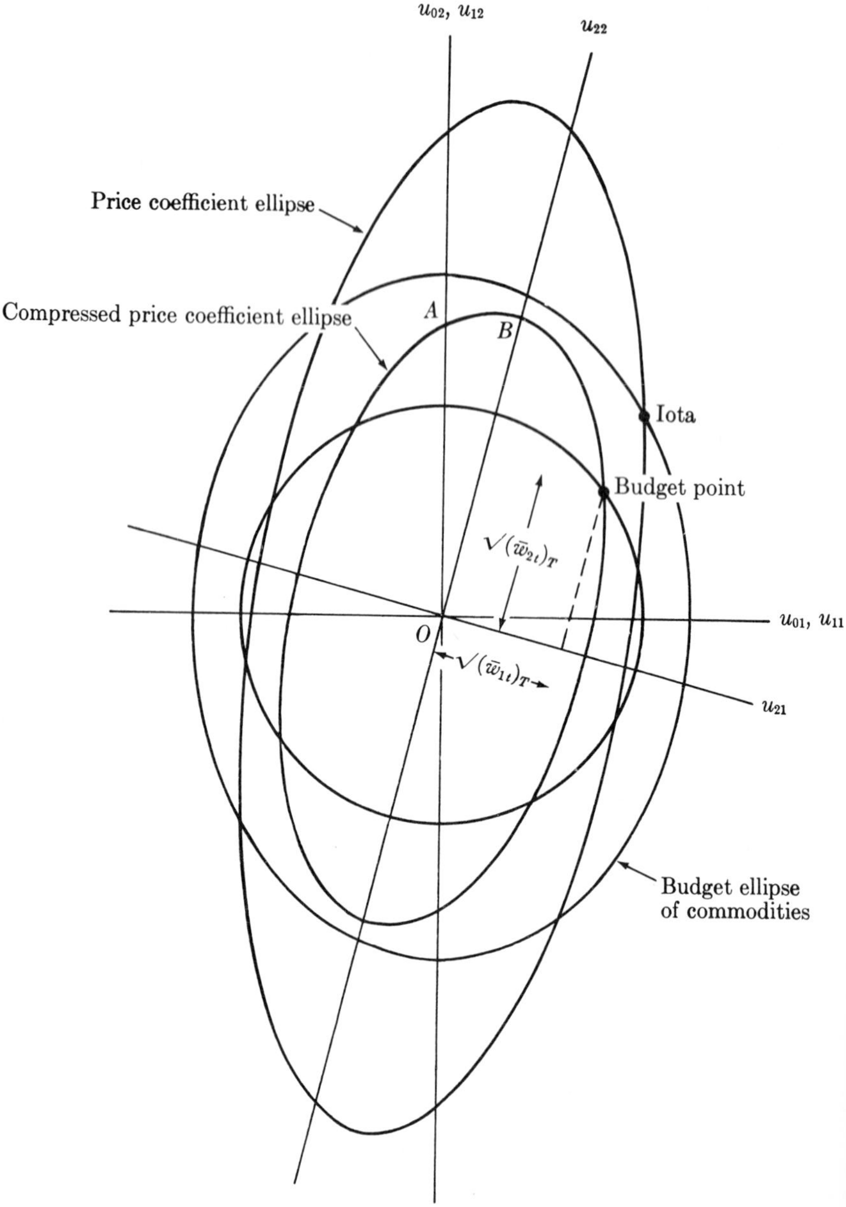

Fig. 12.2 The first two steps of the preference independence transformation

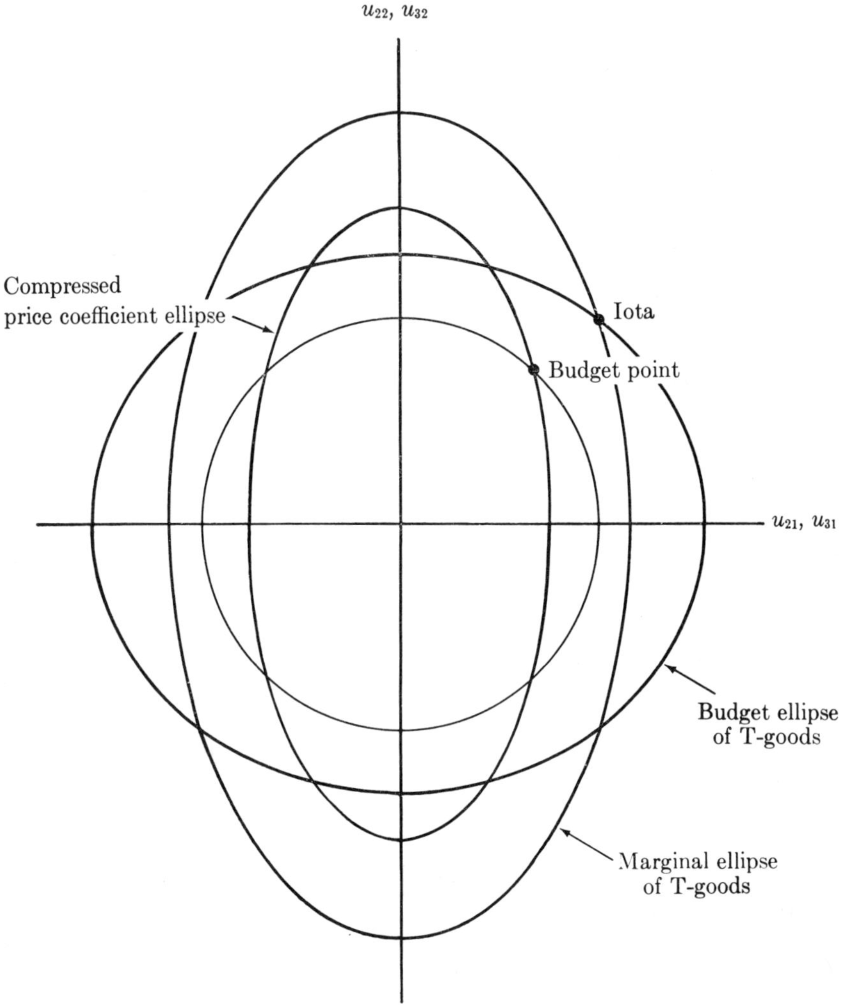

Fig. 12.3 The third step of the preference independence transformation

where use is made of (2.24) and (2.29). Therefore, the decompression (4.9) transforms (4.8) into

(4.10) $$\mathbf{u}_3'(\mathbf{w}_T)_\Delta \mathbf{u}_3 = 1 \qquad \mathbf{u}_3'(\boldsymbol{\mu}_T)_\Delta \mathbf{u}_3 = 1$$

The left-hand sides of both equations are diagonal quadratic forms in $\mathbf{u}_3$, so that both are represented by ellipses whose axes coincide with those of the coordinate system. Thus, the budget share matrix $(\mathbf{w})_\Delta$ and the normalized price coefficient matrix **M** of the commodities in (4.3) have been transformed, in three steps, into the budget share matrix $(\mathbf{w}_T)_\Delta$ and the marginal share matrix $(\boldsymbol{\mu}_T)_\Delta$ of the T-goods. In particular, the price coefficient ellipse has been transformed into the marginal share ellipse or, for short, the marginal ellipse of the T-goods.

Both ellipses of (4.10) and the compressed price coefficient ellipse are shown in Figure 12.3. The budget and marginal ellipses of this figure are identical to those of Figure 11.1 on page 199. The geometric analysis of Section 11.6, which is based on the preference independence assumption, is directly applicable to the preference-dependent case illustrated in Figure 12.1 when it is understood that the preference independence transformation has been performed beforehand.

By combining (4.9) successively with (4.7) and (4.4), we conclude that the preference independence transformation as described here amounts to

$$\mathbf{u}_3 = (\mathbf{w}_T)_\Delta^{-1/2}\,\mathbf{u}_2 = (\mathbf{w}_T)_\Delta^{-1/2}\,\mathbf{K}\mathbf{u}_1 = (\mathbf{w}_T)_\Delta^{-1/2}\,\mathbf{K}\,(\mathbf{w})_\Delta^{1/2}\,\mathbf{u}_0$$

The last member equals $(\mathbf{X}^{-1}\boldsymbol{\iota})_\Delta^{-1}\,\mathbf{X}^{-1}\mathbf{u}_0$ in view of (1.20) and (2.24). Hence, using (2.22) also, we obtain the first equation of

$$\mathbf{u}_3 = \mathbf{S}\mathbf{u}_0 \qquad \mathbf{u}_0 = \mathbf{R}'\mathbf{u}_3 \tag{4.11}$$

while the second equation is obtained from the first by premultiplication by $\mathbf{S}^{-1} = \mathbf{R}'$. A comparison with (3.18) shows that the transformations of (4.11) are identical to those of the income elasticities.

Own-Price Elasticities

When we substitute $\mathbf{u}_1 = [0 \ldots 0 \;\, u_{1i} \;\, 0 \ldots 0]'$ in the second equation of (4.5), we obtain

$$u_{1i}^2 = \frac{\bar{w}_{it}}{\mu_{ii}} \tag{4.12}$$

For $i = 2$ this is equal to the square of OA in Figure 12.2. Similarly, by substituting $\mathbf{u}_2 = [0 \ldots 0 \;\, u_{2i} \;\, 0 \ldots 0]'$ in the second equation of (4.8), we obtain

$$u_{2i}^2 = \frac{1}{\lambda_i} \tag{4.13}$$

For $i = 2$ this equals $(OB)^2$ in Figure 12.2.

The reciprocal of (4.12) is $\mu_{ii}/\bar{w}_{it}$, which is equal to the own-price elasticity of the ith commodity, $\nu_{ii}/\bar{w}_{it}$, divided by the income flexibility ϕ. The reciprocal of (4.13) may similarly be written as $\phi\lambda_i$ divided by ϕ. As we know from the discussion below (3.20), $\phi\lambda_i$ is the own-price elasticity of the ith T-good. Therefore, the squared reciprocals of the distances between the origin and the intersection points of the compressed price coefficient ellipse and the two sets of axes (those before and those after the rotation) are proportional to the own-price elasticities of the commodities and the T-goods.

Multiple Roots

If λ_1 and λ_2 are equal, the compressed price coefficient ellipse of Figure 12.2 is a circle which has no unique pair of axes. The same problem arises for general n when any two (or more) of the n roots are equal. The preference independence transformation is then still possible but it is no longer unique. When λ_1 and λ_2 are not equal but close to each other, the compressed price coefficient ellipse is "almost" a circle. The transformation is then unique, but it is obviously quite sensitive to changes in the price coefficient ellipse (which is determined by **M**) and the budget ellipse of the commodities (which is determined by **w**). This is the geometric version of the algebraic analysis which leads to (3.27) and (3.30). An accurate transformation requires that the roots be well separated.

In the case of Figure 12.2 it does not really matter whether we have $\lambda_1=\lambda_2$, because an obvious rotation choice is not to rotate at all. As is easily verified from this figure, $\lambda_1=\lambda_2$ for $n=2$ implies that the price coefficient ellipse coincides with the budget ellipse, which means that the two commodities are preference independent (and have unitary income elasticities). Also, multiple roots do not really matter under block-independence when these roots correspond to different blocks. Since the preference independence transformation can be applied to each commodity group separately, there is a set of T-goods associated with each group. An indeterminacy which is fundamental from an economic point of view occurs only when multiple roots appear within a group.

T-Goods with Zero Budget Shares

Figure 12.2 also illustrates how T-goods disappear from the consumer's basket. For $n=2$ this is the case in which it just so happens that a rotated axis goes through the budget point. For general n it is the case in which the budget point is located in a space of less than n dimensions spanned by a subset of the rotated axes.

A simple example for $n=2$ is $\bar{w}_{1t}=\bar{w}_{2t}=\frac{1}{2}$, so that $(\mathbf{w})_\Delta=\frac{1}{2}\mathbf{I}$, and

$$\mathbf{M}=\tfrac{1}{4}\begin{bmatrix}1+c & 1-c\\ 1-c & 1+c\end{bmatrix} \tag{4.14}$$

which is a symmetric positive definite matrix whose elements add up to 1 for any $c>0$. The solution of the preference independence transformation is $\lambda_1=1$, $\lambda_2=c$ and

$$\mathbf{X}=\begin{bmatrix}1 & 1\\ 1 & -1\end{bmatrix} \quad \text{implying} \quad \mathbf{X}^{-1}=\tfrac{1}{2}\begin{bmatrix}1 & 1\\ 1 & -1\end{bmatrix} \tag{4.15}$$

This yields $\mathbf{X}^{-1}\boldsymbol{\iota}=[1 \;\; 0]'$, which shows that the second T-good (corresponding to root c) is not represented in the consumer's basket. The budget point of Figure 12.3 is then on the horizontal axis, and the budget and marginal ellipses both become a pair of vertical lines at unit distance from the vertical axis. When the budget point is not on but close to the horizontal axis, the decompression along the vertical axis is quite large. These results are as could be expected, because (4.11) shows that $\mathbf{u}_3$ is obtained by the same $\mathbf{S}$ transformation as that used for the price log-changes, which explodes when the budget share of one of the T-goods moves to zero.

For $n=3$ and $(\bar{w}_{3t})_T=0$, the ellipsoids of the T-goods take the form $au_{31}^2+(1-a)u_{32}^2=1$, where $a=(\bar{w}_{1t})_T$ for the budget ellipsoid and $a=\mu_{1T}$ for the marginal ellipsoid. If the third T-good is measured vertically, these two ellipsoids take the degenerated form of a cylinder around the vertical axis. The intersection of this cylinder and any horizontal plane is an ellipse.

The Two-Commodity Case

As stated below (4.2), the case illustrated here is that of specific substitution, $\nu_{12}>0$ and $\mu_{12}<0$. The two commodities are then *positively* represented in the T-good with the *smaller* income elasticity. Buying this T-good may be viewed as an inexpensive way of satisfying the similar needs associated with these specific substitutes. The T-good with the larger income elasticity is a (relatively) high-quality contrast between these substitutes. In the case of specific complementarity the two commodities are *positively* represented in the T-good with the *larger* income elasticity, which thus corresponds to the basic want which the commodities jointly serve to satisfy. The T-good with the smaller income elasticity is then a contrast between the two complements.

To prove these statements we consider $\mathbf{A}$ of (1.16) for $n=2$,

$$\mathbf{A}=\begin{bmatrix}\mu_{11}/\bar{w}_{1t} & \mu_{12}/\sqrt{\bar{w}_{1t}\bar{w}_{2t}}\\ \mu_{12}/\sqrt{\bar{w}_{1t}\bar{w}_{2t}} & \mu_{22}/\bar{w}_{2t}\end{bmatrix} \tag{4.16}$$

with latent roots equal to

$$\lambda_1, \lambda_2=\tfrac{1}{2}\left(\frac{\mu_{11}}{\bar{w}_{1t}}+\frac{\mu_{22}}{\bar{w}_{2t}}\right)\pm\tfrac{1}{2}\sqrt{\left(\frac{\mu_{11}}{\bar{w}_{1t}}-\frac{\mu_{22}}{\bar{w}_{2t}}\right)^2+4\frac{\mu_{12}^2}{\bar{w}_{1t}\bar{w}_{2t}}} \tag{4.17}$$

where the + sign before the square root corresponds to λ_1, the larger root. [We exclude the trivial case $\mu_{12}=0$ in which no transformation is needed.] Since we have

$$\lambda_1 - \frac{\mu_{11}}{\bar{w}_{1t}} = -\tfrac{1}{2}\left(\frac{\mu_{11}}{\bar{w}_{1t}} - \frac{\mu_{22}}{\bar{w}_{2t}}\right) + \tfrac{1}{2}\sqrt{\left(\frac{\mu_{11}}{\bar{w}_{1t}} - \frac{\mu_{22}}{\bar{w}_{2t}}\right)^2 + 4\frac{\mu_{12}^2}{\bar{w}_{1t}\bar{w}_{2t}}}$$

the implication is

$$\lambda_1 > \frac{\mu_{11}}{\bar{w}_{1t}} \tag{4.18}$$

Next we define

$$\mathbf{K} = \begin{bmatrix} \cos\psi & -\sin\psi \\ \sin\psi & \cos\psi \end{bmatrix} \tag{4.19}$$

which is an orthogonal matrix for any angle ψ. Then apply (1.24) to (4.16) and (4.19):

$$\begin{bmatrix} \mu_{11}/\bar{w}_{1t} & \mu_{12}/\sqrt{\bar{w}_{1t}\bar{w}_{2t}} \\ \mu_{12}/\sqrt{\bar{w}_{1t}\bar{w}_{2t}} & \mu_{22}/\bar{w}_{2t} \end{bmatrix} \begin{bmatrix} \cos\psi & \sin\psi \\ -\sin\psi & \cos\psi \end{bmatrix} = \begin{bmatrix} \lambda_1\cos\psi & \lambda_2\sin\psi \\ -\lambda_1\sin\psi & \lambda_2\cos\psi \end{bmatrix}$$

By equating the leading element on the right to the corresponding vector product on the left we obtain

$$\left(\lambda_1 - \frac{\mu_{11}}{\bar{w}_{1t}}\right)\cos\psi = -\frac{\mu_{12}}{\sqrt{\bar{w}_{1t}\bar{w}_{2t}}}\sin\psi \tag{4.20}$$

On combining this with (4.18), we conclude that $\sin\psi$ and $\cos\psi$ have equal signs when $\mu_{12}<0$; hence the elements of the first row of **K**, corresponding to the T-good with the larger income elasticity (λ_1), have opposite signs, whereas those of the second row have equal signs. For $\mu_{12}>0$ the picture is reversed. The proof is completed by (3.8) and the discussion below that equation, from which we conclude that equal signs of the elements in a row of **K** imply positive elements in the corresponding row of the composition matrix.

12.5 The Principal Components of the Consumer's Basket

The Statistical Principal Component Technique

The objective of principal component analysis in statistics is to summarize the behavior of a set of n observed variables by means of n (or fewer) principal components, which are certain linear combinations of the observed variables.

A brief summary of this statistical technique is in order because of its relationship to the preference independence transformation.[1] Let $\mathbf{M}$ be the (nondiagonal) $n \times n$ matrix of the variances and covariances of the observed variables. This matrix is diagonalized,

$$(\mathbf{M} - \lambda_i \mathbf{I})\,\mathbf{v}_i = \mathbf{0} \qquad i = 1, \ldots, n \tag{5.1}$$

after which the ith principal component ($i = 1, \ldots, n$) is obtained by postmultiplying the observation matrix of the original variables by $\mathbf{v}_i$. Any two components are orthogonal; hence the $n \times n$ covariance matrix of the principal components of the set of observed variables is a diagonal matrix.

The ratio of λ_i to $\sum_j \lambda_j = \operatorname{tr} \mathbf{M}$ may be viewed as the proportion of the total variation of the observed variables which is accounted for by the ith principal component. So, if we arrange the λ's in descending order,

$$\lambda_1 > \lambda_2 > \cdots > \lambda_n \tag{5.2}$$

the first component is the most important in the sense that it accounts for more variation in the observed variables than does any other. Frequently, statisticians use only the first $r < n$ components when $\lambda_1 + \cdots + \lambda_r$ is sufficiently large compared with the sum of the remaining λ's. The observed variables can then be described by a linear combination of the r components to a high degree of approximation. But a complete description of these variables requires all n components if the variables are not linearly dependent, i.e., if $\mathbf{M}$ in (5.1) is nonsingular.

Standardization

A problem with the principal component technique is that the components change in a nontrivial way when the units of measurement of the observed variables are changed. This is not of great concern when these variables have the same dimension, because a change in their common unit does no more than multiply their covariance matrix $\mathbf{M}$ by a scalar, but it is a serious problem when the observed variables have different dimensions.

A frequently used solution is to standardize the observed variables so that they have variances equal to 1. The covariances then become correlation coefficients. If $\mathbf{m}$ is the vector of variances prior to the standardization, so that $(\mathbf{m})_\Delta$ equals $\mathbf{M}$ with the off-diagonal elements replaced by zeros, eq. (5.1) is

[1] The exposition which follows is somewhat simplified; multiple roots are excluded in (5.2) and the length of the principal component vectors is not specified. For a brief account of the technique see, for example, THEIL (1971, pp. 46–56) and, for more details, LAWLEY and MAXWELL (1971).

thus changed into

$$[(\mathbf{m})_\Delta^{-1/2}\,\mathbf{M}(\mathbf{m})_\Delta^{-1/2} - \lambda_i\mathbf{I}]\,\mathbf{v}_i = \mathbf{0} \tag{5.3}$$

The λ_i's and $\mathbf{v}_i$'s obtained from (5.3) are obviously not affected when some or all of the observed variables are measured in different units. So the problem is solved, but note that the solution is artificial in all cases in which there are no good reasons for the choice of the standard deviation as the unit of measurement. If time, population and total personal consumption are three variables for which principal components are computed, this choice may imply a time unit of 1.38 years, a population unit of 151 million, and a consumption unit of 727 million dollars per unit of time (dollars per 1.38 years).

Comparison with the Preference Independence Transformation

A comparison of the preference independence transformation and principal component analysis is particularly appropriate because this transformation does diagonalize the covariance matrix of a random vector. It follows from (1.8) and (3.12) that the covariance matrices of the specific substitution components of the disturbance vectors before and after the transformation are

$$\mathscr{V}(\bar{\boldsymbol{\varepsilon}}_t) = \sigma^2\mathbf{M} \qquad \mathscr{V}(\mathbf{R}\bar{\boldsymbol{\varepsilon}}_t) = \sigma^2(\boldsymbol{\mu}_T)_\Delta \tag{5.4}$$

The second covariance matrix is diagonal, whereas the first is not. This should be compared with the diagonal covariance matrix of the principal components and the nondiagonal covariance matrix $\mathbf{M}$ of the observed variables in (5.1) and (5.3).

There is nevertheless an important difference between principal component analysis and the preference independence transformation. The latter is unique on the basis of the three axioms of Section 12.2, provided only that there are no multiple roots. Principal component analysis has the arbitrariness of the units of the n observed variables even when, as is assumed in (5.2), there are no multiple λ's. To understand this difference it is sufficient to go back to the first subsection of Section 12.2, where we imposed the budget constraint on the T-goods. No constraint of this type is used in principal component analysis. It follows from (2.1) and (2.3) that this budget constraint is responsible for the appearance of the $\bar{w}_{jt}$'s, the budget shares of the commodities, which occur in diagonal matrix form in (1.15),

$$[(\mathbf{w})_\Delta^{-1/2}\,\mathbf{M}(\mathbf{w})_\Delta^{-1/2} - \lambda_i\mathbf{I}]\,\mathbf{v}_i = \mathbf{0} \tag{5.5}$$

where $\mathbf{v}_i$ is given in (1.16). Note the similarity of (5.3) and (5.5), as well as their differences. In (5.3) we standardize $\mathbf{M}$ by means of $\mathbf{m}$, which is the diagonal of $\mathbf{M}$, and in (5.5) we use the budget share vector $\mathbf{w}=[\bar{w}_{it}]$, which is unrelated to the $\mathbf{M}$ of consumption theory. The reason is that the $\bar{w}_{it}$'s describe the expenditure levels – in terms of budget shares – during the transition from $t-1$ to t, and $\mathbf{M}$ describes the (normalized) demand response to changes in relative prices.

A Principal-Component Interpretation of the Transformation

Thus the preference independence transformation avoids the arbitrariness of the standardization of the observed variables in (5.3); this is achieved by the budget constraint which the first axiom imposes on the T-goods. At the same time, this transformation is equivalent to a principal component transformation of a set of random variables, since (5.4) shows that $\bar{\boldsymbol{\varepsilon}}_t$ is transformed into $\mathbf{R}\bar{\boldsymbol{\varepsilon}}_t$ with a diagonal covariance matrix $\sigma^2(\boldsymbol{\mu}_T)_\Delta$. So we conclude that the T-goods may be considered as budget-constrained principal components of the basket of the observed commodities.

The T-good transformation is designed to obtain preference independence, not to approximate the consumer's tastes by means of $r<n$ basic wants – those associated with the T-goods that have the r largest λ's. This is in contrast to the procedure described below (5.2). It is nevertheless of some interest that the sum of the λ's, which is used by the principal component technique to obtain the proportions accounted for by the components, has a simple interpretation in the preference independence transformation. This sum, when multiplied by ϕ, is the sum of the own-price elasticities of the T-goods. As we know from (3.21), the sum of the own-price elasticities is invariant under the transformation.

12.6 The Degree of Utility Interaction Among Commodities

Conditional Price Elasticities

By dividing (3.21) by $n\phi$ we obtain

$$\frac{1}{n}\sum_{i=1}^{n}\lambda_i=\frac{1}{n}\sum_{i=1}^{n}\frac{\mu_{ii}}{\bar{w}_{it}} \tag{6.1}$$

On the right we have the arithmetic average of the own-price elasticities $\nu_{ii}/\bar{w}_{it}$ divided by ϕ. We know from Section 8.7 that ϕ can be identified, under appropriate blockwise dependence conditions in a multiperiod framework, with the own-price elasticity of the demand for total current consumption. Since dividing a price elasticity by the price elasticity of the group is analogous to dividing an income elasticity by the group income elasticity, we may define

$$(6.2) \qquad \frac{\mu_{ij}}{\bar{w}_{it}} = \frac{\nu_{ij}/\bar{w}_{it}}{\phi}$$

as the conditional elasticity of the ith commodity with respect to the jth relative price, given the total amount currently spent. For each i the sum of the n conditional price elasticities equals the ith income elasticity:

$$(6.3) \qquad \sum_{j=1}^{n} \frac{\mu_{ij}}{\bar{w}_{it}} = \frac{\mu_i}{\bar{w}_{it}} \qquad i = 1, \ldots, n$$

Since $\phi\lambda_i$ is the own-price elasticity of the ith T-good, we can interpret λ_i as its conditional own-price elasticity. Equation (6.1) thus states that the arithmetic average of the conditional own-price elasticities is invariant under the preference independence transformation. The geometric mean is not invariant. In the subsection immediately following the next we prove

$$(6.4) \qquad \prod_{i=1}^{n} \lambda_i \leq \prod_{i=1}^{n} \frac{\mu_{ii}}{\bar{w}_{it}}$$

with the equal sign holding if and only if there is preference independence among the commodities. Taking n^{th} roots in (6.4), we conclude that the geometric mean of the conditional own-price elasticities is reduced by the transformation except when the n commodities are preference independent. Later in this section we shall use this reduction to measure the degree of utility interaction among the commodities.

A Geometric Interpretation

It follows from (4.12) and (4.13) that $\mu_{ii}/\bar{w}_{it}$ and λ_i for $i=2$ are equal to $1/(OA)^2$ and $1/(OB)^2$, respectively, in Figure 12.2 on page 254. Therefore, both sides of (6.4) may be viewed as squared reciprocals of rectangular areas. The line segments OA and OB are each one side of such a rectangle.

For general n the picture is extended to n points $A_1, \ldots, A_n$ on the n axes before the rotation, and n points $B_1, \ldots, B_n$ on the n rotated axes. Equations (6.1) and (6.4) then become

$$\frac{1}{n} \sum_{i=1}^{n} \frac{1}{(OB_i)^2} = \frac{1}{n} \sum_{i=1}^{n} \frac{1}{(OA_i)^2}$$

$$\prod_{i=1}^{n} \frac{1}{(OB_i)^2} \leq \prod_{i=1}^{n} \frac{1}{(OA_i)^2}$$

Hence $1/(OB_1)^2$, $1/(OB_2)^2, \ldots$ have the same mean as $1/(OA_1)^2$, $1/(OA_2)^2, \ldots,$ but the product of the former never exceeds that of the latter and it is usually smaller. This suggests that the smallest OB_i is smaller than the smallest OA_i, and that the largest OB_i is larger than the largest OA_i. Indeed, this is true as an inspection of Figure 12.2 shows, because the smallest OB_i corresponds to the smallest axis of the compressed price coefficient ellipsoid and the largest OB_i corresponds to the largest axis. All OA_i's are strictly between these limits except when there is preference independence among the commodities.

Proof of the Inequality of the Geometric Means

It follows from (3.20) that λ_i is a latent root of $(\mathbf{w})_\Delta^{-1}\mathbf{M}$. Hence the product of the λ's is equal to the determinant of this matrix, which equals $|\mathbf{M}|$, the determinant of $\mathbf{M}$, divided by the product of the $\bar{w}_{it}$'s. Therefore, (6.4) is equivalent to

$$|\mathbf{M}| \leq \mu_{11}\mu_{22}\cdots\mu_{nn} \tag{6.5}$$

The proof of (6.5) is elementary and instructive. It is obviously true (with equal sign) for $n=1$, and it is also true for $n=2$:

$$\begin{vmatrix} \mu_{11} & \mu_{12} \\ \mu_{12} & \mu_{22} \end{vmatrix} = \mu_{11}\mu_{22} - \mu_{12}^2 \leq \mu_{11}\mu_{22} \tag{6.6}$$

Assume that (6.5) is true for some n; we proceed to prove that it also holds for $n+1$. For this purpose we augment the $n \times n$ matrix $\mathbf{M}$ by an $(n+1)^{\text{st}}$ row and column so that a symmetric positive definite matrix of order $n+1$ results:

$$\mathbf{M}^* = \begin{bmatrix} \mathbf{M} & \mathbf{b} \\ \mathbf{b}' & \mu_{n+1,n+1} \end{bmatrix} \quad \text{where} \quad \mathbf{b} = [\mu_{1,n+1} \cdots \mu_{n,n+1}]'$$

Write $\mathbf{M}_{ii}$ for the matrix obtained by striking the ith row and column of $\mathbf{M}$. We can then evaluate the determinant of $\mathbf{M}^*$, using the Cauchy expansion,

$$|\mathbf{M}^*| = \mu_{n+1,n+1}\,|\mathbf{M}| - \sum_{i=1}^{n} \mu_{i,n+1}^2\,|\mathbf{M}_{ii}| \leq \mu_{n+1,n+1}\,|\mathbf{M}| \leq \prod_{i=1}^{n+1} \mu_i \tag{6.7}$$

where the second step is based on the positive definiteness of $\mathbf{M}_{ii}$, which is a principal submatrix of $\mathbf{M}$. This completes the proof of (6.5) for any symmetric positive definite matrix $\mathbf{M}$.

The Degree of Utility Interaction

Note that the expressions which are subtracted in the second members of (6.6) and (6.7),

$$\mu_{12}^2 \quad \text{and} \quad \mu_{i,n+1}^2 \, |\mathbf{M}_{ii}| \quad \text{for} \quad i = 1, \ldots, n$$

are positive multiples of the square of μ_{ij} for some $i \neq j$. This illustrates that the difference between the two sides of (6.5) will be large when the off-diagonal elements of the normalized price coefficient matrix are not dominated by the diagonal elements; that is, when the commodities are far from preference-independent.

This feature can be used for the design of a measure of preference dependence. We divide (6.5) by $|\mathbf{M}|$, so that the right-hand side becomes the ratio of the product of the diagonal elements of $\mathbf{M}$ to the determinant value, which equals 1 under preference independence and exceeds 1 otherwise. Then take the logarithm of this ratio:

(6.8) $$\upsilon = \sum_{i=1}^{n} \log \mu_{ii} - \log |\mathbf{M}|$$

This is our measure of the degree of utility interaction among the n commodities. It vanishes when these commodities are preference-independent and it is positive otherwise. Also, applying the developments which precede (6.5), we can write (6.8) as

$$\upsilon = \sum_{i=1}^{n} \log \frac{\mu_{ii}}{\bar{w}_{it}} - \sum_{i=1}^{n} \log \lambda_i$$

which implies

(6.9) $$e^{\upsilon} = \frac{\prod_{i=1}^{n} (\mu_{ii}/\bar{w}_{it})}{\prod_{i=1}^{n} \lambda_i}$$

Hence $e^{\upsilon/n}$ is the ratio of the geometric means of the conditional own-price elasticities of the commodities and the T-goods, and $e^{-\upsilon/2}$ is the ratio of the content of an n-dimensional rectangular area on the axes before the rotation to the content of a similar area after the rotation (see Figure 12.2 for $n=2$).

Write $\mathbf{m} = [\mu_{11} \ldots \mu_{nn}]'$, so that (6.8) can be written in the form $\upsilon = \log |(\mathbf{m})_\Delta \mathbf{M}^{-1}|$ and hence also as

(6.10) $$\upsilon = -\log |(\mathbf{m})_\Delta^{-1/2} \mathbf{M} (\mathbf{m})_\Delta^{-1/2}|$$

The determinant on the right is that of the matrix which is diagonalized in (5.3). Also, this matrix is the correlation matrix of the vector $\bar{\boldsymbol{\varepsilon}}_t$ whose covariance matrix is given in (5.4). Hence the degree of utility interaction is minus the logarithm of the determinant of the correlation matrix of the specific substitution component of the disturbance vector.

Although the properties (6.9) and (6.10) are interesting, the real justification of the definition (6.8) of the degree of utility interaction is in terms of its decomposition within and between groups. This is the topic of the remainder of this section.

Utility Interaction Within Groups Under Block-Independence

Consider the case of block-independence with G groups, $S_1,\ldots, S_G$, so that the $n\times n$ price coefficient matrix can be partitioned as

$$\text{(6.11)} \qquad \mathbf{N} = \begin{bmatrix} \mathbf{N}_1 & \mathbf{0} & \ldots & \mathbf{0} \\ \mathbf{0} & \mathbf{N}_2 & \ldots & \mathbf{0} \\ \vdots & \vdots & & \vdots \\ \mathbf{0} & \mathbf{0} & \ldots & \mathbf{N}_G \end{bmatrix}$$

The sum of the elements of the submatrix $\mathbf{N}_g$ is ϕM_g, where M_g is the marginal share of S_g. Hence the normalized price coefficient matrix within S_g (normalized so that its elements add up to 1) is

$$\text{(6.12)} \qquad \tilde{\mathbf{M}}_g = \frac{1}{\phi M_g}\mathbf{N}_g \qquad g = 1,\ldots, G$$

and the ith diagonal element of $\tilde{\mathbf{M}}_g$ is $\nu_{ii}/\phi M_g = \mu_{ii}/M_g$. Therefore, the definition (6.8) implies the following degree of utility interaction within S_g:

$$\text{(6.13)} \qquad \upsilon_g = \sum_{i\in S_g} \log\frac{\mu_{ii}}{M_g} - \log|\tilde{\mathbf{M}}_g| \qquad g = 1,\ldots, G$$

This υ_g vanishes when $\tilde{\mathbf{M}}_g$ is diagonal and it is positive otherwise.

Decomposition of the Utility Interaction Under Block-Independence

Next multiply (6.11) by $1/\phi$, so that we obtain the normalized price coefficient matrix of order $n\times n$, and use (6.12):

$$\text{(6.14)} \qquad \mathbf{M} = \begin{bmatrix} M_1\tilde{\mathbf{M}}_1 & \mathbf{0} & \ldots & \mathbf{0} \\ \mathbf{0} & M_2\tilde{\mathbf{M}}_2 & \ldots & \mathbf{0} \\ \vdots & \vdots & & \vdots \\ \mathbf{0} & \mathbf{0} & \ldots & M_G\tilde{\mathbf{M}}_G \end{bmatrix}$$

The determinant of this matrix is

$$|\mathbf{M}| = M_1^{n_1} |\tilde{\mathbf{M}}_1| \dots M_G^{n_G} |\tilde{\mathbf{M}}_G|$$

where n_g is the number of commodities of S_g. Hence,

$$\log |\mathbf{M}| = \sum_{g=1}^{G} n_g \log M_g + \sum_{g=1}^{G} \log |\tilde{\mathbf{M}}_g| \tag{6.15}$$

Also consider

$$\sum_{i=1}^{n} \log \mu_{ii} = \sum_{g=1}^{G} \sum_{i \in S_g} \left(\log M_g + \log \frac{\mu_{ii}}{M_g} \right)$$
$$= \sum_{g=1}^{G} n_g \log M_g + \sum_{g=1}^{G} \sum_{i \in S_g} \log \frac{\mu_{ii}}{M_g}$$

By subtracting (6.15) from this equation and using (6.8) and (6.13) we obtain

$$\upsilon = \sum_{g=1}^{G} \upsilon_g \tag{6.16}$$

Hence, under block-independence the degree of utility interaction among the n commodities is equal to the sum of the interactions within the groups.

Utility Interaction Within Groups Under Blockwise Dependence

To extend the above result to blockwise dependence we take the demand equation (2.20) of Section 8.2 as our starting point,

$$\bar{w}_{it} Dq_{it} = \mu_i DQ_t + \sum_{j \in S_g} \nu_{ij} (Dp_{jt} - DP'_t) + \mu_i^g \sum_{h \neq g} N_{gh} (DP'_{ht} - DP'_t) + \varepsilon_{it}$$

where $DP'_t = \sum_k \mu_k Dp_{kt}$. Writing $\tilde{\boldsymbol{\mu}}_g$ for the conditional marginal share vector of S_g, we can thus partition the $n \times n$ price coefficient matrix as

$$\mathbf{N} = \begin{bmatrix} \mathbf{N}_1 & N_{12}\tilde{\boldsymbol{\mu}}_1\tilde{\boldsymbol{\mu}}_2' & \dots & N_{1G}\tilde{\boldsymbol{\mu}}_1\tilde{\boldsymbol{\mu}}_G' \\ N_{21}\tilde{\boldsymbol{\mu}}_2\tilde{\boldsymbol{\mu}}_1' & \mathbf{N}_2 & \dots & N_{2G}\tilde{\boldsymbol{\mu}}_2\tilde{\boldsymbol{\mu}}_G' \\ \vdots & \vdots & & \vdots \\ N_{G1}\tilde{\boldsymbol{\mu}}_G\tilde{\boldsymbol{\mu}}_1' & N_{G2}\tilde{\boldsymbol{\mu}}_G\tilde{\boldsymbol{\mu}}_2' & \dots & \mathbf{N}_G \end{bmatrix} \tag{6.17}$$

It follows from eq. (3.1) of Section 8.3 that the sum of the elements of the within-group submatrix $\mathbf{N}_g$ is N_{gg}. Hence the normalized price coefficient matrix within S_g is

$$\tilde{\mathbf{M}}_g = \frac{1}{N_{gg}} \mathbf{N}_g \qquad g = 1, \dots, G \tag{6.18}$$

which is the extension of (6.12) for blockwise dependence.

Also, given eq. (3.9) of Section 8.3, the sum of the G^2 price coefficients N_{gh} of the commodity groups is ϕ, so that the normalized price coefficients of the groups are

$$M_{gh} = \frac{N_{gh}}{\phi} \qquad g, h = 1, \ldots, G \tag{6.19}$$

and the ith diagonal element of the matrix (6.18) is

$$\frac{\nu_{ii}}{N_{gg}} = \frac{\phi\mu_{ii}}{\phi M_{gg}} = \frac{\mu_{ii}}{M_{gg}}$$

Therefore, the definition (6.8) implies a within-group utility interaction equal to

$$\upsilon_g = \sum_{i \in S_g} \log \frac{\mu_{ii}}{M_{gg}} - \log |\widetilde{\mathbf{M}}_g| \qquad g = 1, \ldots, G \tag{6.20}$$

which is the extension of (6.13).

Decomposition of the Utility Interaction Under Blockwise Dependence

We replace $\mathbf{N}_g$ in the diagonal blocks of (6.17) by $N_{gg}\widetilde{\mathbf{M}}_g = \phi M_{gg}\widetilde{\mathbf{M}}_g$ in accordance with (6.18) and (6.19), and we multiply (6.17) by $1/\phi$:

$$\mathbf{M} = \begin{bmatrix} M_{11}\widetilde{\mathbf{M}}_1 & M_{12}\tilde{\boldsymbol{\mu}}_1\tilde{\boldsymbol{\mu}}_2' & \cdots & M_{1G}\tilde{\boldsymbol{\mu}}_1\tilde{\boldsymbol{\mu}}_G' \\ M_{21}\tilde{\boldsymbol{\mu}}_2\tilde{\boldsymbol{\mu}}_1' & M_{22}\widetilde{\mathbf{M}}_2 & \cdots & M_{2G}\tilde{\boldsymbol{\mu}}_2\tilde{\boldsymbol{\mu}}_G' \\ \vdots & \vdots & & \vdots \\ M_{G1}\tilde{\boldsymbol{\mu}}_G\tilde{\boldsymbol{\mu}}_1' & M_{G2}\tilde{\boldsymbol{\mu}}_G\tilde{\boldsymbol{\mu}}_2' & \cdots & M_{GG}\widetilde{\mathbf{M}}_G \end{bmatrix} \tag{6.21}$$

In the next subsections we prove for the determinant of this matrix:

$$\log |\mathbf{M}| = \sum_{g=1}^{G} \log |\widetilde{\mathbf{M}}_g| + \sum_{g=1}^{G} (n_g - 1) \log M_{gg} + \log |M_{gh}| \tag{6.22}$$

where $|M_{gh}|$ is the determinant of the $G \times G$ normalized price coefficient matrix $[M_{gh}]$ of the commodity groups.

We write (6.8) as

$$\begin{aligned} \upsilon &= \sum_{g=1}^{G} \sum_{i \in S_g} \left(\log \frac{\mu_{ii}}{M_{gg}} + \log M_{gg} \right) - \log |\mathbf{M}| \\ &= \sum_{g=1}^{G} \sum_{i \in S_g} \log \frac{\mu_{ii}}{M_{gg}} + \sum_{g=1}^{G} n_g \log M_{gg} - \log |\mathbf{M}| \\ &= \sum_{g=1}^{G} \left[\sum_{i \in S_g} \log \frac{\mu_{ii}}{M_{gg}} - \log |\widetilde{\mathbf{M}}_g| \right] + \sum_{g=1}^{G} \log M_{gg} - \log |M_{gh}| \end{aligned}$$

where the last step is based on (6.22). The first term in the last line is the sum of υ_g defined in (6.20). For the other terms we write

$$\upsilon_0 = \sum_{g=1}^{G} \log M_{gg} - \log |M_{gh}| \tag{6.23}$$

which is the uppercase version of (6.8) and can thus be identified with the degree of utility interaction among the commodity groups. So we obtain

$$\upsilon = \upsilon_0 + \sum_{g=1}^{G} \upsilon_g \tag{6.24}$$

which states that, under blockwise dependence, the utility interaction among the n commodities is equal to the between-group interaction plus the sum of the within-group interactions.

First Lemma

We write the $G \times G$ determinant $|M_{gh}|$ as

$$|M_{gh}| = \begin{vmatrix} M_{11} & \cdots & M_{1,G-1} & M_{1G} \\ \vdots & & \vdots & \vdots \\ M_{G-1,1} & \cdots & M_{G-1,G-1} & M_{G-1,G} \\ M_{G1} & \cdots & M_{G,G-1} & M_{GG} \end{vmatrix} \tag{6.25}$$

The value of this determinant is not changed when we subtract, for $h=1, \ldots, G-1$, a multiple a_h of the hth column from the Gth column. By selecting these multiples so that

$$\sum_{h=1}^{G-1} M_{gh} a_h = M_{gG} \qquad g = 1, \ldots, G-1 \tag{6.26}$$

the last column of the determinant thus obtained consists of zeros except for the last element, which equals $M_{GG} - \sum_h M_{Gh} a_h$, where the summation is over $h=1, \ldots, G-1$. So we obtain

$$|M_{gh}| = \left(M_{GG} - \sum_{h=1}^{G-1} M_{Gh} a_h \right) \begin{vmatrix} M_{11} & \cdots & M_{1,G-1} \\ \vdots & & \vdots \\ M_{G-1,1} & \cdots & M_{G-1,G-1} \end{vmatrix} \tag{6.27}$$

This is one of the lemmas that will be used for the proof of (6.22). Note that the a's in (6.27) are uniquely determined by (6.26) because the M_{gh}'s in the left-hand side of (6.26) form a nonsingular submatrix of the $G \times G$ matrix $[M_{gh}]$.

Second Lemma

Let $\mathbf{M}=[\mu_{ij}]$ be an arbitrary symmetric matrix and $\boldsymbol{\mu}=[\mu_i]$ be a column vector satisfying $\mathbf{M}\boldsymbol{\iota}=\boldsymbol{\mu}$ and $\boldsymbol{\iota}'\boldsymbol{\mu}=1$. Then

$$|\mathbf{M}-k\boldsymbol{\mu}\boldsymbol{\mu}'|=(1-k)\,|\mathbf{M}| \tag{6.28}$$

holds for any scalar k.

To prove (6.28) for $\mathbf{M}$ of order $n\times n$, we write the left-hand side as

$$\begin{vmatrix} \mu_{11}-k\mu_1^2 & \mu_{12}-k\mu_1\mu_2 & \cdots & \mu_{1n}-k\mu_1\mu_n \\ \mu_{21}-k\mu_2\mu_1 & \mu_{22}-k\mu_2^2 & \cdots & \mu_{2n}-k\mu_2\mu_n \\ \vdots & \vdots & & \vdots \\ \mu_{n1}-k\mu_n\mu_1 & \mu_{n2}-k\mu_n\mu_2 & \cdots & \mu_{nn}-k\mu_n^2 \end{vmatrix}$$

We add the sum of the last $n-1$ columns to the first, so that the ith element of the first column becomes

$$\sum_{j=1}^{n}\mu_{ij}-k\mu_i\sum_{j=1}^{n}\mu_j=(1-k)\,\mu_i$$

Therefore, the result is

$$|\mathbf{M}-k\boldsymbol{\mu}\boldsymbol{\mu}'|=(1-k)\begin{vmatrix} \mu_1 & \mu_{12}-k\mu_1\mu_2 & \cdots & \mu_{1n}-k\mu_1\mu_n \\ \mu_2 & \mu_{22}-k\mu_2^2 & \cdots & \mu_{2n}-k\mu_2\mu_n \\ \vdots & \vdots & & \vdots \\ \mu_n & \mu_{n2}-k\mu_n\mu_2 & \cdots & \mu_{nn}-k\mu_n^2 \end{vmatrix}$$

Next add a multiple $k\mu_i$ of the first column of the right-hand determinant to the ith column for $i=2,\ldots,n$:

$$|\mathbf{M}-k\boldsymbol{\mu}\boldsymbol{\mu}'|=(1-k)\begin{vmatrix} \mu_1 & \mu_{12} & \cdots & \mu_{1n} \\ \mu_2 & \mu_{22} & \cdots & \mu_{2n} \\ \vdots & \vdots & & \vdots \\ \mu_n & \mu_{n2} & \cdots & \mu_{nn} \end{vmatrix}$$

The proof of lemma (6.28) is completed by subtracting the sum of the last $n-1$ columns from the first in the determinant on the right.

Evaluating the Determinant of M

We take antilogs of (6.22):

$$|\mathbf{M}|=|M_{gh}|\prod_{g=1}^{G}M_{gg}^{n_g-1}\,|\tilde{\mathbf{M}}_g| \tag{6.29}$$

Since $|M_{gh}|=1$ for $G=1$, this is obviously true for the one-group case. Therefore, it is sufficient to verify (6.29) for G under the condition that it is true for $G-1$. For this purpose we write the determinant of the matrix (6.21) as

(6.30)
$$|\mathbf{M}| = \begin{vmatrix} M_{11}\widetilde{\mathbf{M}}_1 & \cdots & M_{1,G-1}\tilde{\boldsymbol{\mu}}_1\tilde{\boldsymbol{\mu}}'_{G-1} & M_{1G}\tilde{\boldsymbol{\mu}}_1\tilde{\boldsymbol{\mu}}'_G \\ \vdots & & \vdots & \vdots \\ M_{G-1,1}\tilde{\boldsymbol{\mu}}_{G-1}\tilde{\boldsymbol{\mu}}'_1 & \cdots & M_{G-1,G-1}\widetilde{\mathbf{M}}_{G-1} & M_{G-1,G}\tilde{\boldsymbol{\mu}}_{G-1}\tilde{\boldsymbol{\mu}}'_G \\ M_{G1}\tilde{\boldsymbol{\mu}}_G\tilde{\boldsymbol{\mu}}'_1 & \cdots & M_{G,G-1}\tilde{\boldsymbol{\mu}}_G\tilde{\boldsymbol{\mu}}'_{G-1} & M_{GG}\widetilde{\mathbf{M}}_G \end{vmatrix}$$

We subtract from each of the last n_G columns (corresponding to S_G) an appropriate multiple of a_1 times the sum of the first n_1 columns plus a_2 times the sum of the next n_2 columns and so on, where the a's are given in (6.26). If we set this multiple equal to the corresponding conditional marginal share within S_G and use $\widetilde{\mathbf{M}}_g\boldsymbol{\iota}_g = \tilde{\boldsymbol{\mu}}_g$, we find that the last n_G columns consist of zeros except for the $n_G \times n_G$ submatrix in the lower right, which equals

$$M_{GG}\widetilde{\mathbf{M}}_G - \left(\sum_{h=1}^{G-1} M_{Gh}a_h\right)\tilde{\boldsymbol{\mu}}_G\tilde{\boldsymbol{\mu}}'_G$$

Therefore,

(6.31)
$$|\mathbf{M}| = \left|M_{GG}\widetilde{\mathbf{M}}_G - \left(\sum_{h=1}^{G-1} M_{Gh}a_h\right)\tilde{\boldsymbol{\mu}}_G\tilde{\boldsymbol{\mu}}'_G\right| \times \begin{vmatrix} M_{11}\widetilde{\mathbf{M}}_1 & \cdots & M_{1,G-1}\tilde{\boldsymbol{\mu}}_1\tilde{\boldsymbol{\mu}}'_{G-1} \\ \vdots & & \vdots \\ M_{G-1,1}\tilde{\boldsymbol{\mu}}_{G-1}\tilde{\boldsymbol{\mu}}'_1 & \cdots & M_{G-1,G-1}\widetilde{\mathbf{M}}_{G-1} \end{vmatrix}$$

Since we proceed under the condition that (6.29) is true for $G-1$, the second determinant in the right-hand side of (6.31) can be written as

(6.32)
$$\begin{vmatrix} M_{11} & \cdots & M_{1,G-1} \\ \vdots & & \vdots \\ M_{G-1,1} & \cdots & M_{G-1,G-1} \end{vmatrix} \prod_{g=1}^{G-1} M_{gg}^{n_g-1}\,|\widetilde{\mathbf{M}}_g|$$

The first right-hand determinant in (6.31) may be written as

(6.33)
$$M_{GG}^{n_G}\left|\widetilde{\mathbf{M}}_G - \left(\frac{1}{M_{GG}}\sum_{h=1}^{G-1} M_{Gh}a_h\right)\tilde{\boldsymbol{\mu}}_G\tilde{\boldsymbol{\mu}}'_G\right| = M_{GG}^{n_G}\left(1 - \frac{1}{M_{GG}}\sum_{h=1}^{G-1} M_{Gh}a_h\right)|\widetilde{\mathbf{M}}_G|$$
$$= M_{GG}^{n_G-1}\left(M_{GG} - \sum_{h=1}^{G-1} M_{Gh}a_h\right)|\widetilde{\mathbf{M}}_G|$$

where the first equal sign is based on lemma (6.28). The proof of (6.29) is completed by multiplying (6.32) and (6.33) and using lemma (6.27).

12.7 Summary Measures of the Basket and the Preference Independence Transformation

In this section we return to the summary measures developed in Chapter 11, but now formulated in terms of T-goods. It will appear that, for an important class of coefficients and variables, budget-share-weighted first and second moments are invariant under the preference independence transformation, as are marginally weighted first moments, but marginally weighted second moments are not invariant.

The Price-Quantity Covariance

We consider the price-quantity covariance defined in eq. (1.2) of Section 11.1,

$$\Gamma_t = \sum_{i=1}^{n} \bar{w}_{it}(Dp_{it} - DP_t)(Dq_{it} - DQ_t) \tag{7.1}$$

which we write in the equivalent form

$$\Gamma_t = \sum_{i=1}^{n} \bar{w}_{it} Dp_{it} Dq_{it} - DP_t DQ_t \tag{7.2}$$

The first term on the right is the inner product of $\boldsymbol{\pi}_t = [Dp_{1t} \dots Dp_{nt}]'$ and $\mathbf{z}_t = [\bar{w}_{1t}Dq_{1t} \dots \bar{w}_{nt}Dq_{nt}]'$. Since $\boldsymbol{\pi}_t$ is transformed into $\mathbf{S}\boldsymbol{\pi}_t$ and $\mathbf{z}_t$ into $\mathbf{R}\mathbf{z}_t$, the transformed inner product is $(\mathbf{S}\boldsymbol{\pi}_t)'\,\mathbf{R}\mathbf{d}_t$, which equals $\boldsymbol{\pi}_t'\mathbf{d}_t$ in view of (2.23). Hence this product is invariant. Since DP_t and DQ_t in (7.2) have the same property, this proves that the price-quantity covariance is invariant under the preference independence transformation.

Next consider the components of Γ_t shown in eq. (1.6) of Section 11.1 but with the expression (1.11) of the same section for the substitution term:

(7.3)

$$\Gamma_t = (DP_t' - DP_t)\,DQ_t + \sum_{i=1}^{n}\sum_{j=1}^{n} \nu_{ij}(Dp_{it} - DP_t')(Dp_{jt} - DP_t') + \sum_{i=1}^{n} Dp_{it}\varepsilon_{it}$$

Since DP_t', DP_t and DQ_t are all invariant under the preference independence transformation, so is the real-income component of Γ_t. The substitution component is considered in the next subsection.

The disturbance component in (7.3) is transformed into $(\mathbf{S}\boldsymbol{\pi}_t)'\,\mathbf{R}\boldsymbol{\varepsilon}_t$ and is hence invariant [see (2.23)]. Its variance under the second-moment model

(7.11) of Section 2.7 is

$$\sum_{i=1}^{n}\sum_{j=1}^{n} Dp_{it}Dp_{jt}\operatorname{cov}(\varepsilon_{it},\varepsilon_{jt}) = \sigma^2 \sum_{i=1}^{n}\sum_{j=1}^{n}\left(\frac{\nu_{ij}}{\phi} - \mu_i\mu_j\right) Dp_{it}Dp_{jt}$$
$$= \frac{\sigma^2}{\phi}\sum_{i=1}^{n}\sum_{j=1}^{n} \nu_{ij}Dp_{it}Dp_{jt} - \sigma^2 (DP_t')^2$$

This may be written as

$$\text{(7.4)} \qquad \operatorname{var}\left(\sum_{i=1}^{n} Dp_{it}\varepsilon_{it}\right) = \frac{\sigma^2}{\phi}\sum_{i=1}^{n}\sum_{j=1}^{n} \nu_{ij}(Dp_{it} - DP_t')(Dp_{jt} - DP_t')$$

which amounts to a multiple σ^2/ϕ of the substitution component in (7.3).

The Marginal Variance of the Price Log-changes of the T-Goods

Since $\mathbf{S}\boldsymbol{\pi}_t$ is the vector of the price log-changes of the T-goods and $(\boldsymbol{\mu}_T)_\Delta$ is their diagonal marginal share matrix, the marginally weighted second moment of these log-changes is

$$\text{(7.5)} \qquad (\mathbf{S}\boldsymbol{\pi}_t)'(\boldsymbol{\mu}_T)_\Delta\,\mathbf{S}\boldsymbol{\pi}_t = \boldsymbol{\pi}_t'\mathbf{S}'\mathbf{RMS}^{-1}\mathbf{S}\boldsymbol{\pi}_t = \boldsymbol{\pi}_t'\mathbf{M}\boldsymbol{\pi}_t$$

where the first equal sign is based on (2.29) and the second on (2.23). We obtain the marginally weighted variance from the second moment (7.5) by subtracting the squared marginal mean, $(DP_t')^2$. This gives, as is easily verified,

$$\text{(7.6)} \qquad \sum_{i=1}^{n} \mu_{iT}[(Dp_{it})_T - DP_t']^2 = \sum_{i=1}^{n}\sum_{j=1}^{n} \mu_{ij}(Dp_{it} - DP_t')(Dp_{jt} - DP_t')$$

where the left-hand side is the marginal variance of the price log-changes $(Dp_{1t})_T, \ldots, (Dp_{nt})_T$ of the T-goods.

Consider then (7.3) and (7.4) with $\phi\mu_{ij}$ substituted for ν_{ij}. It follows from (7.6) that these two equations may be written in the original form of eqs. (1.6) and (1.10) of Section 11.1,

$$\text{(7.7)} \qquad \Gamma_t = (DP_t' - DP_t)\,DQ_t + \phi\Pi_t' + \sum_{i=1}^{n} Dp_{it}\varepsilon_{it}$$

$$\text{(7.8)} \qquad \operatorname{var}\left(\sum_{i=1}^{n} Dp_{it}\varepsilon_{it}\right) = \sigma^2\Pi_t'$$

provided that Π_t' is interpreted as the marginal variance of the price log-changes of the T-goods given in (7.6), not as the marginal variance of the price log-changes of the commodities.

Transforming Means, Variances and Covariances

The result obtained above shows that the marginal variance of the price log-changes is not invariant under the preference independence transformation. The left-hand side of (7.6) is this variance for the T-goods, but the right-hand side is not a variance; it is a quadratic form in the marginally deflated price log-changes of the commodities, with a matrix equal to the normalized price coefficient matrix.

This lack of invariance is in agreement with the rule stated in the opening paragraph of this section. To make this rule more precise we consider two n-element vectors, $\mathbf{a}$ and $\mathbf{b}$, which the preference independence transformation changes into

$$\mathbf{a}_T = \mathbf{S}\mathbf{a} \qquad \mathbf{b}_T = \mathbf{S}\mathbf{b} \tag{7.9}$$

Then we have

$$\mathbf{a}_T'(\mathbf{w}_T)_\Delta\, \mathbf{b}_T = \mathbf{a}'(\mathbf{w})_\Delta\, \mathbf{b} \qquad \mathbf{a}_T'(\boldsymbol{\mu}_T)_\Delta\, \mathbf{b}_T = \mathbf{a}'\mathbf{M}\mathbf{b} \tag{7.10}$$

which follows from

$$\mathbf{a}_T'(\mathbf{w}_T)_\Delta\, \mathbf{b}_T = \mathbf{a}'\mathbf{S}'(\mathbf{w}_T)_\Delta\, \mathbf{S}\mathbf{b} = \mathbf{a}'(\mathbf{w})_\Delta\, \mathbf{b} \qquad \text{[see (3.3)]}$$
$$\mathbf{a}_T'(\boldsymbol{\mu}_T)_\Delta\, \mathbf{b}_T = \mathbf{a}'\mathbf{S}'(\boldsymbol{\mu}_T)_\Delta\, \mathbf{S}\mathbf{b} = \mathbf{a}'\mathbf{M}\mathbf{b} \qquad \text{[see (3.14)]}$$

We conclude from (7.10) that the budget-share-weighted cross-moment of the two vectors is invariant under the transformation, but that the marginally weighted cross-moment is not invariant. Next we specify $\mathbf{a}=\boldsymbol{\iota}$, so that $\mathbf{a}_T = \mathbf{S}\boldsymbol{\iota}=\boldsymbol{\iota}$, and substitute this in (7.10):

$$\mathbf{w}_T'\mathbf{b}_T = \mathbf{w}'\mathbf{b} \qquad \boldsymbol{\mu}_T'\mathbf{b}_T = \boldsymbol{\iota}'\mathbf{M}\mathbf{b} = \boldsymbol{\mu}'\mathbf{b}$$

This proves that, when $\mathbf{b}$ is subjected to the $\mathbf{S}$ transformation, both the marginal and the budget-share-weighted means of its elements are invariant.

Write $\bar{b}$ for this budget-share-weighted mean, $\bar{b}'$ for the marginal mean, and $\bar{a}$ and $\bar{a}'$ for those of the elements of $\mathbf{a}$. The following results are easily obtained from (7.10):

$$(\mathbf{a}_T - \bar{a}\boldsymbol{\iota})'\,(\mathbf{w}_T)_\Delta\,(\mathbf{b}_T - \bar{b}\boldsymbol{\iota}) = (\mathbf{a} - \bar{a}\boldsymbol{\iota})'\,(\mathbf{w})_\Delta\,(\mathbf{b} - \bar{b}\boldsymbol{\iota}) \tag{7.11}$$

$$(\mathbf{a}_T - \bar{a}'\boldsymbol{\iota})'\,(\boldsymbol{\mu}_T)_\Delta\,(\mathbf{b}_T - \bar{b}'\boldsymbol{\iota}) = (\mathbf{a} - \bar{a}'\boldsymbol{\iota})'\,\mathbf{M}(\mathbf{b} - \bar{b}'\boldsymbol{\iota}) \tag{7.12}$$

The expressions on the left are both covariances after the transformation. The two equations show that the budget-share-weighted covariance is invariant under the transformation, and that the marginal covariance is not invariant. We obtain (7.6) from (7.12) by specifying $\mathbf{a}=\mathbf{b}=\boldsymbol{\pi}_t$.

Moments of Income Elasticities

It follows from (3.18) that the income elasticity vector of the T-goods is obtained by premultiplying the corresponding vector of the commodities by **S**. Hence the results of the previous subsection are directly applicable to these elasticities. We conclude that the budget-share-weighted mean is invariant (equal to 1) and that the corresponding variance has the same property:

$$\sum_{i=1}^{n} (\bar{w}_{it})_T (\lambda_i - 1)^2 = \sum_{i=1}^{n} \bar{w}_{it} \left(\frac{\mu_i}{\bar{w}_{it}} - 1 \right)^2 \tag{7.13}$$

The marginal mean is also invariant:

$$\sum_{i=1}^{n} \mu_{iT} \lambda_i = \sum_{i=1}^{n} \mu_i \frac{\mu_i}{\bar{w}_{it}} \tag{7.14}$$

Note that this equation can be obtained by adding 1 to both sides of (7.13).

The marginal variance of the income elasticities is not invariant under the transformation. Using (7.12) with $\mathbf{a} = \mathbf{b} = [\mu_i / \bar{w}_{it}]$, we obtain

$$\begin{aligned} \sum_{i=1}^{n} \mu_{iT} \left(\lambda_i - \sum_{k=1}^{n} \mu_{kT} \lambda_k \right)^2 \\ = \sum_{i=1}^{n} \sum_{j=1}^{n} \mu_{ij} \left(\frac{\mu_i}{\bar{w}_{it}} - \sum_{k=1}^{n} \mu_k \frac{\mu_k}{\bar{w}_{kt}} \right) \left(\frac{\mu_j}{\bar{w}_{jt}} - \sum_{k=1}^{n} \mu_k \frac{\mu_k}{\bar{w}_{kt}} \right) \end{aligned} \tag{7.15}$$

Similarly, by specifying $\mathbf{a} = \boldsymbol{\pi}_t$ and $\mathbf{b} = [\mu_i / \bar{w}_{it}]$ we find

$$\sum_{i=1}^{n} \mu_{iT} \left[(Dp_{it})_T - DP'_t \right] \lambda_i = \sum_{i=1}^{n} \sum_{j=1}^{n} \mu_{ij} (Dp_{it} - DP'_t) \frac{\mu_j}{\bar{w}_{jt}} \tag{7.16}$$

which is the marginal covariance of the income elasticities and the price log-changes of the T-goods. Note that the marginal mean of the λ's is not subtracted from λ_i on the left, nor the corresponding mean from $\mu_j / \bar{w}_{jt}$ on the right. Their contributions are both zero.

The Quality Index

We consider the log-change in the quality index defined in eq. (3.2) of Section 11.3:

$$DQ'_t - DQ_t = \sum_{i=1}^{n} (\mu_i - \bar{w}_{it}) \, Dq_{it} \tag{7.17}$$

Recall remark (2) on page 227, according to which quantity log-changes are transformed by premultiplication by **S**. Hence their marginal mean DQ'_t is invariant under the transformation, and so is the log-change in the quality index. [Note that the same argument can be used to establish the invariance of Γ_t by means of (7.11).]

Next consider the components of $DQ'_t - DQ_t$ given in eq. (3.5) of Section 11.3, but with the substitution term in the form (3.13) of the same section:

$$DQ'_t - DQ_t = DQ_t \sum_{i=1}^{n} \bar{w}_{it}\left(\frac{\mu_i}{\bar{w}_{it}} - 1\right)^2 + \sum_{i=1}^{n}\sum_{j=1}^{n} \nu_{ij}(Dp_{it} - DP'_t)\frac{\mu_j}{\bar{w}_{jt}} + \sum_{i=1}^{n}\frac{\mu_i}{\bar{w}_{it}}\varepsilon_{it} \tag{7.18}$$

The variance of the disturbance component under the second-moment model is

$$\sigma^2 \sum_{i=1}^{n}\sum_{j=1}^{n}\left(\frac{\nu_{ij}}{\phi} - \mu_i\mu_j\right)\frac{\mu_i}{\bar{w}_{it}}\frac{\mu_j}{\bar{w}_{jt}}$$

which may be written as

$$\operatorname{var}\left(\sum_{i=1}^{n}\frac{\mu_i}{\bar{w}_{it}}\varepsilon_{it}\right) = \sigma^2 \sum_{i=1}^{n}\sum_{j=1}^{n}\mu_{ij}\left(\frac{\mu_i}{\bar{w}_{it}} - \sum_{k=1}^{n}\mu_k\frac{\mu_k}{\bar{w}_{kt}}\right)\left(\frac{\mu_j}{\bar{w}_{jt}} - \sum_{k=1}^{n}\mu_k\frac{\mu_k}{\bar{w}_{kt}}\right) \tag{7.19}$$

It follows from (7.13) that the real-income component in (7.18) is invariant under the preference independence transformation, and from (7.16) that the substitution component equals ϕ times the marginal covariance of the income elasticities and the price log-changes of the T-goods. The disturbance component is invariant in view of (2.23). The variance (7.19) of this component is σ^2 times the marginal variance (7.15) of the income elasticities of the T-goods. On comparing this with eqs. (3.5) and (3.6) of Section 11.3, we conclude that, mutatis mutandis, we have the same results for $DQ'_t - DQ_t$ as those obtained for Γ_t earlier in this section.

Moments of Budget Share Log-changes

Write $w_{it} = p_{it}q_{it}/m_t$ for $i = 1, \ldots, n$ in log-change vector form:

$$\begin{bmatrix} Dw_{1t} \\ \vdots \\ Dw_{nt} \end{bmatrix} = \begin{bmatrix} Dp_{1t} \\ \vdots \\ Dp_{nt} \end{bmatrix} + \begin{bmatrix} Dq_{1t} \\ \vdots \\ Dq_{nt} \end{bmatrix} - Dm_t \begin{bmatrix} 1 \\ \vdots \\ 1 \end{bmatrix} \tag{7.20}$$

The preference independence transformation premultiplies the first two vectors on the right by $\mathbf{S}$. Since $\mathbf{S}\boldsymbol{\iota} = \boldsymbol{\iota}$, we can apply this to the third also. So we may define the log-changes in the budget shares of the T-goods as S postmultiplied by the corresponding vector prior to the transformation. This implies that the marginal and the budget-share-weighted means of these log-changes are both invariant. As we know from eqs. (2.21) of Section 11.2 and (5.3) of Section 11.5, the budget-share-weighted mean is the allocation discrepancy and the marginal mean is minus the change in the distance from the marginal allocation.

The budget-share-weighted variance of the log-changes in the budget shares is invariant, but the marginal variance is not. It may be verified that the marginal variance of the budget share log-changes of the T-goods is equal to

$$\sum_{i=1}^{n} \sum_{j=1}^{n} \mu_{ij} (Dw_{it} - DW_t') (Dw_{jt} - DW_t') \tag{7.21}$$

This expression allows a decomposition of the form of (5.6) of Section 11.5, with Π_t' interpreted according to (7.6) and K_t' and Γ_t' interpreted similarly. For the budget-share-weighted variance we have the decomposition (2.23) of Section 11.2 in which all four terms are invariant.

12.8 Extensions for the Natural Conjugate Supply Model

From the beginning of Chapter 11 until this point we have assumed that the price log-changes are predetermined in the context of the second-moment model. In this section we extend the most important results of Chapters 11 and 12 for the natural conjugate supply model of Section 10.2.

Review of Some Earlier Results

Our starting point is eqs. (2.4) and (2.6) of Section 10.2:

$$\bar{w}_{it} [Dq_{it} - \mathscr{E}(Dq_{it})] = \sum_{j=1}^{n} \pi_{ij} [Dp_{jt} - \mathscr{E}(Dp_{jt})] + \varepsilon_{it} \tag{8.1}$$

$$\bar{w}_{it} [Dq_{it} - \mathscr{E}(Dq_{it})] = - s_1 \sum_{j=1}^{n} \pi_{ij} [Dp_{jt} - \mathscr{E}(Dp_{jt})] + \eta_{it} \tag{8.2}$$

These are the ith demand equation and the ith natural conjugate supply equation, both written as deviations from their expectations. The covariances involving η_{it}'s are given in eqs. (2.7) and (2.8) of Section 10.2:

$$\text{cov}(\eta_{it}, \eta_{jt}) = s_2 \omega_{ij} \qquad i, j = 1, \ldots, n \tag{8.3}$$

$$\text{cov}(\eta_{it}, \varepsilon_{jt}) = 0 \qquad i, j = 1, \ldots, n \tag{8.4}$$

We shall also use eqs. (2.9) and (2.16) of Section 10.2,

$$(8.5)\qquad \delta_{11}=\frac{s_1^2+s_2}{(1+s_1)^2}\qquad \delta_{12}=\frac{s_1-s_2}{(1+s_1)^2}\qquad \delta_{22}=\frac{1+s_2}{(1+s_1)^2}$$

$$(8.6)\qquad \theta=\delta_{12}+\delta_{22}=\frac{1}{1+s_1}$$

as well as eqs. (2.12) and (2.23) of the same section, which deal with random components of price log-changes:

$$(8.7)\qquad \sum_{j=1}^{n}\pi_{ij}\left[Dp_{jt}-\mathscr{E}(Dp_{jt})\right]=\frac{\eta_{it}-\varepsilon_{it}}{1+s_1}$$

$$(8.8)\qquad \operatorname{cov}(Dp_{it}-DP'_t,\varepsilon_{jt})=\frac{\theta}{\gamma}(1-\mu_j)\quad\text{if}\quad i=j$$

$$-\frac{\theta}{\gamma}\mu_j\qquad\text{if}\quad i\neq j$$

Here $\gamma=-\phi/\sigma^2$ in accordance with eq. (4.4) of Section 7.4.

A Simultaneous Transformation of Demand and Supply Equations

Let us write (8.1) and (8.2) for $i=1,\ldots,n$ in the form of two vector equations. These equations have the same left-hand sides, and the substitution vectors on the right are also the same except for the scalar $-s_1$ in the supply equations. So, by premultiplying both vector equations by the transformation matrix $\mathbf{R}$ and using the matrix $\mathbf{S}$ for the price log-changes, we obtain a transformed demand and supply system, with each demand equation and each supply equation containing only one relative price. In other words, the preference independence transformation yields both a supply and a demand equation of the same form for each T-good. The substitution term of the supply equation of the ith T-good is

$$-\phi s_1\mu_{iT}\left[(Dp_{it})_T-DP_t'\right]$$

where $(Dp_{it})_T=\sum_j s_{ij}Dp_{jt}$ is the price log-change of this good. Note that the deflator DP_t' and the marginal share μ_{iT} are the same as in the demand model. Also note that the price coefficient $-\phi s_1\mu_{iT}$ is positive when s_1 and μ_{iT} are nonzero.

Furthermore, since ω_{ij} in (8.3) is the covariance of ε_{it} and ε_{jt}, we can use (8.3) and (8.4) to extend (3.12) to

$$(8.9)\qquad \mathscr{V}\begin{bmatrix}\mathbf{R}\boldsymbol{\varepsilon}_t\\ \mathbf{R}\boldsymbol{\eta}_t\end{bmatrix}=\begin{bmatrix}\sigma^2 & 0\\ 0 & s_2\sigma^2\end{bmatrix}\otimes\left[(\boldsymbol{\mu}_T)_\Delta-\boldsymbol{\mu}_T\boldsymbol{\mu}_T'\right]$$

where $\boldsymbol{\eta}_t = [\eta_{1t} \dots \eta_{nt}]'$ is the supply disturbance vector prior to the transformation and $\mathbf{R}\boldsymbol{\eta}_t$ is the vector after the transformation. It may be verified that, similarly to $\mathbf{R}\boldsymbol{\varepsilon}_t$, the vector $\mathbf{R}\boldsymbol{\eta}_t$ can be decomposed into specific and general components, which yields $2n$ uncorrelated specific components of supply and demand disturbances whose variances are proportional to the corresponding marginal shares. For the demand disturbances the proportionality constant is σ^2, for the supply disturbances it is $s_2\sigma^2$.

The Price-Quantity Covariance

The three components of the price-quantity covariance shown in (7.3) all contain price log-changes and are therefore all random variables under the natural conjugate supply model. The disturbance component $\sum_i Dp_{it}\varepsilon_{it}$ does not have zero expectation under this model. We use $\varepsilon_{1t} + \dots + \varepsilon_{nt} = 0$ to write this component as

$$\sum_{i=1}^{n} (Dp_{it} - DP'_t)\, \varepsilon_{it} \tag{8.10}$$

Since ε_{it} has zero expectation, we can view the expectation of (8.10) as the sum over i of $\text{cov}(Dp_{it} - DP'_t, \varepsilon_{it})$. Applying (8.8), we thus find

$$\mathscr{E}\left(\sum_{i=1}^{n} Dp_{it}\varepsilon_{it}\right) = \frac{\theta}{\gamma}(n-1) \tag{8.11}$$

Hence the disturbance component of the price-quantity covariance has an expectation proportional to the degree of price-disturbance dependence (θ). This expectation is positive except when $\theta = 0$.

The Quality Index

Next consider (7.18) for the log-change in the quality index, but with Slutsky rather than price coefficients in the substitution term:

$$DQ'_t - DQ_t = DQ_t \sum_{i=1}^{n} \bar{w}_{it}\left(\frac{\mu_i}{\bar{w}_{it}} - 1\right)^2 + \sum_{i=1}^{n} \frac{\mu_i}{\bar{w}_{it}} \sum_{j=1}^{n} \pi_{ij} Dp_{jt} + \sum_{i=1}^{n} \frac{\mu_i}{\bar{w}_{it}}\varepsilon_{it} \tag{8.12}$$

Note that price log-changes do not occur in the real-income and disturbance terms. Hence the real-income term is predetermined under the natural conjugate supply model and the disturbance term has the same distribution as under predetermined price log-changes, with zero mean and variance (7.19). Also, the substitution and disturbance terms of (8.12) are linear functions of random variables (Dp_{it} and ε_{it} for $i = 1, \dots, n$), whereas those of (7.3) are quadratic functions of these variables. This simplicity of (8.12) makes it attractive to derive the variance of its substitution term and the covariance of this term and the disturbance term.

It follows from (8.7) that the random component of the substitution term is

$$(8.13)\qquad \sum_{i=1}^{n} \frac{\mu_i}{\bar{w}_{it}} \sum_{j=1}^{n} \pi_{ij} [Dp_{jt} - \mathscr{E}(Dp_{jt})] = \frac{1}{1+s_1} \sum_{i=1}^{n} \frac{\mu_i}{\bar{w}_{it}} (\eta_{it} - \varepsilon_{it})$$

which has zero expectation when the η_{it}'s and ε_{it}'s have zero expectation. By applying (8.3) and (8.4) and the developments below (7.18), we find that its variance equals $(1+s_2)/(1+s_1)^2$ multiplied by the variance (7.19) of the disturbance term. We use (8.5) to write this as

$$(8.14)\qquad \operatorname{var}\left(\sum_{i=1}^{n} \frac{\mu_i}{\bar{w}_{it}} \sum_{j=1}^{n} \pi_{ij} Dp_{jt}\right) = \delta_{22} \operatorname{var}\left(\sum_{i=1}^{n} \frac{\mu_i}{\bar{w}_{it}} \varepsilon_{it}\right)$$

which shows that the variance of the random component of the substitution term of the quality index is proportional to δ_{22}. Hence this variance vanishes, as it should, under the fixed-price limit of the model ($\delta_{22}=0$).

The covariance of the substitution and disturbance terms of (8.12) is obtained by multiplying the latter by (8.13) and then taking the expectation. Using (8.4) and (8.6), we obtain

$$(8.15)\qquad \operatorname{cov}\left(\sum_{i=1}^{n} \frac{\mu_i}{\bar{w}_{it}} \sum_{j=1}^{n} \pi_{ij} Dp_{jt}, \sum_{i=1}^{n} \frac{\mu_i}{\bar{w}_{it}} \varepsilon_{it}\right) = -\theta \operatorname{var}\left(\sum_{i=1}^{n} \frac{\mu_i}{\bar{w}_{it}} \varepsilon_{it}\right)$$

so that this covariance is nonpositive and proportional to the degree of price-disturbance dependence.

It follows from (8.12) that the random component of $DQ_t' - DQ_t$ has a variance which equals the sum of the variances (7.19) and (8.14) and twice the covariance (8.15). Using (8.6), we find that this amounts to a multiple of the variance (7.19) equal to

$$1 + \delta_{22} - 2(\delta_{12} + \delta_{22}) = 1 - 2\delta_{12} - \delta_{22} = \delta_{11}$$

where the last step is based on $\delta_{11} + 2\delta_{12} + \delta_{22} = 1$ [eq. (1.15) of Section 10.1]. The variance of $DQ_t' - DQ_t$ is thus proportional to δ_{11},

$$(8.16)\qquad \operatorname{var}(DQ_t' - DQ_t) = \delta_{11} \operatorname{var}\left(\sum_{i=1}^{n} \frac{\mu_i}{\bar{w}_{it}} \varepsilon_{it}\right)$$

which implies a zero variance in the fixed-quantity limit ($\delta_{11}=0$). This agrees with the fact that $DQ_t' - DQ_t$ is predetermined in this limit.

The Two Coefficients of the Natural Conjugate Supply Model

It follows from (8.14) and (8.15) that the correlation coefficient of the substitution and disturbance components of $DQ_t'-DQ_t$ is

$$\frac{-\theta}{\sqrt{\delta_{22}}}=\frac{-1}{\sqrt{1+s_2}} \tag{8.17}$$

where the equal sign is based on (8.5) and (8.6). Hence this correlation is close to -1 when s_2 is small, i.e., when the dispersion of the supply disturbances is small compared with that of the demand disturbances, and it moves in zero direction when s_2 takes larger values.

Note that the correlation coefficient (8.17) depends on s_2 but not on s_1, which provides an interesting interpretation of s_2. For this purpose we interpret (8.6) as stating that $1+s_1$ equals the reciprocal of the degree of price-disturbance dependence. In the same way, (8.17) implies that $1+s_2$ is equal to the reciprocal of the squared correlation coefficient of the substitution and disturbance components of the log-change in the quality index.

CHAPTER 13

APPLICATION OF THE PREFERENCE INDEPENDENCE TRANSFORMATION AND ANALYSIS OF PRICE CHANGES

The first objective of this chapter is an application of the preference independence transformation to the 14-commodity model of Chapter 6 and the conditional model for meats of Chapter 7. The second is an analysis of price changes, including the prices of T-goods, the cost of living, the marginal price index, and certain variances of price log-changes. Other summary measures of the consumer's basket are considered in Chapters 14 and 15.

13.1 The Preference Independence Transformation for Meats

The first application concerns the meats of Chapter 7, for which we use the maximum-likelihood estimates of the modified price coefficients given in Table 7.8 on page 41:

$$(1.1)\qquad [v_{ij}^*] = \begin{bmatrix} -.5286 & .0804 & .0109 & 0 \\ & -.2425 & .0282 & 0 \\ & & -.0802 & 0 \\ & & & -.0270 \end{bmatrix} \begin{matrix} \text{Beef} \\ \text{Pork} \\ \text{Chicken} \\ \text{Lamb} \end{matrix}$$

The underlying specification implies that Beef, Pork and Chicken form a three-commodity group in a block-independent framework.

The Conditional Three-Meat Model

We know from Sections 12.1 and 12.2 that under block-independence the preference independence transformation can be applied to each block separately. Two numerical procedures can then be used for this transformation. We may proceed conditionally, with conditional budget shares and price coefficients normalized within the group, or we may use unconditional budget shares and price coefficients divided by ϕ. For meats we shall follow the former route; the latter will be used in the next section for the 14-commodity model of Chapter 6.

For the purpose of the preference independence transformation, we define S_g as the three-meat group, consisting of Beef, Pork and Chicken. Consider then eqs. (3.9) to (3.11) of Section 7.3:

$$\frac{\bar{w}_{it}}{\bar{W}_{gt}} Dq_{it} = \frac{\mu_i}{M_g} DQ_{gt} + \sum_{j \in S_g} v_{ij}^* (Dp_{jt} - DP'_{gt}) + \varepsilon_{it}^* \tag{1.2}$$

$$\sum_{j \in S_g} v_{ij}^* = \frac{\phi \mu_i}{\bar{W}_{gt}} \qquad i \in S_g \tag{1.3}$$

$$\sum_{i \in S_g} \sum_{j \in S_g} v_{ij}^* = \frac{\phi M_g}{\bar{W}_{gt}} \tag{1.4}$$

We can write (1.2) in the equivalent form

$$\frac{\bar{w}_{it}}{\bar{W}_{gt}} Dq_{it} = \frac{\mu_i}{M_g} DQ_{gt} + \frac{\phi M_g}{\bar{W}_{gt}} \sum_{j \in S_g} \mu_{ij}^g (Dp_{jt} - DP'_{gt}) + \varepsilon_{it}^* \tag{1.5}$$

where

$$\mu_{ij}^g = \frac{v_{ij}^*}{\phi M_g / \bar{W}_{gt}} \qquad i, j \in S_g \tag{1.6}$$

is the $(i, j)^{\text{th}}$ price coefficient normalized within S_g. These coefficients satisfy

$$\sum_{j \in S_g} \mu_{ij}^g = \frac{\mu_i}{M_g} \qquad i \in S_g \tag{1.7}$$

$$\sum_{i \in S_g} \sum_{j \in S_g} \mu_{ij}^g = 1 \tag{1.8}$$

which follows directly from (1.3) and (1.4).

The Degree of Utility Interaction Within the Group

The right-hand side of (1.4) is the own-price elasticity of the three-meat group. Using (1.1), we find that it equals $-.6123$.[1] So, writing $\tilde{\mathbf{M}}_g$ for the 3×3 matrix which contains (1.6) as its $(i, j)^{\text{th}}$ element and $\tilde{\boldsymbol{\mu}}_g$ for the corresponding conditional marginal share vector, we obtain from (1.1):

$$[\tilde{\mathbf{M}}_g \quad \tilde{\boldsymbol{\mu}}_g] = \begin{bmatrix} .8633 & -.1313 & -.0178 & \vdots & .7142 \\ & .3960 & -.0461 & \vdots & .2187 \\ & & .1310 & \vdots & .0671 \end{bmatrix} \tag{1.9}$$

[1] This value differs from the own-price elasticity (6.26) of Section 7.6 because the latter refers to the four-meat group with Lamb included. For the same reason the conditional marginal shares shown in (1.9) differ from the corresponding figures in the lower part of Table 7.7 on page 32.

This numerical specification enables us to find the degree of utility interaction of the three meats within their group, as defined in eq. (6.13) of Section 12.6:[1]

$$(1.10) \qquad \upsilon_g = .104$$

As will become clear in Section 13.2, this figure indicates a modest degree of interaction.

The Conditional Design of the Preference Independence Transformation

Equation (1.5) is of the same form as eq. (1.1) of Section 12.1, except for the conditional interpretation and the replacement of ϕ by $\phi M_g/\bar{W}_{gt}$. From a computational point of view, the simplest approach is to diagonalize, in accordance with eq. (1.15) of Section 12.1, the symmetric matrix

$$(1.11) \qquad (\bar{\mathbf{w}}_g)_\Delta^{-1/2}\, \tilde{\mathbf{M}}_g\, (\bar{\mathbf{w}}_g)_\Delta^{-1/2}$$

where $(\bar{\mathbf{w}}_g)_\Delta$ is the 3×3 diagonal matrix which contains the conditional budget shares $\bar{w}_{it}/(\bar{w}_{1t}+\bar{w}_{2t}+\bar{w}_{3t})$ for $i=1, 2$ and 3 in the diagonal. These $\bar{w}_{it}$'s can be obtained from the first three columns of Table 7.2 on page 11.

The diagonalization of the matrix (1.11) yields the latent root matrix $\mathbf{\Lambda}$ and the characteristic vector matrix $\mathbf{X}$. These should be interpreted conditionally, so that the diagonal elements of $\mathbf{\Lambda}$ are the conditional income elasticities of the three transformed meats, and the elements of $\mathbf{X}^{-1}\boldsymbol{\iota}$ are square roots of the conditional budget shares of these meats, in agreement with eqs. (2.32) and (2.25) of Section 12.2. The conditional marginal shares of the transformed meats can be computed as the product of their conditional budget shares and income elasticities, and the matrices $\mathbf{R}$, $\mathbf{S}$ and $\mathbf{T}$ are calculated as shown in eqs. (2.19), (2.22) and (2.20) of Section 12.2.

The Conditional Shares and Income Elasticities of the Transformed Meats

The first three columns of Table 13.1 contain the conditional income elasticities of the three transformed meats for each pair of successive years from 1950 to 1972. Recall from the discussion below eq. (2.32) of Section 12.2 that T-goods are identified by their elasticities. When these elasticities are close to each other, we face a problem when we try to identify T-goods in successive observations. The figures in the first three columns of Table 13.1

[1] The ratio μ_{ii}/M_g in eq. (6.13) of Section 12.6 is to be identified with (1.6) for $i=j$. This is readily verified from the fact that (1.2) is based on the parametrization introduced in Section 7.3.

TABLE 13.1

CONDITIONAL INCOME ELASTICITIES AND BUDGET AND MARGINAL SHARES OF TRANSFORMED MEATS

	T_1	T_2	T_3	T_1	T_2	T_3	T_1	T_2	T_3
	Conditional income elasticities			*Conditional budget shares*			*Conditional marginal shares*		
1950–51	.69	2.06	1.09	.736	.213	.051	.505	.439	.055
1951–52	.69	2.05	1.09	.731	.213	.056	.502	.436	.062
1952–53	.70	1.99	1.11	.723	.210	.066	.508	.418	.074
1953–54	.72	1.95	1.14	.730	.208	.061	.524	.406	.070
1954–55	.74	1.90	1.17	.734	.204	.063	.539	.387	.074
1955–56	.75	1.87	1.18	.726	.196	.078	.542	.366	.093
1956–57	.75	1.85	1.20	.728	.192	.080	.549	.356	.096
1957–58	.76	1.84	1.21	.730	.190	.080	.554	.349	.096
1958–59	.77	1.82	1.23	.740	.184	.075	.572	.335	.093
1959–60	.79	1.79	1.27	.753	.173	.074	.597	.310	.093
1960–61	.81	1.77	1.29	.760	.164	.076	.612	.290	.098
1961–62	.81	1.76	1.30	.765	.161	.074	.620	.284	.096
1962–63	.81	1.76	1.30	.763	.155	.083	.620	.272	.107
1963–64	.82	1.75	1.31	.766	.143	.090	.631	.251	.119
1964–65	.82	1.75	1.30	.758	.138	.104	.624	.240	.136
1965–66	.81	1.76	1.27	.736	.146	.118	.593	.257	.150
1966–67	.81	1.76	1.27	.741	.148	.112	.597	.260	.142
1967–68	.82	1.75	1.30	.756	.136	.108	.622	.237	.140
1968–69	.83	1.74	1.31	.758	.120	.122	.631	.209	.160
1969–70	.84	1.74	1.32	.766	.117	.117	.642	.203	.154
1970–71	.85	1.73	1.34	.779	.109	.112	.661	.188	.151
1971–72	.87	1.72	1.37	.798	.088	.113	.692	.152	.155

indicate that there is no such problem in the case of the transformed meats, since the elasticities are well separated and change slowly over time.

The order in which T-goods are listed is arbitrary. The transformed meats (indicated by T_1, T_2 and T_3 in the heading of Table 13.1) are listed here according to decreasing budget shares in 1950–51. [This order is the same in later years except around 1970.] The conditional budget shares are shown in the middle three columns of the table. The first transformed meat, which has the smallest income elasticity, accounts for about three-quarters of the three-meat budget. The second transformed meat, with the highest income elasticity, has a conditional budget share that gradually declines from 21 to about 10 percent. The third initially has a conditional budget share of only 5 percent, but this share increases gradually until it reaches the same order of magnitude as that of the second transformed meat by the end of the 1960s.

The last three columns of the table contain the conditional marginal shares of the three transformed meats. Since T_1 has an income elasticity less than 1, it is less dominant marginally than at the level of the conditional budget shares. But its conditional marginal share is subject to an increasing trend, from .5 to almost .7, largely because of the increase in its conditional income elasticity. The conditional marginal share of T_3 increases by almost 200 percent due to the increase in both its conditional income elasticity and its conditional budget share. All this occurs at the expense of T_2, whose conditional income elasticity and budget and marginal shares are all subject to declining trends.

The Composition Matrix of 1950-51

The composition matrix for the first observation (1950–51), bordered by row and column sums, takes the following value:

$$\begin{array}{rrr|ll} .119 & .407 & .209 & .736 & (T_1) \\ .295 & -.078 & -.003 & .213 & (T_2) \\ .023 & .092 & -.065 & .051 & (T_3) \\ \hline .438 & .421 & .142 & 1 & \\ \text{(Beef)} & \text{(Pork)} & \text{(Chicken)} & & \end{array} \qquad (1.12)$$

The elements of the first row are all positive; hence each of the three observed meats is positively represented in T_1. This suggests that T_1 corresponds to a basic want for meat in general. But we know from Table 13.1 that T_1 has the smallest income elasticity. Therefore, "meat in general" should be amended in the sense that it refers particularly to the cheaper meats. Accordingly, we shall refer to T_1 as *Inexpensive meat.*

The row of T_2 in (1.12) has a positive entry for Beef and a negative one for Pork, while that of Chicken is virtually zero. This means that T_2 represents the pleasure of consuming Beef rather than Pork, so that we can refer to T_2 as the *Beef/Pork contrast*. As the first three columns of Table 13.1 show, this contrast is the most luxurious of the three transformed meats. The third (T_3), with a conditional budget share of about 5 percent and a conditional income elasticity just over 1 in 1950–51, is a contrast between Beef and Pork on one hand, and Chicken on the other. We shall refer to T_3 as *Antichicken*. The presence of such a transformed meat is not entirely surprising, since Beef and Pork are "regular" meats and Chicken has characteristics of a low-grade fowl.

Recall that we found at the end of Section 12.4 that, in the case of two

TABLE 13.2

COMPOSITION MATRICES AND THE TRANSFORMATION MATRICES **R** AND **S** OF MEATS

	Composition matrix			Sum	R			S		
	B	P	C		B	P	C	B	P	C
					1950–51					
T_1	.119	.407	.209	.736	.27	.97	1.48	.16	.55	.28
T_2	.295	−.078	−.003	.213	.67	−.19	−.02	1.38	−.37	−.01
T_3	.023	.092	−.065	.051	.05	.22	−.45	.46	1.81	−1.27
Sum	.438	.421	.142	1						
					1951–52					
T_1	.119	.398	.213	.731	.27	.95	1.49	.16	.55	.29
T_2	.295	−.079	−.003	.213	.67	−.19	−.02	1.39	−.37	−.01
T_3	.026	.098	−.067	.056	.06	.24	−.47	.46	1.74	−1.20
Sum	.440	.417	.143	1						
					1952–53					
T_1	.127	.382	.215	.723	.28	.95	1.52	.18	.53	.30
T_2	.296	−.084	−.002	.210	.65	−.21	−.01	1.41	−.40	−.01
T_3	.032	.106	−.072	.066	.07	.26	−.51	.49	1.59	−1.08
Sum	.455	.404	.141	1						
					1953–54					
T_1	.137	.387	.207	.730	.29	.97	1.52	.19	.53	.28
T_2	.297	−.087	−.001	.208	.64	−.22	−.01	1.43	−.42	−.01
T_3	.033	.098	−.069	.061	.07	.25	−.51	.53	1.59	−1.13
Sum	.466	.397	.137	1						

					1954–55					
T_1	.148	.383	.202	.734	.31	.99	1.52	.20	.52	.28
T_2	.296	−.092	.000	.204	.61	−.24	.00	1.45	−.45	.00
T_3	.037	.095	−.070	.063	.08	.25	−.52	.59	1.52	−1.11
Sum	.481	.387	.133	1						
					1955–56					
T_1	.155	.365	.207	.726	.31	.97	1.56	.21	.50	.28
T_2	.290	−.096	.001	.196	.59	−.26	.01	1.48	−.49	.01
T_3	.048	.106	−.076	.078	.10	.28	−.57	.61	1.36	−.97
Sum	.493	.375	.132	1						
					1956–57					
T_1	.160	.363	.205	.728	.32	.98	1.57	.22	.50	.28
T_2	.288	−.098	.002	.192	.58	−.26	.02	1.50	−.51	.01
T_3	.051	.106	−.076	.080	.10	.29	−.58	.63	1.32	−.96
Sum	.499	.371	.131	1						
					1957–58					
T_1	.164	.363	.203	.730	.33	.99	1.57	.22	.50	.28
T_2	.286	−.099	.003	.190	.57	−.27	.02	1.51	−.52	.01
T_3	.052	.104	−.076	.080	.10	.28	−.59	.65	1.31	−.96
Sum	.502	.368	.129	1						
					1958–59					
T_1	.176	.368	.196	.740	.34	1.01	1.56	.24	.50	.27
T_2	.282	−.102	.004	.184	.55	−.28	.03	1.53	−.55	.02
T_3	.053	.097	−.075	.075	.10	.27	−.59	.71	1.28	−.99
Sum	.511	.363	.126	1						

TABLE 13.2 *(continued)*

	Composition matrix			Sum	R			S		
	B	P	C		B	P	C	B	P	C
					1959–60					
T_1	.194	.371	.188	.753	.37	1.05	1.56	.26	.49	.25
T_2	.273	−.106	.006	.173	.52	−.30	.05	1.57	−.61	.04
T_3	.058	.089	−.074	.074	.11	.25	−.61	.79	1.21	−1.00
Sum	.524	.355	.121	1						
					1960–61					
T_1	.205	.370	.185	.760	.39	1.06	1.56	.27	.49	.24
T_2	.263	−.108	.008	.164	.49	−.31	.07	1.61	−.66	.05
T_3	.065	.086	−.075	.076	.12	.25	−.63	.85	1.13	−.98
Sum	.533	.348	.118	1						
					1961–62					
T_1	.211	.373	.181	.765	.39	1.07	1.55	.28	.49	.24
T_2	.260	−.108	.009	.161	.49	−.31	.08	1.62	−.67	.06
T_3	.065	.083	−.074	.074	.12	.24	−.63	.88	1.12	−1.00
Sum	.536	.347	.117	1						
					1962–63					
T_1	.213	.365	.185	.763	.40	1.06	1.57	.28	.48	.24
T_2	.254	−.109	.010	.155	.47	−.32	.08	1.64	−.70	.06
T_3	.072	.087	−.077	.083	.13	.25	−.66	.88	1.06	−.93
Sum	.540	.343	.117	1						

					1963–64					
T_1	.223	.359	.184	.766	.41	1.07	1.59	.29	.47	.24
T_2	.241	−.110	.012	.143	.44	−.33	.10	1.68	−.76	.08
T_3	.083	.088	−.080	.090	.15	.26	−.69	.92	.97	−.88
Sum	.547	.337	.116	1						
					1964–65					
T_1	.221	.346	.191	.758	.40	1.04	1.62	.29	.46	.25
T_2	.235	−.109	.012	.138	.43	−.33	.10	1.71	−.79	.09
T_3	.093	.096	−.085	.104	.17	.29	−.72	.90	.92	−.81
Sum	.550	.333	.118	1						
					1965–66					
T_1	.202	.332	.202	.736	.37	.99	1.64	.27	.45	.27
T_2	.244	−.108	.010	.146	.45	−.32	.08	1.67	−.74	.07
T_3	.095	.112	−.089	.118	.18	.33	−.72	.81	.95	−.75
Sum	.541	.336	.123	1						
					1966–67					
T_1	.203	.338	.200	.741	.38	1.00	1.63	.27	.46	.27
T_2	.246	−.108	.010	.148	.46	−.32	.08	1.67	−.73	.07
T_3	.091	.108	−.087	.112	.17	.32	−.71	.82	.96	−.78
Sum	.541	.337	.122	1						
					1967–68					
T_1	.221	.343	.192	.756	.40	1.04	1.63	.29	.45	.25
T_2	.233	−.109	.012	.136	.42	−.33	.10	1.72	−.80	.09
T_3	.096	.097	−.086	.108	.17	.29	−.73	.89	.90	−.80
Sum	.550	.332	.118	1						

TABLE 13.2 *(concluded)*

	Composition matrix B	Composition matrix P	Composition matrix C	Sum	R B	R P	R C	S B	S P	S C
					1968–69					
T_1	.231	.333	.194	.758	.41	1.03	1.65	.30	.44	.26
T_2	.214	−.108	.014	.120	.38	−.33	.12	1.79	−.90	.11
T_3	.113	.099	−.090	.122	.20	.31	−.77	.93	.81	−.74
Sum	.559	.324	.117	1						
					1969–70					
T_1	.238	.338	.190	.766	.42	1.05	1.64	.31	.44	.25
T_2	.211	−.108	.014	.117	.38	−.33	.13	1.80	−.92	.12
T_3	.112	.093	−.088	.117	.20	.29	−.76	.96	.79	−.76
Sum	.561	.323	.116	1						
					1970–71					
T_1	.252	.343	.184	.779	.44	1.07	1.63	.32	.44	.24
T_2	.200	−.107	.016	.109	.35	−.34	.14	1.84	−.99	.15
T_3	.115	.084	−.087	.112	.20	.26	−.77	1.02	.75	−.77
Sum	.567	.320	.113	1						
					1971–72					
T_1	.278	.344	.176	.798	.48	1.10	1.62	.35	.43	.22
T_2	.172	−.103	.019	.088	.30	−.33	.17	1.95	−1.16	.21
T_3	.129	.071	−.086	.113	.22	.23	−.79	1.14	.63	−.76
Sum	.579	.313	.109	1						

commodities which are specific substitutes, both are positively represented in the T-good with the smaller income elasticity; buying this T-good may be viewed as an inexpensive way of satisfying the similar needs associated with these two commodities. In the present case we have three commodities, rather than two, but the result for the T-good with the smallest income elasticity is the same. Beef, Pork and Chicken are described by (1.1) as specific substitutes; all three are positively represented in T_1, Inexpensive meat, which has the smallest income elasticity of the three transformed meats.

Changes in the Composition Matrix Over Time

The first four columns of Table 13.2 contain the bordered composition matrix for each pair of successive years from 1950 to 1972. Some elements of this matrix are relatively stable; others change more drastically. Given that $\tilde{\mathbf{M}}_g$ is treated as a constant matrix in (1.11), these changes (and those shown in Table 13.1 also) are of course due to the changes in $\bar{\mathbf{w}}_g$, the vector of the conditional budget shares of the three observed meats. As the row totals of the composition matrices in Table 13.2 show, the conditional budget share of Beef was subject to an increasing trend. The share of Pork declined from .421 to .313 and that of Chicken from .142 to .109, or about 25 percent for both meats.

The decline of the conditional budget share of Pork is reflected by the decrease of its contribution to Inexpensive meat (T_1) from about .4 in the early 1950s to less than .35 in the mid-1960s, after which it remained approximately constant. This decline is also reflected by the larger negative contribution of Pork to the Beef/Pork contrast (T_2), from about $-.08$ in the early 1950s to a figure between $-.10$ and $-.11$ in the late 1950s and thereafter. The decrease of Pork's contribution to Inexpensive meat was more than compensated by the increase of the contribution of Beef, from about .12 in the early 1950s to more than .20 in the 1960s and still more in the early 1970s. On the other hand, the contribution of Beef to the Beef/Pork contrast declined, from almost .3 in the first half of the 1950s to about .2 around 1970. This decline, combined with the increasing negative contribution of Pork, resulted in a large decrease of the share of this contrast, from about .21 in the first half of the 1950s to around .10 in the early 1970s.

The contribution of Chicken to Inexpensive meat was relatively stable around .2 during most of the period, and that to the Beef/Pork contrast was close to zero. Its negative contribution to Antichicken increased, from about −.07 in the first half of the 1950s to almost −.09 in the period after 1965. This increasing negative contribution was more than compensated by the increasing positive contribution of Beef to Antichicken, from less than .03 in the early 1950s to well over .10 around 1970. The contribution of Pork was not subject to a clear trend, and the result is a 100 percent increase of the conditional budget share of Antichicken, from .05 in 1950–51 to about .11 in the period after 1965.

The Composition Matrix Expressed in Pounds of Meats

The above contributions of the observed meats to their transformed counterparts are all in dollar terms. It is also interesting to consider these contributions in terms of pounds of the various meats involved. So we return to the composition matrix (1.12) of 1950–51, with a conditional budget share of Beef equal to 43.8 percent. Table 7.1 on page 9 shows that the per capita Beef consumption was 50.1 pounds in 1950 and 44.3 pounds in 1951. Since (1.12) refers to 1950–51, we take the average, 47.2 pounds, and consider this the volume counterpart of the share of 43.8 percent. We then distribute these 47.2 pounds over the three transformed meats proportionally to the first column of (1.12) and proceed likewise for Pork and Chicken, which gives the following composition matrix in pounds of meats:

(1.13)

12.9	63.5	31.2	107.6	(T_1)
31.8	−12.2	−.4	19.2	(T_2)
2.5	14.3	−9.6	7.2	(T_3)
47.2	65.6	21.2	134.0	
(Beef)	(Pork)	(Chicken)		

The figures in the fourth column are obtained by summation across rows. They show that the total consumption of the three meats is 134 pounds, about 80 percent of which is accounted for by Inexpensive meat. This percentage exceeds that of (1.12), which agrees with intuition (because a given dollar amount buys more pounds of Inexpensive meat than of expensive meats). However, note that the figures in the last column are in "pounds of meat," whereas those of the three earlier columns are in pounds of Beef or Pork or Chicken. Hence the row totals in (1.13) are primitive volume indexes.

With this qualification in mind, we present the pounds-of-meat composition matrices 10 and 20 years later:

1960–61				1970–71			
25.1	62.6	45.4	133.1	37.3	69.6	67.5	174.4
32.1	−18.2	2.0	15.9	29.5	−21.7	5.9	13.7
7.9	14.6	−18.3	4.2	17.0	17.0	−31.9	2.1
65.1	59.0	29.1	153.2	83.8	64.9	41.5	190.2

Notice the increase in the total number of pounds consumed as well as the increased dominance of Inexpensive meat, to over 90 percent in 1970–71. The consumption of both the Beef/Pork contrast and Antichicken are subject to a declining trend when measured in pounds of meat. In the case of Antichicken the consumption thus measured has virtually disappeared in the early 1970s, which is in sharp contrast to the behavior of the conditional budget share described at the end of the previous subsection. Spending money on Antichicken in the early 1970s amounts to buying certain pounds of Beef and Pork and giving up almost the same number of pounds of Chicken.

The Transformation Matrix R

The last six columns of Table 13.2 contain the transformation matrices **R** of the budget shares and **S** of the price log-changes for each pair of successive years. They are obtained from the composition matrix by dividing each element by the column sum and by the row sum, respectively.

The matrix **R** takes the following value in 1950–51:

$$(1.14) \qquad \begin{bmatrix} .27 & .97 & 1.48 \\ .67 & -.19 & -.02 \\ .05 & .22 & -.45 \end{bmatrix} \begin{matrix} (T_1) \\ (T_2) \\ (T_3) \end{matrix}$$

$$\text{(Beef)} \quad \text{(Pork)} \quad \text{(Chicken)}$$

The first column shows that a dollar spent on Beef implies 27 cents spent on Inexpensive meat, 67 cents spent on the Beef/Pork contrast, and 5 cents spent on Antichicken. The successive values of **R** given in Table 13.2 indicate that the dominant position of the Beef/Pork contrast gradually disappeared. Around 1970 more than 40 cents of a dollar spent on Beef went to Inexpensive meat, between 30 and 40 cents to the Beef/Pork contrast, and about 20 cents to Antichicken.

From the second column of (1.14) we infer that a dollar spent on Pork implies about a dollar spent on Inexpensive meat, 20 cents spent on Antichicken, and 20 cents worth of Pork which is given up in the consumption of the Beef/Pork contrast. Similarly, the third column shows that a dollar spent on Chicken implies about $1\frac{1}{2}$ dollars spent on Inexpensive meat and almost 50 cents worth of Chicken given up in the consumption of Antichicken. We learn from Table 13.2 that the latter two amounts increase gradually over time but that the composition of a dollar spent on Pork did not change very much.

The Transformation Matrix S

The rows of the matrix S describe the content of a dollar spent on each of the transformed meats. The S of 1950–51 is

$$\begin{bmatrix} .16 & .55 & .28 \\ 1.38 & -.37 & -.01 \\ .46 & 1.81 & -1.27 \end{bmatrix} \begin{matrix} (T_1) \\ (T_2) \\ (T_3) \end{matrix} \tag{1.15}$$
$$\begin{matrix} \text{(Beef)} & \text{(Pork)} & \text{(Chicken)} \end{matrix}$$

The first row shows that more than half of a dollar of Inexpensive meat consists of Pork. This meat remains the largest single ingredient of Inexpensive meat until the end of the period considered here, but its share declines to between 40 and 45 percent of a dollar of Inexpensive meat in the early 1970s. The Beef component increases substantially, from 16 cents per dollar of Inexpensive meat to more than 30 cents. The Chicken component fluctuates within much narrower limits.

The second row of (1.15) indicates that in 1950–51 a dollar spent on the Beef/Pork contrast consists of almost \$ 1.40 spent on Beef minus almost 40 cents worth of Pork. Both figures are subject to an increasing trend. In the early 1970s a dollar spent on the Beef/Pork contrast consists of roughly two dollars worth of Beef minus a dollar worth of Pork.

The third row of (1.15) shows that the 1950–51 composition of a dollar worth of Antichicken is 46 cents spent on Beef, about \$ 1.80 spent on Pork, and minus almost \$ 1.30 worth of Chicken. Hence Antichicken is mainly Pork as far as its two positive components are concerned. This changes drastically in the following years; in the early 1970s Antichicken is mainly Beef, the Pork component having declined from \$ 1.80 to around 70 cents. The negative Chicken component gradually declines from almost \$ 1.30 per dollar of Antichicken to about 75 cents in 1965–66, after which it remains virtually constant.

13.2 The Preference Independence Transformation for the 14-Commodity Model

The preferred specification of Section 6.7 is a system of 14 demand equations, with 11 in preference-independent form. The remaining three are the equations for Clothing ($i=10$), Footwear ($i=11$) and Other goods and services ($i=14$). The 3×3 price coefficient submatrix of these commodities, multiplied by 100 and with standard errors in parentheses, is given in eq. (6.4) of Section 6.6 and reproduced here:

$$(2.1)\qquad \begin{bmatrix} -8.74\,(1.17) & -.02\,(.20) & -6.39\;\;(.75) \\ & -.65\,(.22) & -.92\;\;(.18) \\ & & -8.52\,(1.69) \end{bmatrix} \begin{matrix} i=10 \\ i=11 \\ i=14 \end{matrix}$$

The degree of utility interaction within the three-commodity group, based on the point estimates shown in (2.1), is

$$(2.2)\qquad \upsilon_g = 1.192$$

which is more than 10 times as large as (1.10) for the three-meat group. This much higher degree of utility interaction will be our first concern.

The Mixed Estimates of the Preferred Specification Reconsidered

A major cause of the higher degree of utility interaction is the large absolute value of the $\nu_{10,14}$ estimate in (2.1), which is not far below the square root of the product of the corresponding diagonal figures (the estimates of $\nu_{10,10}$ and $\nu_{14,14}$). This means that Clothing and Other goods and services are described as strong specific complements. Although complementarity is not implausible, the question arises whether such a strong degree of complementarity can be considered realistic.

A second reason for doubt is provided by the prediction analysis of Section 6.9. We corrected the predictions by separating House rent from Other goods and services, and postulated that the demand equation for housing is of the preference-independent type. The 3×3 submatrix $[\nu_{ij}]$ thus becomes of order 4×4 and its form is shown below, where H refers to House rent and E to Other goods and services excluding house rent.

$$(2.3)\qquad \begin{bmatrix} \nu_{10,10} & \nu_{10,11} & \nu_{10,14} & 0 \\ \nu_{11,10} & \nu_{11,11} & \nu_{11,14} & 0 \\ \nu_{14,10} & \nu_{14,11} & \nu_{EE} & 0 \\ 0 & 0 & 0 & \nu_{HH} \end{bmatrix} \begin{matrix} \text{Clothing} \\ \text{Footwear} \\ E \\ H \end{matrix}\left.\begin{matrix} \\ \\ \\ \\ \end{matrix}\right\} \text{Other goods}$$

We have $\nu_{HH}=\phi\mu_H$ in view of the preference-independent form of the demand equation for housing. Equation (7.1) of Section 6.7 specifies $-.67$ as the mixed estimate of ϕ, and in the last subsection of Section 6.9 we used .08 for μ_H. The implied estimate of ν_{HH} is thus $-.0536$. When we identify $\nu_{14,14}$ with $\nu_{EE}+\nu_{HH}$ and use the relevant figure in (2.1) for $\nu_{14,14}$, we obtain an estimate of ν_{EE} equal to $-.0852+.0536=-.0316$. A comparison with the point estimates in (2.1) shows that the matrix (2.3) has a principal submatrix of order 2×2, consisting of the first and third rows and columns,

$$\begin{bmatrix} \nu_{10,10} & \nu_{10,14} \\ \nu_{14,10} & \nu_{EE} \end{bmatrix} = \frac{1}{100}\begin{bmatrix} -8.74 & -6.39 \\ -6.39 & -3.16 \end{bmatrix}$$

which is not even negative definite. Although the specification used for the demand equation for housing is not more than a guess, this unfavorable result suggests that it is appropriate to adjust the estimates of the preferred specification.

Revised Estimates of the Preferred Specification

Recall that we started in Chapter 6 by formulating prior judgments on the marginal shares, and that we subsequently allowed the sample to say what it has to say on these parameters. This led to the mixed estimates of the marginal shares, which we shall use in this chapter without any modification. The situation is different for the price coefficients, since no prior judgments were formulated on these.

We shall use the following revised value of the income flexibility:

$$\phi = -.6 \tag{2.4}$$

Given that the original estimate is $-.67$ and the marginal share estimates are unchanged, this implies that the estimates of $\nu_{ii}=\phi\mu_i$ are changed in the same proportion (about 10 percent) for all 11 commodities with a preference-independent demand equation.

The revision of the price coefficients of the three-commodity group shown in (2.1) is confined to the last row and column. Hence the leading 2×2 submatrix of (2.1) remains unchanged. With $\phi=-.6$ and the mixed estimates of the marginal shares, we have implied values of $\phi\mu_i$ equal to $-.1358$ (Clothing), $-.0143$ (Footwear) and $-.1418$ (Other goods and services). These three figures are the successive row and column sums of the revised estimate of the price coefficient submatrix of the three-commodity group. This matrix, multiplied by 100, is

$$\begin{bmatrix} -8.74 & -.02 & -4.82 \\ & -.65 & -.76 \\ & & -8.60 \end{bmatrix} \begin{matrix} \text{Clothing} \\ \text{Footwear} \\ \text{Other goods} \end{matrix} \tag{2.5}$$

A comparison with (2.1) shows that the revision of the last column is minor for $\nu_{14,14}$, about equal to the standard error for $\nu_{11,14}$, and about two standard errors for $\nu_{10,14}$. Given our appraisal of standard errors of price coefficients in Chapter 6, these revisions can be regarded as modest.

The revision of $\nu_{10,14}$ in zero direction has the effect of reducing the specific complementarity of Clothing and Other goods and services. When House rent is introduced as a separate commodity along the lines of (2.3), the estimate (2.5) combined with $\phi=-.6$ and $\mu_H=.08$ yields a negative definite price coefficient matrix of order 4×4. The average information inaccuracy associated with the revised point estimates is within 1 percent of that associated with the original mixed estimates.

The within-group utility interaction computed from (2.5) is

$$\upsilon_g = .527 \tag{2.6}$$

which is more than 50 percent below the value (2.2). This decline results from the fact that the revision is designed to reduce the specific complementarity of Clothing and Other goods and services. However, note that the interaction value (2.6) is still considerably larger than (1.10).

The Unconditional Design of the Preference Independence Transformation

We write S_g for the three-commodity group which consists of Clothing, Footwear and Other goods and services. The demand equation for $i \in S_g$ is

$$\bar{w}_{it} Dq_{it} = \mu_i DQ_t + \phi \sum_{j \in S_g} \mu_{ij} (Dp_{jt} - DP'_t) + \varepsilon_{it} \tag{2.7}$$

where $[\mu_{ij}]=\mathbf{M}_g$ is a 3×3 matrix equal to (2.5) after normalization. This normalization amounts to multiplication by $1/100\phi$, where ϕ is given in (2.4).

We apply eq. (1.29) of Section 12.1,

$$\mathbf{X}'_g (\mathbf{w}_g)_\Delta \mathbf{X}_g = \mathbf{I} \qquad \mathbf{X}'_g \mathbf{M}_g \mathbf{X}_g = \mathbf{\Lambda}_g \tag{2.8}$$

where all matrices are of order 3×3. To implement the transformation we diagonalize the matrix

$$(\mathbf{w}_g)_\Delta^{-1/2} \mathbf{M}_g (\mathbf{w}_g)_\Delta^{-1/2} \tag{2.9}$$

which is the unconditional version of the matrix (1.11). The further developments are all immediate extensions of results described in Section 12.2. In particular, if $\boldsymbol{\iota}$ is a column vector consisting of three unit elements, then $\mathbf{X}_g^{-1}\boldsymbol{\iota}$ consists of square roots of budget shares of T-goods. The sum of these shares is equal to the budget share of the group,

$$(2.10) \qquad (\mathbf{X}_g^{-1}\boldsymbol{\iota})'\,\mathbf{X}_g^{-1}\boldsymbol{\iota} = \boldsymbol{\iota}'(\mathbf{X}_g')^{-1}\,\mathbf{X}_g^{-1}\boldsymbol{\iota} = \boldsymbol{\iota}'(\mathbf{w}_g)_\Delta\,\boldsymbol{\iota} = \sum_{i \in S_g} \bar{w}_{it} = \bar{W}_{gt}$$

which should be compared with eq. (2.26) of Section 12.2. An implication of (2.10) is that the elements of the 3×3 composition matrix do not add up to 1, as they do in Table 13.2, but to the three-commodity budget share $\bar{W}_{gt}$ which changes over time.

Similarly, the marginal shares of the three T-goods are the diagonal elements of the matrix

$$(2.11) \qquad (\boldsymbol{\mu}_{gT})_\Delta = (\mathbf{X}_g^{-1}\boldsymbol{\iota})_\Delta\,\boldsymbol{\Lambda}_g\,(\mathbf{X}_g^{-1}\boldsymbol{\iota})_\Delta$$

and the sum of these shares equals the marginal share of the group:

$$(2.12) \qquad \boldsymbol{\iota}'(\mathbf{X}_g')^{-1}\boldsymbol{\Lambda}_g\mathbf{X}_g^{-1}\boldsymbol{\iota} = \boldsymbol{\iota}'\mathbf{M}_g\boldsymbol{\iota} = \sum_{i \in S_g}\sum_{j \in S_g} \mu_{ij} = M_g$$

The last two equations should be compared with eqs. (2.29) and (2.31) of Section 12.2. The value of the marginal share of the three-commodity group according to the mixed estimates of the preferred specification of Section 6.7 is .4865.

The Shares and Income Elasticities of the T-Goods

Table 13.3 is similar to Table 13.1. The income elasticities are well separated. For all observations, both between the Wars and after World War II, the elasticity of T_2 (the second T-good) is quite small and fluctuates between narrow limits, .20 and .23. The income elasticity of T_1 varies between 1.30 and 1.45 prior to World War II and between 1.17 and 1.31 thereafter. The third T-good has an income elasticity which is subject to larger variations. In particular, the values after World War II are noticeably smaller than the earlier values.

The T-goods are ranked according to decreasing budget shares, with T_1 accounting for as much as 30 to 40 percent of the budget. But in contrast to T_1 of the meats, this dominant T-good is a luxury. The result is that its marginal share, which is the product of the budget share and the income elasticity, accounts for more than 90 percent of the marginal share of the three-commodity group.

TABLE 13.3

INCOME ELASTICITIES AND BUDGET AND MARGINAL SHARES OF THREE T-GOODS OF THE 14-COMMODITY MODEL

	λ_1	λ_2	λ_3	$(\bar{w}_{1t})_T$	$(\bar{w}_{2t})_T$	$(\bar{w}_{3t})_T$	μ_{1T}	μ_{2T}	μ_{3T}
				Between Wars					
1922–23	1.30	.23	.92	.359	.087	.001	.466	.020	.001
1923–24	1.34	.23	.97	.345	.097	.001	.464	.022	.001
1924–25	1.33	.23	.93	.347	.097	.003	.462	.022	.003
1925–26	1.34	.22	.90	.344	.101	.006	.459	.023	.005
1926–27	1.32	.22	.88	.346	.098	.007	.459	.022	.006
1927–28	1.32	.22	.87	.347	.099	.008	.458	.022	.007
1928–29	1.32	.22	.85	.346	.101	.010	.455	.022	.009
1929–30	1.30	.21	.85	.350	.107	.010	.455	.023	.008
1930–31	1.31	.21	.89	.345	.123	.008	.453	.026	.007
1931–32	1.36	.21	.98	.332	.146	.005	.452	.030	.005
1932–33	1.38	.20	1.03	.325	.160	.004	.450	.032	.004
1933–34	1.41	.20	1.05	.317	.170	.005	.448	.034	.005
1934–35	1.45	.20	1.08	.307	.178	.005	.445	.036	.006
1935–36	1.44	.20	1.08	.309	.177	.005	.446	.035	.006
1936–37	1.42	.20	1.06	.315	.166	.005	.448	.034	.005
1937–38	1.43	.21	1.06	.314	.161	.004	.449	.033	.005
1938–39	1.39	.21	.98	.321	.149	.008	.448	.031	.008
				After World War II					
1951–52	1.17	.22	.63	.397	.046	.016	.466	.010	.010
1952–53	1.25	.22	.67	.369	.059	.020	.460	.013	.013
1953–54	1.25	.22	.68	.368	.060	.019	.460	.014	.013
1954–55	1.23	.22	.68	.374	.061	.017	.461	.014	.012
1955–56	1.21	.22	.67	.382	.058	.016	.463	.013	.011
1956–57	1.23	.22	.68	.374	.061	.018	.461	.013	.012
1957–58	1.29	.22	.70	.352	.076	.024	.453	.017	.016
1958–59	1.32	.22	.69	.339	.085	.030	.448	.018	.020
1959–60	1.31	.21	.66	.340	.085	.034	.446	.018	.022
1960–61	1.29	.21	.65	.345	.081	.035	.447	.017	.022
1961–62	1.30	.22	.66	.344	.080	.032	.448	.017	.021
1962–63	1.31	.22	.66	.341	.077	.033	.448	.017	.022

The second T-good had budget shares around .1 in the 1920s, which increased until almost .2 during the depression of the 1930s. Much smaller values are found in the 1950s, after which there was an increase so that around 1960 the level of the early 1920s was almost reached. These figures, in conjunction with the low income elasticity of T_2, imply marginal share values fluctuating between .01 and less than .04.

The third T-good had quite small budget shares in the early 1920s, increasing to .01 around 1930 and then decreasing again. After World War

TABLE 13.4

COMPOSITION MATRICES AND THE TRANSFORMATION MATRICES **R** AND **S** OF THE 14-COMMODITY MODEL, 1922–1939

	Composition matrix			Sum	R			S		
	C	F	O		C	F	O	C	F	O
					1922–23					
T_1	.185	.018	.156	.359	1.36	1.47	.52	.52	.05	.43
T_2	−.045	−.009	.140	.087	−.33	−.72	.47	−.51	−.10	1.61
T_3	−.004	.003	.002	.001	−.03	.26	.01	−4.39	3.33	2.06
Sum	.136	.012	.298	.447						
					1923–24					
T_1	.179	.017	.149	.345	1.37	1.51	.50	.52	.05	.43
T_2	−.045	−.009	.150	.097	−.34	−.75	.50	−.46	−.09	1.55
T_3	−.004	.003	.002	.001	−.03	.25	.01	−4.58	3.48	2.10
Sum	.130	.011	.301	.443						
					1924–25					
T_1	.182	.016	.149	.347	1.39	1.31	.49	.52	.05	.43
T_2	−.045	−.009	.151	.097	−.34	−.76	.50	−.46	−.09	1.55
T_3	−.006	.005	.004	.003	−.05	.45	.01	−2.31	1.94	1.37
Sum	.131	.012	.304	.447						
					1925–26					
T_1	.183	.014	.147	.344	1.41	1.14	.48	.53	.04	.43
T_2	−.045	−.010	.155	.101	−.34	−.78	.50	−.44	−.10	1.54
T_3	−.009	.008	.006	.006	−.07	.64	.02	−1.48	1.37	1.11
Sum	.130	.012	.308	.450						

						1926–27					
T_1	.184	.014	.148	.346		1.41	1.08	.48	.53	.04	.43
T_2	−.044	−.010	.152	.098		−.34	−.77	.49	−.45	−.10	1.55
T_3	−.009	.009	.007	.007		−.07	.69	.02	−1.35	1.28	1.07
Sum	.131	.013	.307	.451							
						1927–28					
T_1	.186	.013	.148	.347		1.41	1.04	.48	.53	.04	.43
T_2	−.044	−.010	.153	.099		−.34	−.77	.49	−.45	−.10	1.55
T_3	−.010	.010	.008	.008		−.07	.74	.03	−1.23	1.20	1.03
Sum	.131	.013	.310	.454							
						1928–29					
T_1	.186	.013	.147	.346		1.42	.95	.47	.54	.04	.42
T_2	−.045	−.010	.156	.101		−.34	−.78	.50	−.44	−.10	1.54
T_3	−.011	.011	.010	.010		−.08	.83	.03	−1.03	1.06	.97
Sum	.131	.013	.313	.458							
						1929–30					
T_1	.188	.013	.149	.350		1.42	.99	.46	.54	.04	.42
T_2	−.046	−.010	.163	.107		−.35	−.79	.51	−.43	−.10	1.53
T_3	−.010	.011	.009	.010		−.08	.80	.03	−1.09	1.10	.98
Sum	.132	.013	.321	.467							
						1930–31					
T_1	.186	.013	.145	.345		1.44	1.06	.43	.54	.04	.42
T_2	−.047	−.010	.181	.123		−.36	−.82	.54	−.38	−.08	1.47
T_3	−.010	.010	.008	.008		−.07	.76	.02	−1.16	1.17	.99
Sum	.129	.013	.334	.476							

TABLE 13.4 *(concluded)*

	Composition matrix			Sum	R			S		
	C	F	O		C	F	O	C	F	O
					1931–32					
T_1	.179	.014	.139	.332	1.45	1.23	.40	.54	.04	.42
T_2	−.048	−.010	.204	.146	−.39	−.86	.59	−.33	−.07	1.39
T_3	−.008	.007	.005	.005	−.06	.63	.02	−1.50	1.42	1.08
Sum	.124	.011	.349	.484						
					1932–33					
T_1	.175	.014	.136	.325	1.46	1.31	.38	.54	.04	.42
T_2	−.048	−.009	.217	.160	−.40	−.87	.61	−.30	−.06	1.36
T_3	−.007	.006	.004	.004	−.05	.57	.01	−1.72	1.58	1.14
Sum	.121	.011	.358	.489						
					1933–34					
T_1	.172	.013	.131	.317	1.47	1.27	.36	.54	.04	.41
T_2	−.048	−.009	.227	.170	−.41	−.89	.62	−.28	−.06	1.34
T_3	−.007	.007	.005	.005	−.06	.62	.01	−1.51	1.44	1.07
Sum	.117	.010	.363	.491						
					1934–35					
T_1	.168	.012	.127	.307	1.48	1.21	.35	.55	.04	.41
T_2	−.047	−.009	.235	.178	−.42	−.91	.64	−.26	−.05	1.32
T_3	−.007	.007	.005	.005	−.06	.69	.01	−1.31	1.30	1.00
Sum	.114	.010	.367	.491						

					1935–36					
T_1	.169	.013	.128	.309	1.48	1.22	.35	.55	.04	.41
T_2	−.047	−.009	.233	.177	−.41	−.90	.64	−.27	−.05	1.32
T_3	−.007	.007	.005	.005	−.06	.68	.01	−1.33	1.32	1.01
Sum	.114	.010	.366	.491						
					1936–37					
T_1	.171	.013	.131	.315	1.47	1.27	.36	.54	.04	.42
T_2	−.047	−.009	.223	.166	−.41	−.89	.62	−.29	−.06	1.34
T_3	−.007	.007	.005	.005	−.06	.62	.01	−1.51	1.44	1.07
Sum	.117	.010	.359	.486						
					1937–38					
T_1	.170	.013	.131	.314	1.46	1.26	.37	.54	.04	.42
T_2	−.047	−.009	.217	.161	−.40	−.88	.62	−.29	−.06	1.35
T_3	−.007	.006	.005	.004	−.06	.62	.01	−1.52	1.44	1.07
Sum	.116	.010	.352	.479						
					1938–39					
T_1	.175	.012	.134	.321	1.46	1.08	.39	.55	.04	.42
T_2	−.047	−.010	.206	.149	−.39	−.87	.59	−.31	−.07	1.38
T_3	−.009	.009	.008	.008	−.07	.79	.02	−1.09	1.14	.95
Sum	.120	.011	.347	.479						

II the values are somewhat larger. The marginal shares of T_2 and T_3 during the years after the War are of the same order of magnitude.

Two Average Composition Matrices

To facilitate the discussion of the composition matrix, we start with the arithmetic average composition matrices of the pre- and postwar observations. These are obtained by summing the 17 prewar composition matrices and multiplying the sum by $\frac{1}{17}$, and proceeding similarly for the 12 postwar matrices. The average prewar composition matrix is

(2.13)

.179	.014	.141	.333	(T_1)
−.046	−.010	.186	.130	(T_2)
−.008	.007	.006	.006	(T_3)
.125	.012	.333	.469	
(Clothing)	(Footwear)	(Other)		

Here "Other" is an abbreviation of Other goods and services. The array shows that, on average, about 47 percent of the budget is spent on the three-commodity group, about 70 percent of which is accounted for by Other goods and services. Notice that T_1 occupies an equally dominant position among the T-goods.

The average postwar composition matrix is

(2.14)

.195	.011	.155	.360	(T_1)
−.039	−.013	.120	.069	(T_2)
−.016	.019	.022	.024	(T_3)
.139	.017	.297	.454	
(Clothing)	(Footwear)	(Other)		

The combined budget share of the three-commodity group is slightly below the figure in (2.13), and the shares of Clothing and Footwear have increased at the expense of that of Other goods and services, so that the dominant position of the latter has declined. On the other hand, the domination of T_1 is even more pronounced than it is in (2.13), which takes place at the expense of T_2. A comparison of the rows of T_2 in (2.13) and (2.14) shows that the decline of T_2 is primarily the result of the reduced contribution of Other goods and services to this T-good.

The first four columns of Table 13.4 contain the individual bordered composition matrix for each of the 17 prewar observations for which (2.13) is the arithmetic average; the letters C, F and O in the heading of the table stand for Clothing, Footwear and Other goods and services. Table 13.5

TABLE 13.5

COMPOSITION MATRICES AND THE TRANSFORMATION MATRICES **R** AND **S** OF THE 14-COMMODITY MODEL, 1951–1963

	Composition matrix			Sum	R			S		
	C	F	O		C	F	O	C	F	O
					1951–52					
T_1	.208	.014	.175	.397	1.34	.76	.61	.52	.04	.44
T_2	−.036	−.011	.093	.046	−.23	−.60	.33	−.80	−.24	2.04
T_3	−.016	.016	.017	.016	−.11	.84	.06	−1.04	.98	1.06
Sum	.155	.018	.285	.459						
					1952–53					
T_1	.197	.012	.160	.369	1.38	.69	.55	.53	.03	.43
T_2	−.038	−.012	.109	.059	−.27	−.68	.38	−.64	−.20	1.84
T_3	−.016	.017	.019	.020	−.11	.98	.07	−.82	.86	.96
Sum	.143	.017	.288	.448						
					1953–54					
T_1	.196	.012	.159	.368	1.38	.71	.55	.53	.03	.43
T_2	−.038	−.012	.110	.060	−.27	−.68	.38	−.63	−.19	1.83
T_3	−.016	.016	.018	.019	−.11	.97	.06	−.84	.87	.96
Sum	.142	.017	.288	.447						
					1954–55					
T_1	.199	.013	.162	.374	1.38	.74	.56	.53	.03	.43
T_2	−.039	−.011	.111	.061	−.27	−.68	.38	−.64	−.19	1.83
T_3	−.015	.016	.017	.017	−.11	.93	.06	−.89	.91	.98
Sum	.145	.017	.290	.452						

TABLE 13.5 *(concluded)*

	Composition matrix C	F	O	Sum	R C	F	O	S C	F	O
					1955–56					
T_1	.202	.013	.166	.382	1.37	.76	.57	.53	.03	.44
T_2	−.039	−.011	.108	.058	−.26	−.66	.37	−.67	−.20	1.87
T_3	−.015	.015	.016	.016	−.10	.89	.06	−.95	.95	1.00
Sum	.148	.017	.290	.456						
					1956–57					
T_1	.199	.013	.162	.374	1.38	.74	.56	.53	.03	.43
T_2	−.039	−.011	.111	.061	−.27	−.67	.38	−.64	−.19	1.83
T_3	−.016	.016	.017	.018	−.11	.93	.06	−.89	.91	.98
Sum	.145	.017	.290	.452						
					1957–58					
T_1	.191	.011	.150	.352	1.41	.64	.50	.54	.03	.43
T_2	−.040	−.012	.128	.076	−.29	−.74	.43	−.53	−.16	1.69
T_3	−.016	.018	.021	.024	−.12	1.10	.07	−.67	.78	.89
Sum	.135	.017	.299	.451						
					1958–59					
T_1	.186	.009	.143	.339	1.43	.55	.47	.55	.03	.42
T_2	−.040	−.013	.138	.085	−.31	−.78	.45	−.47	−.16	1.63
T_3	−.016	.021	.025	.030	−.13	1.23	.08	−.55	.70	.85
Sum	.130	.017	.306	.453						

					1959–60				
T_1	.188	.009	.143	.340	1.43	.51	.46	.55	.03	.42
T_2	−.040	−.014	.138	.085	−.30	−.79	.45	−.47	−.17	1.63
T_3	−.017	.023	.029	.034	−.13	1.28	.09	−.51	.67	.84
Sum	.131	.018	.310	.459						
					1960–61					
T_1	.190	.009	.146	.345	1.43	.51	.47	.55	.03	.42
T_2	−.039	−.014	.135	.081	−.30	−.78	.43	−.48	−.17	1.66
T_3	−.018	.023	.029	.035	−.13	1.27	.09	−.52	.67	.85
Sum	.133	.018	.310	.461						
					1961–62					
T_1	.189	.009	.146	.344	1.43	.53	.48	.55	.03	.42
T_2	−.039	−.014	.132	.080	−.30	−.77	.43	−.49	−.17	1.66
T_3	−.017	.022	.028	.032	−.13	1.25	.09	−.54	.68	.85
Sum	.133	.018	.306	.456						
					1962–63					
T_1	.187	.009	.144	.341	1.43	.52	.48	.55	.03	.42
T_2	−.038	−.014	.129	.077	−.29	−.77	.43	−.50	−.18	1.68
T_3	−.018	.022	.028	.033	−.13	1.25	.09	−.53	.68	.85
Sum	.131	.018	.302	.451						

provides the same information for the 12 postwar observations. In the subsection immediately following the next, we shall use these matrices to draw some tentative conclusions on the nature of the T-goods.

The Effect of the Revision

If we had not revised the mixed estimates shown in (2.1), the income elasticities of the three T-goods would have taken smaller values.[1] The proportionate effect is minor for T_1 and T_3, but the impact on T_2 is more substantial; its income elasticity based on (2.1) is virtually stable around .09, which amounts to a reduction of the λ_2 values of Table 13.3 by more than 50 percent. This result should come as no surprise, because λ_2 is the smallest latent root of the matrix (2.9) and this matrix is closer to singularity under (2.1) than under (2.5). Note that the figure .09 is also smaller than all income elasticity estimates shown in Table 6.14 on page 304 of Volume 1.

The estimate (2.1) yields the following prewar average of the composition matrices:

(2.15)

.179	.015	.166	.360	(T_1)
−.048	−.009	.163	.106	(T_2)
−.006	.005	.003	.003	(T_3)
.125	.012	.333	.469	
(Clothing)	(Footwear)	(Other)		

A comparison with (2.13) shows that the largest differences are in the column of Other goods and services. It seems reasonable to attribute this to the fact that the revision of (2.1) is confined to the column and row which correspond to this commodity. The postwar average composition matrix, shown below, also has a third column whose differences from the corresponding column of (2.14) exceed those of the first and second columns.

(2.16)

.193	.013	.177	.382	(T_1)
−.040	−.010	.106	.056	(T_2)
−.014	.015	.014	.015	(T_3)
.139	.017	.297	.454	
(Clothing)	(Footwear)	(Other)		

[1] It might come as a surprise that the income elasticities of all three T-goods decline, since their budget-share-weighted average must be equal to the income elasticity of the three-commodity group, $M_g/\bar{W}_{gt}$, which takes the same value no matter whether we use (2.1) or (2.5). The point is that the weights of the two averages are not the same. As the pre- and postwar average composition matrices (2.13) to (2.16) show, the budget share of T_1 (which has the highest income elasticity) is larger under (2.1) than under the revised values shown in (2.5), and the budget share of T_2 (with the lowest income elasticity) is smaller under (2.1) than under (2.5).

The first T-good is more dominant in terms of budget shares in (2.15) and (2.16) than in (2.13) and (2.14), respectively. This increased dominance is even more pronounced at the marginal level. In each of the 29 pre- and postwar years, the marginal share of T_1, based on (2.1), accounts for 96 percent or more of the marginal share of the three-commodity group. From now on we shall confine ourselves to the revised estimate (2.5).

A Tentative Interpretation of the T-Goods

It should be stressed at the outset that the interpretation of the present T-goods is much more tentative than that of the transformed meats of Section 13.1. This is unavoidable, since the commodities considered here – particularly Other goods and services with its large budget share – are less narrowly defined than Beef, Pork and Chicken. The arguments which follow below are presented in a series of four remarks and tentative conclusions.

(1) The price coefficient submatrix (2.5) describes the three commodities as specific complements. At the end of Section 12.4 we proved that, for two commodities which are specific complements, both are positively represented in the T-good with the larger income elasticity. This agrees with our findings, because T_1 has the largest income elasticity (see Table 13.3) and all three commodities are positively represented in T_1 for all 29 observations (see Tables 13.4 and 13.5).

(2) The second T-good has a very small income elasticity ($\lambda_2 \approx .2$), so that its basic want is a bare necessity. Clothing and Footwear are both negatively represented; hence buying T_2 implies that the consumer gives up new purchases of Clothing and Footwear. Such purchases can be postponed when the housewife makes and mends the family's clothes and when shoes are repaired frequently instead of replaced by new shoes. Repair services fall under Other goods and services, which are positively represented in T_2. [Repairs were cheap by present-day American standards because of the modest Dutch wage level during most of the period 1922–1963.] Also, Clothing is actually "clothing and other textiles," which includes linens, carpets and curtains, for which new purchases can be postponed and replaced by repairs. The resulting picture of T_2 is that of a transformed good whose function is primarily to keep the household going at a low level of real income, consisting of certain components of Other goods and services such as repair services and partly compensated by negative Clothing and Footwear purchases. Other possible components of Other goods and services represented in T_2 include travel to work and school, parts of medical care

and insurance, minimum contributions to the church and also, as will be argued in the next subsection, part of house rent.

(3) At the other extreme is T_1, the only T-good in which all three commodities are positively represented. Its rather high income elasticity and its substantial marginal share (around .45) may perhaps be viewed as indications that this T-good corresponds to middle-class desires, which involve not only the appearance of the family (Clothing and Footwear) but also expenditures on personal care, housing above minimum standards, the appearance of the house (household textiles), education of children, travel for pleasure, and so on.

(4) The third T-good, with an income elasticity consistently between those of T_1 and T_2, is a contrast between Footwear and Other goods and services on one hand, and Clothing on the other. Tables 13.4 and 13.5 show that T_3 involves about equal absolute amounts of these three commodities in most of the years, but that their levels changed considerably over time, from less than one-half of 1 percent of the budget in the early 1920s to about 2 percent in the early 1960s. A possible interpretation is that T_3 reflects the family's desire to appear in a decent but not expensive manner. This would imply the purchase of shoes but a substitution of the seamstress' services for the purchase of fancy clothes and household textiles. The decline of λ_3 from around 1 before World War II to slightly less than .7 after the War indicates that T_3 changed from a "normal" good to a necessity.

House Rent Further Considered

We concluded from the average composition matrices (2.13) and (2.14) that the decline of the budget share of T_2 is primarily the result of the reduced contribution of Other goods and services to T_2. An inspection of Tables 13.4 and 13.5 shows that this element of the composition matrix increased slowly from .14 to .16 in the 1920s and then more rapidly to around .23 in the mid-1930s, after which there was a modest decline. In the first half of the 1950s we find much smaller values (about .10), followed by a slight increase. Indeed, for this particular element of the composition matrix, the difference between the largest and the smallest value is as much as 14 percent of the budget (.235 in 1934–35 minus .093 in 1951–52). This is by far the largest difference; the next largest is below 5 percent (the contribution of Other goods and services to T_1, .175 in 1951–52 minus .127 in 1934–35).

It seems plausible that these substantial changes are intimately related to the housing sector. In the prewar period the relative price of housing increased steadily until the mid-1930s and then declined slightly.[1] This was a major cause of the following development of the budget share of house rent: an increase from .06 in 1922 to .09 in 1930 to .12 in 1935 and then back to .11 at the end of the prewar period. During and after World War II there was rent control, which reduced the budget share of house rent to .05 in 1951, after which it gradually increased to .07 in 1963. This development is roughly parallel to that of the contribution of Other goods and services to T_2 from the early 1920s to the early 1960s as described in the previous paragraph. Since house rent falls under Other goods and services, it is therefore plausible that at least part of house rent belongs to the contribution of Other goods and services to T_2.

The Transformation Matrix R

The **R** matrix of the first observation (1922–23) is

$$\begin{bmatrix} 1.36 & 1.47 & .52 \\ -.33 & -.72 & .47 \\ -.03 & .26 & .01 \end{bmatrix} \begin{matrix} (T_1) \\ (T_2) \\ (T_3) \end{matrix} \tag{2.17}$$
$$\text{(Clothing)} \quad \text{(Footwear)} \quad \text{(Other)}$$

The first column indicates that a guilder spent on Clothing implies an almost 40 percent larger amount spent on T_1, compensated by negative purchases of the two other T-goods, among which T_2 is by far the most important. Tables 13.4 and 13.5 show that this allocation does not change very much over time, except that T_3 has a larger negative figure in the postwar period.

The second column of (2.17) shows that a guilder spent on Footwear implies almost $1\frac{1}{2}$ guilders spent on T_1, one-quarter of a guilder spent on T_3, and a negative amount spent on T_2. This negative amount remains fairly constant, but the T_3 component increases more than threefold by the end of the 1920s, after which it is at a lower level during the 1930s; in the 1950s it takes larger and increasing values and it is well over a guilder in the 1960s. The T_1 component of Footwear, which is almost six times as large as the T_3 component in 1922–23, remains larger throughout the prewar period, but the difference is less than it was in 1922–23. After World War II the positions of these two components are interchanged, with that of T_3 exceeding T_1.

The third column of (2.17) indicates that a guilder spent on Other goods

[1] See THEIL (1967, Section 5.B) for the statistical data underlying the discussion of this paragraph.

and services is distributed about equally over T_1 and T_2, and that very little is allocated to T_3. This pattern remains in effect during the 1920s. In the decade of the 1930s a larger fraction is allocated to T_2. This changes in the postwar period, when the T_1 component is larger, but the difference between the T_1 and the T_2 components is small around 1960. Notice also that the T_3 component is more prominent in the postwar years than before.

***The Transformation Matrix* S**

The **S** matrix of 1922–23 takes the following value:

$$(2.18) \qquad \begin{bmatrix} .52 & .05 & .43 \\ -.51 & -.10 & 1.61 \\ -4.39 & 3.33 & 2.06 \end{bmatrix} \begin{matrix} (T_1) \\ (T_2) \\ (T_3) \end{matrix}$$
$$\text{(Clothing)} \quad \text{(Footwear)} \quad \text{(Other)}$$

The first row shows that a guilder spent on T_1 consists of about one-half guilder spent on Clothing, slightly less for Other goods and services, and a small amount for Footwear. The subsequent **S** matrices of Tables 13.4 and 13.5 indicate that this pattern was virtually unchanged throughout the period considered here. The second row of (2.18) tells us that a guilder spent on T_2 consists of over $1\frac{1}{2}$ guilders spent on Other goods and services, compensated by a negative one-half guilder worth of Clothing and a smaller negative amount for Footwear. These three amounts are all somewhat smaller in the 1930s, but they are larger in most of the postwar years. In the early 1960s the composition of T_2 is again close to that shown in (2.18) for 1922–23.

The third row of **S** tells a different story. Its elements in (2.18) are quite large and they are even larger in the next year (1923–24), after which they decline sharply. This indicates that the **S** transformation is unstable in the early 1920s. The cause is the very small budget share of T_3 in that period (about one-tenth of 1 percent). This budget share is the third row sum of the composition matrix. So, when we divide the elements of the third row of this matrix by such a small number in order to obtain the third row of **S**, it stands to reason that the latter row is subject to substantial changes over time.

By the end of the 1920s a guilder spent on T_3 consists of about one guilder each spent on Footwear and Other goods and services, compensated by a negative one-guilder contribution of Clothing. In the 1930s the amounts of Clothing and Footwear increase, but both in the last prewar year and in the first postwar year (1938–39 and 1951–52) the composition of a guilder spent on T_3 is rather close to that of the late 1920s. During the later postwar years the three amounts involved are less than a guilder per guilder spent on T_3. On the whole, the composition of T_3 tends to be less stable than that of T_1 and T_2, particularly in the prewar period.

13.3 The Income Elasticities of the Transformed Goods

Since the income elasticities of the T-goods play such a fundamental role in the preference independence transformation, it is appropriate to consider the decomposition of these elasticities given in eq. (3.18) of Section 12.3. In scalar form this equation is

$$\lambda_i = \sum_{j=1}^{n} s_{ij} \frac{\mu_j}{\bar{w}_{jt}} \qquad i = 1, \ldots, n \tag{3.1}$$

which shows that $s_{ij}\mu_j/\bar{w}_{jt}$ may be viewed as the contribution of the jth commodity to the income elasticity of the ith T-good. These contributions are the subject of this section.

The Income Elasticities of the T-Goods of the 14-Commodity Model

For the three T-goods of the 14-commodity model we compute the contributions to their income elasticities by applying (3.1), with the j subscript interpreted as Clothing, Footwear and Other goods and services ($n=3$). The results are given in Table 13.6, which is based on the **S** matrices of Tables 13.4 and 13.5. The first three columns of Table 13.6, which deal with the income elasticity of T_1, show that the contributions of the three observed commodities are relatively stable. That of Clothing varies between .8 and 1.1 except in the first postwar year, and that of Footwear between .07 and .10 in the prewar period and around .05 or a little less in the postwar years. The contribution of Other goods and services varies between .27 and .37.

The contributions to the income elasticity of T_2, shown in the middle three columns, are not so stable. They decline from the early 1920s until the mid-1930s. After World War II they take larger values and then decline again. Notice that the 1962–63 composition of this income elasticity is close to that of 1922–23.

The composition of the income elasticity of T_3 (last three columns of Table 13.6) is quite unstable, particularly in the early 1920s. This is the obvious consequence of the instability of the **S** transformation for this T-good. Recall that we concluded from Table 13.3 that the income elasticity

TABLE 13.6

DECOMPOSITION OF THE INCOME ELASTICITIES OF THE T-GOODS OF THE 14-COMMODITY MODEL

	T_1			T_2			T_3		
	Clothing	Footwear	Other goods	Clothing	Footwear	Other goods	Clothing	Footwear	Other goods
				Between Wars					
1922–23	.86	.10	.34	−.85	−.20	1.28	−7.29	6.58	1.63
1923–24	.90	.10	.34	−.80	−.19	1.22	−7.95	7.27	1.65
1924–25	.91	.09	.33	−.80	−.19	1.21	−4.00	3.87	1.07
1925–26	.93	.08	.33	−.77	−.18	1.18	−2.58	2.64	.85
1926–27	.92	.07	.33	−.78	−.19	1.19	−2.34	2.39	.82
1927–28	.92	.07	.33	−.78	−.19	1.19	−2.11	2.19	.79
1928–29	.93	.07	.32	−.76	−.18	1.16	−1.78	1.90	.73
1929–30	.92	.07	.31	−.73	−.18	1.12	−1.86	1.99	.72
1930–31	.94	.07	.30	−.67	−.16	1.04	−2.02	2.21	.70
1931–32	.99	.09	.28	−.60	−.14	.94	−2.74	2.99	.73
1932–33	1.01	.10	.28	−.57	−.13	.90	−3.22	3.50	.75
1933–34	1.05	.10	.27	−.54	−.13	.87	−2.91	3.27	.69
1934–35	1.09	.09	.27	−.53	−.12	.85	−2.60	3.03	.64
1935–36	1.08	.09	.27	−.53	−.12	.85	−2.63	3.06	.65
1936–37	1.05	.10	.27	−.55	−.13	.88	−2.93	3.29	.70
1937–38	1.05	.10	.28	−.57	−.13	.90	−2.95	3.29	.72
1938–39	1.03	.08	.28	−.59	−.14	.94	−2.05	2.39	.65
				After World War II					
1951–52	.76	.05	.37	−1.16	−.31	1.69	−1.51	1.27	.88
1952–53	.85	.04	.36	−1.01	−.27	1.51	−1.29	1.18	.79
1953–54	.85	.05	.36	−1.01	−.27	1.50	−1.33	1.22	.79
1954–55	.83	.05	.35	−1.00	−.26	1.49	−1.39	1.27	.80
1955–56	.81	.05	.35	−1.03	−.27	1.52	−1.45	1.31	.82
1956–57	.83	.05	.35	−1.00	−.27	1.49	−1.38	1.27	.80
1957–58	.91	.04	.34	−.88	−.23	1.34	−1.12	1.11	.70
1958–59	.96	.04	.33	−.82	−.22	1.26	−.95	.98	.65
1959–60	.95	.04	.32	−.81	−.22	1.25	−.88	.90	.64
1960–61	.94	.03	.32	−.82	−.23	1.27	−.88	.88	.65
1961–62	.94	.04	.33	−.84	−.23	1.29	−.92	.92	.66
1962–63	.95	.04	.33	−.86	−.24	1.31	−.92	.91	.67

of T_3 is subject to larger variations than those of T_1 and T_2. Table 13.6 shows that this elasticity must be viewed as quite stable relative to its unstable components.

The Conditional Income Elasticities of the Transformed Meats

In the case of the three-meat group of Section 13.1 we apply (3.1), with n interpreted as 3, λ_i as the conditional income elasticity of the ith trans-

TABLE 13.7

DECOMPOSITION OF THE CONDITIONAL INCOME ELASTICITIES OF TRANSFORMED MEATS

	Beef	Pork	Chicken	Beef	Pork	Chicken	Beef	Pork	Chicken
		T_1			T_2			T_3	
1950–51	.26	.29	.13	2.26	−.19	−.01	.75	.94	−.60
1951–52	.26	.29	.14	2.25	−.20	−.01	.74	.91	−.56
1952–53	.27	.29	.14	2.21	−.22	−.00	.76	.86	−.51
1953–54	.29	.29	.14	2.18	−.23	−.00	.82	.88	−.55
1954–55	.30	.30	.14	2.16	−.26	.00	.87	.86	−.56
1955–56	.31	.29	.14	2.15	−.29	.00	.88	.79	−.49
1956–57	.32	.29	.14	2.15	−.30	.01	.91	.78	−.49
1957–58	.32	.30	.14	2.14	−.31	.01	.93	.78	−.50
1958–59	.33	.30	.14	2.14	−.33	.01	.99	.77	−.53
1959–60	.35	.30	.14	2.14	−.38	.02	1.08	.74	−.56
1960–61	.36	.31	.14	2.15	−.41	.03	1.13	.71	−.56
1961–62	.37	.31	.14	2.15	−.42	.03	1.17	.71	−.57
1962–63	.37	.30	.14	2.17	−.45	.04	1.16	.67	−.53
1963–64	.38	.30	.14	2.20	−.50	.05	1.19	.63	−.51
1964–65	.38	.30	.14	2.22	−.52	.05	1.16	.60	−.46
1965–66	.36	.29	.15	2.21	−.48	.04	1.06	.62	−.41
1966–67	.36	.30	.15	2.20	−.48	.04	1.08	.63	−.43
1967–68	.38	.30	.14	2.23	−.53	.05	1.16	.60	−.45
1968–69	.39	.30	.15	2.28	−.61	.07	1.19	.55	−.42
1969–70	.40	.30	.14	2.29	−.63	.07	1.22	.54	−.44
1970–71	.41	.30	.14	2.32	−.67	.09	1.29	.51	−.46
1971–72	.43	.30	.14	2.41	−.81	.13	1.40	.44	−.47

formed meat, and $\mu_j/\bar{w}_{jt}$ as the conditional income elasticity of the jth observed meat within the three-meat group.

The results are shown in Table 13.7, based on the **S** matrices of Table 13.2. The first three columns of Table 13.7 contain the components of the conditional income elasticity of Inexpensive meat (T_1). The figures show that the contributions of Pork and Chicken are virtually constant around .30 and .14, respectively. Hence the increasing trend of the conditional income elasticity of Inexpensive meat which is evident in Table 13.1 is almost exclusively due to the increase of its Beef component. It is not really surprising that there is such an increase, given our knowledge [see the discussion below (1.15)] that the Beef component of a dollar of Inexpensive meat increased from 16 to over 30 cents.

The middle three columns of Table 13.7 contain the contributions of the three observed meats to the conditional income elasticity of the Beef/Pork contrast (T_2). The contribution of Chicken is close to zero and that of Beef is relatively stable. The decreasing trend of the conditional income elasticity of this contrast during the 1950s (see Table 13.1) is largely the result of the increasing negative contribution of Pork.

The last three columns of Table 13.7, dealing with the conditional income elasticity of Antichicken, show that Pork was initially the largest positive contributor. This changed when Beef took over in the mid-1950s; from the late 1960s onward the Beef contribution was about twice as large as that of Pork or even larger. This is in qualitative agreement with the changing composition of a dollar of Antichicken described at the end of Section 13.1. The negative contribution of Chicken to the elasticity of Antichicken is more stable; it fluctuated between −.5 and −.6 until the mid-1960s and between −.4 and −.5 thereafter. The increasing trend of the conditional income elasticity of Antichicken during the 1950s mainly results from the increase of the combined contributions of Beef and Pork, from less than 1.7 in the early 1950s to between 1.8 and 1.9 in the early 1960s.

13.4 Changes in Prices

This section describes the price behavior of the T-goods of Sections 13.1 and 13.2 and the following summary measures: the cost-of-living and the marginal price indexes of the associated demand models, and the corresponding variances of the price log-changes.

The Prices of the T-Goods of the 14-Commodity Model

Equation (2.7) of Section 12.2 defines the price log-change of the ith T-good, to be written $(Dp_{it})_T$, as

$$(Dp_{it})_T = \sum_{j=1}^{n} s_{ij} Dp_{jt} \tag{4.1}$$

For the block-independent 14-commodity model we put $n=3$ and use the Dp_{jt}'s of Clothing, Footwear and Other goods and services given in Table 6.4 on page 265 of Volume 1. By applying the **S** matrices of Tables 13.4 and 13.5, we obtain the results shown in the first three columns of Table 13.8. Notice that the price of T_3 is relatively unstable in the period prior to World War II, particularly in the early 1920s. A major cause is the instability of the **S** transformation for this good in this period. [For 1923–24 an additional cause is the sharp decline in the price of Footwear.] Also notice that T_2 is subject to a sizable price increase in the postwar period, especially relative to the price of T_1.

TABLE 13.8

PRICE BEHAVIOR BASED ON THE 14-COMMODITY MODEL

	Price log-change of						
	T_1	T_2	T_3	DP_t	DP'_t	$\sqrt{\Pi_t}$	$\sqrt{\Pi'_t}$
				Between Wars			
1922–23	−5.71	4.77	13.57	−4.27	−5.68 (.13)	4.28	3.43
1923–24	.66	1.81	−89.66	.26	.00 (.10)	4.05	3.65
1924–25	.45	.32	1.05	.69	.11 (.12)	4.08	3.24
1925–26	−5.23	2.67	8.68	−4.75	−5.09 (.13)	4.61	3.57
1926–27	−.12	1.43	4.08	−1.11	−.88 (.10)	2.51	2.20
1927–28	.39	1.88	11.31	.52	.39 (.05)	1.79	1.51
1928–29	−.67	.75	−1.52	−.42	−.15 (.07)	3.43	3.24
1929–30	−8.04	5.39	−.58	−4.44	−4.66 (.20)	5.21	4.44
1930–31	−5.22	1.30	−10.95	−6.51	−6.31 (.20)	5.87	4.87
1931–32	−7.93	−.30	−18.47	−8.62	−9.72 (.21)	6.65	5.71
1932–33	−4.96	−2.18	.55	−3.76	−5.19 (.18)	6.77	5.83
1933–34	−.81	−2.51	−9.09	−1.53	−1.94 (.13)	3.48	3.60
1934–35	−3.04	−2.72	−6.01	−3.43	−3.61 (.06)	1.94	1.73
1935–36	−4.49	−3.79	−5.63	−4.00	−6.15 (.15)	4.22	5.45
1936–37	4.34	−.23	18.59	4.45	5.53 (.11)	3.92	3.60
1937–38	2.67	−.90	−18.89	2.15	2.96 (.13)	4.20	3.47
1938–39	3.99	−1.44	−.31	.88	2.11 (.15)	4.11	3.49
				After World War II			
1951–52	−6.98	20.91	1.62	.17	−1.30 (.32)	7.51	6.21
1952–53	−.82	1.24	3.09	−.94	−1.23 (.05)	2.18	1.86
1953–54	3.27	11.78	4.30	3.79	3.06 (.09)	3.32	2.47
1954–55	.65	6.47	5.17	1.53	1.10 (.08)	2.57	1.79
1955–56	−1.86	9.06	8.01	1.89	1.69 (.17)	5.10	4.66
1956–57	5.31	7.71	1.86	4.50	3.38 (.11)	3.67	4.50
1957–58	1.52	11.02	6.44	1.45	1.10 (.14)	3.58	2.30
1958–59	.23	2.07	4.92	.92	.67 (.05)	1.45	1.21
1959–60	3.22	7.39	5.08	1.76	1.65 (.13)	3.00	2.46
1960–61	1.77	4.48	.74	1.69	1.50 (.05)	1.51	1.18
1961–62	2.33	5.00	2.38	2.20	1.77 (.08)	3.33	2.67
1962–63	2.78	5.97	3.05	2.74	2.30 (.06)	2.05	1.62
				Three-period summary			
1922–39	−33.7	6.3	−103.3	−33.9	−38.3		
1939–51	109.3	17.2	78.0	100.0	110.3		
1951–63	11.4	93.1	46.6	21.7	15.7		

Note. All entries are to be divided by 100.

A Three-Period Summary

The last three lines of Table 13.8 provide a three-period summary. The figures in the 1922–39 row are obtained by summing the 17 prewar price log-changes in the same column, and those of 1951–63 by summing the 12 postwar log-changes; those of 1939–51 are similarly obtained but involve an approximation, which is explained at the end of this subsection. The large negative figure for T_3 in 1922–39 is mainly due to the log-change in 1923–24, when the budget share of T_3 was only one-tenth of 1 percent. The price log-changes from 1924 to 1939 are -28.7 for T_1, $-.3$ for T_2 and -27.2 for T_3 (all to be divided by 100), which amounts to a much smaller dispersion than that shown in the 1922–39 row of Table 13.8.

The last two rows of the table are more interesting. The price of T_2, with its small income elasticity, increased much less than those of T_1 and T_3 from 1939 to 1951. A major cause was the government price control during the War and the early postwar period, which emphasized necessities. After the War controls were relaxed, although not completely abandoned, which led to a sizable increase in the price of T_2. The total price log-change from 1939 to 1963, obtained by adding the last two rows of the table (and dividing by 100), is about 1.10 for T_2 and between 1.20 and 1.25 for T_1 and T_3, which amounts to price increases of about 200 and 240 percent, respectively. Hence the price ratios of the three T-goods in 1963 are relatively close to those of 1939, but the paths of the three prices were quite different in the period between these years.

The figures of the 1939–51 row of Table 13.8 are based on four preference independence transformations: for 1939–48, 1948–49, 1949–50 and 1950–51, followed by adding the price log-changes thus obtained for each T-good. In the case of the 1939–48 transition we interpret each diagonal element of $(\mathbf{w}_g)_\Delta$ in the matrix (2.9) as the average of the corresponding budget shares in 1939 and 1948. No data are available on years between 1939 and 1948. [For the available data see THEIL (1967, Section 5.B).] We shall have more to say about this procedure in Section 13.5.

Means of Price Log-changes of the 14-Commodity Model

The fourth and fifth columns of Table 13.8 contain the log-changes in the cost-of-living and marginal price indexes,

$$DP_t = \sum_{i=1}^{14} \bar{w}_{it} Dp_{it} \qquad DP'_t = \sum_{i=1}^{14} \mu_i Dp_{it} \tag{4.2}$$

where the μ's are approximated by their mixed estimates. Since both indexes are invariant under the preference independence transformation, it is immaterial whether they are computed from the commodity data or from their transformed counterparts. The first method is obviously simpler, but using both methods is a good check on the computations.

The figures in parentheses in the fifth column of Table 13.8 are standard errors of the log-changes in the marginal price index. They measure the uncertainty caused by the use of estimates of the marginal shares and they are computed as the square root of

$$\sum_{i=1}^{14} \sum_{j=1}^{14} Dp_{it} Dp_{jt} \operatorname{cov}(\hat{\mu}_i, \hat{\mu}_j) \tag{4.3}$$

where $\operatorname{cov}(\hat{\mu}_i, \hat{\mu}_j)$ stands for the covariance of the mixed estimates of μ_i and μ_j given in Table 6.15 on page 307 of Volume 1. A majority of the 29 differences $DP'_t - DP_t$ exceeds three times the standard error of DP'_t in absolute value. Nevertheless, these differences tend to be small; in 21 cases out of 29 they are less than .01, and in only one case (1935-36) does it exceed .02. The upper part of Figure 13.1 contains scatters of DP_t and DP'_t for the pre- and postwar periods separately. They indicate that the observations are close to the 45 degree line which has been drawn through the origin.

The last three lines of Table 13.8 provide a three-period summary of the indexes (4.2), obtained by summation as described in the previous subsection. The figures for 1922–39 amount to an average annual decline of about 2 percent for both indexes. During 1939–51 the marginal index increased about 10 percent relative to the cost-of-living index, which is consistent with the more extensive price control of necessities. The postwar development is a reversal of the 1939–51 change and the result is that, in 1963, both indexes are around 350 with base 1939=100.

Variances of Price Log-changes of the 14-Commodity Model

The last two columns of Table 13.8 contain the square roots of Π_t and Π'_t, the budget-share and marginally weighted standard deviations of the price log-changes of the T-goods. Since the former is invariant under the preference independence transformation, we can compute it as

$$\Pi_t = \sum_{i=1}^{14} \bar{w}_{it} (Dp_{it} - DP_t)^2 \tag{4.4}$$

The marginally weighted variance is not invariant. It follows from eq. (7.6)

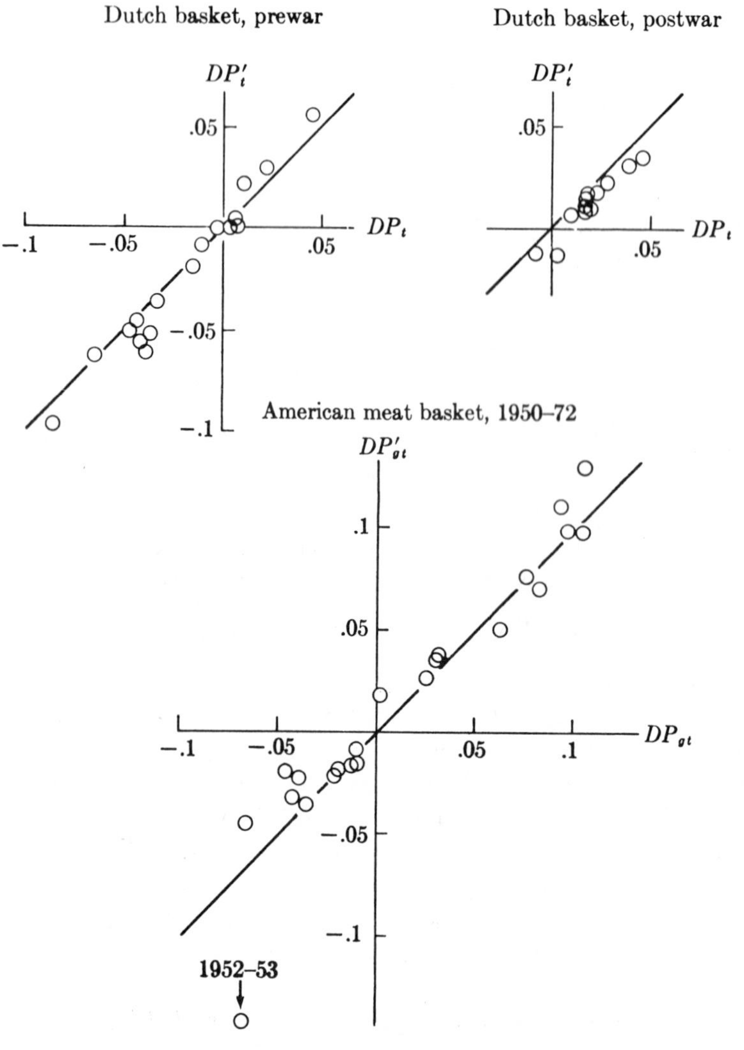

Fig. 13.1 Weighted means of price log-changes

of Section 12.7 that this variance for $n=14$ can be computed as

$$\Pi'_t = \sum_{i=1}^{14} \sum_{j=1}^{14} \mu_{ij} (Dp_{it} - DP'_t)(Dp_{jt} - DP'_t) \tag{4.5}$$

$$= \sum_{i=1}^{14} \sum_{j=1}^{14} \frac{\nu_{ij}}{\phi} (Dp_{it} - DP'_t)(Dp_{jt} - DP'_t)$$

For the model considered here we use the numerical specifications (2.4) and (2.5) when i and j both belong to the three-commodity group; when either i or j is outside this group, ν_{ij}/ϕ vanishes for $i \neq j$ and it is equal to μ_i (to be approximated by its mixed estimate) for $i = j$.

The figures in the last two columns of Table 13.8 show that, with only three exceptions (1933–34, 1935–36 and 1956–57), the budget-share-weighted variance Π_t exceeds the marginally weighted variance Π_t'. This difference between the two variances will be considered in the last two subsections. The largest variance, both budget-share-weighted and marginally weighted, is that of 1951–52. This is a Korean War effect – some prices still going up and others going down. The standard deviations after 1952 tend to be smaller than those between the wars, which means that 1952–1963 was characterized by more price stability than 1922–39 in that there was, on the average, less variation of the individual price changes around the average price change in any given year. This phenomenon should be compared with the smaller range of variation over time of DP_t and DP_t' in the postwar period (see Figure 13.1), which implies that this period was also characterized by more price stability in the sense of less variation of the average price changes from one year to the next.

The Prices of the Transformed Meats

The first three columns of Table 13.9 contain the price log-changes of the transformed meats. They are obtained from (4.1) by specifying $n = 3$ and using the **S** matrices of Table 13.2 combined with the Dp_{jt}'s of Beef, Pork and Chicken given in Table 7.3 on page 12. The year-to-year changes in the price of Inexpensive meat (T_1) are relatively moderate; those of T_2 and T_3 are much larger in several years. In contrast to the case of T_3 of the 14-commodity model in the early 1920s, this is not due to the instability of the **S** transformation. Instead, it is due to the large fluctuations in the prices of the observed meats combined with the unequal signs of s_{i1}, s_{i2} and s_{i3} in the case of T_2 and T_3. For example, take the largest log-change in absolute value, which is that of the price of the Beef/Pork contrast (T_2) in 1952–53. It is computed as

$$s_{21}Dp_{1t} + s_{22}Dp_{2t} + s_{23}Dp_{3t}$$

or, in numerical form,

$$1.41(-.2255) - .40(.0998) - .01(-.0270) = -.3573$$

This large value is evidently due, first, to the substantial decline of the price of Beef and, second, to the increase of the price of Pork.

TABLE 13.9

PRICE BEHAVIOR OF MEATS

	Price log-change of			DP_{gt}	DP'_{gt}	$\sqrt{\Pi_{gt}}$	$\sqrt{\Pi'_{gt}}$
	T_1	T_2	T_3				
1950–51	7.83	19.02	14.36	10.55	13.00	4.57	5.34
1951–52	−1.69	−1.52	−6.32	−1.94	−1.94	1.07	1.12
1952–53	.52	−35.73	7.83	−6.87	−14.14	14.97	18.04
1953–54	−2.09	−2.06	14.81	−.98	−.82	4.01	4.24
1954–55	−8.15	5.43	−30.11	−6.66	−4.45	8.02	9.47
1955–56	−6.49	−1.19	6.39	−4.29	−3.18	3.83	3.98
1956–57	7.89	2.56	26.01	8.24	7.64	5.55	6.32
1957–58	6.22	16.97	19.76	9.31	11.16	5.11	5.60
1958–59	−8.28	10.08	−4.85	−4.66	−1.96	6.95	8.35
1959–60	−.62	−3.01	−3.83	−1.27	−1.64	1.13	1.26
1960–61	−1.14	−7.07	13.71	−1.12	−1.57	4.74	5.58
1961–62	2.77	6.51	−1.08	3.16	3.55	1.83	2.21
1962–63	−3.44	−4.00	−5.62	−3.51	−3.55	1.25	1.45
1963–64	−1.84	−3.56	−1.72	−2.04	−2.20	.63	.79
1964–65	9.57	−4.83	16.53	8.30	7.08	5.59	6.93
1965–66	7.58	−3.59	9.26	6.19	5.08	4.02	4.99
1966–67	−6.43	6.95	−2.99	−3.93	−2.28	4.75	5.65
1967–68	2.63	8.26	1.02	3.29	3.85	2.09	2.58
1968–69	8.92	10.64	13.50	9.65	9.93	1.53	1.68
1969–70	2.01	−.50	8.98	2.58	2.67	2.47	2.88
1970–71	−2.53	20.74	−2.78	.05	1.90	7.20	8.93
1971–72	10.51	−2.40	19.71	10.35	9.86	4.90	6.08
1950-72	23.8	37.7	112.6	34.4	38.0		

Note. All entries are to be divided by 100.

By summing the 22 annual figures in each column we obtain the total price log-change from 1950 to 1972, which is shown in the last row of Table 13.9. This gives .238 for Inexpensive meat, which amounts to a trend increase of about 1 percent per year. For the Beef/Pork contrast the trend is a little steeper, and for Antichicken (T_3) it is much steeper (about 5 percent per year). A major cause of this behavior of the price of T_3 is the decline in the price of Chicken relative to those of Beef and Pork.

Means and Variances of the Price Log-changes of Meats

The summary measures for meats discussed in this and the next chapters refer to the four-meat group, with Lamb included. The log-changes in the cost-of-meat and the marginal meat price indexes are therefore

$$DP_{gt} = \sum_{i=1}^{4} \frac{\bar{w}_{it}}{\bar{W}_{gt}} Dp_{it} \qquad DP'_{gt} = \sum_{i=1}^{4} \frac{\mu_i}{M_g} Dp_{it} \tag{4.6}$$

where $i=1,\dots,4$ stands for Beef, Pork, Chicken and Lamb, respectively, while $\bar{W}_{gt}$ and M_g are the budget and marginal shares of the four-meat group.

The fourth and fifth columns of Table 13.9 show that the differences $DP'_{gt}-DP_{gt}$ tend to be larger than the differences DP'_t-DP_t in Table 13.8. This is also evident from the lower part of Figure 13.1, which contains the scatter of DP_{gt} and DP'_{gt}. The difference $DP'_{gt}-DP_{gt}$ exceeds .01 in absolute value in 10 cases out of 22; the largest difference is $-.073$ (1952–53). Such large differences can occur only when there is a considerable dispersion among the price log-changes of the individual meats. This is pursued in the last two columns of Table 13.9, which give the budget-share and marginally weighted standard deviations of the price log-changes of the transformed meats. The former can be computed from

$$\Pi_{gt} = \sum_{i=1}^{4} \frac{\bar{w}_{it}}{\bar{W}_{gt}} (Dp_{it} - DP_{gt})^2 \tag{4.7}$$

and the latter from

$$\Pi'_{gt} = \sum_{i=1}^{4} \sum_{j=1}^{4} \frac{\nu_{ij}}{\phi M_g} (Dp_{it} - DP'_{gt})(Dp_{jt} - DP'_{gt}) \tag{4.8}$$

Since the numerical specification of the meat model is based on the parame trization of Section 7.3, we can use eq. (3.8) of that section and (1.6),

$$\frac{\nu_{ij}}{\phi M_g} = \frac{\bar{W}_{gt}\nu^*_{ij}}{\phi M_g} = \mu^g_{ij} \tag{4.9}$$

where S_g is now the four-meat group. Hence (4.8) may be written as

$$\Pi'_{gt} = \sum_{i=1}^{4} \sum_{j=1}^{4} \mu^g_{ij} (Dp_{it} - DP'_{gt})(Dp_{jt} - DP'_{gt}) \tag{4.10}$$

A comparison of the last two columns of Tables 13.8 and 13.9 shows that the largest standard deviations of the American meat basket exceed the largest standard deviations of the Dutch 14-commodity basket. In particular, the two standard deviations of 1952–53 in Table 13.9 are quite substantial, enabling DP'_{gt} and DP_{gt} of that year to differ as much as they do.

Comparison of Variances

Recall from the discussion in the paragraph below (4.5) that the budget-share-weighted variances of Table 13.8 exceed the corresponding marginally weighted variances in most cases. In Table 13.9 the picture is exactly the opposite. No simple mathematical relationship exists between these two differently weighted variances, but the developments which follow, based on specific substitution and complementarity considerations, provide interesting insights.

For general n, consider

$$\begin{aligned}\sum_{i=1}^{n}\sum_{j=1}^{n}\mu_{ij}(Dp_{it}-Dp_{jt})^2 &= \sum_{i=1}^{n}\sum_{j=1}^{n}\mu_{ij}[(Dp_{it}-DP'_t)-(Dp_{jt}-DP'_t)]^2\\ &= 2\sum_{i=1}^{n}\mu_i(Dp_{it}-DP'_t)^2-2\sum_{i=1}^{n}\sum_{j=1}^{n}\mu_{ij}(Dp_{it}-DP'_t)(Dp_{jt}-DP'_t)\end{aligned}$$

where the second step is based on $\mu_{i1}+\cdots+\mu_{in}=\mu_i$. Since the second term in the last line equals $-2\Pi'_t$, we have thus proved

$$\Pi'_t=\sum_{i=1}^{n}\mu_i(Dp_{it}-DP'_t)^2-\tfrac{1}{2}\sum_{i=1}^{n}\sum_{j=1}^{n}\mu_{ij}(Dp_{it}-Dp_{jt})^2 \tag{4.11}$$

On the left we have the marginally weighted variance of the price log-changes of the T-goods. The first term on the right is the marginally weighted variance of the price log-changes of the commodities. The second term is a weighted sum of the squares of the differences between the latter price log-changes. In this second term we can confine the summation over i and j to $i\neq j$ (because $Dp_{it}-Dp_{it}=0$), so that it takes the form of $(Dp_{it}-Dp_{jt})^2$ multiplied by $-\frac{1}{2}\mu_{ij}$, summed over i and j with $i\neq j$. If there are some specific complements and no specific substitutes among the commodities [$\nu_{ij}\leq 0$ and hence $\mu_{ij}\geq 0$ for each (i,j)], this second term must be nonpositive, which implies that Π'_t is never larger and usually smaller than the marginally weighted variance of the price log-changes of the commodities. It is then not too surprising to find that Π'_t is also usually smaller than Π_t, the budget-share-weighted variance of the same price log-changes.

Verification for the Two Baskets

Table 13.10 verifies this reasoning for the Dutch basket ($n=14$). It contains Π_t and Π'_t in columns (1) and (2), the first right-hand term of

TABLE 13.10

COMPARISON OF VARIANCES OF PRICE LOG-CHANGES

	Π_t	Π'_t	Components of Π'_t	
	(1)	(2)	(3)	(4)
	Dutch basket, between wars			
1922–23	18.3	11.8	19.2	−7.4
1923–24	16.4	13.4	20.7	−7.4
1924–25	16.7	10.5	10.5	−.0
1925–26	21.3	12.7	17.8	−5.0
1926–27	6.3	4.8	5.1	−.2
1927–28	3.2	2.3	3.2	−.9
1928–29	11.8	10.5	10.7	−.2
1929–30	27.1	19.7	33.6	−13.8
1930–31	34.4	23.7	28.2	−4.5
1931–32	44.2	32.6	40.0	−7.4
1932–33	45.9	33.9	34.8	−.8
1933–34	12.1	13.0	13.5	−.5
1934–35	3.8	3.0	3.1	−.1
1935–36	17.8	29.7	29.7	−.1
1936–37	15.4	13.0	17.2	−4.2
1937–38	17.7	12.1	15.0	−3.0
1938–39	16.9	12.2	15.1	−2.9
	Dutch basket, after World War II			
1951–52	56.5	38.5	66.6	−28.1
1952–53	4.8	3.5	3.8	−.4
1953–54	11.1	6.1	9.6	−3.5
1954–55	6.6	3.2	4.9	−1.7
1955–56	26.0	21.7	27.6	−5.9
1956–57	13.5	20.2	20.7	−.5
1957–58	12.8	5.3	10.6	−5.3
1958–59	2.1	1.5	2.0	−.6
1959–60	9.0	6.0	7.2	−1.1
1960–61	2.3	1.4	1.9	−.5
1961–62	11.1	7.1	7.5	−.4
1962–63	4.2	2.6	3.2	−.6

Π_{gt}	Π'_{gt}	Components of Π'_{gt}		
(5)	(6)	(7)	(8)	
American meat basket				
20.9	28.5	16.9	11.6	1950–51
1.2	1.3	.6	.7	1951–52
224.0	325.6	178.7	146.9	1952–53
16.1	18.0	8.1	9.9	1953–54
64.3	89.7	41.9	47.8	1954–55
14.6	15.8	8.9	6.9	1955–56
30.8	39.9	17.6	22.3	1956–57
26.1	31.4	18.6	12.8	1957–58
48.3	69.7	39.6	30.0	1958–59
1.3	1.6	.9	.6	1959–60
22.5	31.1	14.0	17.1	1960–61
3.3	4.9	2.4	2.5	1961–62
1.6	2.1	1.9	.2	1962–63
.4	.6	.4	.3	1963–64
31.2	48.0	23.1	24.9	1964–65
16.2	24.9	13.1	11.8	1965–66
22.5	31.9	18.4	13.5	1966–67
4.4	6.7	3.4	3.2	1967–68
2.3	2.8	1.6	1.2	1968–69
6.1	8.3	3.7	4.5	1969 70
51.9	79.7	41.4	38.3	1970–71
24.0	36.9	16.5	20.5	1971–72

Note. All entries are to be multiplied by 10^{-4}.

(4.11) in column (3), and the second in column (4). Note that the figures in column (4) are all negative. This is in agreement with the absence of specific substitutes and the specific complementarity of Clothing, Footwear and Other goods and services that is implied by (2.5). The figures in column (4) are necessarily zero when the prices of these three commodities change proportionally (which was almost true in 1924–25); otherwise such a figure is negative. It is interesting to note that Π_t in column (1) is typically closer to the commodity variance in column (3) than to the T-good variance in column (2).

It is easily verified that the four-meat version of (4.11) is

$$\text{(4.12)}\quad \Pi'_{gt} = \sum_{i=1}^{4} \frac{\mu_i}{M_g} (Dp_{it} - DP'_{gt})^2 - \tfrac{1}{2} \sum_{i=1}^{4} \sum_{j=1}^{4} \mu_{ij}^g (Dp_{it} - Dp_{jt})^2$$

The components of this equation, together with Π_{gt}, are shown in columns (5) to (8) of Table 13.10. The second right-hand term of (4.12), given in column (8), is nonnegative because (1.1) specifies that there are no specific complements among the four meats and that Beef, Pork and Chicken are specific substitutes. Note that the figures in column (8) are sometimes quite large, so that the marginally weighted variance of the price log-changes of the observed meats [column (7)] is often considerably below the corresponding variance Π'_{gt} of the transformed meats. In fact, in the period considered here, the former variance is usually smaller than Π_{gt} of column (5), whereas the latter exceeds Π_{gt}.

We conclude by noting that (4.11) and (4.12) are also valid when μ_i is negative for some i, but that the first term on the right in these equations is then an improper variance. In our two applications all marginal shares are positive.

13.5 World War II and the Circular Test

It was mentioned on page 320 that the 1939–51 row of Table 13.8 involves the transition from 1939 to 1948, and that the $\bar{w}_{it}$ of this transition is defined as the arithmetic average of the ith budget share in 1939 and 1948. This procedure is applied throughout this chapter and Chapter 14 when the war transition is discussed. In this section we consider the implied approximation error for the cost-of-living index, which leads to the subject of the circular test for indexes.

The Circular Test

Consider three successive periods, to be written $t=0$, 1 and 2 for notational convenience. The log-changes in the cost-of-living index of these periods are

$$\text{(5.1)}\quad DP_1 = \tfrac{1}{2} \sum_{i=1}^{n} (w_{i0} + w_{i1})\, Dp_{i1} \qquad DP_2 = \tfrac{1}{2} \sum_{i=1}^{n} (w_{i1} + w_{i2})\, Dp_{i2}$$

If we compute the log-change in the index from $t=0$ to $t=2$ directly, using the average of the budget shares of these two periods, we obtain

$$\frac{1}{2}\sum_{i=1}^{n}(w_{i0}+w_{i2})(Dp_{i1}+Dp_{i2}) \tag{5.2}$$

If the expression (5.2) equals DP_1+DP_2, the *circular test* is satisfied, which requires that the index at $t=2$ with base $t=0$ be equal to the product of the index at $t=1$ with base $t=0$ and that at $t=2$ with base $t=1$.

The circular test is not satisfied by (5.1) and (5.2), nor is the discrepancy of a particularly high order of smallness. This discrepancy is obtained by subtracting DP_1+DP_2 from (5.2):

$$\frac{1}{2}\sum_{i=1}^{n}(w_{i2}-w_{i1})Dp_{i1}-\frac{1}{2}\sum_{i=1}^{n}(w_{i1}-w_{i0})Dp_{i2} \tag{5.3}$$

To evaluate this we consider

$$w_{it}-w_{i,t-1}=\bar{w}_{it}(Dp_{it}-DP_t)+\bar{w}_{it}(Dq_{it}-DQ_t)+O_3$$

which we substitute in (5.3) for $t=2$ and $t=1$:

$$\begin{aligned}\frac{1}{2}\sum_{i=1}^{n}&[\bar{w}_{i2}(Dp_{i2}-DP_2)+\bar{w}_{i2}(Dq_{i2}-DQ_2)]Dp_{i1}\\&-\frac{1}{2}\sum_{i=1}^{n}[\bar{w}_{i1}(Dp_{i1}-DP_1)+\bar{w}_{i1}(Dq_{i1}-DQ_1)]Dp_{i2}+O_4\end{aligned} \tag{5.4}$$

It is shown in the next subsection that this expression is of order O_2 under certain conditions. Since (5.2) and DP_1 and DP_2 are all O_1, the relative discrepancy of the circular test is thus O_1.

Derivations for the Circular Test

It is immediately seen that the leading terms in (5.4) are O_2. To verify that (5.4) is actually O_2, it is sufficient to prove that the leading O_2 terms do not cancel each other out. We shall do so under the assumption that DQ_t, $Dp_{1t},\ldots, Dp_{nt}$ are nonstochastic, so that $\bar{w}_{i1}Dq_{i1}$ and $\bar{w}_{i2}Dq_{i2}$ in (5.4) are sums of nonstochastic real-income and substitution terms and a random disturbance (ε_{i1} and ε_{i2}). Hence, apart from the O_4 remainder term, (5.4) has a random component equal to

$$\frac{1}{2}\sum_{i=1}^{n}Dp_{i1}\varepsilon_{i2}-\frac{1}{2}\sum_{i=1}^{n}Dp_{i2}\varepsilon_{i1} \tag{5.5}$$

which has zero expectation. If we succeed in proving that the random variable (5.5) has a standard deviation of order O_2, we can conclude that this variable takes values of that order and that there is no way in which this variable and the nonstochastic O_2 terms of (5.4) cancel each other out.

For this purpose we assume, as usual, that the disturbances have zero lagged covariances and a constant contemporaneous covariance matrix $[\omega_{ij}]$, so that the variance of (5.5) is

$$\tfrac{1}{4}\sum_{i=1}^{n}\sum_{j=1}^{n}\omega_{ij}(Dp_{i1}Dp_{j1}+Dp_{i2}Dp_{j2}) \tag{5.6}$$

The disturbance ε_{it} takes values of order O_1 because the ith demand equation describes ε_{it} as a linear combination of O_1 terms. Hence $\omega_{ii}=\operatorname{var}\varepsilon_{it}$ is of order O_2. Since the expression in parentheses in (5.6) is also O_2, the variance (5.6) is O_4, which proves that the standard deviation of (5.5) is O_2. It may also be verified that, under the second-moment model, (5.6) is equal to $\tfrac{1}{4}\sigma^2(\Pi'_1+\Pi'_2)$, which is O_4 because $\sigma^2=O_2$.

Implications for the War Transition

The transition from 1939 to 1948 may be viewed as consisting of nine year-to-year transitions. Hence, with 1939 written as 0, the log-change in the cost of living is computed as

$$\tfrac{1}{2}\sum_{i=1}^{14}(w_{i0}+w_{i9})\log\frac{p_{i9}}{p_{i0}}=\tfrac{1}{2}\sum_{i=1}^{14}(w_{i0}+w_{i9})\sum_{t=1}^{9}Dp_{it} \tag{5.7}$$

The price increases of the 14 commodities from 1939 to 1948 were substantial and far from proportional. Therefore, the discrepancy of the circular test implies a qualification for the transition from 1939 to 1948 that should be kept in mind.

13.6 Cost-of-Living Comparisons Over Longer Periods at a Constant Utility Level

We know from Section 3.7 that, apart from a remainder term O_3, the cost-of-living index DP_t is evaluated at the utility level which corresponds to the geometric means of the incomes and prices of years $t-1$ and t. This utility level obviously changes over time. The subject considered in this section is that of cost-of-living comparisons at a constant utility level over a period of several years.

Adjusting Budget Shares for Cost-of-Living Comparisons

Consider the transition from $t-1$ to t, with a budget share of the ith good equal to $\bar{w}_{it}$, and imagine that we wish to evaluate the cost of living at either a higher or a lower level of real income than that which prevails in $(t-1, t)$. Such an imagined income change affects the ith budget share. Following THEIL (1967, Section 7.9), we consider this share as a function of the logarithm of income, given fixed prices, and we apply[1]

$$\text{(6.1)} \qquad \frac{\partial w_i}{\partial (\log m)} = \mu_i - w_i$$

as well as lemma (1.7) of Section 2.1. If R_t is the logarithmic change in real income from the $(t-1, t)$ level to that at which the cost of living is to be evaluated, this lemma combined with (6.1) yields $\hat{w}_{it}$, an approximation of the ith budget share at the selected level of real income:

$$\begin{aligned}\hat{w}_{it} - \bar{w}_{it} &= \tfrac{1}{2}[(\mu_i - \bar{w}_{it}) + (\mu_i - \hat{w}_{it})]\, R_t \\ &= \mu_i R_t - \tfrac{1}{2}\bar{w}_{it} R_t - \tfrac{1}{2}\hat{w}_{it} R_t\end{aligned}$$

This implies the following solution for $\hat{w}_{it}$:

$$\text{(6.2)} \qquad \hat{w}_{it} = \bar{w}_{it} + \frac{R_t}{1 + \frac{1}{2}R_t}(\mu_i - \bar{w}_{it})$$

When we use the $\hat{w}_{it}$'s as weights for the price log-changes, we obtain

$$\text{(6.3)} \qquad \sum_{i=1}^{n} \hat{w}_{it} Dp_{it} = DP_t + \frac{R_t}{1 + \frac{1}{2}R_t}(DP_t' - DP_t)$$

The left-hand side is our approximation of the log-change in the true cost-of-living index at the chosen level of real income. Note that the adjustment is an income adjustment, prices remaining as they are observed in both $t-1$ and t.

The index (6.3) is simply a weighted average of the indexes DP_t and DP_t', with weights proportional to $1-\frac{1}{2}R_t$ and R_t. Hence it moves from DP_t in the direction of DP_t' when R_t takes increasing positive values, starting from zero, which is in agreement with eq. (6.13) of Section 3.6 and the discussion below that equation.

---

[1] Take the logarithm of $w_i = p_i q_i / m$ and differentiate with respect to $\log m$. This yields (6.1) after substitution of μ_i / w_i for the income elasticity of the ith commodity.

Extension to the Cost of Meat

Write $i=1,\ldots,4$ for Beef, Pork, Chicken and Lamb, and $i=5,\ldots,n$ for all other (nonmeat) commodities. With $\hat{w}_{it}$ given in (6.2), we define

$$\hat{W}_{gt} = \sum_{i=1}^{4} \hat{w}_{it} \tag{6.4}$$

as the total-meat share at the chosen level of real income. We have

$$\sum_{i=1}^{n} \hat{w}_{it} Dp_{it} = \hat{W}_{gt} \sum_{i=1}^{4} \frac{\hat{w}_{it}}{\hat{W}_{gt}} Dp_{it} + (1 - \hat{W}_{gt}) \sum_{i=5}^{n} \frac{\hat{w}_{it}}{1 - \hat{W}_{gt}} Dp_{it}$$

which shows that we may regard

$$\sum_{i=1}^{4} \frac{\hat{w}_{it}}{\hat{W}_{gt}} Dp_{it} \tag{6.5}$$

as the log-change in the meat price index corresponding to our approximation of the true cost-of-living index, and $(1-\hat{W}_{gt})^{-1} \sum_i \hat{w}_{it} Dp_{it}$, where the summation is over $i=5,\ldots,n$, as the log-change in the index of all nonmeat commodities.

In the next subsection we prove the following within-group version of (6.3) for the index (6.5):

$$\sum_{i=1}^{4} \frac{\hat{w}_{it}}{\hat{W}_{gt}} Dp_{it} = DP_{gt} + \frac{R_t \dfrac{M_g}{\bar{W}_{gt}}}{1 + R_t \left(\dfrac{M_g}{\bar{W}_{gt}} - \frac{1}{2} \right)} (DP'_{gt} - DP_{gt}) \tag{6.6}$$

Note the occurrence of $M_g/\bar{W}_{gt}$, the total-meat income elasticity. This is not surprising, since income changes must be translated into "meat changes" when we design a meat price index. If S_g consists of all commodities of the basket, $M_g/\bar{W}_{gt}$ becomes 1 and (6.6) reduces to (6.3), as it should. Since the block-independence assumption implies $M_g/\bar{W}_{gt}>0$, a departure of R_t from zero in positive (negative) direction causes both sides of (6.6) to move toward (away from) DP'_{gt}, starting from DP_{gt}. This is similar to the conclusion on (6.3) stated at the end of the previous subsection.

Derivations for the Cost of Meat

To obtain the total-meat share (6.4), we sum (6.2) over $i=1,\ldots,4$:

$$\hat{W}_{gt} = \bar{W}_{gt} + \frac{R_t}{1 + \frac{1}{2}R_t} (M_g - \bar{W}_{gt})$$

The implied conditional shares are

$$(6.7)\qquad \frac{\hat{w}_{it}}{\hat{W}_{gt}} = \frac{\bar{w}_{it} + R_t(1+\frac{1}{2}R_t)^{-1}(\mu_i - \bar{w}_{it})}{\bar{W}_{gt} + R_t(1+\frac{1}{2}R_t)^{-1}(M_g - \bar{W}_{gt})}$$

Multiply the numerator and the denominator on the right by $1+\frac{1}{2}R_t$:

$$\frac{(1+\frac{1}{2}R_t)\,\bar{w}_{it} + R_t(\mu_i - \bar{w}_{it})}{(1+\frac{1}{2}R_t)\,\bar{W}_{gt} + R_t(M_g - \bar{W}_{gt})} = \frac{\bar{w}_{it} + R_t(\mu_i - \frac{1}{2}\bar{w}_{it})}{\bar{W}_{gt} + R_t(M_g - \frac{1}{2}\bar{W}_{gt})}$$

$$= \frac{\bar{w}_{it}}{\bar{W}_{gt}} \frac{1 + R_t\left(\dfrac{\mu_i}{\bar{w}_{it}} - \frac{1}{2}\right)}{1 + R_t\left(\dfrac{M_g}{\bar{W}_{gt}} - \frac{1}{2}\right)}$$

The expression in the second line is a multiple $\bar{w}_{it}/\bar{W}_{gt}$ of

$$1 + \frac{R_t\left(\dfrac{\mu_i}{\bar{w}_{it}} - \dfrac{M_g}{\bar{W}_{gt}}\right)}{1 + R_t\left(\dfrac{M_g}{\bar{W}_{gt}} - \frac{1}{2}\right)} = 1 + \frac{R_t\dfrac{M_g}{\bar{W}_{gt}}}{1 + R_t\left(\dfrac{M_g}{\bar{W}_{gt}} - \frac{1}{2}\right)}\left(\frac{\mu_i/M_g}{\bar{w}_{it}/\bar{W}_{gt}} - 1\right)$$

Therefore, (6.7) may be written as

$$(6.8)\qquad \frac{\hat{w}_{it}}{\hat{W}_{gt}} = \frac{\bar{w}_{it}}{\bar{W}_{gt}} + \frac{R_t\dfrac{M_g}{\bar{W}_{gt}}}{1 + R_t\left(\dfrac{M_g}{\bar{W}_{gt}} - \frac{1}{2}\right)}\left(\frac{\mu_i}{M_g} - \frac{\bar{w}_{it}}{\bar{W}_{gt}}\right)$$

which is the conditional version of (6.2). The result (6.6) follows from (6.8) after multiplication by Dp_{it} and summation over $i=1,\ldots,4$.

Applications

Since the differences $DP_t' - DP_t$ shown in Table 13.8 are small, the deviations of the index (6.3) from DP_t are uninteresting unless the real-income level selected differs quite substantially from that of $(t-1, t)$. Such large shifts in real income will tend to lead to a poor quality of the approximation (6.2) of the budget shares. It is more attractive to apply (6.6) to the four meats, because the differences $DP_{gt}' - DP_{gt}$ of Table 13.9 are generally larger than $DP_t' - DP_t$ of Table 13.8.

For this purpose we must select the level of real income at which the cost of meat is to be evaluated. Two levels will be used. The low level is one-half of the real per capita income in 1950. If we define the real per capita income of $(t-1, t)$ as the geometric mean of the levels in $t-1$ and t, the logarithm of real per capita income in 1950–51 exceeds that of 1950 by $\frac{1}{2}DQ_1$, where the subscript 1 refers to the fact that 1950–51 is the first observation. It follows that R_1 in (6.6), the logarithmic real-income change from 1950–51 to one-half of the 1950 level, is

$$R_1 = \log\tfrac{1}{2} - \tfrac{1}{2}DQ_1 \tag{6.9}$$

The geometric mean income definition for pairs of successive years implies that the log-change from $(t-1, t)$ to $(t, t+1)$ equals $\frac{1}{2}(DQ_t+DQ_{t+1})$. Hence the subsequent R_t's can be found recursively:

$$R_{t+1} = R_t - \tfrac{1}{2}(DQ_t + DQ_{t+1}) \qquad t = 1, 2, \ldots \tag{6.10}$$

The higher level of real income is twice the per capita real income of 1950. The only modification required is a replacement of $\log\frac{1}{2}$ by $\log 2$ in (6.9). Real per capita income in each calendar year is shown in the first column of Table 13.11; it is computed as the ratio of total per capita consumption in current dollars to the Bureau of Labor Statistics consumer price index (Table 7.1 on page 9). The figure in 1972 is 159.7 with base 1950=100, so that the higher level of real income used here exceeds the 1972 level by about 25 percent.

Implementation and Discussion

The last four columns of Table 13.11 contain the indexes (6.6) at the two selected values of real income together with DP_{gt} and DP'_{gt}, which are reproduced from Table 13.9 to facilitate the comparison. The implementation of (6.6) requires a numerical specification of $M_g/\bar{W}_{gt}$, the income elasticity of the demand for meat as a group; the value used is .8. The figures show that (6.6) at the higher level of real income is consistently between DP_{gt} and DP'_{gt}. This is as it should be, because the higher real-income level is above the actual per capita real income throughout the period considered. Note also that this index is much closer to DP_{gt} than to DP'_{gt} at the end of the period, whereas it is approximately halfway between DP_{gt} and DP'_{gt} in the beginning. This is caused by the gradual increase of the utility level at which DP_{gt} is evaluated.

The index (6.6) at the low level of real income is always outside the range between DP_{gt} and DP'_{gt}, because the ratio in the right-hand side of (6.6) is negative for this real-income level. The difference between the indexes

TABLE 13.11

THE COST OF MEAT AT TWO LEVELS OF REAL INCOME

	Per capita real income	Cost of meat at low real income	Cost of meat at higher real income	DP_{gt}	Cost of meat at low real income	Cost of meat at higher real income	DP'_{gt}
	Index base 1950 = 100				*Log-changes*		
1951	99.5	109.3	112.4	10.55	8.85	11.68	13.00
1952	100.7	107.2	110.2	−1.94	−1.94	−1.94	−1.94
1953	104.3	105.5	99.6	−6.87	−1.55	−10.11	−14.14
1954	104.7	104.3	98.7	−.98	−1.11	−.91	−.82
1955	110.7	95.9	93.2	−6.66	−8.41	−5.74	−4.45
1956	112.2	91.1	89.7	−4.29	−5.22	−3.85	−3.18
1957	112.3	99.4	97.2	8.24	8.75	8.00	7.64
1958	110.6	107.4	107.5	9.31	7.76	10.05	11.16
1959	115.7	100.1	103.7	−4.66	−6.99	−3.60	−1.96
1960	117.1	99.2	102.2	−1.27	−.93	−1.41	−1.64
1961	117.4	98.5	100.9	−1.12	−.70	−1.29	−1.57
1962	121.3	101.3	104.3	3.16	2.80	3.30	3.55
1963	124.7	97.9	100.7	−3.51	−3.46	−3.52	−3.55
1964	129.8	96.0	98.6	−2.04	−1.88	−2.09	−2.20
1965	136.0	105.8	106.7	8.30	9.65	7.94	7.08
1966	141.0	114.0	113.2	6.19	7.49	5.89	5.08
1967	143.3	107.4	109.3	−3.93	−5.93	−3.52	−2.28
1968	148.4	110.3	113.1	3.29	2.59	3.42	3.85
1969	150.7	121.0	124.7	9.65	9.29	9.71	9.93
1970	149.7	124.0	127.9	2.58	2.46	2.60	2.67
1971	153.2	121.1	128.5	.05	−2.40	.43	1.90
1972	159.7	135.2	142.4	10.35	11.03	10.26	9.86

Notes. See the text for the definition of low and higher real income. The entries in the last four columns are to be divided by 100.

(6.6) for different utility levels can be substantial. For example, the decline of the cost of meat in 1953 at the low real-income level is less than one-sixth of that at the higher level. Also, the indexes do not necessarily move in the same direction. This is illustrated in 1971, where the cost of meat decreased at the low level of real income and increased slightly at the higher level.

The second and third columns of Table 13.11 give (6.6) in index form with base 1950 = 100. They show that the cost of meat was higher in 1972 than in 1950 at both levels of real income, but that the increase was smaller at the low level than at the higher level.

13.7 Predicting the Change in the Cost of Living

In this section we assume that $DP_t = \sum_i \bar{w}_{it} Dp_{it}$, the change in the cost of living evaluated at the utility level which corresponds to the geometric means of the incomes and prices of $t-1$ and t, is the object of our interest. Specifically, we assume that price data for year t have just been published but that – as is frequently the case – detailed quantity data for that year are not yet available. Hence $\bar{w}_{it} = \frac{1}{2}(w_{i,t-1} + w_{it})$ is unknown. Let $w_{1s}, \ldots, w_{ns}$ for some year $s<t$ be the most recent budget shares that are available, so that we can compute $\sum_i w_{is} Dp_{it}$. How close is this to DP_t? Can we use an estimated demand model to improve the approximation?

Updating Lagged Budget Shares

To answer these questions we use the identity

$$DP_t = \sum_{i=1}^{n} w_{is} Dp_{it} + \sum_{i=1}^{n} (\bar{w}_{it} - w_{is})\, Dp_{it} \tag{7.1}$$

and we assume that the behavior of the n prices and of real income is known up to year t. We also introduce, for any positive variable x, the notation

$$(Dx_t)_s = Dx_{s+1} + \cdots + Dx_{t-1} + \tfrac{1}{2} Dx_t \qquad s<t \tag{7.2}$$

so that $(Dp_{it})_s$ for each i and $(DQ_t)_s$ are known. In the next subsection we derive the following estimate of $\bar{w}_{it} - w_{is}$:

(7.3) Estimate of $\bar{w}_{it} - w_{is}$

$$= (\mu_i - w_i)(DQ_t)_s + w_i \left[(Dp_{it})_s - \sum_{j=1}^{n} w_j (Dp_{jt})_s \right] + \sum_{j=1}^{n} \pi_{ij} (Dp_{jt})_s$$

where π_{ij} is the $(i,j)^{\text{th}}$ Slutsky coefficient and w_i on the right is to be determined iteratively. First, we substitute w_{is} for w_i in (7.3), which yields an initial estimate of $\bar{w}_{it}$. The average of this initial estimate and w_{is} is substituted for w_i in the next round, after which the procedure is continued until convergence. Hence, after convergence, w_i in the right-hand side of (7.3) is the average of w_{is} and the converged estimate of $\bar{w}_{it}$. The latter estimate is then substituted in (7.1), which yields a corrected estimate of DP_t.

Derivations for Lagged Budget Shares

The estimate (7.3) is based on the view that $\bar{w}_{it}$ is approximately equal to the ith budget share in the 12-month period from the middle of year $t-1$ until the middle of year t. Hence, according to this view, $\bar{w}_{it} - w_{is}$ is the change in this share from year s until this 12-month period. By extending the familiar decomposition

$$\Delta w_{it} \approx \bar{w}_{it} Dp_{it} + \bar{w}_{it} Dq_{it} - \bar{w}_{it} Dm_t$$

to the transition from s until this period and using the notation (7.2), we obtain

$$\bar{w}_{it} - w_{is} \approx w_i (Dp_{it})_s + w_i (Dq_{it})_s - w_i (Dm_t)_s$$

where w_i on the right is the average of w_{is} and $\bar{w}_{it}$. This result can be written as

$$\text{(7.4)} \qquad \bar{w}_{it} - w_{is} \approx w_i (Dq_{it})_s - w_i (DQ_t)_s + w_i \left[(Dp_{it})_s - \sum_{j=1}^{n} w_j (Dp_{jt})_s \right]$$

when we use the approximation

$$\text{(7.5)} \qquad (Dm_t)_s \approx (DQ_t)_s + \sum_{j=1}^{n} w_j (Dp_{jt})_s$$

Next add the ith demand equations in absolute prices for t and $t-1$:

$$\text{(7.6)} \qquad \bar{w}_{i,t-1} Dq_{i,t-1} + \bar{w}_{it} Dq_{it}$$

$$= \mu_i (DQ_{t-1} + DQ_t) + \sum_{j=1}^{n} \pi_{ij} (Dp_{j,t-1} + Dp_{jt}) + \varepsilon_{i,t-1} + \varepsilon_{it}$$

The left-hand side can be written, for any θ_i, as the sum of three terms:

$$\theta_i (Dq_{i,t-1} + Dq_{it}) + (\bar{w}_{i,t-1} - \theta_i)\, Dq_{i,t-1} + (\bar{w}_{it} - \theta_i)\, Dq_{it}$$

Since $\bar{w}_{i,t-1}$ and $\bar{w}_{it}$ are usually close to each other, the last two terms tend to be small compared with the first when θ_i is between $\bar{w}_{i,t-1}$ and $\bar{w}_{it}$, so that we can use $\theta_i (Dq_{i,t-1} + Dq_{it})$ as an approximation of the left-hand side of (7.6). By extending this equation to the transition considered in (7.4) and specifying θ_i as the w_i of (7.4), we obtain

$$w_i (Dq_{it})_s \approx \mu_i (DQ_t)_s + \sum_{j=1}^{n} \pi_{ij} (Dp_{jt})_s + \varepsilon_{i,s+1} + \cdots + \varepsilon_{i,t-1} + \tfrac{1}{2} \varepsilon_{it}$$

Substitution of this result in (7.4), with the disturbances replaced by their expectations (zero), yields (7.3).

Lagged Conditional Budget Shares

The within-group version of (7.1) is

$$\text{(7.7)} \qquad DP_{gt} = \sum_{i \in S_g} \frac{w_{is}}{W_{gs}} Dp_{it} + \sum_{i \in S_g} \left(\frac{\bar{w}_{it}}{\bar{W}_{gt}} - \frac{w_{is}}{W_{gs}} \right) Dp_{it}$$

To estimate the second term on the right, we extend eqs. (3.4) and (3.16) of Section 7.3 as follows:

$$\text{(7.8)} \qquad \frac{\bar{w}_{it}}{\bar{W}_{gt}} - \frac{w_{is}}{W_{gs}} \approx \frac{w_i}{W_g}\left[(Dp_{it})_s + (Dq_{it})_s - (DP_{gt})_s - (DQ_{gt})_s\right]$$

$$\text{(7.9)} \qquad \frac{w_i}{W_g}(Dq_{it})_s \approx \frac{\mu_i}{M_g}(DQ_{gt})_s + \sum_{j \in S_g} \pi_{ij}^*(Dp_{jt})_s + \text{disturbance}$$

We approximate $(DP_{gt})_s$ by $\sum_j (w_j/W_g)(Dp_{jt})_s$ in (7.8), after which we substitute (7.9) with the disturbance replaced by zero. This yields

$$\text{(7.10)} \qquad \text{Estimate of } \frac{\bar{w}_{it}}{\bar{W}_{gt}} - \frac{w_{is}}{W_{gs}} = \left(\frac{\mu_i}{M_g} - \frac{w_i}{W_g}\right)(DQ_{gt})_s + \frac{w_i}{W_g}\left[(Dp_{it})_s - \sum_{j \in S_g} \frac{w_j}{W_g}(Dp_{jt})_s\right] + \sum_{j \in S_g} \pi_{ij}^*(Dp_{jt})_s$$

which is the within-group version of (7.3). The iteration involves the conditional budget share w_i/W_g, starting at w_{is}/W_{gs} and ending (after convergence is reached) at the average of w_{is}/W_{gs} and the converged estimate of $\bar{w}_{it}/\bar{W}_{gt}$. Note that, when (7.10) is applied to the four meats, the use of $(DQ_{gt})_s$ and $(Dp_{jt})_s$ amounts to assuming that the changes in the volume of total-meat consumption and in the four meat prices are known with adequate precision up to year t.

Uncorrected Predictions of the Change in the Cost of Meat

The first right-hand term of (7.7) may be viewed as a prediction of DP_{gt} conditionally on the Dp_{it}'s and the budget shares of the earlier year s. We use four values of s for the meats, viz., $s=t-k$ for $k=1,\ldots,4$. The first value ($s=t-1$) implies that, when the prices of year t become available, which is sometime in year $t+1$, the most recent budget shares are those of year $t-1$. For the last value the budget shares of $t-4$ are the most recent, which amounts to a five-year time difference relative to year $t+1$ in which the computations are made.

The predictions $\sum_i (w_{is}/W_{gs})\, Dp_{it}$ are shown in the first five columns of Table 13.12, together with the predictand DP_{gt}. Note the dots in the columns of $s=t-2$, $t-3$ and $t-4$. They indicate that the predictions for these years cannot be made because they require data prior to 1950. There are 19 values of DP_{gt} which are predicted for each s (from 1953–54 onward).

A row-by-row comparison of the first five columns of Table 13.12 shows that the predictions are usually close to DP_{gt}. To provide further insight,

TABLE 13.12

UNCORRECTED AND CORRECTED PREDICTIONS OF THE LOG-CHANGES IN THE COST OF MEAT, 1950–1972

	DP_{gt}	$s=t-1$	$s=t-2$	$s=t-3$	$s=t-4$	$s=t-1$	$s=t-2$	$s=t-3$	$s=t-4$
		Uncorrected predictions				*Corrected predictions*			
1950–51	10.55	10.63	.	.	.	10.60	.	.	.
1951–52	−1.94	−1.94	−1.94	.	.	−1.94	−1.95	.	.
1952–53	−6.87	−6.76	−6.03	−6.58	.	−6.86	−6.57	−6.88	.
1953–54	−.98	−1.01	−1.01	−.97	−.97	−.98	−.99	−.95	−.94
1954–55	−6.66	−6.75	−6.83	−6.90	−7.23	−6.67	−6.81	−6.81	−6.97
1955–56	−4.29	−4.29	−4.33	−4.42	−4.46	−4.25	−4.27	−4.33	−4.35
1956–57	8.24	8.21	8.29	8.38	8.38	8.25	8.35	8.35	8.40
1957–58	9.31	9.30	9.26	9.20	9.10	9.31	9.24	9.29	9.24
1958–59	−4.66	−4.73	−4.81	−4.83	−4.97	−4.64	−4.73	−4.85	−4.87
1959–60	−1.27	−1.26	−1.22	−1.22	−1.21	−1.26	−1.25	−1.25	−1.24
1960–61	−1.12	−1.14	−1.06	−1.10	−1.05	−1.13	−1.05	−1.10	−1.01
1961–62	3.16	3.16	3.16	3.12	3.11	3.16	3.16	3.12	3.14
1962–63	−3.51	−3.50	−3.51	−3.50	−3.50	−3.50	−3.51	−3.51	−3.51
1963–64	−2.04	−2.03	−2.03	−2.02	−2.02	−2.04	−2.04	−2.03	−2.04
1964–65	8.30	8.30	8.38	8.44	8.48	8.32	8.37	8.37	8.39
1965–66	6.19	6.16	6.14	6.23	6.27	6.14	6.16	6.22	6.22
1966–67	−3.93	−3.96	−3.88	−3.82	−3.89	−3.91	−3.79	−3.78	−3.81
1967–68	3.29	3.28	3.26	3.28	3.30	3.28	3.30	3.33	3.33
1968–69	9.65	9.65	9.63	9.60	9.63	9.65	9.65	9.64	9.67
1969–70	2.58	2.56	2.58	2.60	2.56	2.57	2.60	2.61	2.60
1970–71	.05	−.04	.04	−.06	−.20	−.01	.12	.03	−.04
1971–72	10.35	10.35	10.42	10.34	10.39	10.35	10.42	10.34	10.40
1953–72	32.69	32.25	32.50	32.34	31.73	32.65	32.92	32.70	32.62

Note. All entries are to be divided by 100.

prediction errors are given in Table 13.13 with an extra decimal place. They are defined as

$$e_{st} = \sum_{i=1}^{4} \frac{w_{is}}{W_{gs}} Dp_{it} - DP_{gt} \tag{7.11}$$

It appears that the prediction errors for $s=t-1$ are negative in 17 cases out of 22, indicating that the associated predictions are too low. This is not entirely surprising. To clarify this we write the log-change in the cost-of-living index as

$$\begin{aligned} DP_t &= \tfrac{1}{2} \sum_{i=1}^{n} w_{i,t-1} Dp_{it} + \tfrac{1}{2} \sum_{i=1}^{n} w_{it} Dp_{it} \\ &= \sum_{i=1}^{n} w_{i,t-1} Dp_{it} + \tfrac{1}{2} \left[\sum_{i=1}^{n} w_{it} Dp_{it} - \sum_{i=1}^{n} w_{i,t-1} Dp_{it} \right] \end{aligned}$$

TABLE 13.13

THE ERRORS OF THE UNCORRECTED AND THE CORRECTED PREDICTIONS

	$\sqrt{\Pi_{gt}}$	$s=t-1$,	$s=t-2$,	$s=t-3$,	$s=t-4$	$s=t-1$,	$s=t-2$,	$s=t-3$,	$s=t-4$
		Uncorrected predictions				*Corrected predictions*			
1950–51	4.57	.079	.	.	.	.052	.	.	.
1951–52	1.07	−.007	−.003	.	.	−.005	−.009	.	.
1952–53	14.97	.101	.840	.286	.	.003	.298	−.019	.
1953–54	4.01	−.021	−.027	.015	.010	.002	−.009	.036	.047
1954–55	8.02	−.092	−.176	−.244	−.572	−.011	−.153	−.150	−.314
1955–56	3.83	−.005	−.043	−.138	−.173	.036	.013	−.044	−.063
1956–57	5.55	−.025	.056	.147	.143	.014	.109	.116	.167
1957–58	5.11	−.011	−.059	−.115	−.214	−.001	−.076	−.025	−.073
1958–59	6.95	−.077	−.151	−.175	−.313	.011	−.079	−.200	−.212
1959–60	1.13	.011	.046	.051	.061	.011	.017	.018	.034
1960–61	4.74	−.020	.060	.019	.071	−.008	.066	.018	.106
1961–62	1.83	−.008	−.000	−.044	−.050	−.005	−.001	−.044	−.029
1962–63	1.25	.004	−.003	.003	.005	.004	−.001	−.002	.001
1963–64	.63	.008	.016	.019	.019	.006	.007	.008	.007
1964–65	5.59	−.000	.087	.138	.182	.022	.077	.072	.095
1965–66	4.02	−.030	−.046	.039	.081	−.046	−.026	.031	.028
1966–67	4.75	−.036	.044	.109	.040	.013	.133	.145	.118
1967–68	2.09	−.017	−.028	−.008	.004	−.009	.009	.042	.036
1968–69	1.53	−.005	−.019	−.053	−.024	−.002	−.008	−.018	.016
1969–70	2.47	−.016	.005	.019	−.015	−.010	.018	.033	.018
1970–71	7.20	−.093	−.014	−.118	−.251	−.062	.070	−.019	−.091
1971–72	4.90	−.008	.067	−.010	.040	−.003	.065	−.009	.041

Note. All entries are to be divided by 100.

The expression in brackets was considered in eq. (2.11) of Section 11.2, from which we concluded that it is normally positive. When we extend this conclusion to the four-meat group, it amounts to a predominance of negative errors (7.11) for $s=t-1$.

It is appropriate to add that this effect is not large in size. When we raise the predictions for $s=t-1$ by 10^{-4}, which amounts to adding .01 to each figure in the second column of Table 13.13, six negative errors in that column become positive, so that the majority of negative values is eliminated. Note also that there is no such dominance of negative errors for values of s other than $t-1$.

Weighted Mean Square Errors

The errors (7.11) are necessarily zero when the prices of the four meats change proportionally. Such errors can be large (positive or negative) only if there is a large dispersion among the four price log-changes. This matter is pursued in Table 13.14, the first three lines of which are based on a grouping of the 22 observations according to the budget-share-weighted standard deviation of $Dp_{1t}, \ldots, Dp_{4t}$. These standard deviations (from Table 13.9) are shown in the first column of Table 13.13; their budget-share-weighted form is a natural choice, given that the predictand DP_{gt} is identically weighted. The figures in line (1) of Table 13.14 are the medians of $|e_{st}|$ over all t for which $\sqrt{\Pi_{gt}}$ is less than .03. Line (2) contains the medians for standard deviations between .03 and .05, and line (3) for standard deviations larger than .05.

It is clear from these lines that there is a systematic tendency towards larger errors when Π_{gt} increases. To take this into consideration, we shall evaluate the accuracy of the predictions by means of the weighted mean square error,

$$(7.12) \qquad \frac{1}{19} \sum_t \frac{e_{st}^2}{\Pi_{gt}}$$

where the summation over t is over the last 19 observations; this insures that we use the same set of observations for each s (from 1953–54 onward).

TABLE 13.14

SUMMARY MEASURES OF PREDICTION ERRORS

	$s=t-1$	$s=t-2$	$s=t-3$	$s=t-4$
	Median absolute errors[a]			
(1) $\sqrt{\Pi_{gt}} < .03$	.01	.01	.02	.02
(2) $.03 < \sqrt{\Pi_{gt}} < .05$	.02	.05	.03	.06
(3) $\sqrt{\Pi_{gt}} > .05$	.08	.09	.15	.23
	Weighted mean square errors[b]			
(4) Uncorrected	.54	2.52	5.47	10.30
(5) Corrected	.31	1.61	2.51	3.92
	Average information inaccuracies[b]			
(6) Uncorrected	.65	4.24	10.18	16.53
(7) Corrected	.50	2.68	5.28	8.04

[a] All entries are to be divided by 100. For even numbers of observations the median is computed by arranging the absolute values of the errors in ascending order and taking the arithmetic average of the two middle values.

[b] All entries are to be multiplied by 10^{-4}.

Line (4) of Table 13.14 contains the mean squares (7.12) for the four values of s. They clearly show how the predictions become less accurate when they are based on less recent budget shares.

The Corrected Predictions

Corrected predictions are obtained from (7.10), based on the estimated price coefficients (1.1) of Section 13.1 and the observed values of $(Dp_{it})_s$ and $(DQ_{gt})_s$. The iterative procedure described below (7.10) converges fast; six or seven iterations are usually sufficient to obtain stability in the first nine digits. To evaluate the merits of this revision of the conditional budget shares, we use the average information inaccuracy. For the shares used by the uncorrected predictions, this average inaccuracy takes the form

$$\frac{1}{19}\sum_t \sum_{i=1}^{4} \frac{\bar{w}_{it}}{\bar{W}_{gt}} \log \frac{\bar{w}_{it}/\bar{W}_{gt}}{w_{is}/W_{gs}} \tag{7.13}$$

where the summation over t is over the last 19 observations. These average inaccuracies are shown in line (6) of Table 13.14. The figures in line (7) are obtained by substituting the converged estimates derived from (7.10) for w_{is}/W_{gs} in (7.13). Line (5) contains the weighted mean square errors of the corrected predictions. They are of the form (7.12), with e_{st} interpreted as the error of the corrected prediction of DP_{gt}. The corrected predictions and their errors are shown in the last four columns of Tables 13.12 and 13.13.

A comparison of lines (4) and (5) and of lines (6) and (7) of Table 13.14 shows that the correction is successful. In particular, the weighted mean square error of the corrected predictions for $s=t-3$ is approximately equal to that of the uncorrected predictions for $s=t-2$. This means that the availability of an estimated demand model is worth one year of data at $s=t-3$. For $s=t-4$ it is worth between one and two years of data, since the corrected mean square error of $s=t-4$ is between the uncorrected mean squares of $s=t-2$ and $s=t-3$.

Also, the correction eliminates the majority of negative errors for $s=t-1$. This follows from Table 13.13, which shows that the errors of the 22 corrected predictions for $s=t-1$ are equally often positive and negative, and from the last row of Table 13.12, which contains the total log-change of the cost of meat from 1953 to 1972 and the eight predictions of this log-change. The error of the uncorrected prediction for $s=t-1$ is $32.25-32.69=-.44$ ($\times 10^{-2}$), and that of the corrected prediction is only a small fraction of this value.

CHAPTER 14

CHANGES IN QUANTITY AND QUALITY AND DECOMPOSITIONS BY COMMODITY GROUPS

This chapter presents numerical evidence on various summary measures of the consumer's basket, in addition to the means and variances of the price log-changes discussed in Section 13.4. A second objective of this chapter is a systematic discussion of the relationship between summary measures of the basket as a whole and the corresponding measures between and within commodity groups. The applications are based, as in Chapter 13, on the Dutch 14-commodity model and the American meat model.

14.1 Changes in Quantity and Quality

The 14-Commodity Basket: Real Income and Quality

Real income is the volume index of the full basket. For $n=14$ its log-change and that of the quality index are

$$DQ_t = \sum_{i=1}^{14} \bar{w}_{it} Dq_{it} \qquad DQ'_t - DQ_t = \sum_{i=1}^{14} (\mu_i - \bar{w}_{it})\, Dq_{it} \tag{1.1}$$

These log-changes, both of which are invariant under the preference independence transformation, are shown in the first two columns of Table 14.1. The figures in parentheses in the second column are standard errors; they describe the inaccuracy of the estimated quality log-changes which results from the use of estimates of the marginal shares in $DQ'_t = \sum_i \mu_i Dq_{it}$. They are computed, similarly to the expression (4.3) of Section 13.4, as the square root of

$$\sum_{i=1}^{14} \sum_{j=1}^{14} Dq_{it} Dq_{jt} \operatorname{cov}(\hat{\mu}_i, \hat{\mu}_j) \tag{1.2}$$

where $\operatorname{cov}(\hat{\mu}_i, \hat{\mu}_j)$ stands for the covariance of the mixed estimates of μ_i and μ_j given in Table 6.15 on page 307 of Volume 1.

The last three lines of Table 14.1 show that the log-change in real per capita income from 1922 to 1939 is .104, which amounts to an average annual increase of .104/17 or about six-tenths of 1 percent, after which

TABLE 14.1

REAL INCOME AND QUALITY OF THE 14-COMMODITY MODEL

	DQ_t	$DQ'_t - DQ_t$	Components of $DQ'_t - DQ_t$		
			Real income	Substitution	Disturbance
		Between Wars			
1922–23	−1.82	−.60 (.11)	−.60	.82	−.83
1923–24	−.59	.10 (.18)	−.21	.01	.30
1924–25	−1.12	.30 (.21)	−.40	.01	.69
1925–26	3.23	.17 (.17)	1.18	.01	−1.02
1926–27	2.27	.91 (.10)	.80	−.24	.35
1927–28	2.76	.15 (.04)	.93	.02	−.80
1928–29	1.40	.31 (.11)	.46	−.23	.08
1929–30	3.89	−.11 (.21)	1.29	−.54	−.86
1930–31	.11	−1.17 (.15)	.04	−.51	−.71
1931–32	−1.03	.17 (.12)	−.39	.42	.14
1932–33	−.76	.77 (.15)	−.30	.96	.10
1933–34	−3.01	−1.86 (.16)	−1.31	.73	−1.28
1934–35	−1.09	−.66 (.08)	−.52	−.05	−.09
1935–36	2.89	2.93 (.20)	1.37	2.03	−.47
1936–37	−1.07	−.83 (.09)	−.49	−.57	.23
1937–38	−.81	−2.27 (.18)	−.39	−.29	−1.60
1938–39	5.19	1.87 (.15)	2.34	−.58	.10
		After World War II			
1951–52	−.94	−1.66 (.14)	−.33	−.13	−1.20
1952–53	4.89	.99 (.09)	1.84	.10	−.96
1953–54	5.35	2.44 (.19)	1.82	.46	.15
1954–55	5.60	2.26 (.20)	1.65	.10	.51
1955–56	6.52	1.39 (.23)	1.68	−.29	−.01
1956–57	−.57	.87 (.22)	−.14	.90	.10
1957–58	−.68	−.80 (.11)	−.18	.00	−.62
1958–59	2.92	.70 (.08)	.80	.14	−.24
1959–60	5.50	1.56 (.13)	1.38	−.08	.26
1960–61	4.20	1.00 (.13)	.94	.07	−.01
1961–62	3.68	.74 (.11)	.78	.18	−.22
1962–63	5.32	1.17 (.16)	1.06	.17	−.06
		Three-period summary			
1922–39	10.4	.2	3.8	2.0	−5.6
1939–51	−6.2	−5.9	−2.4	−4.1	.6
1951–63	41.8	10.7	11.3	1.6	−2.3

Note. All entries are to be divided by 100.

it declined in the period 1939–51. It was not before 1954 that real income exceeded the 1939 level. From 1952 to 1963 there was an almost uninterrupted increase in the standard of living, amounting to an increase in real per capita income of almost 4 percent per year.

The quality index was subject to small year-to-year increases during most of the 1920s, although several of these estimates are not significantly different from zero. The annual changes during the 1930s were larger; among these the negative values tend to dominate. The result is that the change from 1922 to 1939 is virtually zero. From 1939 to 1951 the index declined by about 6 percent, after which there was an increase. It took until 1957 before the quality index returned to the 1939 level.

The Components of the 14-Commodity Quality Index

The log-change in the quality index defined in (1.1) consists of the following three components according to eq. (7.18) of Section 12.7:

(1.3) Real income: $$DQ_t \sum_{i=1}^{14} \bar{w}_{it}\left(\frac{\mu_i}{\bar{w}_{it}} - 1\right)^2$$

(1.4) Substitution: $$\sum_{i=1}^{14} \sum_{j=1}^{14} \nu_{ij}(Dp_{it} - DP'_t)\frac{\mu_j}{\bar{w}_{jt}}$$

(1.5) Disturbances: $$\sum_{i=1}^{14} \frac{\mu_i}{\bar{w}_{it}} \varepsilon_{it}$$

Recall from Section 12.7 that the real-income and disturbance components of the quality index are invariant under the preference independence transformation, and that the substitution component can be identified with ϕ times the marginally weighted covariance of the price log-changes and the income elasticities of the T-goods.

The components (1.3) to (1.5), based on the mixed estimates of the μ's and on the revised estimates (2.4) and (2.5) of Section 13.2, are shown in the last three columns of Table 14.1. The 1922–39 row reveals that the near-zero net change in the quality index from 1922 to 1939 is the result of small positive real-income and substitution contributions and a slightly larger negative disturbance contribution. The result for 1939–51 is more interesting; the decline in quality appears to be largely a matter of substitution, with the real-income effect playing a secondary role. The large substitution component of 1939–51 results mainly from the government price control, which allowed prices of luxuries to increase faster than those of necessities.

The postwar development amounts to a reversal of the change from 1939 to 1951, particularly after 1952, and it is only after this year that the quality index of the Dutch commodity basket was subject to a sustained increase. The total log-change in the index from 1952 to 1963 was .123, which amounts to an average annual increase of the index of about 1.1 percent. This total log-change in quality consists of real-income, substitution and disturbance components equal to .116, .018 and −.011, respectively. The real-income component was the dominant force behind the quality index in the postwar period.

It should be noted that when we cumulate over time, as is done in the last three lines of Table 14.1, the disturbance component may take relatively large values. The reason is that, if the disturbances are serially independent, the sum of (1.5) over t is a random variable with a variance equal to the sum of the variances of the disturbance components that are added.

The Quality Index of a Commodity Group

The within-group extension of DQ'_t is the weighted mean of the Dq_{it}'s with the conditional marginal shares as weights:

$$DQ'_{gt} = \sum_{i \in S_g} \frac{\mu_i}{M_g} Dq_{it} \tag{1.6}$$

This leads immediately to the quality index of the group S_g with the following log-change:

$$DQ'_{gt} - DQ_{gt} = \sum_{i \in S_g} \left(\frac{\mu_i}{M_g} - \frac{\bar{w}_{it}}{\bar{W}_{gt}} \right) Dq_{it} \tag{1.7}$$

Since the right-hand side can be written as

$$\sum_{i \in S_g} \frac{\bar{w}_{it}}{\bar{W}_{gt}} \left(\frac{\mu_i / \bar{w}_{it}}{M_g / \bar{W}_{gt}} - 1 \right) Dq_{it}$$

we conclude that $DQ'_{gt} - DQ_{gt}$ equals the budget-share-weighted covariance of the quantity log-changes and the conditional income elasticities of S_g:

$$DQ'_{gt} - DQ_{gt} = \sum_{i \in S_g} \frac{\bar{w}_{it}}{\bar{W}_{gt}} (Dq_{it} - DQ_{gt}) \left(\frac{\mu_i / \bar{w}_{it}}{M_g / \bar{W}_{gt}} - 1 \right) \tag{1.8}$$

This result should be compared with eq. (3.3) of Section 11.3. It clearly shows that the quality of the S_g basket goes up when its composition shifts in the direction of its more luxurious commodities.

Note that the definition (1.6) presupposes that the conditional marginal shares exist. This is always true under block-independence because M_g is then positive. It is also true under blockwise dependence. Here we proceed under the more restrictive condition; the extension to blockwise dependence is described in Section 14.5.

The Three Components of the Quality Index of a Group

Under block-independence we can use the conditional demand equation (1.6) of Section 7.1:

$$\bar{w}_{it} Dq_{it} = \frac{\mu_i}{M_g} \bar{W}_{gt} DQ_{gt} + \sum_{j \in S_g} \nu_{ij} (Dp_{jt} - DP'_{gt}) + \varepsilon^g_{it} \tag{1.9}$$

It is shown in the next subsection that, when (1.9) is substituted in (1.7), the log-change in the quality index of the group S_g emerges as the sum of a volume, a substitution, and a disturbance component:

$$\text{Volume}: \quad DQ_{gt} \sum_{i \in S_g} \frac{\bar{w}_{it}}{\bar{W}_{gt}} \left(\frac{\mu_i/\bar{w}_{it}}{M_g/\bar{W}_{gt}} - 1 \right)^2 \tag{1.10}$$

$$\text{Substitution}: \quad \frac{\phi M_g}{\bar{W}_{gt}} \sum_{i \in S_g} \sum_{j \in S_g} \frac{\nu_{ij}}{\phi M_g} (Dp_{it} - DP'_{gt}) \frac{\mu_j/\bar{w}_{jt}}{M_g/\bar{W}_{gt}} \tag{1.11}$$

$$\text{Disturbances}: \quad \frac{1}{M_g} \sum_{i \in S_g} \frac{\mu_i}{\bar{w}_{it}} \varepsilon^g_{it} = \frac{1}{\bar{W}_{gt}} \sum_{i \in S_g} \frac{\mu_i/\bar{w}_{it}}{M_g/\bar{W}_{gt}} \varepsilon^g_{it} \tag{1.12}$$

Note that (1.10) is a volume component, not a real-income component, and that the volume log-change DQ_{gt} is multiplied by the budget-share-weighted variance of the conditional income elasticities of the commodities of S_g. The substitution component is equal to the own-price elasticity of the group $(\phi M_g/\bar{W}_{gt})$ multiplied by a bilinear form in the deflated price log-changes and the conditional income elasticities. The matrix of this bilinear form, $[\nu_{ij}/\phi M_g]$, is the price coefficient submatrix normalized within the group. The reader may want to compare this with (1.4) after replacing ν_{ij} in (1.4) by ν_{ij}/ϕ and multiplying the whole expression by ϕ.

Derivation of the Three Components

To verify these components we write (1.7) as

$$DQ'_{gt} - DQ_{gt} = -DQ_{gt} + \sum_{i \in S_g} \frac{\mu_i/M_g}{\bar{w}_{it}} \bar{w}_{it} Dq_{it} \tag{1.13}$$

By substituting the right-hand side of (1.9) for $\bar{w}_{it}Dq_{it}$, we obtain a volume component equal to DQ_{gt} multiplied by

$$-1+\sum_{i\in S_g}\frac{(\mu_i/M_g)^2}{\bar{w}_{it}/\bar{W}_{gt}}=-1+\sum_{i\in S_g}\frac{\bar{w}_{it}}{\bar{W}_{gt}}\left(\frac{\mu_i/\bar{w}_{it}}{M_g/\bar{W}_{gt}}\right)^2$$

The sum on the right is the budget-share-weighted second moment of the conditional income elasticities. Since -1 can be viewed as minus the square of the identically weighted mean of the same elasticities, this proves (1.10).

Similarly, substitution of (1.9) in (1.13) gives the following substitution component:

$$\sum_{i\in S_g}\frac{\mu_i/M_g}{\bar{w}_{it}}\sum_{j\in S_g}\nu_{ij}(Dp_{jt}-DP'_{gt})=\frac{1}{M_g}\sum_{i\in S_g}\sum_{j\in S_g}\nu_{ij}(Dp_{jt}-DP'_{gt})\frac{\mu_i}{\bar{w}_{it}}$$

The right-hand side equals (1.11) in view of the symmetry of $[\nu_{ij}]$. The two alternative expressions in (1.12) for the disturbance component can be derived in the same way.

The Volume and Quality of Meat Consumption

The volume log-change of total-meat consumption, reproduced from Table 7.3 on page 12, is shown in the first column of Table 14.2, followed by the log-change in the quality index of meat consumption and its three components. Using eq. (3.8) of Section 7.3, we can simplify the substitution and disturbance components (1.11) and (1.12) as follows:

$$(1.14)\qquad \text{Substitution:}\quad \sum_{i=1}^{4}\sum_{j=1}^{4}\nu_{ij}^{*}(Dp_{it}-DP'_{gt})\frac{\mu_j/\bar{w}_{jt}}{M_g/\bar{W}_{gt}}$$

$$(1.15)\qquad \text{Disturbances:}\quad \sum_{i=1}^{4}\frac{\mu_i/\bar{w}_{it}}{M_g/\bar{W}_{gt}}\varepsilon_{it}^{*}$$

The first column of Table 14.2 shows that the volume of meat consumption was subject to an annual average increase of $33.93/22\approx 1\frac{1}{2}$ percent per year, with few years of decline. The behavior of the quality index in the second column is quite different. There are as many years in which this index decreased as there are years of an increase. On average the increases are larger than the decreases; the result is an average annual log-change in the quality index from 1950 to 1972 of .0627/22, or less than three-tenths of 1 percent. This does not mean that the index was always subject to small

TABLE 14.2

VOLUME AND QUALITY OF MEAT CONSUMPTION

	DQ_{gt}	$DQ'_{gt} - DQ_{gt}$	Components of $DQ'_{gt} - DQ_{gt}$		
			Volume	Substitution	Disturbances
1950–51	−3.37	−4.53	−1.01	−2.15	−1.37
1951–52	5.57	2.60	1.64	−.06	1.01
1952–53	4.83	8.02	1.26	6.65	.11
1953–54	−.53	1.27	−.13	.06	1.33
1954–55	3.98	−.94	.84	−2.22	.44
1955–56	3.52	−.35	.67	−.80	−.22
1956–57	−3.84	.75	−.70	.76	.69
1957–58	−2.06	−1.45	−.36	−1.50	.41
1958–59	5.05	−1.57	.82	−2.41	.02
1959–60	.23	1.37	.03	.31	1.03
1960–61	.54	.74	.07	.55	.12
1961–62	1.22	−.21	.15	−.38	.02
1962–63	3.92	.33	.47	.05	−.18
1963–64	2.63	.60	.30	.15	.15
1964–65	−3.18	.61	−.37	1.21	−.23
1965–66	3.24	.51	.41	1.04	−.94
1966–67	4.62	−1.02	.59	−1.45	−.16
1967–68	2.60	−.01	.30	−.53	.21
1968–69	.29	−.06	.03	−.19	.10
1969–70	2.67	−.32	.30	−.00	−.61
1970–71	2.53	−1.12	.27	−1.73	.34
1971–72	−.54	1.05	−.05	.58	.52
1950–72	33.93	6.27	5.55	−2.08	2.80

Note. All entries are to be divided by 100.

annual changes. In particular, there was a sizable increase in 1953. The total log-change of .0627 was almost reached in that year; the changes in the 19 subsequent years tend to cancel each other out.

The last row of the table shows that this total log-change from 1950 to 1972 is about equal to its volume component, the substitution and disturbance components both being closer to zero and of opposite signs. However, it would be wrong to conclude that the volume component is the dominant force behind the behavior of the quality index in the separate years. A line-by-line inspection of the table shows that the substitution component is the largest of the three in absolute value in 16 cases out of 22, and the volume component in only three cases. The substitution component of 1952–53 is about four times the largest volume component, and about five times the largest disturbance component. This particular substitution component is mainly the result of the substantial price declines of high-income-elastic Beef and Lamb relative to low-income-elastic Pork (see Table 7.3 on page 12); or, equivalently, of the equally substantial price declines of the Beef/Pork contrast and Lamb relative to Inexpensive meat (see Table 13.9 on page 324).

Also, there are four other substitution components besides that of 1952–53 which exceed the largest volume component in absolute value. Thus we conclude that, although the net change in the quality index of meat consumption from 1950 to 1972 is mainly the result of the volume component, it is the substitution component which dominates the behavior of the index in most of the separate years.

The Variance of the Conditional Income Elasticities

Another feature of interest is the behavior of the variance of the conditional income elasticities in the volume component. As (1.10) shows, this component is obtained by multiplying the variance by DQ_{gt}. On comparing the first and third columns of Table 14.2, we find that this variance is about .3 in the early 1950s and that it gradually decreases to about .1 in the early 1970s. This is largely the result of the increasing conditional budget share of Beef and the decreasing share of Pork, which jointly account for between 80 and 90 percent of the expenditure on the four-meat basket (see Table 7.2 on page 11). When the conditional budget share of Beef increases, its conditional marginal share remaining constant by assumption, the conditional income elasticity of Beef declines in the direction of 1. Similarly, when the conditional budget share of Pork decreases, its conditional income elasticity moves upward in the direction of 1. Hence both changes contribute to a smaller variance of the conditional income elasticities. It follows from (1.10) that the effect on the quality index of a given log-change in total-meat consumption will then decrease over time.

14.2 Price-Quantity Covariances

Covariances of the 14-Commodity Basket

For $n=14$ the price-quantity covariance takes the form

$$\Gamma_t = \sum_{i=1}^{14} \bar{w}_{it}(Dp_{it} - DP_t)(Dq_{it} - DQ_t) \tag{2.1}$$

which consists of three components according to eq. (7.3) of Section 12.7:

(2.2) Real income: $(DP'_t - DP_t)\,DQ_t$

(2.3) Substitution: $\sum_{i=1}^{14}\sum_{j=1}^{14} \nu_{ij}(Dp_{it} - DP'_t)(Dp_{jt} - DP'_t)$

(2.4) Disturbances: $\sum_{i=1}^{14} Dp_{it}\varepsilon_{it}$

We proved in Section 12.7 that Γ_t and its real-income and disturbance components are invariant under the preference independence transformation, and that the substitution component can be written as $\phi\Pi'_t$, with Π'_t defined as the marginally weighted variance of the price log-changes of the T-goods.

The first four columns of Table 14.3 contain Γ_t and its components for each of the 29 observations on the 14-commodity basket. The covariances are negative except in two cases and the largest values are of the order of -20×10^{-4}. The two exceptions (1922–23 and 1926–27) are of minor numerical importance; in both cases Γ_t would have been negative if its real-income component had vanished. The substitution component, which is equal to $\phi = -.6$ multiplied by the relevant entry in column (2) of Table 13.10 (page 327), plays a dominant role for most observations. The disturbance component tends to be second in numerical importance.

The real-income component (2.2) is generally small; it is less in absolute value than 4×10^{-4} in all cases except two (1935–36 and 1938–39). The reason is that DQ_t and $DP'_t - DP_t$ are usually close to zero. However, note the predominance of the negative signs among the postwar real-income components of Γ_t. This is the combined effect of the increase in real income ($DQ_t > 0$) in most of the postwar years and the increase in the cost of living relative to the marginal price index ($DP_t > DP'_t$, see Table 13.8 on page 319).

The Price-Quantity Covariance of a Commodity Group

The price-quantity covariance of the group S_g is defined as

(2.5)
$$\Gamma_{gt} = \sum_{i\in S_g} \frac{\bar{w}_{it}}{\bar{W}_{gt}}(Dp_{it} - DP_{gt})(Dq_{it} - DQ_{gt})$$
$$= \frac{1}{\bar{W}_{gt}} \sum_{i\in S_g} (Dp_{it} - DP_{gt})\,\bar{w}_{it} Dq_{it}$$

Using (1.9), we find that under block-independence Γ_{gt} is the sum of three components:

(2.6) Volume: $(DP'_{gt} - DP_{gt})\,DQ_{gt}$

TABLE 14.3

PRICE-QUANTITY COVARIANCES OF THE DUTCH 14-COMMODITY BASKET AND THE AMERICAN MEAT BASKET

Dutch basket, between wars

	Γ_t	Components of Γ_t: Real income	Substitution	Disturbances
1922–23	2.1	2.6	−7.1	6.6
1923–24	−9.9	.2	−8.0	−2.0
1924–25	−15.2	.6	−6.3	−9.6
1925–26	−13.9	−1.1	−7.6	−5.2
1926–27	.1	.5	−2.9	2.5
1927–28	−1.0	−.4	−1.4	.7
1928–29	−3.7	.4	−6.3	2.2
1929–30	−18.1	−.9	−11.8	−5.4
1930–31	−11.8	.0	−14.2	2.4
1931–32	−19.5	1.1	−19.6	−1.1
1932–33	−22.3	1.1	−20.4	−3.0
1933–34	−1.8	1.2	−7.8	4.8
1934–35	−1.5	.2	−1.8	.1
1935–36	−22.3	−6.2	−17.8	1.7
1936–37	−6.0	−1.2	−7.8	2.9
1937–38	−13.0	−.7	−7.2	−5.1
1938–39	−3.6	6.4	−7.3	−2.8

Dutch basket, after World War II

	Γ_t	Real income	Substitution	Disturbances
1951–52	−8.3	1.4	−23.1	13.5
1952–53	−5.5	−1.4	−2.1	−2.0
1953–54	−12.5	−3.9	−3.7	−4.8
1954–55	−5.4	−2.4	−1.9	−1.0
1955–56	−24.3	−1.3	−13.0	−10.0
1956–57	−12.0	.6	−12.1	−.5
1957–58	−3.3	.2	−3.2	−.3
1958–59	−1.5	−.7	−.9	.1
1959–60	−1.9	−.6	−3.6	2.3
1960–61	−3.7	−.8	−.8	−2.1
1961–62	−10.2	−1.6	−4.3	−4.3
1962–63	−6.6	−2.4	−1.6	−2.7

American meat basket

Γ_{gt}	Components of Γ_{gt}: Volume	Substitution	Disturbances	
−36.6	−8.2	−18.2	−10.1	1950–
.2	.0	−.8	1.0	1951–
−244.9	−35.1	−208.1	−1.6	1952–
−11.7	−.1	−11.5	−.2	1953–
−45.1	8.8	−57.3	3.4	1954–
−13.7	3.9	−10.1	−7.5	1955–
−25.9	2.3	−25.5	−2.7	1956–
−24.0	−3.8	−20.1	−.1	1957–
−32.5	13.6	−44.5	−1.6	1958–
−3.4	−.1	−1.0	−2.3	1959–
−18.4	−.2	−19.9	1.8	1960–
−1.7	.5	−3.1	.9	1961–
−2.4	−.2	−1.3	−.9	1962–
−2.1	−.4	−.4	−1.3	1963–
−31.1	3.9	−30.7	−4.3	1964–
−10.3	−3.6	−15.9	9.2	1965–
−15.1	7.6	−20.4	−2.4	1966–
−.9	1.4	−4.3	1.9	1967–
−1.4	.1	−1.8	.4	1968–
−2.9	.2	−5.3	2.1	1969–
−33.0	4.7	−51.0	13.3	1970–
−22.4	.3	−23.6	.9	1971–

Note. All entries are to be multiplied by 10^{-4}.

(2.7) Substitution : $$\frac{\phi M_g}{\bar{W}_{gt}} \sum_{i \in S_g} \sum_{j \in S_g} \frac{\nu_{ij}}{\phi M_g} (Dp_{it} - DP'_{gt})(Dp_{jt} - DP'_{gt})$$

(2.8) Disturbances : $$\frac{1}{\bar{W}_{gt}} \sum_{i \in S_g} Dp_{it}\varepsilon_{it}^{g}$$

These three components should be compared with (2.2) to (2.4) and also with the components (1.10) to (1.12) of the within-group quality index.

Covariances of the Meat Basket

It follows from eq. (3.8) of Section 7.3 that the components (2.7) and (2.8) can be written as follows for the four meats:

$$\text{(2.9)} \qquad \text{Substitution}: \quad \sum_{i=1}^{4}\sum_{j=1}^{4} v_{ij}^{*}(Dp_{it}-DP'_{gt})(Dp_{jt}-DP'_{gt})$$

$$\text{(2.10)} \qquad \text{Disturbances}: \quad \sum_{i=1}^{4} Dp_{it}\varepsilon_{it}^{*}$$

These two expressions may be compared with (1.14) and (1.15).

The last four columns of Table 14.3 contain Γ_{gt} and its three components for the American meat basket. All covariances except one are negative. Their absolute values tend to be larger than those of Γ_t of the 14-commodity basket in the first column of the table. The substitution component of Γ_{gt} is the largest of the three in 19 cases out of 22, but the volume component is not as small as its real-income counterpart in the second column. In particular, the 1952–53 volume component takes a large negative value. This is due to the large decline in the marginal meat price index relative to the cost-of-meat index ($DP'_{gt}-DP_{gt}=-.073$) combined with the rather large increase in the volume of meat consumption ($DQ_{gt}=.048$), as may be verified from Tables 13.9 and 14.2 on pages 324 and 349, respectively.

14.3 Decomposition of Volume and Price Indexes by Commodity Groups

In Sections 14.1 and 14.2 we introduced within-group extensions of the quality index and the price-quantity covariance. The remainder of this chapter is devoted to a more systematic analysis of groupwise decompositions. In this section we consider price and volume indexes (DP_t, DP'_t, DQ_t), which provide the simplest decompositions.

Three Commodity Groups for the 14-Commodity Basket

Our numerical illustrations will be based on the 14-commodity model, for which we specify the following three commodity groups:

Food (S_1) consisting of six commodities: Bread; Groceries; Dairy products; Vegetables and fruit; Meat; Fish.

Beverages and tobacco (S_2) consisting of three: Beverages; Tobacco; Pastry, chocolate and ice cream.

Durables/Remainder (S_3) consisting of five: Clothing; Footwear; Other durables; Water, light and heat; Other goods and services.

These three groups are identical to those used in Chapter 5 except that Durables and Remainder are combined. The present grouping has the advantage that it agrees with the block structure of the preferred specification of Section 6.7. The budget shares $\bar{W}_{gt}$ of the three groups change over time, but they are approximately .3 for S_1, .1 for S_2 and .6 for S_3. The mixed estimates of the marginal shares are $M_1 = .1689$, $M_2 = .0859$ and $M_3 = .7452$. This shows that the Durables/Remainder group dominates considerably when marginal weights are used.

Volume and Price Indexes of Three Groups

The first three columns of Table 14.4 contain the log-changes in the volume indexes,

$$DQ_{gt} = \sum_{i \in S_g} \frac{\bar{w}_{it}}{\bar{W}_{gt}} Dq_{it} \tag{3.1}$$

where $g = 1$, 2 and 3. The last six columns contain the log-changes in the price indexes of the three groups, budget-share-weighted and marginally weighted:

$$DP_{gt} = \sum_{i \in S_g} \frac{\bar{w}_{it}}{\bar{W}_{gt}} Dp_{it} \qquad DP'_{gt} = \sum_{i \in S_g} \frac{\mu_i}{M_g} Dp_{it} \tag{3.2}$$

The figures in parentheses in the last three columns are standard errors, which measure the uncertainty of the corresponding DP'_{gt} due to the use of estimates of the conditional marginal shares. Their derivation is described in the next subsection. It will be noticed that the standard errors of the first two groups (Food and Beverages and tobacco) tend to be larger than those of the third.

The relationship between the group indexes (3.1) and (3.2) and the corresponding index of the basket is

(3.3)

$$DQ_t = \sum_{g=1}^{3} \bar{W}_{gt} DQ_{gt} \qquad DP_t = \sum_{g=1}^{3} \bar{W}_{gt} DP_{gt} \qquad DP'_t = \sum_{g=1}^{3} M_g DP_{gt}$$

Table 14.5 provides a three-period summary of the left-hand sides of these three equations (reproduced from Tables 13.8 and 14.1) and the corresponding group indexes. The three 1922–39 rows show that, both for volumes and for prices, the net changes in the group indexes during the prewar period are rather close to each other. The postwar development of the volumes

	DQ_{1t}	DQ_{2t}	DQ_{3t}	DP_{1t}	DP_{2t}	DP_{3t}	DP'_{1t}	DP'_{2t}	DP'_{3t}
					Between Wars				
1922–23	.14	−3.46	−2.66	−4.75	−1.23	−4.47	−5.04 (.32)	−1.30 (.13)	−6.32 (.18)
1923–24	−1.12	2.14	−.73	.57	.23	.09	−.19 (.34)	.75 (.28)	−.04 (.12)
1924–25	−5.67	−1.45	1.48	3.31	−.87	−.51	2.34 (.30)	−.97 (.24)	−.27 (.13)
1925–26	4.69	8.55	1.57	−6.88	−6.37	−3.33	−6.94 (.32)	−5.83 (.69)	−4.59 (.14)
1926–27	2.52	−.15	2.53	−3.59	−.34	.10	−4.53 (.24)	−.24 (.10)	−.13 (.03)
1927–28	2.03	3.54	3.02	.94	−.58	.48	1.12 (.11)	−.49 (.10)	.32 (.06)
1928–29	−1.17	2.05	2.61	−.15	−4.87	.13	1.23 (.37)	−5.90 (.48)	.19 (.04)
1929–30	2.24	2.00	4.98	−6.50	−1.21	−3.91	−5.47 (.41)	−1.13 (.22)	−4.88 (.24)
1930–31	3.12	−2.59	−.89	−12.79	−2.26	−4.23	−13.91 (.54)	−1.91 (.22)	−5.10 (.13)
1931–32	2.36	−6.53	−1.74	−14.73	−6.21	−6.25	−17.03 (.58)	−5.16 (.39)	−8.59 (.18)
1932–33	−3.80	−2.41	.79	−1.11	−4.99	−4.73	−1.69 (.80)	−3.64 (.56)	−6.17 (.10)
1933–34	−2.67	−3.88	−3.04	.47	−1.56	−2.40	1.30 (.35)	−.79 (.41)	−2.81 (.09)
1934–35	.21	.22	−1.85	−3.71	−5.42	−3.03	−4.87 (.22)	−4.61 (.26)	−3.21 (.01)
1935–36	−1.43	1.56	5.01	−.97	−2.82	−5.53	−1.84 (.20)	−2.09 (.22)	−7.59 (.17)
1936–37	−.66	1.14	−1.56	6.93	1.20	3.78	8.40 (.32)	.68 (.24)	5.44 (.12)
1937–38	.25	3.13	−1.86	4.21	.38	1.43	5.68 (.45)	.89 (.15)	2.58 (.10)
1938–39	4.44	4.56	5.63	−1.28	.36	1.97	−1.60 (.39)	.29 (.02)	3.16 (.11)
					After World War II				
1951–52	.54	.88	−1.99	4.02	1.12	−1.92	4.07 (.31)	3.53 (.44)	−3.08 (.34)
1952–53	5.05	4.65	4.85	−1.25	−.61	−.84	−2.17 (.28)	−.07 (.12)	−1.15 (.05)
1953–54	4.21	3.69	6.22	3.52	2.30	4.19	3.53 (.31)	1.83 (.29)	3.09 (.12)
1954–55	1.22	2.75	8.22	1.27	.46	1.83	.84 (.23)	.46 (.00)	1.23 (.09)
1955–56	3.10	8.22	7.84	3.94	−.74	1.34	5.09 (.49)	−.71 (.09)	1.19 (.18)
1956–57	−2.44	2.96	−.28	4.74	6.97	4.00	4.38 (.16)	7.78 (.28)	2.65 (.15)
1957–58	2.47	−1.39	−1.99	−2.11	3.87	2.65	−2.24 (.14)	3.64 (.04)	1.56 (.15)
1958–59	1.56	3.64	3.41	1.83	−.17	.70	2.20 (.13)	−.02 (.04)	.40 (.04)
1959–60	3.33	4.02	6.68	−1.01	−.32	3.30	−1.80 (.23)	−.20 (.03)	2.64 (.08)
1960–61	4.21	5.94	3.92	2.02	.47	1.75	2.33 (.16)	.38 (.06)	1.44 (.05)
1961–62	2.45	3.52	4.23	2.95	.82	2.10	2.66 (.44)	.65 (.05)	1.69 (.06)
1962–63	3.40	4.87	6.18	3.32	1.30	2.73	3.18 (.20)	1.18 (.03)	2.22 (.06)

Notes. All entries are to be divided by 100. The standard error of DP'_{2t} in 1954–55 is .003 in three decimal places (also to be divided by 100).

TABLE 14.5

SUMMARY OF VOLUME AND PRICE CHANGES OF THE 14-COMMODITY MODEL

	Complete basket	Food	Beverages and tobacco	Durables/ Remainder
		Volume		
1922–39	10.4	5.5	8.4	13.3
1939–51	−6.2	−9.6	−2.8	−5.4
1951–63	41.8	29.1	43.7	47.3
		Cost of living		
1922–39	−33.9	−40.0	−36.6	−30.4
1939–51	100.0	104.7	112.9	96.0
1951–63	21.7	23.2	15.5	21.8
		Marginal price index		
1922–39	−38.3	−43.1	−31.5	−38.0
1939–51	110.3	113.0	107.1	110.0
1951–63	15.7	22.1	18.5	13.9

Note. All entries are to be divided by 100.

shows a larger range of variation, with Food consumption lagging behind the general trend. This is due partly to the smaller income elasticity of Food relative to those of the two other groups, partly to the faster increase in the marginal price index of Food from 1939 to 1951.

Indeed, the block-independence specification implies that the demand equation for each group can be written as

$$DQ_{gt} = \frac{M_g}{\bar{W}_{gt}} DQ_t + \frac{\phi M_g}{\bar{W}_{gt}} (DP'_{gt} - DP'_t) + \frac{E_{gt}}{\bar{W}_{gt}} \tag{3.4}$$

so that each DQ_{gt} equals the sum of a real-income, a substitution and a disturbance component. We shall not display this in numerical form since (3.4) is equivalent to the sum of a subset of demand equations which were discussed extensively in Section 6.7.

Derivation of Standard Errors

The index DP'_{gt} defined in (3.2) is a nonlinear function of the marginal shares. Let us write it as

$$DP'_{gt} = \frac{\sum_{i \in S_g} \mu_i Dp_{it}}{M_g} = \frac{\sum_{i \in S_g} \mu_i Dp_{it}}{\sum_{i \in S_g} \mu_i} \tag{3.5}$$

Hence the partial derivative of DP'_{gt} with respect to μ_i is $(i \in S_g)$

$$\frac{\partial (DP'_{gt})}{\partial \mu_i} = \frac{M_g Dp_{it} - \sum_{j \in S_g} \mu_j Dp_{jt}}{M_g^2} = \frac{Dp_{it} - DP'_{gt}}{M_g}$$

We approximate DP'_{gt} by a linear function of the μ's, so that its variance becomes

$$\text{(3.6)} \qquad \frac{1}{M_g^2} \sum_{i \in S_g} \sum_{j \in S_g} (Dp_{it} - DP'_{gt})(Dp_{jt} - DP'_{gt}) \operatorname{cov}(\hat{\mu}_i, \hat{\mu}_j)$$

The standard error of DP'_{gt} in Table 14.4 is computed as the square root of (3.6), with M_g and DP'_{gt} approximated by their point estimates and the covariance of $\hat{\mu}_i$ and $\hat{\mu}_j$ by the relevant entry of Table 6.15 on page 307 of Volume 1. Note that the factor $(1/M_g)^2$ before the summation signs in (3.6) has the tendency to yield large standard errors for groups with small M_g's. This applies particularly to Food and to Beverages and tobacco ($g=1$ and 2).

14.4 Means and Variances of Log-changes in Budget Shares

In Section 11.5 we considered $DW'_t = \sum_i \mu_i Dw_{it}$, the marginally weighted mean of the log-changes in the budget shares. Let us write eq. (5.5) of that section as

$$\text{(4.1)} \qquad DW'_t = (DP'_t - DP_t) + (DQ'_t - DQ_t) + O_3$$

where use is made of $DP_t + DQ_t = Dm_t + O_3$. Since the right-hand side of (4.1) contains DP'_t, DP_t and DQ_t, for which we just considered groupwise decompositions, it is natural to ask whether there is a similar decomposition for DW'_t.

The Marginally Weighted Mean of the Budget Share Log-changes

For this purpose we write DW'_t as

$$\begin{aligned} DW'_t &= \sum_{i=1}^{n} \mu_i (\log w_{it} - \log w_{i,t-1}) \\ &= \sum_{g=1}^{G} M_g \sum_{i \in S_g} \frac{\mu_i}{M_g} \left(\log \frac{W_{gt}}{W_{g,t-1}} + \log \frac{w_{it}/W_{gt}}{w_{i,t-1}/W_{g,t-1}} \right) \end{aligned}$$

or, more simply, as

$$\text{(4.2)} \qquad DW'_t = \sum_{g=1}^{G} M_g DW_{gt} + \sum_{g=1}^{G} M_g \left[\sum_{i \in S_g} \frac{\mu_i}{M_g} D\left(\frac{w_{it}}{W_{gt}}\right) \right]$$

where $DW_{gt} = \log W_{gt} - \log W_{g,t-1}$ is the log-change in the budget share of S_g from $t-1$ to t, and

$$D\left(\frac{w_{it}}{W_{gt}}\right) = \log \frac{w_{it}}{W_{gt}} - \log \frac{w_{i,t-1}}{W_{g,t-1}}$$

is the log-change in the conditional budget share of the ith good within its group S_g. It will be noted that the term in brackets in (4.2) requires that the conditional marginal shares exist.

Equation (4.2) is the decomposition between and within groups of the marginal mean of the log-changes in the budget shares. Note that there is no between-group term in the simpler decompositions (3.3), but recall that we did have such a term in eq. (6.24) of Section 12.6 for the degree of utility interaction. We shall shortly see that such terms appear more frequently. The between-group term in (4.2) is the average log-change in the budget shares of the groups, and the within-group term is the average log-change in the conditional budget shares of the commodities within each group, averaged over all groups. All averages are marginally weighted.

Recall from the end of Section 12.7 that DW_t' is invariant under the preference independence transformation. Also recall eq. (5.3) of Section 11.5, which shows that $-DW_t'$ is the change in the distance from the marginal allocation. Hence we obtain a between- and within-group decomposition of this change by simply multiplying (4.2) by -1.

Price and Volume Components of the Marginal Means

The following results are proved in the next subsection:

$$DW_{gt} = (DP_{gt} - DP_t) + (DQ_{gt} - DQ_t) + O_3 \tag{4.3}$$

$$D\left(\frac{w_{it}}{W_{gt}}\right) = (Dp_{it} - DP_{gt}) + (Dq_{it} - DQ_{gt}) + O_3 \tag{4.4}$$

By multiplying (4.3) by M_g and summing over g we obtain

$$\sum_{g=1}^{G} M_g DW_{gt} = \left(\sum_{g=1}^{G} M_g DP_{gt} - DP_t\right) + \left(\sum_{g=1}^{G} M_g DQ_{gt} - DQ_t\right) + O_3 \tag{4.5}$$

which shows that the between-group term of (4.2) can be expressed, apart from an O_3 term, as the sum of a price and a volume component. This is similar to (4.1). Note that $\sum_g M_g DP_{gt}$ and $\sum_g M_g DQ_{gt}$ are both marginally weighted means of group indexes ($DP_{1t}, \ldots, DP_{Gt}$ and $DQ_{1t}, \ldots, DQ_{Gt}$), each of which is budget-share-weighted within its group.

Similarly, by multiplying (4.4) by μ_i/M_g and summing over $i\in S_g$, we obtain

$$\sum_{i\in S_g}\frac{\mu_i}{M_g}D\left(\frac{w_{it}}{W_{gt}}\right)=(DP'_{gt}-DP_{gt})+(DQ'_{gt}-DQ_{gt})+O_3 \tag{4.6}$$

which is the within-group version of (4.1). By adding the price component of (4.5) to the marginally weighted average of the corresponding component of (4.6) for $g=1,\dots,G$, we obtain the price component of (4.1):

$$\left(\sum_{g=1}^{G}M_gDP_{gt}-DP_t\right)+\sum_{g=1}^{G}M_g(DP'_{gt}-DP_{gt})=DP'_t-DP_t \tag{4.7}$$

It may be verified that the volume components have the same property. Hence the between- and within-group decomposition (4.2), with marginal shares used as weights for the within-group term, applies to the price and volume components separately.

Note also that the volume component in (4.1) is the log-change in the quality index of the basket, and that the corresponding component in (4.6) is the log-change in the quality index within S_g defined in (1.7). This raises the question of whether the volume component in (4.5) has a similar interpretation with respect to commodity groups. We shall resolve this question in Section 14.5.

Derivations

We divide eq. (3.2) of Section 7.3 by $\bar{W}_{gt}$,

$$\begin{aligned}\frac{\Delta W_{gt}}{\bar{W}_{gt}}&=DP_{gt}+DQ_{gt}-Dm_t+O_3\\&=(DP_{gt}-DP_t)+(DQ_{gt}-DQ_t)+O_3\end{aligned} \tag{4.8}$$

where the second step is based on $Dm_t=DP_t+DQ_t+O_3$. Next we apply lemma (1.7) of Section 2.1 to W_g as a function of $\log W_g$. Since the derivative of this function is

$$\frac{d(e^{\log W_g})}{d(\log W_g)}=e^{\log W_g}=W_g$$

the lemma implies

$$\Delta W_{gt}=\tfrac{1}{2}(W_{g,t-1}+W_{gt})\log\frac{W_{gt}}{W_{g,t-1}}+O_3=\bar{W}_{gt}DW_{gt}+O_3 \tag{4.9}$$

This result combined with (4.8) yields (4.3) directly. To prove (4.4) we write the left-hand side as $Dw_{it}-DW_{gt}$, after which we use (4.3) for DW_{gt} and $Dw_{it}=Dp_{it}+Dq_{it}-Dm_t$.

Other Means of Budget Share Log-changes

Consider the information expectation

$$I(w_t : w_{t-1}) = \sum_{i=1}^{n} w_{it} \log \frac{w_{it}}{w_{i,t-1}} = \sum_{i=1}^{n} w_{it} Dw_{it} \tag{4.10}$$

The third member is equivalent to $DW'_t = \sum_i \mu_i Dw_{it}$, except that the marginal shares are replaced by current budget shares as weights. So, applying the developments which lead to (4.2), we obtain

$$\sum_{i=1}^{n} w_{it} Dw_{it} = \sum_{g=1}^{G} W_{gt} DW_{gt} + \sum_{g=1}^{G} W_{gt} \left[\sum_{i \in S_g} \frac{w_{it}}{W_{gt}} D\left(\frac{w_{it}}{W_{gt}}\right) \right] \tag{4.11}$$

This may be viewed as a between- and within-group decomposition of the information inaccuracy of no-change extrapolation of budget shares (with w_{it} predicted by $w_{i,t-1}$). In fact, we considered such decompositions in the last subsection of Section 6.4. Note further that the expression in brackets in (4.11) can be written as

$$\sum_{i \in S_g} \frac{w_{it}}{W_{gt}} \log \frac{w_{it}/W_{gt}}{w_{i,t-1}/W_{g,t-1}}$$

which is similar to that used in (7.13) of Section 13.7 for the evaluation of the accuracy of estimates of the conditional budget shares $\bar{w}_{it}/\bar{W}_{gt}$.

When we replace the weight w_{it} by $\bar{w}_{it}$ in the third member of (4.10), we obtain the allocation discrepancy $DW_t = \sum_i \bar{w}_{it} Dw_{it}$. Its decomposition, similar to (4.2) and (4.11), is

$$DW_t = \sum_{g=1}^{G} \bar{W}_{gt} DW_{gt} + \sum_{g=1}^{G} \bar{W}_{gt} \left[\sum_{i \in S_g} \frac{\bar{w}_{it}}{\bar{W}_{gt}} D\left(\frac{w_{it}}{W_{gt}}\right) \right] \tag{4.12}$$

In contrast to (4.11), the two components of (4.12) are of the order O_3.

A Variance Decomposition of Budget Share Log-changes

Consider the following identity:

$$Dw_{it} - DW_t = \left(\sum_{j \in S_g} \frac{\bar{w}_{jt}}{\bar{W}_{gt}} Dw_{jt} - DW_t \right) + \left(Dw_{it} - \sum_{j \in S_g} \frac{\bar{w}_{jt}}{\bar{W}_{gt}} Dw_{jt} \right)$$

We square both sides, multiply by $\bar{w}_{it}$, sum over $i \in S_g$ and then over $g = 1, \ldots, G$, so that we obtain $\sum_i \bar{w}_{it}(Dw_{it} - DW_t)^2$ on the left (sum over $i = 1, \ldots, n$).

The right-hand side becomes

$$\sum_{g=1}^{G} \bar{W}_{gt}\left(\sum_{j\in S_g} \frac{\bar{w}_{jt}}{\bar{W}_{gt}} Dw_{jt} - DW_t\right)^2 + \sum_{g=1}^{G} \bar{W}_{gt} \sum_{i\in S_g} \frac{\bar{w}_{it}}{\bar{W}_{gt}}\left(Dw_{it} - \sum_{j\in S_g} \frac{\bar{w}_{jt}}{\bar{W}_{gt}} Dw_{jt}\right)^2$$

plus the expression

$$2\sum_{g=1}^{G} \bar{W}_{gt}\left(\sum_{j\in S_g} \frac{\bar{w}_{jt}}{\bar{W}_{gt}} Dw_{jt} - DW_t\right) \sum_{i\in S_g} \frac{\bar{w}_{it}}{\bar{W}_{gt}}\left(Dw_{it} - \sum_{j\in S_g} \frac{\bar{w}_{jt}}{\bar{W}_{gt}} Dw_{jt}\right)$$

which is zero. Therefore, the result is

(4.13)

$$\sum_{i=1}^{n} \bar{w}_{it}(Dw_{it} - DW_t)^2 = \sum_{g=1}^{G} \bar{W}_{gt}\left(\sum_{j\in S_g} \frac{\bar{w}_{jt}}{\bar{W}_{gt}} Dw_{jt} - DW_t\right)^2 + \sum_{g=1}^{G} \bar{W}_{gt}\left[\sum_{i\in S_g} \frac{\bar{w}_{it}}{\bar{W}_{gt}}\left(Dw_{it} - \sum_{j\in S_g} \frac{\bar{w}_{jt}}{\bar{W}_{gt}} Dw_{jt}\right)^2\right]$$

This is a between- and within-group decomposition of the weighted variance of the budget share log-changes, with $\bar{w}_{1t}, \ldots, \bar{w}_{nt}$ as weights.

It is interesting that this variance decomposition is close to the decomposition (4.11), which uses the current budget shares $w_{1t}, \ldots, w_{nt}$ as weights. To show this we write the left-hand side of (4.11) as

(4.14)
$$\begin{aligned}\sum_{i=1}^{n} w_{it}Dw_{it} &= \sum_{i=1}^{n} (\bar{w}_{it} + \tfrac{1}{2}\Delta w_{it})\, Dw_{it} \\ &= \tfrac{1}{2}\sum_{i=1}^{n} \Delta w_{it}Dw_{it} + DW_t \\ &= \tfrac{1}{2}\sum_{i=1}^{n} \bar{w}_{it}(Dw_{it})^2 + DW_t + O_4\end{aligned}$$

where the last step is based on $\Delta w_{it} = \bar{w}_{it}Dw_{it} + O_3$, which is the one-commodity version of (4.9). Also,

(4.15)
$$\sum_{i=1}^{n} \bar{w}_{it}(Dw_{it})^2 - \sum_{i=1}^{n} \bar{w}_{it}(Dw_{it} - DW_t)^2 = (DW_t)^2 = O_6$$

because $DW_t = O_3$. By combining (4.14) and (4.15), we find that the leading term of the left-hand side of (4.11) is one-half the leading term of the corresponding side of (4.13). It is shown in the last subsection that the leading term of the between-group component of (4.11) is also one-half that of (4.13), and that the same holds for the average within-group components. See THEIL (1967, Sections 5.7 and 5.C) for a verification based on Dutch data.

The Informational Divergence

When we use $w_{i,t-1}$ instead of w_{it} in (4.14), we obtain

$$\sum_{i=1}^{n} w_{i,t-1} Dw_{it} = \sum_{i=1}^{n} (\bar{w}_{it} - \tfrac{1}{2}\Delta w_{it})\, Dw_{it}$$
$$= -\tfrac{1}{2} \sum_{i=1}^{n} \bar{w}_{it} (Dw_{it})^2 + DW_t + O_4$$

We subtract this from (4.14),

$$(4.16) \qquad \sum_{i=1}^{n} (w_{it} - w_{i,t-1})\, Dw_{it} = \sum_{i=1}^{n} \bar{w}_{it} (Dw_{it})^2 + O_4$$
$$= \sum_{i=1}^{n} \bar{w}_{it} (Dw_{it} - DW_t)^2 + O_4$$

where the second step is based on (4.15). The left-hand side of (4.16) is the informational divergence of the budget shares in t and $t-1$ defined in eq. (2.15) of Section 11.2, and the expression in the second line confirms eq. (2.24) of that section. Note that the remainder term in (4.16) is O_4, whereas in (4.14) we have DW_t, which is O_3.

The variance $\sum_i \bar{w}_{it}(Dw_{it} - DW_t)^2$ was written as the sum of Π_t, K_t and $2\Gamma_t$ in eq. (2.23) of Section 11.2. Each of these three terms can be decomposed along the lines of (4.13); see Section 14.6 for price-quantity covariances between and within groups.

More Derivations

We write the between-group component of (4.11) as

$$(4.17) \qquad \sum_{g=1}^{G} W_{gt} DW_{gt} = \sum_{g=1}^{G} (\bar{W}_{gt} + \tfrac{1}{2}\Delta W_{gt})\, DW_{gt}$$
$$= \tfrac{1}{2} \sum_{g=1}^{G} \bar{W}_{gt} (DW_{gt})^2 + \sum_{g=1}^{G} \bar{W}_{gt} DW_{gt} + O_4$$

where the second step is based on (4.9). Also,

$$\sum_{j \in S_g} \frac{\bar{w}_{jt}}{\bar{W}_{gt}} Dw_{jt} = \frac{1}{\bar{W}_{gt}} \sum_{j \in S_g} \Delta w_{jt} + O_3 = \frac{\Delta W_{gt}}{\bar{W}_{gt}} + O_3 = DW_{gt} + O_3$$

where the first and the last steps are based on (4.9) and its one-commodity version. We combine this with $DW_t = O_3$ to conclude that the between-group component of (4.13) is equal to

$$\sum_{g=1}^{G} \bar{W}_{gt}(DW_{gt} + O_3)^2 = \sum_{g=1}^{G} \bar{W}_{gt}(DW_{gt})^2 + O_4 \tag{4.18}$$

Since $\sum_g \bar{W}_{gt} DW_{gt}$ in (4.17) is O_3, this proves that the leading term of the between-group component of (4.11) is one-half that of (4.13). The proof for the average within-group components then follows by simply subtracting the between-group components from both sides of (4.11) and (4.13) and taking the leading terms.

14.5 Quality Changes Between and Within Commodity Groups

The groupwise decomposition of the quality index of the basket requires consideration of the quality change between groups, which is the first topic of this section. The decomposition is applied to the 14-commodity model, after which its real-income, substitution and disturbance components are analyzed under the assumption of blockwise dependence. This leads to a two-dimensional decomposition of the quality index of the basket.

Quality Change Between Groups

Consider the log-change in the quality index of the basket,

$$DQ'_t - DQ_t = \sum_{i=1}^{n} (\mu_i - \bar{w}_{it})\, Dq_{it} \tag{5.1}$$

as well as the uppercase version of the right-hand side:

$$\sum_{g=1}^{G} (M_g - \bar{W}_{gt})\, DQ_{gt} = \sum_{g=1}^{G} M_g DQ_{gt} - DQ_t \tag{5.2}$$

Note that the expression on the right equals the volume component of (4.5). In the paragraph below (4.7) we surmised that it measures the quality change between groups. This seems to be corroborated by the fact that (5.2) is the uppercase version of (5.1).

To verify this interpretation we write the left-hand side of (5.2) as

$$\sum_{g=1}^{G} \bar{W}_{gt}\left(\frac{M_g}{\bar{W}_{gt}} - 1\right) DQ_{gt} = \sum_{g=1}^{G} \bar{W}_{gt}(DQ_{gt} - DQ_t)\left(\frac{M_g}{\bar{W}_{gt}} - 1\right) \tag{5.3}$$

The expression on the right is the budget-share-weighted covariance of the volume log-changes and the income elasticities of the commodity groups.

Hence it takes a positive (negative) value if the composition of the consumer's basket changes so that the volume log-changes of groups with high income elasticities are algebraically larger (smaller) than those of groups with low income elasticities. On comparing this with (1.8) and eq. (3.3) of Section 11.3, we conclude that (5.3) or, equivalently, (5.2) does measure the change in quality between the groups.

The Groupwise Decomposition of the Quality Index

To establish the relationship between (5.1), (5.2) and the quality indexes within the groups, we use (1.6) in

$$DQ'_t = \sum_{g=1}^{G} M_g DQ'_{gt} \tag{5.4}$$

Therefore,

$$DQ'_t - DQ_t = \sum_{g=1}^{G} M_g DQ'_{gt} - \sum_{g=1}^{G} \bar{W}_{gt} DQ_{gt}$$

which can also be written as

$$DQ'_t - DQ_t = \sum_{g=1}^{G} (M_g - \bar{W}_{gt})\, DQ_{gt} + \sum_{g=1}^{G} M_g (DQ'_{gt} - DQ_{gt}) \tag{5.5}$$

The first term on the right is the between-group quality change (5.2) and the second is, in view of (1.7), the average within-group quality change, marginally weighted. Hence (5.5) provides a between- and within-group decomposition of the log-change in the quality index of the basket. It should be compared with (4.2), which also uses marginal shares as weights in the average within-group term.

Application to the 14-Commodity Model

Table 14.6 contains the decomposition (5.5) for the $G=3$ groups of the 14-commodity basket that were described in the first subsection of Section 14.3. The first column is reproduced from Table 14.1 on page 344. The figures in parentheses are standard errors; their derivation is described in the next subsection.

The table shows that until 1933 the between-group and the average within-group components are of the same order of magnitude, but that the latter dominates in most of the later years. The 1922-39 row in the lower part of the table indicates that the near-zero net change in the basket's quality index during the prewar period is the result of small opposite changes in the between-group and the average within-group indexes, the former

TABLE 14.6

QUALITY DECOMPOSITION BETWEEN AND WITHIN COMMODITY GROUPS OF THE 14-COMMODITY MODEL

	$DQ'_t - DQ_t$	Between	Average within	Food	Beverages and Tobacco	Durables/ Remainder
			Between Wars			
1922–23	−.60 (.11)	−.44 (.05)	−.16 (.10)	−.12 (.23)	−.53 (.35)	−.13 (.11)
1923–24	.10 (.18)	.04 (.02)	.06 (.17)	−.50 (.21)	−.91 (.50)	.30 (.20)
1924–25	.30 (.21)	1.14 (.15)	−.83 (.15)	−.41 (.42)	.79 (.93)	−1.11 (.12)
1925–26	.17 (.17)	−.53 (.10)	.71 (.13)	.02 (.15)	−.98 (.61)	1.06 (.14)
1926–27	.91 (.10)	.03 (.02)	.88 (.10)	−.03 (.26)	−.04 (.18)	1.19 (.10)
1927–28	.15 (.04)	.14 (.02)	.01 (.04)	.58 (.19)	−.15 (.09)	−.10 (.04)
1928–29	.31 (.11)	.53 (.07)	−.21 (.08)	−.57 (.34)	−.17 (.26)	−.14 (.06)
1929–30	−.11 (.21)	.37 (.07)	−.48 (.18)	−1.31 (.28)	−.79 (.38)	−.26 (.22)
1930–31	−1.17 (.15)	−.47 (.07)	−.71 (.11)	1.28 (.29)	−.26 (.21)	−1.21 (.12)
1931–32	.17 (.12)	−.42 (.07)	.59 (.09)	.75 (.22)	−1.38 (.50)	.79 (.11)
1932–33	.77 (.15)	.50 (.10)	.27 (.11)	−1.09 (.48)	−1.47 (.51)	.77 (.06)
1933–34	−1.86 (.16)	−.04 (.01)	−1.83 (.16)	−1.41 (.29)	−.97 (.42)	−2.02 (.18)
1934–35	−.66 (.08)	−.24 (.05)	−.42 (.06)	−.50 (.16)	−.88 (.38)	−.35 (.03)
1935–36	2.93 (.20)	.73 (.14)	2.19 (.15)	.38 (.25)	−1.35 (.45)	3.01 (.23)
1936–37	−.83 (.09)	−.11 (.04)	−.72 (.09)	−1.71 (.39)	.41 (.20)	−.63 (.09)
1937–38	−2.27 (.18)	−.27 (.07)	−2.00 (.15)	−.35 (.33)	−.71 (.21)	−2.53 (.17)
1938–39	1.87 (.15)	.15 (.03)	1.72 (.15)	−.12 (.35)	−.13 (.30)	2.35 (.17)
			After World War II			
1951–52	−1.66 (.14)	−.38 (.06)	−1.28 (.13)	−.63 (.21)	−5.61 (.99)	−.92 (.10)
1952–53	.99 (.09)	−.02 (.00)	1.01 (.09)	1.55 (.39)	.78 (.14)	.92 (.10)
1953–54	2.44 (.19)	.32 (.05)	2.12 (.18)	.41 (.25)	1.34 (.52)	2.60 (.23)
1954–55	2.26 (.20)	.97 (.16)	1.29 (.12)	.49 (.29)	.43 (.09)	1.58 (.15)
1955–56	1.39 (.23)	.56 (.09)	.83 (.20)	.16 (.40)	1.27 (.31)	.93 (.25)
1956–57	.87 (.22)	.20 (.04)	.67 (.21)	.22 (.30)	.14 (.06)	.83 (.27)
1957–58	−.80 (.11)	−.51 (.09)	−.29 (.05)	.32 (.10)	.62 (.12)	−.53 (.05)
1958–59	.70 (.08)	.20 (.03)	.50 (.07)	−.22 (.17)	1.42 (.28)	.56 (.08)
1959–60	1.56 (.13)	.39 (.08)	1.17 (.11)	.59 (.17)	.17 (.05)	1.42 (.14)
1960–61	1.00 (.13)	−.06 (.02)	1.06 (.12)	−.11 (.23)	1.88 (.40)	1.23 (.13)
1961–62	.74 (.11)	.18 (.04)	.56 (.11)	.03 (.33)	1.62 (.38)	.55 (.13)
1962–63	1.17 (.16)	.28 (.06)	.89 (.16)	−.36 (.27)	1.46 (.45)	1.11 (.19)
			Three-period summary			
1922–39	.2	1.1	−.9	−5.1	−9.5	1.0
1939–51	−5.9	.4	−6.2	−2.0	−3.5	−7.5
1951–63	10.7	2.1	8.5	2.5	5.5	10.3

Notes. All entries are to be divided by 100. The standard error of the between-group index in 1952–53 is .003 in three decimal places (also to be divided by 100).

going up and the latter going down, both by about 1 percent. Note that when we use index levels instead of log-changes, the quality index of the basket is the product of the between-group and the average within-group indexes, and the latter index is the marginally weighted geometric mean of the quality indexes within the separate groups.

The 1939–51 row of the table shows that the quality decline during that period is wholly due to changes within groups, with Durables/Remainder playing a dominant role. The last row indicates that the postwar behavior of the basket's quality index is also mainly the result of changes within the groups. All three groups contributed, but particularly Durables/Remainder.

The numerical conclusions stated in the two previous paragraphs are subject to the qualification that the individual within-group indexes tend to have relatively large standard errors, especially for Food and Beverages and tobacco. The groupwise decomposition exposes the limitations of the 14-commodity model.

Derivation of Standard Errors

It follows from (5.2) that

$$\sum_{g=1}^{G} M_g DQ_{gt} = \sum_{g=1}^{G} DQ_{gt} \sum_{i \in S_g} \mu_i$$

is the part of the between-group quality index which involves marginal shares. So, with $G=3$, we obtain the standard error of this component as the square root of

$$\sum_{g=1}^{3} \sum_{h=1}^{3} DQ_{gt} DQ_{ht} \sum_{i \in S_g} \sum_{j \in S_h} \operatorname{cov}(\hat{\mu}_i, \hat{\mu}_j) \tag{5.6}$$

with $\operatorname{cov}(\hat{\mu}_i, \hat{\mu}_j)$ as specified in Table 6.15 on page 307 of Volume 1.

We turn to the average within-group component in (5.5), which we write for $G=3$ as

$$\begin{aligned}\sum_{g=1}^{3} M_g (DQ'_{gt} - DQ_{gt}) &= \sum_{g=1}^{3} \sum_{i \in S_g} \mu_i Dq_{it} - \sum_{g=1}^{3} M_g DQ_{gt} \\ &= \sum_{g=1}^{3} \sum_{i \in S_g} (Dq_{it} - DQ_{gt})\, \mu_i\end{aligned}$$

Hence the standard error of this component is the square root of

$$\sum_{g=1}^{3} \sum_{h=1}^{3} \sum_{i \in S_g} \sum_{j \in S_h} (Dq_{it} - DQ_{gt})(Dq_{jt} - DQ_{ht}) \operatorname{cov}(\hat{\mu}_i, \hat{\mu}_j) \tag{5.7}$$

To evaluate the standard error of the within-group index (1.7) we note that $DQ'_{gt}=\sum_i(\mu_i/M_g)Dq_{it}$ is the part which involves marginal shares. This expression is of the same form as (3.5), so that we can use (3.6) after replacing Dp_{it}, Dp_{jt}, DP'_{gt} by Dq_{it}, Dq_{jt}, DQ'_{gt}.

The Three Components of the Between-Group Quality Index

We return to the between-group index (5.2), which we write as

$$\sum_{g=1}^{G} \frac{M_g}{\bar{W}_{gt}} \bar{W}_{gt} DQ_{gt} - DQ_t \tag{5.8}$$

Under block-independence the demand equation for the group S_g is

$$\bar{W}_{gt} DQ_{gt} = M_g DQ_t + \phi M_g (DP'_{gt} - DP'_t) + E_{gt} \tag{5.9}$$

which we substitute in (5.8). The result is that the between-group component of $DQ'_t - DQ_t$ equals the sum of three terms:

$$\text{Real income}: \quad DQ_t \sum_{g=1}^{G} \bar{W}_{gt} \left(\frac{M_g}{\bar{W}_{gt}} - 1\right)^2 \tag{5.10}$$

$$\text{Substitution}: \quad \phi \sum_{g=1}^{G} M_g (DP'_{gt} - DP'_t) \frac{M_g}{\bar{W}_{gt}} \tag{5.11}$$

$$\text{Disturbances}: \quad \sum_{g=1}^{G} \frac{M_g}{\bar{W}_{gt}} E_{gt} \tag{5.12}$$

Note that these three components are the uppercase versions of the successive terms in the right-hand side of eq. (3.5) of Section 11.3.

If, in addition, the second-moment model in the block-independent form of eq. (7.31) of Section 2.7 holds, the variance of the disturbance component (5.12) is

$$\sigma^2 \sum_{g=1}^{G} M_g \left(\frac{M_g}{\bar{W}_{gt}} - \sum_{h=1}^{G} M_h \frac{M_h}{\bar{W}_{ht}}\right)^2 \tag{5.13}$$

This is a multiple σ^2 of the marginally weighted variance of the income elasticities of the G groups, which amounts to the uppercase version of eq. (3.6) of Section 11.3.

Extension to Blockwise Dependence

The components (5.10) to (5.12) have been derived under the block-independence assumption (5.9). When we have blockwise dependence, we replace (5.9) by eq. (3.4) of Section 8.3,

$$\bar{W}_{gt}DQ_{gt} = M_g DQ_t + \sum_{h=1}^{G} N_{gh}(DP'_{ht} - DP'_t) + E_{gt} \tag{5.14}$$

which shows that only the substitution component (5.11) is affected. Under the present weaker condition we can write this component as

$$\sum_{g=1}^{G}\sum_{h=1}^{G} N_{gh}(DP'_{gt} - DP'_t)\frac{M_h}{\bar{W}_{ht}} \tag{5.15}$$

which is the uppercase version of the bilinear form (3.13) of Section 11.3.

Alternatively, we can use the absolute price version (4.7) of Section 8.4:

$$\bar{W}_{gt}DQ_{gt} = M_g DQ_t + \sum_{h=1}^{G} \Pi_{gh} DP'_{ht} + E_{gt} \tag{5.16}$$

By substituting the right-hand side in (5.8), we obtain the following decomposition of the between-group component of $DQ'_t - DQ_t$:

$$\sum_{g=1}^{G}(M_g - \bar{W}_{gt})DQ_{gt} = DQ_t \sum_{g=1}^{G} \bar{W}_{gt}\left(\frac{M_g}{\bar{W}_{gt}} - 1\right)^2 + \sum_{g=1}^{G}\frac{M_g}{\bar{W}_{gt}}\sum_{h=1}^{G}\Pi_{gh}DP'_{ht} + \sum_{g=1}^{G}\frac{M_g}{\bar{W}_{gt}}E_{gt} \tag{5.17}$$

The Three Components of the Average Within-Group Quality Index

Under blockwise dependence we write the log-change in the quality index of S_g as

$$DQ'_{gt} - DQ_{gt} = \sum_{i \in S_g}\left(\mu_i^g - \frac{\bar{w}_{it}}{\bar{W}_{gt}}\right)Dq_{it} \tag{5.18}$$

and we use the conditional demand equation (4.11) of Section 8.4:

$$\bar{w}_{it}Dq_{it} = \mu_i^g \bar{W}_{gt} DQ_{gt} + \sum_{j \in S_g}\pi_{ij}^g Dp_{jt} + \varepsilon_{it}^g \tag{5.19}$$

Substitution of (5.19) in (5.18) gives

$$DQ'_{gt} - DQ_{gt} = DQ_{gt}\sum_{i \in S_g}\frac{\bar{w}_{it}}{\bar{W}_{gt}}\left(\frac{\mu_i^g}{\bar{w}_{it}/\bar{W}_{gt}} - 1\right)^2 + \sum_{i \in S_g}\frac{\mu_i^g}{\bar{w}_{it}}\sum_{j \in S_g}\pi_{ij}^g Dp_{jt} + \sum_{i \in S_g}\frac{\mu_i^g}{\bar{w}_{it}}\varepsilon_{it}^g \tag{5.20}$$

The three components on the right should be compared with the corresponding terms in (5.17) and also with the components of $DQ'_{gt} - DQ_{gt}$ derived under block-independence as shown in (1.10) to (1.12).

The average within-group term in (5.5) is obtained by multiplying the left-hand side of (5.20) by M_g and summing over g. When we apply this to the right-hand side also, we find that this average within-group term consists of a volume, a substitution, and a disturbance component:

$$\text{(5.21)} \qquad \text{Volume:} \quad \sum_{g=1}^{G} M_g DQ_{gt} \sum_{i \in S_g} \frac{\bar{w}_{it}}{\bar{W}_{gt}} \left(\frac{\mu_i^g}{\bar{w}_{it}/\bar{W}_{gt}} - 1 \right)^2$$

$$\text{(5.22)} \qquad \text{Substitution:} \quad \sum_{g=1}^{G} \sum_{i \in S_g} \frac{\mu_i}{\bar{w}_{it}} \sum_{j \in S_g} \pi_{ij}^g Dp_{jt} \qquad \text{(because } M_g \mu_i^g = \mu_i\text{)}$$

$$\text{(5.23)} \qquad \text{Disturbances:} \quad \sum_{g=1}^{G} \sum_{i \in S_g} \frac{\mu_i}{\bar{w}_{it}} \varepsilon_{it}^g$$

The Three Subcomponents of the Volume Component of the Average Within-Group Quality Index

Note that (5.21) is not a real-income but a volume component, which itself consists of three components, to be called subcomponents: one for real income, one for substitution, and one for disturbances. To derive these we use the identity

$$\text{(5.24)} \qquad \sum_{i \in S_g} \frac{\bar{w}_{it}}{\bar{W}_{gt}} \left(\frac{\mu_i^g}{\bar{w}_{it}/\bar{W}_{gt}} \right)^2 = \sum_{i \in S_g} \mu_i^g \frac{\mu_i^g}{\bar{w}_{it}/\bar{W}_{gt}}$$

which states that the budget-share-weighted second moment of the conditional income elasticities of S_g is equal to their marginally weighted first moment. [This is the within-group version of eqs. (3.9) and (3.10) of Section 11.3.] So, by subtracting from (5.24) the square of the budget-share-weighted mean of these elasticities, which is 1, we obtain the corresponding variance on the left:

$$\sum_{i \in S_g} \frac{\bar{w}_{it}}{\bar{W}_{gt}} \left(\frac{\mu_i^g}{\bar{w}_{it}/\bar{W}_{gt}} - 1 \right)^2 = \sum_{i \in S_g} \mu_i^g \frac{\mu_i^g}{\bar{w}_{it}/\bar{W}_{gt}} - 1$$

Next we multiply this by M_g,

$$\text{(5.25)} \qquad M_g \sum_{i \in S_g} \frac{\bar{w}_{it}}{\bar{W}_{gt}} \left(\frac{\mu_i^g}{\bar{w}_{it}/\bar{W}_{gt}} - 1 \right)^2 = \sum_{i \in S_g} \mu_i^g \frac{\mu_i}{\bar{w}_{it}/\bar{W}_{gt}} - M_g$$

$$= \bar{W}_{gt} \left(\sum_{i \in S_g} \mu_i^g \frac{\mu_i}{\bar{w}_{it}} - \frac{M_g}{\bar{W}_{gt}} \right)$$

and we multiply (5.25) by $M_g/\bar{W}_{gt}$, starting with the expression in the second line:

$$(5.26)\qquad M_g\left(\sum_{i\in S_g}\mu_i^g\frac{\mu_i}{\bar{w}_{it}}-\frac{M_g}{\bar{W}_{gt}}\right)=\frac{M_g^2}{\bar{W}_{gt}}\sum_{i\in S_g}\frac{\bar{w}_{it}}{\bar{W}_{gt}}\left(\frac{\mu_i^g}{\bar{w}_{it}/\bar{W}_{gt}}-1\right)^2$$

$$=\bar{W}_{gt}\sum_{i\in S_g}\frac{\bar{w}_{it}}{\bar{W}_{gt}}\left(\frac{\mu_i}{\bar{w}_{it}}-\frac{M_g}{\bar{W}_{gt}}\right)^2$$

We conclude from (5.25) that the volume component (5.21) can be written as

$$\sum_{g=1}^{G}\bar{W}_{gt}DQ_{gt}\left(\sum_{i\in S_g}\mu_i^g\frac{\mu_i}{\bar{w}_{it}}-\frac{M_g}{\bar{W}_{gt}}\right)$$

Then substitute (5.16) for $\bar{W}_{gt}DQ_{gt}$. This yields the three subcomponents of the volume component (5.21), with the expression (5.27) for the real-income subcomponent based on (5.26):

$$(5.27)\qquad \text{Real income:}\quad DQ_t\sum_{g=1}^{G}\bar{W}_{gt}\left[\sum_{i\in S_g}\frac{\bar{w}_{it}}{\bar{W}_{gt}}\left(\frac{\mu_i}{\bar{w}_{it}}-\frac{M_g}{\bar{W}_{gt}}\right)^2\right]$$

$$(5.28)\qquad \text{Substitution:}\quad \sum_{g=1}^{G}\sum_{h=1}^{G}\Pi_{gh}DP'_{ht}\sum_{i\in S_g}\mu_i^g\frac{\mu_i}{\bar{w}_{it}}-\sum_{g=1}^{G}\frac{M_g}{\bar{W}_{gt}}\sum_{h=1}^{G}\Pi_{gh}DP'_{ht}$$

$$(5.29)\qquad \text{Disturbances:}\quad \sum_{g=1}^{G}E_{gt}\sum_{i\in S_g}\mu_i^g\frac{\mu_i}{\bar{w}_{it}}-\sum_{g=1}^{G}\frac{M_g}{\bar{W}_{gt}}E_{gt}$$

The Two-Dimensional Decomposition of the Quality Index of the Basket

By adding (5.27) to the real-income component of (5.17), we obtain a multiple DQ_t of

(5.30)

$$\sum_{g=1}^{G}\bar{W}_{gt}\left(\frac{M_g}{\bar{W}_{gt}}-1\right)^2+\sum_{g=1}^{G}\bar{W}_{gt}\left[\sum_{i\in S_g}\frac{\bar{w}_{it}}{\bar{W}_{gt}}\left(\frac{\mu_i}{\bar{w}_{it}}-\frac{M_g}{\bar{W}_{gt}}\right)^2\right]=\sum_{i=1}^{n}\bar{w}_{it}\left(\frac{\mu_i}{\bar{w}_{it}}-1\right)^2$$

where the equal sign is based on the between- and within-group decomposition of the variance of the income elasticities [compare (4.13)]. Since the right-hand side of (5.30), when multiplied by DQ_t, is the real-income component of the log-change in the quality index of the basket, we have thus proved that this component is equal to the real-income component of the between-group index plus the real-income subcomponent of the volume component of the average within-group index.

Next consider the disturbance subcomponent (5.29) and note that its second term is equal (apart from sign) to the disturbance component of (5.17). Let us add the latter component to the sum of (5.29) and (5.23),

$$\sum_{g=1}^{G} \sum_{i \in S_g} \frac{\mu_i}{\bar{w}_{it}} (\mu_i^g E_{gt} + \varepsilon_{it}^g) = \sum_{i=1}^{n} \frac{\mu_i}{\bar{w}_{it}} \varepsilon_{it}$$

where the equal sign is based on eq. (3.26) of Section 8.3. The right-hand side is the disturbance component of $DQ'_t - DQ_t$, so that we have proved that this component is the sum of (1) the disturbance component of the between-group index, (2) the disturbance component of the average within-group index, and (3) the disturbance subcomponent of the volume component of the average within-group index.

TABLE 14.7

THE TWO-DIMENSIONAL DECOMPOSITION OF THE LOG-CHANGE IN THE QUALITY INDEX OF THE BASKET

	Between groups	Within groups
Real income	R	VR
Substitution	S	S and VS
Disturbances	D	D and VD

In the next subsection we prove a similar property for the substitution components. The result can be conveniently summarized in two-dimensional form as shown in Table 14.7. The three rows of the table correspond to the real-income, substitution and disturbance components of $DQ'_t - DQ_t$, and the two columns to its between-group and average within-group components. The letters R, S and D in the first column stand for the real-income, substitution and disturbance components of the between-group quality index; they fall under the corresponding component of the basket as a whole. The letters S and D in the second column have the same interpretation (but within groups), and the letter combinations VR, VS and VD stand for the real-income, substitution and disturbance subcomponents of the volume component of the average within-group index.

Derivations for the Substitution Components

The second term of the substitution subcomponent (5.28) equals minus the substitution component in (5.17). Hence the sum of the substitution components and subcomponent shown in the second line of Table 14.7 is

$$(5.31)\quad \sum_{g=1}^{G}\sum_{i\in S_g}\frac{\mu_i}{\bar{w}_{it}}\sum_{j\in S_g}\pi_{ij}^{g}Dp_{jt}+\sum_{g=1}^{G}\sum_{h=1}^{G}\Pi_{gh}DP'_{ht}\sum_{i\in S_g}\mu_i^{g}\frac{\mu_i}{\bar{w}_{it}}$$
$$=\sum_{g=1}^{G}\sum_{i\in S_g}\frac{\mu_i}{\bar{w}_{it}}\left(\sum_{j\in S_g}\pi_{ij}^{g}Dp_{jt}+\sum_{h=1}^{G}\sum_{j\in S_h}\Pi_{gh}\mu_i^{g}\mu_j^{h}Dp_{jt}\right)$$

It follows from eq. (4.15) of Section 8.4 that the expression in parentheses equals $\sum_j \pi_{ij}Dp_{jt}$, where the summation is over $j=1,\ldots,n$. Therefore, the right-hand side of (5.31) is equal to

$$\sum_{i=1}^{n}\frac{\mu_i}{\bar{w}_{it}}\sum_{j=1}^{n}\pi_{ij}Dp_{jt}$$

which is the substitution component of the log-change in the quality index of the basket written in terms of Slutsky rather than price coefficients. This confirms the second line of Table 14.7.

14.6 Price-Quantity Covariances Between and Within Commodity Groups

This section extends the results obtained for the quality index in Section 14.5 to the price-quantity covariance. It is assumed from the second subsection onward that there is either block-independence or blockwise dependence.

The Groupwise Decomposition of the Price-Quantity Covariance

The covariance Γ_t has a groupwise decomposition similar to (4.13) and (5.30). Consider, for $i\in S_g$, the identity

$$(Dp_{it}-DP_t)(Dq_{it}-DQ_t)$$
$$=[(DP_{gt}-DP_t)+(Dp_{it}-DP_{gt})]\,[(DQ_{gt}-DQ_t)+(Dq_{it}-DQ_{gt})]$$

We multiply both sides by $\bar{w}_{it}$ and sum first over $i\in S_g$ and then over $g=1,\ldots,G$, so that the left-hand side becomes Γ_t. The result is

$$(6.1)\quad \Gamma_t=\sum_{g=1}^{G}\bar{W}_{gt}(DP_{gt}-DP_t)(DQ_{gt}-DQ_t)$$
$$+\sum_{g=1}^{G}\bar{W}_{gt}\left[\sum_{i\in S_g}\frac{\bar{w}_{it}}{\bar{W}_{gt}}(Dp_{it}-DP_{gt})(Dq_{it}-DQ_{gt})\right]$$

We define

$$(6.2)\quad \Gamma_{0t}=\sum_{g=1}^{G}\bar{W}_{gt}(DP_{gt}-DP_t)(DQ_{gt}-DQ_t)$$

as the price-quantity covariance between the groups. Hence, using (2.5), we can write (6.1) in the simple form

$$\Gamma_t = \Gamma_{0t} + \sum_{g=1}^{G} \bar{W}_{gt}\Gamma_{gt} \tag{6.3}$$

which states that the price-quantity covariance of the basket is the sum of the between-group covariance and the average within-group covariance, budget-share-weighted. See THEIL (1967, Section 5.6) for applications of this decomposition and of similar decompositions of the variances of the price and quantity log-changes.

The Between-Group Covariance Under Block-Independence

We write (6.2) in the form $\Gamma_{0t} = \sum_g (DP_{gt} - DP_t)\bar{W}_{gt}DQ_{gt}$ and substitute (5.9) for $\bar{W}_{gt}DQ_{gt}$. This shows that under block-independence the price-quantity covariance between groups consists of three components:

$$\text{Real income:} \quad \left(\sum_{g=1}^{G} M_g DP_{gt} - DP_t\right) DQ_t \tag{6.4}$$

$$\text{Substitution:} \quad \phi \sum_{g=1}^{G} M_g (DP_{gt} - DP_t)(DP'_{gt} - DP'_t) \tag{6.5}$$

$$\text{Disturbances:} \quad \sum_{g=1}^{G} DP_{gt}E_{gt} \tag{6.6}$$

The real-income component (6.4) is similar to the corresponding expression in eq. (1.6) of Section 11.1; note the price index $\sum_g M_g DP_{gt}$, which we met earlier in (4.5). The substitution component (6.5) is not ϕ times a variance, as it is in eq. (1.6) of Section 11.1, but ϕ times a covariance, viz., the marginally weighted covariance of two sets of price indexes of commodity groups:

$$\begin{matrix} DP_{1t} & DP_{2t} & \dots & DP_{Gt} \\ DP'_{1t} & DP'_{2t} & \dots & DP'_{Gt} \end{matrix}$$

This interpretation follows from the fact that (6.5) is identical to

$$\phi \sum_{g=1}^{G} M_g \left(DP_{gt} - \sum_{h=1}^{G} M_h DP_{ht}\right)(DP'_{gt} - DP'_t) \tag{6.7}$$

It is easily verified that the difference between (6.5) and (6.7) is zero.

The variance of the disturbance component (6.6) under the second-moment model (7.31) of Section 2.7 is

$$\text{var}\left(\sum_{g=1}^{G} DP_{gt}E_{gt}\right) = \sigma^2 \sum_{g=1}^{G} M_g \left(DP_{gt} - \sum_{h=1}^{G} M_h DP_{ht}\right)^2 \tag{6.8}$$

The right-hand side is a multiple σ^2 of the variance which corresponds to the mean $\sum_g M_g DP_{gt}$. This result should be compared with eq. (1.10) of Section 11.1.

Extension to Blockwise Dependence

The substitution component (6.5) is affected when we replace block-independence by blockwise dependence. Using (5.14), we find that this component becomes

$$\sum_{g=1}^{G} \sum_{h=1}^{G} N_{gh}(DP_{gt} - DP_t)(DP'_{ht} - DP'_t) \tag{6.9}$$

This is a bilinear form in two sets of deflated price indexes of commodity groups, to be compared with the quadratic form (1.11) of Section 11.1.

When we use the absolute price version (5.16), the decomposition of Γ_{0t} becomes

(6.10)

$$\Gamma_{0t} = \left(\sum_{g=1}^{G} M_g DP_{gt} - DP_t \right) DQ_t + \sum_{g=1}^{G} \sum_{h=1}^{G} \Pi_{gh} DP_{gt} DP'_{ht} + \sum_{g=1}^{G} DP_{gt} E_{gt}$$

where $\sum_g \Pi_{gh} = 0$ is used to simplify the substitution component [see eq. (4.8) of Section 8.4].

Components and Subcomponents of the Average Within-Group Covariance

We write the within-group term of (6.3) as

$$\begin{aligned} \sum_{g=1}^{G} \bar{W}_{gt} \Gamma_{gt} &= \sum_{g=1}^{G} \sum_{i \in S_g} \bar{w}_{it} (Dp_{it} - DP_{gt})(Dq_{it} - DQ_{gt}) \\ &= \sum_{g=1}^{G} \sum_{i \in S_g} (Dp_{it} - DP_{gt}) \bar{w}_{it} Dq_{it} \end{aligned} \tag{6.11}$$

Using (5.19), we obtain the three components of the average within-group covariance shown below. The substitution component is simplified by means of eq. (4.12) of Section 8.4.

$$\text{Volume:} \quad \sum_{g=1}^{G} (DP'_{gt} - DP_{gt}) \bar{W}_{gt} DQ_{gt} \tag{6.12}$$

$$\text{Substitution:} \quad \sum_{g=1}^{G} \sum_{i \in S_g} \sum_{j \in S_g} \pi_{ij}^{g} Dp_{it} Dp_{jt} \tag{6.13}$$

$$\text{Disturbances:} \quad \sum_{g=1}^{G} \sum_{i \in S_g} Dp_{it} \varepsilon_{it}^{g} \tag{6.14}$$

Next, using (5.16), we obtain the three subcomponents of the volume component (6.12):

$$\text{(6.15)} \qquad \text{Real income:} \quad \left(DP'_t - \sum_{g=1}^{G} M_g DP_{gt}\right) DQ_t$$

$$\text{(6.16)} \qquad \text{Substitution:} \quad \sum_{g=1}^{G} \sum_{h=1}^{G} \Pi_{gh} (DP'_{gt} - DP_{gt})\, DP'_{ht}$$

$$\text{(6.17)} \qquad \text{Disturbances:} \quad \sum_{g=1}^{G} (DP'_{gt} - DP_{gt})\, E_{gt}$$

The Two-Dimensional Decomposition of the Covariance of the Basket

We obtain $(DP'_t - DP_t)DQ_t$ by adding (6.15) to the real-income component of (6.10), so that the real-income component of Γ_t is equal to the corresponding component of Γ_{0t} plus the real-income subcomponent of the volume component of $\sum_g \bar{W}_{gt}\Gamma_{gt}$. This means that the first line of Table 14.7 applies not only to the quality index but also to the price-quantity covariance. We prove below that the two other lines of this table are also applicable to Γ_t.

The sum of the substitution component of (6.10) and the expressions (6.13) and (6.16) is

$$\sum_{g=1}^{G} \sum_{i \in S_g} \sum_{j \in S_g} \pi^g_{ij} Dp_{it} Dp_{jt} + \sum_{g=1}^{G} \sum_{h=1}^{G} \Pi_{gh} DP'_{gt} DP'_{ht}$$
$$= \sum_{g=1}^{G} \sum_{i \in S_g} \left(\sum_{j \in S_g} \pi^g_{ij} Dp_{it} Dp_{jt} + \sum_{h=1}^{G} \sum_{j \in S_h} \Pi_{gh} \mu^g_i \mu^h_j Dp_{it} Dp_{jt} \right)$$

It follows from eq. (4.15) of Section 8.4 that the right-hand side of this equation equals $\sum_i \sum_j \pi_{ij} Dp_{it} Dp_{jt}$, where the summation is over $i, j = 1, \ldots, n$, and it is easily verified (by means of $\sum_i \pi_{ij} = 0$) that this is the substitution component of Γ_t expressed in terms of Slutsky coefficients.

Similarly, the sum of the disturbance component of (6.10) and the expressions (6.14) and (6.17) is

$$\sum_{g=1}^{G} \sum_{i \in S_g} Dp_{it} \varepsilon^g_{it} + \sum_{g=1}^{G} DP'_{gt} E_{gt} = \sum_{g=1}^{G} \sum_{i \in S_g} Dp_{it} (\varepsilon^g_{it} + \mu^g_i E_{gt})$$

which equals $Dp_{1t}\varepsilon_{1t} + \cdots + Dp_{nt}\varepsilon_{nt}$, the disturbance component of Γ_t, in view of eq. (3.26) of Section 8.3. This completes the proof.

14.7 Demand and Supply of Groups and Within Groups Under the Natural Conjugate Supply Model

In this section we use the natural conjugate supply model of Section 10.2

to formulate (1) demand and supply equations for commodity groups and (2) conditional demand and supply equations for commodities within their groups. Blockwise dependence is assumed throughout.

Demand and Supply Equations of Commodity Groups

Consider the demand equation (4.7) of Section 8.4:

$$\bar{W}_{gt}DQ_{gt} = M_g DQ_t + \sum_{h=1}^{G} \Pi_{gh} DP'_{ht} + E_{gt} \tag{7.1}$$

Since this equation is obtained by adding the n_g demand equations of the goods of S_g, we have

$$\begin{aligned} \bar{W}_{gt}DQ_{gt} &= \sum_{i \in S_g} \bar{w}_{it} Dq_{it} \\ \sum_{h=1}^{G} \Pi_{gh} DP'_{ht} &= \sum_{i \in S_g} \sum_{j=1}^{n} \pi_{ij} Dp_{jt} \end{aligned} \tag{7.2}$$

Also consider eqs. (2.4) and (2.6) of Section 10.2:

$$\bar{w}_{it}[Dq_{it} - \mathscr{E}(Dq_{it})] = \sum_{j=1}^{n} \pi_{ij}[Dp_{jt} - \mathscr{E}(Dp_{jt})] + \varepsilon_{it} \tag{7.3}$$

$$\bar{w}_{it}[Dq_{it} - \mathscr{E}(Dq_{it})] = -s_1 \sum_{j=1}^{n} \pi_{ij}[Dp_{jt} - \mathscr{E}(Dp_{jt})] + \eta_{it} \tag{7.4}$$

By summing (7.3) over $i \in S_g$ and using (7.2) we obtain

$$\bar{W}_{gt}[DQ_{gt} - \mathscr{E}(DQ_{gt})] = \sum_{h=1}^{G} \Pi_{gh}[DP'_{ht} - \mathscr{E}(DP'_{ht})] + E_{gt} \tag{7.5}$$

which is the demand equation (7.1) written as a deviation from its expectation. Similarly, when we define

$$H_{gt} = \sum_{i \in S_g} \eta_{it} \tag{7.6}$$

and sum (7.4) over $i \in S_g$, we obtain

$$\bar{W}_{gt}[DQ_{gt} - \mathscr{E}(DQ_{gt})] = -s_1 \sum_{h=1}^{G} \Pi_{gh}[DP'_{ht} - \mathscr{E}(DP'_{ht})] + H_{gt} \tag{7.7}$$

which is the supply equation of S_g, also written as a deviation of its expectation, with H_{gt} as the supply disturbance of the group.

Next consider eqs. (2.11) and (2.12) of Section 10.2:

$$\bar{w}_{it}[Dq_{it} - \mathscr{E}(Dq_{it})] = \frac{\eta_{it} + s_1 \varepsilon_{it}}{1 + s_1} \tag{7.8}$$

$$(7.9)\qquad \sum_{j=1}^{n} \pi_{ij}\left[Dp_{jt} - \mathscr{E}(Dp_{jt})\right] = \frac{\eta_{it} - \varepsilon_{it}}{1 + s_1}$$

By summing over $i \in S_g$ and using (7.2) and (7.6), we obtain

$$(7.10)\qquad \bar{W}_{gt}\left[DQ_{gt} - \mathscr{E}(DQ_{gt})\right] = \frac{H_{gt} + s_1 E_{gt}}{1 + s_1}$$

$$(7.11)\qquad \sum_{h=1}^{G} \Pi_{gh}\left[DP'_{ht} - \mathscr{E}(DP'_{ht})\right] = \frac{H_{gt} - E_{gt}}{1 + s_1}$$

Note that (7.5) and (7.7), as well as (7.10) and (7.11), are straightforward uppercase versions of the corresponding equations for the individual goods.

Demand and Supply Disturbances of Commodity Groups

Since η_{it} has zero expectation by assumption, so has the supply disturbance of the group defined in (7.6). For the second moments we use eqs. (2.7) and (2.8) of Section 10.2,

$$(7.12)\qquad \begin{aligned} \operatorname{cov}(\eta_{it}, \eta_{jt}) &= s_2 \omega_{ij} \qquad & i, j = 1, \ldots, n \\ \operatorname{cov}(\eta_{it}, \varepsilon_{jt}) &= 0 \qquad & i, j = 1, \ldots, n \end{aligned}$$

This implies

$$(7.13)\qquad \operatorname{cov}(H_{gt}, \varepsilon_{jt}) = \operatorname{cov}(H_{gt}, E_{ht}) = \operatorname{cov}(\eta_{it}, E_{ht}) = 0$$

for all values of the subscripts.

The covariances of the H's and η's implied by (7.6) and (7.12) are

$$\operatorname{cov}(H_{gt}, \eta_{jt}) = s_2 \sum_{i \in S_g} \omega_{ij} \qquad \operatorname{cov}(H_{gt}, H_{ht}) = s_2 \sum_{i \in S_g} \sum_{j \in S_h} \omega_{ij}$$

This can be simplified to

$$(7.14)\qquad \operatorname{cov}(H_{gt}, \eta_{jt}) = s_2 \sigma^2 \mu_j^h \frac{\Pi_{gh}}{\phi} \qquad j \in S_h$$

$$(7.15)\qquad \operatorname{cov}(H_{gt}, H_{ht}) = s_2 \sigma^2 \frac{\Pi_{gh}}{\phi}$$

which follows from $\omega_{ij} = \sigma^2 \pi_{ij}/\phi$ and eqs. (4.16) and (4.17) of Section 8.4.

Conditional Demand and Supply Equations

In Section 8.3 we derived conditional demand equations by subtracting the group demand equation, multiplied by the ith conditional marginal share, from the ith unconditional demand equation. We write the result in the absolute price form of eq. (4.11) of Section 8.4:

$$\bar{w}_{it} Dq_{it} = \mu_i^g \bar{W}_{gt} DQ_{gt} + \sum_{j \in S_g} \pi_{ij}^g Dp_{jt} + \varepsilon_{it}^g \qquad i \in S_g$$

Since DQ_{gt} is predetermined in the conditional demand model of S_g, the ith conditional demand model written as a deviation from its conditional expectation is

$$\text{(7.16)} \qquad \bar{w}_{it} \left[Dq_{it} - \mathscr{E}_g(Dq_{it}) \right] = \sum_{j \in S_g} \pi_{ij}^g \left[Dp_{jt} - \mathscr{E}_g(Dp_{jt}) \right] + \varepsilon_{it}^g$$

where $\mathscr{E}_g$ stands for the conditional expectation, given what is predetermined in the conditional model of S_g. This is further elaborated in the next subsection.

We proceed in the same way for the supply model by multiplying (7.7) by the ith conditional marginal share and subtracting the result from (7.4). This yields the ith conditional supply equation written as a deviation from its conditional expectation,

$$\text{(7.17)} \quad \bar{w}_{it} \left[Dq_{it} - \mathscr{E}_g(Dq_{it}) \right] = - s_1 \sum_{j \in S_g} \pi_{ij}^g \left[Dp_{jt} - \mathscr{E}_g(Dp_{jt}) \right] + \eta_{it}^g$$

where

$$\text{(7.18)} \qquad \eta_{it}^g = \eta_{it} - \mu_i^g H_{gt} \qquad i \in S_g;\ g = 1, \ldots, G$$

is the ith conditional supply disturbance. The solution of the system (7.16) and (7.17) is

$$\text{(7.19)} \qquad \bar{w}_{it} \left[Dq_{it} - \mathscr{E}_g(Dq_{it}) \right] = \frac{\eta_{it}^g + s_1 \varepsilon_{it}^g}{1 + s_1}$$

$$\text{(7.20)} \qquad \sum_{j \in S_g} \pi_{ij}^g \left[Dp_{jt} - \mathscr{E}_g(Dp_{jt}) \right] = \frac{\eta_{it}^g - \varepsilon_{it}^g}{1 + s_1}$$

which may be verified along the lines of eqs. (2.10) to (2.12) of Section 10.2.

Conditional Demand and Supply Disturbances

It follows from (7.18) that each conditional supply disturbance is a linear function of unconditional supply disturbances (η_{it} and H_{gt}). This is also true, mutatis mutandis, for the demand disturbances. Therefore, since all unconditional demand disturbances are uncorrelated with all unconditional supply disturbances, the conditional disturbances have the same property.

The conditional supply disturbance (7.18) satisfies

$$\text{(7.21)} \qquad \operatorname{cov}(\eta_{it}^{g}, \eta_{jt}^{h}) = \begin{cases} s_2\sigma^2 \dfrac{\pi_{ij}^{g}}{\phi} & \text{if} \quad i\in S_g, j\in S_h, g=h \\ 0 & \text{if} \quad i\in S_g, j\in S_h, g\neq h \end{cases}$$

as well as

$$\text{(7.22)} \qquad \operatorname{cov}(\eta_{it}^{g}, H_{ht})=0 \qquad i\in S_g;\ g, h=1,\ldots, G$$

Equations (7.21) and (7.22) are the supply version of eqs. (4.21) and (4.22) of Section 8.4; they can be derived along similar lines by means of specific and general components of supply disturbances.

We conclude from (7.22) that the conditional supply disturbances are uncorrelated with the supply disturbances of the commodity groups. We know from eq. (4.22) of Section 8.4 that the demand disturbances have the same property. Also, the conditional supply disturbances are uncorrelated with the demand disturbances of the groups [see (7.18) and (7.13)], and the conditional demand disturbances are uncorrelated with the supply disturbances of the groups. Hence all conditional demand *and* supply disturbances are uncorrelated with all group demand *and* supply disturbances. Therefore, if the disturbance distribution is multivariate normal, the left-hand variables of (7.10) and (7.11) are predetermined in the conditional equations (7.16) and (7.17). The symbol $\mathscr{E}_g$ in the latter equations should thus be read as the conditional expectation, given DQ_{gt} and DP'_{ht} for all pairs (g, h).

Random Components of Deflated Price Log-changes

Consider eq. (2.20) of Section 10.2,

$$\text{(7.23)} \qquad Dp_{it} - DP'_t - \mathscr{E}(Dp_{it} - DP'_t) = \frac{1}{1+s_1}\sum_{j=1}^{n} \nu^{ij}(\eta_{jt} - \varepsilon_{jt})$$

and write N^{gh} for the $(g, h)^{\text{th}}$ element of the inverse of the $G\times G$ price coefficient matrix of the groups, and ν^{gij} for the $(i, j)^{\text{th}}$ element of the inverse of the $n_g\times n_g$ price coefficient matrix of the goods of S_g. In the next paragraph we prove the following group and within-group versions of (7.23):

$$\text{(7.24)} \qquad DP'_{gt} - DP'_t - \mathscr{E}(DP'_{gt} - DP'_t) = \frac{1}{1+s_1}\sum_{h=1}^{G} N^{gh}(H_{ht} - E_{ht})$$

$$\text{(7.25)} \qquad Dp_{it} - DP'_{gt} - \mathscr{E}_g(Dp_{it} - DP'_{gt}) = \frac{1}{1+s_1}\sum_{j\in S_g} \nu^{gij}(\eta_{jt}^{g} - \varepsilon_{jt}^{g})$$

We use eqs. (4.6) of Section 8.4 and (6.10) of Section 9.6 to obtain

$$\sum_{k=1}^{G} N^{gk}\Pi_{kh} = \begin{cases} 1 - M_h & \text{if } g = h \\ -M_h & \text{if } g \neq h \end{cases} \tag{7.26}$$

When we write (7.11) in the form of a G-element vector equation and premultiply by $[N^{gh}]$, we obtain (7.24) from (7.26). By similarly premultiplying (7.20) by $[\nu^{gij}]$ we obtain (7.25), using

$$\sum_{k \in S_g} \nu^{gik}\pi^g_{kj} = \begin{cases} 1 - \mu^g_j & \text{if } i = j \\ -\mu^g_j & \text{if } i \neq j \end{cases} \tag{7.27}$$

which follows from eqs. (4.10) of Section 8.4 and (6.11) of Section 9.6.

Covariance Matrices of Deflated Price Log-changes

Next consider eqs. (2.9) and (2.22) of Section 10.2:

$$\delta_{11} = \frac{s_1^2 + s_2}{(1+s_1)^2} \qquad \delta_{12} = \frac{s_1 - s_2}{(1+s_1)^2} \qquad \delta_{22} = \frac{1 + s_2}{(1+s_1)^2} \tag{7.28}$$

$$\operatorname{cov}(Dp_{it} - DP'_t, Dp_{jt} - DP'_t) = \delta_{22}\sigma^2 \frac{\pi^{ij}}{\phi} \tag{7.29}$$

In the next paragraph we prove the following group and within-group versions of (7.29), both involving reciprocal Slutsky coefficients:

$$\operatorname{cov}(DP'_{gt} - DP'_t, DP'_{ht} - DP'_t) = \delta_{22}\sigma^2 \frac{\Pi^{gh}}{\phi} \tag{7.30}$$

$$\operatorname{cov}(Dp_{it} - DP'_{gt}, Dp_{jt} - DP'_{ht}) = \begin{cases} \delta_{22}\sigma^2 \dfrac{\pi^{gij}}{\phi} & \text{if } i \in S_g, j \in S_h, g = h \\ 0 & \text{if } i \in S_g, j \in S_h, g \neq h \end{cases} \tag{7.31}$$

These equations are generalizations of the second-moment results for the reciprocal equations given in eqs. (6.25) and (6.26) of Section 9.6 [compare the paragraph below eq. (2.22) of Section 10.2].

We multiply (7.24) by the same equation, but with g replaced by h, and take the expectation. It follows from (7.13), (7.15) and eq. (4.19) of Section 8.4 that this yields the $(g, h)^{\text{th}}$ element of the matrix

$$\frac{1 + s_2}{(1+s_1)^2} \frac{\sigma^2}{\phi} [N^{gh}] [\Pi_{gh}] [N^{gh}]$$

after which (7.28) and eq. (6.23) of Section 9.6 confirm (7.30). Similarly, we multiply (7.25) by the same equation with i replaced by j ($i, j \in S_g$), and take the expectation. Application of (7.21) and eq. (4.21) of Section 8.4 shows that this gives the $(i, j)^{\text{th}}$ element of

$$\frac{1+s_2}{(1+s_1)^2} \frac{\sigma^2}{\phi} [v^{gij}] [\pi^g_{ij}] [v^{gij}]$$

This element equals the right-hand side of (7.31) for $g=h$ in view of eq. (6.24) of Section 9.6. For $g \neq h$ we proceed in the same way, using the second line of (7.21) and the corresponding property of the conditional demand disturbances.

Note that the left-hand side of (7.31) is a conditional covariance, given $DQ_{1t}, \ldots, DQ_{Gt}$, $DP'_{1t}, \ldots, DP'_{Gt}$. From now on we shall no longer use subscripts attached to expectation signs to indicate conditional expected values. It should simply be understood that when we operate within a commodity group, an expectation is a conditional expectation, given the variables (DQ_{gt} and DP'_{gt}) of all groups.

Covariances of Deflated Price Log-changes and Demand Disturbances

Finally consider eqs. (2.16) and (2.23) of Section 10.2,

$$\theta = \delta_{12} + \delta_{22} = \frac{1}{1+s_1} \tag{7.32}$$

$$\operatorname{cov}(Dp_{it} - DP'_t, \varepsilon_{jt}) = \begin{cases} \dfrac{\theta}{\gamma}(1-\mu_j) & \text{if } i=j \\ -\dfrac{\theta}{\gamma}\mu_j & \text{if } i \neq j \end{cases} \tag{7.33}$$

where γ is defined in eq. (4.4) of Section 7.4:

$$\gamma = -\frac{\phi}{\sigma^2} \tag{7.34}$$

Equation (7.33) implies

$$\operatorname{cov}(Dp_{it} - DP'_t, E_{ht}) = \begin{cases} \dfrac{\theta}{\gamma}(1-M_h) & \text{if } i \in S_g, g=h \\ -\dfrac{\theta}{\gamma}M_h & \text{if } i \in S_g, g \neq h \end{cases} \tag{7.35}$$

This is immediately clear for $g \neq h$. For $g=h$ we write the left-hand side of

(7.35) in the following form, where $\sum_j$ stands for summation over $j \in S_h$ excluding $j = i$:

$$\operatorname{cov}(Dp_{it} - DP'_t, \varepsilon_{it}) + \sum_j \operatorname{cov}(Dp_{it} - DP'_t, \varepsilon_{jt})$$
$$= \frac{\theta}{\gamma}(1 - \mu_i - \sum_j \mu_j) = \frac{\theta}{\gamma}(1 - \mu_i - M_h + \mu_i) = \frac{\theta}{\gamma}(1 - M_h)$$

This completes the proof of (7.35). Next consider

$$\operatorname{cov}(DP'_{gt} - DP'_t, E_{ht}) = \sum_{i \in S_g} \mu_i^g \operatorname{cov}(Dp_{it} - DP'_t, E_{ht})$$

and apply (7.35):

$$\operatorname{cov}(DP'_{gt} - DP'_t, E_{ht}) = \begin{cases} \frac{\theta}{\gamma}(1 - M_h) & \text{if } g = h \\ -\frac{\theta}{\gamma} M_h & \text{if } g \neq h \end{cases} \tag{7.36}$$

In the same way, using

$$\operatorname{cov}(DP_{gt} - DP'_t, E_{ht}) = \sum_{i \in S_g} \frac{\bar{w}_{it}}{\bar{W}_{gt}} \operatorname{cov}(Dp_{it} - DP'_t, E_{ht})$$

we obtain

$$\operatorname{cov}(DP_{gt} - DP'_t, E_{ht}) = \begin{cases} \frac{\theta}{\gamma}(1 - M_h) & \text{if } g = h \\ -\frac{\theta}{\gamma} M_h & \text{if } g \neq h \end{cases} \tag{7.37}$$

Equations (7.36) and (7.37) are two group versions of (7.33).

The within-group version takes a similar form ($i, j \in S_g$):

$$\operatorname{cov}(Dp_{it} - DP'_{gt}, \varepsilon_{jt}^g) = \begin{cases} \frac{\theta}{\gamma}(1 - \mu_j^g) & \text{if } i = j \\ -\frac{\theta}{\gamma} \mu_j^g & \text{if } i \neq j \end{cases} \tag{7.38}$$

To prove this result we write the left-hand side as

$$\operatorname{cov}(Dp_{it} - DP'_t, \varepsilon_{jt}^g) - \operatorname{cov}(DP'_{gt} - DP'_t, \varepsilon_{jt}^g)$$

The second covariance vanishes in view of (7.24) and the zero correlations of the conditional disturbances and the disturbances of the groups. Hence we can write the left-hand side of (7.38) as

$$\operatorname{cov}(Dp_{it} - DP'_t, \varepsilon_{jt}) - \mu_j^g \operatorname{cov}(Dp_{it} - DP'_t, E_{gt})$$

The proof of (7.38) then follows from (7.33) and (7.35).

14.8 Two-Dimensional Decompositions Under the Natural Conjugate Supply Model

This section applies the theory of Section 14.7 to the two-dimensional decomposition shown in Table 14.7 on page 371. The first application concerns the price-quantity covariance; it extends eq. (8.11) of Section 12.8,

$$\mathscr{E}\left(\sum_{i=1}^{n} Dp_{it}\varepsilon_{it}\right) = \frac{\theta}{\gamma}(n-1) \tag{8.1}$$

to the disturbance terms of the components of Γ_t which we derived in Section 14.6. The second application concerns the quality index. Blockwise dependence is again assumed.

Expected Disturbance Components of Price-Quantity Covariances

Consider the decomposition (6.10) of the between-group covariance Γ_{0t}. In the next subsection we derive the expectation of its disturbance component,

$$\mathscr{E}\left(\sum_{g=1}^{G} DP_{gt}E_{gt}\right) = \frac{\theta}{\gamma}(G-1) \tag{8.2}$$

and also the expectation of the disturbance component of the within-group covariance Γ_{gt}:

$$\mathscr{E}\left(\frac{1}{\bar{W}_{gt}}\sum_{i\in S_g} Dp_{it}\varepsilon_{it}^{g}\right) = \frac{\theta}{\gamma\bar{W}_{gt}}(n_g-1) \tag{8.3}$$

This implies that the disturbance component (6.14) of the average within-group covariance $\sum_g \bar{W}_{gt}\Gamma_{gt}$ has the following expectation:

$$\mathscr{E}\left(\sum_{g=1}^{G}\sum_{i\in S_g} Dp_{it}\varepsilon_{it}^{g}\right) = \frac{\theta}{\gamma}(n-G) \tag{8.4}$$

The disturbance subcomponent of the volume component of $\sum_g \bar{W}_{gt}\Gamma_{gt}$ is given in (6.17). We shall prove that this subcomponent has zero expectation:

$$\mathscr{E}\left[\sum_{g=1}^{G}(DP'_{gt} - DP_{gt})E_{gt}\right] = 0 \tag{8.5}$$

The two-dimensional decomposition of Γ_t implies that its disturbance component equals the sum of (1) the disturbance component of Γ_{0t}, (2) the disturbance component of $\sum_g \bar{W}_{gt}\Gamma_{gt}$, and (3) the disturbance subcomponent of the volume component of $\sum_g \bar{W}_{gt}\Gamma_{gt}$. Therefore, the sum of (8.2), (8.4) and

(8.5) must be equal to the expected disturbance component of Γ_t. This is confirmed by (8.1).

Derivations for Price-Quantity Covariances

We have $E_{1t}+\cdots+E_{Gt}=0$, so that the disturbance component of (6.10) can be written as

$$\sum_{g=1}^{G} DP_{gt}E_{gt} = \sum_{g=1}^{G} (DP_{gt} - DP'_t)\, E_{gt}$$

The expectation of the right-hand side can be viewed as the sum over g of $\operatorname{cov}(DP_{gt}-DP'_t,\, E_{gt})$, because E_{gt} has zero expectation. Hence (7.37) yields the expectation

$$\frac{\theta}{\gamma} \sum_{g=1}^{G} (1 - M_g) = \frac{\theta}{\gamma}(G-1)$$

which confirms (8.2). When we replace DP_{gt} by DP'_{gt}, we use (7.36), which yields the same expectation $\theta(G-1)/\gamma$. By combining this result with (8.2) we obtain (8.5).

The disturbance component of Γ_{gt} is given in (2.8); it was derived there under block-independence, but it takes the same form under blockwise dependence. We can write this component as

$$\frac{1}{\overline{W}_{gt}} \sum_{i \in S_g} (Dp_{it} - DP'_{gt})\, \varepsilon_{it}^{g}$$

because the conditional demand disturbances add up to zero when summed over $i \in S_g$. The result (8.3) then follows directly from (7.38).

The Quality Change Between and Within Groups

The results summarized below, which are proved in the next subsection, concern variances and covariances of the substitution and disturbance components of the between- and within-group quality log-changes.

The variance of the disturbance term in the between-group decomposition (5.17) is

$$\text{(8.6)} \quad \operatorname{var}\left(\sum_{g=1}^{G} \frac{M_g}{\overline{W}_{gt}} E_{gt}\right) = \sigma^2 \sum_{g=1}^{G} \sum_{h=1}^{G} M_{gh} \left(\frac{M_g}{\overline{W}_{gt}} - \sum_{k=1}^{G} M_k \frac{M_k}{\overline{W}_{kt}}\right)\left(\frac{M_h}{\overline{W}_{ht}} - \sum_{k=1}^{G} M_k \frac{M_k}{\overline{W}_{kt}}\right)$$

where $M_{gh}=N_{gh}/\phi$ is the normalized price coefficient of the groups S_g and S_h defined in eq. (6.19) of Section 12.6. The result (8.6) is the uppercase version of eq. (7.19) of Section 12.7. Also,

$$\text{(8.7)} \qquad \operatorname{var}\left(\sum_{g=1}^{G} \frac{M_g}{\bar{W}_{gt}} \sum_{h=1}^{G} \Pi_{gh} DP'_{ht}\right) = \delta_{22} \operatorname{var}\left(\sum_{g=1}^{G} \frac{M_g}{\bar{W}_{gt}} E_{gt}\right)$$

$$\text{(8.8)} \qquad \operatorname{cov}\left(\sum_{g=1}^{G} \frac{M_g}{\bar{W}_{gt}} \sum_{h=1}^{G} \Pi_{gh} DP'_{ht}, \sum_{g=1}^{G} \frac{M_g}{\bar{W}_{gt}} E_{gt}\right) = -\theta \operatorname{var}\left(\sum_{g=1}^{G} \frac{M_g}{\bar{W}_{gt}} E_{gt}\right)$$

$$\text{(8.9)} \qquad \operatorname{var}\left[\sum_{g=1}^{G} (M_g - \bar{W}_{gt}) DQ_{gt}\right] = \delta_{11} \operatorname{var}\left(\sum_{g=1}^{G} \frac{M_g}{\bar{W}_{gt}} E_{gt}\right)$$

These are the group versions of eqs. (8.14) to (8.16) of Section 12.8.

Next consider the within-group quality index (5.20). The variance of its disturbance component is

$$\text{(8.10)} \qquad \operatorname{var}\left(\sum_{i \in S_g} \frac{\mu_i^g}{\bar{w}_{it}} \varepsilon_{it}^g\right) = \frac{\sigma^2 M_{gg}}{\bar{W}_{gt}^2} \sum_{i \in S_g} \sum_{j \in S_g} \mu_{ij}^g x_i^g x_j^g$$

where

$$\text{(8.11)} \qquad x_i^g = \frac{\mu_i^g}{\bar{w}_{it}/\bar{W}_{gt}} - \sum_{k \in S_g} \mu_k^g \frac{\mu_k^g}{\bar{w}_{kt}/\bar{W}_{gt}}$$

which is the conditional income elasticity of the ith good within its group, measured as a deviation from the marginally weighted mean of all conditional income elasticities of this group. The variance (8.10), which should be compared with (8.6), is a positive definite quadratic form in the elasticities thus measured. The matrix of this form is $\tilde{\mathbf{M}}_g$, the $n_g \times n_g$ price coefficient matrix normalized within S_g [see eq. (6.18) of Section 12.6], multiplied by the positive scalar $(\sigma/\bar{W}_{gt})^2 M_{gg}$.

For the substitution component in (5.20) we have

$$\text{(8.12)} \qquad \operatorname{var}\left(\sum_{i \in S_g} \frac{\mu_i^g}{\bar{w}_{it}} \sum_{j \in S_g} \pi_{ij}^g Dp_{jt}\right) = \delta_{22} \operatorname{var}\left(\sum_{i \in S_g} \frac{\mu_i^g}{\bar{w}_{it}} \varepsilon_{it}^g\right)$$

$$\text{(8.13)} \qquad \operatorname{cov}\left(\sum_{i \in S_g} \frac{\mu_i^g}{\bar{w}_{it}} \sum_{j \in S_g} \pi_{ij}^g Dp_{jt}, \sum_{i \in S_g} \frac{\mu_i^g}{\bar{w}_{it}} \varepsilon_{it}^g\right) = -\theta \operatorname{var}\left(\sum_{i \in S_g} \frac{\mu_i^g}{\bar{w}_{it}} \varepsilon_{it}^g\right)$$

and for the index $DQ'_{gt} - DQ_{gt}$ itself:

$$\text{(8.14)} \qquad \operatorname{var}(DQ'_{gt} - DQ_{gt}) = \delta_{11} \operatorname{var}\left(\sum_{i \in S_g} \frac{\mu_i^g}{\bar{w}_{it}} \varepsilon_{it}^g\right)$$

These three equations should be compared with (8.7) to (8.9). In particular, the substitution and disturbance components have a correlation coefficient equal to $-\theta/\sqrt{\delta_{22}}$, both for groups and within groups. Hence the conclusions drawn from eq. (8.17) of Section 12.8 apply not only to the quality index of the n-commodity basket, but also to the between- and within-group indexes.

Derivations for Quality Changes

We have $\Pi_{gh}/\phi=(N_{gh}-\phi M_g M_h)/\phi=M_{gh}-M_g M_h$ in view of eq. (4.6) of Section 8.4. Hence we can write (7.15) and eq. (4.19) of Section 8.4 as

$$\begin{aligned} \operatorname{cov}(H_{gt}, H_{ht}) &= s_2\sigma^2(M_{gh}-M_g M_h) \\ \operatorname{cov}(E_{gt}, E_{ht}) &= \sigma^2(M_{gh}-M_g M_h) \end{aligned} \tag{8.15}$$

The variance in the left-hand side of (8.6) is thus σ^2 multiplied by

$$\sum_{g=1}^{G}\sum_{h=1}^{G}(M_{gh}-M_g M_h)\frac{M_g}{\overline{W}_{gt}}\frac{M_h}{\overline{W}_{ht}} = \sum_{g=1}^{G}\sum_{h=1}^{G} M_{gh}\frac{M_g}{\overline{W}_{gt}}\frac{M_h}{\overline{W}_{ht}} - \left(\sum_{g=1}^{G} M_g \frac{M_g}{\overline{W}_{gt}}\right)^2$$

It follows from $\sum_h M_{gh}=\sum_h M_{hg}=M_g$ that the right-hand side of this equation agrees with that of (8.6).

We use (7.11) to write the random component of the substitution term in (5.17) as

$$\sum_{g=1}^{G}\frac{M_g}{\overline{W}_{gt}}\sum_{h=1}^{G}\Pi_{gh}[DP'_{ht}-\mathscr{E}(DP'_{ht})] = \frac{1}{1+s_1}\sum_{g=1}^{G}\frac{M_g}{\overline{W}_{gt}}(H_{gt}-E_{gt}) \tag{8.16}$$

When we square both sides and take the expectation, using (7.28) for δ_{22} and (8.15), we obtain the variance (8.7). The covariance (8.8) can be similarly verified by means of (7.32) for θ. The variance (8.9) is obtained by adding the variances (8.6) and (8.7) to twice the covariance (8.8) and using eq. (1.15) of Section 10.1.

Next we apply eq. (4.10) of Section 8.4 in

$$\frac{\pi_{ij}^g}{\phi} = \frac{N_{gg}}{\phi}\,\frac{\nu_{ij}-N_{gg}\mu_i^g\mu_j^g}{N_{gg}} = M_{gg}(\mu_{ij}^g-\mu_i^g\mu_j^g) \tag{8.17}$$

where

$$\mu_{ij}^g = \frac{\nu_{ij}}{N_{gg}} \tag{8.18}$$

is the $(i, j)^{\text{th}}$ price coefficient normalized within S_g. Using (8.17), we can thus write the covariance (4.21) of Section 8.4 for $g=h$ as

$$\text{cov}(\varepsilon_{it}^g, \varepsilon_{jt}^g) = \sigma^2 M_{gg}(\mu_{ij}^g - \mu_i^g \mu_j^g) \tag{8.19}$$

The variance in the left-hand side of (8.10) is therefore

$$\sigma^2 M_{gg} \sum_{i \in S_g} \sum_{j \in S_g} (\mu_{ij}^g - \mu_i^g \mu_j^g) \frac{\mu_i^g}{\bar{w}_{it}} \frac{\mu_j^g}{\bar{w}_{jt}}$$

which is identical to the right-hand side of (8.10). This may be verified by means of (8.18) and eq. (2.14) of Section 8.2.

Finally, we use (7.20) to obtain the following expression for the substitution term of (5.20) measured as a deviation from its conditional expectation:

$$\frac{1}{1+s_1} \sum_{i \in S_g} \frac{\mu_i^g}{\bar{w}_{it}} (\eta_{it}^g - \varepsilon_{it}^g)$$

The results (8.12) and (8.13) can then be verified along the lines of the derivations for (8.7) and (8.8) described below (8.16). For (8.14) we can proceed similarly to the proof of (8.9) given below (8.16).

14.9 The Conditional Demand and Supply of Meats

Section 14.7 shows how the natural conjugate approach can be used to formulate a conditional demand and supply model for a group of commodities. In this section we extend the approach to the parametrization of Section 7.3, so that it applies directly to the analysis of meats described in Sections 10.4 to 10.6.

The Conditional Demand for Meats

Since Section 14.7 is based on the blockwise dependence assumption, we take the exposition of Section 8.6 as our starting point. With S_g interpreted as the four-meat group, we consider eqs. (6.2), (6.6) and (6.7) of that section:

$$\frac{\bar{w}_{it}}{\bar{W}_{gt}} Dq_{it} = \mu_i^g DQ_{gt} + \sum_{j \in S_g} \pi_{ij}^* Dp_{jt} + \varepsilon_{it}^* \qquad i \in S_g \tag{9.1}$$

$$\pi_{ij}^* = \frac{\pi_{ij}^g}{\bar{W}_{gt}} \qquad \varepsilon_{it}^* = \frac{\varepsilon_{it}^g}{\bar{W}_{gt}} \qquad i, j \in S_g \tag{9.2}$$

We obtain (9.1) by dividing eq. (4.11) of Section 8.4 by $\bar{W}_{gt}$. Since $\bar{W}_{gt}$ is treated as predetermined, we can use (7.16), which is derived from the latter equation, to write (9.1) as a deviation from its conditional expectation:

$$\text{(9.3)} \qquad \frac{\bar{w}_{it}}{\bar{W}_{gt}}[Dq_{it} - \mathscr{E}_g(Dq_{it})] = \sum_{j \in S_g} \pi_{ij}^*[Dp_{jt} - \mathscr{E}_g(Dp_{jt})] + \varepsilon_{it}^*$$

Note the use of the g subscript attached to $\mathscr{E}$; this is appropriate in view of the developments in the next subsection.

The Supply of Meats

With S_g again interpreted as meats and $i \in S_g$, we divide the supply equations (7.4) and (7.7) by $\bar{W}_{gt}$:

$$\text{(9.4)} \qquad \frac{\bar{w}_{it}}{\bar{W}_{gt}}[Dq_{it} - \mathscr{E}(Dq_{it})] = -s_1 \sum_{j=1}^{n} \frac{\pi_{ij}}{\bar{W}_{gt}}[Dp_{jt} - \mathscr{E}(Dp_{jt})] + \frac{\eta_{it}}{\bar{W}_{gt}}$$

$$\text{(9.5)} \qquad DQ_{gt} - \mathscr{E}(DQ_{gt}) = -s_1 \sum_{h=1}^{G} \frac{\Pi_{gh}}{\bar{W}_{gt}}[DP'_{ht} - \mathscr{E}(DP'_{ht})] + \frac{H_{gt}}{\bar{W}_{gt}}$$

Next we proceed as in the developments leading to (7.17) by multiplying (9.5) by the ith conditional marginal share and subtracting the result from (9.4). It follows from (9.2) and eq. (4.15) of Section 8.4 that this yields

$$\text{(9.6)} \qquad \frac{\bar{w}_{it}}{\bar{W}_{gt}}[Dq_{it} - \mathscr{E}_g(Dq_{it})] = -s_1 \sum_{j \in S_g} \pi_{ij}^*[Dp_{jt} - \mathscr{E}_g(Dp_{jt})] + \eta_{it}^*$$

where

$$\text{(9.7)} \qquad \eta_{it}^* = \frac{\eta_{it} - \mu_i^g H_{gt}}{\bar{W}_{gt}} = \frac{\eta_{it}^g}{\bar{W}_{gt}} \qquad \text{[see (7.18)]}$$

Equation (9.6) is the conditional supply equation of the ith meat, written as a deviation from its conditional expectation, under the parametrization of Section 7.3. When we combine it with (9.3) and proceed along the lines of eqs. (2.10) to (2.12) of Section 10.2, we obtain

$$\text{(9.8)} \qquad \frac{\bar{w}_{it}}{\bar{W}_{gt}}[Dq_{it} - \mathscr{E}_g(Dq_{it})] = \frac{\eta_{it}^* + s_1\varepsilon_{it}^*}{1 + s_1}$$

$$\text{(9.9)} \qquad \sum_{j \in S_g} \pi_{ij}^*[Dp_{jt} - \mathscr{E}_g(Dp_{jt})] = \frac{\eta_{it}^* - \varepsilon_{it}^*}{1 + s_1}$$

This result is the extension of (7.19) and (7.20) under the present parametrization.

The Implied Variance-Covariance Specification

The disturbance covariance structure of (9.1) and (9.3) is given in eq. (6.8) of Section 8.6,

$$\operatorname{cov}(\varepsilon_{it}^*, \varepsilon_{jt}^*) = \frac{\sigma^2}{\phi \bar{W}_{gt}} \pi_{ij}^* = -\frac{\pi_{ij}^*}{\gamma} \tag{9.10}$$

where the second step is based on eq. (4.3) of Section 7.4. For (9.6) we have

$$\operatorname{cov}(\eta_{it}^*, \eta_{jt}^*) = \frac{\operatorname{cov}(\eta_{it}^g, \eta_{jt}^g)}{\bar{W}_{gt}^2} = s_2\sigma^2 \frac{\pi_{ij}^g}{\phi \bar{W}_{gt}^2} = -s_2 \frac{\pi_{ij}^*}{\gamma} \tag{9.11}$$

where the first step is based on (9.7), the second on (7.21), and the third on (9.2) and (9.10).

The results (9.10) and (9.11) combined with the zero correlation of the conditional demand and supply disturbances provide a complete description of all disturbance variances and covariances of the model (9.3) and (9.6). When we apply it to (9.8) and (9.9), we obtain

$$\operatorname{cov}\left(\frac{\bar{w}_{it}}{\bar{W}_{gt}} Dq_{it}, \frac{\bar{w}_{jt}}{\bar{W}_{gt}} Dq_{jt}\right) = \frac{s_1^2 + s_2}{(1+s_1)^2}\left(-\frac{\pi_{ij}^*}{\gamma}\right)$$

$$\operatorname{cov}\left(\textstyle\sum_k \pi_{ik}^* Dp_{kt}, \sum_k \pi_{jk}^* Dp_{kt}\right) = \frac{1+s_2}{(1+s_1)^2}\left(-\frac{\pi_{ij}^*}{\gamma}\right)$$

$$\operatorname{cov}\left(\frac{\bar{w}_{it}}{\bar{W}_{gt}} Dq_{it}, \textstyle\sum_k \pi_{jk}^* Dp_{kt}\right) = -\frac{s_1 - s_2}{(1+s_1)^2}\left(-\frac{\pi_{ij}^*}{\gamma}\right)$$

where $\sum_k$ stands for summation over $k \in S_g$. This result is equivalent to eqs. (2.13) to (2.15) of Section 10.2 under the conditional interpretation of eq. (4.1) of Section 10.4, so that the covariance specification (1.12) of Section 10.1 is valid under this interpretation. This covariance specification is the basis of the estimation procedure described in Sections 10.4 to 10.6.

CHAPTER 15

EQUIVALENT INCOME CHANGES

The purpose of the preference independence transformation is to represent the consumer's preferences in the simplest possible way, with marginal utilities of T-goods which are independent of the consumption levels of other T-goods in the neighborhood of the budget-constrained utility maximum. Since the Rotterdam Model is formulated in terms of changes over time, it is thus natural to analyze the changes in the marginal utilities of these T-goods. This is the subject of the equivalent income changes, which leads to valuable insights into other matters as well, including the quality index, the price-quantity covariance, and certain problems of statistical inference. It is assumed throughout this chapter, except when otherwise stated, that there is preference independence or that the preference independence transformation has been applied.

15.1 Equivalent Income and Volume Changes

Definition of an Equivalent Income Change

Under preference independence the ith demand equation takes the form

$$\bar{w}_{it} Dq_{it} = \mu_i DQ_t + \phi\mu_i (Dp_{it} - DP'_t) + \varepsilon_{it} \tag{1.1}$$

where $\mu_i > 0$. Let us divide the variable on the left by μ_i:

$$\frac{\bar{w}_{it} Dq_{it}}{\mu_i} = \frac{Dq_{it}}{\mu_i / \bar{w}_{it}} \tag{1.2}$$

The right-hand side indicates that the resulting expression is equal to the ratio of the ith quantity log-change to the ith income elasticity. This ratio equals the log-change in real income which would yield the observed Dq_{it} if the change in real income were the only change, i.e., if all relative prices were constant and if the disturbances were zero; this may be verified by equating the last two terms in (1.1) to zero and solving for DQ_t. The expression (1.2) was therefore referred to by THEIL (1967, Section 7.8) as the *equivalent income change* of the ith good from $t-1$ to t.

There are n equivalent income changes, one for each good. Their marginally weighted mean is equal to the log-change in real income:

$$\sum_{i=1}^{n} \mu_i \frac{\bar{w}_{it} Dq_{it}}{\mu_i} = DQ_t \tag{1.3}$$

The Three Components of an Equivalent Income Change

By dividing both sides of (1.1) by μ_i, we obtain

$$\frac{\bar{w}_{it} Dq_{it}}{\mu_i} = DQ_t + \phi\,(Dp_{it} - DP'_t) + \frac{\varepsilon_{it}}{\mu_i} \tag{1.4}$$

Note that this equation is much simpler than (1.1). The real-income components of all n equivalent income changes are equal to the log-change in real income, and their own-price coefficients are all equal to the income flexibility.

If the second-moment model holds for (1.1),

$$\operatorname{cov}(\varepsilon_{it}, \varepsilon_{jt}) = \begin{cases} \sigma^2 \mu_i (1 - \mu_i) & \text{if } i = j \\ -\sigma^2 \mu_i \mu_j & \text{if } i \neq j \end{cases} \tag{1.5}$$

the implication for the disturbance component of (1.4) is

$$\operatorname{cov}\left(\frac{\varepsilon_{it}}{\mu_i}, \frac{\varepsilon_{jt}}{\mu_j}\right) = \begin{cases} \sigma^2 \left(\dfrac{1}{\mu_i} - 1\right) & \text{if } i = j \\ -\sigma^2 & \text{if } i \neq j \end{cases} \tag{1.6}$$

This covariance structure is simpler than (1.5) in that all covariances ($i \neq j$) take the same value. Hence the only features in the right-hand sides of (1.4) and (1.6) which are specific for the ith good are Dp_{it} in the substitution component and the variance of the disturbance component.

Log-changes in Marginal Utilities of T-Goods

Consider eq. (6.6) of Section 1.6:

$$d\left(\log \frac{\partial u}{\partial q_i}\right) = \sum_{j=1}^{n} v^{ij}(m, \mathbf{p})\, w_j\, d(\log q_j)$$

Under preference independence this can be simplified to

$$d\left(\log \frac{\partial u}{\partial q_i}\right) = \frac{w_i\, d(\log q_i)}{\phi \mu_i} \tag{1.7}$$

where $(m, \mathbf{p})$ is deleted for notational convenience. Since the right-hand side is the infinitesimal version of $\bar{w}_{it} Dq_{it}/\phi\mu_i$, we conclude that the equivalent income change of the ith good may be identified with the log-change in its marginal utility, multiplied by the income flexibility. In most cases we have to apply a preference independence transformation to obtain demand equations of the form (1.1), so that the ith equivalent income change is then equal to ϕ multiplied by the log-change in the marginal utility of the ith T-good. It follows from (1.3) that the marginally weighted mean of the log-changes in the marginal utilities of the T-goods equals DQ_t divided by ϕ. The corresponding variance is considered in Section 15.3.

It is also instructive to consider the reciprocal equation of the Rotterdam Model which is given in eqs. (5.4) and (5.5) of Section 9.5. In the case of preference independence this equation can be written as

$$(1.8) \qquad Dp_{it} - DP'_t = \frac{\bar{w}_{it} Dq_{it}}{\phi \mu_i} - \frac{DQ_t}{\phi} - \frac{\varepsilon_{it}}{\phi \mu_i}$$

which is equivalent to (1.4). Given the conclusion drawn from (1.7), this result should come as no surprise, since we know from the discussion below eq. (5.10) of Section 9.5 that the ith reciprocal equation is equivalent to $\partial u / \partial q_i = \lambda p_i$ written in log-change form.

The Geometry of Equivalent Income Changes

We return to Figure 11.5 on page 207 and its point Q^{**} whose i^{th} coordinate equals $\bar{w}_{it} Dq_{it}$. To obtain the vector of equivalent income changes, we apply the reciprocal marginal transformation to Q^{**} twice, so that the ith coordinate becomes

$$\frac{1}{\sqrt{\mu_i}} \frac{1}{\sqrt{\mu_i}} \bar{w}_{it} Dq_{it} = \frac{\bar{w}_{it} Dq_{it}}{\mu_i}$$

which equals (1.2). This yields the boldface vector OE in Figure 15.1, where E is the point whose i^{th} coordinate equals $\bar{w}_{it} Dq_{it} / \mu_i$. The real-income component in (1.4) is represented by the vector OR_E, with R_E defined as the point whose coordinates are all equal to DQ_t. This point is always on the straight line through the origin and Iota. The substitution component in (1.4) for $i = 1, \ldots, n$ is obtained by multiplying $Dp_{1t} - DP'_t, \ldots, Dp_{nt} - DP'_t$, which are the coordinates of the deflated price point (P_d in Figures 11.5 and 15.1), by the negative scalar ϕ. This yields the vector OS_E in Figure 15.1.

The disturbance component in (1.4) is represented by the vector OD_E in Figure 15.1, and the point indicated by $D_E + S_E$ is obtained by adding the vectors OD_E and OS_E, after which OE emerges from the parallelogram on O, R_E and $D_E + S_E$. Note that the points P_d, O, D_E and S_E are all on the

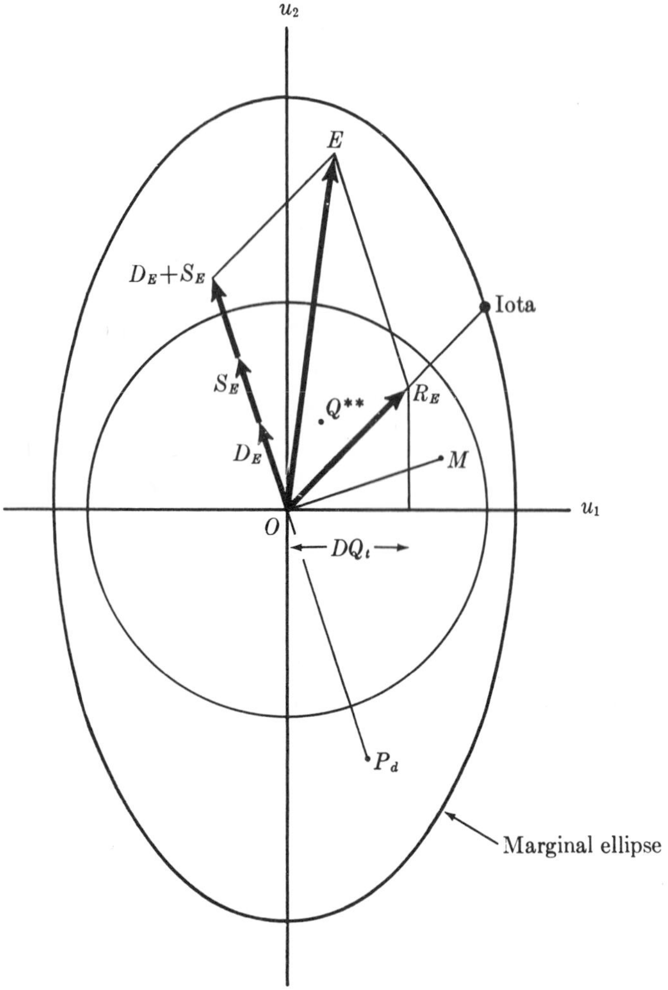

Fig. 15.1 The vector of equivalent income changes and its components

straight line $\sum_i \mu_i u_i = 0$, which is perpendicular to the line from the origin to M (see also Figure 11.5). For general n the equation $\sum_i \mu_i u_i = 0$ is represented by an $(n-1)$-dimensional plane through the origin which is perpendicular to OM.

Equivalent Income Changes of Commodity Groups

Recall from (1.3) that the marginally weighted mean of the n equivalent income changes is equal to the log-change in real income. Consider now the equivalent income changes of the goods of S_g only, and weight them with conditional marginal shares:

$$\sum_{i \in S_g} \frac{\mu_i}{M_g} \frac{\bar{w}_{it} Dq_{it}}{\mu_i} = \frac{\bar{W}_{gt} DQ_{gt}}{M_g} \tag{1.9}$$

The right-hand side is the uppercase version of $\bar{w}_{it} Dq_{it}/\mu_i$, which suggests that it should be interpreted as the equivalent income change of the group S_g. To verify this interpretation, we consider the preference-independent demand equation for this group:

$$\bar{W}_{gt} DQ_{gt} = M_g DQ_t + \phi M_g (DP'_{gt} - DP'_t) + E_{gt} \tag{1.10}$$

If the relative prices are unchanged ($DP'_{gt} - DP'_t = 0$) and the disturbance E_{gt} vanishes, this amounts to $\bar{W}_{gt} DQ_{gt} = M_g DQ_t$ which, when solved for DQ_t, yields the right-hand side of (1.9). Going back to the developments below (1.2), we conclude that this corroborates our interpretation. Note also that, since $\bar{W}_{gt}$ and M_g are both 1 when S_g consists of all n commodities, (1.9) implies that DQ_t, the log-change in real income, may be interpreted as the equivalent income change of the complete basket.

By dividing (1.10) by M_g we obtain

$$\frac{\bar{W}_{gt} DQ_{gt}}{M_g} = DQ_t + \phi (DP'_{gt} - DP'_t) + \frac{E_{gt}}{M_g} \tag{1.11}$$

which is the commodity group version of (1.4). The analogous extension of (1.3) is

$$\sum_{g=1}^{G} M_g \frac{\bar{W}_{gt} DQ_{gt}}{M_g} = DQ_t \tag{1.12}$$

and that of (1.6) is

$$\operatorname{cov}\left(\frac{E_{gt}}{M_g}, \frac{E_{ht}}{M_h}\right) = \begin{cases} \sigma^2 \left(\dfrac{1}{M_g} - 1\right) & \text{if } g = h \\ -\sigma^2 & \text{if } g \neq h \end{cases} \tag{1.13}$$

which may be verified from eq. (7.31) of Section 2.7.

Equivalent Income Changes Within a Commodity Group

Under preference independence we can write the conditional demand equation (1.6) of Section 7.1 as

$$\bar{w}_{it} Dq_{it} = \frac{\mu_i}{M_g} \bar{W}_{gt} DQ_{gt} + \phi \mu_i (Dp_{it} - DP'_{gt}) + \varepsilon_{it}^g \tag{1.14}$$

By dividing both sides by μ_i we obtain

$$\text{(1.15)} \qquad \frac{\bar{w}_{it} Dq_{it}}{\mu_i} = \frac{\bar{W}_{gt} DQ_{gt}}{M_g} + \phi\,(Dp_{it} - DP'_{gt}) + \frac{\varepsilon^g_{it}}{\mu_i}$$

This equation, which should be compared with (1.4), describes the ith equivalent income change as the sum of a volume, a price and a disturbance component, all within S_g. The volume component is the equivalent income change of the group. The deflator in the substitution component is the marginally weighted price index of the group. For all $i \in S_g$, the volume components are the same and the own-price coefficients are equal to ϕ, which is similar to the real-income and substitution components of (1.4).

We use eqs. (1.10) and (1.17) of Section 7.1 to write the second-moment model of the disturbances of the conditional equations in the following preference-independent form:

$$\text{(1.16)} \qquad \operatorname{cov}(\varepsilon^g_{it}, \varepsilon^g_{jt}) = \begin{cases} \sigma^2 \mu_i \left(1 - \dfrac{\mu_i}{M_g}\right) & \text{if} \quad i = j \\[2ex] -\sigma^2 \dfrac{\mu_i \mu_j}{M_g} & \text{if} \quad i \neq j \end{cases}$$

The implied variance-covariance structure of the disturbance component in (1.15) is

$$\text{(1.17)} \qquad \operatorname{cov}\left(\frac{\varepsilon^g_{it}}{\mu_i}, \frac{\varepsilon^g_{jt}}{\mu_j}\right) = \begin{cases} \sigma^2 \left(\dfrac{1}{\mu_i} - \dfrac{1}{M_g}\right) & \text{if} \quad i = j \\[2ex] -\dfrac{\sigma^2}{M_g} & \text{if} \quad i \neq j \end{cases}$$

This shows that the covariances ($i \neq j$) are equal for all commodity pairs of the group. As in (1.4) and (1.6), the only commodity-specific features in (1.15) and (1.17) are Dp_{it} in the substitution component and the variance of the disturbance component. Note that (1.11) and (1.13) have a similar property.

Note further that the disturbance component in (1.15) is uncorrelated with that of a good j in any other group ($j \in S_h$, $g \neq h$), and also with the disturbance components $E_{1t}/M_1, \ldots, E_{Gt}/M_G$ of the groups. This follows from eqs. (1.17) and (1.18) of Section 7.1.

Equivalent Volume Changes Within a Commodity Group

Recall from (1.2) that the ith equivalent income change equals Dq_{it} divided by the ith income elasticity. Let us now divide Dq_{it} by the ith conditional income elasticity:

$$Dq_{it}\left(\frac{\mu_i/\bar{w}_{it}}{M_g/\bar{W}_{gt}}\right)^{-1} = \frac{M_g}{\bar{W}_{gt}}\frac{\bar{w}_{it}Dq_{it}}{\mu_i} \qquad i \in S_g \tag{1.18}$$

The right-hand side indicates that this amounts to multiplying the ith equivalent income change by the income elasticity of the group. We shall refer to (1.18) as the *equivalent volume change* of the ith good within its group. To clarify this terminology we multiply (1.15) by $M_g/\bar{W}_{gt}$:

$$\frac{M_g}{\bar{W}_{gt}}\frac{\bar{w}_{it}Dq_{it}}{\mu_i} = DQ_{gt} + \frac{\phi M_g}{\bar{W}_{gt}}(Dp_{it} - DP'_{gt}) + \frac{\varepsilon_{it}^g/\bar{W}_{gt}}{\mu_i/M_g} \tag{1.19}$$

By equating $Dp_{it} - DP'_{gt}$ and the conditional disturbance to zero and solving for DQ_{gt}, we find that (1.18) is the volume log-change of S_g which would yield the observed Dq_{it} if there were no changes in the relative prices of the goods of S_g and the conditional disturbance were zero. This is identical to the reasoning below (1.2) except that we now operate within S_g and the volume log-change DQ_{gt} plays the role of DQ_t.

Equation (1.19) is a straightforward extension of (1.4), with DQ_t replaced by DQ_{gt} and ϕ by $\phi M_g/\bar{W}_{gt}$, the own-price elasticity of the group. Note further that the marginally weighted mean of the equivalent volume changes of the goods of S_g equals the volume log-change of S_g:

$$\sum_{i \in S_g} \frac{\mu_i}{M_g}\left(\frac{M_g}{\bar{W}_{gt}}\frac{\bar{w}_{it}Dq_{it}}{\mu_i}\right) = DQ_{gt} \tag{1.20}$$

This is a within-group extension of (1.3).

Recall also from the discussion below (1.7) that $\bar{w}_{it}Dq_{it}/\mu_i$ can be identified with ϕ multiplied by the log-change in the marginal utility of the ith T-good. It follows from (1.18) that the ith equivalent volume change within its group equals the log-change in the same marginal utility, but multiplied by the own-price elasticity of the group.

15.2 Equivalent Volume and Quantity Changes of Meats

In this section we discuss the equivalent volume changes of the American meats from 1950 to 1972. Since they are obtained by dividing quantity log-changes by conditional income elasticities, it is convenient to discuss both sets of changes here.

TABLE 15.1

QUANTITY LOG-CHANGES AND EQUIVALENT VOLUME CHANGES OF MEATS

	Quantity log-changes			Equivalent volume changes			Components of equivalent volume changes						
							Volume	Substitution			Disturbances		
	T_1	T_2	T_3	T_1	T_2	T_3		T_1	T_2	T_3	T_1	T_2	T_3
1950–51	1.60	−18.47	−5.40	2.36	−9.11	−5.01	−3.37	3.30	−3.85	−.87	2.42	−1.89	−.77
1951–52	2.70	13.90	4.08	3.98	6.88	3.78	5.57	−.16	−.26	2.80	−1.43	1.57	−4.59
1952–53	−3.42	36.59	−9.40	−4.93	18.61	−8.55	4.83	−9.37	13.81	−14.04	−.38	−.02	.67
1953–54	−1.33	5.99	−12.03	−1.88	3.11	−10.67	−.53	.81	.80	−9.99	−2.16	2.84	−.15
1954–55	4.07	−2.32	24.80	5.60	−1.23	21.43	3.98	2.36	−6.32	16.40	−.74	1.10	1.05
1955–56	4.99	4.72	−10.02	6.77	2.56	−8.56	3.52	2.11	−1.27	−6.12	1.14	.31	−5.97
1956–57	−3.89	2.41	−17.90	−5.23	1.32	−15.16	−3.84	−.16	3.25	−11.75	−1.22	1.92	.43
1957–58	.66	−7.36	−14.98	.89	−4.06	−12.60	−2.06	3.16	−3.72	−5.50	−.21	1.72	−5.04
1958–59	6.64	−5.61	12.46	8.71	−3.12	10.25	5.05	4.04	−7.70	1.85	−.38	−.48	3.35
1959–60	−1.72	8.35	.92	−2.20	4.73	.74	.23	−.65	.88	1.40	−1.78	3.62	−.89
1960–61	−.10	7.16	−9.82	−.12	4.09	−7.71	.54	−.28	3.52	−9.77	−.38	.04	1.52
1961–62	1.42	−.75	3.41	1.77	−.43	2.65	1.22	.50	−1.90	2.96	.05	.24	−1.53
1962–63	3.51	6.95	5.79	4.37	4.00	4.50	3.92	−.07	.29	1.32	.52	−.20	−.74
1963–64	1.86	9.60	3.79	2.29	5.57	2.93	2.63	−.23	.87	−.31	−.11	2.08	.61
1964–65	−3.24	8.46	−16.02	−4.00	4.93	−12.51	−3.18	−1.60	7.61	−6.04	.77	.50	−3.29
1965–66	2.99	8.98	−2.97	3.79	5.19	−2.38	3.24	−1.60	5.54	−2.67	2.15	−3.60	−2.95
1966–67	5.82	−3.26	8.77	7.35	−1.89	7.00	4.62	2.66	−5.90	.46	.07	−.61	1.92
1967–68	2.44	2.67	5.09	3.02	1.56	3.98	2.60	.78	−2.82	1.81	−.36	1.79	−.43
1968–69	.64	3.89	−3.82	.79	2.28	−2.97	.29	.65	−.45	−2.28	−.15	2.44	−.99
1969–70	3.27	3.17	−.26	3.99	1.87	−.20	2.67	.42	2.03	−4.04	.90	−2.83	1.17
1970–71	3.90	−10.42	6.62	4.70	−6.17	5.05	2.53	2.83	−12.04	2.99	−.67	3.35	−.48
1971–72	−1.82	15.29	−4.85	−2.14	9.07	−3.62	−.54	−.41	7.84	−6.30	−1.19	1.76	3.21
1950–72	31.0	89.9	−31.8	39.9	49.8	−27.6	33.9	9.1	.2	−47.7	−3.1	15.7	−13.9

Note. All entries are to be divided by 100.

Quantity Log-changes of Transformed Meats

The first three columns of Table 15.1 contain the quantity log-changes of Inexpensive meat (T_1), the Beef/Pork contrast (T_2), and Antichicken (T_3). It follows from remark (2) on page 227 that these log-changes can be computed as $\sum_j s_{ij} Dq_{jt}$, with $[s_{ij}]$ as given in Table 13.2 on pages 288–292. Table 15.1 shows that the year-to-year changes in the consumption of Inexpensive meat are small, whereas those of the two other transformed meats are much larger in several years. This is mainly the result of prices; we observed a similar difference between T_1 on one hand and T_2 and T_3 on the other when we discussed the price log-changes of Table 13.9 on page 324.

By dividing the figures in the last row of Table 15.1 by 22, we obtain an average annual percentage change in consumption of almost $1\frac{1}{2}$ for T_1, about 4 for T_2, and about $-1\frac{1}{2}$ for T_3. This amounts to a large difference between these three meats, and it is not surprising. We know from Table 13.9 that the price of Antichicken increased substantially relative to the marginal meat price index, which implies a negative substitution effect on its consumption. The price of Inexpensive meat declined from 1950 to 1972 relative to the marginal index, leading to a positive substitution effect, and the net change in the price of the Beef/Pork contrast in this period is virtually the same as that in the marginal index. The major cause of the trend in the consumption of this contrast is its high conditional income elasticity (Table 13.1 on page 286) combined with the increase in the volume of total meat consumption. It will be convenient to discuss these components for the equivalent volume changes, which – in contrast to the quantity log-changes – have the same volume component. For this purpose we must return to the preference independence transformation.

The Commodity Interpretation of the Equivalent Income Changes

Assume that there is no preference independence among the commodities, so that the preference independence transformation must be applied for the computation of the equivalent income changes. Each such change is obtained by dividing the left-hand variable of a transformed demand equation by the corresponding marginal share. These shares are the diagonal elements of $(\boldsymbol{\mu}_T)_\Delta$ and the vector of left-hand variables is $\mathbf{Rz}_t$, so that we can find the vector of equivalent income changes by premultiplying $\mathbf{Rz}_t$ by the inverse of $(\boldsymbol{\mu}_T)_\Delta$.

To evaluate this vector we use eqs. (2.19) and (2.29) of Section 12.2:

$$(\boldsymbol{\mu}_T)_\Delta^{-1}\,\mathbf{R} = (\mathbf{X}^{-1}\boldsymbol{\iota})_\Delta^{-1}\,\boldsymbol{\Lambda}^{-1}\,(\mathbf{X}^{-1}\boldsymbol{\iota})_\Delta^{-1}\,(\mathbf{X}^{-1}\boldsymbol{\iota})_\Delta\,\mathbf{X}' = (\mathbf{X}^{-1}\boldsymbol{\iota})_\Delta^{-1}\,\boldsymbol{\Lambda}^{-1}\mathbf{X}'$$

The third member can be written, in view of eqs. (2.22) of Section 12.2 and

(1.23) of Section 12.1, as

$$(\mathbf{X}^{-1}\boldsymbol{\iota})_{\Delta}^{-1}\,\mathbf{X}^{-1}(\mathbf{X}\boldsymbol{\Lambda}^{-1}\mathbf{X}') = \mathbf{S}\mathbf{M}^{-1}$$

so that the vector of equivalent income changes becomes

$$(\boldsymbol{\mu}_T)_{\Delta}^{-1}\,\mathbf{R}\mathbf{z}_t = \mathbf{S}\mathbf{M}^{-1}\mathbf{z}_t \tag{2.1}$$

The marginally weighted mean of the elements of this vector is

$$\boldsymbol{\mu}_T'(\boldsymbol{\mu}_T)_{\Delta}^{-1}\,\mathbf{R}\mathbf{z}_t = \boldsymbol{\iota}'\mathbf{R}\mathbf{z}_t = \boldsymbol{\iota}'\mathbf{z}_t = DQ_t \tag{2.2}$$

where use is made of eq. (2.1) of Section 12.2 in the second step. This result agrees with (1.3) and the invariance of DQ_t under the preference independence transformation.

Note the premultiplication of $\mathbf{z}_t$ by $\mathbf{M}^{-1}$ in the right-hand side of (2.1), and compare this with the premultiplication by $\mathbf{N}^{-1} = (\phi\mathbf{M})^{-1}$ which was performed in Section 9.5 to derive the reciprocal equations. Recall also that we concluded below (1.8) that under preference independence the ith reciprocal equation is equivalent to (1.4). This is confirmed by (2.1), since we can specify $\mathbf{S}=\mathbf{I}$ when there is preference independence.

Extension to the Equivalent Volume Changes of Meats

We use eq. (3.8) of Section 7.3 to simplify the disturbance term in (1.19), so that this equation becomes

$$\frac{M_g}{\bar{W}_{gt}}\frac{\bar{w}_{it}Dq_{it}}{\mu_i} = DQ_{gt} + \frac{\phi M_g}{\bar{W}_{gt}}(Dp_{it} - DP_{gt}') + \frac{\varepsilon_{it}^*}{\mu_i/M_g} \tag{2.3}$$

It is to be understood that the symbols involving the subscript i in this equation refer to the ith transformed meat. Also, in order to make the results comparable with earlier tables and those which follow later in this chapter, we interpret S_g as the four-meat group (with Lamb included). Hence DQ_{gt} in (2.3) is as shown in Table 14.2 on page 349 and the own-price elasticity is specified as

$$\frac{\phi M_g}{\bar{W}_{gt}} = -.6393 \tag{2.4}$$

which agrees with eq. (6.26) of Section 7.6. The conditional version of (2.1) is then

$$\begin{bmatrix} s_{11} & s_{12} & s_{13} & 0 \\ s_{21} & s_{22} & s_{23} & 0 \\ s_{31} & s_{32} & s_{33} & 0 \\ 0 & 0 & 0 & 1 \end{bmatrix} \begin{bmatrix} \mu_{11}^g & \mu_{12}^g & \mu_{13}^g & 0 \\ \mu_{21}^g & \mu_{22}^g & \mu_{23}^g & 0 \\ \mu_{31}^g & \mu_{32}^g & \mu_{33}^g & 0 \\ 0 & 0 & 0 & \mu_4/M_g \end{bmatrix}^{-1} \begin{bmatrix} \bar{w}_{1t}Dq_{1t}/\bar{W}_{gt} \\ \bar{w}_{2t}Dq_{2t}/\bar{W}_{gt} \\ \bar{w}_{3t}Dq_{3t}/\bar{W}_{gt} \\ \bar{w}_{4t}Dq_{4t}/\bar{W}_{gt} \end{bmatrix} \tag{2.5}$$

where the second matrix is the inverse of $\tilde{\mathbf{M}}_g$, the price coefficient matrix normalized within the four-meat group; the $(i, j)^{\text{th}}$ element of $\tilde{\mathbf{M}}_g$ is given in eq. (4.9) of Section 13.4. The equivalent volume changes of T_1, T_2 and T_3 are the first three elements of the vector (2.5). The fourth element refers to Lamb; it can be obtained directly from Tables 7.2 and 7.3 (pages 11–12) and $\mu_4/M_g = .0422$.

The ratios of the quantity log-changes in the first three columns of Table 15.1 to the corresponding equivalent volume changes (shown in the next three columns) are conditional income elasticities. These elasticities differ slightly from those of Table 13.1 on page 286 because of the four-meat interpretation of S_g which is used here. If λ_i for $i=1$, 2 or 3 is a conditional income elasticity of Table 13.1, we can write it under the present interpretation as

$$\lambda_i = \frac{\mu_{iT}/(M_g - \mu_4)}{(\bar{w}_{it})_T/(\bar{W}_{gt} - \bar{w}_{4t})} = \frac{1 - \dfrac{\bar{w}_{4t}}{\bar{W}_{gt}}}{1 - \dfrac{\mu_4}{M_g}} \frac{\mu_{iT}/M_g}{(\bar{w}_{it})_T/\bar{W}_{gt}} \tag{2.6}$$

Hence λ_i of the three-meat group equals the conditional income elasticity within the four-meat group, multiplied by 1 minus the conditional budget share of Lamb and divided by 1 minus the conditional marginal share of Lamb. Since the latter share is .0422 and the former is smaller (see Table 7.2 on page 11), λ_i is a little larger than the corresponding elasticity within the four-meat group.

Discussion of the Equivalent Volume Changes and Their Components

The 1950–51 row of Table 15.1 shows that the equivalent volume changes of T_1, T_2 and T_3 in that year are .0236, −.0911 and −.0501, respectively. Alternatively, using (2.4) and the interpretation given in the paragraph below (1.20), we can say that the marginal utility of Inexpensive meat declined by $2.36/(.6393) \approx 3.7$ percent in 1951, whereas the marginal utilities of the Beef/Pork contrast and Antichicken increased. Note that the equivalent volume changes of Inexpensive meat are all larger than the corresponding quantity log-changes, and that the opposite is true for the other two transformed meats. This is due to the fact that the latter two meats have conditional income elasticities exceeding 1, whereas that of Inexpensive meat is less than 1. The result is that the order of magnitude of the equivalent volume changes of the three meats is much less different than that of the quantity log-changes in the first three columns of the table.

The substitution term in (2.3) is obtained by combining (2.4) with the price log-changes and the marginal price index of Table 13.9 on page 324. The disturbance term is computed from (2.5) with $\bar{w}_{it}Dq_{it}/\bar{W}_{gt}$ replaced by ε_{it}^{*}. It will come as no surprise that the substitution components take large absolute values in 1952–53, leading to large equivalent volume changes (particularly for the Beef/Pork contrast) and hence also to large changes in the marginal utilities of the transformed meats. The importance of substitution is also illustrated by the fact that 16 of the 66 substitution components exceed the largest volume component in absolute value. The sum of the equivalent volume changes of Antichicken from 1950 to 1972 is negative, which amounts to a net increase of the marginal utility of this meat. The major force behind this change is price substitution, which more than compensated the effect of the increase in the volume of total meat consumption. The two other transformed meats have a net decrease in their marginal utility from 1950 to 1972, mainly caused by the volume component.

15.3 The Variance of the Equivalent Income Changes

The budget-share-weighted variance of the n quantity log-changes is

$$K_t = \sum_{i=1}^{n} \bar{w}_{it}(Dq_{it} - DQ_t)^2 \tag{3.1}$$

This variance was introduced in eq. (2.13) of Section 11.2 as a measure of the change in the relative composition of the consumer's basket, but we found in Section 11.5 that its decomposition in terms of real-income, substitution and disturbance components leads to as many as six terms, including three interaction terms. The variance of the equivalent income changes, which performs a similar but not identical function, is much simpler in this respect.

The Mean and the Variance of the Equivalent Income Changes

Recall from (1.3) that the marginally weighted mean of the equivalent income changes is equal to the log-change in real income. The corresponding variance is therefore

$$V_t = \sum_{i=1}^{n} \mu_i\left(\frac{\bar{w}_{it}Dq_{it}}{\mu_i} - DQ_t\right)^2 \tag{3.2}$$

To interpret this variance we compare it with K_t, which measures the degree to which the n quantity log-changes differ from the log-change in real income. In contrast to this, we have in V_t a measure of the extent to which the change in real income fails to account for the n quantity log-changes, taking into consideration that different goods have different income elasticities. This interpretation follows from eq. (1.4), which shows that the expression in parentheses in (3.2) involves only a relative price change and a disturbance.

Recall also from the discussion below (1.7) that the ith equivalent income change is a multiple ϕ of the log-change in the marginal utility of the ith T-good. Hence the variance (3.2) is a multiple ϕ^2 of the marginally weighted variance of the log-changes in these marginal utilities.

The Three Components of the Variance

By substituting (1.4) in (3.2) we obtain

$$V_t = \phi^2 \sum_{i=1}^{n} \mu_i (Dp_{it} - DP_t')^2 + 2\phi \sum_{i=1}^{n} (Dp_{it} - DP_t')\, \varepsilon_{it} + \sum_{i=1}^{n} \frac{\varepsilon_{it}^2}{\mu_i}$$

which can be simplified to

$$V_t = \phi^2 \Pi_t' + 2\phi \sum_{i=1}^{n} Dp_{it}\varepsilon_{it} + \sum_{i=1}^{n} \frac{\varepsilon_{it}^2}{\mu_i} \tag{3.3}$$

The first term on the right concerns price substitution exclusively, the third concerns disturbances exclusively, and the second describes the interaction effect of substitution and disturbances. This decomposition is evidently much more attractive than the six terms of K_t which result from eq. (5.10) of Section 11.5.

To simplify the terminology we shall refer to the first right-hand term in (3.3) as the substitution component of V_t, to the second as the linear disturbance component, and to the third as the quadratic disturbance component. Note that the substitution component is a multiple ϕ of the corresponding component of Γ_t given in eq. (1.6) of Section 11.1, and that the linear disturbance component is a multiple 2ϕ of the disturbance component of Γ_t. The expectation of the quadratic disturbance component under the second-moment model is

$$\mathscr{E}\left(\sum_{i=1}^{n} \frac{\varepsilon_{it}^2}{\mu_i}\right) = \sigma^2 \sum_{i=1}^{n} \frac{\mu_i(1-\mu_i)}{\mu_i} = \sigma^2 (n-1) \tag{3.4}$$

which is a multiple σ^2 of the number of linearly independent demand equations.

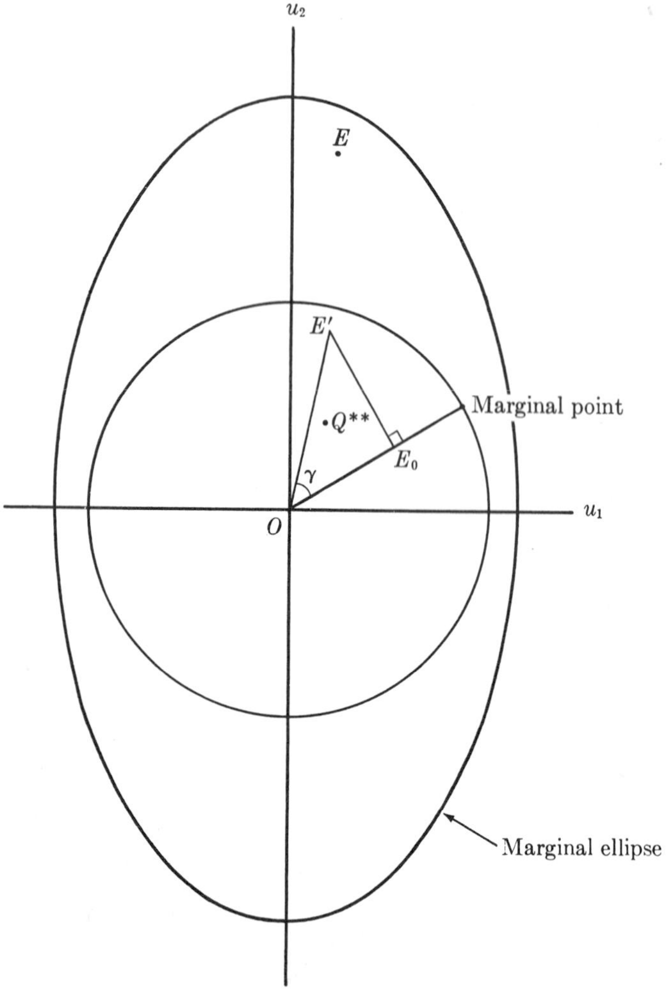

Fig. 15.2 The variance of the equivalent income changes

The Geometry of the Variance

In Figure 15.2 we apply the marginal transformation to point E of Figure 15.1 on page 394, which yields E' with $\bar{w}_{it}Dq_{it}/\sqrt{\mu_i}$ as i^{th} coordinate. [Note that E' is also obtained by applying the reciprocal marginal transformation to Q^{**}.] Point E_0 is the perpendicular projection of E' on the straight line from the origin to the marginal point (see Figure 11.4 on page 205). The ith coordinate of the marginal point is $\sqrt{\mu_i}$, so that the angle γ between the lines which connect the origin with E' and the marginal point has the following cosine:

$$\cos\gamma = \frac{\sum_{i=1}^{n} \sqrt{\mu_i}\,\frac{\bar{w}_{it}Dq_{it}}{\sqrt{\mu_i}}}{\sqrt{\sum_{i=1}^{n}(\sqrt{\mu_i})^2 \sum_{i=1}^{n}\left(\frac{\bar{w}_{it}Dq_{it}}{\sqrt{\mu_i}}\right)^2}} = \frac{DQ_t}{\sqrt{\sum_{i=1}^{n}\frac{(\bar{w}_{it}Dq_{it})^2}{\mu_i}}}$$

Since the denominator in the third member is the length of the vector OE', this proves that the line segment OE_0 represents DQ_t, the marginally weighted mean of the equivalent income changes, and that the variance V_t is equal to the square of the distance $E'E_0$. The reader may want to compare this with eqs. (6.6) and (6.7) of Section 11.6 to check the details.

The Decomposition of the Variance by Commodity Groups

Let each of the n commodities belong to one of G groups, $S_1, \ldots, S_G$. The variance of the equivalent income changes within S_g is

$$V_{gt} = \sum_{i\in S_g} \frac{\mu_i}{M_g}\left(\frac{\bar{w}_{it}Dq_{it}}{\mu_i} - \frac{\bar{W}_{gt}DQ_{gt}}{M_g}\right)^2 \tag{3.5}$$

which is related to V_t by

$$V_t = V_{0t} + \sum_{g=1}^{G} M_g V_{gt} \tag{3.6}$$

where

$$V_{0t} = \sum_{g=1}^{G} M_g\left(\frac{\bar{W}_{gt}DQ_{gt}}{M_g} - DQ_t\right)^2 \tag{3.7}$$

is the variance of the equivalent income changes of the groups. Using (1.11) and (1.15), we find that both V_{0t} and V_{gt} can be written as the sum of three components:

$$V_{0t} = \phi^2\Pi'_{0t} + 2\phi\sum_{g=1}^{G} DP'_{gt}E_{gt} + \sum_{g=1}^{G}\frac{E_{gt}^2}{M_g} \tag{3.8}$$

$$V_{gt} = \phi^2\Pi'_{gt} + \frac{2\phi}{M_g}\sum_{i\in S_g} Dp_{it}\varepsilon_{it}^g + \frac{1}{M_g}\sum_{i\in S_g}\frac{(\varepsilon_{it}^g)^2}{\mu_i} \tag{3.9}$$

where

$$\Pi'_{0t} = \sum_{g=1}^{G} M_g(DP'_{gt} - DP'_t)^2 \tag{3.10}$$

$$\Pi'_{gt} = \sum_{i\in S_g}\frac{\mu_i}{M_g}(Dp_{it} - DP'_{gt})^2 \tag{3.11}$$

Equations (3.8) and (3.9) describe each variance as the sum of a substitution component and a linear and a quadratic disturbance component, which is similar to (3.3). Also, using (1.13) and (1.16), we find that under the second-moment model the expectations of the quadratic disturbance components are

$$\mathscr{E}\left(\sum_{g=1}^{G} \frac{E_{gt}^2}{M_g}\right) = \sigma^2 (G-1) \tag{3.12}$$

$$\mathscr{E}\left(\frac{1}{M_g} \sum_{i \in S_g} \frac{(\varepsilon_{it}^g)^2}{\mu_i}\right) = \frac{\sigma^2}{M_g} (n_g - 1) \tag{3.13}$$

where n_g is the number of commodities of S_g. These expectations should be compared with (3.4).

The Two-Dimensional Decomposition of the Variance of the Basket

In (3.6) we have a decomposition of V_t between and within groups, and in (3.8) and (3.9) we have decompositions of these groupwise components. This enables us to find the two-dimensional decomposition of V_t, by groups and by substitution and linear and quadratic disturbance components. For the substitution components we use the groupwise decomposition of the variance of the price log-changes, marginally weighted:

$$\Pi_t' = \Pi_{0t}' + \sum_{g=1}^{G} M_g \Pi_{gt}' \tag{3.14}$$

On comparing this with (3.6) and the substitution components in (3.3), (3.8) and (3.9), we conclude that the substitution component of V_t is the sum of the corresponding components of the between-group variance V_{0t} and the average within-group variance $\sum_g M_g V_{gt}$.

This applies to the linear and quadratic disturbance components also. For the linear disturbance component we use eq. (1.7) of Section 7.1, so that the sum of these components of V_{0t} and $\sum_g M_g V_{gt}$ can be written as a multiple 2ϕ of

$$\begin{aligned}\sum_{g=1}^{G} DP_{gt}' E_{gt} + \sum_{g=1}^{G} \sum_{i \in S_g} Dp_{it} \varepsilon_{it}^g &= \sum_{g=1}^{G} \sum_{i \in S_g} Dp_{it} \left(\frac{\mu_i}{M_g} E_{gt} + \varepsilon_{it} - \frac{\mu_i}{M_g} E_{gt}\right) \\ &= \sum_{g=1}^{G} \sum_{i \in S_g} Dp_{it} \varepsilon_{it} = \sum_{i=1}^{n} Dp_{it} \varepsilon_{it}\end{aligned}$$

The last member is, apart from the factor 2ϕ, the linear disturbance component in (3.3). For the quadratic disturbance component we also use eq. (1.7) of Section 7.1:

$$\sum_{g=1}^{G} \frac{E_{gt}^2}{M_g} + \sum_{g=1}^{G} \sum_{i \in S_g} \frac{\left(\varepsilon_{it} - \dfrac{\mu_i}{M_g} E_{gt}\right)^2}{\mu_i}$$
$$= \sum_{g=1}^{G} \left[\frac{E_{gt}^2}{M_g} + \sum_{i \in S_g} \frac{\varepsilon_{it}^2}{\mu_i} - 2\frac{E_{gt}}{M_g} \sum_{i \in S_g} \varepsilon_{it} + \frac{E_{gt}^2}{M_g^2} \sum_{i \in S_g} \mu_i\right]$$

Since the first, third and fourth terms inside the brackets cancel each other out, this gives $\sum_i \varepsilon_{it}^2/\mu_i$, which is the quadratic disturbance component in (3.3).

The result is thus that (3.6) applies to the substitution and linear and quadratic disturbance components separately. Note how much simpler this two-dimensional decomposition is than those of the quality index and the price-quantity covariance described in Sections 14.5 and 14.6, where we had to consider subcomponents of volume components. The cause of this simplicity is the fact that variances of equivalent income changes have neither a volume nor a real-income component.

The Variance of the Equivalent Volume Changes of a Commodity Group

The variance of the equivalent volume changes of a group S_g will be indicated by a superscript g (rather than g as a subscript) in order to distinguish it from V_{gt}, the variance of the equivalent income changes within S_g. So, using (1.18) and (1.20), we have

$$V_t^g = \sum_{i \in S_g} \frac{\mu_i}{M_g} \left(\frac{M_g}{\bar{W}_{gt}} \frac{\bar{w}_{it} Dq_{it}}{\mu_i} - DQ_{gt}\right)^2 \tag{3.15}$$

which equals V_{gt}, defined in (3.5), multiplied by $(M_g/\bar{W}_{gt})^2$:

$$V_t^g = \left(\frac{M_g}{\bar{W}_{gt}}\right)^2 V_{gt} \tag{3.16}$$

This is an obvious result, because each equivalent volume change is a multiple $M_g/\bar{W}_{gt}$ of the corresponding equivalent income change.

The components of (3.16) are thus obtained by multiplying (3.9) by the square of the income elasticity of the group:

$$V_t^g = \left(\frac{\phi M_g}{\bar{W}_{gt}}\right)^2 \Pi'_{gt} + 2\frac{\phi M_g}{\bar{W}_{gt}} \sum_{i \in S_g} Dp_{it} \frac{\varepsilon_{it}^g}{\bar{W}_{gt}} + \sum_{i \in S_g} \frac{(\varepsilon_{it}^g/\bar{W}_{gt})^2}{\mu_i/M_g} \tag{3.17}$$

When S_g stands for the four-meat group, we can use eq. (3.8) of Section 7.3 to simplify this to

$$V_t^g = \left(\frac{\phi M_g}{\bar{W}_{gt}}\right)^2 \Pi'_{gt} + 2\,\frac{\phi M_g}{\bar{W}_{gt}} \sum_{i=1}^{4} Dp_{it}\varepsilon_{it}^* + \sum_{i=1}^{4} \frac{\varepsilon_{it}^{*2}}{\mu_i/M_g} \tag{3.18}$$

Note that this is a within-group version of (3.3), with ϕ replaced by the own-price elasticity of the meat group.

Variances of Quantity Log-changes of Meats

In Section 15.2 we discussed the quantity log-changes of the transformed meats prior to the equivalent volume changes. Here we proceed in the same way by starting with the budget-share-weighted variance of the quantity log-changes of the transformed meats, which is the within-group version of (3.1). It can be computed as

$$K_{gt} = \sum_{i=1}^{4} \frac{\bar{w}_{it}}{\bar{W}_{gt}} (Dq_{it} - DQ_{gt})^2 \tag{3.19}$$

because this variance is invariant under the preference independence transformation. The results are shown in column (1) of Table 15.2. They indicate that K_{gt} fluctuated between .0001 in 1961–62 and .0268 in 1952–53.

Column (2) of the table contains the marginally weighted variance of the quantity log-changes of the transformed meats. It is computed, similarly to the corresponding price variance given in eq. (4.10) of Section 13.4, as

$$K'_{gt} = \sum_{i=1}^{4} \sum_{j=1}^{4} \mu_{ij}^g (Dq_{it} - DQ'_{gt})(Dq_{jt} - DQ'_{gt}) \tag{3.20}$$

The figures in column (2) exceed those in column (1). To clarify this we extend eq. (4.12) of Section 13.4 to quantity log-changes:

$$K'_{gt} = \sum_{i=1}^{4} \frac{\mu_i}{M_g} (Dq_{it} - DQ'_{gt})^2 - \tfrac{1}{2} \sum_{i=1}^{4} \sum_{j=1}^{4} \mu_{ij}^g (Dq_{it} - Dq_{jt})^2 \tag{3.21}$$

The first term on the right is shown in column (3) and the second in column (4). The figures in the latter column are positive because there are no specific complements among the meats and Beef, Pork and Chicken are specific substitutes. This positive sign raises the left-hand side of (3.21), shown in column (2), above the first term on the right, which is the marginally weighted variance of the quantity log-changes of the observed meats [column (3)]. Note that in most years the latter variance is smaller than the corresponding budget-share-weighted variance in column (1).

TABLE 15.2

VARIANCES OF QUANTITY LOG-CHANGES AND EQUIVALENT VOLUME CHANGES OF MEATS

	K_{gt}	K'_{gt}	Components of K'_{gt}		V_t^g	Components of V_t^g		
						Substitution	Linear disturbance	Quadratic disturbance
	(1)	(2)	(3)	(4)	(5)	(6)	(7)	(8)
1950–51	68.7	92.9	54.9	38.0	31.6	11.6	12.9	7.1
1951–52	25.9	34.6	22.2	12.4	4.6	.5	−1.3	5.5
1952–53	268.0	389.6	215.2	174.4	135.7	133.1	2.1	.6
1953–54	17.1	24.3	11.8	12.5	13.1	7.3	.2	5.5
1954–55	34.5	44.7	19.8	24.9	33.3	36.7	−4.4	1.0
1955–56	17.5	20.3	10.5	9.8	20.6	6.5	9.6	4.5
1956–57	22.7	31.0	14.0	17.0	21.8	16.3	3.4	2.1
1957–58	23.4	26.7	15.2	11.5	16.3	12.8	.1	3.4
1958–59	27.8	42.6	23.5	19.1	31.8	28.5	2.1	1.3
1959–60	13.9	19.9	11.3	8.6	9.4	.6	3.0	5.8
1960–61	16.2	23.4	11.2	12.2	10.9	12.7	−2.3	.4
1961–62	1.0	1.5	.7	.8	1.1	2.0	−1.2	.3
1962–63	4.8	6.8	5.8	.9	3.0	.9	1.2	1.0
1963–64	16.1	24.8	20.2	4.5	9.0	.3	1.7	7.1
1964–65	36.7	55.3	26.7	28.6	27.5	19.6	5.5	2.3
1965–66	9.4	13.9	6.5	7.4	5.7	10.2	−11.8	7.3
1966–67	13.2	19.8	10.8	9.1	17.2	13.0	3.0	1.1
1967–68	1.7	2.6	2.2	.4	1.6	2.7	−2.4	1.3
1968–69	5.2	8.2	5.3	2.9	3.5	1.2	−.5	2.8
1969–70	2.7	4.4	3.6	.8	3.7	3.4	−2.7	3.0
1970–71	21.8	33.9	17.2	16.7	18.2	32.6	−17.0	2.6
1971–72	25.6	40.5	20.0	20.5	16.9	15.1	−1.2	3.0

Note. All entries are to be multiplied by 10^{-4}.

Columns (1) to (4) are the quantity version of columns (5) to (8) of Table 13.10 on page 327. We can therefore refer to the last two subsections of Section 13.4 for more detailed explanations. Our next step is the preference independence transformation, which is needed to obtain the variance of the equivalent volume changes of the meats.

The Commodity Interpretation of the Variance of the Equivalent Income Changes

We know from Section 12.7 that marginally weighted second moments are not invariant under the preference independence transformation. We should therefore not expect that the variance of $\bar{w}_{1t}Dq_{1t}/\mu_1, \ldots, \bar{w}_{nt}Dq_{nt}/\mu_n$ has the invariance property. In fact, these ratios can be infinitely large because a commodity can have a zero income elasticity.

The marginally weighted second moment (around zero) of the elements of the vector (2.1) is

$$[(\boldsymbol{\mu}_T)_\Delta^{-1}\,\mathbf{Rz}_t]'\,(\boldsymbol{\mu}_T)_\Delta\,(\boldsymbol{\mu}_T)_\Delta^{-1}\,\mathbf{Rz}_t = \mathbf{z}_t'\mathbf{R}'\,(\boldsymbol{\mu}_T)_\Delta^{-1}\,\mathbf{Rz}_t = \mathbf{z}_t'\mathbf{M}^{-1}\mathbf{z}_t$$

where the second step is based on eq. (3.11) of Section 12.3. We conclude that the variance of the equivalent income changes can be expressed in terms of commodity coefficients and variables as

$$V_t = \sum_{i=1}^{n}\sum_{j=1}^{n} \mu^{ij}\,(\bar{w}_{it}Dq_{it})\,(\bar{w}_{jt}Dq_{jt}) - (DQ_t)^2 \tag{3.22}$$

where μ^{ij} is the $(i,j)^{\text{th}}$ element of $\mathbf{M}^{-1}$. This result can also be written as

$$V_t = \sum_{i=1}^{n}\sum_{j=1}^{n} \mu^{ij}\,(\bar{w}_{it}Dq_{it} - \mu_i DQ_t)\,(\bar{w}_{jt}Dq_{jt} - \mu_j DQ_t) \tag{3.23}$$

which amounts to a quadratic form, with $\mathbf{M}^{-1}$ as matrix, in the vector of left-hand variables of the Rotterdam Model corrected for the effect of the change in real income.

To verify that (3.22) and (3.23) are equivalent, we write the right-hand side of the latter equation as the sum of four terms:

$$\sum_{i=1}^{n}\sum_{j=1}^{n} \mu^{ij}\,(\bar{w}_{it}Dq_{it})\,(\bar{w}_{jt}Dq_{jt}) - DQ_t \sum_{i=1}^{n}\left(\sum_{j=1}^{n}\mu^{ij}\mu_j\right)\bar{w}_{it}Dq_{it}$$
$$- DQ_t \sum_{j=1}^{n}\left(\sum_{i=1}^{n}\mu^{ij}\mu_i\right)\bar{w}_{jt}Dq_{jt} + (DQ_t)^2 \sum_{i=1}^{n}\sum_{j=1}^{n}\mu_i\mu^{ij}\mu_j$$

The last three terms are equal to $-(DQ_t)^2$, $-(DQ_t)^2$ and $(DQ_t)^2$, respectively. This follows from $\mathbf{M}^{-1}\boldsymbol{\mu}=\boldsymbol{\iota}$ and $\boldsymbol{\mu}'\mathbf{M}^{-1}\boldsymbol{\mu}=1$, which is implied by $\mathbf{M}\boldsymbol{\iota}=\boldsymbol{\mu}$ and $\boldsymbol{\iota}'\boldsymbol{\mu}=1$.

The Variance of the Equivalent Volume Changes of Meats

The subscript i in (3.15) and (3.18) refers to the ith transformed meat. The expression in terms of observed meats is a conditional version of (3.23),

$$V_t^g = \sum_{i=1}^{4}\sum_{j=1}^{4} \mu^{gij}\left(\frac{\bar{w}_{it}}{\bar{W}_{gt}}Dq_{it} - \frac{\mu_i}{M_g}DQ_{gt}\right)\left(\frac{\bar{w}_{jt}}{\bar{W}_{gt}}Dq_{jt} - \frac{\mu_j}{M_g}DQ_{gt}\right) \tag{3.24}$$

where

$$[\mu^{gij}] = [\mu_{ij}^g]^{-1} \tag{3.25}$$

The quadratic disturbance component of (3.18) is similarly computed from the ε^*'s of the observed meats as

$$\sum_{i=1}^{4} \sum_{j=1}^{4} \mu^{gij} \varepsilon_{it}^* \varepsilon_{jt}^*$$

and the substitution and linear disturbance components are obtained by combining (2.4) with the substitution and disturbance components of Γ_{gt} given in Table 14.3 on page 352.

The results are shown in the last four columns of Table 15.2. The variance of the equivalent volume changes is considerable in 1952–53, which is due almost wholly to its large substitution component. From 1960 onward the variance is less than .002 with one exception, whereas a majority exceeds .002 in the 1950s. This amounts to a decreasing dispersion of the log-changes in the marginal utilities of the transformed meats. The substitution component plays a dominant role; it exceeds both the linear and the quadratic disturbance component in 14 cases out of 22.

15.4 Covariances and a Regression Involving Equivalent Income Changes

In this section we consider two covariances involving equivalent income changes and a regression based on one of them. As in the case of the mean (1.3) and the variance (3.2), these covariances are marginally weighted.

Equivalent Income Changes and Income Elasticities

The covariance of the equivalent income changes and the income elasticities is

$$\sum_{i=1}^{n} \mu_i \left(\frac{\bar{w}_{it} Dq_{it}}{\mu_i} - DQ_t \right) \left(\frac{\mu_i}{\bar{w}_{it}} - \sum_{j=1}^{n} \mu_j \frac{\mu_j}{\bar{w}_{jt}} \right) \tag{4.1}$$

which is equal to

$$\sum_{i=1}^{n} \mu_i \left(\frac{\bar{w}_{it} Dq_{it}}{\mu_i} - DQ_t \right) \frac{\mu_i}{\bar{w}_{it}} = DQ'_t - DQ_t \sum_{i=1}^{n} \frac{\mu_i^2}{\bar{w}_{it}}$$

The right-hand side of this equation can be written as

$$\begin{aligned}(DQ'_t - DQ_t) - DQ_t \left[\sum_{i=1}^{n} \bar{w}_{it} \left(\frac{\mu_i}{\bar{w}_{it}} \right)^2 - 1 \right] \\ = (DQ'_t - DQ_t) - DQ_t \sum_{i=1}^{n} \bar{w}_{it} \left(\frac{\mu_i}{\bar{w}_{it}} - 1 \right)^2\end{aligned}$$

On comparing this with eq. (3.5) of Section 11.3, we conclude that the covariance (4.1) is equal to the log-change in the quality index minus the real-income component of this log-change. Therefore, (4.1) can be written as

$$\sum_{i=1}^{n} \mu_i\left(\frac{\bar{w}_{it}Dq_{it}}{\mu_i} - DQ_t\right)\left(\frac{\mu_i}{\bar{w}_{it}} - \sum_{j=1}^{n} \mu_j \frac{\mu_j}{\bar{w}_{jt}}\right) = \phi \sum_{i=1}^{n} \mu_i (Dp_{it} - DP_t')\frac{\mu_i}{\bar{w}_{it}} + \sum_{i=1}^{n} \frac{\mu_i}{\bar{w}_{it}}\varepsilon_{it} \tag{4.2}$$

Hence, the covariance of the equivalent income changes and the income elasticities consists of a substitution and a disturbance component which are equal to the corresponding components of the log-change in the quality index.

Equivalent Income Changes and Price Log-changes

Next consider the covariance of the equivalent income changes and the price log-changes:

$$C_t = \sum_{i=1}^{n} \mu_i\left(\frac{\bar{w}_{it}Dq_{it}}{\mu_i} - DQ_t\right)(Dp_{it} - DP_t') \tag{4.3}$$

This can be written as

$$\sum_{i=1}^{n} \mu_i\left(\frac{\bar{w}_{it}Dq_{it}}{\mu_i} - DQ_t\right)Dp_{it} = \sum_{i=1}^{n} \bar{w}_{it}Dp_{it}Dq_{it} - DP_t'DQ_t$$

The first term on the right is equal to the price-quantity covariance Γ_t plus DP_tDQ_t. Therefore,

$$C_t = \Gamma_t - (DP_t' - DP_t)\, DQ_t \tag{4.4}$$

In view of eq. (1.6) of Section 11.1, this implies that C_t equals Γ_t minus the real-income component of Γ_t. So we have

$$C_t = \phi\Pi_t' + \sum_{i=1}^{n} Dp_{it}\varepsilon_{it} \tag{4.5}$$

which states that the covariance of the equivalent income changes and the price log-changes consists of a substitution and a disturbance component identical to those of the price-quantity covariance.

Note the similarity of this result to that obtained in the previous subsection. We conclude that, for the Dutch 14-commodity model, we obtain the covariance in the left-hand side of (4.2) by adding the last two columns of Table 14.1 on page 344, and we obtain C_t by adding the third and fourth columns of Table 14.3 on page 352.

A Regression of the Equivalent Income Changes on the Price Log-changes

Let us write (1.4) in the following form:

$$\frac{\bar{w}_{it} Dq_{it}}{\mu_i} - DQ_t = \phi\,(Dp_{it} - DP'_t) + \frac{\varepsilon_{it}}{\mu_i} \tag{4.6}$$

The left-hand side is the ith equivalent income change measured as a deviation from the marginally weighted mean of all n such changes. The first term on the right is a multiple ϕ of the ith price log-change measured as a deviation from the marginally weighted mean of all n price log-changes.

Imagine that we know $\mu_1, \ldots, \mu_n$, so that the left-hand side of (4.6) and DP'_t are also known, but that ϕ is unknown. We want to estimate ϕ, and use for this purpose the marginally weighted least-squares regression of the left-hand variable of (4.6) on $Dp_{it} - DP'_t$ for $i = 1, \ldots, n$. This yields a ϕ estimator in the form of a ratio, with denominator equal to

$$\sum_{i=1}^{n} \mu_i (Dp_{it} - DP'_t)^2 = \Pi'_t$$

and numerator equal to

$$\sum_{i=1}^{n} \mu_i (Dp_{it} - DP'_t) \left(\frac{\bar{w}_{it} Dq_{it}}{\mu_i} - DQ_t \right) = C_t$$

where the equal sign is based on (4.3). So the estimator of ϕ is

$$\hat{\phi}_t = \frac{C_t}{\Pi'_t} \tag{4.7}$$

The subscript t on the left indicates that the n observations on which the estimator is based are confined to the transition $(t-1, t)$.

Optimum Properties of the Regression

To evaluate the properties of the estimator (4.7), we assume that the second-moment model is valid and use eq. (7.24) of Section 2.7 to separate the specific and the general substitution components of the disturbance in (4.6):

$$\frac{\bar{w}_{it} Dq_{it}}{\mu_i} - DQ_t + \bar{E}_t = \phi\,(Dp_{it} - DP'_t) + \frac{\bar{\varepsilon}_{it}}{\mu_i}$$

Next multiply both sides by $\sqrt{\mu_i}$:

$$\sqrt{\mu_i} \left(\frac{\bar{w}_{it} Dq_{it}}{\mu_i} - DQ_t + \bar{E}_t \right) = \phi \sqrt{\mu_i}\,(Dp_{it} - DP'_t) + \frac{\bar{\varepsilon}_{it}}{\sqrt{\mu_i}} \tag{4.8}$$

Under the second-moment model in preference-independent form, $\bar{\varepsilon}_{1t}, \ldots, \bar{\varepsilon}_{nt}$

are uncorrelated random variables with zero means and variances $\sigma^2\mu_1,\ldots,\sigma^2\mu_n$, so that the disturbances of (4.8) for $i=1,\ldots,n$ are uncorrelated with zero means and the same variance σ^2. This suggests that least squares applied to (4.8) provides a best linear unbiased estimator of ϕ. The unobservable $\bar{E}_t$ on the left presents a problem, but let us ignore this aspect for the moment. So we run a least-squares regression of the left-hand variable of (4.8) on $(Dp_{it}-DP_t')\sqrt{\mu_i}$ for $i=1,\ldots,n$. It is readily verified that this yields $\hat{\phi}_t$ defined in (4.7). Since this does not involve $\bar{E}_t$, we are justified in ignoring it as we did. Also, by applying standard least-squares theory to (4.8), we find that the variance of the estimator is

$$\text{var}\,\hat{\phi}_t = \frac{\sigma^2}{\Pi_t'} \tag{4.9}$$

In the previous paragraph we assumed that (1) there is preference independence, (2) the second-moment model is valid, (3) the marginal shares are known, and (4) the price log-changes are nonstochastic or, at least, stochastically independent of the disturbances. Under these four conditions, the marginally weighted least-squares regression of the equivalent income changes on the price log-changes (both variables measured as deviations from their means) provides a best linear unbiased estimator of the income flexibility. If, in addition, the disturbance distribution is multivariate normal, as it is under the theory of rational random behavior of Section 2.8, the restriction "linear" can be dropped and the estimator $\hat{\phi}_t$ is also normally distributed; see, for example, THEIL (1971, p. 390).

A Multiperiod Estimator of the Income Flexibility

Note that (4.7) provides a one-period estimator of ϕ; it is obtained from the transition $(t-1, t)$, based on n demand equations. If we have T periods and the disturbances are uncorrelated over time, an optimal estimator is obtained by weighting the one-period estimators inversely proportionally to their variances. This yields

$$\hat{\phi} = \frac{\sum_{t=1}^{T} \Pi_t'\hat{\phi}_t}{\sum_{t=1}^{T} \Pi_t'} = \frac{\sum_{t=1}^{T} C_t}{\sum_{t=1}^{T} \Pi_t'} \tag{4.10}$$

which is an unbiased estimator of ϕ with the following variance:

$$\text{var}\,\hat{\phi} = \frac{\sigma^2}{\sum_{t=1}^{T} \Pi_t'} \tag{4.11}$$

The variance σ^2 in (4.11) is unknown. It is shown in the next subsection that

$$\hat{\sigma}_t^2 = \frac{V_t - \hat{\phi}_t C_t}{n-2} \tag{4.12}$$

is an unbiased one-period estimator of σ^2, and that

$$\hat{\sigma}^2 = \frac{1}{(n-1)\,T-1} \sum_{t=1}^{T} (V_t - \hat{\phi} C_t) \tag{4.13}$$

is an unbiased estimator based on (4.10). Note the occurrence of the variance of the equivalent income changes in (4.12) and (4.13), in addition to the covariance C_t.

Estimation of the Variance of the Regression

The following result is obtained from (3.3) and (4.5):

(4.14)
$$V_t - \hat{\phi}_t C_t = (\phi - \hat{\phi}_t)\,\phi \Pi'_t + 2\phi \sum_{i=1}^{n} Dp_{it}\varepsilon_{it} + \sum_{i=1}^{n} \frac{\varepsilon_{it}^2}{\mu_i} - \hat{\phi}_t \sum_{i=1}^{n} Dp_{it}\varepsilon_{it}$$

The expectations of the first two terms on the right vanish and that of the third is $\sigma^2(n-1)$ in view of (3.4). For the last term we have

$$\mathscr{E}\left(\hat{\phi}_t \sum_{i=1}^{n} Dp_{it}\varepsilon_{it}\right) = \sigma^2 \tag{4.15}$$

from which the unbiasedness of the estimator (4.12) follows immediately. To prove (4.15) we use (4.5) to write (4.7) as

$$\hat{\phi}_t = \phi + \frac{1}{\Pi'_t} \sum_{i=1}^{n} Dp_{it}\varepsilon_{it} \tag{4.16}$$

The left-hand side of (4.15) thus equals the variance of $\sum_i Dp_{it}\varepsilon_{it}$ divided by Π'_t; the proof then follows from eq. (1.10) of Section 11.1.

Next replace $\hat{\phi}_t$ by $\hat{\phi}$ in (4.14) and sum over t:

$$\begin{aligned}\sum_{t=1}^{T} (V_t - \hat{\phi} C_t) = (\phi - \hat{\phi})\,\phi \sum_{t=1}^{T} \Pi'_t &+ 2\phi \sum_{t=1}^{T} \sum_{i=1}^{n} Dp_{it}\varepsilon_{it} \\ &+ \sum_{t=1}^{T} \sum_{i=1}^{n} \frac{\varepsilon_{it}^2}{\mu_i} - \hat{\phi} \sum_{t=1}^{T} \sum_{i=1}^{n} Dp_{it}\varepsilon_{it}\end{aligned} \tag{4.17}$$

The expectations of the first two terms on the right are zero, as in (4.14), and that of the third is $\sigma^2(n-1)T$. For the fourth term we have

$$\mathscr{E}\left(\hat{\phi}\sum_{t=1}^{T}\sum_{i=1}^{n} Dp_{it}\varepsilon_{it}\right) = \sigma^2 \tag{4.18}$$

which completes the proof of the unbiasedness of the estimator (4.13). To prove (4.18) we substitute (4.5) in (4.10),

$$\hat{\phi} = \phi + \frac{\sum_{t=1}^{T}\sum_{i=1}^{n} Dp_{it}\varepsilon_{it}}{\sum_{t=1}^{T} \Pi'_t} \tag{4.19}$$

which shows that the left-hand side of (4.18) equals

$$\frac{\sum_{s=1}^{T}\sum_{t=1}^{T}\sum_{i=1}^{n}\sum_{j=1}^{n} Dp_{is}Dp_{jt}\,\mathscr{E}(\varepsilon_{is}\varepsilon_{jt})}{\sum_{t=1}^{T} \Pi'_t} = \frac{\sum_{t=1}^{T}\left[\sum_{i=1}^{n}\sum_{j=1}^{n} Dp_{it}Dp_{jt}\,\mathscr{E}(\varepsilon_{it}\varepsilon_{jt})\right]}{\sum_{t=1}^{T} \Pi'_t}$$

where the equal sign is based on the zero lagged covariances of the disturbances. The proof of (4.18) then follows from eq. (1.10) of Section 11.1.

Three Remarks

(1) Write e_{it} for the residual corresponding to ε_{it} which is obtained when $\hat{\phi}_t$ is substituted for ϕ in (4.6):

$$\frac{e_{it}}{\mu_i} = \frac{\bar{w}_{it}Dq_{it}}{\mu_i} - DQ_t - \hat{\phi}_t(Dp_{it} - DP'_t) \tag{4.20}$$

This implies

$$\begin{aligned}\sum_{i=1}^{n}\mu_i\left(\frac{e_{it}}{\mu_i}\right)^2 &= \sum_{i=1}^{n}\mu_i\left(\frac{\bar{w}_{it}Dq_{it}}{\mu_i} - DQ_t\right)^2 + \hat{\phi}_t^2\sum_{i=1}^{n}\mu_i(Dp_{it} - DP'_t)^2 \\ &\quad - 2\hat{\phi}_t\sum_{i=1}^{n}\mu_i\left(\frac{\bar{w}_{it}Dq_{it}}{\mu_i} - DQ_t\right)(Dp_{it} - DP'_t) \\ &= V_t + \hat{\phi}_t^2\Pi'_t - 2\hat{\phi}_t C_t\end{aligned}$$

Using (4.7), we can simplify this to

$$\sum_{i=1}^{n}\frac{e_{it}^2}{\mu_i} = V_t - \hat{\phi}_t C_t \tag{4.21}$$

On comparing this result with (4.12), we conclude that the one-period estimator of σ^2 is equal to the residual sum of squares, divided by $n-2$, of the least-squares regression based on (4.8). Hence $\hat{\sigma}_t$ exists and is nonnegative for $n>2$. If the disturbance distribution is multivariate normal, $(n-2)\hat{\sigma}_t^2/\sigma^2$ is distributed as $\chi^2(n-2)$, and $\hat{\sigma}_t$ and $\hat{\phi}_t$ are independent.

(2) The left-hand side of (4.21) is the residual version of the quadratic disturbance component of V_t [see (3.3)]. This version has expectation $\sigma^2(n-2)$, whereas the component itself has expectation $\sigma^2(n-1)$ [see (3.4)]. The difference is due, in view of (4.15), to the degree of freedom which is sacrificed for the estimation of ϕ.

(3) The above results can be extended straightforwardly for $\hat{\sigma}$ defined in (4.13); we use $\hat{\phi}$ rather than $\hat{\phi}_t$ in (4.20) and sum both sides of (4.21) thus modified over t. Note that $\hat{\sigma}^2$ is not the average of the one-period estimator (4.12) over t. This average sacrifices T degrees of freedom for ϕ, whereas $\hat{\sigma}^2$ sacrifices only one. Under multivariate normality $\hat{\sigma}$ and $\hat{\phi}$ are independent and $\hat{\sigma}^2/\sigma^2$ multiplied by $(n-1)T-1$ has a χ^2 distribution, because $\hat{\phi}$ can be viewed as the least-squares estimator of ϕ obtained from (4.8) for all nT pairs (i, t).

The Geometry of the Regression

The regression of the equivalent income changes on the price log-changes is illustrated in Figure 15.3. The left-hand side of (4.6) for $i=1$ and 2 is represented by E_d, which is obtained from point E of Figure 15.1 on page 394 by subtracting DQ_t from both coordinates. The line EE_d is parallel to that from the origin to Iota; these are the two broken lines in Figure 15.3. Since the right-hand side of (4.6) is the sum of the substitution and disturbance components of $\bar{w}_{it}Dq_{it}/\mu_i$, E_d coincides with the point indicated by D_E+S_E in Figure 15.1.

We apply the marginal transformation to E_d, which yields E_d', whose i^{th} coordinate is

$$\sqrt{\mu_i}\left(\frac{\bar{w}_{it}Dq_{it}}{\mu_i} - DQ_t\right)$$

We also apply the marginal transformation to P_d in Figure 15.1, which yields P_d' with $(Dp_{it}-DP_t')\sqrt{\mu_i}$ as i^{th} coordinate. [Note that this point is identical to P_d' in Figure 11.4 on page 205.] The points E_d' and P_d' correspond to the two variables of (4.8) except for $\bar{E}_t$ on the left, but this has no consequences for $\hat{\phi}_t$, which is independent of $\bar{E}_t$. Since $\hat{\phi}_t$ is obtained by applying least squares to (4.8), it is geometrically described by the perpendicular projection

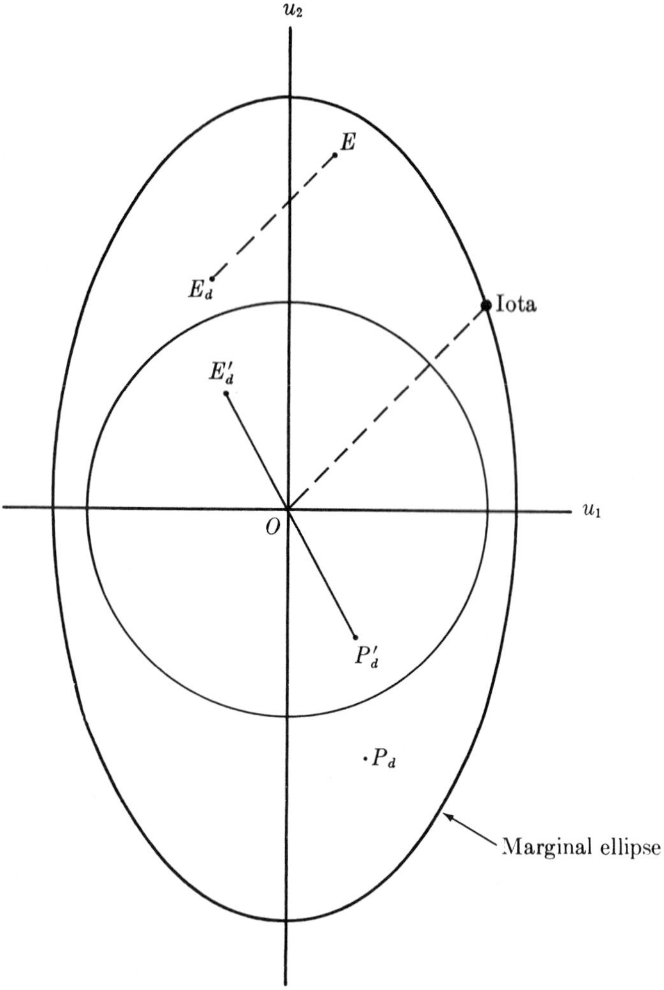

Fig. 15.3 The regression of the equivalent income changes on the price log-changes

of E'_d on OP'_d. In the case illustrated here, with $n=2$, E'_d is on OP'_d and $\hat{\phi}_t$ is equal to the ratio of OE'_d to OP'_d; this ratio is negative because E'_d and P'_d are on opposite sides of the origin. For $n>2$ the point E'_d will usually not be on OP'_d; the squared distance of E'_d from this line is the geometric version of the left-hand side of (4.21).

Applications

PAULUS (1972) used the 12-equation aggregated model described in Section 6.8, which is in preference-independent form. He extended the Rotterdam Model in accordance with eqs. (3.29) and (3.30) of Section 3.3 in order to verify Frisch's conjecture on the dependence of the income flexibility on the level of real income (see page 30 of Volume 1). This amounts to the specification

$$\log(-\phi_t) = \alpha_0 + \alpha \log Q_t \tag{4.22}$$

where Q_t is the geometric mean of the per capita real incomes of years $t-1$ and t. Paulus proceeded conditionally on the mixed estimates of the marginal shares and computed the income flexibility estimate (4.7) for each of the 29 annual observations, followed by a weighted least-squares regression based on (4.22).[1] This yields a positive estimate of α, in agreement with Frisch's conjecture, but with a standard error almost as large as the estimate.

The weighted least-squares procedure assumes the validity of the second-moment model, which certainly cannot be guaranteed for the data of Chapter 6. An alternative procedure was used by THEIL and BROOKS (1970–71), based on the Dutch four-commodity block-independent model described in Section 5.4. They operated conditionally on the marginal share estimates of this model (so that μ_{34}, corresponding to Durables and Remainder, is the only unconstrained normalized price coefficient) and also on the estimated disturbance covariance matrix. For the dependence of the income flexibility on the level of real income they used

$$-\phi_t = \alpha_0 + \alpha \log Q_t \tag{4.23}$$

which has the absolute value of the income flexibility [not its logarithm as in (4.22)] on the left. Given the conditions imposed, the only unconstrained parameters are α_0, α and the normalized price coefficient μ_{34}. A maximum-likelihood procedure under the normality assumption yields the following estimates, with asymptotic standard errors in parentheses:

$$\hat{\alpha}_0 = .64\ (.17) \qquad \hat{\alpha} = -.9\ (1.3) \qquad \hat{\mu}_{34} = .129\ (.026) \tag{4.24}$$

[1] Two of the 29 estimates (4.7) are positive; for these the left-hand side of (4.22) cannot be computed. This problem was solved by grouping the 29 observations into five groups according to increasing values of Q_t. The weighted least-squares regression was computed from the group averages, based on the variance (4.9) and a Taylor approximation for the variances of the logarithms of minus the income flexibility estimates.

The estimate of μ_{34} is significantly positive; it is close to the converged estimate of ν_{34}/ϕ obtained in Section 5.4 (see Table 5.12 on page 205 of Volume 1). But the estimate of α is negative, which points in a direction opposite to that of Frisch's conjecture, although the standard error indicates that the estimate is far from significant. Clearly, the data present no reason to depart from the hypothesis that the income flexibility is independent of income ($\alpha=0$). This result is not due to a lack of variation of per capita real income; for the data used here the highest value exceeds the lowest by about two-thirds.

15.5 Groupwise Extensions

Equivalent Income Changes and Price Log-changes

Let there be G groups of goods, $S_1, \ldots, S_G$. We multiply

$$\left(\frac{\bar{W}_{gt}DQ_{gt}}{M_g} - DQ_t\right) + \left(\frac{\bar{w}_{it}Dq_{it}}{\mu_i} - \frac{\bar{W}_{gt}DQ_{gt}}{M_g}\right)$$

by

$$\mu_i[(DP'_{gt} - DP'_t) + (Dp_{it} - DP'_{gt})]$$

and sum the product over $i \in S_g$ and then over $g=1,\ldots, G$. This shows that the covariance C_t has a between- and within-group decomposition, similar to (3.6) for the variance, of the form

$$C_t = C_{0t} + \sum_{g=1}^{G} M_g C_{gt} \tag{5.1}$$

where C_{0t} is the covariance of the equivalent income changes and the marginally weighted price indexes of the groups,

$$C_{0t} = \sum_{g=1}^{G} M_g \left(\frac{\bar{W}_{gt}DQ_{gt}}{M_g} - DQ_t\right)(DP'_{gt} - DP'_t) \tag{5.2}$$

and C_{gt} is the corresponding covariance within S_g:

$$C_{gt} = \sum_{i \in S_g} \frac{\mu_i}{M_g}\left(\frac{\bar{w}_{it}Dq_{it}}{\mu_i} - \frac{W_{gt}DQ_{gt}}{M_g}\right)(Dp_{it} - DP'_{gt}) \tag{5.3}$$

It follows from (1.11) and (3.10) that the between-group covariance (5.2) consists of a substitution and a disturbance component:

$$C_{0t} = \phi\Pi'_{0t} + \sum_{g=1}^{G} DP'_{gt}E_{gt} \tag{5.4}$$

Similarly, using (1.15) and (3.11), we find for (5.3):

$$C_{gt} = \phi \Pi'_{gt} + \frac{1}{M_g} \sum_{i \in S_g} Dp_{it} \varepsilon^g_{it} \tag{5.5}$$

It is readily verified from (3.14) that the substitution component $\phi\Pi'_t$ of C_t equals the substitution component of C_{0t} plus the substitution component of the average within-group term $\sum_g M_g C_{gt}$. We conclude from the paragraph below (3.14) that this is also true for the disturbance components. Hence the two-dimensional decomposition of C_t is as simple as that of V_t.

Equivalent Volume Changes and Price Log-changes

The covariance of the equivalent volume changes and the price log-changes of a group S_g will be denoted, similarly to the variance (3.15), by a superscript g in order to distinguish it from the covariance defined in (5.3). We thus have, by applying (1.18) and (1.20),

$$C^g_t = \sum_{i \in S_g} \frac{\mu_i}{M_g} \left(\frac{M_g}{\bar{W}_{gt}} \frac{\bar{w}_{it} Dq_{it}}{\mu_i} - DQ_{gt} \right) (Dp_{it} - DP'_{gt}) \tag{5.6}$$

which satisfies

$$C^g_t = \frac{M_g}{\bar{W}_{gt}} C_{gt} \tag{5.7}$$

in view of (5.3). Hence (5.5) implies

$$C^g_t = \frac{\phi M_g}{\bar{W}_{gt}} \Pi'_{gt} + \frac{1}{\bar{W}_{gt}} \sum_{i \in S_g} Dp_{it} \varepsilon^g_{it} \tag{5.8}$$

When S_g is the four-meat group, we use eq. (3.8) of Section 7.3 to simplify this to

$$C^g_t = \frac{\phi M_g}{\bar{W}_{gt}} \Pi'_{gt} + \sum_{i=1}^{4} Dp_{it} \varepsilon^*_{it} \tag{5.9}$$

which is a within-group version of (4.5) in the same way that (3.18) is a within-group version of (3.3).

Comparison with Price-Quantity Covariances

Recall from (4.4) that C_t equals the price-quantity covariance Γ_t minus the real-income component of Γ_t. Do the between- and within-group components of C_t shown in (5.1) have the same property?

The disturbance component in (5.5) is not, but that in (5.8) is equal to the corresponding component of Γ_{gt} shown in (2.8) of Section 14.2. It may be verified (by means of $\nu_{ij}=\phi\mu_i$ for $i=j$ and 0 for $i \neq j$) that under preference independence the substitution component of Γ_{gt}, given in (2.7) of Section 14.2, equals the substitution component in (5.8). Hence the covariance of the equivalent volume (not income!) changes and the price log-changes of S_g is equal to the price-quantity covariance Γ_{gt} minus the volume component of Γ_{gt}:

$$C_t^g = \Gamma_{gt} - (DP'_{gt} - DP_{gt})\, DQ_{gt} \tag{5.10}$$

This is the within-group version of (4.4). Note also that (5.1) and (5.7) imply

$$C_t = C_{0t} + \sum_{g=1}^{G} \bar{W}_{gt} C_t^g \tag{5.11}$$

The weights of the within-group term (the $\bar{W}_{gt}$'s) are the same as those which occur in eq. (6.3) of Section 14.6 for the groupwise decomposition of Γ_t.

The between-group covariance C_{0t} should be related to both Γ_{0t} and the volume component of the average within-group term $\sum_g \bar{W}_{gt}\Gamma_{gt}$. Specifically, the disturbance term in (5.4) is the sum of the disturbance component of Γ_{0t} and the disturbance subcomponent of the volume component of $\sum_g \bar{W}_{gt}\Gamma_{gt}$, which may be verified by adding the expressions (6.6) and (6.17) of Section 14.6. For the substitution term in (5.4) we have an analogous result, which the reader may want to verify by adding the expressions (6.5) and (6.16) of the same section and applying the preference independence specification which is used here.

Group Regressions and Regressions Within Groups

Write (1.11) and (1.15) in the following form:

$$\frac{\bar{W}_{gt} DQ_{gt}}{M_g} - DQ_t = \phi\,(DP'_{gt} - DP'_t) + \frac{E_{gt}}{M_g} \tag{5.12}$$

$$\frac{\bar{w}_{it} Dq_{it}}{\mu_i} - \frac{\bar{W}_{gt} DQ_{gt}}{M_g} = \phi\,(Dp_{it} - DP'_{gt}) + \frac{\varepsilon_{it}^g}{\mu_i} \tag{5.13}$$

A comparison with (4.6) and the developments below that equation shows that we can estimate ϕ from (5.12) for $g=1,\ldots, G$, and also from (5.13) for all $i \in S_g$. If the four conditions stated below (4.9) are satisfied, marginally weighted least-squares regressions based on (5.12) and (5.13) yield unbiased

ϕ estimators equal to C_{0t}/Π'_{0t} and C_{gt}/Π'_{gt}, respectively. It is shown in the next subsection that the variances of these estimators are

$$\text{(5.14)} \qquad \text{var}\,\frac{C_{0t}}{\Pi'_{0t}} = \frac{\sigma^2}{\Pi'_{0t}} \qquad \text{var}\,\frac{C_{gt}}{\Pi'_{gt}} = \frac{\sigma^2}{M_g\Pi'_{gt}}$$

By running within-group regressions for all groups, we obtain G within-group estimators of ϕ in addition to the group estimator C_{0t}/Π'_{0t}. These $G+1$ estimators are uncorrelated because of the zero-correlation properties of the disturbances in (5.12) and (5.13). When they are weighted inversely proportionally to their variances shown in (5.14), we obtain $\hat{\phi}_t$ defined in (4.7),

$$\text{(5.15)} \qquad \frac{\Pi'_{0t}\dfrac{C_{0t}}{\Pi'_{0t}} + \sum_{g=1}^{G} M_g\Pi'_{gt}\dfrac{C_{gt}}{\Pi'_{gt}}}{\Pi'_{0t} + \sum_{g=1}^{G} M_g\Pi'_{gt}} = \frac{C_t}{\Pi'_t} = \hat{\phi}_t$$

where the first step is based on (5.1) and (3.14).

Derivations

The proof of the first variance in (5.14) is a straightforward extension of that of (4.9). For the second variance we use eq. (1.19) of Section 7.1 to write (5.13) as

$$\frac{\bar{w}_{it}Dq_{it}}{\mu_i} - \frac{\bar{W}_{gt}DQ_{gt}}{M_g} + \frac{\bar{E}_{gt}}{M_g} = \phi\,(Dp_{it} - DP'_{gt}) + \frac{\bar{\varepsilon}_{it}}{\mu_i}$$

which we multiply by $\sqrt{\mu_i/M_g}$:

$$\text{(5.16)} \qquad \sqrt{\mu_i/M_g}\left(\frac{\bar{w}_{it}Dq_{it}}{\mu_i} - \frac{\bar{W}_{gt}DQ_{gt}}{M_g} + \frac{\bar{E}_{gt}}{M_g}\right) = \phi\sqrt{\mu_i/M_g}\,(Dp_{it} - DP'_{gt}) + \frac{\bar{\varepsilon}_{it}}{\sqrt{M_g\mu_i}}$$

The variance of the disturbance on the right is σ^2/M_g, which is the same for each $i\in S_g$. So we apply least squares to (5.16), which yields a ϕ estimator equal to C_{gt}/Π'_{gt} whose variance is as shown in (5.14).

It is also easily verified that the regression based on (5.12) yields an unbiased estimator of σ^2 equal to the residual version of the quadratic disturbance component in (3.8) divided by $G-2$. The within-group regression similarly yields

$$\text{(5.17)} \qquad \sum_{i\in S_g} \frac{\mu_i}{M_g}\left(\frac{e_{it}^g}{\mu_i}\right)^2 = \frac{1}{M_g}\sum_{i\in S_g}\frac{(e_{it}^g)^2}{\mu_i}$$

where the e's are residuals corresponding to the ε's in (5.13). The right-hand side of (5.17) is the residual version of the quadratic disturbance component in (3.9). It may be verified that (5.17) provides an unbiased estimator of σ^2 after multiplication by $M_g/(n_g-2)$.

Equivalent Income Changes and Income Elasticities

Using (1.11) and (1.15), we obtain the following results for the covariances of the equivalent income changes and the income elasticities between and within groups:

$$(5.18) \quad \sum_{g=1}^{G} M_g\left(\frac{\bar{W}_{gt}DQ_{gt}}{M_g} - DQ_t\right)\left(\frac{M_g}{\bar{W}_{gt}} - \sum_{h=1}^{G} M_h \frac{M_h}{\bar{W}_{ht}}\right) = \phi \sum_{g=1}^{G} M_g(DP'_{gt} - DP'_t)\frac{M_g}{\bar{W}_{gt}} + \sum_{g=1}^{G} \frac{M_g}{\bar{W}_{gt}} E_{gt}$$

$$(5.19) \quad \sum_{i\in S_g} \frac{\mu_i}{M_g}\left(\frac{\bar{w}_{it}Dq_{it}}{\mu_i} - \frac{\bar{W}_{gt}DQ_{gt}}{M_g}\right)\left(\frac{\mu_i}{\bar{w}_{it}} - \sum_{j\in S_g} \frac{\mu_j}{M_g}\frac{\mu_j}{\bar{w}_{jt}}\right) = \phi \sum_{i\in S_g} \frac{\mu_i}{M_g}(Dp_{it} - DP'_{gt})\frac{\mu_i}{\bar{w}_{it}} + \frac{1}{M_g}\sum_{i\in S_g} \frac{\mu_i}{\bar{w}_{it}} \varepsilon_{it}^g$$

Under preference independence the right-hand side of (5.19) is equal to the sum of the expressions (1.11) and (1.12) of Section 14.1, which proves that the within-group covariance of the equivalent income changes and the income elasticities is equal to the within-group quality change minus the volume component of this change. This is the within-group version of (4.2). Similarly, (5.18) is the group version of (4.2), because its right-hand side is the sum of the expressions (5.11) and (5.12) of Section 14.5. Note that this result is simpler than that for C_{0t}, described in the paragraph below (5.11) of this section, which involves the volume component of the average within-group term $\sum_g \bar{W}_{gt}\Gamma_{gt}$.

It is not true that the sum of (5.18) and the marginally weighted mean of (5.19) is equal to the covariance (4.1) of the basket, which can be clarified by means of Table 14.7 on page 371. Since (4.1) equals $DQ'_t - DQ_t$ minus the real-income component, it is equal to the sum of the S and D components between the groups plus the sum of the S, D, VS and VD components within the groups. In (5.18) we have the S and D components between the groups and in (5.19) the S and D components within a group. Hence the covariance (4.1) exceeds the sum of the between-group covariance (5.18) and the marginally weighted mean of the within-group covariance (5.19) by the sum of the VS and VD components, i.e., the substitution and disturbance sub-components of the volume component of the average within-group quality index.

15.6 The Own-Price Elasticity of Meat Under Predetermined Price Changes

We return to the meats and write (1.19) in the form

$$\frac{M_g}{\bar{W}_{gt}} \frac{\bar{w}_{it} Dq_{it}}{\mu_i} - DQ_{gt} = \psi (Dp_{it} - DP'_{gt}) + \frac{\varepsilon^g_{it}/\bar{W}_{gt}}{\mu_i/M_g} \tag{6.1}$$

where

$$\psi = \frac{\phi M_g}{\bar{W}_{gt}} \tag{6.2}$$

is the own-price elasticity of meat.

The Regression of the Equivalent Volume Changes

We run a marginally weighted least-squares regression of the left-hand variable of (6.1) on $Dp_{it} - DP'_{gt}$ for each $i \in S_g$. This yields an estimator of ψ which involves the covariance (5.6):

$$\hat{\psi}_t = \frac{C^g_t}{\Pi'_{gt}} \tag{6.3}$$

Since this exceeds C_{gt}/Π'_{gt} by a factor $M_g/\bar{W}_{gt}$ in view of (5.7), we obtain the variance of $\hat{\psi}_t$ from that of C_{gt}/Π'_{gt}, shown in (5.14), by multiplication by $(M_g/\bar{W}_{gt})^2$:

$$\operatorname{var} \hat{\psi}_t = \frac{\sigma^2 M_g}{\bar{W}^2_{gt} \Pi'_{gt}} \tag{6.4}$$

The marginally weighted residual sum of squares of this regression is

$$\sum_{i \in S_g} \frac{\mu_i}{M_g} \left(\frac{e^g_{it}/\bar{W}_{gt}}{\mu_i/M_g} \right)^2 = \sum_{i \in S_g} \frac{(e^g_{it}/\bar{W}_{gt})^2}{\mu_i/M_g} \tag{6.5}$$

which is the residual version of the quadratic disturbance component in (3.17).

Note that (6.1) is obtained from (5.13) by multiplication by $M_g/\bar{W}_{gt}$ and that both M_g and $\bar{W}_{gt}$ are assumed to be known in the regressions of the equivalent income and volume changes. This means that the regressions based on (5.13) and (6.1) are equivalent, so that we are justified in using the same symbols for the residuals in (5.17) and (6.5).

Extension for the Parametrization of Section 7.3

Consider the preference-independent version of eq. (3.9) of Section 7.3,

(6.6)
$$\frac{\bar{w}_{it}}{\bar{W}_{gt}} Dq_{it} = \frac{\mu_i}{M_g} DQ_{gt} + \psi \frac{\mu_i}{M_g} (Dp_{it} - DP'_{gt}) + \varepsilon^*_{it} \quad \text{where} \quad \varepsilon^*_{it} = \frac{\varepsilon^g_{it}}{\bar{W}_{gt}}$$

so that under this parametrization (6.1) becomes

(6.7)
$$\frac{M_g}{\bar{W}_{gt}} \frac{\bar{w}_{it} Dq_{it}}{\mu_i} - DQ_{gt} = \psi (Dp_{it} - DP'_{gt}) + \frac{\varepsilon^*_{it}}{\mu_i/M_g}$$

This modification does not affect the estimator (6.3), but it does have an effect on the variance (6.4). Recall from the discussion preceding eq. (4.2) of Section 7.4 that the parametrization of Section 7.3 implies that σ varies proportionally to $\bar{W}_{gt}$, so that $\sigma/\bar{W}_{gt}$ becomes constant. We define

(6.8)
$$\sigma_g^2 = \frac{\sigma^2 M_g}{\bar{W}^2_{gt}}$$

which is then also constant (because the constancy of M_g is not affected by the parametrization of Section 7.3). The variance (6.4) thus becomes

(6.9)
$$\operatorname{var} \hat{\psi}_t = \frac{\sigma_g^2}{\Pi'_{gt}}$$

which is an immediate within-group extension of (4.9). Note that in (6.9) the variance of $\hat{\psi}_t$ is inversely proportional to Π'_{gt} with a constant proportionality coefficient, and that this is not so in (6.4) when σ is treated as a constant.

The ith residual of the regression based on (6.7) is

(6.10)
$$\frac{e^*_{it}}{\mu_i/M_g} = \frac{M_g}{\bar{W}_{gt}} \frac{\bar{w}_{it} Dq_{it}}{\mu_i} - DQ_{gt} - \hat{\psi}_t (Dp_{it} - DP'_{gt})$$

By proceeding along the lines of (4.20) to (4.21), we obtain the marginally weighted sum of squares of these residuals:

(6.11)
$$\sum_{i \in S_g} \frac{e^{*2}_{it}}{\mu_i/M_g} = V_t^g - \hat{\psi}_t C_t^g$$

The expression on the left is the residual version of the quadratic disturbance component in (3.18). The ratio of (6.11) to $n_g - 2$,

(6.12)
$$\hat{\sigma}^2_{gt} = \frac{V_t^g - \hat{\psi}_t C_t^g}{n_g - 2}$$

is an unbiased one-period estimator of the parameter (6.8). The reader may want to verify this proposition along the lines of (4.14) to (4.16) by subtracting $\hat{\psi}_t$ times (5.8) from (3.17) and using (3.13) and (1.16).

Annual Estimates of the Own-Price Elasticity of Meat

The first column of Table 15.3 contains the estimate (6.3) of the own-price elasticity of meat for each pair of successive years from 1950 to 1972. It follows from (5.10) that the covariance in the numerator of (6.3) can be obtained by subtracting the volume component from Γ_{gt} in Table 14.3 on page 352; the denominator is shown in column (6) of Table 13.10 on page 327.

The annual estimates of the own-price elasticity in Table 15.3 are a within-group version of the annual income flexibility estimates that were mentioned below (4.22). They deserve more confidence, however, because the meat data are in better agreement with the second-moment model than the Dutch consumption data of Chapter 6. This model determines the standard errors which are shown in parentheses in the first column. They are obtained from (6.9) with σ_g estimated by $\hat{\sigma}_g$, which is defined in (6.14) below. Column (3) contains $\hat{\sigma}_{gt}$, the annual estimate of σ_g whose square is defined in (6.12) with $n_g=4$. The other columns of Table 15.3 are discussed later in this section and in Section 15.7.

Eleven of the 22 estimates of the own-price elasticity in column (1) are between $-.50$ and $-.75$. The others are almost equally (five against six) divided between values smaller than $-.75$ and larger than $-.50$. The median estimate is $-.64$. Some estimates differ substantially from the median, including one positive estimate, but these typically have large standard errors caused by a small value of Π'_{gt}. The annual estimates of σ_g in column (3) fluctuate between .002 and .017.

The 22-Year Estimate of the Own-Price Elasticity

The within-group version of (4.10) and (4.11) is

$$\hat{\psi} = \frac{\sum_{t=1}^{T} C_t^g}{\sum_{t=1}^{T} \Pi'_{gt}} \qquad \operatorname{var} \hat{\psi} = \frac{\sigma_g^2}{\sum_{t=1}^{T} \Pi'_{gt}} \tag{6.13}$$

and that of (4.13) is

$$\hat{\sigma}_g^2 = \frac{1}{(n_g - 1)\,T - 1} \sum_{t=1}^{T} (V_t^g - \hat{\psi} C_t^g) \tag{6.14}$$

TABLE 15.3

ANNUAL ESTIMATES OF THE OWN-PRICE ELASTICITY OF MEAT AND ITS RECIPROCAL

	$\hat{\psi}_t$ (1)	Precision contribution (2)	$\hat{\sigma}_{gt}$ (3)	$1/\tilde{\psi}_t$ (4)	Precision contribution (5)	$\tilde{\sigma}_{gt}/\lvert\tilde{\psi}_t\rvert$ (6)	$\tilde{\psi}_t$ (7)	$\tilde{\sigma}_{gt}$ (8)
	Predetermined price changes			*Predetermined quantity changes*				
1950–51	−.99 (.19)	.032	.013	−.90 (.26)	.072	.013	−1.12	.014
1951–52	.19 (.91)	.001	.015	.05 (.69)	.011	.008	19.84	.157
1952–53	−.64 (.06)	.362	.005	−1.55 (.13)	.311	.008	−.65	.005
1953–54	−.65 (.24)	.020	.017	−.89 (.41)	.030	.019	−1.12	.022
1954–55	−.60 (.11)	.100	.007	−1.62 (.26)	.076	.011	−.62	.007
1955–56	−1.11 (.26)	.018	.007	−.86 (.33)	.047	.006	−1.17	.007
1956–57	−.71 (.16)	.044	.010	−1.29 (.32)	.050	.013	−.77	.010
1957–58	−.64 (.18)	.035	.013	−1.24 (.37)	.037	.018	−.81	.015
1958–59	−.66 (.12)	.077	.008	−1.45 (.26)	.072	.012	−.69	.008
1959–60	−2.10 (.82)	.002	.011	−.36 (.48)	.022	.004	−2.82	.013
1960–61	−.58 (.18)	.035	.004	−1.67 (.45)	.025	.007	−.60	.004
1961–62	−.45 (.47)	.005	.002	−1.99 (1.40)	.003	.005	−.50	.002
1962–63	−1.07 (.71)	.002	.006	−.74 (.85)	.007	.005	−1.35	.006
1963–64	−2.74 (1.31)	.001	.015	−.19 (.49)	.021	.004	−5.30	.020
1964–65	−.73 (.15)	.053	.010	−1.27 (.28)	.063	.013	−.78	.010
1965–66	−.27 (.21)	.028	.014	−1.19 (.62)	.013	.029	−.84	.025
1966–67	−.71 (.18)	.035	.007	−1.33 (.36)	.039	.009	−.75	.007
1967–68	−.36 (.40)	.007	.006	−1.51 (1.18)	.004	.012	−.66	.008
1968–69	−.51 (.61)	.003	.012	−.41 (.79)	.008	.011	−2.43	.026
1969–70	−.38 (.36)	.009	.011	−.86 (.77)	.008	.017	−1.16	.019
1970–71	−.47 (.12)	.089	.004	−2.07 (.35)	.042	.009	−.48	.005
1971–72	−.61 (.17)	.041	.012	−1.34 (.36)	.039	.018	−.75	.013

which is an unbiased estimator of σ_g^2. For the meats ($n_g=4$, $T=22$) this yields

(6.15) $$\hat{\psi} = -.639\ (.034) \qquad \hat{\sigma}_g = .0103$$

The point estimate of ψ is in good agreement with (2.4), which is not surprising. Its standard error is obtained from the variance given in (6.13) after substituting $\hat{\sigma}_g$ for σ_g.

By comparing the variances shown in (6.9) and (6.13), we conclude that the ratio of Π'_{gt} to $\Pi'_{g1}+\cdots+\Pi'_{gT}$ may be viewed as the contribution of the tth one-period estimate ($\hat{\psi}_t$) to the precision of the T-period estimate ($\hat{\psi}$). These ratios are shown in column (2) of Table 15.3. The 1952–53 estimate contributes more than 36 percent to the precision of $\hat{\psi}$, followed by the 1954–55 and 1970–71 estimates, both of which contribute about 10 percent. The contribution of some estimates (1951-52 and 1963–64) is only one-tenth of 1 percent.

We should add that it is probably realistic to consider the standard errors in Table 15.3 and in (6.15) as optimistic from the viewpoint of the precision of the estimates, because the regression based on (6.7) treats ψ as the only unknown parameter. It ignores the random variability of the estimates of the conditional marginal shares of the transformed meats by proceeding as if these estimates coincide with the corresponding parameters. In fact, the procedure ignores the random variability of the estimate of the normalized price coefficient matrix from which the transformed meats have been derived.

Is the Own-Price Elasticity Constant Over Time?

The parametrization of Section 7.3 treats the own-price elasticity of meat as a constant. The annual estimates in the first column of Table 15.3 enable us to test this constancy conditionally on the normalized price coefficient matrix just mentioned. For this purpose we must formulate an alternative hypothesis.

The price coefficient matrix of the four meats was derived in Section 7.6 under the assumption that these meats are block-independent of all other commodities. The demand equation for meat as a whole then involves real income and the relative price of meat. Our alternative hypothesis therefore postulates that the own-price elasticity of meat depends on real income and the relative price of meat. The form chosen is

(6.16) $$\psi_t = \alpha_0 + \alpha_1 \log P_{gt} + \alpha_2 \log Q_t$$

where ψ_t is the own-price elasticity of meat during the transition from $t-1$

to t, and P_{gt} and Q_t are the relative price of meat and real per capita income, respectively, during the same transition. The last variable is shown for each calendar year in the first column of Table 15.4 (reproduced from Table 13.11 on page 335). We express it as an index with base 1 in 1950 and define Q_t as the geometric mean of the index values in $t-1$ and t. To obtain the relative

TABLE 15.4

EXPLANATORY VARIABLES FOR THE OWN-PRICE ELASTICITY OF MEAT

	Per capita real income	Relative price of meat P_g	Relative price of meat P'_g	Per capita consumption of meat
	Index base 1950 = 100			
1951	99.5	102.9	105.5	96.7
1952	100.7	98.7	101.2	102.2
1953	104.3	91.5	87.2	107.3
1954	104.7	90.2	86.1	106.7
1955	110.7	84.7	82.6	111.1
1956	112.2	79.9	78.9	115.0
1957	112.3	83.9	82.3	110.7
1958	110.6	89.6	89.5	108.4
1959	115.7	84.8	87.1	114.1
1960	117.1	82.5	84.3	114.3
1961	117.4	80.7	82.1	114.9
1962	121.3	82.3	84.1	116.3
1963	124.7	78.5	80.2	121.0
1964	129.8	76.0	77.4	124.2
1965	136.0	81.2	81.8	120.3
1966	141.0	83.9	83.6	124.3
1967	143.3	78.5	79.5	130.2
1968	148.4	77.8	79.2	133.6
1969	150.7	81.3	83.1	134.0
1970	149.7	78.8	80.5	137.6
1971	153.2	75.6	78.7	141.1
1972	159.7	81.2	84.1	140.4

price of meat we should ideally use the marginal price index as deflator, but since this is not available we use the Bureau of Labor Statistics consumer price index (Table 7.1 on page 9). So we cumulate DP_{gt} over time (Table 13.9 on page 324) and take antilogs for each year, after which we divide by the BLS index to obtain the relative price of meat shown in the second column of Table 15.4. The variable P_{gt} in (6.16) is defined as the geometric mean of the index values in $t-1$ and t with base 1 in 1950.

Our null hypothesis is $\alpha_1 = \alpha_2 = 0$. The maintained hypothesis includes (6.9) as well as the serial independence of the conditional demand disturbances, so that $\hat{\psi}_1, \hat{\psi}_2, \ldots$ are also independent. These annual estimates thus have a diagonal covariance matrix $\mathbf{D}$ whose t^{th} diagonal element is given in (6.9). So, if $\mathbf{X}$ is a $T \times 3$ matrix ($T = 22$) with 1, $\log P_{gt}$ and $\log Q_t$ as successive elements of the tth row, we obtain weighted least-squares estimates of the α's by postmultiplying $(\mathbf{X}'\mathbf{D}^{-1}\mathbf{X})^{-1}\,\mathbf{X}'\mathbf{D}^{-1}$ by the column vector of the $\hat{\psi}_t$'s; their standard errors under the null hypothesis are equal to the square roots of the diagonal elements of $(\mathbf{X}'\mathbf{D}^{-1}\mathbf{X})^{-1}$. The result is

$$\psi_t = -\underset{(.075)}{.654} + \underset{(.94)}{.61}\log P_{gt} + \underset{(.52)}{.66}\log Q_t \tag{6.17}$$

The standard errors of the estimates of α_1 and α_2 leave little doubt about their significance.

Further Experiments

A comparison of the first two columns of Table 15.4 shows that the relative price of meat is lower at the end of the period than at the beginning, whereas the opposite is true for per capita real income. This suggests a certain degree of multicollinearity among the right-hand variables in (6.17), which could be the cause of the large standard errors. It is true that the increase in per capita real income is a gradual increase and that the decrease in the relative price of meat was essentially completed in 1956; nevertheless, it is worthwhile to consider the weighted least-squares regressions with one of the two variables (P_{gt} or Q_t) deleted. This yields

$$\psi_t = -\underset{(.048)}{.691} + \underset{(.23)}{.36}\log Q_t \tag{6.18}$$

$$\psi_t = -\underset{(.065)}{.701} - \underset{(.42)}{.46}\log P_{gt} \tag{6.19}$$

The standard errors in (6.18) and (6.19) are indeed smaller than the corresponding standard errors in (6.17), but still so large that the associated point estimates are not significant. Note also the difference in sign of the coefficients of $\log P_{gt}$ in (6.17) and (6.19).

An alternative procedure consists of using DP'_{gt} rather than DP_{gt} for the relative price of meat. The resulting index (deflated by the BLS index) is shown in the third column of Table 15.4. For this price specification (6.17) and (6.19) become

$$\psi_t = -.673 + .23 \log P'_{gt} + .45 \log Q_t \tag{6.20}$$
$$\qquad (.079) \quad (.79) \qquad\qquad (.39)$$

$$\psi_t = -.708 - .51 \log P'_{gt} \tag{6.21}$$
$$\qquad (.073) \quad (.47)$$

These results indicate that the data provide no evidence against the assumption that the own-price elasticity of meat is a constant.

15.7 The Case of Predetermined Quantity Changes

In this section we assume that the quantity changes are predetermined, so that the equivalent income and volume changes have the same property.

Equivalent Income Changes and Price Log-changes

We write (4.6) in the form

$$Dp_{it} - DP'_t = \frac{1}{\phi}\left(\frac{\bar{w}_{it}Dq_{it}}{\mu_i} - DQ_t\right) - \frac{\varepsilon_{it}}{\phi\mu_i} \tag{7.1}$$

which is the ith reciprocal equation under preference independence [see eq. (5.24) of Section 9.5]. We multiply both sides by

$$\phi\mu_i\left(\frac{\bar{w}_{it}Dq_{it}}{\mu_i} - DQ_t\right)$$

and sum over i, which yields

$$\phi C_t = V_t - \sum_{i=1}^{n} \frac{\bar{w}_{it}Dq_{it}}{\mu_i}\varepsilon_{it} \tag{7.2}$$

This shows that under predetermined quantity changes, ϕC_t has expectation V_t and a random component equal to minus the inner product of the vectors of disturbances and equivalent income changes. The variance of this component is

$$\operatorname{var}\left(\sum_{i=1}^{n} \frac{\bar{w}_{it}Dq_{it}}{\mu_i}\varepsilon_{it}\right) = \sigma^2 V_t \tag{7.3}$$

The proof of (7.3) is analogous to that of eq. (1.10) of Section 11.1.

Next square both sides of (7.1), multiply by $\phi^2\mu_i$, and sum over i. This yields

$$\phi^2 \Pi'_t = V_t - 2\sum_{i=1}^{n} \frac{\bar{w}_{it}Dq_{it}}{\mu_i}\varepsilon_{it} + \sum_{i=1}^{n} \frac{\varepsilon_{it}^2}{\mu_i} \tag{7.4}$$

which shows that $\phi^2 \Pi'_t$ consists of a predetermined component equal to that of ϕC_t in (7.2), a linear disturbance component which is twice the disturbance component of ϕC_t, and a quadratic disturbance component which is identical to the quadratic disturbance component of V_t under predetermined price changes [see (3.3)].

A Regression of Price Log-changes on Equivalent Income Changes

We write (7.1) in a form similar to (4.8):

$$\text{(7.5)} \qquad \sqrt{\mu_i}\left(Dp_{it} - DP'_t - \frac{\bar{E}_t}{\phi}\right) = \frac{1}{\phi}\sqrt{\mu_i}\left(\frac{\bar{w}_{it}Dq_{it}}{\mu_i} - DQ_t\right) - \frac{\bar{\varepsilon}_{it}}{\phi\sqrt{\mu_i}}$$

The disturbance term on the right has variance σ^2/ϕ^2, independent of i. So we apply least squares to (7.5) for $i=1,\ldots,n$ to obtain a one-period estimator of $1/\phi$ (the income elasticity of the marginal utility of income):

$$\text{(7.6)} \qquad \frac{1}{\tilde{\phi}_t} = \frac{C_t}{V_t}$$

Under predetermined quantity changes this is a best linear unbiased one-period estimator of $1/\phi$ (linear in the equivalent income changes) with a variance equal to

$$\text{(7.7)} \qquad \text{var}\,\frac{1}{\tilde{\phi}_t} = \frac{\sigma^2}{\phi^2 V_t}$$

It may also be verified along the lines of (4.14) to (4.16) that

$$\text{(7.8)} \qquad \frac{\Pi'_t - C_t/\tilde{\phi}_t}{n-2}$$

is an unbiased one-period estimator of σ^2/ϕ^2.

To describe the regression based on (7.5) geometrically, we go back to Figure 15.3 on page 418, where we projected E'_d on the line OP'_d. For (7.5) we have to project P'_d on OE'_d. This makes no difference for $n=2$ because O, P'_d and E'_d are then on a straight line, but it does make a difference for $n>2$.

Groupwise Extensions

Next write (5.12) and (5.13) in the form

$$\text{(7.9)} \qquad DP'_{gt} - DP'_t = \frac{1}{\phi}\left(\frac{\bar{W}_{gt}DQ_{gt}}{M_g} - DQ_t\right) - \frac{E_{gt}}{\phi M_g}$$

$$\text{(7.10)} \qquad Dp_{it} - DP'_{gt} = \frac{1}{\phi}\left(\frac{\bar{w}_{it}Dq_{it}}{\mu_i} - \frac{\bar{W}_{gt}DQ_{gt}}{M_g}\right) - \frac{\varepsilon^g_{it}}{\phi\mu_i}$$

These are the preference-independent versions of the reciprocal equation of S_g and of the ith conditional reciprocal equation [see eqs. (5.28) and (5.30) of Section 9.5]. By applying operations analogous to those leading to (7.2) and (7.4), we obtain expressions for the covariances of the price log-changes and the equivalent income changes between and within groups,

$$\phi C_{0t} = V_{0t} - \sum_{g=1}^{G} \frac{\bar{W}_{gt} DQ_{gt}}{M_g} E_{gt} \tag{7.11}$$

$$\phi C_{gt} = V_{gt} - \frac{1}{M_g} \sum_{i \in S_g} \frac{\bar{w}_{it} Dq_{it}}{\mu_i} \varepsilon_{it}^g \tag{7.12}$$

and the following expressions for the variances of the price log-changes:

$$\phi^2 \Pi'_{0t} = V_{0t} - 2 \sum_{g=1}^{G} \frac{\bar{W}_{gt} DQ_{gt}}{M_g} E_{gt} + \sum_{g=1}^{G} \frac{E_{gt}^2}{M_g} \tag{7.13}$$

$$\phi^2 \Pi'_{gt} = V_{gt} - \frac{2}{M_g} \sum_{i \in S_g} \frac{\bar{w}_{it} Dq_{it}}{\mu_i} \varepsilon_{it}^g + \frac{1}{M_g} \sum_{i \in S_g} \frac{(\varepsilon_{it}^g)^2}{\mu_i} \tag{7.14}$$

The last terms of (7.13) and (7.14) are identical to the quadratic disturbance components in (3.8) and (3.9); the two other terms should be compared with the corresponding terms of (7.11) and (7.12).

Marginally weighted least-squares regressions based on (7.9) and (7.10) can be designed along the lines of (7.5). If the quantity changes are predetermined, these regressions yield unbiased estimators of $1/\phi$ equal to C_{0t}/V_{0t} for groups and to C_{gt}/V_{gt} for the goods of S_g, with variances equal to $\sigma^2/\phi^2 V_{0t}$ and $\sigma^2/\phi^2 M_g V_{gt}$, respectively. By weighting the group estimator and the G within-group estimators inversely proportionally to their variances we obtain the estimator (7.6):

$$\frac{V_{0t} \dfrac{C_{0t}}{V_{0t}} + \sum_{g=1}^{G} M_g V_{gt} \dfrac{C_{gt}}{V_{gt}}}{V_{0t} + \sum_{g=1}^{G} M_g V_{gt}} = \frac{C_t}{V_t} = \frac{1}{\tilde{\phi}_t}$$

This result should be compared with (5.15).

A Regression of Price Log-changes on Equivalent Volume Changes

Next write (6.1) as

$$Dp_{it} - DP'_{gt} = \frac{1}{\psi}\left(\frac{M_g}{\bar{W}_{gt}} \frac{\bar{w}_{it} Dq_{it}}{\mu_i} - DQ_{gt}\right) - \frac{\varepsilon_{it}^g/\bar{W}_{gt}}{\psi \mu_i/M_g} \tag{7.15}$$

or, equivalently, as

$$(7.16)\quad \sqrt{\mu_i/M_g}\left(Dp_{it} - DP'_{gt} - \frac{\bar{E}_{gt}}{\psi \bar{W}_{gt}}\right) = \frac{1}{\psi}\sqrt{\mu_i/M_g}\left(\frac{M_g}{\bar{W}_{gt}}\frac{\bar{w}_{it}Dq_{it}}{\mu_i} - DQ_{gt}\right) - \frac{\bar{\varepsilon}_{it}/\bar{W}_{gt}}{\psi\sqrt{\mu_i/M_g}}$$

where use is made of eq. (1.19) of Section 7.1. For the disturbance term in the right-hand side of (7.16) we have

$$(7.17)\quad \operatorname{var}\left(\frac{\bar{\varepsilon}_{it}/\bar{W}_{gt}}{\psi\sqrt{\mu_i/M_g}}\right) = \frac{\sigma^2 M_g}{\psi^2 \bar{W}_{gt}^2}$$

which is the same for each $i \in S_g$. Therefore, if the quantity changes are predetermined, we obtain an unbiased one-period estimator of $1/\psi$ from the least-squares regression based on (7.16),

$$(7.18)\quad \frac{1}{\tilde{\psi}_t} = \frac{C_t^g}{V_t^g}$$

whose variance equals $\sigma^2 M_g/\psi^2 \bar{W}_{gt}^2 V_t^g$ in view of (7.17). When the parametrization of Section 7.3 is selected, we can use (6.8) to simplify this to

$$(7.19)\quad \operatorname{var}\frac{1}{\tilde{\psi}_t} = \frac{\sigma_g^2}{\psi^2 V_t^g}$$

The results (7.18) and (7.19) are within-group extensions of (7.6) and (7.7).

Application to Meats

Column (4) of Table 15.3 on page 428 contains the annual estimates (7.18) of $1/\psi$, the reciprocal of the own-price elasticity of meat. The variance and covariance in the right-hand side of (7.18) are specified numerically in the same way as they are in Section 15.6, and are therefore based on the parameter estimates obtained in Section 7.6 under the condition of predetermined price changes. Since the approach of this section is based on predetermined quantity changes, this qualification should be kept in mind.

The figures in column (7) of Table 15.3 are the reciprocals of (7.18); they are the implied estimates of the own-price elasticity of meat. They all have the same sign as those of $\hat{\psi}$ in column (1), but they are larger in absolute value. The signs are determined by that of the covariance in the numerators of (6.3) and (7.18). To verify the difference in absolute value, we multiply (6.3) and (7.18),

$$\frac{\hat{\psi}_t}{\tilde{\psi}_t} = \frac{(C_t^g)^2}{\Pi'_{gt} V_t^g} \leq 1 \tag{7.20}$$

where the inequality sign is based on the fact that the second ratio is the square of the marginally weighted correlation coefficient of the price log-changes and the equivalent volume changes. Given that $\hat{\psi}_t$ and $\tilde{\psi}_t$ have the same sign, we thus conclude from (7.20) that $\tilde{\psi}_t$ exceeds $\hat{\psi}_t$ in absolute value except when a ψ exists such that the residuals in the regression based on (7.16) are zero for all $i \in S_g$.

It is not really surprising that the ψ estimates under predetermined quantity changes are larger in absolute value than those obtained under predetermined price changes. We know from eq. (3.9) of Section 9.3 that the estimated price sensitivity in terms of conditional Slutsky coefficients is greater under predetermined quantity changes than under predetermined price changes. The result (7.20) extends this to the estimated price sensitivity in terms of the own-price elasticity of the demand for meat as a group.

Estimates of the Variance of the Regression

Column (6) of Table 15.3 contains the annual estimate of $\sigma_g/|\psi|$, computed as the square root of

$$\frac{\tilde{\sigma}_{gt}^2}{\tilde{\psi}_t^2} = \frac{\Pi'_{gt} - C_t^g/\tilde{\psi}_t}{n_g - 2} \tag{7.21}$$

where $n_g = 4$. This is the within-group version of the ratio (7.8); it fluctuates between .004 and .029.

By multiplying (7.21) by the square of $\tilde{\psi}_t$, we obtain the implied estimate of the square of σ_{gt}. Using (7.18), we write the result as

$$\tilde{\sigma}_{gt}^2 = \frac{\tilde{\psi}_t^2 \Pi'_{gt} - V_t^g}{n_g - 2} \tag{7.22}$$

The estimates $\tilde{\sigma}_{gt}$ are shown in column (8) of Table 15.3. Note the very large value of 1951–52, which results from the large $\tilde{\psi}_t$. The other $\tilde{\sigma}_{gt}$'s are much closer to the corresponding $\hat{\sigma}_{gt}$'s in column (3), but they, too, are systematically larger. We have

$$\frac{\hat{\sigma}_{gt}}{\tilde{\sigma}_{gt}} \leq 1 \tag{7.23}$$

which should be compared with (7.20). To prove (7.23) we use (7.20) to conclude that, if $\hat{\psi}_t \neq \tilde{\psi}_t$,

$$\left(\frac{\sqrt{\Pi'_{gt}V_t^g}}{C_t^g} - \frac{C_t^g}{\sqrt{\Pi'_{gt}V_t^g}}\right)^2 > 0$$

This can be written as

$$V_t^g\left[\frac{\Pi'_{gt}V_t^g}{(C_t^g)^2} - 1\right] > V_t^g\left[1 - \frac{(C_t^g)^2}{\Pi'_{gt}V_t^g}\right]$$

which is equivalent to $\tilde{\sigma}_{gt} > \hat{\sigma}_{gt}$ in view of eqs. (7.18), (7.22), (6.3) and (6.12). The equal sign in (7.23) holds if and only if the equal sign holds in (7.20).

Estimating the Income Flexibility from Several Observations

Assume that T observations are available and that the disturbances are serially independent. Under predetermined quantity changes we obtain an optimal estimator of $1/\phi$ by weighting the one-period estimator (7.6) inversely proportionally to its variance (7.7). This yields

$$\frac{1}{\tilde{\phi}} = \frac{\sum_{t=1}^{T} V_t/\tilde{\phi}_t}{\sum_{t=1}^{T} V_t} = \frac{\sum_{t=1}^{T} C_t}{\sum_{t=1}^{T} V_t} \tag{7.24}$$

with variance

$$\text{var}\,\frac{1}{\tilde{\phi}} = \frac{\sigma^2}{\phi^2 \sum_{t=1}^{T} V_t} \tag{7.25}$$

The T-period extension of (7.8) is

$$\frac{\tilde{\sigma}^2}{\tilde{\phi}^2} = \frac{1}{(n-1)\,T-1}\sum_{t=1}^{T}\left(\Pi'_t - \frac{C_t}{\tilde{\phi}}\right) \tag{7.26}$$

which may be shown [see (4.17) to (4.19)] to be an unbiased estimator of σ^2/ϕ^2. The implied estimator of σ^2 is

$$\tilde{\sigma}^2 = \frac{1}{(n-1)\,T-1}\sum_{t=1}^{T}(\tilde{\phi}^2\Pi'_t - V_t) \tag{7.27}$$

which is obtained by multiplying (7.26) by $\tilde{\phi}^2$ and using (7.24).

The 22-Year Estimate of the Own-Price Elasticity of Meat

The within-group version of (7.24) to (7.27) for the meats is

$$\frac{1}{\tilde{\psi}} = \frac{\sum_{t=1}^{T} C_t^g}{\sum_{t=1}^{T} V_t^g} \qquad \operatorname{var} \frac{1}{\tilde{\psi}} = \frac{\sigma_g^2}{\psi^2 \sum_{t=1}^{T} V_t^g} \tag{7.28}$$

$$\frac{\tilde{\sigma}_g^2}{\tilde{\psi}^2} = \frac{1}{(n_g - 1)\,T - 1} \sum_{t=1}^{T} \left(\Pi'_{gt} - \frac{C_t^g}{\tilde{\psi}} \right) \tag{7.29}$$

$$\tilde{\sigma}_g^2 = \frac{1}{(n_g - 1)\,T - 1} \sum_{t=1}^{T} (\tilde{\psi}^2 \Pi'_{gt} - V_t^g) \tag{7.30}$$

For the meats ($n_g = 4$, $T = 22$) this yields

$$\frac{1}{\tilde{\psi}} = -\,1.317\ (.071) \qquad \frac{\tilde{\sigma}_g}{|\tilde{\psi}|} = .0148 \tag{7.31}$$

This result may be viewed as the predetermined-quantity counterpart of (6.15). The standard error of $1/\tilde{\psi}$ is obtained from the variance shown in (7.28) after substituting $(\tilde{\sigma}_g/\tilde{\psi})^2$ for $(\sigma_g/\psi)^2$. The same substitution is also applied to the standard errors in column (4) of Table 15.3, which are obtained from the variance (7.19).

The estimates of ψ and σ_g implied by (7.31) are

$$\tilde{\psi} = -\,.759\ (.041) \qquad \tilde{\sigma}_g = .0112 \tag{7.32}$$

Both point estimates exceed the corresponding values of (6.15) in absolute value, but the t ratios of the two ψ estimates are about equal.

Two Remarks

(1) The standard error of $\tilde{\psi}$ shown in (7.32) is an asymptotic approximation. Write $x = 1/\psi$ and interpret $dx = d(1/\psi)$ as the sampling error of $1/\tilde{\psi}$. The implied error of $\tilde{\psi}$ is

$$d\tilde{\psi} = d\left(\frac{1}{x}\right) = -\frac{dx}{x^2} = -\,\psi^2 d\left(\frac{1}{\psi}\right)$$

Accordingly, the asymptotic variance is computed as $\tilde{\psi}^4 \operatorname{var}(1/\tilde{\psi})$.

(2) Column (5) of Table 15.3 on page 428 contains the ratio

$$\frac{V_t^g}{V_1^g + \cdots + V_T^g} \tag{7.33}$$

It follows from (7.19) and (7.28) that this ratio measures the contribution of $1/\tilde{\psi}_t$ to the precision of $1/\tilde{\psi}$. The largest contribution is from 1952–53. This is similar to the analogous contributions in column (2), although 1952–53 is not as dominant in column (5) as in column (2). Also, there are two other contributions exceeding .08 in column (2) but none in (5). On the other hand, there are four observations in column (2) whose contribution is as small as one or two-tenths of 1 percent, but none in column (5). This suggests that the contributions of the 22 observations to the precision of $1/\tilde{\psi}$ are more equal than those to the precision of $\hat{\psi}$. A simple way of measuring this is by means of the entropy of these contributions. So we multiply the ratio (7.33) by the logarithm of its reciprocal and sum over $t=1,\ldots,22$, which gives an entropy of 2.53 nits. The entropy of column (2) is 2.31 nits, which is indeed smaller.

Is the Own-Price Elasticity of Meat Constant Over Time?

At the end of Section 15.6 we verified the constancy of ψ under predetermined price changes. When the quantity changes are predetermined, we can use the reciprocal equation for meat as a group, which describes the change in the relative price of meat in terms of the changes in real income and the volume of meat consumption. So we change (6.16) into

$$\frac{1}{\psi_t} = \beta_0 + \beta_1 \log Q_{gt} + \beta_2 \log Q_t \tag{7.34}$$

where Q_{gt} is the volume of meat consumption during the transition from $t-1$ to t. This volume is shown as an index in the last column of Table 15.4; it is obtained by cumulating DQ_{gt} of Table 14.2 on page 349. The variable Q_{gt} in (7.34) is defined as the geometric mean of these index values in $t-1$ and t with base 1 in 1950.

The estimation procedure for (7.34) is weighted least squares, similar to that used for (6.16), but with the variances of the $\hat{\psi}_t$'s replaced by those of $1/\tilde{\psi}_t$. The result is

$$\frac{1}{\psi_t} = \underset{(.14)}{-\,1.14} - \underset{(4.1)}{6.9} \log Q_{gt} + \underset{(2.9)}{4.7} \log Q_t \tag{7.35}$$

When either Q_{gt} or Q_t is deleted, we obtain

$$\frac{1}{\psi_t} = \underset{(.10)}{-\,1.31} - \underset{(.5)}{.1} \log Q_t \tag{7.36}$$

$$\frac{1}{\psi_t} = \underset{(.11)}{-\,1.28} - \underset{(.7)}{.3} \log Q_{gt} \tag{7.37}$$

The t ratios of $\log Q_{gt}$ and $\log Q_t$ in these three regressions indicate that we may accept $1/\psi$ as a constant. Note the large standard errors in (7.35), which result from the substantial positive correlation of $\log Q_{gt}$ and $\log Q_t$ over time.

15.8 Extensions of the Regressions for the Natural Conjugate Supply Model

In this section we generalize the regressions of Sections 15.4 to 15.7 for the natural conjugate supply model along the lines of Sections 10.4 to 10.6. For this purpose we use eqs. (8.1) and (8.3) of Section 14.8,

$$\mathscr{E}\left(\sum_{i=1}^{n} Dp_{it}\varepsilon_{it}\right) = \frac{\theta}{\gamma}(n-1) \tag{8.1}$$

$$\mathscr{E}\left(\sum_{i \in S_g} Dp_{it}\varepsilon_{it}^g\right) = \frac{\theta}{\gamma}(n_g-1) \tag{8.2}$$

where γ is defined in eq. (7.34) of Section 14.7:

$$\gamma = -\frac{\phi}{\sigma^2} \tag{8.3}$$

We shall also use

$$\mathscr{E}\left(\sum_{g=1}^{G} DP'_{gt}E_{gt}\right) = \frac{\theta}{\gamma}(G-1) \tag{8.4}$$

which follows from eqs. (8.2) and (8.5) of Section 14.8.

Two Estimation Equations

It will be convenient to denote the averages of Π'_t, C_t and V_t over time by

$$\bar{\Pi}' = \frac{1}{T}\sum_{t=1}^{T} \Pi'_t \qquad \bar{C} = \frac{1}{T}\sum_{t=1}^{T} C_t \qquad \bar{V} = \frac{1}{T}\sum_{t=1}^{T} V_t \tag{8.5}$$

so that after averaging over t, (3.3) and (4.5) can be written as

$$\bar{V} = \phi^2\bar{\Pi}' + \frac{2\phi}{T}\sum_{t=1}^{T}\sum_{i=1}^{n} Dp_{it}\varepsilon_{it} + \frac{1}{T}\sum_{t=1}^{T}\sum_{i=1}^{n}\frac{\varepsilon_{it}^2}{\mu_i} \tag{8.6}$$

$$\bar{C} = \phi\bar{\Pi}' + \frac{1}{T}\sum_{t=1}^{T}\sum_{i=1}^{n} Dp_{it}\varepsilon_{it} \tag{8.7}$$

It follows from (8.1) and (8.3) that the disturbance term in (8.7) has expectation $\theta(n-1)/\gamma = -\sigma^2\theta(n-1)/\phi$. Using (3.4) also, we thus obtain the following result after substituting expectations for the three disturbance terms in (8.6) and (8.7):

$$\bar{V} = \phi^2 \bar{\Pi}' + \sigma^2 (1 - 2\theta)(n - 1) \tag{8.8}$$

$$\bar{C} = \phi \bar{\Pi}' - \frac{\sigma^2 \theta (n - 1)}{\phi} \tag{8.9}$$

These are two estimation equations for ϕ and σ^2. Note that ϕ and σ^2 are estimates in (8.8) and (8.9).

The Solution for Two Special Cases

By substituting $\theta = 0$ in (8.9) we obtain $\phi = \bar{C}/\bar{\Pi}'$, which is identical to the T-period estimator $\hat{\phi}$ which we obtained in (4.10) under predetermined price changes. The associated σ^2 estimator, based on (8.8), is

$$\frac{\bar{V} - \hat{\phi}^2 \bar{\Pi}'}{n - 1} = \frac{\bar{V} - \hat{\phi} \bar{C}}{n - 1}$$

which agrees with (4.13) except for the degree of freedom which is subtracted from $(n-1)T$ in (4.13).

By multiplying (8.9) by ϕ and subtracting the result from (8.8), we obtain

$$\bar{V} - \phi \bar{C} = \sigma^2 (1 - \theta)(n - 1) \tag{8.10}$$

This yields $\phi = \bar{V}/\bar{C}$ at $\theta = 1$, in agreement with $\tilde{\phi}$ which we derived in (7.24) under predetermined quantity changes. Substitution of $\tilde{\phi}$ in (8.8) gives the σ^2 estimator $(\tilde{\phi}^2 \bar{\Pi}' - \bar{V})/(n-1)$ at $\theta = 1$, which agrees with (7.27) except for the degree of freedom which is subtracted from $(n-1)T$ in (7.27).

In the sequel we shall assume

$$\bar{C} < 0 \tag{8.11}$$

in order to insure that the ϕ estimates at $\theta = 0$ and $\theta = 1$ are both negative.

A Conditional Estimator of the Income Flexibility

Since the case $\theta = 1$ has been disposed of, we can assume that

$$\theta < 1 \tag{8.12}$$

We thus have $\sigma^2(n-1) = (\bar{V} - \phi \bar{C})/(1 - \theta)$ in view of (8.10), which we substitute in (8.8):

$$\bar{V} - \phi^2 \bar{\Pi}' = \frac{1 - 2\theta}{1 - \theta} (\bar{V} - \phi \bar{C})$$

This can be written as

(8.13) $$\phi^2(1-\theta)\,\bar{\Pi}' - \phi(1-2\theta)\,\bar{C} - \theta\bar{V} = 0$$

which is a quadratic equation in ϕ with the following roots:

$$\phi = \frac{(1-2\theta)\,\bar{C} \pm \sqrt{(1-2\theta)^2\,\bar{C}^2 + 4\theta(1-\theta)\,\bar{\Pi}'\bar{V}}}{2(1-\theta)\,\bar{\Pi}'}$$

To verify which solution is to be selected we put $\theta=0$, so that the solution pair becomes $(\bar{C}\pm\sqrt{\bar{C}^2})/2\bar{\Pi}' = [\bar{C}\pm(-\bar{C})]/2\bar{\Pi}'$, where the equal sign is based on (8.11). This equals $\hat{\phi}=\bar{C}/\bar{\Pi}'$ if and only if we take the negative square root, so that we have to take this root for each θ. Using the identity

$$(1-2\theta)^2\,\bar{C}^2 + 4\theta(1-\theta)\,\bar{\Pi}'\bar{V} = \bar{C}^2 + 4\theta(1-\theta)\,(\bar{\Pi}'\bar{V} - \bar{C}^2)$$

we thus obtain

(8.14) $$\phi(\theta) = \frac{(1-2\theta)\,\bar{C} - \sqrt{\bar{C}^2 + 4\theta(1-\theta)\,(\bar{\Pi}'\bar{V} - \bar{C}^2)}}{2(1-\theta)\,\bar{\Pi}'}$$

which is a conditional estimator of the income flexibility, given the degree of price-disturbance dependence. The reader may want to prove the consistency of this estimator by verifying (under conditions similar to those used in Section 10.4) that the terms which have been replaced by their expectations in (8.6) and (8.7) converge in probability to these expectations as $T\to\infty$.

Groupwise Extensions

Next consider the averages (8.5) between groups,

(8.15) $$\bar{\Pi}_0' = \frac{1}{T}\sum_{t=1}^{T} \Pi_{0t}' \qquad \bar{C}_0 = \frac{1}{T}\sum_{t=1}^{T} C_{0t} \qquad \bar{V}_0 = \frac{1}{T}\sum_{t=1}^{T} V_{0t}$$

and average (3.8) and (5.4) over t:

$$\bar{V}_0 = \phi^2\bar{\Pi}_0' + \frac{2\phi}{T}\sum_{t=1}^{T}\sum_{g=1}^{G} DP_{gt}'E_{gt} + \frac{1}{T}\sum_{t=1}^{T}\sum_{g=1}^{G}\frac{E_{gt}^2}{M_g}$$

$$\bar{C}_0 = \phi\bar{\Pi}_0' + \frac{1}{T}\sum_{t=1}^{T}\sum_{g=1}^{G} DP_{gt}'E_{gt}$$

When we replace the three disturbance terms in these two equations by their expectations, using (3.12), (8.3) and (8.4), we obtain

(8.16) $$\bar{V}_0 = \phi^2\bar{\Pi}_0' + \sigma^2(1-2\theta)(G-1)$$

$$\bar{C}_0 = \phi \bar{\Pi}'_0 - \frac{\sigma^2 \theta (G-1)}{\phi} \tag{8.17}$$

which is identical to (8.8) and (8.9), except for the replacement of n by G and the zero subscripts added to $\bar{\Pi}'$, $\bar{C}$ and $\bar{V}$.

Similarly, when we define

$$\bar{\Pi}'_g = \frac{1}{T} \sum_{t=1}^{T} \Pi'_{gt} \qquad \bar{C}_g = \frac{1}{T} \sum_{t=1}^{T} C_{gt} \qquad \bar{V}_g = \frac{1}{T} \sum_{t=1}^{T} V_{gt} \tag{8.18}$$

and average (3.9) and (5.5) over t, we find

$$\bar{V}_g = \phi^2 \bar{\Pi}'_g + \frac{2\phi}{M_g T} \sum_{t=1}^{T} \sum_{i \in S_g} Dp_{it} \varepsilon_{it}^g + \frac{1}{M_g T} \sum_{t=1}^{T} \sum_{i \in S_g} \frac{(\varepsilon_{it}^g)^2}{\mu_i}$$

$$\bar{C}_g = \phi \bar{\Pi}'_g + \frac{1}{M_g T} \sum_{t=1}^{T} \sum_{i \in S_g} Dp_{it} \varepsilon_{it}^g$$

Again, replace the three disturbance terms by their expectations, using (3.13), (8.2) and (8.3),

$$\bar{V}_g = \phi^2 \bar{\Pi}'_g + \frac{\sigma^2}{M_g} (1 - 2\theta)(n_g - 1)$$

$$\bar{C}_g = \phi \bar{\Pi}'_g - \frac{\sigma^2 \theta (n_g - 1)}{\phi M_g}$$

and multiply these two equations by M_g:

$$M_g \bar{V}_g = \phi^2 (M_g \bar{\Pi}'_g) + \sigma^2 (1 - 2\theta)(n_g - 1) \tag{8.19}$$

$$M_g \bar{C}_g = \phi (M_g \bar{\Pi}'_g) - \frac{\sigma^2 \theta (n_g - 1)}{\phi} \tag{8.20}$$

This result is identical to (8.8) and (8.9), except for the replacement of n, $\bar{\Pi}'$, $\bar{C}$ and $\bar{V}$ by n_g, $M_g \bar{\Pi}'_g$, $M_g \bar{C}_g$ and $M_g \bar{V}_g$, respectively. It is easily verified how the conditional estimator (8.14) is to be modified when it is based on (8.16) and (8.17) or on (8.19) and (8.20).

Extension to Equivalent Volume Changes

For the equivalent volume changes under the parametrization of Section 7.3, we proceed in the same way. We use (8.2) and (8.3) in

$$\mathscr{E}\left(\sum_{i \in S_g} Dp_{it} \frac{\varepsilon_{it}^g}{\bar{W}_{gt}} \right) = - \frac{\sigma^2 \theta (n_g - 1)}{\phi \bar{W}_{gt}} = - \frac{\sigma_g^2 \theta (n_g - 1)}{\psi} \tag{8.21}$$

where the last step is based on (6.2) and (6.8). We define

$$\bar{V}^g = \frac{1}{T}\sum_{t=1}^{T} V_t^g \qquad \bar{C}^g = \frac{1}{T}\sum_{t=1}^{T} C_t^g \tag{8.22}$$

and average (3.17) and (5.8) over t:

$$\bar{V}^g = \psi^2 \bar{\Pi}'_g + \frac{2\psi}{T}\sum_{t=1}^{T}\sum_{i\in S_g} Dp_{it}\frac{\varepsilon_{it}^g}{\bar{W}_{gt}} + \frac{1}{T}\sum_{t=1}^{T}\sum_{i\in S_g}\frac{(\varepsilon_{it}^g/\bar{W}_{gt})^2}{\mu_i/M_g}$$

$$\bar{C}^g = \psi\bar{\Pi}'_g + \frac{1}{T}\sum_{t=1}^{T}\sum_{i\in S_g} Dp_{it}\frac{\varepsilon_{it}^g}{\bar{W}_{gt}}$$

We replace the three disturbance terms by their expectations, using (8.21) as well as (3.13) and (6.8):

$$\bar{V}^g = \psi^2\bar{\Pi}'_g + \sigma_g^2(1-2\theta)(n_g-1) \tag{8.23}$$

$$\bar{C}^g = \psi\bar{\Pi}'_g - \frac{\sigma_g^2\theta(n_g-1)}{\psi} \tag{8.24}$$

This is the within-group version of (8.8) and (8.9). The conditional estimator of ψ is therefore obtained directly from (8.14),

$$\psi(\theta) = \frac{(1-2\theta)\bar{C}^g - R(\theta)}{2(1-\theta)\bar{\Pi}'_g} \tag{8.25}$$

where $R(\theta)$ is the positive square root of

$$[R(\theta)]^2 = (\bar{C}^g)^2 + 4\theta(1-\theta)\,[\bar{\Pi}'_g\bar{V}^g - (\bar{C}^g)^2] \tag{8.26}$$

Conditional Estimates of the Own-Price Elasticity of Meat

The values of the average variances and covariance for the meats are

$$\bar{\Pi}'_g = .004088 \qquad \bar{C}^g = -.002613 \qquad \bar{V}^g = .001984$$

Note the negative sign of $\bar{C}^g$, in agreement with (8.11).

The first column of Table 15.5 contains the estimate (8.25) of the own-price elasticity of meat for θ increasing from 0 to 1 at intervals of .1. The figures show that the estimate of this elasticity increases in absolute value from $\hat{\psi}$ to $\tilde{\psi}$ given in (6.15) and (7.32), respectively. Note also that (8.25) and (8.26) imply that at $\theta=\frac{1}{2}$ the estimate equals the negative square root of $\bar{V}^g/\bar{\Pi}'_g$, independent of $\bar{C}^g$.

TABLE 15.5

ESTIMATES OF THE OWN-PRICE ELASTICITY OF MEAT AT DIFFERENT DEGREES OF PRICE-DISTURBANCE DEPENDENCE

θ	ψ	σ_g	$-\psi/\sigma_g^2$
0	−.639	.0102	6128
.1	−.651	.0102	6230
.2	−.663	.0102	6307
.3	−.674	.0103	6361
.4	−.685	.0104	6393
.5	−.697	.0104	6403
.6	−.708	.0105	6393
.7	−.720	.0106	6361
.8	−.732	.0108	6307
.9	−.745	.0109	6230
1	−.759	.0111	6128

To estimate σ_g we use (8.24),

$$-\frac{\sigma_g^2\theta(n_g-1)}{\psi} = \bar{C}^g - \psi\bar{\Pi}_g' = \frac{2(1-\theta)\,\bar{C}^g - (1-2\theta)\,\bar{C}^g + R(\theta)}{2(1-\theta)}$$

where the second step is based on (8.25). This result implies

$$\text{(8.27)} \qquad \frac{\sigma_g^2(n_g-1)}{-\psi} = \frac{\bar{C}^g + R(\theta)}{2\theta(1-\theta)}$$

provided $0<\theta<1$. So for the meats, with $n_g=4$, we obtain $\sigma_g(\theta)$ by multiplying the right-hand side of (8.27) by $-\frac{1}{3}\psi(\theta)$ and taking the square root. The result is shown in the second column of Table 15.5, which indicates that the σ_g estimate increases slowly with θ. Note that $\sigma_g(0)$ and $\sigma_g(1)$ are slightly lower than the values given in (6.15) and (7.32), respectively, because the present procedure ignores the degree of freedom which is needed for the estimation of ψ (see the second subsection of this section).

The last column of Table 15.5 contains the estimate of $-\psi/\sigma_g^2$, which is a symmetric function of θ around $\theta=\frac{1}{2}$ in view of (8.27) and (8.26). It follows from (6.2) and (6.8) that $-\psi/\sigma_g^2$ equals $-\phi\bar{W}_{gt}/\sigma^2$, which is the connecting parameter for meats defined in eq. (4.3) of Section 7.4. The symmetry of the estimate of this parameter around $\theta=\frac{1}{2}$ may be compared with the analogous behavior of the estimates in the first column of Table 10.2 on page 160.

15.9 Equivalent Income and Volume Changes Under the Natural Conjugate Supply Model

In Section 15.8 we showed how the regressions based on equivalent income changes are to be modified under the conditions of the natural conjugate supply model, but we did not consider the implications of this model for the equivalent income changes themselves. This is the topic of the present section. It will appear that the results are quite close to those obtained for the quality index in Sections 12.8 and 14.8.

Reciprocal Slutsky Coefficients Under Preference Independence

Reciprocal Slutsky coefficients play a role in what follows. Since this chapter is based on the preference independence specification, we use eq. (5.25) of Section 9.5 to write these coefficients, multiplied by ϕ, as

$$(9.1) \qquad \phi\pi^{ij} = \begin{cases} \dfrac{1}{\mu_i} - 1 & \text{if} \quad i = j \\ -1 & \text{if} \quad i \neq j \end{cases}$$

Similarly, eq. (6.17) of Section 9.6 may then be written as

$$(9.2) \qquad \phi\Pi^{gh} = \begin{cases} \dfrac{1}{M_g} - 1 & \text{if} \quad g = h \\ -1 & \text{if} \quad g \neq h \end{cases}$$

For the conditional reciprocal Slutsky coefficients we combine (9.1) and (9.2) with eq. (6.22) of Section 9.6:

$$(9.3) \qquad \phi\pi^{gij} = \begin{cases} \dfrac{1}{\mu_i} - \dfrac{1}{M_g} & \text{if} \quad i = j \\ -\dfrac{1}{M_g} & \text{if} \quad i \neq j \end{cases}$$

Here i and j are both part of S_g.

The Random Substitution Components of Equivalent Income Changes

Consider eqs. (7.29) to (7.31) of Section 14.7:

$$(9.4) \qquad \operatorname{cov}(Dp_{it} - DP'_t, Dp_{jt} - DP'_t) = \delta_{22}\sigma^2 \frac{\pi^{ij}}{\phi}$$

$$(9.5) \qquad \operatorname{cov}(DP'_{gt} - DP'_t, DP'_{ht} - DP'_t) = \delta_{22}\sigma^2 \frac{\Pi^{gh}}{\phi}$$

(9.6)
$$\operatorname{cov}(Dp_{it}-DP'_{gt}, Dp_{jt}-DP'_{ht}) = \begin{cases} \delta_{22}\sigma^2 \dfrac{\pi^{gij}}{\phi} & \text{if} \quad i \in S_g,\, j \in S_h,\, g = h \\ 0 & \text{if} \quad i \in S_g,\, j \in S_h,\, g \neq h \end{cases}$$

The substitution component of the ith equivalent income change in (1.4) is $\phi(Dp_{it}-DP'_t)$. We conclude from (9.4) and (9.1) that its variance under the natural conjugate supply model is

$$\text{(9.7)} \qquad \operatorname{var}[\phi(Dp_{it}-DP'_t)] = \delta_{22}\sigma^2\left(\frac{1}{\mu_i}-1\right) = \delta_{22} \operatorname{var}\frac{\varepsilon_{it}}{\mu_i}$$

where the second step is based on (1.6). For the substitution component of the equivalent income change of S_g in (1.11) we use (9.2), (9.5) and (1.13):

$$\text{(9.8)} \qquad \operatorname{var}[\phi(DP'_{gt}-DP'_t)] = \delta_{22} \operatorname{var}\frac{E_{gt}}{M_g}$$

We proceed similarly for the substitution component of the equivalent income change within S_g, given in (1.15), using (9.3), (9.6) and (1.17):

$$\text{(9.9)} \qquad \operatorname{var}[\phi(Dp_{it}-DP'_{gt})] = \delta_{22} \operatorname{var}\frac{\varepsilon^g_{it}}{\mu_i}$$

We conclude from (9.7) to (9.9) that in each case the variance of the substitution component is a multiple δ_{22} of the variance of the corresponding disturbance component. Note the similarity to eqs. (8.14) of Section 12.8 and (8.7) and (8.12) of Section 14.8.

Covariances of Substitution and Disturbance Components

Next consider eqs. (7.33), (7.36) and (7.38) of Section 14.7:

$$\text{(9.10)} \qquad \operatorname{cov}(Dp_{it}-DP'_t, \varepsilon_{jt}) \doteq \begin{cases} \dfrac{\theta}{\gamma}(1-\mu_j) & \text{if} \quad i = j \\ -\dfrac{\theta}{\gamma}\mu_j & \text{if} \quad i \neq j \end{cases}$$

$$\text{(9.11)} \qquad \operatorname{cov}(DP'_{gt}-DP'_t, E_{ht}) = \begin{cases} \dfrac{\theta}{\gamma}(1-M_h) & \text{if} \quad g = h \\ -\dfrac{\theta}{\gamma}M_h & \text{if} \quad g \neq h \end{cases}$$

$$\text{(9.12)} \qquad \operatorname{cov}(Dp_{it}-DP'_{gt}, \varepsilon^g_{jt}) = \begin{cases} \dfrac{\theta}{\gamma}(1-\mu^g_j) & \text{if} \quad i = j \\ -\dfrac{\theta}{\gamma}\mu^g_j & \text{if} \quad i \neq j \end{cases}$$

We apply (9.10) to obtain the covariance of the substitution and disturbance components of the ith equivalent income change,

$$\operatorname{cov}\left[\phi(Dp_{it} - DP'_t), \frac{\varepsilon_{it}}{\mu_i}\right] = \frac{\theta\phi}{\gamma}\left(\frac{1}{\mu_i} - 1\right) = -\theta\sigma^2\left(\frac{1}{\mu_i} - 1\right)$$

where the second step is based on (8.3). We use (1.6) to write this as

$$\operatorname{cov}\left[\phi(Dp_{it} - DP'_t), \frac{\varepsilon_{it}}{\mu_i}\right] = -\theta \operatorname{var}\frac{\varepsilon_{it}}{\mu_i} \tag{9.13}$$

Similarly, by applying (9.11) to (1.11) and (9.12) to (1.15), we obtain

$$\operatorname{cov}\left[\phi(DP'_{gt} - DP'_t), \frac{E_{gt}}{M_g}\right] = -\theta \operatorname{var}\frac{E_{gt}}{M_g} \tag{9.14}$$

$$\operatorname{cov}\left[\phi(Dp_{it} - DP'_{gt}), \frac{\varepsilon^g_{it}}{\mu_i}\right] = -\theta \operatorname{var}\frac{\varepsilon^g_{it}}{\mu_i} \tag{9.15}$$

By combining these three covariances with the variances (9.7) to (9.9), we find that the correlation coefficient of the substitution and disturbance components of an equivalent income change equals $-\theta/\sqrt{\delta_{22}}$. This correlation is the same for each of the n equivalent income changes and also for that of each S_g [(9.14) and (9.8)] and for each such change within a group [(9.15) and (9.9)], and it is equal to the correlation coefficient of the substitution and disturbance components of the log-change in the quality index given in eq. (8.17) of Section 12.8. Recall from the discussion below eq. (8.14) of Section 14.8 that this correlation also applies to the quality change between groups and within each group.

The Variances of the Equivalent Income Changes

We have

$$1 + \delta_{22} - 2\theta = \delta_{11} \tag{9.16}$$

which follows from eq. (1.16) of Section 10.1. Consider then (4.6), which implies that the random component of $\bar{w}_{it}Dq_{it}/\mu_i - DQ_t$ has a variance equal to the sum of the variances of the disturbance and substitution components and twice their covariance. Using (9.7) and (9.13) as well as (9.16), we obtain

$$\operatorname{var}\left(\frac{\bar{w}_{it}Dq_{it}}{\mu_i} - DQ_t\right) = \delta_{11} \operatorname{var}\frac{\varepsilon_{it}}{\mu_i} \tag{9.17}$$

This result should be compared with eq. (8.16) of Section 12.8.

Equations (5.12) and (5.13) similarly imply

$$\text{(9.18)} \qquad \operatorname{var}\left(\frac{\bar{W}_{gt}DQ_{gt}}{M_g} - DQ_t\right) = \delta_{11} \operatorname{var}\frac{E_{gt}}{M_g}$$

$$\text{(9.19)} \qquad \operatorname{var}\left(\frac{\bar{w}_{it}Dq_{it}}{\mu_i} - \frac{\bar{W}_{gt}DQ_{gt}}{M_g}\right) = \delta_{11} \operatorname{var}\frac{\varepsilon_{it}^g}{\mu_i}$$

which should be compared with eqs. (8.9) and (8.14) of Section 14.8. Note that (9.19) differs from (9.17) in that (9.19) provides the conditional variance of the ith equivalent income change within S_g.

Covariances Involving Different Equivalent Income Changes

For $i \neq j$, consider the ith and j^{th} equivalent income changes. The covariance of their substitution components is obtained from (9.4) and (9.1):

$$\text{(9.20)} \qquad \operatorname{cov}[\phi(Dp_{it} - DP_t'),\ \phi(Dp_{jt} - DP_t')] = -\delta_{22}\sigma^2 \qquad i \neq j$$

Hence these covariances are independent of i and j, which is analogous to the second line of (1.6) for the disturbance covariances. Similarly,

$$\text{(9.21)} \qquad \operatorname{cov}[\phi(DP_{gt}' - DP_t'),\ \phi(DP_{ht}' - DP_t')] = -\delta_{22}\sigma^2 \qquad g \neq h$$

$$\text{(9.22)} \qquad \operatorname{cov}[\phi(Dp_{it} - DP_{gt}'),\ \phi(Dp_{jt} - DP_{gt}')] = -\frac{\delta_{22}\sigma^2}{M_g} \qquad i \neq j$$

which may be verified by means of (9.2) to (9.6). When $Dp_{jt} - DP_{gt}'$ in (9.22) is replaced by $Dp_{jt} - DP_{ht}'$ with $g \neq h$, we obtain a zero covariance in view of (9.6).

The covariance of the substitution and disturbance components of two different equivalent income changes is obtained from (9.10) and (8.3):

$$\text{(9.23)} \qquad \operatorname{cov}\left[\phi(Dp_{it} - DP_t'),\ \frac{\varepsilon_{jt}}{\mu_j}\right] = \theta\sigma^2 \qquad i \neq j$$

The groupwise versions are derived from (9.11) and (9.12):

$$\text{(9.24)} \qquad \operatorname{cov}\left[\phi(DP_{gt}' - DP_t'),\ \frac{E_{ht}}{M_h}\right] = \theta\sigma^2 \qquad g \neq h$$

$$\text{(9.25)} \qquad \operatorname{cov}\left[\phi(Dp_{it} - DP_{gt}'),\ \frac{\varepsilon_{jt}^g}{\mu_j}\right] = \frac{\theta\sigma^2}{M_g} \qquad i \neq j$$

The covariance of the ith and j^{th} equivalent income changes ($i \neq j$) can now be derived by combining (4.6) with (9.20), (9.23) and (1.6). Using (9.16), we write the result as

$$\text{(9.26)} \qquad \operatorname{cov}\left(\frac{\bar{w}_{it}Dq_{it}}{\mu_i} - DQ_t, \frac{\bar{w}_{jt}Dq_{jt}}{\mu_j} - DQ_t\right) = -\delta_{11}\sigma^2 \qquad i \neq j$$

The groupwise versions are

$$\text{(9.27)} \qquad \operatorname{cov}\left(\frac{\bar{W}_{gt}DQ_{gt}}{M_g} - DQ_t, \frac{\bar{W}_{ht}DQ_{ht}}{M_h} - DQ_t\right) = -\delta_{11}\sigma^2 \qquad g \neq h$$

$$\text{(9.28)} \qquad \operatorname{cov}\left(\frac{\bar{w}_{it}Dq_{it}}{\mu_i} - \frac{\bar{W}_{gt}DQ_{gt}}{M_g}, \frac{\bar{w}_{jt}Dq_{jt}}{\mu_j} - \frac{\bar{W}_{gt}DQ_{gt}}{M_g}\right) = -\frac{\delta_{11}\sigma^2}{M_g}$$

where $i, j \in S_g$ and $i \neq j$.

Extensions for Equivalent Volume Changes

Since (1.19) is obtained by multiplying (1.15) by $M_g/\bar{W}_{gt}$, the formulation of the analogous properties for the components of the equivalent volume changes is straightforward. In particular, using (6.2) and (6.8), we obtain the following results by multiplying (9.22), (9.25) and (9.28) by $(M_g/\bar{W}_{gt})^2$:

$$\text{(9.29)} \qquad \operatorname{cov}\left[\psi(Dp_{it} - DP'_{gt}), \psi(Dp_{jt} - DP'_{gt})\right] = -\delta_{22}\sigma_g^2 \qquad i \neq j$$

$$\text{(9.30)} \qquad \operatorname{cov}\left[\psi(Dp_{it} - DP'_{gt}), \frac{\varepsilon_{jt}^g/\bar{W}_{gt}}{\mu_j/M_g}\right] = \theta\sigma_g^2 \qquad i \neq j$$

$$\text{(9.31)} \qquad \operatorname{cov}\left(\frac{M_g}{\bar{W}_{gt}}\frac{\bar{w}_{it}Dq_{it}}{\mu_i} - DQ_{gt}, \frac{M_g}{\bar{W}_{gt}}\frac{\bar{w}_{jt}Dq_{jt}}{\mu_j} - DQ_{gt}\right) = -\delta_{11}\sigma^2$$

where $i \neq j$. These three covariances, which refer to (6.1), are within-group extensions of (9.20), (9.23) and (9.26), respectively.

CHAPTER 16

TRANSITIONS BETWEEN BUDGET SHARES

A considerable part of the discussion from Chapter 11 onward has been devoted to statistical summary measures which describe certain aspects of the consumer's basket and its changes over time. In this chapter we proceed in the opposite direction by asking for *more* rather than less detail. As in Chapter 15, it is assumed (unless otherwise stated) that there is preference independence or that the preference independence transformation has been applied.

16.1 Transitions and Net Flows Between Budget Shares

Under preference independence the jth demand equation takes the form

$$\bar{w}_{jt}Dq_{jt} = \mu_j DQ_t + \phi\mu_j(Dp_{jt} - DP_t') + \varepsilon_{jt} \tag{1.1}$$

The left-hand variable is the quantity component of the change in the jth budget share. Since these shares play such a prominent role in the analysis, we may ask whether it is possible to describe their changes over time in terms of flows from one commodity to another. That is, if we observe that the first commodity has a budget share increase equal to .012, we ask whether this increase can be described as being caused by a share flow of (say) .015 from the second commodity to the first, perhaps partly compensated by a negative flow from the third to the first, and so on.

One might react by saying that such a bivariate flow analysis is artificial, arguing that the budget share of a commodity goes up or down and that there is no way of identifying where the increase came from or to which particular commodities the loss must be ascribed. However, such an outright dismissal goes too far. In the preference independence transformation we replace commodities by T-goods so that the demand equations are preference-independent. Such a replacement of a commodity basket by a T-good basket need not necessarily be formulated in bivariate form, but we did find that the approach yields a bivariate array in the form of the composition matrix which, as we saw in Sections 13.1 and 13.2, is useful for the interpretation of the T-goods. We shall show in this section, which is based – apart from several modifications and extensions – on an article by THEIL (1970), that an equally instructive picture of transitions between budget shares can be presented.

Transitions and Net Flows

Consider the decomposition of the change in the jth budget share,

$$\Delta w_{jt} = \bar{w}_{jt} Dp_{jt} + \bar{w}_{jt} Dq_{jt} - \bar{w}_{jt} Dm_t + O_3$$

or, equivalently,

$$(1.2) \qquad \Delta w_{jt} = \bar{w}_{jt}(Dp_{jt} - DP_t) + \bar{w}_{jt}(Dq_{jt} - DQ_t) + O_3$$

The right-hand side consists of a *price term*, $\bar{w}_{jt}(Dp_{jt} - DP_t)$, a *quantity term*, $\bar{w}_{jt}(Dq_{jt} - DQ_t)$, and a remainder term of order O_3.

In the next two subsections we use (1.1) and (1.2) to define the *transition* from the ith budget share to the jth in $(t-1, t)$, which we shall indicate by $(ij)_t$. We refer to i as the *origin* of this transition and to j as the *destination*. The transition from the jth budget share to the ith is thus $(ji)_t$, and the *net flow* from the ith share to the jth is defined as

$$(1.3) \qquad (iji)_t = (ij)_t - (ji)_t$$

Hence the net flow from i to j is the excess of the transition from i to j over the reverse transition. For this net flow, too, we refer to i as the origin and to j as the destination. The net flow from j to i is minus the net flow from i to j,

$$(jij)_t = (ji)_t - (ij)_t = -(iji)_t$$

which shows that the net flows are the elements of a skew-symmetric matrix of order $n \times n$.

An Axiomatic Approach to Budget Share Transitions

The definition of $(ij)_t$ is based on an axiom which insures that the corresponding net flow depends only on Dp_{it} and Dp_{jt} as far as prices are concerned. This axiom implies that $(ij)_t$ agrees with the decomposition (1.2) of the budget share change, as it obviously should.

Specifically, the axiom states that (1) the transition $(ij)_t$ consists of a price and a quantity term, (2) the price term is a proportion A_i of the price term $\bar{w}_{jt}(Dp_{jt} - DP_t)$ of the budget share change of the destination,

$$(1.4) \qquad A_i \bar{w}_{jt}(Dp_{jt} - DP_t)$$

and, similarly, (3) the quantity term of $(ij)_t$ is a proportion B_i of the quantity term of the same budget share change,

$$B_i \bar{w}_{jt}(Dq_{jt} - DQ_t) \tag{1.5}$$

in such a way that (4) the price and quantity terms of the corresponding net flow, $(iji)_t$, are both independent of the price log-changes of all goods other than the ith and the jth. The word "proportion" is used for the A_i's and the B_i's to indicate that they must add up to 1.

The Solution

It is shown in the next subsection that the solution is

$$A_i = \bar{w}_{it} \qquad B_i = \mu_i \tag{1.6}$$

Hence the proportion used for the price term of Δw_{jt} is the budget share of the origin, and the proportion used for the quantity term is the corresponding marginal share. These shares are, of course, all positive under the preference independence specification stated in the opening paragraph of this chapter.

Substitution of (1.6) in (1.4) and (1.5) yields the following definition of the transition $(ij)_t$:

$$(ij)_t = \bar{w}_{it}\bar{w}_{jt}(Dp_{jt} - DP_t) + \mu_i \bar{w}_{jt}(Dq_{jt} - DQ_t) \tag{1.7}$$

Summation over j gives

$$\sum_{j=1}^{n} (ij)_t = \bar{w}_{it}(DP_t - DP_t) + \mu_i(DQ_t - DQ_t) = 0 \tag{1.8}$$

Hence the sum of all transitions with origin i vanishes identically, for any i. Next sum (1.7) over i:

$$\sum_{i=1}^{n} (ij)_t = \bar{w}_{jt}(Dp_{jt} - DP_t) + \bar{w}_{jt}(Dq_{jt} - DQ_t) \tag{1.9}$$

The right-hand side equals Δw_{jt} in view of (1.2), apart from an O_3 term. Finally, interchange i and j in (1.8), and apply (1.9) and (1.2) also:

$$\sum_{i=1}^{n} [(ij)_t - (ji)_t] = \sum_{i=1}^{n} (iji)_t = \Delta w_{jt} + O_3 \tag{1.10}$$

The second member is the total net flow with destination j, which should obviously be equal to the change in the jth budget share. The equation states that this is true except for an O_3 term. We shall ignore remainder terms of this order in the sequel.

Verification of the Solution

Consider the price term (1.4) and subtract the same expression, but with i and j interchanged, to obtain the price term of $(iji)_t$:

$$A_i\bar{w}_{jt}(Dp_{jt} - DP_t) - A_j\bar{w}_{it}(Dp_{it} - DP_t) \tag{1.11}$$

The axiom requires that (1.11) be independent of all price log-changes except Dp_{it} and Dp_{jt}. This means that the coefficient of DP_t in (1.11) must vanish, $-A_i\bar{w}_{jt} + A_j\bar{w}_{it} = 0$. Hence the A_i's must be proportional to the $\bar{w}_{it}$'s, which implies $A_i = \bar{w}_{it}$ as stated in (1.6) in view of the unit-sum constraint on the A_i's. The price term (1.11) of $(iji)_t$ is thus simplified to

$$\bar{w}_{it}\bar{w}_{jt}(Dp_{jt} - Dp_{it}) \tag{1.12}$$

The quantity term of $(iji)_t$ implied by (1.5) is

$$B_i\bar{w}_{jt}(Dq_{jt} - DQ_t) - B_j\bar{w}_{it}(Dq_{it} - DQ_t)$$

Substitution of the demand equation (1.1) for i and j gives

$$\begin{aligned} &B_i[(\mu_j - \bar{w}_{jt})\,DQ_t + \phi\mu_j(Dp_{jt} - DP_t') + \varepsilon_{jt}] \\ &\qquad - B_j[(\mu_i - \bar{w}_{it})\,DQ_t + \phi\mu_i(Dp_{it} - DP_t') + \varepsilon_{it}] \end{aligned} \tag{1.13}$$

Prices occur only in the substitution terms. The required independence of all price log-changes (except Dp_{it} and Dp_{jt}) implies that DP_t' must have a zero coefficient: $-\phi(B_i\mu_j - B_j\mu_i) = 0$. Hence the B_i's must be proportional to the μ_i's, which gives $B_i = \mu_i$ in view of $\sum_i B_i = 1$.

The Four Components of a Transition

So far the analysis has been formulated in terms of price and quantity terms, but it is at least equally instructive to separate the quantity terms into real-income, substitution and disturbance components. So we substitute (1.1) in (1.7):

(1.14)
$$(ij)_t = \bar{w}_{it}\bar{w}_{jt}(Dp_{jt} - DP_t) + \mu_i(\mu_j - \bar{w}_{jt})\,DQ_t + \phi\mu_i\mu_j(Dp_{jt} - DP_t') + \mu_i\varepsilon_{jt}$$

The transition $(ij)_t$ thus consists of a real-income component, a disturbance component, and two price components. To distinguish between the latter components we shall from now on refer to the price term (1.12), which is the first right-hand term in (1.14), as the *direct price component* of $(ij)_t$, and to the third right-hand term in (1.14) as the *substitution component*. The direct price component measures the effect on $(ij)_t$ of changes in relative prices which is unrelated to changes in quantities. The substitution component is an indirect price component in the sense that it describes the effect of changes in relative prices via the quantities bought.

The Four Components of a Net Flow

Consider again (1.14). By subtracting the same equation, but with i and j interchanged, we obtain

$$(1.15)\qquad (iji)_t = \bar{w}_{it}\bar{w}_{jt}(Dp_{jt} - Dp_{it}) + (\bar{w}_{it}\mu_j - \bar{w}_{jt}\mu_i)\, DQ_t + \phi\mu_i\mu_j(Dp_{jt} - Dp_{it}) + \mu_i\varepsilon_{jt} - \mu_j\varepsilon_{it}$$

which shows that the net flow consists of four components similar to (1.14). Note that this result can also be obtained by substituting μ's for the B's in (1.13) and adding (1.12).

We may interpret (1.15) in the sense that *the consumer behaves as if his allocation decision is based on pairwise comparisons of all goods.* The two price components require knowledge of the relative price change of two goods and the real-income component requires that he knows the change in his real income. That is all the information needed. The consumer then adds these three components (which will be further discussed in the next subsection), after which he proceeds to other pairwise comparisons. At the end he applies (1.10) to obtain the change in the budget share of each good, which completes the allocation decision.

The interpretation of the previous paragraph ignores the disturbance component in (1.15). It will appear in the subsection immediately following the next that this component has a fundamental zero-correlation property, which is strengthened to stochastic independence when the distribution of the disturbances is multivariate normal, as it is under the theory of rational random behavior of Section 2.8. This independence obviously simplifies the pairwise comparisons.

The Real-Income and Price Components of a Net Flow

The real-income component in (1.15) can be written as

$$\bar{w}_{it}\bar{w}_{jt}\left(\frac{\mu_j}{\bar{w}_{jt}} - \frac{\mu_i}{\bar{w}_{it}}\right) DQ_t$$

which shows that the coefficient of DQ_t is positive (negative) if and only if the jth income elasticity is larger (smaller) than the ith. This means that an increase in real income generates a positive net flow to the good with the higher income elasticity, which is intuitively plausible.

The two price components of (1.15) have opposite signs. The direct price component of a net flow is dominated by the substitution component if and only if the product of the income elasticities of the two goods exceeds the absolute value of the income elasticity of the marginal utility of income:

$$\text{(1.16)} \qquad \frac{\mu_i}{\bar{w}_{it}} \frac{\mu_j}{\bar{w}_{jt}} > \frac{1}{|\phi|}$$

Recall that we concluded from eqs. (5.24) and (5.25) of Section 1.5 that the substitution component dominates the change in the budget share if and only if the commodity has an income elasticity exceeding that of the marginal utility of income in absolute value. This is similar to (1.16), but note that there is a subtle difference, because we had to make the simplifying assumption $DP_t' \approx DP_t$ in Section 1.5. Such a restriction is unnecessary in (1.15), where DP_t' and DP_t play no role.

The Disturbance Component of a Net Flow

The disturbance component in (1.15) involves only the disturbances of the two goods involved (i and j), which is similar to the analogous property of the two price components with respect to the price log-changes.

The variances and covariances of the disturbance components of the net flows have a very simple structure under the second-moment model. It is shown in the next subsection that two net flows, from i to j and from h to k, have uncorrelated disturbance components when the four commodities are all different:

$$\text{(1.17)} \qquad \operatorname{cov}(\mu_i\varepsilon_{jt} - \mu_j\varepsilon_{it}, \mu_h\varepsilon_{kt} - \mu_k\varepsilon_{ht}) = 0 \qquad \text{(all subscripts } i, j, h \text{ and } k \text{ different)}$$

Hence two net flows have correlated disturbance components only if the pairs (i, j) and (h, k) have at least one commodity in common. When they have either the origin or the destination in common ($i = h$ or $j = k$), the covariance of the disturbance components is proportional to the product of the three marginal shares involved:

$$\text{(1.18)} \qquad \operatorname{cov}(\mu_i\varepsilon_{jt} - \mu_j\varepsilon_{it}, \mu_i\varepsilon_{kt} - \mu_k\varepsilon_{it}) = \operatorname{cov}(\mu_i\varepsilon_{jt} - \mu_j\varepsilon_{it}, \mu_k\varepsilon_{jt} - \mu_j\varepsilon_{kt}) = \sigma^2\mu_i\mu_j\mu_k \qquad \text{(all subscripts } i, j \text{ and } k \text{ different)}$$

If the origin of one net flow coincides with the destination of the other, we can apply (1.18) after reversing the direction of either flow and multiplying by -1. This follows directly from the skew-symmetric property of the matrix $[\mu_i\varepsilon_{jt}-\mu_j\varepsilon_{it}]$.

When the pairs (i, j) and (h, k) have two commodities in common ($i=h$, $j=k$ or $i=k, j=h$), the covariance becomes a variance or minus a variance. As is shown in the next subsection, the variance of a net-flow disturbance is proportional to the product of the two marginal shares and their sum:

$$\text{var}(\mu_i\varepsilon_{jt}-\mu_j\varepsilon_{it})=\sigma^2\mu_i\mu_j(\mu_i+\mu_j) \qquad i\neq j \tag{1.19}$$

The simplicity of this covariance structure, particularly the zero-correlation property (1.17), adds to the plausibility of the net-flow definition. For large n a vast majority of the covariances vanishes. To show this we note that, although there are n^2 net flows, it is sufficient to confine the attention to $\frac{1}{2}n(n-1)$ such flows for all commodity pairs (i, j) with $i<j$, given the skew symmetry. These pairs are displayed below for $n=5$.

(1, 2)	(1, 3)	(1, 4)	(1, 5)
	(2, 3)	(2, 4)	(2, 5)
		(3, 4)	(3, 5)
			(4, 5)

For each pair (i, j), there are $n-2$ pairs with the same i and $n-2$ pairs with the same j. Hence the covariance matrix of all net flows, which is square of order $\frac{1}{2}n(n-1)$, contains $n(n-1)(n-2)$ elements of the form (1.18), or (1.18) multiplied by -1. Since the total number of elements of the covariance matrix is $\frac{1}{4}n^2(n-1)^2$, this means that only a fraction $4/n$ of these elements is nonzero for large n.

Derivations for the Second-Moment Model

We separate the specific and general substitution components of the disturbances in (1.15) along the lines of eq. (7.24) of Section 2.7:

$$\mu_i(\bar{\varepsilon}_{jt}-\mu_j\bar{E}_t)-\mu_j(\bar{\varepsilon}_{it}-\mu_i\bar{E}_t)=\mu_i\bar{\varepsilon}_{jt}-\mu_j\bar{\varepsilon}_{it}$$

Hence,

$$\mu_i\varepsilon_{jt}-\mu_j\varepsilon_{it}=\mu_i\bar{\varepsilon}_{jt}-\mu_j\bar{\varepsilon}_{it} \tag{1.20}$$

which shows that the disturbance component of each net flow is the same function of the specific substitution components of the two disturbances as it is of these disturbances themselves.

We apply eq. (7.22) of Section 2.7 in preference-independent form,

$$\text{cov}(\bar{\varepsilon}_{it}, \bar{\varepsilon}_{jt}) = \begin{cases} \sigma^2 \mu_i & \text{if} \quad i=j \\ 0 & \text{if} \quad i \neq j \end{cases} \tag{1.21}$$

from which (1.17) and (1.18) follow immediately. The variance in the left-hand side of (1.19) is a multiple σ^2 of

$$\mu_i^2 \mu_j + \mu_j^2 \mu_i = \mu_i \mu_j (\mu_i + \mu_j)$$

which proves (1.19).

The Order of Magnitude of a Net Flow

When we imagine that μ_i and μ_j increase, the variance (1.19) also increases. More specifically, the standard deviation of the disturbance component of the net flow from i to j increases faster than the geometric mean of μ_i and μ_j. Alternatively, consider two commodity pairs, (i, j) and (h, k), and take $\mu_h = 2\mu_i$, $\mu_k = 2\mu_j$; then the standard deviation of the disturbance component of the net flow from h to k is $\sqrt{8}$ or almost three times as large as the standard deviation corresponding to the pair (i, j). This shows that disturbance components of net flows tend to take values which increase faster than the size of the origin and the size of the destination as measured by their marginal shares.

The other components of the net flow have, at least qualitatively, the same property. As (1.15) shows, these three components take the form of DQ_t or $Dp_{jt} - Dp_{it}$ multiplied by an expression which contains the product of budget and/or marginal shares. This indicates that, when the ith and j^{th} commodities increase in importance, their budget and marginal shares both moving upward, the net flows and their four components tend to increase more than proportionally.

The Geometry of Transitions and Net Flows

To provide a geometric interpretation of the transition $(ij)_t$ we return to (1.14), which shows that each of its four components can be written as the product $a_i b_j$ for appropriate specifications of a_i and b_j. For example, in the case of the substitution component we may specify

$$a_i = \mu_i \qquad b_j = \phi \mu_j (Dp_{jt} - DP_t') \tag{1.22}$$

The vectors $\mathbf{a} = [a_i]$ and $\mathbf{b} = [b_j]$ defined by (1.22) are equal to OM and OS, respectively, in Figure 11.5 on page 207. The points M and S, together with their projections M_1, M_2, S_1 and S_2 on the two axes, are shown in Figure

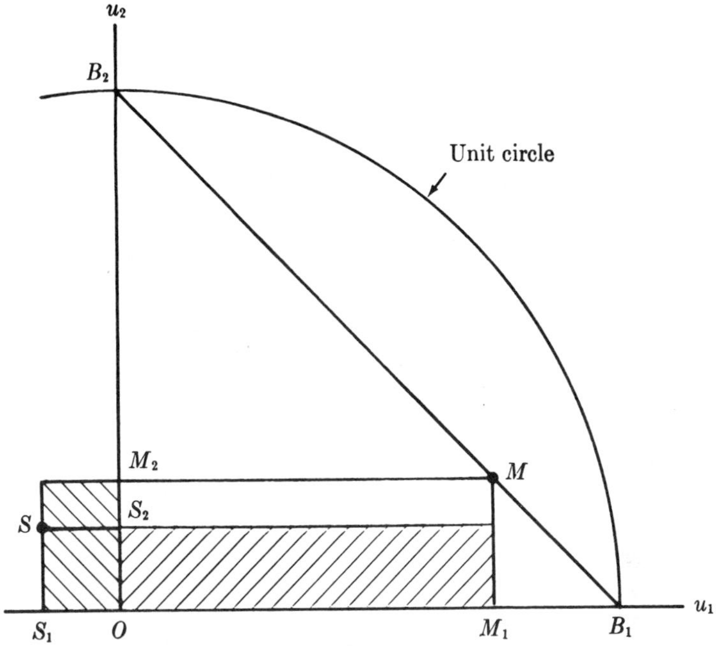

Fig. 16.1 Substitution components of a budget share transition and a net flow

16.1 on an enlarged scale. The coordinates of M_1 and M_2 are the elements of the successive columns of $(\mathbf{a})_\Delta$ and those of S_1 and S_2 are column elements of $(\mathbf{b})_\Delta$, where $(\mathbf{a})_\Delta$ and $(\mathbf{b})_\Delta$ are diagonal matrices whose diagonal elements are defined in (1.22). Each product $a_i b_j$ is represented by the area of a rectangle. For example, $a_1 b_2$ corresponds to the rectangle on OM_1 and OS_2, and $a_2 b_1$ to that on OM_2 and OS_1, both of which are shaded in Figure 16.1. Note that the latter area is to be counted negatively because OS_1 is negative and OM_2 is positive. In the case illustrated here the substitution component of the transition $(12)_t$ is positive and that of $(21)_t$ is negative, so that there is a positive net flow from 1 to 2 as far as price substitution is concerned.

The other three components in (1.14) can be similarly described as (positive or negative) areas of rectangles; the corresponding component of the net flow (1.15) is then obtained from a pair of such areas. For general n we have to extend this to every pair of (u_i, u_j)-axes, but the cases $i = j$ may be left out if we are interested only in the net flows (because the net flow from i to i is trivially zero).

16.2 Budget Share Transitions Between and Within Commodity Groups

Transitions Between Commodity Groups

The transition from the budget share of group S_g to that of group S_h, written $(gh)_{0t}$ with $g, h=1,\ldots, G$, is defined as the sum of the transitions from all commodities of S_g to all commodities of S_h:

(2.1) $$(gh)_{0t} = \sum_{i\in S_g} \sum_{j\in S_h} (ij)_t$$

Using $\sum_j \bar{w}_{jt}Dp_{jt}=\bar{W}_{ht}DP_{ht}$ and $\sum_j \bar{w}_{jt}Dq_{jt}=\bar{W}_{ht}DQ_{ht}$, where the summations are over $j\in S_h$, we obtain the following commodity group version of (1.7):

(2.2) $$(gh)_{0t}=\bar{W}_{gt}\bar{W}_{ht}(DP_{ht}-DP_t)+M_g\bar{W}_{ht}(DQ_{ht}-DQ_t)$$

The first term on the right is the price term of $(gh)_{0t}$ and the second is the quantity term. Summation of (2.2) over h and over g gives

(2.3) $$\sum_{h=1}^{G} (gh)_{0t} = \bar{W}_{gt}(DP_t - DP_t) + M_g(DQ_t - DQ_t) = 0$$

(2.4) $$\sum_{g=1}^{G} (gh)_{0t} = \bar{W}_{ht}(DP_{ht} - DP_t) + \bar{W}_{ht}(DQ_{ht} - DQ_t)$$

These results are the group versions of (1.8) and (1.9), respectively, and the right-hand side of (2.4) is equal to the change in the budget share of S_h, apart from an O_3 term. This may be verified by summing (1.2) over $j\in S_h$.

By substituting the demand equation for S_h in (2.2), we obtain

(2.5) $$(gh)_{0t}=\bar{W}_{gt}\bar{W}_{ht}(DP_{ht}-DP_t)+M_g(M_h-\bar{W}_{ht})\,DQ_t + \phi M_g M_h(DP'_{ht}-DP'_t)+M_gE_{ht}$$

This is the commodity group version of (1.14). It is easily verified that the sum over $i\in S_g$ and $j\in S_h$ of each of the four components of (1.14) is equal to the corresponding component of (2.5).

Net Flows Between Commodity Groups

The net flow from S_g to S_h, written $(ghg)_{0t}$, is defined as the transition from S_g to S_h minus the reverse transition. So, using (2.1) and (1.3), we have

(2.6) $$(ghg)_{0t} = (gh)_{0t} - (hg)_{0t} = \sum_{i\in S_g} \sum_{j\in S_h} (iji)_t$$

Hence the net flow from S_g to S_h is equal to the sum of the net flows from all commodities of S_g to all commodities of S_h. By applying (2.5) we find

$$(2.7)\qquad (ghg)_{0t} = \bar{W}_{gt}\bar{W}_{ht}(DP_{ht} - DP_{gt}) + (\bar{W}_{gt}M_h - \bar{W}_{ht}M_g)\, DQ_t + \phi M_g M_h(DP'_{ht} - DP'_{gt}) + M_g E_{ht} - M_h E_{gt}$$

which is the group version of (1.15). By summing each component of (1.15) over $i \in S_g$ and $j \in S_h$, we obtain the corresponding component of (2.7). The real-income component of (2.7) is similar to that of (1.15) in that a positive DQ_t generates a positive net flow to the commodity group with the higher income elasticity. It is also easily verified that the variances and covariances of the net-flow disturbance components of the groups are similar to (1.17) through (1.19):

$$(2.8)\qquad \operatorname{cov}(M_g E_{ht} - M_h E_{gt},\, M_k E_{lt} - M_l E_{kt}) = 0 \qquad \text{(all subscripts } g, h, k \text{ and } l \text{ different)}$$

$$(2.9)\qquad \operatorname{cov}(M_g E_{ht} - M_h E_{gt},\, M_g E_{kt} - M_k E_{gt}) = \operatorname{cov}(M_g E_{ht} - M_h E_{gt},\, M_k E_{ht} - M_h E_{kt}) = \sigma^2 M_g M_h M_k \qquad \text{(all subscripts } g, h \text{ and } k \text{ different)}$$

$$(2.10)\qquad \operatorname{var}(M_g E_{ht} - M_h E_{gt}) = \sigma^2 M_g M_h (M_g + M_h) \qquad g \neq h$$

The only major difference between (2.7) and (1.15) is the way in which prices occur in the price components. In (1.15) we have price log-changes of individual commodities, but in (2.7) different price indexes are used in the direct price component and the substitution component. If the differences $DP'_{gt} - DP_{gt}$ and $DP'_{ht} - DP_{ht}$ can be ignored, the direct price component of (2.7) is dominated by the substitution component if and only if

$$(2.11)\qquad \frac{M_g}{\bar{W}_{gt}} \frac{M_h}{\bar{W}_{ht}} > \frac{1}{|\phi|}$$

This is similar to (1.16), but note the proviso on group indexes that must be made here.

Conditional Transitions Within a Commodity Group

Next we extend the transition (1.7) to a conditional transition within the group S_g for two goods (i and j) which belong to S_g. This transition, written $(ij)_{gt}$, is defined as

$$(2.12)\qquad (ij)_{gt} = \frac{\bar{w}_{it}}{\bar{W}_{gt}} \frac{\bar{w}_{jt}}{\bar{W}_{gt}} (Dp_{jt} - DP_{gt}) + \frac{\mu_i}{M_g} \frac{\bar{w}_{jt}}{\bar{W}_{gt}} (Dq_{jt} - DQ_{gt})$$

which is obtained from (1.7) by replacing DP_t and DQ_t by DP_{gt} and DQ_{gt}, respectively, and the budget and marginal shares by their conditional versions.

It may be verified that the sum of (2.12) over $j \in S_g$ vanishes, which is similar to (1.8) and (2.3). The sum of (2.12) over $i \in S_g$ is

$$\frac{\bar{w}_{jt}}{\bar{W}_{gt}}(Dp_{jt} - DP_{gt}) + \frac{\bar{w}_{jt}}{\bar{W}_{gt}}(Dq_{jt} - DQ_{gt})$$

On comparing this with eq. (3.4) of Section 7.3, we conclude that

$$\sum_{i \in S_g} (ij)_{gt} = \Delta\left(\frac{w_{jt}}{W_{gt}}\right) + O_3 \tag{2.13}$$

which is the within-group version of (1.9) combined with (1.2).

Under preference independence we can write the conditional demand equation (1.6) of Section 7.1 so that it contains only one relative price. The jth equation ($j \in S_g$) then becomes

$$\bar{w}_{jt}Dq_{jt} = \frac{\mu_j}{M_g}\bar{W}_{gt}DQ_{gt} + \phi\mu_j(Dp_{jt} - DP'_{gt}) + \varepsilon^g_{jt} \tag{2.14}$$

which we substitute in (2.12):

$$(ij)_{gt} = \frac{\bar{w}_{it}}{\bar{W}_{gt}}\frac{\bar{w}_{jt}}{\bar{W}_{gt}}(Dp_{jt} - DP_{gt}) + \frac{\mu_i}{M_g}\left(\frac{\mu_j}{M_g} - \frac{\bar{w}_{jt}}{\bar{W}_{gt}}\right)DQ_{gt} + \frac{\phi M_g}{\bar{W}_{gt}}\frac{\mu_i}{M_g}\frac{\mu_j}{M_g}(Dp_{jt} - DP'_{gt}) + \frac{\mu_i}{M_g}\frac{\varepsilon^g_{jt}}{\bar{W}_{gt}} \tag{2.15}$$

This result should be compared with (1.14). The successive terms on the right in (2.15) are the direct price component, the volume component (rather than the real-income component) and the substitution and disturbance components. Note that all shares of the two commodities have become conditional shares and that ϕ of (1.14) is replaced by $\phi M_g/\bar{W}_{gt}$, the own-price elasticity of the demand for the group.

Conditional Net Flows Within a Commodity Group

The conditional net flow from i to j is defined as

$$(iji)_{gt} = (ij)_{gt} - (ji)_{gt} \qquad i, j \in S_g \tag{2.16}$$

The equation for this flow is obtained by subtracting the reverse transition from (2.15). Since eq. (1.7) of Section 7.1 implies

$$\text{(2.17)}\qquad \mu_i\varepsilon_{jt}^g - \mu_j\varepsilon_{it}^g = \mu_i\left(\varepsilon_{jt} - \frac{\mu_j}{M_g}E_{gt}\right) - \mu_j\left(\varepsilon_{it} - \frac{\mu_i}{M_g}E_{gt}\right)$$
$$= \mu_i\varepsilon_{jt} - \mu_j\varepsilon_{it}$$

we can write the result as

$$\text{(2.18)}\qquad (iji)_{gt} = \frac{\bar{w}_{it}}{\bar{W}_{gt}}\frac{\bar{w}_{jt}}{\bar{W}_{gt}}(Dp_{jt} - Dp_{it}) + \left(\frac{\bar{w}_{it}}{\bar{W}_{gt}}\frac{\mu_j}{M_g} - \frac{\bar{w}_{jt}}{\bar{W}_{gt}}\frac{\mu_i}{M_g}\right)DQ_{gt}$$
$$+ \frac{\phi M_g}{\bar{W}_{gt}}\frac{\mu_i}{M_g}\frac{\mu_j}{M_g}(Dp_{jt} - Dp_{it}) + \frac{\mu_i\varepsilon_{jt} - \mu_j\varepsilon_{it}}{M_g\bar{W}_{gt}}$$

The volume component shows that an increase in the demand for S_g generates a positive conditional net flow to the commodity with the higher income elasticity. The sign of the direct price component is always opposite that of the substitution component, as it is in (1.15). The present substitution component dominates the direct price component if and only if the product of the two conditional income elasticities exceeds the reciprocal of the absolute value of the own-price elasticity of the group:

$$\text{(2.19)}\qquad \frac{\mu_i/\bar{w}_{it}}{M_g/\bar{W}_{gt}}\,\frac{\mu_j/\bar{w}_{jt}}{M_g/\bar{W}_{gt}} > \frac{1}{|\phi M_g/\bar{W}_{gt}|}$$

Note that, as in the analogous case (1.15) and (1.16) [but unlike (2.7) and (2.11)], no assumptions on price indexes are needed.

Recall from eqs. (1.17) and (1.18) of Section 7.1 that the disturbances of the conditional model (2.14) are uncorrelated across commodity groups and are also uncorrelated with the disturbances $E_{1t}, \ldots, E_{Gt}$ of the groups. Applying (2.17) for the disturbance component of (2.18), we conclude that this component and that of (2.7) have the same zero-correlation properties. Within the group S_g, the disturbance component of (2.18) satisfies the covariance results (1.17) to (1.19), except that (obviously) the right-hand sides of the latter equations are to be divided by $(M_g\bar{W}_{gt})^2$.

16.3 Comparison of Conditional and Unconditional Net Flows

A more detailed comparison of the conditional net flow (2.18) and its unconditional counterpart (1.15) is in order. It will appear that the equivalent income and volume changes described in Chapter 15 play an interesting role in this comparison.

Equivalent Income Changes of the Origin and the Destination

We subtract eq. (1.4) of Section 15.1 from the same equation with i replaced by j, which yields the difference between the jth and i^{th} equivalent income changes, and then multiply by $\mu_i\mu_j$:

$$(3.1) \qquad \mu_i\mu_j\left(\frac{\bar{w}_{jt}Dq_{jt}}{\mu_j} - \frac{\bar{w}_{it}Dq_{it}}{\mu_i}\right) = \phi\mu_i\mu_j(Dp_{jt} - Dp_{it}) + \mu_i\varepsilon_{jt} - \mu_j\varepsilon_{it}$$

A similar procedure applied to eq. (1.11) of Section 15.1 gives

$$(3.2) \qquad M_gM_h\left(\frac{\bar{W}_{ht}DQ_{ht}}{M_h} - \frac{\bar{W}_{gt}DQ_{gt}}{M_g}\right) = \phi M_gM_h(DP'_{ht} - DP'_{gt}) + M_gE_{ht} - M_hE_{gt}$$

On comparing (3.1) and (3.2) with (1.15) and (2.7), respectively, we conclude that, both for individual goods and for groups of goods, the sum of the substitution and disturbance components of a net flow is equal to the difference between the equivalent income changes of the destination and the origin, multiplied by the product of their marginal shares.

In the same way we have from eq. (1.19) of Section 15.1:

$$(3.3) \qquad \frac{\mu_i}{M_g}\frac{\mu_j}{M_g}\left(\frac{M_g}{\bar{W}_{gt}}\frac{\bar{w}_{jt}Dq_{jt}}{\mu_j} - \frac{M_g}{\bar{W}_{gt}}\frac{\bar{w}_{it}Dq_{it}}{\mu_i}\right)$$
$$= \frac{\phi M_g}{\bar{W}_{gt}}\frac{\mu_i}{M_g}\frac{\mu_j}{M_g}(Dp_{jt} - Dp_{it}) + \frac{\mu_i}{M_g}\frac{\varepsilon^g_{jt}}{\bar{W}_{gt}} - \frac{\mu_j}{M_g}\frac{\varepsilon^g_{it}}{\bar{W}_{gt}}$$

The left-hand side is the difference between the jth and i^{th} equivalent volume changes within their group (S_g), multiplied by the product of their conditional marginal shares. The expression on the right is, in view of (2.17) and (2.18), the sum of the substitution and disturbance components of the conditional net flow from i to j.

First Comparison of Conditional and Unconditional Net Flows

To compare the flows (2.18) and (1.15) it is important to recognize that the former is the net flow from the ith conditional budget share to the jth (from w_i/W_g to w_j/W_g), whereas the latter is the net flow from w_i to w_j. This suggests that it is appropriate to divide (1.15) by the square of $\bar{W}_{gt}$. Using (3.1) for the substitution and disturbance components, we can write the result as

$$(3.4)\qquad \frac{(iji)_t}{\bar{W}_{gt}^2} = \frac{\bar{w}_{it}}{\bar{W}_{gt}}\frac{\bar{w}_{jt}}{\bar{W}_{gt}}(Dp_{jt} - Dp_{it}) + \frac{\bar{w}_{it}}{\bar{W}_{gt}}\frac{\bar{w}_{jt}}{\bar{W}_{gt}}\left(\frac{\mu_j}{\bar{w}_{jt}} - \frac{\mu_i}{\bar{w}_{it}}\right) DQ_t + \frac{M_g}{\bar{W}_{gt}}\frac{\mu_i}{M_g}\frac{\mu_j}{M_g}\left(\frac{M_g}{\bar{W}_{gt}}\frac{\bar{w}_{jt}Dq_{jt}}{\mu_j} - \frac{M_g}{\bar{W}_{gt}}\frac{\bar{w}_{it}Dq_{it}}{\mu_i}\right)$$

In the same way, using (3.3), we write (2.18) as

$$(3.5)\qquad (iji)_{gt} = \frac{\bar{w}_{it}}{\bar{W}_{gt}}\frac{\bar{w}_{jt}}{\bar{W}_{gt}}(Dp_{jt} - Dp_{it}) + \frac{\bar{w}_{it}}{\bar{W}_{gt}}\frac{\bar{w}_{jt}}{\bar{W}_{gt}}\left(\frac{\mu_j}{\bar{w}_{jt}} - \frac{\mu_i}{\bar{w}_{it}}\right)\frac{\bar{W}_{gt}DQ_{gt}}{M_g} + \frac{\mu_i}{M_g}\frac{\mu_j}{M_g}\left(\frac{M_g}{\bar{W}_{gt}}\frac{\bar{w}_{jt}Dq_{jt}}{\mu_j} - \frac{M_g}{\bar{W}_{gt}}\frac{\bar{w}_{it}Dq_{it}}{\mu_i}\right)$$

Note that the direct price components in (3.4) and (3.5) are identical. By subtracting we find

$$(3.6)\qquad (iji)_{gt} - \frac{(iji)_t}{\bar{W}_{gt}^2} = \frac{\bar{w}_{it}}{\bar{W}_{gt}}\frac{\bar{w}_{jt}}{\bar{W}_{gt}} A_{ijt} - \frac{\mu_i}{M_g}\frac{\mu_j}{M_g} B_{ijt}$$

where

$$(3.7)\qquad A_{ijt} = \left(\frac{\mu_j}{\bar{w}_{jt}} - \frac{\mu_i}{\bar{w}_{it}}\right)\left(\frac{\bar{W}_{gt}DQ_{gt}}{M_g} - DQ_t\right)$$

$$(3.8)\qquad B_{ijt} = \left(\frac{M_g}{\bar{W}_{gt}} - 1\right)\left(\frac{M_g}{\bar{W}_{gt}}\frac{\bar{w}_{jt}Dq_{jt}}{\mu_j} - \frac{M_g}{\bar{W}_{gt}}\frac{\bar{w}_{it}Dq_{it}}{\mu_i}\right)$$

Since DQ_t may be viewed as the equivalent income change of the basket, A_{ijt} can be described as the difference between the equivalent income changes of the group and the basket, multiplied by the difference between the income elasticities of the destination and the origin. Similarly, B_{ijt} equals the difference between the equivalent volume changes of the destination and the origin, multiplied by the difference between the income elasticities of the group and the basket.

Second Comparison

In (3.6) we made $(iji)_t$ and $(iji)_{gt}$ comparable by dividing the former by the square of $\bar{W}_{gt}$. Alternatively, multiply the latter by $M_g\bar{W}_{gt}$, so that (2.18) yields

$$(3.9)\qquad M_g\bar{W}_{gt}(iji)_{gt} = \frac{M_g}{\bar{W}_{gt}}\bar{w}_{it}\bar{w}_{jt}(Dp_{jt} - Dp_{it}) + (\bar{w}_{it}\mu_j - \bar{w}_{jt}\mu_i)\,DQ_{gt} + \phi\mu_i\mu_j(Dp_{jt} - Dp_{it}) + \mu_i\varepsilon_{jt} - \mu_j\varepsilon_{it}$$

Note that the substitution and disturbance components are now identical to those of (1.15) but that the direct price components differ. By subtracting (1.15) from (3.9) we obtain

(3.10) $$M_g \bar{W}_{gt}(iji)_{gt} - (iji)_t = \bar{w}_{it}\bar{w}_{jt}(C_{ijt} + D_{ijt})$$

where C_{ijt} is a price term and D_{ijt} a volume term:

(3.11) $$C_{ijt} = \left(\frac{M_g}{\bar{W}_{gt}} - 1\right)(Dp_{jt} - Dp_{it})$$

(3.12) $$D_{ijt} = \left(\frac{\mu_j}{\bar{w}_{jt}} - \frac{\mu_i}{\bar{w}_{it}}\right)(DQ_{gt} - DQ_t)$$

Note that both terms involve differences between income elasticities similar to those which occur in (3.7) and (3.8).

16.4 The Commodity Interpretation of the Transitions

In this section we assume that there is no preference independence, so that the preference independence transformation has to be used. Our objective is to express the net flow (1.15) and its components in terms of the commodities prior to the transformation.

The Direct Price Component of a Net Flow

The direct price component in (1.15) is the $(i, j)^{\text{th}}$ element of the $n \times n$ matrix

(4.1) $$[\bar{w}_{it}\bar{w}_{jt}(Dp_{jt} - Dp_{it})]_T = [\bar{w}_{it}\bar{w}_{jt}Dp_{jt}]_T - [\bar{w}_{it}\bar{w}_{jt}Dp_{it}]_T$$

where the subscript T is added to indicate that all symbols refer to T-goods. Since $(Dp_{jt})_T$ is the jth element of the vector $\mathbf{S}\boldsymbol{\pi}_t$, we can write the first matrix in the right-hand side of (4.1) as

$$\begin{aligned}\mathbf{w}_T[(\mathbf{w}_T)_\Delta \mathbf{S}\boldsymbol{\pi}_t]' &= (\mathbf{X}^{-1}\boldsymbol{\iota})_\Delta^2 \boldsymbol{\iota}[(\mathbf{X}^{-1}\boldsymbol{\iota})_\Delta^2 (\mathbf{X}^{-1}\boldsymbol{\iota})_\Delta^{-1} \mathbf{X}^{-1}\boldsymbol{\pi}_t]' \\ &= (\mathbf{X}^{-1}\boldsymbol{\iota})_\Delta \mathbf{X}^{-1}\boldsymbol{\iota}[(\mathbf{X}^{-1}\boldsymbol{\iota})_\Delta \mathbf{X}^{-1}\boldsymbol{\pi}_t]'\end{aligned}$$

where the first equal sign is based on eqs. (2.22) and (2.24) of Section 12.2. Applying eq. (2.20) of that section also, we obtain

(4.2) $$[\bar{w}_{it}\bar{w}_{jt}Dp_{jt}]_T = \mathbf{T}\boldsymbol{\iota}(\mathbf{T}\boldsymbol{\pi}_t)'$$

Since the second matrix in the right-hand side of (4.1) is the transpose of the first, we thus have

(4.3) $$[\bar{w}_{it}\bar{w}_{jt}(Dp_{jt} - Dp_{it})]_T = \mathbf{T}(\boldsymbol{\iota}\boldsymbol{\pi}_t' - \boldsymbol{\pi}_t\boldsymbol{\iota}')\mathbf{T}'$$

which expresses the matrix of the direct price components of the net flows as a simple function of the composition matrix and the price log-changes of the commodities.

The Real-Income Component of a Net Flow

The real-income component in (1.15) is the $(i, j)^{\text{th}}$ element of

$$DQ_t[\bar{w}_{it}\mu_j]_T - DQ_t[\bar{w}_{jt}\mu_i]_T \tag{4.4}$$

Using eqs. (2.24) and (2.30) of Section 12.2, we write the first matrix in (4.4) as a multiple DQ_t of

$$\begin{aligned}\mathbf{w}_T\boldsymbol{\mu}_T' &= (\mathbf{X}^{-1}\boldsymbol{\iota})_\Delta^2\,\boldsymbol{\iota}\,[(\mathbf{X}^{-1}\boldsymbol{\iota})_\Delta\,\boldsymbol{\Lambda}\mathbf{X}^{-1}\boldsymbol{\iota}]' \\ &= (\mathbf{X}^{-1}\boldsymbol{\iota})_\Delta\,\mathbf{X}^{-1}\boldsymbol{\iota}\,[(\mathbf{X}^{-1}\boldsymbol{\iota})_\Delta\,\mathbf{X}^{-1}(\mathbf{X}\mathbf{X}')\,(\mathbf{X}')^{-1}\boldsymbol{\Lambda}\mathbf{X}^{-1}\boldsymbol{\iota}]' \\ &= \mathbf{T}\boldsymbol{\iota}\,[\mathbf{T}(\mathbf{w})_\Delta^{-1}\,\mathbf{M}\boldsymbol{\iota}]'\end{aligned}$$

where the last step is based on eqs. (2.20) of Section 12.2 and (1.21) and (1.23) of Section 12.1. Next we use $\mathbf{M}\boldsymbol{\iota}=\boldsymbol{\mu}$ to conclude that the first matrix in (4.4) equals

$$DQ_t[\bar{w}_{it}\mu_j]_T = (DQ_t)\,\mathbf{T}\boldsymbol{\iota}\,[\mathbf{T}(\mathbf{w})_\Delta^{-1}\,\boldsymbol{\mu}]' \tag{4.5}$$

which differs from the corresponding matrix (4.2) for the direct price component in that the price log-change vector $\boldsymbol{\pi}_t$ is replaced by the income elasticity vector of the commodities multiplied by DQ_t. The real-income component (4.4) of the net flows is then obtained from (4.5) by subtracting its transpose.

The Substitution and Disturbance Components

The substitution component in (1.15) is the $(i, j)^{\text{th}}$ element of

$$\phi\,[\mu_i\mu_j Dp_{jt}]_T - \phi\,[\mu_i\mu_j Dp_{it}]_T \tag{4.6}$$

The first matrix is a multiple ϕ of

$$\begin{aligned}&(\mathbf{X}^{-1}\boldsymbol{\iota})_\Delta\,\boldsymbol{\Lambda}\mathbf{X}^{-1}\boldsymbol{\iota}\,[(\mathbf{X}^{-1}\boldsymbol{\iota})_\Delta\,\boldsymbol{\Lambda}(\mathbf{X}^{-1}\boldsymbol{\iota})_\Delta\,\mathbf{S}\boldsymbol{\pi}_t]' \\ &\qquad = \boldsymbol{\Lambda}(\mathbf{X}^{-1}\boldsymbol{\iota})_\Delta\,\mathbf{X}^{-1}\boldsymbol{\iota}\,[\boldsymbol{\Lambda}(\mathbf{X}^{-1}\boldsymbol{\iota})_\Delta\,\mathbf{X}^{-1}\boldsymbol{\pi}_t]' = \boldsymbol{\Lambda}\mathbf{T}\boldsymbol{\iota}(\boldsymbol{\Lambda}\mathbf{T}\boldsymbol{\pi}_t)'\end{aligned}$$

where the first equal sign is based on the commutative multiplication property of diagonal matrices. Hence,

$$\phi\,[\mu_i\mu_j Dp_{jt}]_T = \boldsymbol{\Lambda}\mathbf{T}\boldsymbol{\iota}\,[\boldsymbol{\Lambda}\mathbf{T}(\phi\boldsymbol{\pi}_t)]' \tag{4.7}$$

which differs from (4.2) in that the composition matrix is premultiplied by the diagonal matrix of the income elasticities of the T-goods and the price log-change vector $\boldsymbol{\pi}_t$ is multiplied by the income flexibility.

Finally, the disturbance component in (1.15) is an element of the matrix $[\mu_i \varepsilon_{jt}]_T - [\mu_j \varepsilon_{it}]_T$, where

$$[\mu_i \varepsilon_{jt}]_T = (\mathbf{X}^{-1}\boldsymbol{\iota})_\Delta \, \boldsymbol{\Lambda}\mathbf{X}^{-1}\boldsymbol{\iota}(\mathbf{R}\boldsymbol{\varepsilon}_t)' = \boldsymbol{\Lambda}\mathbf{T}\boldsymbol{\iota}\left[\mathbf{T}(\mathbf{w})_\Delta^{-1}\,\boldsymbol{\varepsilon}_t\right]' \tag{4.8}$$

The last step is based on eq. (2.11) of Section 12.2. Note that the vector $\boldsymbol{\Lambda}\mathbf{T}\boldsymbol{\iota}$ in the third member also occurs in (4.7), and that the row vector by which $\boldsymbol{\Lambda}\mathbf{T}\boldsymbol{\iota}$ is postmultiplied in (4.8) has a form similar to the row in (4.5).

16.5 Transition Analysis of Meats

For the meats we use the conditional net flow and its components shown in (2.18). Applying (2.17) and the disturbance notation of eqs. (3.8) and (3.9) of Section 7.3, we can write this conditional net flow as

$$(iji)_{gt} = \frac{\bar{w}_{it}}{\bar{W}_{gt}}\frac{\bar{w}_{jt}}{\bar{W}_{gt}}(Dp_{jt} - Dp_{it}) + \left(\frac{\bar{w}_{it}}{\bar{W}_{gt}}\frac{\mu_j}{M_g} - \frac{\bar{w}_{jt}}{\bar{W}_{gt}}\frac{\mu_i}{M_g}\right) DQ_{gt} + \frac{\phi M_g}{\bar{W}_{gt}}\frac{\mu_i}{M_g}\frac{\mu_j}{M_g}(Dp_{jt} - Dp_{it}) + \frac{\mu_i}{M_g}\varepsilon_{jt}^* - \frac{\mu_j}{M_g}\varepsilon_{it}^* \tag{5.1}$$

This is the conditional version of (1.15) with DQ_t replaced by DQ_{gt}, ϕ by $\phi M_g / \bar{W}_{gt}$, and budget and marginal shares by their within-group counterparts. So, subject to these modifications, we can apply the commodity interpretation of Section 16.4 directly. In the analysis which follows this is done for the four meats (with Lamb included), similarly to eqs. (2.3) to (2.5) of Section 15.2.

The Conditional Net Flows of 1950-51

The conditional net flows of the first observation are shown in 4×4 matrix form below, with a fifth row added which contains the changes in the conditional budget shares.

$$\begin{array}{c} \left[\begin{array}{rrrr} 0 & -.0135 & -.0001 & -.0025 \\ .0135 & 0 & .0008 & -.0005 \\ .0001 & -.0008 & 0 & -.0002 \\ .0025 & .0005 & .0002 & 0 \end{array}\right] \begin{array}{l} (T_1) \\ (T_2) \\ (T_3) \\ (\text{Lamb}) \end{array} \\ \begin{array}{rrrr} .0161 & -.0138 & .0009 & -.0032 \\ (T_1) & (T_2) & (T_3) & (\text{Lamb}) \end{array} \end{array} \tag{5.2}$$

The first column of this conditional net flow matrix shows that there are positive net flows to Inexpensive meat (T_1) from each of the three other meats in 1950–51, leading to an increase in the conditional budget share of Inexpensive meat of about 1.6 percent. By far the largest net flow is that between T_1 and T_2 (Beef/Pork contrast). As we shall shortly see, this is the usual pattern; it is in agreement with the discussion of the order of magnitude of a net flow in Section 16.1, because T_1 and T_2 are the dominant transformed meats during most of the period.

The changes in the conditional budget shares of the transformed meats can be computed either by premultiplying the corresponding untransformed vector by the transformation matrix **R**, or by adding the elements of the conditional net flow matrix of each column. These two procedures lead to the same result except for a remainder term O_3. In the applications discussed in this section, such remainder terms play no role in the decimal places shown.

The Flow Components of 1950-51

The conditional net flow matrix (5.2) is obtained by computing its four components and taking their sum. One of these is the volume component, which takes the following value:

$$\text{(5.3)} \qquad \begin{bmatrix} 0 & -.0067 & -.0005 & -.0006 \\ .0067 & 0 & .0003 & .0001 \\ .0005 & -.0003 & 0 & -.0000 \\ .0006 & -.0001 & .0000 & 0 \end{bmatrix} \begin{matrix} (T_1) \\ (T_2) \\ (T_3) \\ \text{(Lamb)} \end{matrix}$$

The first column shows that, as far as the change in the volume of total-meat consumption is concerned, there is a positive net flow to Inexpensive meat from each of the three other meats. This results from the decline in total-meat consumption ($DQ_{gt}<0$) in 1950–51 combined with the fact that Inexpensive meat has a smaller conditional income elasticity than the other meats.

The substitution component of (5.2) is

$$\text{(5.4)} \qquad \begin{bmatrix} 0 & -.0146 & -.0011 & -.0004 \\ .0146 & 0 & .0007 & .0010 \\ .0011 & -.0007 & 0 & .0001 \\ .0004 & -.0010 & -.0001 & 0 \end{bmatrix} \begin{matrix} (T_1) \\ (T_2) \\ (T_3) \\ \text{(Lamb)} \end{matrix}$$

and the direct price component is

$$\text{(5.5)} \qquad \begin{bmatrix} 0 & .0166 & .0023 & .0006 \\ -.0166 & 0 & -.0005 & -.0005 \\ -.0023 & .0005 & 0 & -.0001 \\ -.0006 & .0005 & .0001 & 0 \end{bmatrix} \begin{matrix} (T_1) \\ (T_2) \\ (T_3) \\ \text{(Lamb)} \end{matrix}$$

TABLE 16.1

CONDITIONAL NET FLOWS AND THEIR COMPONENTS AMONG MEATS, 1950–1972

	1950–51			1951–52			1952–53			1953–54			1954–55			1955–56		
									Volume components									
T_2	67			−110			−88			9			−64			−52		
T_3	5	−3		−9	6		−9	5		1	−1		−7	3		−8	3	
Lamb	6	−1	0	−9	2	−0	−7	2	−0	1	−0	0	−6	1	−0	−5	1	−0
									Substitution components									
T_2	146			2			−452			0			166			62		
T_3	11	−7		−8	−8		16	79		36	28		−51	−59		38	15	
Lamb	4	−10	−1	−1	−1	1	−20	22	−4	4	3	−3	7	−9	5	10	2	−1
									Direct price components									
T_2	−166			−2			518			−0			−191			−71		
T_3	−23	5		18	5		−33	−57		−71	−20		95	43		−69	−11	
Lamb	−6	5	1	2	1	−1	33	−13	4	−6	−2	3	−11	5	−5	−15	−1	1
									Disturbance components									
T_2	88			−60			−7			−98			−35			15		
T_3	8	−3		9	15		−4	−2		−7	8		−7	0		33	20	
Lamb	21	11	2	−18	−10	−3	−8	−6	−1	−4	5	0	3	5	1	11	6	−1
									Conditional net flows									
T_2	135			−170			−28			−88			−124			−46		
T_3	1	−8		10	19		−29	25		−41	15		30	−13		−6	27	
Lamb	25	5	2	−26	−9	−3	−2	5	−1	−6	6	0	−6	3	1	1	8	−1
									Changes in conditional budget shares									
T_1, T_2, T_3	161	−138	9	−186	181	−32	−60	59	3	−135	110	26	−100	114	−16	−52	82	−22
Lamb			−32			38			−2			−1			2			−8

TABLE 16.1 *(continued)*

	1956–57			1957–58			1958–59			1959–60			1960–61			1961–62		
								Volume components										
T_2	55			29			−67			−3			−6			−13		
T_3	9	−4		5	−2		−12	4		−1	0		−1	0		−3	1	
Lamb	6	−1	0	3	−0	0	−7	1	−0	−0	0	−0	−1	0	−0	−2	0	−0
								Substitution components										
T_2	−61			122			206			−26			−62			39		
T_3	56	47		42	5		11	−27		−10	−1		52	35		−13	−12	
Lamb	−3	3	−5	3	−8	−3	4	−13	−0	−1	1	1	−7	1	−5	4	−1	2
								Direct price components										
T_2	70			−141			−236			29			69			−43		
T_3	−99	−34		−74	−4		−18	20		17	1		−81	−24		20	8	
Lamb	5	−2	5	−5	4	2	−6	8	0	1	−1	−1	10	−1	4	−7	0	−1
								Disturbance components										
T_2	−56			−34			2			−92			−7			−3		
T_3	−8	5		24	21		−18	−11		−5	12		−10	−4		9	4	
Lamb	−0	4	1	−0	2	−2	−4	−3	1	−6	4	−1	−5	−2	−0	−2	−1	−1
								Conditional net flows										
T_2	8			−24			−95			−91			−5			−21		
T_3	−42	14		−3	20		−38	−15		1	12		−40	7		12	1	
Lamb	7	5	0	1	−1	−2	−13	−7	0	−5	4	−0	−2	−1	−1	−6	−1	−1
								Changes in conditional budget shares										
T_1, T_2, T_3	−27	11	29	−26	44	−19	−146	73	53	−95	107	−13	−48	11	33	−15	22	−15
Lamb			−12			2			20			2			4			8

TABLE 16.1 *(continued)*

	1962–63			1963–64			1964–65			1965–66			1966–67			1967–68		
									Volume components									
T_2	−41			−25			29			−31			−45			−23		
T_3	−11	2		−8	1		11	−2		−12	3		−17	3		−9	2	
Lamb	−5	1	−0	−4	0	−0	5	−0	0	−5	0	−0	−8	0	−1	−4	−0	−0
									Substitution components									
T_2	−6			−16			−127			−100			122			49		
T_3	−9	−3		1	3		35	41		9	29		17	−22		−8	−14	
Lamb	10	5	2	1	2	0	−3	8	−3	0	8	−1	13	−3	2	6	−1	2
									Direct price components									
T_2	6			18			143			114			−139			−55		
T_3	13	2		−1	−2		−52	−29		−14	−21		−27	16		13	10	
Lamb	−14	−3	−2	−2	−1	−0	4	−4	2	−0	−4	0	−15	2	−1	−7	1	−1
									Disturbance components									
T_2	11			−32			4			80			10			−29		
T_3	8	1		−5	4		32	11		42	−2		−14	−9		1	7	
Lamb	12	5	2	30	14	6	11	4	0	−0	−6	−3	9	3	3	7	5	2
									Conditional net flows									
T_2	−29			−55			49			64			−53			−58		
T_3	1	3		−13	6		25	21		24	8		−41	−11		−5	4	
Lamb	3	7	2	26	15	6	16	7	−0	−5	−2	−4	−1	1	3	2	4	2
									Changes in conditional budget shares									
T_1, T_2, T_3	−25	38	−2	−42	76	13	90	−20	−47	82	−58	−36	−95	43	55	−61	67	2
Lamb			−11			−47			−23			12			−4			−8

TABLE 16.1 *(concluded)*

	1968–69			1969–70			1970–71			1971–72			1950–72		
	Volume components														
T_2	−2			−20			−18			3			−416		
T_3	−1	0		−11	1		−10	1		2	−0		−97	26	
Lamb	−1	−0	−0	−5	−0	−0	−5	−0	−0	1	0	0	−52	5	−3
	Substitution components														
T_2	13			−19			170			−80			149		
T_3	27	6		41	17		−1	−39		58	31		347	144	
Lamb	−1	−1	−2	4	3	−2	11	−8	3	−6	4	−5	39	5	−17
	Direct price components														
T_2	−15			22			−189			87			−171		
T_3	−40	−4		−60	−12		2	28		−80	−21		−565	−104	
Lamb	1	1	1	−4	−1	1	−10	4	−2	5	−2	3	−45	−4	14
	Disturbance components														
T_2	−31			45			−46			−29			−305		
T_3	8	11		−2	−12		−2	10		−43	−3		46	84	
Lamb	15	7	3	13	1	3	5	5	1	−7	0	1	84	55	14
	Conditional net flows														
T_2	−35			27			−83			−18			−742		
T_3	−7	12		−32	−5		−11	−0		−63	6		−268	150	
Lamb	14	6	2	9	2	2	1	−0	2	−6	2	−1	26	62	8
	Changes in conditional budget shares														
T_1, T_2, T_3	−28	54	−3	3	−30	40	−93	82	14	−87	27	56	−985	954	127
Lamb			−23			−13			−3			5			−95

Note that the corresponding elements of the matrices (5.4) and (5.5) have opposite signs; this is always the case. The positive elements in the first column of (5.4) result from the price decline of Inexpensive meat relative to the other meats in 1950–51 (see Table 13.9 on page 324 and Table 7.3 on page 12 for the price of Lamb). The corresponding negative elements in the first column of (5.5) are all larger in absolute value. This results from the small income elasticity of Inexpensive meat, which implies that $<$ rather than $>$ holds in (2.19) for i = Inexpensive meat and j = any other meat.

The disturbance component of (5.2) is

$$\begin{bmatrix} 0 & -.0088 & -.0008 & -.0021 \\ .0088 & 0 & .0003 & -.0011 \\ .0008 & -.0003 & 0 & -.0002 \\ .0021 & .0011 & .0002 & 0 \end{bmatrix} \begin{matrix} (T_1) \\ (T_2) \\ (T_3) \\ (\text{Lamb}) \end{matrix} \tag{5.6}$$

By far the largest disturbance component is that of T_1 and T_2. This agrees with the variance expression (1.19) combined with the fact that T_1 and T_2 have the largest conditional marginal shares.[1]

The Other Net Flows and Their Components

Since each net-flow matrix and its four components are skew-symmetric, it is sufficient to show only the triangle below the main diagonal. These triangles are displayed in Table 16.1 for each pair of successive years from 1950 to 1972. The rows of each triangle correspond to T_2, T_3 and Lamb; the columns correspond to T_1, T_2 and T_3. The bottom of the table contains the annual changes in the conditional budget shares, with those of Lamb inserted in the last row.

The dominant position of T_1 and T_2 (Inexpensive meat and the Beef/Pork contrast) is illustrated by the fact that the conditional net flow between these two meats is the largest of all net flows for 17 of the 22 annual observations. In the other five cases the largest conditional net flow is that between T_1 and T_3 (Antichicken). During the 1950s the volume components of the flows between T_1 and T_2 were frequently in excess of .005, but later on the volume components of all net flows were typically close to zero. This reflects the declining dispersion of the conditional income elasticities (see the end of Section 14.1).

[1] Recall from the discussion at the end of Section 16.2 that (1.19) is to be divided by $(M_g \bar{W}_{gt})^2$ for a conditional net flow. It may be verified that, under the parametrization of Section 7.3, eqs. (1.17) to (1.19) apply to the disturbance component of (5.1), provided we use conditional marginal shares on the right and replace σ by σ_g defined in eq. (6.8) of Section 15.6.

The substitution and direct price components take large values in several instances, but since they have opposite signs, they tend to cancel each other out. An interesting case is presented by 1952–53 with its large changes in relative prices. The substitution and direct price components of that year are accordingly large, particularly for the net flow between T_1 and T_2. But since these components have the tendency to cancel each other out, both the conditional net flows of 1952–53 and the changes in the conditional budget shares of that year are actually quite modest compared with the corresponding figures in the other years of the first half of the 1950s.

The Sum of the 22 Net-Flow Matrices

The last three columns of Table 16.1 contain the total net flows from 1950 to 1972, obtained by summing the corresponding annual figures, and the four components of each total net flow. This total net flow from T_2 to T_1 is about $-.074$, with the negative volume component (about $-.042$) as the largest single contributor. The total net flow from T_3 to T_1 is also negative and the result for T_1 is a total decline in the conditional budget share of about .1. For T_2 there is an increase in the conditional share of the same order of magnitude; for T_3 and Lamb the changes are of the order of .01 and $-.01$, respectively.

It is instructive to compare these computed 22-year changes in the conditional budget shares with the actual behavior of these shares. The last column of Table 7.2 on page 11 reveals that the conditional budget share of Lamb declined from .0299 in 1950 to .0204 in 1972. This agrees with the 22-year change of $-.0095$ shown in the last column of Table 16.1. [It may be verified that all annual budget share changes for Lamb in Table 16.1 agree with Table 7.2.] Table 13.1 on page 286 indicates that the conditional budget shares of T_1 and T_3 increased from 1950–51 to 1971–72, whereas that of T_2 decreased. This is not in agreement with the computed 22-year changes of Table 16.1. How can this discrepancy be explained?

The Computed 22-Year Changes in Shares, Prices and Quantities

Before resolving this question we first show that the computed 22-year changes of Table 16.1 agree with the behavior of prices and quantities. For this purpose we use eq. (3.4) of Section 7.3,

$$\Delta\left(\frac{w_{it}}{W_{gt}}\right) = \frac{\bar{w}_{it}}{\bar{W}_{gt}}\,(Dp_{it} - DP_{gt} + Dq_{it} - DQ_{gt}) + O_3 \tag{5.7}$$

where i is interpreted as Inexpensive meat. We apply (5.7) to the total change (the net change) from 1950 to 1972. For the first two terms in the expression in parentheses on the right we use the relevant entries in the last row of Table 13.9 on page 324; for the last two terms we use Tables 15.1 and 14.2 (pages 398 and 349). The result is that the expression in parentheses, interpreted as a 22-year log-change, becomes

$$.238 - .344 + .310 - .339 = -.135 \tag{5.8}$$

Similarly, when i in (5.7) is the Beef/Pork contrast, we obtain

$$.377 - .344 + .899 - .339 = .593 \tag{5.9}$$

and for $i =$ Antichicken:

$$1.126 - .344 - .318 - .339 = .125 \tag{5.10}$$

It follows from (5.7) that the right-hand sides of (5.8) to (5.10) must be multiplied by the corresponding conditional budget shares in order to yield (approximately) the changes in these shares from 1950 to 1972. Table 13.1 on page 286 shows that the average values of these conditional budget shares are of the order .75, .16 and .09. By multiplying these three figures by $-.135$, .593 and .125, respectively, we obtain about $-.1$ for Inexpensive meat, almost .1 for the Beef/Pork contrast, and a little over .01 for Antichicken. This is in reasonable agreement with the corresponding figures in the last three columns of Table 16.1. It is true that the conditional budget shares of Table 13.1 which are used here refer to the three-meat group, but this is of minor numerical importance, because the conditional budget share of Lamb (within the four-meat group) is only about 2 or 3 percent.

The Changing Composition of the Transformed Meats

We now turn to the question: Why is there agreement between the computed 22-year change in the conditional budget share of Lamb and the observed behavior of this share, but not for the three other meats?

The answer is that the composition of the transformed meats changes gradually over time. Although Lamb may be viewed as a transformed meat, it is also an observed meat. It is of constant composition as measured by its row in the 4×4 transformation matrix **S**, because this row consists of one unit element and three zero elements for each annual observation. This is the reason why the computed 22-year change in the conditional budget share of Lamb agrees with the observed behavior of this share.

If Inexpensive meat were of constant composition, we should expect that its conditional budget share is subject to a declining trend due to the increase in the volume of total-meat consumption, because its conditional income elasticity is less than 1. This is in agreement with the three negative volume components in the third-last column of Table 16.1. However, we know from Section 13.1 that Inexpensive meat was not at all of constant composition. It was "beefed up" considerably. This meat consisted of less than 20 cents of Beef per dollar in the early 1950s, but of much more Beef in the early 1970s; its conditional income elasticity increased during this period from less than .7 to almost .9. The conditional net flows and their components shown in Table 16.1 refer to a pair of successive years during which the composition of the transformed meats is treated as constant. When such net flows and their components are added, as they are in the last three columns of this table, the aspect of composition change is not incorporated. In other words, in Table 16.1 we consider only the effect of volume and price changes and disturbances on the conditional budget shares of the transformed meats, but there is also an effect caused by the change in the composition of these meats.

Composition Variables

One way of handling the latter effect is by means of composition variables. Write the expenditure on the ith good as $p_i q_i c_i$, where c_i is a positive variable which measures the effect of the composition of this good on its expenditure. Total expenditure is then $m = \sum_i p_i q_i c_i$, and the budget share of this good becomes $w_i = p_i q_i c_i / m$. The infinitesimal change in this share is

$$dw_i = w_i d(\log p_i) + w_i d(\log q_i) + w_i d(\log c_i) - w_i d(\log m)$$

which is an immediate extension of eq. (5.1) of Section 1.5. The finite-change version of this result is

$$\text{(5.11)} \qquad \Delta w_{it} = \bar{w}_{it} Dp_{it} + \bar{w}_{it} Dq_{it} + \bar{w}_{it} Dc_{it} - \bar{w}_{it} Dm_t + O_3$$

The log-change in the composition variable of the meat group (S_g) is defined, similarly to DP_{gt} and DQ_{gt}, as

$$\text{(5.12)} \qquad DC_{gt} = \sum_{i \in S_g} \frac{\bar{w}_{it}}{\bar{W}_{gt}} Dc_{it}$$

Let us first interpret i in (5.11) as the ith observed meat and postulate that observed goods are of constant composition. Hence $Dc_{it} = 0$ and also $DC_{gt} = 0$ in view of (5.12). Next interpret i in (5.11) as the ith transformed meat, so that Dc_{it} may take nonzero values. This does not affect the zero value of DC_{gt}, because (5.12) is a budget-share-weighted mean which is invariant under the preference independence transformation.[1] We then extend the first two subsections of Section 7.3 to include the term $\bar{w}_{it}Dc_{it}$ of (5.11), which yields the following version of (5.7) with a fifth term in parentheses on the right:

$$(5.13) \qquad \Delta\left(\frac{w_{it}}{W_{gt}}\right) = \frac{\bar{w}_{it}}{\bar{W}_{gt}}(Dp_{it} - DP_{gt} + Dq_{it} - DQ_{gt} + Dc_{it}) + O_3$$

This fifth term can be used to reconcile the differences between Table 13.1 (page 286) and the last three columns of Table 16.1. The former table shows that the conditional budget share of Inexpensive meat increased by .798 $-$.736=.062 from 1950–51 to 1971–72. This involves 22 pairs of successive years and hence a time span of 21 years, so that the average annual increase in this share is .062/21≈.003. The corresponding computed 22-year change of Table 16.1 is $-$.0985, which amounts to an average annual change of $-$.0985/22≈$-$.0045. Thus there is a discrepancy of about .0075 to be explained, which (5.13) does by means of Dc_{it}. Using $\bar{w}_{it}/\bar{W}_{gt} \approx .75$ [see the discussion below (5.10)], we find that the average annual log-change in the composition variable of Inexpensive meat is about .010. By performing similar computations for the two other transformed meats, we obtain the following (approximate) average annual log-changes in the composition variables:

$$(5.14) \qquad T_1\colon .010 \qquad T_2\colon -.064 \qquad T_3\colon .027$$

Composition Variables and Income Elasticities

The result (5.14) becomes more interesting if we can relate it to other characteristics of the transformed meats. An obvious comparison is with the conditional income elasticities, because if a transformed meat changes in composition so that it becomes more luxurious, we may expect that this change makes this meat more expensive, thus leading to a larger c_i in the expenditure $p_iq_ic_i$. Table 13.1 shows that the conditional income elasticity of Inexpensive meat increased by .87$-$.69=.18 from 1950–51 to 1971–72, and hence by .18/21≈.009 per year on the average. The average annual changes in the conditional income elasticities of the three meats are

$$(5.15) \qquad T_1\colon .009 \qquad T_2\colon -.016 \qquad T_3\colon .013$$

[1] By applying remark (2) on page 227 to Dc_{it} in (5.11), we find that the Dc_{it}'s are subjected to the **S** transformation. The invariance of their budget-share-weighted mean then follows from Section 12.7.

A comparison of these three figures with those in (5.14) suggests that the 22-year changes in the conditional budget shares of the transformed meats, insofar as they cannot be ascribed to volume and price changes and disturbances, can be ascribed – at least in part – to the changes in the desirability of these meats measured by their conditional income elasticities. More evidence is needed before a statement can be made on the general validity of this proposition.

16.6 Extensions for the Natural Conjugate Supply Model

The axiomatic approach of Section 16.1 is not affected when price log-changes are endogenous, but the substitution and direct price components obviously become random and correlated with the disturbance components. This is analyzed below under the conditions of the natural conjugate supply model.

The Random Substitution Component of a Net Flow

The following results are proved in the next paragraph for $i \neq j$:

$$\text{var}\left[\phi\mu_i\mu_j(Dp_{jt} - Dp_{it})\right] = \delta_{22}\sigma^2\mu_i\mu_j(\mu_i + \mu_j) \tag{6.1}$$

$$\text{cov}\left[\phi\mu_i\mu_j(Dp_{jt} - Dp_{it}),\, \mu_i\varepsilon_{jt} - \mu_j\varepsilon_{it}\right] = -\,\theta\sigma^2\mu_i\mu_j(\mu_i + \mu_j) \tag{6.2}$$

A comparison of (6.1) with (1.15) and (1.19) shows that the variance of the substitution component of the net flow $(iji)_t$ equals a multiple δ_{22} of the variance of the disturbance component of this flow. Similarly, (6.2) implies that the covariance of these two components is a multiple $-\theta$ of the variance (1.19). The correlation coefficient of the two components is therefore equal to $-\theta/\sqrt{\delta_{22}}$, which holds for any pair of goods. Note the similarity of these results to those obtained for the quality index in Section 12.8 and the equivalent income changes in Section 15.9.

To prove (6.1) we use the identity

$$Dp_{jt} - Dp_{it} = (Dp_{jt} - DP'_t) - (Dp_{it} - DP'_t)$$

as well as eqs. (9.1) and (9.4) of Section 15.9:

$$\begin{aligned} \text{var}\,(Dp_{jt} - Dp_{it}) &= \delta_{22}\sigma^2\,\frac{\pi^{ii} + \pi^{jj} - 2\pi^{ij}}{\phi} \\ &= \frac{\delta_{22}\sigma^2}{\phi^2}\left(\frac{1}{\mu_i} + \frac{1}{\mu_j}\right) \end{aligned} \tag{6.3}$$

Multiplication by $(\phi\mu_i\mu_j)^2$ yields (6.1). Next use eq. (9.10) of Section 15.9 in

$$\operatorname{cov}(Dp_{jt} - DP'_t, \mu_i\varepsilon_{jt} - \mu_j\varepsilon_{it}) = \frac{\theta}{\gamma}[\mu_i(1-\mu_j) + \mu_i\mu_j]$$

$$\operatorname{cov}(Dp_{it} - DP'_t, \mu_i\varepsilon_{jt} - \mu_j\varepsilon_{it}) = \frac{\theta}{\gamma}[-\mu_i\mu_j - \mu_j(1-\mu_i)]$$

By subtracting the second equation from the first and multiplying the difference by $\phi\mu_i\mu_j$, we obtain (6.2) by means of $\gamma = -\phi/\sigma^2$ [eq. (8.3) of Section 15.8].

Groupwise Extensions

The conditional net flow $(iji)_{gt}$ defined in (2.18) has substitution and disturbance components equal to $1/M_g\bar{W}_{gt}$ times the corresponding components of $(iji)_t$. The extension of the variance (6.1) and the covariance (6.2) to the conditional flow $(iji)_{gt}$ is therefore straightforward. In particular, the correlation coefficient of the substitution and disturbance components of $(iji)_{gt}$ takes the value $-\theta/\sqrt{\delta_{22}}$. This holds for all pairs of goods within any group.

For the net flow between groups, $(ghg)_{0t}$ defined in (2.7), we prove the following results in the next paragraph $(g \neq h)$:

$$\text{(6.4)} \qquad \operatorname{var}[\phi M_g M_h(DP'_{ht} - DP'_{gt})] = \delta_{22}\sigma^2 M_g M_h(M_g + M_h)$$

(6.5)

$$\operatorname{cov}[\phi M_g M_h(DP'_{ht} - DP'_{gt}), M_g E_{ht} - M_h E_{gt}] = -\theta\sigma^2 M_g M_h(M_g + M_h)$$

These equations are the uppercase versions of (6.1) and (6.2). Using (2.10) also, we conclude that the correlation $-\theta/\sqrt{\delta_{22}}$ applies to any pair of groups as well.

Equation (6.5) can be derived from eq. (9.11) of Section 15.9 in the same way that (6.2) is derived at the end of the previous subsection. For (6.4) we use

$$\text{(6.6)} \qquad \operatorname{var}(DP'_{ht} - DP'_{gt}) = \frac{\delta_{22}\sigma^2}{\phi^2}\left(\frac{1}{M_g} + \frac{1}{M_h}\right) \qquad g \neq h$$

after which multiplication by $(\phi M_g M_h)^2$ yields (6.4). To prove (6.6), which is the uppercase version of (6.3), we consider

$$DP'_{gt} - DP'_t = \sum_{i \in S_g} \frac{\mu_i}{M_g}(Dp_{it} - DP'_t)$$

which has the following variance in view of eqs. (9.1) and (9.4) of Section 15.9:

$$\frac{\delta_{22}\sigma^2}{\phi}\sum_{i\in S_g}\sum_{j\in S_g}\frac{\mu_i}{M_g}\frac{\mu_j}{M_g}\pi^{ij}=\frac{\delta_{22}\sigma^2}{\phi^2}\left[\sum_{i\in S_g}\frac{\mu_i^2}{M_g^2}\frac{1}{\mu_i}-\sum_{i\in S_g}\sum_{j\in S_g}\frac{\mu_i}{M_g}\frac{\mu_j}{M_g}\right]$$

Since the expression in brackets equals $1/M_g-1$, this proves the first line of

$$\text{(6.7)}\quad \operatorname{cov}(DP'_{gt}-DP'_t,\ DP'_{ht}-DP'_t)=\begin{cases}\dfrac{\delta_{22}\sigma^2}{\phi^2}\left(\dfrac{1}{M_g}-1\right) & \text{if } g=h\\[2ex] -\dfrac{\delta_{22}\sigma^2}{\phi^2} & \text{if } g\neq h\end{cases}$$

The second line may be verified similarly. The result (6.6) follows directly from (6.7).

The Random Direct Price Components

The direct price component of $(iji)_t$ in (1.15) is equal to the substitution component multiplied by $\bar{w}_{it}\bar{w}_{jt}/\phi\mu_i\mu_j<0$. Hence the covariance of the direct price and disturbance components is obtained by multiplying (6.2) by the same number, and the variance of the direct price component is found by multiplying (6.1) by the square of this number. The correlation coefficient of the direct price and disturbance components takes the nonnegative value $\theta/\sqrt{\delta_{22}}$. The results for the direct price component of the conditional net flow in (2.18) are completely analogous.

The case of the direct price component of $(ghg)_{0t}$ in (2.7) is more complicated, because the component involves the budget-share-weighted price indexes DP_{gt} and DP_{ht}. The following results are proved in the next subsection:

$$\text{(6.8)}\quad \operatorname{var}[\bar{W}_{gt}\bar{W}_{ht}(DP_{ht}-DP_{gt})]=\frac{\delta_{22}\sigma^2}{\phi^2}\left[\bar{W}_{gt}^2\sum_{j\in S_h}\frac{\bar{w}_{jt}^2}{\mu_j}+\bar{W}_{ht}^2\sum_{i\in S_g}\frac{\bar{w}_{it}^2}{\mu_i}\right]$$

(6.9)

$$\operatorname{cov}[\bar{W}_{gt}\bar{W}_{ht}(DP_{ht}-DP_{gt}),\ M_gE_{ht}-M_hE_{gt}]=-\frac{\theta\sigma^2}{\phi}\bar{W}_{gt}\bar{W}_{ht}(M_g+M_h)$$

The variance (6.8) has no simple relationship to the variance (2.10) of the disturbance component of $(ghg)_{0t}$, but the covariance (6.9) does have a simple relationship to the latter variance. The ratio of (6.9) to (2.10) is

$$\text{(6.10)}\qquad \frac{-\theta/\phi}{(M_g/\bar{W}_{gt})(M_h/\bar{W}_{ht})}$$

which is the product of the degree of price-disturbance dependence (θ) and the absolute value of the income elasticity of the marginal utility of income ($-1/\phi$), divided by the product of the income elasticities of the two groups. It is interesting to compare the roles of these three elasticities in (6.10) and (2.11).

Derivations for the Direct Price Components

We consider

$$DP_{gt} - DP'_t = \sum_{i \in S_g} \frac{\bar{w}_{it}}{\bar{W}_{gt}} (Dp_{it} - DP'_t)$$

which has the following variance in view of eqs. (9.1) and (9.4) of Section 15.9:

$$\begin{aligned} \operatorname{var}(DP_{gt} - DP'_t) &= \frac{\delta_{22}\sigma^2}{\phi} \sum_{i \in S_g} \sum_{j \in S_g} \frac{\bar{w}_{it}}{\bar{W}_{gt}} \frac{\bar{w}_{jt}}{\bar{W}_{gt}} \pi^{ij} \\ &= \frac{\delta_{22}\sigma^2}{\phi^2} \left[\sum_{i \in S_g} \frac{\bar{w}_{it}^2}{\bar{W}_{gt}^2} \frac{1}{\mu_i} - 1 \right] \end{aligned}$$

Similarly, for $g \neq h$,

$$\operatorname{cov}(DP_{gt} - DP'_t, DP_{ht} - DP'_t) = -\frac{\delta_{22}\sigma^2}{\phi^2}$$

The result (6.8) follows when these two results are combined.

For (6.9) we use eq. (7.37) of Section 14.7. This equation implies, for $g \neq h$,

$$\operatorname{cov}(DP_{ht} - DP_{gt}, M_g E_{ht} - M_h E_{gt}) = \frac{\theta}{\gamma} (M_g + M_h)$$

from which we derive (6.9) by means of $\gamma = -\phi/\sigma^2$.

BIBLIOGRAPHY

BARNETT, W. A. (1974). *Labor Supply and the Allocation of Consumption Expenditure*. Doctoral dissertation, Carnegie-Mellon University.

BARTEN, A. P. (1971). "Preference and Demand Interactions Between Commodities," pp. 1–18 of *Schaarste en welvaart*. Leiden: H. E. Stenfert Kroese, N. V.

BECKER, G. S. (1965). "A Theory of the Allocation of Time." *The Economic Journal*, **75**, pp. 493–517.

BORTKIEWICZ, L. VON (1923). "Zweck und Struktur einer Preisindexzahl (Erster Artikel)." *Nordisk Statistisk Tidskrift*, **2**, pp. 369–408.

BROOKS, R. B. (1970). *Diagonalizing the Hessian Matrix of the Consumer's Utility Function*. Doctoral dissertation, The University of Chicago.

CHOW, G. C. (1968). "Two Methods of Computing Full-Information Maximum Likelihood Estimates in Simultaneous Stochastic Systems." *International Economic Review*, **9**, pp. 100–112.

CRAMER, J. S. (1966). "Een prijsindex van nieuwe personenauto's, 1950–1965." *Statistica Neerlandica*, **20**, pp. 215–239.

CRAMER, J. S. (1973). "Interaction of Income and Price in Consumer Demand." *International Economic Review*, **14**, pp. 351–363.

DEATON, A. S. (1974). "The Analysis of Consumer Demand in the United Kingdom, 1900–1970." *Econometrica*, **42**, pp. 341–367.

FINIZZA, A. J. (1971). *Estimation of Demand Equations for a Subgroup of Meat Commodities*. Doctoral dissertation, The University of Chicago.

FOX, K. A. (1958). *Econometric Analysis for Public Policy*. Ames, Iowa: The Iowa State University Press.

FOX, K. A. (1968). "Demand and Supply: Econometric Studies," pp. 104–111 of *International Encyclopedia of the Social Sciences*, Vol. 4, Crowell Collier and Macmillan, Inc.

GANTMACHER, F. R. (1959). *The Theory of Matrices*. Volume One. New York: Chelsea Publishing Company.

GOLDMAN, S. M., and H. UZAWA (1964). "A Note on Separability in Demand Analysis." *Econometrica*, **32**, pp. 387–398.

GRILICHES, Z. (1971, editor). *Price Indexes and Quality Change*. Cambridge, Mass.: Harvard University Press.

HOUTHAKKER, H. S. (1952–53). "Compensated Changes in Quantities and Qualities Consumed." *The Review of Economic Studies*, **19**, pp. 155–164.

KENDALL, M. G., and A. STUART (1967). *The Advanced Theory of Statistics*, Vol. 2. Second edition. New York: Hafner Publishing Company.

KOOPMANS, T. C. (1960). "Stationary Ordinal Utility and Impatience." *Econometrica*, **28**, pp. 287–309.

KOOPMANS, T. C., P. A. DIAMOND and R. E. WILLIAMSON (1964). "Stationary Utility and Time Perspective." *Econometrica*, **32**, pp. 82–100.

KULLBACK, S. (1968). *Information Theory and Statistics*. New York: Dover Publications, Inc.

LANCASTER, K. J. (1966). "A New Approach to Consumer Theory." *Journal of Political Economy*, **74**, pp. 132–157.

LANCASTER, K. J. (1971). *Consumer Demand: A New Approach.* New York and London: Columbia University Press.

LAWLEY, D. N., and A. E. MAXWELL (1971). *Factor Analysis as a Statistical Method.* Second edition. New York: American Elsevier Publishing Company.

MALINVAUD, E. (1970). *Statistical Methods of Econometrics.* Second edition. New York: American Elsevier Publishing Company, and Amsterdam: North-Holland Publishing Company.

MALINVAUD, E. (1972). *Lectures on Microeconomic Theory.* New York: American Elsevier Publishing Company, and Amsterdam: North-Holland Publishing Company.

PAULUS, J. D. (1972). *The Estimation of Large Systems of Consumer Demand Equations Using Stochastic Prior Information.* Doctoral dissertation, The University of Chicago.

PEARCE, I. F. (1961). "An Exact Method of Consumer Demand Analysis." *Econometrica,* **29**, pp. 499–516.

PEARCE, I. F. (1964). *A Contribution to Demand Analysis.* Oxford: Clarendon Press.

POLLAK, R. A. (1971). "Conditional Demand Functions and the Implications of Separable Utility." *Southern Economic Journal,* **37**, pp. 423–433.

POWELL, M. J. D. (1964). "An Efficient Method for Finding the Minimum of a Function of Several Variables Without Calculating Derivatives." *The Computer Journal,* **7**, pp. 155–162.

STEWERT, G. W. (1967). "A Modification of Davidon's Minimization Method to Accept Difference Approximations of Derivatives." *Journal of the Association for Computing Machinery,* **14**, pp. 72–83.

STIGLER, G. J. (1954). "The Early History of Empirical Studies of Consumer Behavior." *Journal of Political Economy,* **62**, pp. 95–113.

THEIL, H. (1952–53). "Qualities, Prices and Budget Enquiries." *The Review of Economic Studies,* **19**, pp. 129–147.

THEIL, H. (1967). *Economics and Information Theory.* New York: American Elsevier Publishing Company, and Amsterdam: North-Holland Publishing Company.

THEIL, H. (1970). "Value Share Transitions in Consumer Demand Theory." *Econometrica,* **38**, pp. 118–127.

THEIL, H. (1971). *Principles of Econometrics.* New York: John Wiley and Sons, Inc., and Amsterdam: North-Holland Publishing Company.

THEIL, H. (1973a). "Measuring the Quality of the Consumer's Basket." *De Economist,* **121**, pp. 333–346.

THEIL, H. (1973b). "Some Recent Developments in Consumer Demand Analysis," pp. 41–73 of *Economic Structure and Development: Essays in Honour of Jan Tinbergen,* edited by H. C. Bos, H. Linnemann and P. de Wolff. Amsterdam: North-Holland Publishing Company.

THEIL, H. (1975). "The Theory of Rational Random Behavior and Its Application to Demand Analysis." *European Economic Review,* **6**, pp. 217–226.

THEIL, H., and R. B. BROOKS (1970-71). "How Does the Marginal Utility of Income Change When Real Income Changes?" *European Economic Review,* **2**, pp. 218–240.

TURNBULL, H. W. (1947). *Theory of Equations.* Edinburgh and London: Oliver and Boyd.

WOLD, H. O. (1969). "E. P. Mackeprang's Question Concerning the Choice of Regression: A Key Problem in the Evolution of Econometrics," pp. 325–341 of *Economic Models, Estimation and Risk Programming: Essays in Honor of Gerhard Tintner,* edited by K. A. Fox, J. K. Sengupta and G. V. L. Narasimham. Berlin, Heidelberg and New York: Springer Verlag.

INDEX